Praise f<

"Israel is in deep trouble at ... that is executing a genocide in ... ... ~, ~~, ~~~ does an outstanding job explaining the causes and the evolution of the disastrous path that Israel is on. This book deserves to be widely read by anyone interested in understanding contemporary Israel."

JOHN J. MEARSHEIMER is the R. Wendell Harrison Distinguished
Service Professor of Political Science at the University of Chicago, the pioneer
of "offensive realism" and co-author of *The Israel Lobby and U.S. Foreign Policy*

"This impressive book provides a comprehensive and incisive answer to the question how we got to where we are in Israel and Palestine today. In a very accessible manner, Steinbock narrates the making of a messianic and theocratic Israel which is a menace for the Palestinians, the region and no less important to itself. Its downfall as the book predicts is neigh, but on the way, it wreaks havoc and destruction. This is the picture world leaders must be aware of and challenge before it is too late."

ILAN PAPPÉ, Director, European Centre for Palestine Studies, Exeter University,
Author, *The Ethnic Cleansing of Palestine*

"Eight years ago I said that Israel would not be a state in 20 years; today I reaffirm that prognosis adding only that it won't take 12 more years. Many of my reasons for reaching that conclusion—and indeed far more—are elaborated in *The Fall of Israel*. Apparently, not many Americans want to know these truths—they're too nuanced, complex, and damning; but if you happen to be in that group of us who believe strongly in the rule of law—U.S. domestic law and international humanitarian and criminal law in particular—and in democracy, then you need to read this book. When you finish, I hope you will understand that our current national path leads us straight to hell."

LAWRENCE WILKERSON, Col., USA (Ret.) is former
chief of staff to Secretary of State Colin Powell

"*The Fall of Israel* is one of the most comprehensive books on the Palestinian crisis. As a Middle East specialist at Princeton University, after reading the book, I gained a better and broader understanding of the root causes of 70 years of failures to resolve this crisis. It accurately explains significant facts about the objectives and crimes of Zionism, the likes of which are rarely found in previous academic works. Moreover, this book demonstrates that the idea of only One Jewish State has been the primary agenda of global Zionism from the beginning, advancing toward the complete elimination of Palestine by prolongation and dragging out decades of negotiations. More disappointing, the United States, which has led the peace process in recent decades and has played a central role in vetoing UN resolutions, facilitated this strategy by giving 'carte blanche' to Israel, effectively becoming part of the problem rather than the solution."

SEYED HOSSEIN MOUSAVIAN is Middle East Security and
Nuclear Policy Specialist at Princeton University and a former
head of Iran's national security foreign relations committee

"*The Fall of Israel* attempts the gigantic task of making sense out of the current situation in Israel/Palestine. It is ambitious in its scope and breadth, yet it successfully creates a context in which we can understand the rapidly shifting and moving events in the Middle East. Vital reading for anyone concerned with this issue and provides perceptive insight that is sorely needed."

JONATHAN KUTTAB, international human rights attorney,
Co-founder of Nonviolence International and Al-Haq for Palestinian human rights,
Author, *Beyond the Two-State Solution* and *The Truth Shall Set You Free*

"Dr. Steinbock's research illuminates what the public is reluctant to digest: Namely that Israel operates in open rebellion against international law, refusing to live in peace with Palestine's native population and with neighbouring states including Lebanon and Syria. Israel's apartheid and genocidal policies have made it a pariah on the international stage, as manifested in countless UN Resolutions and in the International Court of Justice's Orders and two Advisory Opinions, which Israel has ignored, hitherto with impunity, thanks to the connivance of the U.S., UK and EU, and the complicity of the media. The concept known as Zionism was already obsolete when formulated in the 19th century and the attempt to implement it has led to countless wars in the Middle East. Not without reason, the UN General Assembly called Zionism "a form of racism" in its Resolution 3379 of 10 November 1975. Whereas the resolution was withdrawn in 1991, when it seemed that Israel was ready to negotiate in good faith to allow a Palestinian state to emerge, the human rights situation has worsened significantly with the illegal blockade and bombardment of Gaza, the ongoing theft of Palestinian lands and relentless construction of 'settlements.' In a very real sense, Israel is a failed state, but one that through its hubris and lack of control could embroil the entire world in a nuclear confrontation."

ALFRED-MAURICE DE ZAYAS is UN Independent Expert on the Promotion of a
Democratic and Equitable International Order,
international expert on human rights and ethnic expulsions

"Dr Steinbock's book *The Fall of Israel*, is an illuminating and intelligent contribution to our understanding of the events in the Middle East. It makes clear the long roots of the conflict in which the atrocious attacks in October 2023 were a predictable consequence of decisions taken and policies implemented by Israel during many decades. Only through an honest and open recognition of this history will peace in the region become possible."

DR. ERKKI TUOMIOJA is a historian and the longest serving Minister for Foreign
Affairs, Finland, who also had a prominent role as the spokesman of European foreign policy

"*The Fall of Israel* explains excellently how 76 years of repression and suffering for the Palestinians has been facilitated by the unconditional American support for Israel. The response from the extremist Israeli government to the terror of October 2023 has caused total destruction of Gaza, mass-killing of civilians and an accelerating, violent colonization of the West Bank. This further destabilizes the whole Middle East Region and can lead to implosion of Israel itself."

MOGENS LYKKETOFT is former Danish Foreign Minister and
President of the United Nations General Assembly 2015–2016

THE FALL OF ISRAEL

The Degradation of Israel's Politics, Economy & Military

Dan Steinbock

Clarity Press, Inc.

©2025 Dan Steinbock

ISBN: 978-1-963892-00-0
EBOOK ISBN: 978-1-963892-01-7

In-house editor: Diana G. Collier
Book design: Becky Luening

Library of Congress Control Number: 2024944097

Clarity Press, Inc.
2625 Piedmont Rd. NE, Ste. 56
Atlanta, GA 30324, USA
https://www.claritypress.com

PREFACE

Not so long ago, Rimal, a coastal neighborhood in Gaza City, was considered one of the more prosperous neighborhoods in the Strip. When several Palestinian militant groups led by Hamas launched a coordinated offensive against the nearby Israeli towns and settlements, Gaza border crossings and adjacent military installations on October 7, 2023, it triggered Israel's mass mobilization and a lethal ground assault. In just four days, Israeli bombs pummeled the neighborhood into nothingness. Today Rimal remains on the map, but most of the built environment has been reduced to rubble and ruin. As this book's top cover photo attests, Rimal is just one of the many neighborhoods in the Gaza Strip that has been leveled into oblivion.

How could this happen? Why would Israel impose collective punishment on the Palestinian people for the offensive of a few? Why would such a sentence be allowed to unfold, day after day and night after night, by the international community? Why would tens of thousands of women, children and elderly have to die for the attack by the militants? Why would the United States, Israel's powerful military ally, not intervene to ensure at least a semblance of proportionality? Why would the European Union, so proud of upholding "human rights" elsewhere, tacitly permit the carnage? And why would the international community proclaim, "the whole world is watching," while looking the other way?

Not so long ago, the state of Israel was established as a "Jewish and democratic state." And yet, the months leading to October 7 were characterized by massive Israeli demonstrations, the largest in Israel's history, against the proposed judicial reforms by the Netanyahu cabinet, as the book's lower cover photo attests. Aiming to turn a secular democracy into a Jewish autocracy – while some of its extreme members would prefer a theocracy – the most far-right government in the history of Israel has continued to push this judicial coup amid the fog of war. These cleavages in the Israeli society figure large in its political disintegration.

These are some of the haunting questions that led to title of this book, *The Fall of Israel*. The common denominator of the destruction of the Gaza Strip and the mass protests against Jewish autocracy is the fall of Israel. Today, it pervades the Israeli economy, politics, society and the military and thereby its very moral fiber.

The path to the obliteration of Gaza was paved by the confluence of a set of longstanding forces. It is this great conjuncture that has transformed Israel and the occupied Palestinian territories while driving the region to the edge.

The Fall of Israel connects the dots among these lethal headwinds. It outlines the central drivers of this simmering tinderbox: the successive expulsions of Palestinians, the aggressive expansion of Jewish settlements in the occupied territories, a half century of failed U.S. diplomacy in the Middle East, and Israel's militarization, enabled by the symbiotic bilateral ties with Washington and massive U.S. military aid. In the Gaza War, these ties fostered paradigms of devastation, such as the Dahiya doctrine, the Hannibal Directive and mass assassination factories, backed by pioneering artificial intelligence.

What makes the book unique is its comprehensive scope. It addresses the efforts to institute a Jewish rather than a secular state. It shows how the postwar labor alignments fueled by labor Zionism were replaced by the hard-right coalitions driven by revisionist Zionism, thanks to U.S. neoliberal economic policies, assertive neoconservatism and Jewish-American donors. It also explains the causes behind the rise of the Messianic far-right, centrist parties, and the failure of the Left.

The Fall of Israel covers the country's political and ethnic divides, economic polarization, social and military changes, the shifts in the Palestinian struggle for sovereignty, the apartheid regime in the occupied territories and the genocidal atrocities, the regional and global reverberations, and the ensuing human and economic costs, both prior and subsequent to Israel's fatal war on Gaza. There, the nightmarish Israeli actions have led to the engagement of the International Court of Justice and the International Criminal Court, international calls for international boycotts, and massive domestic and international protests. In the long view, the ethnic expulsions and the settlements have contributed to the destabilization of the broader region since the early 1970s and are now compounding its politico-economic and geopolitical crisis.

The corrosion of Israeli society and politics was already reflected in and constrained by extraordinary economic polarization, as reflected by the liabilities of its high-tech cluster, the talent "brain drain," the undermined welfare state, rising poverty and the subsidized religious sector. But now, the already evident political, economic and military costs to Israel of the Gaza war have set the stage for extraordinary uncertainty in the foreseeable future. Should Israel continue its present trajectory, it will bankrupt its economy.

In a 1968 essay titled "The Territories," Yeshayahu Leibowitz, an Israeli Orthodox Jew, polymath and public intellectual, envisioned a nightmarish future. What the West puffed up as Israel's glorious triumph in the 1967 Six-Day War, Leibowitz saw as a dark prelude to endless colonial wars that could turn Israel into a police state, subvert democratic institutions, foster corruption, transform Palestinians into an exploited underclass and the Israeli military into suffering from the kind of colonial demoralization seen previously in Algeria and Vietnam (and more recently in Iraq and Afghanistan).

Despite his stunning prevision, even Leibowitz failed to see the occupation as an effect of the prior Palestinian expulsions since the 1940s. Until recently, many attributed the fall of Israel mainly to the occupation of the Palestinian territories in the 1967 War and the subsequent expansion of Jewish settlements. Even though colonization and the settlements have played a central role in the conflict, they are its proximate effect. It is the ethnic expulsions of the Palestinian Arabs that is the modus operandi of the conflict – from the late 1940s to contemporary Gaza and the West Bank.

Against the prevailing conventional wisdom, *The Fall of Israel* shows why the rise and fall of the two-state solution between the Israeli Jews and Palestinian Arabs is not a recent phenomenon, and how it actually had already unfolded in the mid-1950s – hence the eight decades of missed opportunities, lost peace prospects, and unwarranted "forever wars."

Due to its military might and catastrophic complicity, the United States is today both a part of the solution and the problem. Conversely, Chinese efforts to counter military force with diplomacy and economic development reflect a ray of hope after decades of wasted opportunities and generations of lost lives.

In the region, an equitable and enduring solution can no longer come from within. It must come from without. What is needed is international cooperation – not by the prosperous West alone, but by both the leading advanced economies led by Washington and Brussels, and by the largest emerging economies, spearheaded by Beijing. Unipolar solutions are doomed in the increasingly multipolar world economy.

On October 24, 2023, in the wake of weeks of genocidal atrocities in the Gaza Strip, UN Secretary-General António Guterres condemned the Hamas offensive while pointing out that "Hamas did not happen in a vacuum."

What follows is the story of this dark vacuum.

CONTENTS

Chapter 2   Settlement Expansion..................38

Chapter 4   Perils of Militarization 104

Part II   THE TRANSFORMATION OF ISRAEL

Chapter 6   The Fall of Israeli Politics 179

Part III REPERCUSSIONS IN THE MIDDLE EAST AND BEYOND

Chapter 8 The Struggle for a Sovereign Palestine.. 245

Chapter 9   From Ultra-Apartheid to Genocide.... 286

Chapter 10   Prospects of Regional Escalation ... 320

LIST OF FIGURES

Part I
THE GREAT CONJUNCTURE

Chapter 1

LEGACIES OF ETHNIC EXPULSIONS

In March 2024, amid ongoing genocidal atrocities, Jared Kushner, former president Trump's son-in-law, said that the Gaza waterfront property could be very valuable, suggesting that Israel should remove civilians as it "cleans up" the Strip. As Trump's senior foreign policy adviser, Kushner had been tasked with preparing a peace plan for the Middle East. His comments unleashed a tsunami of international indignation.

Kushner's credentials had little to do with the Middle East. Heading the family business, he was married to Trump's daughter Ivanka and took over the company after his property tycoon father had been convicted for 18 criminal charges, including illegal campaign contributions, tax evasion, and witness tampering in 2005. Charles Kushner was controversially pardoned by President Trump in 2020.

Jared Kushner did have a direct stake in the outcome of the Gaza War. After his time at the White House, he founded a private equity firm deriving most of its funds from Saudi government's sovereign wealth fund. He invested the millions into Israeli high-tech, which plays a central role in the military and security equipment used in the occupied territories, including during the Gaza War.[1]

Kushner characterized the Gaza atrocities as "a little bit of an unfortunate situation there, but from Israel's perspective I would do my best to move the people out and then clean it up."[2] After all, genocides come and go, but great beachfronts are hard to ignore.

There was little new in the issue, though, as it concerned removing Palestinians and taking their land. These ethnic expulsions began years before the establishment of Israel in 1948 and has been clouded by misrepresentations ever since.

ETHNIC CLEANSING

Elusive Legal Status of Ethnic Cleansing

What complicates *legal* accounts of ethnic expulsions are the elusive terms used to understand them. *Crimes against humanity* feature systematic attacks against civilians involving inhumane means, such as extermination, forcible population transfer, torture, rape, and disappearances. *War crimes* are grave breaches of the Geneva Conventions including willful killing, willfully causing great suffering or serious injury, extensive destruction and appropriation of property, and torture. *Ethnic cleansing* is the removal of a particular group of people from a state or region using such means as forced migration and/or mass killing.[3] Nonetheless, ethnic cleansing is not defined as an atrocity crime under the Rome Statute of the International Criminal Court. However, Article 7 of the Statute, which outlines crimes against humanity, includes as one of its listed acts "deportation or forcible transfer of population." And that is understood to mean "forced displacement of the persons concerned by expulsion or other coercive acts from the area in which they are lawfully present."[4] As a consequence, ethnic expulsions are typically included as a distinct category of mass atrocity, despite the absence of a formal legal definition.

Legal scholars refer to these crimes collectively, including ethnic cleansing, as atrocity crimes; that is, *mass atrocities*.

Despite the elusive legal status of the concept, ethnic expulsions of the Palestinians have been the not-so-secret secret among Israelis since the 1940s. S. Yizhar opened his controversial novella *Khirber Khizeh* (1949), "True, it all happened a long time ago, but it has haunted me ever since." Struggling to forget but compelled to remember, the narrator goes back to the original scene of crime, "astonished at how easy it had been to be seduced, to be knowingly led astray and join the great general mass of liars – that mass compounded of crass ignorance, utilitarian indifference, and shameless self-interest – and exchange a single great truth for the cynical shrug of a hardened sinner."[5] No conventional wisdom could repress the original sin indefinitely. So, instead of staying silent, he decides to tell the story. It is a fictionalized narrative of the expulsion of Palestinians from their village, home and land during the 1948 War. It is also the story of S. Yizhar, the celebrated Israeli postwar author and veteran labor politician. Serving as an intelligence officer in the IDF, he moved with a group of soldiers into a Palestinian village whose women, children and old people were rounded up, herded into trucks and sent across the border. At what cost, Yizhar asked:

My guts cried out. Colonizers, they shouted. Lies, my guts shouted. Khirbet Khizeh is not ours. The Spandau gun never gave us any rights. Oh, my guts screamed. . . . Those we were driving out – that was a totally different matter. Wait. Two thousand years of exile. The whole story. Jews being killed. Europe. We were the masters now. . . .

Long live Hebrew Khizeh! Who, then, would ever imagine that once there had been some Khirbet Khizeh that we emptied out and took for ourselves. We came, we shot, we burned; we blew up, expelled, drove out, and sent into exile.

What in God's name were we doing in this place![6]

After two millennia of persecution, Yizhar saw the new Israelis as "peddlers of exile." The old slaves were the new masters. The Judeocide legitimized the Palesticide. It was a dual offense, implying the Jews perpetrating against the Palestinians the cruelties of their own history and the new nation invoking divine sanction in order to do so. But to Yizhar, it felt like a double-bind. The novella struck a chord among Israelis and became a best-seller. In 1964, it was included in the Israeli high school curriculum. And when it was dramatized for the Israeli TV in the late 1970s, it sparked still another wave of controversy.

If *Khirbet Khizeh* was controversial in 1948, today the remembrance is criminalized. "We needed an Eleventh Commandment," Yizhar might say today. In 2009, Israel's Education Ministry declared that the term "Nakba," which had been introduced two years previously into Palestinian-Israeli textbooks, was to be removed because its use amounted to spreading anti-Israeli propaganda. A year later, the "Nakba Law" ensued that withdraws government funding from any group that commemorates the Nakba. It effectively criminalizes remembrance.

Intriguingly, it was only in 2014 that Yizhar's novella was first officially published in the United States; that is, more than half a century after the release of Leon Uris's *Exodus* (1958) and nearly four decades after the Holocaust literature became recognized in America.[7] Revised histories and even a genocide were easier to sell to American readers than the naked, cold truth about the birth of Israel.

Nonetheless, even Israeli leaders have refused to be quiet about what revisionist Israel would like to repress into nothingness.

Furor over Rabin's Memoirs

When Yitzhak Rabin, the late Israeli political leader and promoter of the peace process until his assassination, published his memoirs in 1979, his blunt style unleashed several public debacles.[8] One of these focused on the expulsion of Arabs in contested regions when he served as commander of the Harel Brigade during Israel's Independence War. Rabin's narrative opened with a meeting including himself, Israel's first prime minister Ben-Gurion and Yigal Allon, later foreign minister. It focused on the 50,000 civilians of two Palestinian cities, Lod and Ramla originally known as Lydda and ar-Ramleh:

> Clearly, we could not leave Lod's hostile and armed populace in our rear, where it could endanger the supply route to Yiftach [another brigade], which was advancing eastward.
>
> We walked outside, Ben-Gurion accompanying us. [Yigal Allon, who later became Foreign Minister] repeated his question: "What is to be done with the population?" B.G. waved his hand in a gesture which said, "Drive them out!" ...
>
> "Driving out" is a term with a harsh ring. Psychologically, this was one of the most difficult actions we undertook. The population of Lod did not leave willingly. There was no way of avoiding the use of force and warning shots.[9]

Even then, Rabin acknowledged the devastation that was imposed on the Palestinians. He also recognized the distress that the expulsion inflicted upon his soldiers taking part in the eviction action, including youth-movement graduates, who had been inculcated with values like international brotherhood and humaneness. Some of these soldiers "refused to take part in the expulsion action."[10] It was a remarkable admission by the man who eventually would recognize the futility of military responses in a conflict that required peace and understanding on both sides.

And yet, every paragraph pertaining to Rabin's expulsion narrative was suppressed from his memoirs by the censorship board. Under Israeli law, those who have served in government must submit written material to two sets of censors: the military, which cleared the paragraphs in question, and then a board of cabinet ministers headed by the justice minister, which prohibited Rabin from including in his memoirs the first-person account. However, when a copy of the manuscript was provided to the *New York Times,* the newspaper did publish the relevant paragraphs. Hence, the furor.

Deir Yassin and Restricted Archives

At the time, the narrative of ethnic expulsion was painfully familiar to Palestinian historians, but they were still largely ignored in the West. In his memoir *The Revolt,* then-prime minister Menachem Begin, Rabin's conservative nemesis, depicted a very different picture of the turmoil of the late 1940s. As the leader of the far-right paramilitary Irgun, which participated in both expulsions and atrocities, Begin flatly denied that any atrocities had been committed by his followers in Deir Yassin, the site of a notorious massacre, or in other Palestinian villages. Such stories were just a "lie" spread by "Jew-haters all over the world."[11]

Subsequently, the *New York Times* published an open letter charging Begin, the Irgun and its Herut ("Freedom") party for the massacre. The letter characterized Herut as "a political party closely akin in its organization, methods, political philosophy and social appeal to the Nazi and Fascist parties." The signatories included the physicist Albert Einstein and philosopher Hannah Arendt.[12]

As Deir Yassin testimonies suggest, bodies were piled and burned, a young man was tied to a tree and set on fire, girls were lined up against a wall and shot with a submachine gun, and so on.[13] Citing national security, Israel has kept the army file (No. 681-922/1975) on Palestinian refugees sealed. The classified documents include research commissioned by Ben Gurion to "prove" that the refugees were not expelled in 1948.[14] In effect, "the researchers were told in advance what they were supposed to prove – that the Arabs fled with the encouragement of Palestinian and Arab leaders, and that Arab armies aided those fleeing, whereas the Jewish forces tried to prevent the flight."[15] They were to twist history in the name of history.

The foreign, defense and justice ministries were all adamantly opposed to releasing the file, arguing that it could affect Israel's ability to deal with future talks with the Palestinians or decisions by the UN Security Council on core issues of a permanent arrangement like the refugee issue.[16] The discussions were led by then-justice minister Ayelet Shaked, the influential leader of Israel's New Right, which opposes the establishment of a Palestinian state. Indeed, the story of the ministerial committee obstructing access to the restricted archives is a strange mix of Kafka's *The Castle* and *The Trial.*[17]

As long as such practices of disinformation are allowed to prevail, they tend to foster efforts at denial and disavowal. Denial builds on a psychological defense representing the refusal to acknowledge disturbing aspects of external reality and the existence of disturbing events, such as thoughts, memories, or feelings. Like denial, disavowal builds on an archaic defense in which the subject refuses to recognize the reality of a traumatic perception.

It is layered on a primal defense mechanism for dealing with distressing external reality. To rationalize such a defense mechanism, the subject is compelled to hold two incompatible positions at the same time.[18] So the subject resolves it in ways such as this: "Sure, ethnic cleansing does happen, but Jews have been its victims and thus can't be its perpetrators." It is this logic that seeks to prevent the return of the repressed: the inconvenient truth that ethnic expulsions paved the way to Israeli independence. In the post-apartheid South Africa, Nelson Mandela and Desmond Tutu authorized a truth and reconciliation commission, which invited witnesses, identified as victims of severe human rights violations, to give statements about their experiences in public hearings. In Israel, such realities remain under repression that was legalized with the 2011 "Nakba Law" authorizing the withdrawal of state funds from organizations that commemorate the day on which the state of Israel was established as a day of mourning, or that deny the existence of Israel as a "Jewish and democratic state."[19]

Truth is seldom clean and rarely simple. It will set one free but not without pain. Deir Yassin is a shocking example of ethnic expulsions, but it was not the only massacre undertaken to advance expulsions. Hundreds of Palestinian towns witnessed ethnic expulsions.

ONE COIN, TWO SIDES

Two Historical Narratives

For three decades after the 1948 establishment of the state of Israel, the mainstream version of Israeli history remained largely unchallenged. One of the nodal points of this narrative was Israel's role in the Palestinian displacement and flight, and the unwillingness of proximate Arab nations to engage in peace talks with Israel. But as the Israeli government has declassified new primary source materials, cracks have surfaced in the narrative. Ever since the late 1980s, Israeli "new historians" – a loosely-defined group of Israeli historians, initially led by Benny Morris, who coined the term – began to challenge the traditional narrative. Featuring Benny Morris, Ilan Pappé, Avi Shlaim, Simha Flapan and other many historians have since revised Israel's role in the 1948 Palestinian expulsion and flight in light of historical facts. Nonetheless, most neo-Zionist and revisionist Zionist historians continue to vehemently dispute these historical facts.[20]

In contrast to their precursors, the Israeli new historians argued that ethnic cleansing triggered what the Palestinians call the Nakba, or the "Catastrophe"; that is, the displacement and dispossession of Palestinians, and the devastation of their society, economy, polity and culture. These exposés had been preceded by Palestinian disclosures years before, when the Nakba had been described as ethnic cleansing by many Palestinian scholars, including Rashid Khalidi, Adel Manna, Nur Masalha and others. But whereas the voice of the Israeli historians mattered in the West, their Palestinian precursors were largely ignored.

And so, the once-monolithic, simple and heroic tale of the Israeli founding fathers began to crumble. It became coupled with another narrative that has proved far more nuanced, complicated and human. In their essentials, the two can compared and contrasted.[21]

The Traditional Narrative	The Revised Narrative
Prior to the partition of Palestine by the newly established UN, Britain tried to prevent the founding of a Jewish state.	Actually, in the pre-partition era, Britain sought to prevent the establishment of a Palestinian state.
Palestinians fled from their homes voluntarily, of their own free will.	On the contrary, the Palestinians were expelled and chased out.
After the partition, the balance of power in Israel/Palestine was overwhelmingly in favor of the Arabs.	Despite its small population size, Israel enjoyed an advantage both in arms and human capital.
Israel was surrounded by many hostile Arab countries, which had a coordinated plan and purpose to destroy Israel.	Israel was surrounded by several Arab countries, but they had different motives and objectives, and they were divided among themselves.
The military odds favored Arab countries, which enjoyed an overwhelming advantage in manpower and arms. David beat Goliath.	The balance of military power favored Israel, which enjoyed an advantage in manpower and arms during most rounds of fighting. David was the Goliath.
Israel did whatever it could for peace in the region. It was the intransigence of Arabs that undermined it.	No, things were far more complicated. The primary responsibility of the "dead end" should be assigned to Israel.
Israel did not engage in systematic ethnic cleansing. It was committed to a two-state solution. A few extremists were the exception.	Israel initiated ethnic cleansing even before the 1947 partition. It saw a two-state solution as a stepping-stone to a Jewish one-state reality, over time.
Arab countries, not Israel, are responsible for the Palestinian refugee problem.	Israel and Arab countries have their share of responsibility for the Palestinian flight.

If there is a divide between old and new Israeli historians, there is another divide *among* the new historians. The chasm pertains to the question whether the Palestinian expulsions were intentionally planned or collateral damage of the 1947 UN Partition Plan and the 1948 Israeli Independence. The damage idea was promoted by Benny Morris; the intentional expulsion interpretation by Ilan Pappé.[22] Morris argued that the displacement took place in the heat of the Israeli Independence War. It was not a pre-planned, coordinated objective but rather the outcome of a confluence of unintended tragic circumstances. By contrast, Ilan Pappé has argued that the early Zionist leaders deliberately intended to ethnically cleanse most Palestinian Arabs.

Even today, the intentionalist interpretation by Pappé remains controversial in the West. In 2008, Pappé, the son of two German Holocaust survivors who has long engaged in left-wing peace politics, left Israel after receiving several death threats. During the Gaza War, these pressures intensified. When the 70-year-old academic arrived in the United States for lecturing, he was detained by the FBI for two hours, his phone was seized, and he was subjected to what felt to him like a surreal interrogation: "Who are my Arab and Muslim friends in America . . . how long do I know them, what kind of relationship I have with them. . . . am I a Hamas supporter? do I regard the Israeli actions in Gaza a genocide? What is the solution to the 'conflict'?" Both perplexed and amused, Pappé did not think he was "threatening America's national security."[23]

Transfers and Partitions as Imperial Legacies

In effect, the ethnic expulsions were not just a Palestinian phenomenon. They cast a dark shadow over much of the Middle East in the post–World War I era. During Britain and France's interwar occupation of Iraq, Palestine, and Syria, the British and French mandate governments, in cooperation with the League of Nations, undertook a series of campaigns of ethnic removal and separation.

As historian Laura Robson has shown, "Within its first two decades, the League involved itself in several other plans for ethnically based mass transfer: forced population exchange between Greece and Türkiye, large-scale Armenian resettlement in the border areas of Syria, redistribution of territory by ethnicity in Palestine, and the relocation of European Jews to any available empty space."[24]

As "mandate" states, Iraq, Palestine, Syria, and Lebanon – the former British and French colonial holdings – were, in theory, being supervised by their European masters on the road to national independence. In practice, the system was designed to legitimize European intervention in the Middle East, even if it meant a series of lethal plans for ethnic engineering. By the late 1930s, these schemes of partition and transfer served "as a practical method of controlling colonial subjects and a rationale for imposing a neo-imperial form of international governance, with long-standing consequences for the political landscape."[25]

When the empires of Britain and France were dismantled in the postwar era, the United States took over their role, seeking to impose *its* "rules-based international order" in the region. America did not question ethno-nationalism; it sought to recast the system to legitimize U.S. interventions in the Middle East, despite the anticipated fatal costs in human lives and economic devastation.

As a result, what you see is not necessarily what you get in Israel. Appearances can be deceiving.

Father of the Forests, Architect of the Transfers

When I attended the Jewish school, every Friday the teacher would bring to the class a white-and-blue charity box, known as a *pushke*. It was from the Jewish National Fund (JNF). As we put our coins into the box, we saw ourselves contributing to a peaceful future in which sandy deserts would be transformed into beautiful forest gardens. The realities were and remain different.

Since 1901, the JNF has planted more than 250 million trees, developed over 250,000 acres of land, created more than 2,000 parks and provided the infrastructure for over 1,000 communities.[26] It is a part of the story, but not the full narrative. Yosef Weitz, head of its land and afforestation department, made the Fund a central player in the pre-state Yishuv in the 1930s. At the time, Jews represented barely a tenth of the population, owning just 2 percent of the land. If there was to be a Jewish state, Weitz thought, that was grossly inadequate. The solution was Arab emigration or "transfer," which could rely on voluntary departure or, if necessary, on force; that is, expulsion. As we have seen, in the early decades of the 20th century, the idea was very much in the air. In the new normal, ethnic minorities were expunged amid the disintegration of European empires and the rise of new nation-states. However, the Zionist founding fathers were thinking of "a massive 'strategic' transfer."[27] Weitz was rather blunt about the objectives. As he wrote in his diary in 1940:

> ...there is no room in Palestine for these two peoples. No "development" will bring us to our goal of independent nationhood in this small country. Without the Arabs, the land will become wide and spacious for us; with the Arabs, the land will remain sparse

and cramped. . . . The only solution is Palestine, at least Western
Palestine, without Arabs. There is no room here for compromises!
. . . The way is to transfer the Arabs from here to the neighboring
countries, all of them, except perhaps those from Bethlehem,
Nazareth and the Old City of Jerusalem.

Not one village, not one tribe should be left. And the form of
the transfer needs to be the creation of a refuge for them in Iraq,
in Syria and even in Transjordan. There is no other way out."[28]

As far as Weitz was concerned, the land of Israel would be adequate for
Jews, "if only the Arabs were removed, and its frontiers enlarged a little, to
the north up to the [Litani River (in southern Lebanon)] and to the east including the Golan Heights . . . with the Arabs transferred to northern Syria and
Iraq."[29] Weitz's views anticipated the Greater Israel territorial ambitions of
the hard-right Likud, and those of Netanyahu's far-right cabinet in 2023–24,
as they hoped to consolidate a "security zone" 30 km up to the Litani River, to
"destroy Hezbollah," but also to exploit the critical water resources. Hence,
the Israeli demand in early June 2024 that Hezbollah pull their forces back
behind the Litani, even at the risk of regional escalation.

Weitz had been the key member of the Jewish Agency "transfer committee" in the late 1930s and he was willing to walk the talk. Despite the
ambiguous status of the committee, he arranged the destruction of several
villages in June 1948. In practice, his agents determined which Arab villages
would be destroyed and which preserved for Jewish settlement.[30] Obviously,
the expelled Palestinians would try to return to their lands after the 1948
War, Weitz said to Ben-Gurion. What was needed was a policy of relentless
harassment by every available means to quash any such return. The empty
Palestinian homes and villages had to be razed to prevent the return of the
refugees. Hence, Weitz's work in afforestation, which often clashed with
the ecological objectives of the Israeli conservation movement, served to
cover up the destruction of the Palestinian villages, and to preempt efforts of
rebuilding them.[31] Though portrayed as "environmentalism," the JNF's goal
in actuality has been nation-building via afforestation, despite its harm to
local biomes and unique biodiversity.

Importantly, the JNF has approved a proposal, operative since 2021,
to formally start purchasing land for Jewish settlement expansion in the
West Bank. Responding to the consequent uproar, the JNF suggested that
its mandate had not changed, that "redeeming land" had always been the
JNF's role on both sides of Green Line: "The only change is [that] we're done
with the Israbluff."[32] In the past, the JNF efforts to take Palestinian land were

conducted in the shadows or via subsidiaries. Henceforth it would happen out in the open.

So why are ethnic expulsions still a source of a remarkable controversy, intense denials and threats?

Plan *Dalet*

Armed with abundant historical evidence, Ilan Pappé and other historians have shown that ethnic expulsion has accompanied Jewish colonization in Palestine since the beginning of the modern Zionist movement. These expulsions were not decided on an *ad hoc* basis, as mainstream historians claim. After the Peel Report, a decade before the UN Partition Plan, Ben-Gurion tasked Tel Aviv's Haganah commander to prepare a plan for the military conquest of Palestine. Following subsequent adjustments for future plans (A, B, C), this rudimentary plan provided a blueprint for Plan D, or Plan *Dalet* in Hebrew. In this view, the Israeli strategic objective was "to take over as much of Palestine as possible with as few Palestinians as possible."[33]

According to Israeli new historians, the purpose of Plan *Dalet* was primarily defensive. It was an extreme response to extreme circumstances. By contrast, according to Pappé and Palestinian historians, the plan was offensive. It was an extreme response, aiming to ensure Jewish presence in strategic areas Israeli leaders deemed pivotal, within and outside the UN-defined borders.

Following the UN Partition of Palestine in 1947, the subsequent Arab Jerusalem Riots and the broader escalation, the hostilities led the United States to withdraw its support for the partition plan. Alarmed by the increasing resistance, Ben-Gurion convened what Pappé calls the "Consultancy," a group of a dozen senior military and security figures that prepared the plans for the ethnic cleansing and supervised its execution until the job of uprooting half of Palestine's native Arab population had been completed. It featured the best and brightest of the Israeli military, including Yigael Yadin, Moshe Dayan, Yigal Allon and Yitzhak Rabin, as well as Isser Harel, the first to head the Mossad.[34]

As hardened as these men of the Consultancy were, the expulsions and the violent birth of Israel impacted them, even Harel, Israel's pioneering spy chief, whom I met in suburban Tel Aviv in the mid-1970s. Taking it for granted that all parties in the Middle East had dirty hands, he avoided abstract terms, such as humanity and morality. He had lived his life in the concrete. After our meeting, Harel led me to his beautiful garden, with lavish and bold roses and tulips, where he liked to spend his free time. "I like flowers," he said. "They have their thorns, but they won't sting you on purpose. They get no pleasure from bloodletting."

Even before Plan *Dalet* was implemented in early 1948, more than 250,000 Palestinians had fled, with most still expecting or at least hoping they could return after the hostilities. In the following months, altogether over 700,000 Palestinian Arabs were expelled from their homes by Zionist paramilitaries and later the Israeli army or fled. The expulsion and flight fractured Palestinian society with its attendant dispossession, displacement and devastation.[35] As some 400–600 Palestinian villages were destroyed, the devastation went hand in hand with dozens of massacres and looting to prevent Palestinians from returning to their homes. That latter objective even included poisoning village wells.[36]

With new trees hiding broken Arab towns, many were renamed in Hebrew. Physical devastation wasn't enough; any sign of the past Palestinian society and culture, any possibility of memory was suppressed. Out of sight, out of mind. It wasn't inevitable. It was planned.

SEPARATE AND UNEQUAL

In 2022, Alon Schwarz's documentary film *Tantura* featured a number of Israelis who acknowledged they had witnessed a massacre in the Palestinian village following its surrender. Assigned to the Jewish state by the UN Partition Plan, the village of 1,500 people near Haifa was taken over as part of Plan *Dalet,* a week after the declaration of Israeli independence. Based on the testimonies of the villagers, historian Walid Khalidi in 1961 estimated that 40 men from Tantura were shot and buried in a mass grave.[37] Four decades later, Khalidi's estimate was corroborated by a Haifa graduate Theodore Katz, who had interviewed the survivors. But his MA thesis, defended by historian Ilan Pappé, was met with a denial campaign.

Subsequently, Mustafa al-Wali gathered more testimonies and Pappé provided new evidence. Nevertheless, the denial campaign continued as Israeli historian Yoav Gelber sought to discredit Katz's research, Pappé's new findings and the *Tantura* documentary.[38]

In the *Tantura* documentary, one survivor estimated that more than 200 Palestinians were killed in the massacre. In 2023, a Forensic Architecture investigation suggested that the victims of the massacre were buried in three grave sites beneath what is now a car park for a nearby beach resort.[39]

The suppression of the Tantura massacre reflects decades of concerted denial, compounded by ideological agendas. Gelber is no exception. Just days after October 7, the historian was asked how Israel should deal with

2.3 million Gazans. "I see no solution other than dispersing them across the world," Galber said.[40]

Yet, in the big picture, Tantura was just one of the many depopulated locations.

Decades of Palestinian Expulsions

During the tumultuous years of 1947–1949, several hundred Arab towns and villages were forcibly depopulated in what should have become the state of Palestine, according to the UN Plan. Along with Walid Khalidi, Nur Masalha and other Palestinian historians conclude that

> Mountains of archival documents and other evidence show a strong correlation between the Zionist "transfer" solution (which became central to Jewish strategy in the 1930s and 1940s) and the Palestinian Nakba, the creation of the Palestinian refugee problem, the willful and systematic destruction of hundreds of Arab villages. By the end of the 1948 war, hundreds of villages had been completely depopulated. Their houses were blown up or bulldozed, with the main objective of preventing the return of the refugees to their homes and villages (in addition to helping perpetuate the Zionist myth that Palestine was virtually an "empty territory" before the Jews entered it). . . .
>
> Of the 418 depopulated villages, 293 (70 percent) were totally destroyed and 90 (22 percent) were largely destroyed. . . . While an observant traveler can still see some evidence of these villages, in the main all that remains is a scattering of stones and rubble.[41]

Following conquest, most of the Palestinian towns and villages were deliberately destroyed to prevent the return of the original population, which in many cases was replaced by Jewish immigrants moving to locations that now carried Hebrew names to eradicate memories associated with the Palestinian past. A fraction of the original Arab population remained in small numbers in a few cities. Jerusalem was divided between Jordan and Israel. Some 30,000 Palestinians remained in East Jerusalem (Jordan), coupled with an estimated 30,000 relocated non-Jewish refugees, while 5,000 Jewish refugees moved from the Old City to West Jerusalem (Israel). Most Arab residents in major cities, which were renamed and made an integral part of Israel, fled and/or were expelled from urban hubs like Acre, Haifa, Safad, Tiberias, Ashkelon, Be'er Sheva, and Jaffa (Figure 1-1).[42]

Figure 1-1   Depopulated Palestinian Locations in Israel

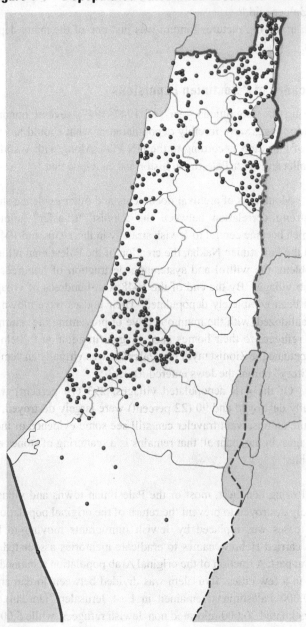

During the 1947–1949 Palestine war around 400 Palestinian Arab towns and villages were forcibly depopulated, with a majority being destroyed and left uninhabitable. Today these locations are all in Israel.

Source: Wikimedia Commons

Ethnic cleansings did not end with the ceasefire agreements between Israel and its Arab neighbors in 1949. As Israel consolidated its new territories and borders, it displaced and expunged tens of thousands of Palestinians and Bedouins, while numerous villages along the Lebanese border were also emptied and resettled by Jewish immigrants. During 1948–1950, the number of Arabs expunged or persuaded to leave from the country in the border-clearing operations and in the internal anti-infiltration sweeps was around 20,000, 30,000–40,000 if the expelled northern Negev Bedouins are included.[43]

The forced expulsions were also premised on Israeli efforts to expand its control in the demilitarized zones with Egypt (Gaza), Jordan (West Bank), Syria (Golan Heights) and Lebanon (southern border areas). The failure to negotiate peace deals among these parties has paved the way for Israel's present-day conflicts with non-state actors like Hamas (Gaza), Hezbollah (Lebanon) as well as Palestinian Authority (West Bank), and Syria, a sovereign state. Furthermore, the right-wing Herut Party, the precursor of the present-day Likud, and its leader Menachem Begin retained the vision of a Jewish state from the Mediterranean Sea to the Jordan River.[44]

In 1965, when Israel implemented the demolition of more than 100 of the abandoned Arab villages, "a clear policy was established to 'level' the abandoned villages with the aim of 'clearing' the country."[45] Two years later, the Six-Day War resulted in another Palestinian exodus from the occupied territories. By December 1967, a further 245,000 had fled from the West Bank and the Gaza Strip into Jordan; 116,000 from the Golan Heights to Syria; 11,000 from Gaza to Egypt. Of the total 145,000 became UNRWA refugees. To them it was the second catastrophe in a single generation.[46]

In Israel, the continued emergency regulations legitimized these displacements in the name of national security.

The Long Emergency

In May 1948 Israel's Provisional Council of State passed an ordinance that gave the Council power to declare a state of emergency, which the Council did immediately. Since its very establishment, Israel has seen itself as facing conditions justifying the declaration of a state of emergency, although its rationale was formally acknowledged only in 1991:

> Since its establishment, the State of Israel has been the victim of continuous threats and attacks on its very existence as well as on the life and property of its citizens.

These have taken the form of threats of war, of actual armed
attacks, and campaigns of terrorism resulting in the murder of and
injury to human beings ...
    In view of the above, the State of Emergency which was
proclaimed in May 1948 has remained in force ever since.[47]

Due to the continuous state of emergency, Israel has been able to apply
a set of extraordinary provisions, which were initially adopted for Mandatory
Palestine by Great Britain. These emergency regulations have a long colonial
history. In the 19th century, the British had used a variety of legal and institutional approaches in Ireland, which refused to submit to British authority.
Subsequently, these repressive measures were exported to other parts of the
empire, including India, South Africa, and Nigeria. In each case, they served
to reduce and displace the potential for more direct violence by the indigenous
populations, but at the cost of legitimizing repressive practices.[48] In Palestine,
the British Army had already deployed them with devastating effect in the
suppression of the Arab Revolt of 1936–1939, following its "long tradition
of pacification."[49] After World War II, the British used such emergency laws
to suppress independence fighters in their colonies; this was portrayed as
a struggle against communism during the early Cold War. Effectively, the
repression was war. However, the term "emergency" was preferred since
London's insurers did not pay out in instances of civil war.[50]
    In Mandatory Palestine, the emergency laws permitted detention with-
out trial along with deportation, curfew, and suppression of publications. First
propagated in 1945, the British repealed the regulations before withdrawing
from Palestine in 1948. Nonetheless, most were incorporated into Israel's
domestic legislation. The state of emergency was originally authorized under
Section 9 of the 1948 Law and Administration Ordinance and has been in
continuous effect since. As amended, these regulations form a central part
of the legal system in the West Bank, permitting military tribunals, prohibi-
tions on books and newspapers, house demolitions, indefinite administrative
detention, extensive powers of search and seizure, the sealing off of territories
and the imposition of curfews.[51]
    In the postwar decades, a comparable "strategy of tension" was
exploited in several countries considered vital to the U.S.-led West. In Italy,
it resulted in two decades of extraordinary social turmoil, political violence
and economic volatility. It was also marked by a wave of false flag terror,
originally attributed to the far-left but later linked with far-right, as well as
Italian and U.S. intelligence agencies.[52] The strategic objective was to use
a general sense of insecurity related to targeted groups and to buttress an

increasingly repressive government. As geopolitics replaces development, economic welfare suffers, but the perceived common enemy is expected to "unite the nation."[53] Historically, the strategy of tension paved way to neo-liberal economic policies; for example, the 1973 Pinochet regime relying on U.S.-trained Chicago economists in Chile.[54]

In the aftermath of the 1973 Yom Kippur War and the rise of U.S.-Israeli military ties, the long emergency in Israel contributed to extra-parliamentary efforts at violent ethnic expulsions in the West Bank, thanks to Messianic far-right militants and their American-Jewish idol, Meir Kahane.

Rabbi Meir Kahane's Legacy of Hate

Born in Brooklyn, rabbi Meir Kahane (1932–90) came from an established rabbinical family. His father was a staunch supporter of Ze'ev Jabotinsky, revisionist Zionism and the Irgun, their extremist armed group.[55] Jabotinsky and Peter Bergson (Hillel Kook) were frequent guests in his parents' home, and he idolized them as a teen. Subsequently, Kahane served as a rabbi at Howard Beach, a Queens neighborhood that later gained notoriety for racial tensions. Thanks to his rapid anti-communism, he became an informant with the FBI. With Joseph Churba, an American-Syrian-Jewish "intelligence expert" and later one of president Reagan's Middle East specialists, he promoted U.S. involvement in the Vietnam War among Jewish college students.[56] Mimicking the Black Panthers, Kahane launched the Jewish Defense League (JDL), which led to friction with black communities. Concurrently, he was pursuing a plan to launch a terrorist attack against Soviet officials in the U.S. with biological weapons.[57] By then, he had been convicted of domestic terrorism leading to a suspended five-year prison sentence. Despite the severity of the offenses, he served his sentence mainly in a hotel, due to concessions over the provision of kosher food.[58]

In the early '70s, Kahane moved to Israel. That's when I met him in Jerusalem. With the Jewish Defense League in the U.S. as a blueprint, he established the ultra-radical Kach Party in Israel. Both relied on terror to advance their aims. "Israel can only be sustained by a permanent Jewish majority and a small, and docile Arab minority," he said. "The Land of Israel should not be committed to national suicide."[59] The Jews were the "chosen people" and the "promised land" belonged to the Jews because God had given it to them. Whoever thought otherwise could go to hell. "We Jews should not allow demography, geography, and democracy to push Israel ever closer to an abyss," he would say. Democracy was a Hellenic invention, a "*goy* thing." Israeli Arabs could accept non-citizenship, leaving with compensation, or be forcibly expelled. What if Arabs refused to leave? It's not a matter of a dialogue, he said. "In Israel, there is only one solution for Jews and Arabs and that's separation."

Never in my life had I met anyone as full of hate. Kahane couldn't utter the word "Arab" without a hint of disgust. I fully expected him to face a violent death (Figure 1-2).

Figure 1-2   Intimidation by Terror: "Gas the Arabs"

(*Above, top*) "Gas the Arabs" painted on the gate outside a Palestinian home in Hebron by Israeli settlers. It is signed "JDL" for Jewish Defense League (June 2008 by Magne Hagesæter). (*Above, bottom*) Kahane speaking before his followers in Tel Aviv in June 1984. (Dan Hadani collection / National Library of Israel)
Source: Wikimedia Commons

Fast forward to November 1990. In the early evening, I was walking to Grand Central in midtown-Manhattan. Meanwhile, Kahane was giving a speech in the Marriott East Side hotel to a mainly Orthodox-Jewish audience. Disguised as an Orthodox Jew, El Sayyid Nosair, an Egyptian-born American, approached him and reportedly shot him from close range with a .357-caliber pistol. As I heard the shots, I saw a man running from the hotel. When he tried to take over a taxi at gunpoint, an on-duty postal police drew his pistol and ordered the assassin to freeze. Nosair shot and hit him in the chest, but the officer returned fire and arrested him.[60] Oddly, the jury acquitted Nosair of Kahane's murder but convicted him of assault and possession of an illegal firearm.[61] Serving time in state prison, Nosair was later convicted as part of the federal trial of the "Blind Sheik" Omar Abdel-Rahman and involvement in the alleged and far broader New York City landmark bomb plot.[62]

Assassination made Kahane a martyr and attracted even more supporters.

The Long Displacement

Though the U.S. debate on the "alleged Israeli ethnic cleansing" intensified with the Gaza War in 2023–24, it is over a century old. Several historical landmarks punctuate this long campaign, in which the countervailing force has been "the Palestinians' continuing resistance, against heavy odds."[63] The first of these landmarks was issued on behalf of the British cabinet by Foreign Secretary Arthur James Balfour in 1917 when British troops were conquering Palestine. Coupled with the subsequent League of Nations Mandate, the Balfour Declaration arrogated national rights in Palestine exclusively to Jews, who constituted 6 percent of the population at the time, thereby denying the rights of the vast majority of Arab Palestinians as the "existing non-Jewish communities in Palestine."[64]

Another landmark ensued with Article 22 of the Covenant of the League of Nations, promulgated in 1919, which described the Arab peoples of the regions of the former Ottoman Empire as "independent nations." With the exclusion of Arab Palestine, this provision was subsequently violated by both Britain and the League of Nations. As the Jewish immigration flows soared, Palestinians launched the 1936–1939 Great Revolt, which was ruthlessly crushed by the British, who "killed, wounded, deported or imprisoned an estimated 10 percent of the adult male Palestinian Arab population."[65]

The first postwar landmark ensued in November 1947 via UN General Assembly Resolution 181 for the partition of Palestine, supported by the United States and the Soviet Union. The two superpowers hoped to use the new states to weaken the old regional colonial powers, Britain and France, and ensure access to the remarkable energy resources in the Gulf.[66] The partition handed over most of the Arab-majority country to its Jewish minority without the consent of that majority, thereby violating the principle of self-determination of the UN Charter. The Arabs were left a broken territory in three noncontiguous segments. Even before the onset of the Arab-Israeli War in May 1948, as many as 300,000 Palestinians had been driven from their homes. In the subsequent year, another 400,000 Palestinians were expelled.

The next superpower-mandated postwar landmark was UN Security Council Resolution 242 of November 1967, which did not mention the Palestinians as a people, or even as a party to the conflict. Instead, it framed the entire issue as a conflict between the Arab states and Israel; a stance reflected by the U.S. and Israeli efforts at "normalization" with Arab countries even today. What about the peace process? In consequence of these factors, the regime that emerged from the Oslo Accords did not bring about Palestinian self-determination yet permitted the continued occupation and settlement expansion. Furthermore, the long campaign took a new "internationalized" step after the joint U.S.–European Union (EU) and Israeli refusal to recognize the results of the 2006 Palestinian elections won by Hamas. This non-recognition and particularly the subsequent economic blockade paved the way to incessant conflicts and atrocities in the occupied territories, thereby burying whatever was left of the peace process.

Today, the Palestinians in Israel, occupied territories, neighboring Arab countries and worldwide are the descendants of the hundreds of thousands who once lived in areas that became Israel. In the process, the demographic conditions in Israel/Palestine have turned upside down as a result of colonization, conquest, wars and expulsions. Prior to the British Mandate, the Palestinians still comprised some 90 percent of the total population and the Jews the rest. In the 1947 Partition Plan, the UN granted 55 percent of Palestine to the new Jewish state and only 45 percent to a non-contiguous Arab state, with Jerusalem to be under international control. By the time of Israel's 1948 creation, the Jewish forces had already expelled some 750,000 Palestinians while capturing 78 percent of the historic Palestine. The remaining 22 percent was split into the West Bank and Gaza Strip until the 1967 War, at which time Israel occupied all historic Palestine and expelled still another 300,000 Palestinians (Figure 1-3).

Figure 1-3   Mapping a Century of Ethnic Cleansing

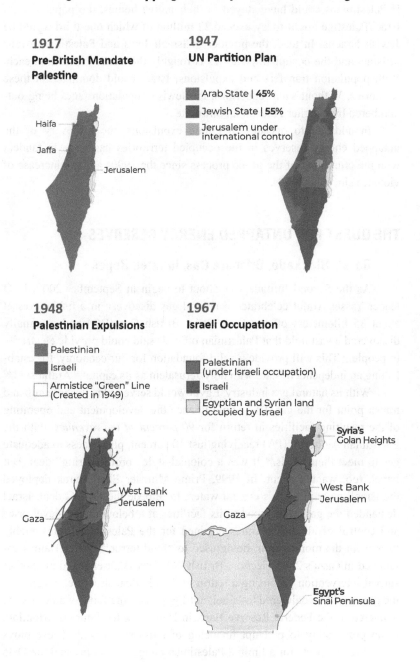

1917
Pre-British Mandate Palestine

Haifa

Jaffa

Jerusalem

1947
UN Partition Plan

- Arab State | **45%**
- Jewish State | **55%**
- Jerusalem under international control

1948
Palestinian Expulsions

- Palestinian
- Israeli
- Armistice "Green" Line (Created in 1949)

Gaza

West Bank
Jerusalem

1967
Israeli Occupation

- Palestinian (under Israeli occupation)
- Israeli
- Egyptian and Syrian land occupied by Israel

Syria's Golan Heights

West Bank
Jerusalem

Gaza

Egypt's Sinai Peninsula

Source: Al Jazeera

Today, there are almost 15 million Palestinians around the world. If Palestinians could have stayed in their native homes, the population of Israel/Palestine might today exceed 22 million of which one-third would be Jewish Israelis. Instead, the number of Israeli Jews and Palestinian Arabs in Israel and the occupied territories is roughly the same, 7.2 million each. With population transfers and expulsions, Israel could dominate all these territories. Without such reductions, the Jewish population faces being out-numbered by a higher Palestinian birth rate.

In addition to decades of ethnic expulsions, the discovery of the untapped energy reserves in the occupied territories has gone in tandem with the crumbling of the peace process since the 1990s and the increase of violence since the 2000s.

THE QUEST FOR UNTAPPED ENERGY RESERVES

Gaza's Blockade, Offshore Gas, Inflated Hopes

As the Second Intifada was about to begin in September 2000, PLO leader Yasser Arafat celebrated a natural gas discovery in a fishing vessel about 35 kilometers off the Gaza Strip. British Gas (BG) had eventually discovered a vast field that Palestinian officials said could provide electricity to people. "This will provide a solid foundation for our economy, for estab-lishing an independent state with holy Jerusalem as its capital," Arafat said.[67]

With its natural gas industry, Egypt would serve as the onshore hub and transit point for the gas. BG would finance the development and operating of the resulting facilities in return for *90 percent of the revenues,* with the Palestinian Authority (PA) receiving just 10 percent, plus access to adequate gas to meet their needs.[68] It was a colonial-style "profit-sharing" deal. But Israel, too, wanted a cut. In 1999, Prime Minister Ehud Barak deployed the Israeli navy in Gaza's coastal waters to impede the PA-BG deal. Israel demanded the gas to be piped to its facilities at a below-market-level price and control of all the revenues destined for the Palestinians, presumably to prevent the monies from being used to "fund terror."[69] After Hamas tri-umphed in Gaza's 2006 election, British PM Tony Blair engaged in another surreal intervention proposing a return to the old deal structure, except that the gas would be delivered to Israel, not Egypt, and the funds would first be delivered to the Federal Reserve Bank in New York for future distribution, again presumably to preempt financing of terrorist attacks.[70] These ploys killed the prospects for a limited Palestinian budget autonomy and the Oslo

Accords, while a path was paved for new wars, which would then be blamed on the Palestinians.

When the Hamas-led Palestinian unity government refused the impossible offer, Israeli PM Ehud Olmert imposed a blockade on Gaza. The economic warfare was hoped to result in a political crisis with an uprising against Hamas. Israel put the Palestinians "on a diet, but not to make them die of hunger."[71] It was an old colonial ploy. Imperial Britain had used it in India where British policies compounded the severity of the famines and chronic malnutrition, killing some 6 to 10 million people during the Great Famine of 1876–1878 alone.[72] In Gaza, such attrition games would have taken too long. Hence, the launch of Israel's 2008–2009 Gaza War to subject the Strip to a "Shoah" (Hebrew for *Holocaust*), as Deputy Defense Minister Matan Vilnai warned.[73] The idea was to "send Gaza decades into the past," said commanding general Yoav Gallant, who 15 years later would serve as Netanyahu's defense minister pledging to "wipe this thing called Hamas off the face of the earth."[74] This latest starvation experiment resulted in the International Criminal Court's genocide case against Netanyahu and Gallant in May 2024.[75]

The 2008–2009 War did cause devastation in Gaza but failed to transfer the control of the gas fields to Israel. So, as the West was swept by the financial crisis of 2008–2009, the Netanyahu government found itself also struggling with an energy crisis. Amid the Arab Spring in the region, Israel lost 40 percent of its gas supplies and faced soaring energy prices, which sparked the 2011 cost-of-living mass protests, the largest in decades.[76] Ironically, Netanyahu's government was saved by the discovery of a huge field of recoverable natural gas in the Levantine Basin: the Tamar and Leviathan fields near Israel, the Aphrodite field off Cyprus and Zohr close to Egypt. Israel claimed "most" of the newly confirmed gas reserves lay within Israeli territory, which led to increasing tensions with Lebanon, Syria, Cyprus, and the Palestinians.[77] To ease tensions, the U.S. pioneered its "gas diplomacy," hoping to use the region's new energy wealth to bring countries in conflict back to the negotiating table (Figure 1-4).

But even before October 7, the inflated gas diplomacy visions and the pipeline project proved outsized.[78] As a result, the offshore Gaza Marine gas field, discovered in 1999–2000, a decade before Israel's Tamar and Leviathan, "remains inaccessible due to Israeli restrictions, and thus offers no relief to the people in Gaza suffering under a stifling Israeli siege."[79] In theory, the timing was favorable, due to the high gas prices and Europe's need to diversify gas resources. Yet, the gas Levantine ecosystem lacked pipelines out of

Figure 1-4 Eastern Mediterranean Gas Fields

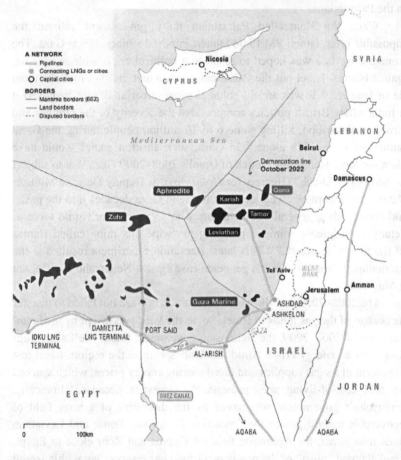

Source: International Crisis Group

the sub-region, remaining dependent on limited gas liquefaction capabilities in Egypt, while progress was slow, due to elevated tensions in the region.[80]

In addition to energy discoveries, there was still more at stake: the alternative distribution channels that ran right next to Gaza.

An Alternative to the Suez Canal

Some 12 percent of the world's trade passes through the Suez Canal, which connects the Red Sea and the Gulf of Suez with the Mediterranean Sea. That translates to $9.4 billion in annual revenues to Egypt.[81] But the traffic hasn't always been smooth. In March 2021, the canal was blocked for six days by a container ship that had run aground.[82] The closure required oil tankers to divert around the Cape of Good Hope near the southern tip of Africa, adding over 4,000 kilometers to the transit from Saudi Arabia to the United States. Amid the Gaza War, media buzz intensified about an Israeli canal initiative. It wasn't a new idea.

In the ancient era, there were a number of famous routes passing through the Negev desert. The city of Eilat functioned as a key port during the reign of Solomon, as the trading point with Africa and the Orient. In the mid-19th century, British Rear-Admiral William Allen championed construction of a canal between the Mediterranean and the Red Sea, as an alternative to the proposed Suez Canal.[83] As Allen failed to attract the powers-to-be behind his dream plan, the Suez Canal was built. It reduced the journey from London to the Arabian Sea by some 8,900 kilometers. Yet, the dream of an alternative to the Suez Canal retained its position in the early Zionist visions. In his novel *The Old-New Land* (1902), Theodor Herzl, the father of political Zionism, saw the Jewish land as a nodal point between two massive regional blocs and envisioned a future when "traffic between Europe and Asia had taken a new route – via Palestine."[84] It was this idea that PM Netanyahu was promoting with his map of the "new Middle East" in the UN General Assembly just two weeks before the Hamas offensive of October 7, 2023. With Palestine and Palestinians effectively erased from the map, the speech caused an international firestorm.

In the 1950s, Israel had a deep-water port constructed at Eilat, while a modern port was built on the southern coast of the Mediterranean at Ashdod, just 60 kilometers from the Gaza border. In the 1960s, the Suez Canal had also become vital to U.S. interests, as evidenced by a plan of the Lawrence Livermore Laboratory (LLL) that was declassified only at the end of the Cold War. One proposed project built on a memorandum by H. D. MacCabee, advocating the use of 520 2-megaton nuclear explosions to excavate a canal through the Negev desert.[85] In 1970, the Israeli shipping line ZIM set up a subsidiary to provide service for cargoes transported cross-country between Ashdod and Eilat, while construction started on a 42-inch oil pipeline through Negev from Eilat to Ashkelon, just 12 kilometers from the Gaza Strip.[86]

These visions leaped ahead in October 2020, when the Israeli state-owned Europe Asia Pipeline Company (EAPC) and the UAE-based MED-RED Land Bridge inked a deal to use the Eilat-Ashkelon pipeline to move oil from the Red Sea to the Mediterranean; just *1 month after* the Abraham Accords (Figure 1-5).[87]

Figure   1-5   Ben Gurion Canal Project

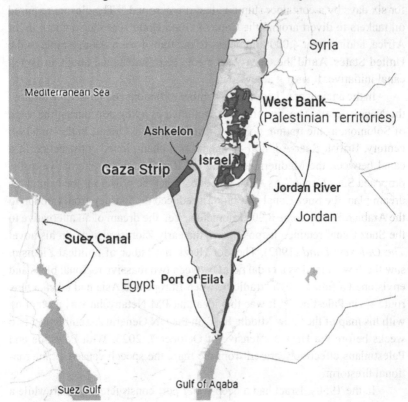

The trajectory in red [or dark gray].
Source: The New Arab, created with Datawrapper

In April 2021, Israel announced that the Ben Gurion Canal would connect to the Mediterranean Sea by getting around the Gaza Strip. Unlike the Suez Canal, the Israeli dual-canal would handle ships going in both directions. It would be almost one-third longer than the 193-km Suez Canal. The costs of the 5-year project would amount to $16 billion to $55 billion. The canal was projected to generate $6 billion or more in annual income.[88] Whoever controls the proposed canal would have enormous influence over the global supply routes for commodities shipping.

Before October 7, the only thing that stood between the Netanyahu government and the massive canal project was Gaza and Hamas. The challenge was to get rid of both.

Denying Palestinians Their Energy Wealth

Sizeable reservoirs of oil and natural gas wealth are located in Area C of the occupied West Bank and the Mediterranean coast off the Gaza Strip. And yet, the Israeli occupation continues to prevent Palestinian efforts to develop their energy fields, to exploit and benefit from such assets. In 2019, the United Nations Conference on Trade and Development (UNCTAD) reported that the occupied territories lie above sizeable reservoirs of oil and natural gas wealth in Area C of the occupied West Bank and the Mediterranean coast off the Gaza Strip. However, as UNCTAD warned, the occupation continues to *prevent* Palestinians from developing their energy fields so as to exploit and benefit from such assets. Israel was "either preventing them from exploiting or is exploiting without due regard for international law."[89]

> As such, the Palestinian people have been denied the benefits of using this natural resource to finance socioeconomic development and meet their need for energy. The accumulated losses are estimated in the billions of dollars. The longer Israel prevents Palestinians from exploiting their own oil and natural gas reserves, the greater the opportunity costs and the greater the total costs of the occupation borne by Palestinians become.
> Also critical are the new oil and natural gas finds in the Eastern Mediterranean that Israel has begun to exploit for its own benefit, while these resources may be considered shared resources, whereby the oil and natural gas exist in common pools.[90]

Based on the 2010 U.S. Geological survey, the discoveries of oil and natural gas in the Levant Basin amounted to 122 trillion cubic feet of natural gas and 1.7 billion barrels of recoverable oil.[91] In 2023 U.S. dollars, the value of these resources translated to $557 billion and $87 billion, respectively. That's about $644 billion in total.[92] Together, these offered an opportunity to distribute and share the total among the different parties, in addition to many other advantages of energy security and cooperation among the longstanding belligerents.

By 2018, 18 years had passed since the drilling of Marine 1 and Marine 2. As the Palestinian Authority had not been able to exploit these fields, the accumulated losses were already in the billions of dollars. In the West, the Israeli stance was seen as needlessly harsh.[93] The Palestinian people have been denied the benefits of using this natural resource to finance socioeconomic development and meet their need for energy for decades to come. However, as UNCTAD has cautioned, these reservoirs could also function as a source of additional conflict and violence if the stakeholders seek to exploit these resources without due regard for the fair share of others and "without due regard for international law and norms."[94] Such disregard was indicated by the "secret memorandum" to expunge Gazans, widely supported by Israeli conservatives and Messianic far-right.

ISRAEL'S SECRET MEMORANDUM

Gaza's Population Transfer

Barely a week after October 7, Israel's intelligence ministry prepared a secret memorandum. Tasked with supporting Israel's national security in coordination with and under the guidance of the prime minister, the ministry oversees policies related to the intelligence organizations Mossad and Shin Bet, also known as the Shabak (Israel Security Agency). Despite its small size, the ministry has an important role in defining national agendas and priorities. In fall of 2023, the intelligence ministry was headed by Gila Gamliel, a veteran member of Netanyahu's Likud Party, who had been criticized for taking bribes, fraud and violation of trust; although investigations had been halted in the absence of sufficient evidence.

The memorandum sought to persuade the United States and other countries to support Israel goals, enumerated thus:

a. Overthrow of Hamas' rule.
b. Evacuation of the population outside of the combat zone for the benefit of the citizens of the Gaza Strip.
c. It is necessary to plan for and channel international aid to reach the area in accordance with the chosen policy.
d. In every policy, it is necessary to carry out a deep process of implementing an ideological change (de-Nazification).
e. The selected policy will support the state's political goal regarding the future of the Gaza Strip and the final picture of the war.[95]

Oddly, the ministry associated its efforts to achieve ideological change in Gaza with a process of "de-Nazification." Though fully misaligned with the realities of Gaza, the terminology reflected the Likud's longstanding efforts to use the Holocaust in ideological efforts to identify Hamas with al-Qaeda and both with the German Nazis.

The secret document outlined three possible options:

a. Option A: The population remaining in Gaza and the import of Palestinian Authority (PA) rule.
b. Option B: The population remaining in Gaza along with the emergence of a local Arab authority.
c. Option C: The evacuation of the civilian population from Gaza to Sinai.[96]

Of these three, the memo recommended C: the forcible transfer of Gaza's 2.3 million residents to Egypt's Sinai as the preferred course of action. It encouraged Israel's government to lead a public campaign in the West to promote the transfer plan "in a way that does not incite or vilify Israel." This would be done by presenting the expulsion of Gaza's population as a "humanitarian necessity." The challenge was to enlist Washington to exert pressure on Egypt, along with other countries in Europe and the Middle East, to absorb the Palestinian residents of Gaza. During the war, Israel should "evacuate the civilian population to Sinai"; establish tent cities and later more permanent cities in the northern Sinai that would absorb the expelled population; and then create "a sterile zone of several kilometers...within Egypt and [prevent] the return of the population to activities/residences near the border with Israel." Targeting the civilians in Gaza was framed as vital to "motivate" Palestinians to accept the plan and give up their land.[97]

Despite objections by all these proposed destination countries, Gamliel and other Israeli authorities had a clear vision of what they intended for the "day after in Gaza," or as she put it:

> At the end of the war Hamas rule will collapse, there are no municipal authorities, the civilian population will be entirely dependent on humanitarian aid. There will be no work, and 60% of Gaza's agricultural land will become security buffer zones.[98]

The classified memo was distributed exclusively to the Israeli defense elite. But it was soon leaked to the Israeli business newspaper *Calcalist* and the international media.[99] While the leak sparked a global firestorm over the "advocacy for ethnic cleansing," Gamliel claimed members of the Knesset were backing the proposal.[100] Meanwhile, a pro-Likud think tank, previously a partner with the intelligence ministry, was working on the economic opportunities "for resettlement and final rehabilitation in Egypt of the entire population of Gaza."[101]

Investing in the Cleansed Gaza Beachfronts

Just days after October 7, the Misgav Institute for National Security & Zionist Strategy released a curious policy paper that also called for the forced transfer of Gaza's population to the Sinai. But unlike the intelligence ministry, it saw ethnic cleansing as an extraordinary commercial opportunity. The hawkish right-wing think tank was headed by Meir Ben-Shabbat, Netanyahu's close associate and an ex-head of Israel's national security council. In the Shin Bet, Ben-Shabbat had tackled Hamas during Operation Cast Lead (Gaza War 2008–2009). He had also played a role in establishing bilateral ties with the United Arab Emirates, Morocco and Bahrain, as part of the U.S.-brokered Abraham Accords. To Netanyahu's hawks, these accords were the first step in ejecting Palestine from the Middle East talks.

Released in Hebrew on Misgav's website, the report was written by Amir Weitman, an investment manager and visiting researcher. Leading the Likud's libertarian faction, Weitmann was close to intelligence minister Gamliel. His asset management company had a largely U.S.-trained, American-Jewish and Israeli team aligned with U.S. multinationals and Silicon Valley. In his report, Weitmann argued that there were 10 million vacant housing units in Egypt that could be "immediately" filled with Palestinians. Stunningly, Weitman envisioned Israel purchasing Gazan properties at a cost of $5 to 8 billion dollars, which represented only 1 to 1.5 percent of Israel's GDP. He saw it as "an innovative, cheap and sustainable solution." Buying the Gaza Strip was a worthwhile investment that would "add a lot of value over time," thanks to local land conditions, and it would provide many Israeli settlers a high standard of living.[102]

Actually, the idea of using investment to turn Gaza around was not a new one. In 2012, Dr. Yacov Sheinin, a veteran economist with extensive experience in the U.S. and Israel, proposed that a $10 billion investment would turn Gaza into the Riviera. "The economic significance for the Gazans is more than $35,000 per family in aid," Scheinin argued. "This amount should make possible the economic recovery of Gaza and let it achieve an annual growth rate of 10%, so that, within 15 years, the GDP per capita will reach $8,000. Gaza could even become a Mediterranean Riviera between Lebanon and Egypt."[103] However, Sheinin was thinking of the *Gazans'* welfare as fostering Israeli security, whereas the Israeli hard-right and the settlers were thinking of the takeover and resettlement of Gaza, which they saw necessary for Israeli security.

Furthermore, Weitman argued that his "sustainable plan ... aligns well with the economic and geopolitical interests of the State of Israel, Egypt, the USA and Saudi Arabia," despite the stated opposition of all these Arab countries.[104] In Egypt's view, however, that meant a Gazan Nakba that could endanger the al-Sisi regime. Hence, Cairo's absolute rejection of the plan. Yet, Weitman claimed Western Europe would welcome "the transfer of the entire Gaza population to Egypt," since it would significantly "reduce the risk of illegal immigration," while Saudi Arabia would embrace the move because the "evacuation of the Gaza Strip means the elimination of a significant ally of Iran."[105]

In reality, Western European capitals had little desire for the kind of huge migration crisis they had coped with as a result of the Arab Spring and the Syrian Civil War. Similarly, Saudi Arabia premised further normalization of bilateral ties with Israel on peaceful progress in Gaza and the West Bank. In spring 2023, Riyadh had agreed to the China-brokered reconciliation with Iran, which drove a wave of détente and reconciliation in the Middle East. It had little incentive to inflame regional escalation, which would penalize *Saudi Vision 2030*, its huge modernization and diversification program. In effect, all regional countries opposed any Israeli plan to forcefully transfer Palestinians from Gaza.

Nonetheless, Weitman and his proponents claimed, "closing the Gaza issue will ensure a stable and increased supply of Israeli gas to Egypt and its liquefaction."[106] In March 2024, he was seconded by Jared Kushner, Trump's son-in-law, who was promoting the (cleansed) Gaza as a property opportunity, although his private equity operation was dependent on investment by Saudi Arabia, which opposed forceful population transfer.[107]

As the leak of Weitman's report unleashed uniform international censure, the Misgav Institute deleted the post from Twitter and from its website. But that did not stop Weitman, who interviewed on his Facebook page Likud MK Ariel Kallner, who supported his ideas. After October 7, Kallner called on Israel to bring about a "second Nakba" in Gaza that would "overshadow the Nakba of '48."[108]

"Settlement Brings Security"

In January 2024, the far-right Israeli settler organization, Nachala, hosted a "Settlement Brings Security" conference featuring the head of the Samaria Council, Yossi Dagan, and Nachala chairwoman Daniella Weiss. The two had been busy re-establishing previously dismantled outposts, with the backing of the Netanyahu cabinet. Now they petitioned for the creation of Israeli settlements in Gaza after the Israel-Hamas War. "It's the end of the presence of Arabs in Gaza," Weiss said to reporters. "Many, many Jews that will return to the settlements, that will build new settlements."[109]

Projected on the wall during Weiss' presentation was her vision of postwar Gaza, a map with six nucleus groups laying claim to settlements spanning the entire length and width of the Strip. It featured no areas for Gaza's 2.3 million Palestinians. "The Arabs will move," said Weiss. Israel should give them no food, "so they will have to move. The world will accept this." (Figure 1-6).

> It is not to a foreign land that we are returning, but rather
> to the golden sands of our Gaza. There is no "day after"—the
> day after is today, it's every day in which the Jewish people is
> victorious and returns to settle in Gaza.[110]

Figure 1-6   "Returning to Gaza"

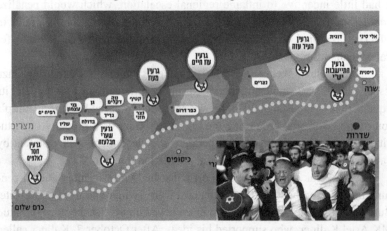

Attended by Israeli cabinet ministers and members of parliament, the "Return to Gaza Conference," held on January 28, 2024, presented a map showing plans for the re-establishment of 15 Israeli settlements and the addition of 6 new ones (map). Netanyahu cabinet's national security minister Itamar Ben-Gvir was seen dancing at the conference. *Source: Al Jazeera/AJ Labs* (Jan 29, 2024)

It reflected the old, ominous practice of renaming Palestinian locations, "Zeitoun" to "Shivat Zion" and "Shu'iya" to "Gibor Oz" and so on, one which, ever since 1947 has trailed the destruction of the Palestinians' society, economy, and infrastructure.

Portrayed as the "godmother of the Zionist settler movement" by CNN, Weiss claimed that 500 families had already signed up to resettle through Nachala.[111] Nachala received support from U.S. groups, including from "rich Americans," as Weiss called them. These groups included Americans for a

Safe Israel, founded in 1970 as an American counterpart to the Land of Israel Movement – a euphemism for the movement for Greater Israel – asserting Israel's historic, religious, and legal rights to the land reclaimed in the 1967 war.

Representing the far-right Israeli orthodox settlers, Weiss's parents belonged to Lehi or the Stern group, the pre-independence far-right terrorist gang excelling in assassinations of Arabs, British, and occasionally Jews. Lehi had a track record in the ethnic cleansing of Palestinians. In the 1970s, Weiss had played a vital role in the Gush Emunim, the pioneer settler movement that gave rise to the violent Jewish Underground and years of terror in the occupied territories. She had been sentenced and fined for anti-Palestinian vigilante violence and assault against Israeli police.[112] Seeking to exploit October 7, her Nachala, which has been involved with at least one killing, raised funds via crowdfunding to annex the West Bank and Gaza under Israeli leadership.[113]

These specifics have been habitually ignored in Weiss's interviews, in which she is typically portrayed as a grandmotherly figure.

The Compensation Challenge

The efforts at expulsions are not just a reflection of mob violence and nationalist hatred. They reflect the quest for power and property. Historically, material incentives have fueled ethnic expulsions, which are not some sort of unplanned convulsions of society, but net effects of deliberate policy choices. Typically, it was the "lure of property and social mobility, as well as economic necessities"[114] that shaped the course and consequences of ethnic cleansing in the wake of World War II and that also marks the efforts at population transfer in the Gaza Strip.

In *Hitler's Beneficiaries* (2005), German genocide historian Götz Aly showed how Hitler won the allegiance of ordinary Germans by engaging in a campaign of theft and by channeling the proceeds into generous social programs. Hitler did not just force his people's consent. He "bought" it. While Jews and other citizens of the Nazi-occupied lands suffered crippling taxation, mass looting, enslavement, and destruction, most Germans enjoyed an improved standard of living. Reservations were swept away by tax breaks and government handouts.[115] Despite a very different historical context, Israeli settlers benefit from extraordinary handouts, subsidies and tax breaks, while Palestinians cope with rampages, looting and occasionally war and devastation. With developers in the West Bank working intimately with the Likud coalitions, the racket has been lucrative. Property buyers in sought-after settlements have paid full price, while the developers are benefi-ciaries of state-subsidized land in less desirable areas.[116]

Prejudice, hatred and distrust play a major role in ethnic cleansing, but the latter cannot be explained away with psychology or abnormality. It is the political economy of ethnic cleansing that accounts for the genocidal atrocities illuminating the dark side of democracy and the nation-state, or as Michael Mann has argued: "All cases of cleansing involve material interests. Usually, members of an ethnic group come to believe they have a collective economic interest against an out-group."[117]

A durable resolution of the Middle East conflict requires a comprehen-sive settlement of the Palestinian refugee issue writ large, the net effect of these expulsions. It is reflected by three sets of inter-linked issues: repatria-tion, resettlement, and compensation. *Repatriation* focuses on the Palestinian refugees' right of return, which Israel vehemently opposes, preferring that the registered Palestinian refugees accept permanent civil status in their current countries, or relocation elsewhere. *Resettlement* is favored by Israel, which would prefer to see most of the registered Palestinian refugees required to accept permanent civil status of in their present homes in Syria, Lebanon and Jordan, or re-location elsewhere. By contrast, Palestinians resist this option because it would abolish their legal right to return and mitigate decades of suffering in exile. *Compensation* focuses on the individual and collective claims of the Palestinian refugees and the displaced for the restitution of or indemnification for their lost homes and properties in present-day Israel, and monetary damages for related losses.[118]

The effort to secure compensation or reparations for the Palestinians who were forcibly displaced during the establishment of the state of Israel began with the UN General Assembly Resolution, UNGAR 194. Approved in December 1948, it proposed that

> refugees wishing to return to their homes and live at peace
> with their neighbors should be permitted to do so at the earliest
> practicable date, and that compensation should be paid for the
> property of those choosing not to return and for loss of or damage
> to property which, under the principles of international law or in
> equity, should be made good by the Governments or authorities
> responsible.[119]

A Committee established by the General Assembly spent years gather-ing data on Palestinian refugee property losses, while in Israel the Absentees' Property Law (1950) acknowledged the property seizures. As there was little progress toward peace in the region, the issue was largely suspended in the subsequent decades, except for some scholarly studies.[120] It was only after the Cold War that refugee repatriation, property restitution, and other refugee claims were seen as vital for conflict resolution, particularly after the violent ethnic cleansing in Bosnia. Yet, the Palestinian case lingered until the peace process took off and several international conferences on the matter ensued. And so, the Pandora's Box was finally opened and tentatively addressed in the Camp David talks and by the Clinton Parameters (2000) and particularly the Taba Negotiations (2001). Palestinians identified more than 31 separate clauses on refugee property and other claims, whereas Israelis excluded any restitution, focusing on compensation.[121] Furthermore, progress in these talks was overshadowed by the inception of the Second Intifada (2000–2005) in the occupied territories and the 2008–2009 Gaza War. After Benjamin Netanyahu returned to power in 2009, Israeli-Palestinian talks went nowhere.

At the time, based on international compensation standards, one comprehensive review estimated Palestinian material losses in 1948 at $3.4 billion; that is, equivalent to $297 billion in 2009 dollars when interest is assessed on the total, at a rate of 1.7 percent over inflation. Valued conservatively, that could amount up to about $435 billion today.[122] Another review put the estimate of these losses at a total of $3 billion, equivalent to $295 billion at 2008; or up to about $430 billion today.[123] Unsurprisingly, most such reviews have identified a huge gap between the estimated refugee losses and Israel's willingness to compensate these losses. In the Taba Negotiations, Israeli negotiators reportedly thought that some $2–3 billion might be made available for compensation.

Even though these talks focus only on the losses in the late 1940s, they are no minor issue. The issue of refugee compensation is highly complex, sensitive and contested.[124] Both sides perceive such restorative issues as a Pandora's Box. To one, it is a metaphor for hope; to the other, a source of great potential misfortune.

Conflicts are a convenient way to defer the reckoning.

Chapter 2
SETTLEMENT EXPANSION

At the beginning of 2024, Zvi Sukkot, Knesset member of the Religious Zionist Party, urged the government to "occupy, annex, and demolish all the houses [in Gaza], and build large neighborhoods and settlements."[1] It sounded harsh, but at least he was truthful. Since 2010, Sukkot had been arrested in an investigation of a mosque arson and expelled from the West Bank for violent anti-Palestinian attacks. He had defended Jews suspected of firebombing a Palestinian family and been arrested for alleged involvement in "price tagging"; that is, vandalism and violent settler attacks against Palestinians. And the list goes on. By early 2023, Sukkot was in the Knesset. After October 7 he chaired the Knesset Subcommittee for Judea and Samaria (read: the West Bank).[2] Inspired by rabbi Meir Kahane, he had once belonged to a violent zealot group, Revolt, advocating dismantling the state of Israel to establish a Judaic theocracy.[3] Now he was in a position to shape the future of the land.

How did the Messianic far-right march into institutions they hoped to then pull to pieces? Ironically, the Israeli settlement policy was first developed by the Labor governments, which paved the way for the foxes to take over the henhouse.

RISE OF THE SETTLEMENTS

When Hassan bin Talal, then-Crown Prince of Jordan, published his report on *Palestinian Self-Determination* (1981), he opened his work aptly: "Historically, seldom have unity, self-determination, statehood and security been so bedeviled as in the case of Palestine."[4] Compressed into a single sentence, the opening illustrated the arrogance of ambitions embedded in Israel's Zionist enterprise and why this hubris, though initially so certain of itself and so confident of its inevitable future, could result in its own doom. Israel controlled the occupied territories, but it wasn't in control of the events that would transform those contested ancient areas, even Israel itself.

When the dominant Labor coalition set out to consolidate politically the role of the occupied Palestinian territories, it was at the peak of its power and confident it could resolve the status of the West Bank and Gaza in an internationally acceptable way. Barely a decade later, the Labor alignment was defeated politically by the hard-right Likud coalition. It had failed to resolve the status of the occupied territories and it had alienated the international community.

Labor's Allon Plan

Following the Six-Day War in June 1967, the Israeli settlement policy was first outlined by the Labor coalition of Levi Eshkol (1895–1969). Born in Kiev, present-day Ukraine, Eshkol joined the Zionists as a teen and immigrated to Palestine where he became a founder of the Labor Party and led many key institutions of the pre-state Yishuv, including the powerful labor federation Histadrut and the paramilitary Haganah. His government also created the foundation for the special political and military relationship with the United States prior to the Six-Day War.[5]

Known for caution, gradualism and consensus-building, Eshkol was not a man of extremes. Yet, during the 1967 war, he established the national unity government, which gave the conservative Israeli right its first foothold in the cabinet. After the War, he allowed the construction of the first settlements in the name of national security. Though a labor man and a kibbutznik, Eshkol's parents came from religious families. He wasn't immune to Messianic sentiments. As he noted after the Six-Day War,

> For the first time since the establishment of the State, Jews pray at the Western Wall, the relic of our holy Temple and our historic past, and at Rachel's Tomb. For the first time in our generation, Jews can pray at the Cave of Machpela in Hebron, the city of the Patriarchs. The prophecy has been fulfilled: "There is recompense for the work, the sons have returned to their borders."[6]

Eshkol's approach to the settlements was defined by Yigal Allon (1918–80), who grew of age in a family of immigrants from today's Belarus. Allon was one of the early leaders of the pre-state terrorist group, Haganah, and its elite Palmach, and the military leader of several subsequent wars. But he was also a skillful labor politician, and as a co-founder of the left-wing Mapam Party, who contributed to the founding of the Labor Party itself. Just days after the June 1967 War, Allon introduced his settlement plan to the cabinet. Though not adopted officially, it became the *de facto* guideline for the early settlement policy. Essentially, the Allon Plan sought to end Israeli occupation of parts of the West Bank with a negotiated partition of territories, in the name of the "historical right to settle the land of Israel."[7] To Israel's neighbors, the Plan was dead on arrival. They urged Israel's immediate withdrawal from the Jordanian-annexed West Bank, Syria's Golan Heights, the Egyptian-occupied Gaza Strip and Egypt's Sinai Peninsula. In the view of the Palestinians, the Six-Day War, or what they called the Naksa (lit. "Setback"), was a déjà vu of the original Catastrophe of Nakba in 1947–48.

Suspending the issue of the refugees, the Allon Plan advocated a partitioning of the West Bank between Israel and Jordan, the creation of a sovereign Druze state in the Golan Heights, and the return of most of the Sinai Peninsula to Egypt. It supported an Israeli annexation of East Jerusalem; Gush Etzion, a set of Judean settlements that had been lost with the 1949 armistice lines; and most of the Jordan Valley. All remaining parts of the West Bank, containing the majority of Palestinians, were to be returned to Jordan, linked to the country by a corridor through Jericho (Jordanian option), or reorganized as Palestinian autonomous territory (Palestinian option) (Figure 2-1).

The majority of the government seemed to favor the Palestinian option, including Allon: "The last thing we must do is to return one inch of the West Bank."[8] He was skeptical of the staying power of Jordan's King Hussein. Hence, the preference for Palestinians' "quasi-independent autonomy." Hussein found the Allon Plan "insulting." After all, the Plan retained a third to nearly half of the West Bank through settlements and military outposts along the Jordan Valley. Presumably, these settlements and installations would protect Israel from potential invasion. The Plan also called for the development of Jewish neighborhoods in East Jerusalem, the rehabilitation of the Old City's Jewish Quarter, and the annexation of Gaza, whose Arab inhabitants would have to be resettled elsewhere, although the Israeli government did not rule out discussions on its future, according to Hussein.[9]

Unsurprisingly, the Plan was opposed by the Palestinians in both the West Bank and Gaza, and by the right-wing and ultra-religious Israelis.

A Covert Military Plan to Confiscate Land for Settlements

As the Allon Plan was officially introduced in the Israeli cabinet in September 1967, a group of young Bnei Akiva religious-Zionists, who later morphed into the ultra-orthodox group called Gush Emunim, took up residence in Gush Etzion, south of Jerusalem and Bethlehem in the West

Figure 2-1   The Allon Plan, 1967

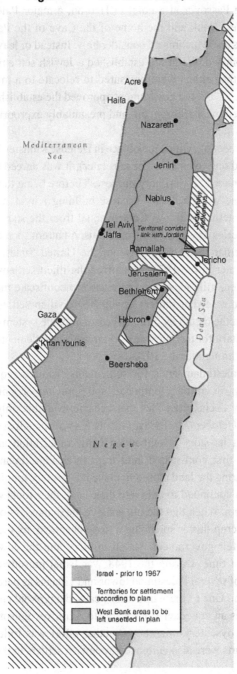

Source: Palestinian Academy for the Study of International Affairs

Bank. In April 1968, another group received a permission from the military to celebrate the Passover at a hotel in Hebron, a major Palestinian city in the southern West Bank and the home of the Cave of the Patriarchs which Jews, Christians and Muslims all consider holy. Instead of leaving afterwards as they had promised, the group established a Jewish settlement in Hebron. A month later, the settlers were pressured to relocate to a military building and in December 1968, the government approved the establishment of Kiryat Arba, a settlement near Hebron, on land presumably expropriated for "security needs."

In a 1970 meeting, which took place in Defense Minister Moshe Dayan's office (disclosed only over four decades later), it was agreed that the houses would be constructed "for military purposes" before being turned over to the settlers. The ruse was necessary because building Kiryat Arba constituted a violation of international law. Controversial from the start, the settlement would spark a series of violent confrontations. A pattern soon emerged. Since neither the international community nor the United States, Israel's major superpower partner in the 1970s, penalized the illicit settlement expansion, it prevailed. Then, military orders were used to confiscate more Palestinian land in which the Jewish settlers established civilian settlements. Though suppressed from the media by military censorship, the system of confiscating land by the military for the purpose of establishing settlements "was an open secret in Israel throughout the 1970s."[10]

Seizing Palestinian lands for settlements featured requisitioning the land, ostensibly for military purposes, and spraying of land with poison, as evidenced by declassified files that became available only in 2023, just months before October 7.[11] Today, Gitit is a small Israeli settlement in the West Bank, but its story is embedded with colonization and biowarfare. In 1972, Israel first confiscated land from three Palestinian villages from Al-Jiftlik, declaring the land closed to make it a military training zone. When the Palestinians continued to cultivate their land, their tools were sabotaged by Israeli soldiers. When that did not achieve the dispossession, the area was sprayed with a crop duster spreading a toxic chemical, by the joint decision of the Golda Meir government, Israeli military and the Jewish Agency. It was not the first time. During the 1948 War Israel poisoned the wells and water supplies of several Palestinian towns and villages as part of a biological warfare program. One of these operations caused a typhoid epidemic in Acre in May 1948, as an aqueduct from Kabri to Acre was poisoned with flasks of typhoid and dysentery microbes. Another effort was foiled by Egypt in Gaza. Such efforts were also embraced by Jewish settlers in the West Bank in the early 2000s, when Israeli police suspected militant Jews were behind the poisoning of the only water source of Tatwana, a Palestinian village.[12]

Until the Yom Kippur War, the Israeli Defense Force (IDF) had tacitly contributed to the building of new settlements. Why did the labor government permit effective collusion with the settlers?

Golda Meir's cabinet was on the defensive, coping with increasing criticism by the right-wing and the religious parties due to the 1973 War losses. Settlers seized the moment. Their settlements began to expand from Gush Etzion and the Hebron Hills in the southern West Bank toward the north, which brought them in closer proximity to Palestinian cities like Nablus, Ramallah and Jenin. At the same time, the settlers began to infiltrate the institutions, merging with a faction of the National Religious Party and forming the Gush Emunim ("Bloc of the Faithful"), which soon emerged as the ideological core of the settler movement. Furthermore, even as the government sought to distance itself from the settlers, private money began to pour in, particularly from the United States.

First Wave of Settlement Expansion

In the course of the 1970s, the primacy of national security considerations began to shift from security per se toward dreams of national redemption. The rise of Ofra, the flagship settlement of Gush Emunim, tells the story. While Shimon Peres (1923–2016), the preeminent labor leader serving as defense secretary in the late 1970s, did not permit the military to provide assistance other than basic protection, he didn't prevent private aid that transformed Gush Emunim's camp into Ofra. Confiscated from three nearby Palestinian villages and towns of Ein Yabrud, Silwad and Taybeh, much of Ofra was built on privately-owned Palestinian land, which was illegal even by Israeli law.[13] While trying to avoid an open conflict with the settlers in the area, Peres's "compromise" was opposed by his own prime minister, Yitzhak Rabin, because it effectively fostered Jewish settlements amid densely-populated Palestinian areas, which Labor governments had resisted in the past.[14]

Why did Peres compromise? Born Szymon Perski in present-day Belarus, the smart, smooth and shrewd young man was soon noticed by the strongman Ben Gurion, who became his mentor. Though serving in Rabin's government, the ambitious Peres was Rabin's old nemesis. In the early 1960s, Peres had a central role in the talks with President John F. Kennedy on the first sale of U.S. military equipment to Israel. Subsequently, he moved smoothly like a ballerina within and among multiple labor and centrist parties, including Mapai, Rafi, the Labor and its Alignment, and the centrist

Kadima. Hence, too, the new blueprint. Since land occupation was deemed illegal under international law, Peres shunned military assistance by the government in settler expansion, at least in public. However, the influx of private aid was tacitly encouraged, which transformed military camps into civilian settlements. The blueprint included a window for *foreign* private capital by mainly American-Jewish donors, effectively enabling a chunk of settlement funding to be gleaned from offshore sources.

If the idea of appeasement was to bring settlers into the labor camp, it failed. But it made Peres more acceptable among the settler zealots. After the 1977 right-wing election triumph, the Begin government recognized Ofra as an official community.[15] Moreover, the right-wing Likud coalition was augmented by the National Religious Party, including its extremist Gush Emunim faction, and the conservative and ultra-orthodox Agudat Yisrael party. The odd threesome was the settlers' dream come true. Far from fostering national security, Peres's compromise brought far-right and ultra-religious zealots into close proximity with Palestinians, which compounded friction, confrontation and conflict. That was very much in the interests of the settlers, who aimed to disrupt any disengagement from the settlements. Effectively, it was "strategy of tension," settler style. As aggressive settler expansion inflamed tensions with indigenous Palestinians, it was depicted as a security threat against Israel, which was then used as a pretext for further expansion. At the same time, successive American presidents turned a blind eye and were tacitly resigned to settlement expansion in the occupied territories. The international community did a lot of barking, but little biting.

Despite all its liabilities, the original Allon Plan was motivated mainly by considerations of national security, as defined by the Israeli military and intelligence, not by mythologies of national redemption concocted by rabbinical mystics and religious zealots. When the first peace protests took place against Gush Emunim, there were barely 2,000 settlers. By the end of the 1970s, the number of settlers had increased to more than 5,000. In the past, wars for survival had united the Israelis. Starting in the 1980s, wars to maintain the occupation would divide the nation.

It was a pivotal moment for Israel. And it left an irreversible mark on its national security doctrine as its wars with Arab states gave way to counterinsurgencies seeking to sustain colonization. With the Lebanon War (1982) and the subsequent First Intifada (1987–93), Israel found itself in a new status quo. The uprising started spontaneously in the occupied territories, but it was structurally over-determined: the Palestinians saw themselves detached from their leadership, neglected by other Arab powers and the international community. After all, the PLO had fought Israel within its borders via Egypt,

Jordan, Syria and Lebanon, and internationally, yet without much tangible progress. And by 1987, after two decades of settler expansion, Arafat and PLO leadership were in Tunis. Palestinians saw themselves under a tightening squeeze with no progress in sight. That's when in December 1987, an Israeli truck collided with a civilian car in the Jabalia refugee camp, killing four Palestinian workers. Israel saw the collision as an accident; Palestinians, as a purposeful response for the killing of an Israeli in Gaza days earlier. Appropriate conflict resolution might have contained the turmoil. But as the occupying power, Israel saw it as a major security threat and deployed 80,000 soldiers in response. Coupled with the use of lethal force, the disproportionate reaction poured more oil into the flames.[16]

The Intifada had little in common with Israel's past wars with the adjacent Arab states. It was more akin to counterinsurgencies in Algeria in the 1950s, in Vietnam in the 1960s or perhaps in South Africa in the apartheid era. Yet, there was continuity as well. Israeli counterinsurgency operations did not start with the First Intifada. They could be dated from Israel's border wars around 1949–56, particularly Israel's retaliatory responses at the time, including the Qibya massacre in which almost 70 civilians were killed.[17] These wars set patterns of conduct that would mark the subsequent uprisings in the occupied territories. Except for the brief peace process in the 1990s, the effective march to darkness began already in the late 1940s, not in 1987. And the stage was set for that march with the 1917 Balfour Declaration. The two-state solution that Israel accepted in 1947 had been mainly tactical, as Ben-Gurion suggested at the time.

THE WAR ON PEACE

The Turn to the (Hard) Right

As long as Labor coalitions dominated the governments, national security dominated settlement discussions. After the Likud coalitions took over in the late 1970s, national security gave way to visions of national redemption in those debates. A broad secular transformation ensued in Israeli politics, economy and security. It wasn't just about the turn to the (neo)conservative right, which took place in many Western democracies with their goodbyes to the Keynesian policies that had supported the long, postwar economic expansion. It was also about the re-emergence of the hard-right revisionist Zionism aiming to establish "Iron Wall" security arrangements between Israel and its proximate Arab neighbors. As the head of the right wing, Menachem Begin (1913–1992) had struggled long for government responsibility. Born in today's Belarus, he joined the revisionist youth movement, Betar, as a teen and became a disciple of Ze'ev Jabotinsky, the founder of the revisionist Zionism. Having lost his family in the Holocaust, Begin subsequently assumed the leadership of the paramilitary Irgun. After terrorism and assassinations of the British and the Arabs, he ordered the bombing of the British military HQ at the King David Hotel in Jerusalem. By June 1948, the dissension between Ben Gurion's Labor government and Irgun's revisionists climaxed in a violent confrontation between the two, nearly unleashing a civil war.[18] After Irgun gave in, Begin launched the conservative Herut ("Freedom") party that would linger in opposition for three long decades.[19]

Unlike the mainstream Zionists, Begin and his supporters believed in Greater Israel, which would comprise not just the occupied territories but Transjordan and much of the Sinai Peninsula. During his campaign, he captured the hearts and minds of the settlers with his pledge to create "many Elon Morehs." The phrase referred to an orthodox Jewish settlement close to Nablus. Created on land confiscated by the Israeli military from two Palestinian villages, Elon Moreh was another offspring of Ofra. The pledge for many more Elon Morehs was precisely the promise the settlers wanted to hear.

Begin made Ariel Sharon, the maverick military hawk, the chief of Likud's settlement surge. Sharon's plan was premised on settlement expansion but also on their strategic locations to preempt the establishment of a Palestinian state. The plan was torpedoed by the High Court of Justice, which limited the state's ability to expropriate land on security grounds in the Elon Moreh ruling. As a result, Sharon exploited the 1858 Ottoman Land Code, which still guides the Israeli land regime in the West Bank. In Israeli hands, "non-cultivated lands have been declared 'state lands,' an act that allowed them to be used for settlement expansion."[20]

Yet, the initial settler euphoria dimmed when Begin signed the Israel-Egypt peace treaty, which led to the removal of the Jewish settlements from Sinai. Gush Emunim saw it as a possible precedent for a withdrawal from the West Bank since the Camp David Accords included a deal on Palestinian autonomy. So, the settlers focused on the Yamit settlement, located in the Rafah Plain region south of the Gaza Strip. Though it had just 2,500 residents, it was envisioned as a hub of 200,000 people with ambitious plans for a port and a Dead Sea canal.[21]

The settlers tried to make Yamit into a point of resistance, even civil war, which was somewhat ironic in light of Yamit's history. It had actually been built in 1975 on Bedouin land from which some 1,500 tribal families had been expelled under direct orders by then-defense minister Moshe Dayan and the then-head of southern command, Ariel Sharon. The idea of settling northeastern Sinai was touted by Dayan and subsequently proposed in a document on the occupied territories. Presumably, it was the last nail in Egyptian President Sadat's decision to launch the Yom Kippur War so that Egypt might regain Sinai and begin peace talks.[22]

Booming "Lifestyle" Settlements

When Begin's Likud replaced Golda Meir's Labor Party in 1977, East Jerusalem and a number of surrounding villages had already been effectively incorporated into Jerusalem. Under Begin, Likud rejected relinquishing Israeli control over the occupied territories. After the Likud government got its second term in 1981, Begin described his overriding goal as "to ensure that Judea, Samaria [i.e., the West Bank], and the Gaza Strip are never handed over to foreign rule." Exploiting a set of loopholes in the Supreme Court's ruling on expropriation of privately-owned land in the West Bank and Gaza, it engaged in a series of land seizures.[23]

And so, the Likud coalition rushed ahead with all the elegance of a megalomaniacal rhinoceros in a porcelain store. The dawn of the Likud era fostered the outflow of tens of thousands of Arabs from the West Bank, while the demographic increase of those who stayed declined dramatically,[24] reflecting the social unease that burst into flames with the First Intifada in 1987.

The second wave of settlement expansion ensued after the Camp David Accords and lasted until the Oslo Accords in the early 1990s. These years saw the expansion of Gush Emunim and their settler peers, the emergence of the Jewish Underground, Kahane's loyalists and the subsequent Kahanite movements. And yet, the most important force fueling the settlement expansion had little to do with the Messianic far-right. Instead, it involved the heavily publicized and lavishly funded government campaign to flood the territories with new settlers. It was not ideology but subsidies and tax relief that drove the soaring "lifestyle settlement." These were a new breed of Jewish settlers representing

> apolitical middle class urban dwellers, willing to move to sub-urban settlements in the West Bank and Gaza where dreams of a detached house, clean surroundings, and a comfortable commute could be realized at affordable prices. Launched in November 1982 this campaign was supported by an elaborate array of discounts, subsidies, and tax breaks. Businesses were offered tax benefits

equivalent to the highest available in various underdeveloped regions within the Green Line, generous investment assistance made available—40% of total in low interest loans and 35% in grants, as well as insurance against losses that might be associated with change in the territory's political status. Contractors were sold land at a 95% discount and given generous guarantees and the full cooperation of government ministries in return for rapid development of selected sites. Individuals could choose to build their own home at reduced rates on lots sold at discounted prices. Alternatively, apartments could be purchased at subsidized prices—well below what they would cost within the Green Line (exact prices varied depending on location and the income level of the purchaser). According to the director general of the Ministry of Housing and Construction, that ministry spent 44% of its entire budget for 1982 to support these and other settlement projects in the West Bank.[25]

While these settlers sympathized with the Messianic settlers, most were not motivated by religious dreams. They had no intention to get their hands dirty in biblical lands in the heat of the desert sun. They were largely white-collar employees commuting from coastal Israel. Some had had enough of austerity. Others had grown weary of harsh life in cities where jobs were harder to find and development towns offered few venues for mobility. Trading security for benefits, they had little interest in reclaiming ancient Judea or Samaria. What inspired them was a lifestyle dream of being able to live in a spacious villa just a half-hour drive from Israel, cushioned with state subsidies that made transportation, housing and living significantly less costly.

With these attractive villas for sale in the middle of the West Bank "at the price of a small apartment in Jerusalem," influential journalists like Amos Elon thought it possible that by 1985, 100,000 settlers would live in Judea and Samaria. Presumably, the opposition no longer had the will or the ability to resist annexation. Rather, the question was "whether there is any territory left to compromise. It would appear not."[26]

Bur had the settlement expansion reached the inflection point of irreversibility?

The Irreversibility Thesis

In the Allon Plan, the settlements were a bargaining chip, designed primarily to boost Israel's national security. As such, a simple annexation of the West Bank wasn't an option because it would have drastically changed Israel's demographic balance from a Jewish majority toward a Palestinian Arab majority. Hence, the renewed efforts at the depopulation of Palestinian lands in tandem with Jewish settler expansion in those lands. What the Labor coalitions had legitimized in terms of national security, the Likud governments justified as national redemption.

Though beneficiaries of the Likud government's policies, the settlers were concerned over the future. Located near Hebron, Elon Moreh was a settlement that had been transferred following an appeal and a court decision in 1979. Built on Bedouin land, Yamit was evacuated in 1982, despite a 45-day hunger strike by Gush Emunim. Feeling betrayed by Begin, the settlers saw no assurance of Jewish rule over Judea, Samaria and Gaza. Nonetheless, former deputy mayor Dr. Meron Benvenisti announced *de facto* annexation was in full swing, due to the Begin government's huge changes in the West Bank.[27] He argued that a *de facto* annexation of the West Bank and the Gaza Strip had become "irreversible."[28] Though known as a moderate center-left dove, his conclusions were rejected by the Labor leadership, fearing they could turn into a self-fulfilling prophecy.

In the first decade of the Israeli occupation, Arab unwillingness to accede to further losses was presented as the major obstacle to resolving the Arab-Israeli conflict. After 1982 the question was no longer "whether the Arabs can make a credible commitment to territorial compromise, but whether the Israelis, as a result of their increased presence in the West Bank and Gaza, can do so."[29]

But did the data back up the irreversibility thesis? During the second wave of settlement expansion from the late 1970s to early 1990s, the number of settlers in the West Bank increased more than tenfold from 10,000 to more than 136,000. Even the First Intifada (1987–93) did little to halt their inflow. But despite settlement expansion and high natural increase, the settlers still account for barely 14 percent of the West Bank's total population today

In the aftermath of the Israel-Egypt peace treaty (1979), the most radical settler fringe went underground. They wanted to ensure an irreversible settler future through violence.[30]

SETTLEMENTS FOR NATIONAL REDEMPTION

The Jewish Underground, Gush Emunim and American Donors

The Jewish Underground was inspired by rabbi Meir Kahane's clandestine activities in Israel. "Arab terrorism must be met with an eye for an eye," he said during our meeting in 1974. What was not known at the time was that he had already launched his clandestine group, "Terror Against Terror" (*Terror K-Neged Terror* – TNT). TNT militants engaged in violent attacks against Palestinians ranging from simple vandalism to mass shooting and murder. Originating from Kahane's Jewish Defense League (JDL) in New York City and Kach in Israel, the hard-core acolytes comprised three dozen hardline Jewish-American settlers based in Hebron.[31]

With the Underground's covert attacks, a vicious cycle of violence ensued in the West Bank and Jerusalem, including burning of Arab vehicles and newspaper offices, beatings of residents, Molotov cocktails thrown at homes, firing on busses of Arab workers and hand-grenade attacks against both Muslim and Christian holy sites.[32] By 1984, the members of the Underground were "very close" to carrying out a planned multiple bombing against Muslim holy sites on the Temple Mount. Possible actions included an effort to crash a drone packed with explosives on the Temple Mount, or a manned suicide attack with a light aircraft during mass Muslim worship on the Mount, or assassination of a prominent Temple Mount Muslim leader (Figure 2-2).[33]

Figure 2-2   The Temple Mount Tinderbox

The Dome of the Rock (*left*), the Western Wall (*center*) and Al-Aqsa Mosque (*right*).
Source: Wikimedia Commons

These extremists launched car bomb attacks against several Palestinian mayors, including the mayor of Nablus, Bassam Shakaa (who lost both of his legs); of Ramallah, Karim Khalaf (who lost one of his legs); and of El Bireh, Ibrahim Tawil (the planted explosive device was discovered). When the co-founder of Gush Emunim, rabbi Haim Drukman, heard about the attacks, he rejoiced, citing the Bible, "Thus, may all Israel's enemies perish!"[34]

The Underground was not the only terrorist group of its kind. At the turn of the 1990s, the *Sicarii* followed in its footprints, engaging in a series of terrorist attacks on Palestinians and Jewish political figures sympathetic to the plight of the Palestinians. Like drug gangs in Latin America, they sent threatening letters to public media figures, judges, and moderate right and left-wing parties. In their view, any peace initiative was an abomination, and any peacemaker fair game. By 1990, they were threatening the family of deputy PM Shimon Peres, labor members of the Knesset and a dozen activists of the Peace Now movement.[35] In May 1989, eight Kach party activists were arrested over the *Sicarii* attacks, but then released on bail. Most served short terms and the ringleaders were pardoned.[36] The pattern – severe offenses, soft sentences, lax enforcement – turned these fanatic criminals into the rock stars of the Messianic far-right.

Meanwhile, financial intermediaries steered increasing money flows to settlement groups. Take, for example, Russian oligarch Roman Abramovich, whose companies donated $100 million to Elad, a settler organization in East Jerusalem. These funds came to light only through a leak of bank documents.[37]

In Hebron, Menachem Livni, former chair of a Jewish settlement, and other vigilantes hoped to inspire fear among Arabs, while American Jews spearheaded fund-raising for the group's covert activities. In 2003, when Livni was convicted for shooting at a Palestinian truckdriver, he founded a winery to produce Cabernet Sauvignon in Kiryat Arba.[38] But it wasn't a real business. He received a monthly salary from the Brooklyn-based Hebron Fund. U.S. tax-deductible donations supported Jewish terrorists persecuting and killing Palestinians.

For a period of over half a decade, these donors alone gave the settlements more than $220 million in tax-exempt funds.[39] Livni's mentor, Moshe Levinger, an orthodox rabbi and Gush Emunim principal participated in multiple violent acts against Palestinians.[40] He got minimal sentences, serving only short periods. When Levinger died in 2015, Prime Minister Netanyahu, courting the constituency, sent a letter of condolence to the family, describing Levinger as "an outstanding example of a generation that sought to realize the Zionist dream, in deed and in spirit, after the Six-Day War."[41]

Ultimately, this lethal zealotry was inspired by an ailing, fragile rabbi who swore in the name of God, but relied on American dollars.

Rabbi Kook's Apocalyptic Jewish Redemption

In early June 2024, thousands of Messianic far-right Israelis paraded through East Jerusalem as part of an annual Jerusalem Day flag march. Rejoicing in Israel's conquest of the city and its holy sites in the 1967 War, some chanted racist slogans, "Death to the Arabs!" and "May your village burn!"; these calls were darkly reminiscent of "Death to the Jews!" amid pogroms a century before. Still others called for dismantling the Al-Aqsa Mosque to make way for the ancient Jewish temple. A mob of religious Jewish students attacked Palestinian journalist Saif Kwasmi after it had tried to get at a female journalist.

The popular parade began in 1968, a year after the Six-Day War. It was the creation of rabbi Zvi Yehuda Kook, the spiritual founder of Israel's Messianic far-right. Born into an influential rabbinical family in modern-day Lithuania, he was the son of the legendary rabbi, Abraham Isaac Kook.

Rabbi Zvi Yehuda Kook (1891–1982) lived his life in anticipation of the Apocalypse. In his magic kingdom, the first stage of the messianic redemption arrived with the establishment of the state of Israel in 1948. It was the reincarnation of the Davidic Kingdom. The second stage ensued after the 1967 War with the redemptive process premised on extending Jewish rule over the occupied territories on the back of the settlements. The third stage would come with the establishment of the Third Temple Mount on the holy Muslim sites of Al-Aqsa Mosque and the Dome of the Rock in East Jerusalem.[42] Hence, the recurring high-profile visits by sympathetic Israeli leaders to the Temple Mount to escalate the end of times. To the faithful, such turmoil was a divine sign because they expected the redemptive process to climax in the restoration of Jewish sovereignty over Amalek, the enemy nation of the Israelites. Hence, too, the coded references to "Amalek" by Israeli soldiers and Prime Minister Netanyahu during the Gaza War.[43]

In Kook's view, international condemnations of Israel were an offense to God. Due to his hostility to Christianity, he was particularly critical of protests by Christian leaders.[44] He condemned as illegitimate Begin's peace talks with Egypt, Israel's withdrawal from Sinai and Palestinians' administrative autonomy.[45] God desired the territorial integrity of the land of Israel; a singular sanctified unity superseding all negotiated compromises. The laws of the Torah, the first five books of the Hebrew bible, took precedence over secular law.[46] Intellectually, it was supernatural hogwash, but in the minds of the rabbi's supporters these mystical musings to replace the rule of law with the rule of Torah was pure Jewish fundamentalism.

Despite the Messianic sound and fury of Kook's proponents since the 1970s, such ideas just didn't sell in Israel as long as labor leaders still shunned religious hocus-pocus. So, the fortunes of Kook's Mercaz HaRav yeshiva waned in Jerusalem as it struggled to survive with just a few students.[47] The Six-Day War unleashed the sweet sound of the cash register. Kook's apocalyptic visions resonated with the graduates of Bnei Akiva at a time when their efforts to change the course of the centrist National Religious Party were still being snubbed. A frustrated and secretive fraternity called *Gahelet*, a nucleus of Torah pioneers, transformed the fringe teachings into an actionable platform for radical zealotry. By adopting Kook as their spiritual leader, the members of Gahelet propelled him "from the status of a forgotten, ridiculed figure at the margins of the Torah and Zionist worlds into an outstanding Israeli personality with a magnetic influence on a broad circle."[48]

Networks of Hate

As time went by, Kook's acolyte networks proliferated. Until 2014, his student Dov Lior, one of the most vocal rabbis to demand the ethnic cleansing of Palestinians, served as chief rabbi of extremist Jewish settlers in "Judea and Samaria" (the West Bank). In the late 1980s, Israel's attorney general had to bar Lior's election to Israel's supreme rabbinical council after a wild public outcry over his comment that captured Arab terrorists could be exploited as guinea pigs in medical experiments. But the extremist rabbi was on a roll. He met rabbi Meir Kahane's associate, Baruch Goldstein, whose massacre in the Cave of the Patriarchs would leave 29 Palestinian worshippers dead while wounding 125 people. This was followed by the first revenge suicide attack by Hamas. Lior declared Goldstein "as holy as the martyrs of the Holocaust." The next year, Lior released rulings in which Prime Minister Rabin was targeted as a *rodef*, as a traitor who endangers Jewish lives and thereby can be executed in the name of public good. After the religious Kahanist extremist Yigal Amir met Lior, he used that ruling to legitimize the premeditated assassination of Rabin in 1995. By the early 2010s, Lior was being questioned by police on suspicion of inciting violence, legitimizing the killing by Jews of innocent Palestinians, including children since, as the argument went, they may pose a future threat by growing up to be evil like their parents. So, it was permissible in some situations to kill non-Jews according to Jewish law. The incitement to mass murder of non-Jewish children was based on Messianic rabbi Yitzhak Shapira's *The King's Torah* (2009), which was distributed by rabbi Meir Kahane's followers. Before retirement, Lior stated that it was permissible to kill Palestinian civilians and destroy the entire Gaza Strip to protect Jewish people in the South.[49] Inspired by Kook's teachings, rabbi Lior's rulings resonated among the hateful Messianic far-right.

In the United States, extremist financiers donated monies to settlers that was used in anti-Palestinian violence. But Lior was just one of the many acolytes of rabbi Zvi Yehuda Kook, including rabbi Moshe Levinger, one of the principals of the extremist settler movement, Gush Emunim. Starting in 1975, the spiritual father of the terrorist Jewish Underground was arrested and charged numerous times, in relation to settler violence in Hebron or Kiryat Arba.

The list also featured Haim Drukman, a veteran Knesset member and the influential proponent of modern-day hard-right Religious Zionism. He fought against Israeli withdrawal from Sinai, the Oslo Accords and Gaza. In his later years he championed Naftali Bennett and, eventually, the self-proclaimed fascist, Bezalel Smotrich. What made Drukman different from extremists like Lior who lit fires in the shadows was his influence as a legislator and teacher of a generation of Israeli political, military and intelligence leaders, including Bennett, a business millionaire and former PM of the hard-right Jewish Home party, who is often interviewed by mainstream media as a seasoned voice of Israeli policies; Israel Katz, a minister of Netanyahu's far-right cabinet infamous for his promotion of the obliteration of Gaza; Benny Gantz, the retired Army general and war cabinet's center-right opposition leader whom the White House was selling as Netanyahu's moderate alternative in summer 2024. And then, there was Yossi Cohen, former chief of Mossad who had been responsible for the multiyear covert operation to suppress the International Criminal Court's investigations on Israel's activities in the occupied territories; a high-profile debacle his predecessor at the head of Mossad characterized as "Mafia-like."[50] These are just some samples of Kook's broad and deep influence networks that permeate Israeli society and politics, military and intelligence (Figure 2-3).

But even oracles must eat. Where did the money that financed rabbi Zvi Yehuda Kook and his yeshivas come from? The short answer is: the promised land. Not Israel, of course, but Florida.

Figure 2-3 Rabbi Zvi Yehuda Kook's Acolyte Networks

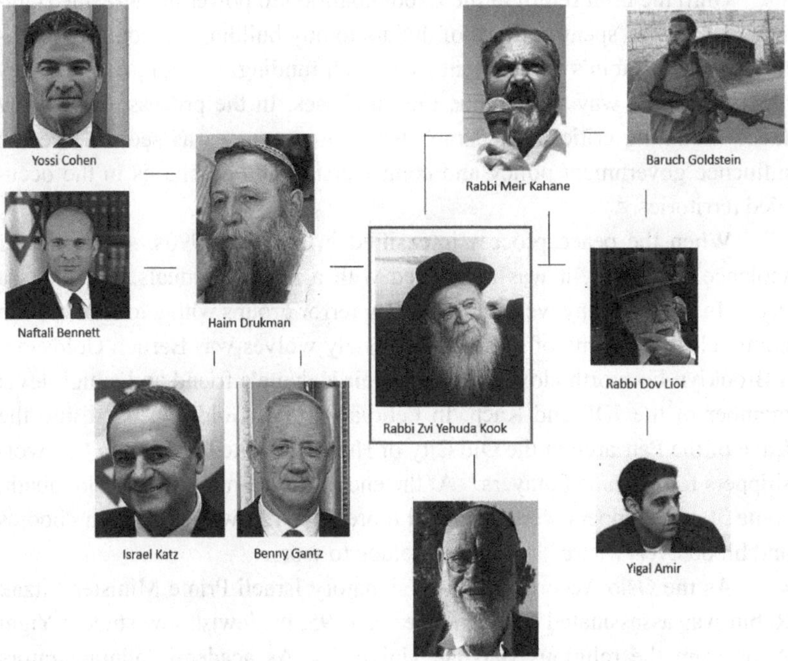

Yossi Cohen

Naftali Bennett

Haim Drukman

Israel Katz

Benny Gantz

Rabbi Meir Kahane

Baruch Goldstein

Rabbi Zvi Yehuda Kook

Rabbi Dov Lior

Yigal Amir

Financial Proxy Revisionism

One of Kook's generous supporters was Irving I. Moskowitz, a Florida-based bingo and gambling billionaire who had lost his extended family in the Holocaust. The retired doctor built his wealth by buying and selling hospitals. After the Six-Day War, he began assisting Jewish settlements in the occupied territories.[51] These activities reached a new level in 1988, when he bought the Hawaiian Gardens bingo parlor in a small, largely Hispanic city near Los Angeles, California. Sued unsuccessfully for alleged abuses of its workers, he launched the Irving I. Moskowitz Foundation. Yet only a small chunk of the money went to charities on location, whereas millions went to the occupied territories, including Jerusalem, and to campaigns to defeat peace plans.[52]

Most American Jews focus on "non-political" humanitarian and philanthropical pursuits in the United States. Like American Zionists, Moskowitz favored Israel as a beneficiary. But unlike them, he preferred *revisionist* Zionism. The right-wing pathos was better aligned with his economic position in America. His settlement financing represents what might be called financial proxy revisionism. By the mid-1990s, his foundation had dispersed more than $18 million in bingo profits to various causes. Today it is one of the top 1,000 private foundations in America.[53]

Until the brief return of the Labor coalition to power in 1992, the right-wing Likud had spent millions of dollars to buy buildings in contested territories. When Rabin's government froze such funding, foreign private money emerged as the way to continue the purchases. In the process, Moskowitz faced mounting criticism in Israel, where his money was seen as used to influence government policy and controversial land purchases in the occupied territories.[54]

When the peace process intensified in the mid-1990s, so did settler violence. Officially, it was associated with a few individuals. But that's a myth. In reality, many were supported by terror groups with a long history in ethnic cleansing. One of these not-so-lonely wolves was Baruch Goldstein, a Brooklyn-born orthodox Jew, rabbi Meir Kahane's friend and a high-level member of the JDL and Kach. In February 1994, Goldstein burst into the Cave of the Patriarch in the Old City of Hebron, packed with up to 800 worshippers for Ramadan prayers.[55] At the end of the 10-minute-long bloodbath, some 30 worshippers were dead and more than 125 wounded, with "bodies and blood everywhere."[56] It was a prelude to worse.

As the Oslo Accords took off, signatory Israeli Prime Minister Yitzak Rabin was assassinated on November 4, 1995, by Jewish law student Yigal Amir from the religious Bar-Ilan University. As academic administrators took a serious, critical look at this religious institution in Israel, financial proxy revisionists in America celebrated it. Condemning the peace process as a "slide toward concessions, surrender and Israeli suicide," Moskowitz had his foundation give $100,000 to the Bar Ilan University.[57] A year later, Moskowitz persuaded Netanyahu to open a controversial tunnel next to the Al-Aqsa Mosque compound, one of the most sacred sites of the Arab world.[58] When the tunnel was opened in September 1996, it unleashed days of rioting, causing the first conflict between the Israeli military and the just-created Palestinian National Security Forces (NSF). After Jerusalem, the turmoil spread across the West Bank and Gaza. Almost 80 people, mainly Palestinians but also Israelis, were killed and hundreds wounded.[59]

Some saw the Temple Mount riots as the end of the Oslo Accords and the peace process. To Moskowitz, they likely meant a glorious new beginning. He gave millions of dollars to the American Friends of Ateret Cohanim, which owned more than 70 buildings in the Muslim Quarter of Jerusalem.[60] Promoting a Jewish majority in the Arab neighborhoods in East Jerusalem, it is dedicated to rebuilding the destroyed temple. The only way to accomplish that objective is to tear down the Dome of the Rock and Al-Aqsa Mosque. Furthermore, Likud's rising star, Benjamin Netanyahu, ardently supported the U.S. billionaire's land purchases in Jerusalem after Moskowitz donated funds to a think tank dedicated to his brother. Even after his death, Moskowitz's funds continue to boost settlement construction projects in the West Bank, while settler organizations like City of David Foundation, commonly known as El'ad, and Ateret Cohanim seek a Jewish majority in Palestinian neighborhoods of Jerusalem. The recipients of his annual Moskowitz Prize for Zionism feature a set of the who's-who among the Messianic far-right.[61]

In the United States, Moskowitz sponsored neoliberal economic policies and neoconservative initiatives, including the Project for the New American Century that inspired the Bush Jr. administration's War on Terror, uber-hawkish think tanks engaging in climate denialism, such as the Hudson Institute, and their geopolitically driven peers fostering American hegemony around the world.[62]

SETTLEMENT ESCALATION

The Third Wave of Settler Expansion

Israel's undertaking in the Oslo Accords was predicated on the idea that facts on the ground would not be altered, yet the settlement expansion continued. The Rabin government did not allow new settlement building, but it permitted old ones to be expanded. Hence, the proliferation of new neighborhoods, which were effectively new settlements. With the subsequent Netanyahu government, there was no halt to settler expansion. Through 1995–2000, the number of settlers in the West Bank soared by 50,000 people, up to more than 203,000. As Israeli voters opted for the hardline right-wing, Palestinians saw no alternative but armed struggle. The fading prospects of peace unleashed the Second Intifada (1987–1993), sparked by Ariel Sharon's provocative intrusion into the Al-Aqsa compound. At the same time, the number of settlers increased by another 50,000, with the total climbing to a quarter of million.

Although Ariel Sharon's election win in 2001 was thought to undermine efforts at settlement removal, growing international pressure pushed him to the negotiating table. At the end of 2003, Sharon announced his intention to unilaterally withdraw from Gaza. Did it change the status of the Gaza Strip as an occupied territory? Yes and no. Yes: Israelis no longer controlled Gaza from within. No: Israelis controlled the Strip from without. The form of the occupation had changed, not its substance. Or as Israeli journalist Gideon

Levy put it back in 2010: "The jailer pulled out of the jail and was now holding its prisoners captive from without. Yes, Gaza was and still is the largest prison on earth, a gruesome experiment performed on living human beings."[63]

The decision had been motivated by the 2003 Geneva Accord, President Bush's Roadmap initiative and particularly the weary views of his veteran military peers. In addition to the settlements in Gaza, Israel dismantled four settlements to enable Palestinians' territorial contiguity from Jenin to Nablus in the northern West Bank, as part of the disengagement. However, he had second thoughts about the occupation, overall. Intriguingly, Sharon was one of those military leaders who, since the late 1940s, had done his utmost to achieve Greater Israel, often by using lethal force, including massacres. It was amid the violence of the Second Intifada that some of his equally hawkish military colleagues began to express skepticism about Israel's hardline politics. So, Sharon began to draft plans for a unilateral pullout that would leave two-thirds of the West Bank to Palestinians. In January 2006, four months after Israel's unilateral disengagement from the Gaza Strip, Sharon was on the phone with Rafi Eitan (1926–2019), his security adviser. A former Mossad operative who had been in charge of Eichmann's capture from Argentina in the early 1960s and Jonathan Pollard's spy debacle in the U.S. in the 1980s (and thus subject to an arrest warrant by the FBI), Eitan had cooperated with the Thatcher government in counter-terrorism and tracking the Irish Republican Army (IRA), which led to Irish orders to find and kill him. He had played a key role in the first exports of surveillance software exports and nuclear triggers. Eitan was a lot of things, but no dove.

Just a month before his stroke, Sharon discussed with Eitan a preliminary plan to leave the West Bank, while maintaining the maximum number of settlements under Israeli control. "Sharon knew that we must disengage from the Palestinians in the West Bank too; that we can't continue occupying a foreign people," Eitan acknowledged in 2013. Sharon dubbed his plan "the mosaic separation," because it left most Israeli settlements intact, while only allowing isolated Palestinian villages access to large urban centers through an intricate system of underpasses and tunnels. As Eitan put it: "Arik [Sharon] said: 'Let's divide Judea and Samaria and take roughly one-third for ourselves, leaving two-thirds for the Arabs.' Under this plan, the Jordan Valley and the Judean Desert would remain ours." Subsequently, Eitan advised Netanyahu to implement the Sharon plan immediately. "We must disconnect from them [the Palestinians] as much as possible," he said, favoring a plan to hand over the area known as "the Triangle" in northwest Israel (Israeli Arab towns and villages adjacent to the Green Line) with its up to 300,000 Arab citizens to the future Palestinian state.[64] The move would have turned some 15 percent of Israeli Arabs into Palestinian citizens.

Once again, the settlers protested vehemently, predicting a "civil war." Yet, most Israelis welcomed Sharon's disengagement from Gaza. But as he moved ahead to implement a similar disengagement from the West Bank, his health gave in. After two strokes, he fell into coma, passing away a few years later. Another historic opportunity for peace was missed.

Following Sharon, Netanyahu retook his place as Likud's leader. Initially, his hands were tied by the Obama administration seeking to contain settlement expansion. But as Obama's first term ended, Netanyahu's government began to re-issue building permits in the occupied territories. Hence, the simmering turmoil some termed the "silent Intifada" set the stage for the 2015–16 violence, and so on.

U.S. Charities and Settler Funding

Through these decades, the settlement expansion has been fueled by Jewish-American money. The early investigative reports on these funding flows went hand in hand with the Obama years, when the administration still tried to contain the settlement expansion. In 2010, a *New York Times* examination of public records in the U.S. and Israel identified some 40 American groups that had collected more than $200 million in tax-deductible gifts for Jewish settlements in the West Bank and East Jerusalem over the prior decade. Most of the funds went to schools, synagogues, recreation centers and the like, but they also paid for housing, guard dogs, bulletproof vests, rifle scopes and vehicles to secure outposts deep in occupied areas. Israel had ended tax breaks for contributions to settlement-building in the West Bank a decade ago; the U.S. hadn't.[65]

Did the naming and shaming halt the money flows? Not at all. In 2015, a *Ha'aretz* investigation demonstrated how tax-free U.S. donations had enriched the settlements by more than $224 million in the past five years. In turn, these money flows were coupled by Israeli corporations that were giving millions of dollars to the West Bank settlements: from corporate giants like the Delek energy group and Israel Petrochemical Enterprises and dairy conglomerate Tnuva, cellular carrier Cellcom and Bank Hapoalim to smaller companies like chocolate manufacturer Hashachar Ha'ole and Leo Shachter Diamonds."[66]

Following in the footprints of financiers like Moskowitz, tax-exempt U.S. non-profits were driving the settler organizations seeking to evict Palestinians from their homes in East Jerusalem. Typically, the Israel Land

Fund was relying on the help of private American donors, who got tax deductions for the money they gave to U.S.-based nonprofits, which then funneled the money to Israeli settlements. Most of the Israel Land Fund's budget came from the Central Fund of Israel, a U.S.-based nonprofit.[67] Pro-Israel money – read: pro-Netanyahu, pro-Likud – has also been used to unseat Democratic progressives in congressional races.[68] These monies did not emerge out of the blue during the Gaza War. After decades of influence efforts, such operations intensified with the rise of neoconservatives in the U.S. and Israel some two to three decades ago. This merry-go-round has been going round and round until today. The only thing that has gradually changed is public awareness, particularly since October 2023 in the aftermath of Israel's ground assault on Gaza. Not all Americans wanted to fund – or be seen as funding – settler violence in the West Bank or genocidal atrocities in the Gaza Strip. Furthermore, the role of U.S. charities funding the settlements and thus Palestinian expulsions and dispossession had become far too blatant to ignore any longer. Hence, the public campaigns against such funding drives (Figure 2-4).

The Rise of the Settlements

In 2016, the number of settlers exceeded 400,000. And when the Trump administration stepped in, the settler expansion accelerated. Under his "peace to prosperity plan," *all* settlements would remain under Israeli sovereignty and not a single settlement would be removed. It was a plan for, of and by the settler interests, designed to appeal to Trump's wealthy pro-Zionist financiers, the Israeli lobby and evangelical Christians in the U.S. Once again, Palestinians served as collateral damage in the raising of U.S. campaign finance. The return of a Democrat to the White House made no difference and resulted in no reset. Relying on stated multilateralism, President Biden, the self-proclaimed "American Zionist," and his administration offered more of the same.

Indeed, as globalization gave way to U.S.-led trade protectionism and American efforts to contain the rise of China, the expected global recovery in 2017 fell apart and geopolitical conflicts proliferated. Following the COVID-19 pandemic-induced global depression, the proxy war in Ukraine unleashed an energy and food crisis. Preoccupied with quarantines, the world looked inward. It was a perfect cover for elevated settlement expansion. Between 2015 and 2023, the settlers' numbers soared from 386,000 to almost 520,000 (Figure 2-5a).

Under the 1947 UN Partition Plan, Jerusalem was seen as a distinct but unified international city. After the 1948–1949 War, it became divided

Figure 2-4 How U.S. Charities Fund Israeli Settlements

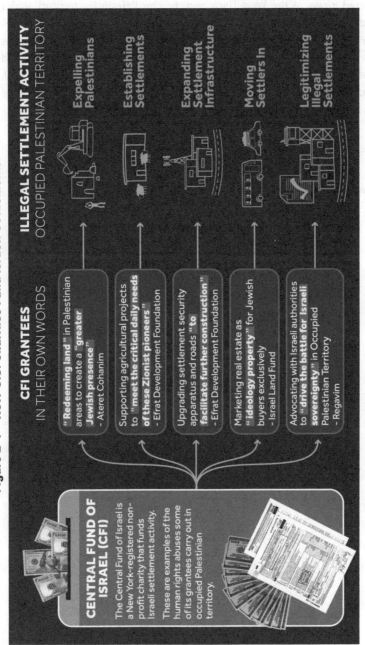

Source: Visualizing Palestine, May 2023 (https://visualizingpalestine.org/)

between Israel (West Jerusalem) and Jordan (East Bank). East Jerusalem is considered a part of the West Bank and thereby Palestinian territory under international law. Occupied by Israel since the Six-Day War, Palestinians see the city as the capital of their presumptive state of Palestine. Yet, it was effectively integrated into Jerusalem in 1980; an act that was condemned internationally. In 2020, East Jerusalem had a population of nearly 600,000, of which over 60 percent were Palestinian Arabs and nearly 40 percent were Jewish settlers (Figure 2-5b).

Figures 2-5a-e   Settlements and Expansion

(a) Jewish Settlers in the West Bank, 1970–2024

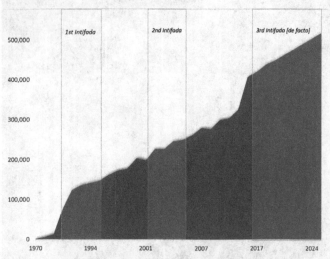

(b) Number of Israelis in East Jerusalem

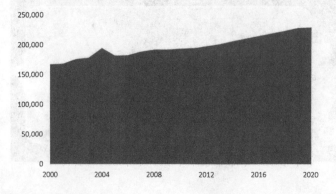

(c) Rise of Illegal Outposts, 1991–2023

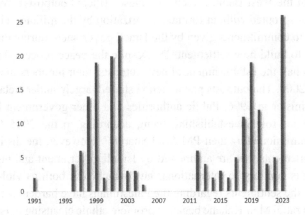

(d) Declarations of State Lands

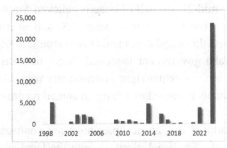

(e) Settler Violence Incidents*

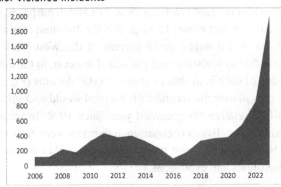

*Includes Palestinian property damage and/or casualties in settler-initiated incidents.

Source: (a) Data from Peace Now, author; (b) Peace Now (ICBS/JIIS); (c,d) Data from Peace Now, author; (e) Data from OCHA, author.

According to Israeli law, an outpost is an unauthorized or illegal Israeli settlement in the West Bank. Effectively, these "[illegal outposts] were settlements that sprouted without formal authorization by the military administration, due to commitments given by the Israeli government during the Oslo process not to build new settlements."[69] Despite the peace process that was supposed to halt the establishment of new outposts, their numbers increased fivefold by 2000. The outposts phenomenon started largely under Netanyahu as prime minister in 1996. Public authorities and other government bodies played a major role in establishing them, according to the 2005 *Sasson Report*, commissioned by then-PM Ariel Sharon.[70] However, the distinction between settlements that are authorized by Israeli government and outposts that are not is contrary to international law, which sees both as violations. Meanwhile, the sentiments regarding the Palestinians have hardened accordingly. When rabbi Meir Kahane began to promote ethnic cleansing in Israel in the 1970s, his doctrines and successors were described as "foreign imports" well into the 1990s. By the mid-2010s, half of Israelis believed Arabs should be expelled or transferred from Israel.[71] Increasing U.S. and international pressure brought the numbers down and kept them at zero around 2005–2011. Subsequently, the Netanyahu government launched illegal outposts again, despite international pressure. As center-right governments were surpassed by far-right cabinets, the numbers soared, reaching an annual record of 26 in 2023 (Figure 2-5c).

According to international law, an occupier must not confiscate land for the needs of the occupier. So, Israel came up with the legal acrobatics of "declaring" instead of "confiscating" land. This declaration is based on a subversion of the Ottoman land law from 1858. For Israeli purposes, it allows land confiscation by another name. Through this bizarre interpretation, Israel has taken over 900,000 dunams, or 16 percent of the West Bank prior to October 7. That is 500 to 5,000 dunams per year. However, in the first half of 2024, declarations of state land shot to almost *24,000* dunams (Figure 2-5d). If the pace will prevail over the second half, the total would soar up to 48,000 dunams, or 10-fold relative any recorded year since 1998. In other words, while Gaza was burning, Israeli occupation authorities were rushing to take over the West Bank, which, if past is any guidance, could result in a major round of new hostilities and expulsions.

Settler Violence

Since the 1970s there has been a tacit collusion between the Israeli state and the settlers. It is a functional, symbiotic system. The state takes

of dollars within just days.[78] By May that year, Secretary of State Blinken told Congress he had determined the punishments for the soldiers and officers in all four cases to be adequate.[79] It was yet another example of the slap-on-the-hand approach to ensure effective impunity. More than a century ago, Jews knew only too well the consequences of mobs rushing into Jewish neighborhoods while calling for "Death to the Jews!" Today, Palestinians know exactly what will follow when Jewish settlers burst into Arab neighborhoods crying for "Death to the Arabs!"

These dark calls did not come out of the blue. When I met Kahane in Israel in the mid-1970s, his followers had already adopted them. In the 1980s, the slogans were discovered at the University of Haifa, along with swastikas.[80] By the 1990s, those shouts were often heard in Israeli soccer stadiums. In the 2000s, they became common in graffiti, price tag attacks and mob violence, and today they are a common occurrence in the annual Jerusalem Day marches commemorating the 1967 War and occupation of East Jerusalem.

If or when a Messianic far-right effort to destroy the Temple Mount succeeds, it is likely to be accompanied with that haunting plea for blood and fire: "Death to the Arabs!"

Settlements as a Security Burden

By the 2020s, there were almost 7 million Israeli Jews and 7 million Palestinians, respectively. Of the Jews, more than 460,000 were settlers living in the West Bank, over 220,000 in East Jerusalem. Both lived in a relatively small proximate area. But where the Israelis enjoyed their liberal democracy and rule of law (in turn, Israeli Arabs lived under military rule from 1948 to 1966 and see themselves as second-class citizens in Israel), Palestinians were subject to a harsh military autocracy and suppressive emergency laws. Israeli Jews were free to pursue their dreams of happiness; Palestinians lived under an apartheid regime, as acknowledged by an increasing number of Israel's elite military, intelligence and police authorities.[81]

Ever since the 1970s, the settlers and their financiers have argued that the settlements ensure Israel's security. In this view, settlers allow the residents of Tel Aviv to breathe easy because the settlements are good for national security. Until recently, more than half of Israelis believed the settlements were good for national security.[82] Yet, in contrast to conventional wisdom, the settlements have been a security burden for Israel. Their presence in the West Bank depends on civilians (Jewish settlements) and security (military and intelligence). For decades, the settler lobby has portrayed the settlements as a kind of protection provided by the Israeli military and intelligence. In reality, the settlements cannot provide their own protection. Worse, when Israel's security forces have to service the settlements, it distracts from their mission, compounds their challenges and causes a security-deficit within Israel.[83]

In the past four decades, there had been no major war between Israel and its Arab neighbors. Prior to October 7, peace treaties were prevailing with Egypt and Jordan and there was a semblance of normalization with some Gulf states. Israel's military prowess had been superior, thanks to U.S. military aid. Furthermore, the Palestinian resistance had expressed willingness to engage in peace talks, as the PLO had done since the 1980s and as Hamas had signaled since the late 1990s, but to no avail. Nevertheless, due to the Separation Wall and fragmentation of the West Bank, the line of defense that the Israeli Defense Force (IDF) is required to protect is today about five times the length it would be without the settlements. Moreover, the shift from the Open Bridges policy, which contributed to Palestinian jobs and rising living standards during the era of Labor coalitions, has been replaced by the Likud's Iron Wall policy, which undermined Palestinian jobs, living standards, indeed their very future.

Stunningly, again pre-October 7, the IDF had to deploy more than half its active forces, and in crisis situations even two-thirds of them, in the West Bank. And that was more than the forces allocated to guarding all other fronts combined (Lebanon, Syria, Gaza, and the Jordanian border along the Arava). Worse, these allocations had to be coupled with a large contingent required to protect the settlements themselves. According to estimates, some 80 percent of IDF forces in the West Bank were allocated to settlement guard duty, while only the remaining 20 percent focused on defending Israel proper within the 1967 borders.[84] Furthermore, the IDF presence and operations contributed to several major uprisings, which penalized economic prospects in Israel as well. If Israeli military presence in southern Lebanon was the architect of Hezbollah, its presence in the West Bank and use in the suppression of Gaza has served as the midwife of Hamas.

In the old status quo, the Israeli military was compelled to misspend its resources to protect settlers by compromising security in Israel proper, whose protection should have been its primary task. The military strategy was self-destructive. The political strategy was short-sighted and untenable. The economic consequences remain adverse. Furthermore, after October 7, more than 250,000 Israelis were evacuated from their homes on the southern and northern fronts, according to Israeli estimates.[85] In summer 2024, the number of Israelis displaced was still estimated at close to 90,000, most of them from northern Israel, due to Hezbollah strikes in support of Gaza. Not only did the costs soar, but the socio-economic gap between those living in central Israel and border communities deepened.

JUDEOCIZING PALESTINE

The Israeli Legal Simulacrum to Legitimize the Occupation

Today, most countries condemn Israeli settlements in the occupied territories, whereas Israel repudiates the condemnation. The former rely on international law, particularly the Fourth Geneva Convention.[86] By contrast, Israel argues that the West Bank does not fall under the definition of "occupied territory" by international law. Rather, it is a "disputed territory" since the previous occupying power (Jordan) lacked an internationally recognized claim to it. In light of the demise of the Ottoman Empire at the end of World War I and the end of the British Mandate in 1948, Israel argues that no international actor has superior legal claim to it.

The same goes, Israel argues, for the Gaza Strip, but for a different reason. In this view, Israel no longer occupies Gaza because it does not exercise effective control or authority over any land or institutions *inside* the Strip. Furthermore, Israel argues that Gaza does not belong to any sovereign state. In reality, the 1948 War left Egypt in control of the Strip, which Israel took over in 1967 and controlled until its unilateral withdrawal in 2005. The disengagement left the internal control of the Strip to the Palestinians, but it was effectively negated by the many tactics whereby Israel exerted external control of the Strip: through the airspace, coastline, and the supply of the critical infrastructure, including water, communication, electricity and sewage networks. Hence, Israel's effective sovereignty over Gaza.

In the 1967 War, Israel also occupied the strategically pivotal Golan Heights. In 1981, the Likud government passed the Golan Heights Law, which amounted to a *de facto* annexation of the territory. In 2019, the Trump administration recognized the area as being under the sovereignty of Israel. But it was a unilateral declaration. Adopted in 1981, UN Security Council Resolution 497 holds that the Israeli-controlled area in the Golan Heights is occupied territory belonging to Syria.

For decades, international public sentiment echoed these legal and effective realities, but mainly in rhetoric. In the aftermath of October 7, such voices have strengthened and grown more vocal, particularly in the case of the International Criminal Court (ICC) and International Court of Justice (ICJ).

The Extra-Legal Effort to Annex the West Bank

In December 2022 the UN General Assembly (UNGA) requested the International Court of Justice (ICJ) to issue an advisory opinion on the legal status and consequences of Israel's control of the occupied Palestinian territories, thereby pushing the doctrinal and theoretical gap regarding the definition of annexation to a boiling point. The UNGA resolution addressed two possible classifications for Israel's control of the territory: annexation and unlawful occupation.[87] But what qualified as annexation? In fact, had Israel already annexed the West Bank or was the prolonged control over the territory still below the "annexation threshold" as Israel asserts, pending its formal declaration of annexation? Presumably that's why the Israeli far-right moved fast in early 2023, to create irreversible "facts on the ground."

When Smotrich first floated his plan in February 2023, some Israeli jurists warned that transferring powers from the military would amount to annexation in law. The prohibition on the annexation of territory is a cornerstone of modern international law. However, since annexation has not been clearly defined, it is uncertain what would qualify as annexation, while a formal declaration by the annexing state clearly would do so. Obviously, official annexation was bound to result international backlash and vocal U.S. protests. So the Messianic far-right chose to use Israeli democracy to subvert that. In the dual state, while the normative regime operated by its democratic rules, its prerogative aspect facilitated achieving the desired objectives with minimal resistance.[88] The war on Gaza diverted attention away from Smotrich's appointments, order and transfer of responsibilities in the West Bank. Officially, the Biden administration opposed annexation policies, yet Smotrich's administrative decisions were seen as internal Israeli measures. Preoccupied by the election year, the international spillovers of the Gaza War, and its own political survival, the West Bank was not a White House priority.

In early 2023, several Israeli jurists had warned that the existing ideas of *de facto* annexation and unlawful occupation were framed in such a manner that by the time the situation crossed a critical threshold, it had already become annexation *de jure*. In their view, the organizational changes we are now witnessing qualify as Israeli annexation of the West Bank."[89] When Smotrich moved ahead with the transfer of powers, the jurists described the order as "a step toward *de jure* annexation – even though Israel may not have officially annexed the territories."[90]

To the Messianic far-right and many center-right parties, the prior Jewish nation-state bill, the proposed judicial reforms, the Gaza War and the parallel administrative changes in the West Bank had a common denominator: seizure of the historical opportunity to finally annex the occupied territories – Judea,

Samaria and Azza (Hebrew for Gaza). These efforts moved to a new phase in April 2024, when as Netanyahu's minister, Bezalel Smotrich appointed his ideological ally, Hillel Roth, as the deputy in the civil administration with responsibility for enforcing building regulations in settlements and outposts. It was still another win for prerogative action. Roth had studied at Od Yosef Chai Yeshiva in the Yitzhar settlement in the northern West Bank. Both are notorious for their extremism; the vanguard of the settlers' retaliatory attacks against Palestinians, according to Shin Bet.[91] After studies in this racist environment, Roth served as a senior official in the notorious Honenu organization providing legal representation to far-right Israelis in ethno-nationalist and anti-Arab crimes.[92]

In the West Bank, the governance of civilian affairs used to be under the authority of the Civil Administration and the military. As a result, the pro-settler Religious Zionism Party, led by Smotrich, could not exercise political control over the settlements. All of this changed in late May 2024, when the outgoing head of the IDF Central Command, Maj. Gen Yehuda Fuchs, signed an order permitting the head of the Civil Administration to delegate his areas of authority to the newly created position of "deputy head" of the Civil Administration, whereby Roth replaced Fuchs. In a highly controversial move, the IDF thereby quietly transferred effective responsibility from the civil administration – the Israeli body governing in the West Bank – to officials led by Smotrich at the defense ministry. In a private pro-settler event, Smotrich acknowledged that a separate civilian system "will be easier to swallow in the international and legal context. So that they won't say that we are doing annexation here."[93] Which, of course, is what they were doing.

During the creation of the far-right cabinet, Smotrich and his allies had insisted on the control of the administration in the West Bank in order to extend Israeli sovereignty over the West Bank. The transfer served as an instrument to suppress legal checks on settlement expansion. In July 2024, Israel's government approved the largest land seizure in the West Bank since the 1993 Oslo Accords. The land declaration covered 1,270-hectare (3,138 acre) section of the Jordan Valley near Jericho. It was followed by the approval of 5,000 new housing units in dozens of Jewish settlements. As before, the strategic goal was to prevent the West Bank from becoming a part of a sovereign Palestine and thus, as Minister Smotrich liked to put it, to "thwart" its statehood preemptively.

To the secular critics, the transfer arrangements, land declarations and housing approvals were the beginning of the end of the old "land for peace" approach. If the land couldn't be traded, peace couldn't be achieved. To the Messianic far-right, they were a step closer toward national redemption; Israeli sovereignty of all biblical lands.

From a Buffer Zone to Smotrich's "Decisive Plan" in Gaza

In 2017, Bezalel Smotrich, then still a young Knesset member, presented his "Decisive Plan." It represented an endgame of sorts for the Israeli-Palestinian conflict, which he proposed in closed religious Zionist circles.[94] The plan portrayed the conflict as devoid of any reconciliation, or partition. Smotrich envisioned a singular state from the sea to the river, for one nation only: the Jewish people. True to his beliefs, he built on biblical allegories, which to him were no allegories at all:

> When Joshua entered the land, he sent three letters to its inhabitants: Those who want to accept [our rule] will accept; those who want to leave, will leave; those who want to fight, will fight. ... When they have no hope and no outlook, they will leave, just as they left in 1948.[95]

Since October 7, Smotrich had championed what he described as a "humane" solution for Gazan non-combatants: a voluntary population transfer.[96] The two-state model was a dead end. Smotrich's solution was simpler: Eliminate the adversary, resolve the dilemma.

A month after October 7, U.S. Secretary of State Antony Blinken presented his outline of what America would *not* accept as the "day after" in Gaza:

> No forcible displacement of Palestinians from Gaza. No use of Gaza as a platform for launching terrorism or other attacks against Israel. No diminution of the territory in Gaza and a commitment to Palestinian land governance for Gaza and the West Bank and in a unified way.[97]

In light of the on-the-ground realities, Blinken was living in a parallel universe. Most Gazans had already been displaced, the attacks continued, the infrastructure had been leveled and the path was paved for mass starvation and worse. To the Messianic far-right in Israel, the White House was a convenient asset in God's plan for Israel; not more, not less. In their view, America was not just rich and powerful, but soft and manipulable. What the White House needed was a legal pretext for Israeli activities, ideally spiced with ethical dressing.

Setting aside international optics, Israel, as the White House knew quite well, had already informed several countries in the region, including Jordan, the UAE, Türkiye, and Saudi Arabia, that it was planning to establish a buffer zone between Israel and Gaza upon conclusion of the war. In early 2024, these were the new facts on the ground threatening to endanger Israel's border coordination with Egypt, economic deals with Jordan, normalization with Saudi Arabia and ultimately its peace treaties with Egypt and Jordan. So, while the Netanyahu cabinet's official emissaries paid tribute to their American sponsors by regularly bowing to liturgical phrases, such as a "two-state solution" and "no displacement," they were tenaciously building the institutional framework for a singular Jewish state and for displacing almost 2 million Palestinians. The envisioned buffer zone was projected to be 1 kilometer wide, stretching along the entire 60-km border with Israel, featuring military posts, paved roads and surveillance devices. It would be off limits to Palestinians, including the residents who had lived or cultivated fields in it before the war. Effectively, it was a "security zone," and as such its creation constituted a war crime.[98]

To create the buffer zone, Israel was destroying almost everything in the area, including residential buildings, public structures such as schools, medical clinics and mosques, fields, groves and greenhouses. Upon completion, the zone would encompass 16 percent of the already-overcrowded Gaza Strip. Moreover, Israel was building a control corridor by splitting the Strip into two parts allowing the IDF to control traffic on strategic roads. Such a projected long-term presence was ominously reminiscent of Israel's initial infiltration of the West Bank, which was split into three areas in the 1990s and then isolated with a Separation Barrier and further effectively sub-divided by check points.

It was death by thousand cuts – adverse change which occurs seemingly gradually in the kind of neglected increments that can be ignored internationally.

Chapter 3
THE TIES THAT BLIND

On October 10, 2023, just three days after the calibrated yet brutal military offensive by Hamas and other Palestinian militants against Israeli military and civilians, U.S. President Joe Biden addressed the nation in the White House pledging unwavering support for Israel, even as Israeli military was pummeling Gaza.

When the pure, unadulterated evil is unleashed on this world . . . we must be crystal clear: We stand with Israel. . . .[1]

To cope against "unadulterated evil," America would ensure Israel had the military assets it needed to thwart the "sheer evil" that he compared with "painful memories and the scars left by a millennium of antisemitism and genocide of the Jewish people."[2] There was no effort at context, history, or balance; only the certitude of a Manichean world of good and evil, legitimate and illegitimate, Israel and Hamas. It was the beginning of those missteps that paved the way to what Senator Bernie Sanders would later call "Biden's Vietnam."

Where Biden still cautioned Israel not to repeat America's military excesses after September 11, 2001, the Republicans had fewer such inhibitions. Following more than half a year of atrocities, Nikki Haley, South Carolina's former Republican governor and failed presidential nominee, visited Israel and its northern border with Lebanon, in tandem with Israel's disastrous Rafah offensive. Criticizing the Biden administration for temporarily withholding weapons to discourage attack on Rafah, Haley signed Israeli artillery shells with the inscription "Finish Them!" and "America loves Israel." Accompanied by Danny Danon, Israel's hawkish ex-UN ambassador, she was then off to visit West Bank settlements, which are not recognized under international law.[3] A decade before the Gaza War, the ambitious Danon had championed punitive attacks against Palestinian civilians and infrastructure. Opposing any peace agreement with the Palestinians, he had proposed cutting off all electricity and fuel supplies to Gaza to force Hamas into a cease-fire. When an Israeli soldier was kidnapped, he proposed "leveling Gaza." After October 7, he welcomed the far-right minister Smotrich's proposal to expunge Palestinians ("voluntary immigration of Gaza Arabs").[4] Haley had served as Trump's, and Danon Netanyahu's UN ambassador, respectively. Shunning exemplars of multilateral diplomacy, both were advocates of uni-lateral militarization and dispossession. Great minds thought alike.

Indeed, Israel's lethal counter-offensive was underwritten by America's longstanding massive military aid. Over decades, the ties between the two had grown into a symbiotic alliance. Since 1950, Israel has received more than $120 billion in U.S. aid, most of it in military aid. At the same time, Palestinians got a total of $11 billion in aid, mainly via refugee assistance. Israel's support is over tenfold that of the Palestinians (Figure 3-1a). Furthermore, while Israel has been receiving more than $4 billion annually, Palestinian aid has plunged to around $200 to $300 million (Figure 3-1b). And unlike the Palestinians, Israel has benefited from wealthy Jewish-American donors for almost a century.

Figure 3-1   The Great Imbalance:
U.S. Foreign Aid to Israel and Palestine

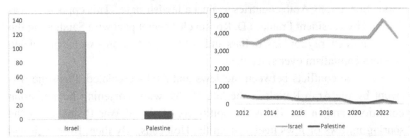

Source: USAID, UNRWA, CRS, author

Due to its ongoing, indiscriminate military aid to Israel, American cred-ibility in the Middle East has steadily eroded. This outcome wasn't inevitable. It was the net effect of the Cold War and U.S. domestic politics.

HEDGING BETS

Toward the UN Partition Plan

Initially, the U.S. diplomacy was cautious and divided regarding the Middle East. Despite stated internationalism, Woodrow Wilson exemplified this tradition. Sympathetic to the British Balfour Declaration (1917), he supported a "national home for Jewish people" in Palestine with safeguards for Palestinian Arabs' civil and religious rights.[5] The Declaration was aligned with his stated self-determination doctrine, which conveniently permitted Washington to benefit from the eclipse of Imperial Britain in the region and elsewhere. However, Wilson's priorities focused on his domestic "New Freedom" agenda with the proposed progressive economic reforms, and internationally on the effort to consolidate the League of Nations to make the world safe for American capitalism. In these efforts, Mandatory Palestine was but a footnote.

Up to the interwar period, American Jewry was not committed to Zionism as a national project in Palestine. But things began to change with increasing immigration to Israel in the 1910s, U.S. immigration quotas in the mid-1920s, xenophobic isolationism in America, and rise of Fascism and Nazism in Western Europe in the 1930s.[6] It was then, in 1942, that America's Zionist movement, for the first time, explicitly called for the creation of "a Jewish Commonwealth integrated in the structure of the new democratic world."[7] However, efforts by the Congress to pass resolutions to support a Jewish state in Palestine were still habitually torpedoed by the realists of the War Department and the Arabists of the State Department, due to the broad opposition among Arab countries against a Jewish state.[8] This opposition was fostered by President Franklin D. Roosevelt's secret pact with Saudi King Ibn Saud – gulf energy for U.S. dollars and military protection – which has fueled Western capitalism ever since then.[9]

As the conflicts between the Jews and Arabs escalated, Palestine was swept by the Arab Revolt in the late 1930s, with worsening humanitarian conditions and in the 1940s the spillovers of World War II, including the soaring inflows of Jews fleeing from the Holocaust. By then, Roosevelt had passed away and been replaced by President Harry S. Truman who knew little about foreign policy and was thus useful to the national security state with ensued in 1947. That November, the General Assembly of the newly created United Nations (UN) adopted the Partition Plan for Palestine. The idea was to have a mainly Jewish state and a largely Arab state, and a primarily international Jerusalem. Perhaps most importantly, the Partition Plan was premised on *economic integration.*[10] The economic union was understood to be critical for the survival of the entire population in the area. Promoted by the Jews and rejected by Arab countries, the Plan was adopted with U.S. support. Barely half a year later, on May 4, 1948, David Ben-Gurion declared unilaterally "the establishment of a Jewish state in Eretz Israel, to be known as the State of Israel."[11]

Even then, the White House struggled to hedge its bets.

From Recognition to Trusteeship to Recognition

According to the conventional mythology, the United States was the first country to recognize Israel. In reality, an uneasy hesitation and intense lobbying marked the last-minute decision-making in the White House. As President Truman subsequently acknowledged, "I do not think I ever had as much pressure and propaganda aimed at the White House as I had in this instance. The persistence of a few of the extreme Zionist leaders actuated by a political motive and engaging in political threats disturbed and annoyed me."[12] On March 18, 1948, just months after the partition resolution supported by the U.S., the UN Special Committee on Palestine reported it had failed to achieve a truce and proposed a temporary trusteeship for Palestine to restore peace. As a result, UN Ambassador Warren Austin declared that the partition of Palestine was no longer a viable option. It was a view seconded by the U.S. Secretary of State George C. Marshall. Hence, the U.S. Proposal for Temporary UN Trusteeship for Palestine. Without appropriate framework conditions, they thought that "open warfare" was inevitable:

> Unless emergency action is taken, there will be no public authority in Palestine on that date capable of preserving law and order. Violence and bloodshed will descend upon the Holy Land. Large-scale fighting among the people of that country will be the inevitable result. Such fighting would infect the entire Middle East and could lead to consequences of the gravest sort involving the peace of this Nation and of the world.
>
> These dangers are imminent. Responsible governments in the United Nations cannot face this prospect without acting promptly to prevent it.[13]

The issue of the recognition of the Jewish state divided Truman, his domestic and campaign adviser Clark Clifford, and the State and Defense Departments. Truman's concern centered on the plight of the displaced Jews from Europe. He had less concern for the Palestinians displaced by the Jewish forces in 1947–48. They were not his constituency and had no meaningful U.S. lobby. With Truman hesitating, Clifford argued that the U.S. should recognize the Jewish state in accordance with the partition resolution. By contrast, Secretary of State George C. Marshall dismissed such arguments as motivated by domestic politics. Marshall believed that siding with a Jewish state could harm U.S. relations with Arab countries, thereby pushing them toward the Soviet Union while limiting access to Middle Eastern oil and destabilizing the region.[14] For months, the U.S. delegation had worked hard on the trusteeship plan. But in the election year, Truman erred on the side of domestic politics. Marshall had no alternative but to send a State Department official to the UN to prevent the delegates from resigning.

Within hours of Israel's Independence Declaration, Truman recognized Israel. But it was only a *de facto* acknowledgement. Joseph Stalin's Soviet Union became the first country to recognize Israel *de jure* on May 17, 1948.[15] The U.S. extended its official recognition only in 1949; a year later. Effectively, the U.S. was "less firm, less consistent, and less consequential in supporting the establishment of the state of Israel than were the Soviet Union and the Communist states of Eastern Europe, especially Czechoslovakia and Poland."[16] Stalin, like George C. Marshall and George F. Kennan, expected the creation of the Jewish state to accelerate the demise of British influence in the Middle East and foster Moscow's access to the region's huge, untapped energy reserves. That was also the guiding light of U.S. policy regarding the Middle East, based on Roosevelt's bilateral alliance with Saudi Arabia that would supply oil to the U.S. in exchange for American military protection of the Saudi regime, setting the stage for the petrodollar, requiring Saudi oil to be purchased only by dollars.[17]

CHOOSING SIDES

Reverse Course and the Cold War

Following the death of Roosevelt along with his plans for international peace and stability in the post-1945 world, the subsequent Cold War sealed America's reverse course. In the name of Cold War, America's wartime allies – the Soviet Union and China – were now regarded as enemies, while wartime enemies – Germany, Italy and Japan – were embraced as allies. In Western Europe, the Marshall Plan served as economic instrument to reverse course. Structured to support European recovery, which had already begun, the Plan intensified convergence among the major already-developed Western European economies. The funds came with strings attached: membership in the U.S.-led North Atlantic Treaty Organization (NATO). The wartime pledges to the developing economies were set aside. As a result, the Marshall Plan sped up economic convergence *among* developed countries in the West, while intensifying divergence *between* advanced and developing economies and thus deepening the gap between the two. These developing economies of the Global South included most countries of the Middle East.[18]

Israel was something of an exception, however. Though established within the developing Middle East, it enjoyed relatively high-level human capital, thanks to huge immigration inflows from the relatively prosperous industrialized countries. More importantly, Israel benefited hugely from the Reparations Agreement with West Germany in the early 1950s when, as a newly-established country, it was in dire need for investment and foreign currency. If postwar West Germany saved Israel's economy in the 1950s, France served as its main arms supplier. While Israel was still setting up its U.S. ties, it was secretly building a large nuclear reactor near Dimona in the Negev desert, with French support. These bilateral ties peaked in 1956 when Israel invaded Egypt, in cooperation with France and Britain. Responding strongly, the Eisenhower administration forced an end to the intervention.

Under Eisenhower, the U.S. still sought to maintain its neutrality to ensure its access to oil, fostering ties with Arab countries with a view to containing Moscow's access to the oil fields.

Palestinians as a "Refugee Problem"

In May 2024, Israeli settlers launched several attacks on the head-quarters of the UN Relief and Works Agency for Palestine Refugees in the Near East (UNRWA), setting fire to the perimeter of the building in East Jerusalem. Given the ongoing security risk to the UNRWA staff, the attack forced the agency to shut down the compound, which had also been hit just a day before.[19] Some of the settlers came from Efrat, which, like other illegal settlements, has been funded by an Israeli crowdfunding platform, IsraelGives. The attacks against UNRWA came after months of far-right settler protests outside of the building, following months of Israeli claims of UNRWA-Hamas links; accusations that lacked verification, according to U.S. intelligence.[20] The UN's humanitarian agency reported at least 800 Israeli settler attacks against Palestinians since October 7 resulting in either casualties or property damage.[21] Among the protesters was Aryeh King, a deputy mayor of Jerusalem and a prominent advocate for settlements, who called Palestinian Gazans "Muslim Nazis," described them as "sub-human" calling for captured Palestinians to be "buried alive.[22]

Targeting UNRWA is synonymous with efforts to dismantle the long-standing lifeline of U.S. humanitarian aid to Palestinians. To Palestinian Arabs, the establishment of Israel in 1948 meant catastrophic displacement, dispossession and devastation. Subsequently, their numbers in the area were halved to 750,000. In U.S. postwar foreign policy, they were largely a second thought, framed as a "refugee problem."

A year after Israel's independence, the UN General Assembly established the UNRWA. With a temporary mandate, it was to provide humanitarian assistance and protection to registered Palestinian refugees in the West Bank, Gaza Strip, Jordan, Lebanon, and Syria. Today, the number of Palestinian refugees amounts to almost 6 million. UNRWA is critical to most Palestinians in the region because it provides food and other essential supplies, health care, education, and other services, coupled with public services provided by the host authorities. In Gaza alone, some 1.7 million of 2.3 million residents are registered Palestinian refugees. Without the enforcement of UN resolutions, many have relied on humanitarian assistance for decades.

Historically, the United States has been UNRWA's largest financial contributor, with more than $7.1 billion since 1950.[23] From the start, U.S. contributions to UNRWA have been subject to a variety of legislative conditions and oversight measures, however. As Palestinians began to fight for their rights, these conditions, which were used as leverage, grew tighter.[24] Launched in 1964, the PLO did not receive any official recognition from the U.S. government, although an unofficial PLO Information Office was allowed to be established in New York. Run by Sadat Hassan, who served as Yemen's Permanent Representative to the UN, it, too, was closed in 1968.

Ironically, American humanitarian support was predicated on a status quo that all stakeholders, including the U.S., regarded as untenable.

Origins of the U.S.-Israel "Special Relationship"

Like Truman, President John F. Kennedy kept a certain distance from the State Department and its efforts to cement ties with the Arab world. Like Truman, he relied on his advisors and was ultimately motivated by domestic political considerations. But unlike Truman, he did begin to build security ties with Israel and a bilateral alliance. Despite their sympathies with Holocaust survivors and Israel, both Truman and Eisenhower had enforced an arms embargo on Israel. Kennedy ended it. Engaged in a delicate balancing act, the early postwar presidents – Truman, Eisenhower, Kennedy and Lyndon B. Johnson – courted Arab states to contain Soviet communism and ensure access to oil, *while* bolstering Israel's economic and military strength. In the process, America's "special relationship" with Israel moved gradually from semi-detached neutrality to a full-blown commitment. As one perceptive observer put it:

> The Eisenhower administration's single-minded anticommunist framework made policy less prone to domestic influences regarding Israel. His first term sought Arab allies as well as positive Israeli ties but, when this proved untenable, sought instead

to deny both camps much in the way of aid or favor. Kennedy attempted balance, like Eisenhower, but by courting both Arabs and Israel rather than distancing both. Johnson increasingly turned from the impartial approach to one identifying Israel explicitly as a friend and speaking of a "special relationship." This included the delivery of aid and arms that previous presidents had refused to grant. By the end of this period, with Arabs and Israelis poised for war, the U.S. was positioned to be a decisive factor in the outcome of such conflicts.[25]

In 1962 the Kennedy administration sold Israel the Hawk anti-aircraft missile. It was a major weapon system, but defensive rather than offensive. Military ties were not a source of bilateral friction; Israel's nuclear program was. The U.S. concern was that Israel's program could unleash a nuclear arms-race in the Middle East.[26]

Mired in Vietnam, Johnson tipped the balance of U.S. foreign policy toward greater support of Israel, while seeking to avoid tensions with the Soviet Union in the Middle East. As his legislative agenda for the "Great Society" crumbled under increasing domestic divisions, war protests and civil rights turmoil, Nixon took over the White House.

Meanwhile, in late 1967, UN Resolution 242 had called for Israeli withdrawal from the occupied territories, which Israel shunned, and mutual recognition of each state's sovereignty, which Arab states rejected in the absence of Israeli withdrawal. What followed was the War of Attrition with continuous fighting between Israel and Egypt, Jordan and, for the first time, a new non-state actor, the Palestine Liberation Organization (PLO), an umbrella organization of several resistance movements. Seeking to preempt escalation, the Rogers Plan pushed for a ceasefire and military standstill around the Suez Canal without success. After Nasser's death, President Sadat expelled Soviet advisers from Egypt in preparation for a shift toward Washington. But the U.S. and Israel ignored this signal for peace talks. As a result, Sadat began to plan a surprise attack that would ensure leverage in future talks.

Oil-for-Protection and the Petrodollar

It was Roosevelt's oil-for-protection bargain that set the stage for President Nixon's decisions some three decades later. After the Bretton Woods conference in 1944, the U.S. dollar continued to be pegged to gold at $35 per ounce from 1941 to 1971. However, the dire U.S. economic prospects led President Nixon to unilaterally cancel the U.S. dollar's convertibility to gold in 1971. In the absence of a fixed value convertibility to gold, the U.S. dollar deteriorated in value relative to other currencies. As a result, the Middle East's producers received less real income for the same price.[27] Yet, oil remained priced in dollars in the new world of freely floating fiat currencies. As the Organization of Petroleum Exporting Countries (OPEC) priced the barrel of oil against gold, the quadrupled price caused a supply shock in the world economy.[28] Following the 1973 Yom Kippur War, oil exporters amassed big surpluses of what then became called "petrodollars," which U.S.-led financial intermediaries steered to attractive developing countries, particularly in Latin America. So, Nixon negotiated another deal so that Saudi Arabia would denominate future oil sales in dollars in exchange for U.S. arms and protection. As other OPEC countries agreed to similar deals, the demand for "petrodollars" soared and revenues were then recycled into the U.S. and Latin America through arms purchases. In the U.S., that contributed to stagflation, which in turn fueled record-high interest rates and the monetarism of the Reagan era. In Latin America, the huge boom fostered a massive bubble that resulted in *La Década Perdida* ("The Lost Decade") of stagnation, hyperinflation and crushing foreign debt.[29]

But Nixon's deals failed to preempt what loomed ahead.

DEEPENING TIES

Yom Kippur War: At the Edge of a Nuclear War

Israel first crossed the nuclear threshold on the eve of the Six-Day War in May 1967, when Prime Minister Levi Eshkol secretly ordered the nuclear reactor scientists in Dimona to assemble two crude nuclear devices. The crude atomic bombs "were readied for deployment on trucks that could race to the Egyptian border for detonation in the event Arab forces overwhelmed Israeli defenses."[30]

At the eve of Yom Kippur in 1973, despite advance intelligence about the impending attack, Prime Minister Golda Meir decided not to launch a pre-emptive strike fearing the U.S. response could prove adverse as it had in 1956. Mobilization proved grossly inadequate; for a few days, Israel faced an existential threat. Even the normally sober Defense Minister Moshe Dayan was rattled enough to later tell Meir that "this is the end of the Third Temple." It was a reference to the collapse of the state of Israel. But "Temple" was also the code word for nuclear weapons.[31]

On the night of October 8, Meir and her kitchen cabinet had thirteen 20-kiloton atomic bombs assembled. Their destructive potential was higher than that of the atom bomb dropped on Hiroshima, with an explosive yield of the equivalent of about 15 kilotons of dynamite.[32] The Israelis planned to use the bombs against Egyptian and Syrian targets *if* Arab forces would advance too far. Leaks suggest that the primary purpose was strategic deterrent; but it also signaled a tentative "Samson Option"; that is, a massive *potential* Israeli retaliation as a "last resort" option. At the time, the implications of the devastating aftermath of even tactical nuclear strikes were not well-known.[33] As the Soviets began to resupply Arab forces, particularly Syria, Meir requested Nixon for help with military supply. After the full nuclear alert, Israelis began to load the warheads into waiting planes. Cognizant of the potential implications, Nixon ordered a full-scale strategic airlift operation to deliver weapons and supplies to Israel. By the time the aid arrived, Israel was gaining the upper hand in the war.[34]

After those days on a nuclear edge, nothing would ever remain the same in the Middle East. American military aid to Israel contributed to the 1973 OPEC embargo against the United States, which was lifted in March 1974, and subsequently to the overthrow of the Shah in Iran 1979, followed by another oil crisis. The twin crises and the postwar economic expansion ended with devastating stagflation, which led to record-high interest rates. As the Keynesian era faded away, monetarism coupled with Reagan's rearmament drives ensued.

An Emerging U.S.-Palestinian Dialogue

Before the Yom Kippur War, the U.S. saw the PLO and Fatah under Yasser Arafat as a terrorist organization, opposing PLO aspirations at the UN. In the Nixon era, this stance was quite explicit and U.S. diplomats in the Middle East were ordered by the State Department to avoid contacts with Arafat and his representatives.[35] However, the realists of the State Department began to see the Palestinian role as vital to the peace process, particularly to efforts at an Israeli-Jordanian deal on the West Bank. Behind the official façade, U.S. intelligence officials created clandestine contacts with the PLO, after the organization in 1970 expressed willingness to recognize the state of Israel in exchange for U.S. support of a Palestinian state.[36]

Following the Yom Kippur War, the deputy chief of the CIA, Vernon A. Walters, and Khaled al-Hassan, Arafat's right-hand and the PLO's *de facto* foreign minister, discussed the possibility of integrating the PLO into the peace process. As the organization refrained from attacks against U.S. targets, al-Hassan advocated Israel's withdrawal from the occupied territories, deployment of UN forces and the creation of a Palestinian state.[37] President

Gerald Ford deemed that the PLO's integration into the nascent peace process was possible, though not probable.[38] Unlike Ford, President Jimmy Carter thought that this "very serious roadblock" was surmountable.

As the Carter administration took an active role in the peace talks between Egypt and Israel, the PLO, after a decade of its closure, was allowed to open the Palestine Information Office (PIO) in Washington, D.C. The Camp David Accords ended the war between Israel and Egypt, stirring great domestic opposition in both Egypt and Israel. Ironically, while trying to break with traditional U.S. policy, Carter "ended up fulfilling the goals of that tradition, which had been to break up the Arab alliance, sideline the Palestinians, build an alliance with Egypt, weaken the Soviet Union and secure Israel."[39] And it was *that* legacy, not the peace process, that the Reagan and Bush administrations would build upon. And in that legacy, the key role belonged to the Gulf. And so it was that, in the aftermath of the twin oil crises of the 1970s, Roosevelt's oil-for-protection pact with Saudi Arabia in 1944 was extended across much of the Gulf. According to the consequent Carter Doctrine (1980),

> An attempt by any outside force to gain control of the Persian Gulf region will be regarded as an assault on the vital interests of the United States of America, and such an assault will be repelled by any means necessary, including military force.[40]

In an attempt to stress continuity, Carter's national security adviser Zbigniew Brzezinski portrayed the doctrine as modeled on the postwar Truman Doctrine. In reality, its substance mimicked Imperial Britain's 1903 declaration to keep Russia and Germany out of the Gulf. Ostensibly, the doctrine was a response to Soviet intervention in Afghanistan. Effectively, the purpose was to sustain U.S. hegemony in the Persian Gulf. Geopolitics followed economics.

With Reagan, Strategic Military Partnership

After Carter's departure from the White House, there was great concern in Israel about the Reagan administration's extensive ties with Arab countries. Nonetheless, Reagan's rearmament drive, which supported wide-ranging cooperation with and military supplies to Israel, and his neoliberal policies, echoed by the Israeli right-wing Likud's liberalization efforts, strengthened bilateral ties. Despite Operation Opera, Israel's preemptive air strike on Iraq's

Osirak nuclear reactor, coupled with its 1982 Lebanon War and devastating siege of Beirut, the bilateral relationship prevailed and the ties deepened with

- the Strategic Cooperation Agreement (1981);
- joint military exercises (since 1984);
- war reserve stock facilities in Israel for military equipment, intended for U.S. use in the Middle East but transferable to Israeli use when necessary;
- a free trade agreement (1985);
- support for Israel's economic stabilization via $1.5 billion in loan guarantees
- and the creation of a U.S.-Israel bilateral economic forum, the U.S.-Israel Joint Economic Development Group (1985).

And when the U.S. launched a dialogue with the PLO in 1988, Israel was granted a "major non-NATO ally" status, ensuring access to expanded weapons systems and opportunities to bid on U.S. defense contracts. Meanwhile, U.S. aid to Israel climbed to $3 billion annually.

Following the Israel-Egypt peace treaty and the 1982 Lebanon War, Palestinians felt betrayed by the Arab states. They took their fate in their own hands, unleashing the First Intifada (Uprising) in the occupied territories. The George H. W. Bush administration (1989–93) still sought to recalibrate its ties with Israel by criticizing Israel's "expansionist policies" and declaring that East Jerusalem was not a part of Israel. However, during the Iraq-Kuwait crisis and the subsequent Persian Gulf War, Bush repeated the U.S. commitment to Israel's security. Despite being a target of over 30 Iraqi Scud missiles, as instructed, Israel did not respond. That kept Bush's coalition united, while boosting Israel's leverage in the subsequent peace conference in Madrid. A political showdown with the Bush administration ensued only when Israeli Prime Minister Yitzhak Shamir, former head of the pre-state terrorist group, the Stern Gang, requested $10 billion in U.S. loan guarantees.

Toward the Oslo Accords

To the Reagan and Bush administrations, efforts at peace between Israel and the PLO were secondary to bilateral state-to-state peace treaties. In 1980, the Republican party platform had stated unambiguously that

Republicans reject any call for the involvement of the PLO as not in keeping with the long-term interests of either Israel or the Palestinian Arabs. The imputation of legitimacy to organizations not yet willing to acknowledge the fundamental right to existence of the State of Israel is wrong. ... [T]he establishment of a Palestinian State on the West Bank would be destabilizing and harmful to the peace process.[41]

Instead, the Reagan administration preferred the idea of Palestinian autonomy under Jordanian supervision; a stance mimicking that of the Likud. At the end of Reagan's second term, the U.S. Anti-Terrorism Act declared the PLO a terrorist organization, thereby banning any assistance to it and ordering the closure of its information office. For its part, the Reagan administration's marginalization of the PLO contributed to the First Intifada, which the administration portrayed as an external import rather than a broad, popular rebellion that it really was.

With the looming implosion of the Soviet Union, long a patron of the PLO, the Palestinian leadership shifted its policy positions to adjust to U.S. hegemony in the Middle East. With the Palestinian Declaration of Independence in late 1988, the PLO accepted the UN Security Council Resolutions 242 and 338, recognizing Israel's right to exist and renouncing terrorism. That, finally, paved the way for a dialogue with the U.S. and a degree of normalization in the PLO's institutional presence in Washington D.C. Following the establishment of the Palestinian National Authority in 1994 under the Oslo Agreement, the PLO Mission was renamed. The normalization was expected to accelerate during the George H. W. Bush administration. Then Arafat chose to support Saddam Hussein in the Persian Gulf War. Bush responded by stepping back from the PLO, stating that "They've lost credibility."[42]

In 1991, the Madrid Peace Conference did welcome a Palestinian delegation, though not explicit PLO participation, thus paving the way to the Oslo Accords.

Rabin's Assassination

Returning to power, the labor coalition in Israel approved a partial freeze of housing construction in the occupied territories, which paved the way for rapprochement with the Clinton administration. While the U.S.-PLO dialogue was suspended in 1990–1993, the Israelis and Palestinians took the initiative to proceed with direct talks, starting with back channels in Oslo and from there to exchanges between Arafat's PLO and Rabin's government. It was only in fall 1993 that the U.S. was brought back into the process, while in

1994, the Israel-Jordan peace treaty came into effect. With President Clinton announcing the resumption of the U.S.-PLO dialogue, Rabin, Clinton, and Arafat signed the Oslo Accords at the White House in September 1993. It was a great photo opportunity for Clinton who was portrayed as the architect of a deal that only became viable when the U.S. was insulated from the process (Figure 3-2).

Figure 3-2   The 1993 Oslo Accords

(*Above, top*) Rabin, Clinton and Arafat signing the Oslo Accords in 1993. (*Above, bottom*) A poster of Rabin proclaiming him a traitor to Israel.

Source: Wikimedia Commons; PPPA

In Israel, the Oslo Accords unleashed a massive wave of protests by the far-right and ultra-religious, which the Likud's new head, Benjamin Netanyahu, tacitly instigated. (This is why when Rabin's family was mourning his loss at their Tel Aviv home, Yasser Arafat was welcomed to offer his condolences, whereas Netanyahu was advised not to show up.) Rabin became Enemy Number 1 of Israel's Messianic far-right. Netanyahu, then head of the vocal right-wing opposition, directly contributed to and reinforced the incendiary political climate in which protesters branded Rabin a "traitor," "murderer," even "Nazi" for signing the peace agreement with the Palestinians. To them, "Rabin and his ilk" brought shame on Zionism and were an embarrassment to Judaism. It was amid this tumultuous historical moment that the orthodox Jewish zealot Yigal Amir, after careful and long planning, seized his semi-automatic Beretta and assassinated Rabin. Influenced by previous anti-Arab massacres, particularly the Cave of Machpelah mass murder by the ex-Kahanite leader Baruch Goldstein, Amir was closely linked with extremists influenced by Kahanism. Upon hearing that Rabin was dead, he said to the police he had "no regrets" because he was acting on the "orders of God." Rabin was a "pursuer" endangering Jewish lives, he said. According to some far-right Messianic rabbis, the concept of din rodef ("law of the pursuer") is a part of traditional Jewish law. Amir believed the assassination was not just legitimate but his responsibility as an observant Jew.[43] Subsequently, he has expressed no regret for his actions. Why should he, when believing God is on his side.

Like the Hamas offensive three decades later, the assassination was initially attributed to an "intelligence failure." Shin Bet, Israel's internal security, could have stopped the killer in advance but didn't.[44] So, was the assassination "allowed" to happen, the critics asked? Whatever the case, Rabin's assassination was the Israeli mirror-image of the prior Sadat assassination. The latter has been attributed to the Egyptian Islamic Jihad, including Ayman al-Zawahiri, subsequently Osama bin Laden's deputy; both of whom later figured among the fedayeen in Afghanistan who were armed, trained and financed by the CIA's Operation Cyclone to fight the Soviet intervention.[45]

At first, the assassination of Rabin in 1995 did not seem to halt history. But the peace momentum was crumbling. Furthermore, Rabin had been in talks even with Syria, which his successor, Shimon Peres, failed to continue. It didn't help that the chemistry between Bill Clinton and Netanyahu was minimal. As they first sat down in the Oval Office, Clinton wanted assurances that Netanyahu would continue the Oslo process. Instead, Netanyahu gave a protracted lecture on the Arabs and why his government would honor previous agreements, but first needed to review outstanding issues with the

Palestinians. After Netanyahu was gone, an exasperated Clinton could hardly believe what he had witnessed, "Who the fuck does he think he is? Who's the fucking superpower here?"[46] But outwardly, the president remained all smiles and compliments to his guest. As Israelis came to hear news about Rabin outside the Tel Aviv hospital, they had less inhibitions. They were shouting, "Bibi the murderer!"

A year later, the Clinton administration brokered the Israel-Palestine ceasefire agreement, while assisting in building the institutions of the new Palestinian Authority (PA). In 1998, Clinton became the first U.S. president to visit the PA. To keep the peace process going, the Clinton administration offered Israel $100 million in aid for anti-terror activities, $200 million for Arrow anti-missile deployment, and about $50 million for an anti-missile laser weapon.[47] Not only was it too little too late. It strengthened the hand of Netanyahu's Likud, which won the subsequent election. Another effort to deepen the peace process ensued at the end of the 1990s, when Clinton mediated meetings between Prime Minister Ehud Barak and PLO chairman Arafat. By then, Israeli labor and centrist leaders were in bed with American political consultants, with Clinton's 1992 wizard James Carville and pollster strategist Stan Greenberg advising Barak, who was also supported by Philip Gould, Tony Blair's pollster. Barak was a great fan of the 1997 "New Labor" campaign.

As efforts to capitalize on the peace momentum failed, Likud consolidated its power, Vice President Al Gore's presidential bid failed, Arafat's ailing health gave in, Gaza saw the rise of Hamas and the U.S. faced September 11, 2001. And three years later, Arafat's ailing health gave in, although many believe he was poisoned. The latter are typically explained away as "conspiracy theories." Yet, Israel had tried to assassinate Arafat multiple times, typically with Palestinian assets and poison.[48] While polonium has been mentioned as a likely poison by Arafat's personal doctor and aide, both Israelis and some Palestinian officials have denied such claims.[49] The investigation of Al Jazeera and a Swiss medical expert analysis, however, suggests that Arafat *could* have died of polonium poisoning.[50]

All things considered, there are critical holes in the official narratives of the deaths of those who have tried to advance the peace process, including Sadat's assassins in 1981; the absence of Rabin's security detail and delays in his transportation to emergency in 1995; Arafat's death in 2004; Sharon's second and lethal stroke which may have been medication-induced, right before the planned unilateral disengagement from the West Bank.

Obviously, the Holy Land is not immune to God working in mysterious ways.

SYMBIOSIS

The George W. Bush Mobilization

Even before September 11, 2001, the George W. Bush administration (2001–2009) had distanced itself from Arafat, keeping the relationship with the Palestinian Authority largely on a technical level. After 9/11, Clinton's pursuit of globalization was replaced by the Bush administration's world-wide struggle against terrorism. In 2000, the Camp David Summit between Clinton, Arafat and Prime Minister Ehud Barak was to end with a final agreement on the peace process. But it failed to do so, largely due to differences on the status of Jerusalem. This added fuel to the Second Intifada, sparked by Ariel Sharon's provocative visit to the Al-Aqsa compound.[51] Seeking to avoid further escalation in the region, Bush gave his support for a Palestinian state, while pushing for more "pragmatic" Palestinian leaders:

> My vision is two states living side by side in peace and security. There is simply no way to achieve that peace until all parties fight terror. . . . Peace requires a new and different Palestinian leadership, so that a Palestinian state can be born.[52]

The idea lingered in the hollow rhetoric on the need to "reform the Palestinian Authority"; that is, to replace it with malleable pro-West proxy leaders, a bit like Venezuela's Juan Guaidó. To preempt Arafat's participation in peace talks, Bush established ties with Palestinian Authority President Mahmoud Abbas, whom the administration saw as manageable. Meanwhile, as the Bush administration launched its War on Terrorism after the September 11 attacks, Israel's Prime Minister Ariel Sharon launched an extensive campaign of targeted assassinations against Palestinian militants. This was supported by the Bush administration as long as Israel restrained from building new settlements in the West Bank. When Israel was coping with a challenging economic downturn and the Second Intifada (2000–2005), the U.S. provided Israel with $9 billion in conditional loan guarantees through 2011. Revising the longstanding U.S. stance toward Jewish settlements, the Bush administration stressed the need to make note of "Israel's security concerns" and changed "realities on the ground."

Though avoiding direct involvement in Israeli-Palestinian talks, the U.S. administration welcomed Israel's disengagement from Gaza in 2005 as a step toward the two-state solution. With the 2006 Lebanon War, the U.S. Congress was notified of a potential sale of $210 million worth of jet fuel to Israel, presumably "to keep peace and security in the region." In practice, this U.S. support enabled Israel's War, and included "bunker buster" bombs, presumably to target Hezbollah's leaders, although Israel reportedly used them also against civilian targets. However, when Israel proposed to bomb Iranian nuclear facilities in summer 2008, the U.S. vetoed the plan.[53]

Critics like former president Jimmy Carter warned that U.S. was enabling Israel's occupation policies, which amounted to South African–style apartheid.[54] In *The Israel Lobby and U.S. Foreign Policy* (2006), John Mearsheimer and Stephen Walt, proponents of realism in international affairs, proposed that the impact of America's "Israel lobby," comprised mainly of Jewish Americans but also of Christian Zionists and neoconservatives, had a "negative effect on American interests" and was "unintentionally harmful to Israel as well."[55] But the dissenting voices had little impact on the policymaking in the White House, which was supported by the powerful, conservative American-Jewish lobby, AIPAC, that sponsored the administration's proponents and their agendas.

President Mahmoud Abbas was elected in 2005 to serve as president of the Palestinian National Authority with a four-year term to end in 2009. Hamas won Gaza's elections in 2006, after which Abbas and the PLO Central Council then remained in office while refusing elections thereafter. What the Bush administration saw as steady progress with a "moderate" PA, Palestinians in Gaza saw as quisling-like collaboration with an Islamophobic enemy. It was at this point that U.S. bilateral aid to the Palestinians peaked. As the support of Hamas broadened, U.S. aid began to decline (Figure 3-3).

Figure 3-3   U.S. Bilateral Aid to the Palestinians, 1988–2023

In millions (constant 2013 dollars), 1990–2015

Source: U.S. State Department, USAID

Obama's Diplomatic Caution

Like Carter, President Obama made a concerted effort to halt settlement expansion in the occupied territories, facilitated more aid, and allowed the PLO mission to be upgraded to the PLO General Delegation to the U.S. But unlike Carter, Obama had to deal with the realities of Jewish settlement expansion. During Carter's peace talks in the late 1970s, there were up to 15,000 settlers in the occupied territories. After Rabin was assassinated, the figure had climbed nine-fold to almost 135,000. By the time Obama began to pressure Prime Minister Netanyahu, it had more than doubled to some 300,000.[56] Responding to the heat, Israel imposed a 10-month freeze on settlement construction in the West Bank. Obama oiled the pressure by authorizing the secret sale of bunker buster bombs to Israel.

Yet, Obama's settlement ban included neither East Jerusalem nor some 3,000 pre-approved housing units under construction nor dismantling already-built Israeli outposts. In the Palestinian view, U.S. ambivalence was part of the problem. In May 2011, Obama called for a return to the pre-1967 Israeli borders with mutually agreed land swaps, which allowed bargaining space for "security considerations." Yet, his administration vetoed a UN resolution declaring Israeli settlements illegal, while contributing $235 million to the funding of the Iron Dome missile system for Israel.[57]

The Palestinian Authority saw its future threatened both in the occupied territories and internationally. And so, in 2011 the PA sought UN membership for the Palestinian state yet was opposed by both the U.S. and Israel. After Obama told Abbas the U.S. would veto any effort at Palestinian recognition in the UN Security Council, Abbas turned to the UN General Assembly, which made Palestine an observer state, with the U.S. voting against the resolution and refusing to recognize Palestine as a sovereign state.

Though often critical in public, the Obama administration fostered the bilateral militarized ties with Israel. Concurrently, Israeli exports to the U.S. surpassed those to the EU, which in the past had been the top destination for Israeli exports. Despite friction areas, the bilateral ties were growing increasingly symbiotic. Of course, it was not a mutualism of equals, but it was mutually beneficial. At times, though, it wasn't entirely clear who was in charge of the symbiosis. What Netanyahu thought was no secret. As he put it in 2001: "I know what America is; America is a thing you can move very easily, move it in the right direction. They won't get in the way."[58]

Mutual concern regarding Iran had a way of fostering U.S.-Israeli ties. After years of negotiations led by the Obama administration and the P-5+1 nations, an Iran deal designed to constrain any Iranian progress towards development of a nuclear weapon was finally in the works. In the U.S., the

Likud's critical reaction to the Geneva interim agreement was to be expected. To restrain Netanyahu's inclination to preempt Iran's nuclear plans by more dangerous means, Congress passed the United States–Israel Strategic Partnership Act of 2013, which is seen as a notch above the "major non-NATO ally" classification, thereby adding even further support for defense, energy, and cooperation in business and sciences. The bill also increased the U.S. war reserve stock held in Israel to $1.8 billion.[59] Meanwhile, in the occupied territories, the West's economic blockade was strangling Gaza even as settlement expansion prevailed in the West Bank, despite increasing opposition and turmoil.

Despite his diplomatic caution, President Obama greenlighted increasing U.S.-Israeli military cooperation in advanced technology.

Iron Dome Interceptor: Developed by Israel, Co-produced in America

As Israel's capabilities in advanced technology increased through learning-by-doing, it had moved from imitation to innovation, which further fostered its indigenous technological innovation. The Iron Dome is a case in point. After Hamas's military-style offensive on October 7, Biden pledged America would replenish the Dome to intercept the barrages of al-Qaddam missiles hitting Israel. Yet, the interceptor had actually been developed by an Israeli contractor, Rafael Advanced Defense Systems, and Israel Aerospace Industries, a state-owned colossus (Figure 3-4).

Figure 3-4   The Iron Dome

Israel's "Iron Dome" air defense system, Operation Guardian of the Walls, 2021 (IDF Spokesperson's Unit photographer).

Source: Wikimedia Commons

In the 1990s, Hezbollah, a Shia militant group in southern Lebanon that had emerged in response to the Israeli attack on that country after 1982, began to fire rockets into northern Israel's population centers. Consequently, Israelis began to develop the idea of a short-range anti-missile system of their own. The initial effort was killed by U.S. defense officials who claimed it was "doomed to fail."[60] When "Danny" was appointed the head of the IDF R&D, however, the idea was revived. In the 2006 Second Lebanon War, Hezbollah fired some 4,000 rockets reaching Haifa, Israel's third-largest city with more than 1 million people in the metro area. The net effect? Over 40 deaths, 250,000 citizens evacuated and relocated, and 1 million confined to bomb shelters. In the south, 4,000 rockets and 4,000 mortar bombs were fired from Gaza between 2000 to 2008, mainly by Hamas.[61] (In late 2023, the rockets by Hamas and Hezbollah again caused 250,000 Israelis to be evacuated.)

Gold hustled to secure financing and the requisite political support for the antimissile project. In early 2007, Defense Minister Amir Peretz selected the Iron Dome for Israel's defense against the short-range rocket threats. The development was commissioned to Israeli contractor Rafael over the U.S. giant Lockheed Martin. In Israeli style, the system remarkably went from the drawing board to combat readiness in less than four years. Constrained by schedule and low-cost settings constraints, the lead developers took some missile components from a toy car sold by Toys "R" Us.[62]

Initially named "Anti-Qassam," the Iron Dome was first deployed in April 2011. But soon it faced improved Qassam missiles, requiring increasing its range of interceptions from 70 to 250 kilometers and greater versatility to respond to rockets coming from two directions simultaneously. Following President Obama's request in 2010, the U.S. contributed $1.6 billion to the defense system, with another $1 billion approved by the U.S. Congress in 2022.[63] As the U.S. was boosting funding for the Iron Dome, calls ensued for technology transfer and co-production in America. The U.S.-Israel co-production of the Israeli Arrow 3 missile system with Boeing manufacturing served as a precedent. In Washington, the Iron Dome project was seen as the next stage to further strengthen the bilateral ties, a sort of made-in-Israel coupled with buy-American. And so, Raytheon, a major U.S. defense contractor, was made Israel's U.S. partner in co-production of major components.[64]

The Trump Reversal

When the Trump administration arrived in the White House in early 2017, any remaining Palestinian hopes faded as Trump made David M. Friedman U.S. ambassador to Israel. They knew each other well. With a

GOP pedigree from the Reagan era, Friedman had a way of turning Trump's losses to his own gains. He had advised and represented Trump and The Trump Organization in bankruptcies involving his Atlantic City casinos. As a revisionist Zionist, Friedman called members of the pro-peace Israel group J Street "far worse" than *kapos*, Nazi prison guards. He walked the talk, pumping tens of millions of dollars into West Bank settlements through his own fund, particularly Beit El, the flagship of the Messianic far-right, Gush Emunim.[65] A day later, Netanyahu announced Israel would lift all restrictions on settlement construction in the West Bank. Initially Trump had doubts about the Israeli PM. But during a visit to Israel in May 2017, Netanyahu showed Trump tapes with Abbas presumably calling for killing Israeli children. "And that's the guy you want to help?" Netanyahu asked. Secretary of State Rex Tillerson believed the tapes were faked or manipulated. Yet, next day, at a meeting in Bethlehem, the outraged Trump lashed out at Abbas. "Murderer!" he said. "Liar! I thought you were this grandfatherly figure that I could trust. Now, I realize you're nothing but a murderer. You tricked me!"[66]

Subsequently, the U.S. announced its first permanent military base in Israel and recognized Jerusalem as the capital of Israel, moving the U.S. Embassy from Tel Aviv to the Holy City. Decades of U.S. policy toward Israel and the occupied territories, however ambiguous, was reversed almost overnight, as the administration chose to violate several UN resolutions on East Jerusalem. But that was only a prelude. In May 2018, Trump withdrew the U.S. from the Iran nuclear deal that had taken years to achieve. In fall 2018, he ordered the closure of the PLO office in Washington, D.C. and canceled nearly all U.S. aid to the West Bank and Gaza, plus $360 million in annual aid previously given to the UNRWA. The U.S. ambassador to the UN called Hamas "one of the greatest obstacles to resolving the Israeli-Palestinian conflict."[67] In 2019, the administration unilaterally recognized the Golan Heights as part of Israel, in full violation with UN Security Council Resolution 497 (1981).

Presumably, Trump's greatest coup ensued in August 2020, when the U.S., Israel and the United Arab Emirates formalized Israel-UAE relations in a set of bilateral deals, followed by Bahrain, Sudan and Morocco. But it was not divine faith that united the signatories of the "Abraham Accords," but longstanding intelligence relations, collaboration with the U.S. and increasingly with Israel, pledges of U.S. economic and military aid, and good-old arm twisting behind the official façade. For decades, Palestine had been a second thought in U.S. policy. Now it was fading away from the map.

Biden's "Iron-Clad Ties"

When the Biden administration took office, the expectation was that it would steer away from the Trump administration's disastrous trade, technology and Middle East policies. The Biden administration did send an early signal by restoring relations with Palestine's leaders and aid flows to Palestinians. But Biden did not want to rock the boat. Building on Trump's "normalization," the old political fox hoped to hedge his bets. In mid-2022, the renamed "U.S. Office of Palestinian Affairs" would report directly to Washington "on substantive matters."

Yet, in the West Bank where Israeli raids and settler violence were broadening, and in Gaza, where people were struggling for survival amid the West's economic siege, it all sounded like "no sovereignty, no statehood." The U.S. Embassy would stay in Jerusalem. The Biden administration hoped to build on the Abraham Accords. In the aftermath of a violent Al-Aqsa Mosque conflict, the administration opted for calculated distance, which both the Israelis and Palestinians called "lame and late." Loyal to the Pentagon and Big Defense, President Biden and Secretary of State Antony Blinken signed a joint declaration in Jerusalem in 2022, extending the 10-year, $38 billion defense package to Israel, while both sides committed to preventing Iran from obtaining a nuclear weapon. Concurrently, the White House was pushing Israel into greater cooperation with India, seeking to drag the Israelis into the Indo-Pacific alliance against China.

It was only months after the Netanyahu cabinet's accelerated settlement expansion, a legal effort to move Israeli democracy toward autocracy and the broadest mass protests in Israeli history that the Biden administration cautiously signaled its discontent with Netanyahu's proposed "judicial reforms." But the calculated caution turned on its head following the Hamas offensive of October 7, 2023. Declaring himself a Zionist, Biden issued a statement condemning the attacks, pledging "all appropriate means of support to the government and people of Israel." Concurrently, his administration called on Congress to pass $14.3 billion in emergency military aid to Israel, which enabled the genocidal bombing of Gaza by the most far-right government in Israel's history.[68] After the Hamas operation of October 7, 2023, all gloves were off.

The longer the Gaza War and its genocidal atrocities prevailed, the greater was the unease among the Arab states Biden and Netanyahu saw as their normalization partners. Indeed, the prolonged era of oil-for-protection and the petrodollar – from Roosevelt's original to the 1970s reformulation and the 2023–2024 Gaza War – seemed to terminate in early June 2024, when the Crown Prince of Saudi Arabia made a pivotal decision *not* to renew the

50-year-old petrodollar agreement with the United States. Riyadh was not renouncing its ties with Washington, but it was hedging its bets. The Saudi move towards de-dollarization was well-aligned with its growing ties to the BRICS, the coalition of large emerging economies. By opting not to renew the petrodollar pact, Saudi Arabia signaled its intention to foster its modernization program, diversify its economic partnerships and reduce reliance on the U.S. It was the end of the era that had begun with the deal aboard the *Quincy* toward the end of World War II, setting the stage for a new economic and political realignments on a global scale while impacting international trade and financial stability.[69]

MILITARY DIPLOMACY

In fall 2015, I met retired U.S. Army lieutenant general Karl W. Eikenberry at a Shanghai conference. In a dinner conversation on Israel and the 2014 Gaza War, I suggested that due to U.S. military diplomacy the status quo was likely to get a lot worse. "How could we change the course?" Eikenberry asked. "Freeze the flow of U.S. military aid," I said. "Make U.S. aid conditional on progress in the enforcement of UN resolutions and Israeli withdrawal from the occupied territories." Eikenberry smiled faintly. "Yes, it may be a just solution," I acknowledged, "but the least likely to materialize in any scenario."

Israel's occupation is not an undesired side-effect of U.S. foreign policy. It reflects the general militarization of American diplomacy. Eikenberry is one of the few who understood this paradoxical, lethal effect.

The Militarization of U.S. Foreign Policy

In September 2012, Karl W. Eikenberry, former U.S. ambassador to and commanding general of Afghanistan, warned of "the erosion of appropriate levels of executive, congressional, and media oversight of the American armed forces." The conclusion of the 35-year army veteran? In the past 50 years, American foreign policy has become "excessively reliant on military power."[70] By the early 2010s, America had engaged in over 300 conflict-related military deployments since 1798. As Eikenberry noted, half of these took place after World War II when the U.S. became a superpower with global security interests, and that rate had continued to rise, reflecting the increased use of American coercive power.[71]

In effect, these trends have got much worse since Eikenberry's address. With 800 military bases in almost 90 countries, plus hundreds of such bases within the U.S., America has the "biggest collection of military bases occupying foreign lands in history."[72] The military presence abroad seems to correlate with U.S. forces engaging in military conflicts, which lead to more bases, which foster more conflicts. Most stunningly, supported by this global web, the U.S. has been in war, engaged in combat, or has otherwise employed its forces in foreign countries in all but 11 years of its existence.[73]

Let's quantify the argument and update it from Eikenberry's 2012 address a decade ago to the present, with congressional data. From 1776 to the 1970s, U.S. Armed Forces were deployed in up to 20 instances per year. Between 1969 and 1999, these tripled to 34 annually. And in the past two decades, they almost quadrupled to 140.[74] Another indicator of this escalation is the grossly unbalanced ratio of the level of resources available to the military versus those offered to diplomacy.[75] As former defense secretary Robert Gates once put it, the U.S. military has more musicians in its marching bands than the State Department has diplomats.[76] By the early 2020s, the total number of foreign service members from all foreign service agencies (State Department, USAID, etc.) was about 15,600, including about 8,000 foreign service officers, or "generalist" diplomats.[77] These numbers pale in comparison with military capacity in terms of personnel, communications, logistics, transportation, organizational capability, and discretionary funds. The U.S. Department of Defense has over 1.3 million active-duty service members, including soldiers, marines, sailors, airmen, and guardians. Adding the reserve military, the figure increases to 2.1 million, right behind India, China and Russia (Figure 3-5).[78]

Figure 3-5   America's Military Diplomacy

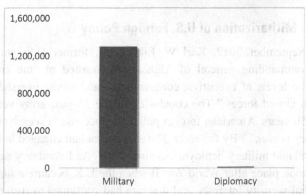

Resources of U.S. Military and Diplomacy

Source: (a) Data from reports by Congressional Research Service, author; (b) U.S. State Department, U.S. Defense Department, author.

However, these figures should be reviewed on a per capita basis. In that case, the big picture is very different: the highest rankings belong to North Korea (49 per 1,000 active military), Eritrea (34) and Israel (20), whereas Russia ranks 19th (8), the U.S. 56th (3.9) and China 133rd (1.4). There is a caveat, however. Even in aggregate terms, the U.S. figure is an understatement because it does not include the employees of the U.S. Homeland Security (about 260,000), intelligence community (100,000 directly; eight times more if those with top-secret clearances are included) and several other major organizations with significant input in the U.S. foreign policy.[79]

When Truman and Eisenhower carried out their [economic] reforms, both presidents still allocated defense outlays using the "remainder method"; that is, they subtracted necessary domestic spending from tax revenues and gave everything else to defense. But at least they were "conscious of the ill effects of being a debtor nation."[80] Today, the long-term impact of America's mounting fiscal woes, due to military expenditures on domestic welfare and international security, is ignored. The neglect comes with grave long-term consequences. The Middle East and the Israel-Palestine conflict are a case in point.

The Rise of U.S. Military Aid to Israel—and in Israel

For all practical purposes, the U.S.-Israeli military ties are locked in for years, even decades ahead. In 2016, the two governments signed their third 10-year Memorandum of Understanding (MOU) on military aid, covering fiscal years from 2019 to 2028. Under these terms, the U.S. has pledged to provide, with congressional approval, $38 billion to Israel in military aid; that is, $33 billion in Foreign Military Financing (FMF) grants plus $5 billion in missile defense appropriations.

The symbiotic ties are reflected by an ever deepening technology relationship and Israel's role as a U.S. military priority. The latter includes Israel's privileged role as the first international operator of the F-35 Joint Strike Fighter, the Pentagon's fifth-generation stealth aircraft, perhaps the most technologically advanced fighter jet ever made. To date, Israel has purchased 50 F-35s in three separate contracts, funded with U.S. assistance. For fiscal 2023, Congress also authorized $520 million for joint U.S.-Israel defense programs, including $500 million for missile defense. Congress appropriated an annual $3.8 billion for Israel (FMF and missile defense), adding almost $100 million in funding for other cooperative defense and nondefense programs. With the Gaza War, the aid skyrocketed (Figure 3-6).[81]

Figure 3-6   U.S. Aid to Israel, 1949–2023

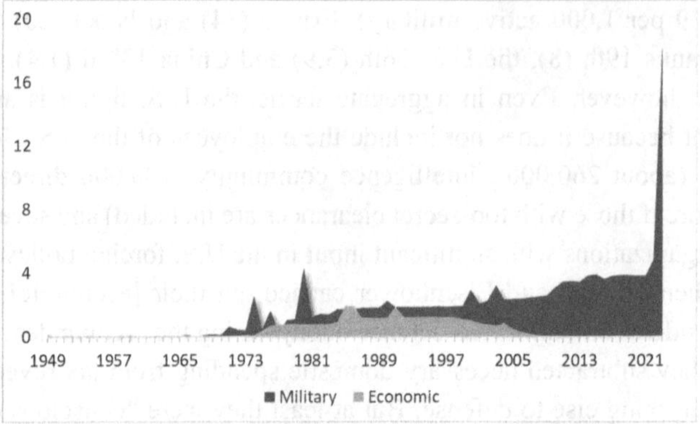

Sources: Data from ForeignAssistance.gov; author

In May 2012, a year before the talks began with Iran on a nuclear deal, the U.S. had an early missile warning radar station on Mt. Keren in Israel. The radar could detect a Shahab-3 missile launched toward Israel from Tehran 1,000 miles away to the northwest within seconds into its flight; or 6–7 minutes earlier than Israel would know from its own radar. Those additional minutes increased the time Israeli officials would have to sound sirens by 60 percent, as well as its chances of launching interceptors to knock down the incoming missile before it reached Israel. This discreet complex and the 100 U.S. service members who staffed it also posed "a compelling argument against any notion that the Jewish state will launch an attack on Iran without the United States."[82] When the radar installation was announced in 2008, it was the first permanent foreign military installation on Israeli soil. Wary of the U.S. presence, some top officials compared the early warning system to "a pair of golden handcuffs on Israel."[83] After all, the responses would be dictated by the *U.S.* national security considerations. That said, the cooperation was a prelude of more to come.

In September 2017, Israel and the U.S. inaugurated the first official American military base on Israeli soil with dozens of soldiers operating a missile defense system. The launch of the Bislach Air Base near Be'er Sheva occurred in parallel with the Trump administration's sparring with Iran and Israeli unease about Tehran's long-range missiles. Just weeks before October 7, the Pentagon awarded a multimillion-dollar contract to expand U.S. troop facilities for a secret military facility within Israel's Negev desert, only 20 miles from Gaza. Code-named "Site 512," the U.S. base was a radar facility monitoring the skies for missile attacks on Israel. Ironically, when thousands of Hamas rockets were launched on October 7 from Gaza, Site 512 saw nothing. It was focused on Iran.[84]

Built in cooperation with the U.S., Israel's multilayered system of defenses includes the Arrow, designed to intercept long-range ballistic missiles in the stratosphere with an eye on Iran; the Iron Dome, against short-range rockets from the Gaza Strip; and David's Sling, to counter the medium-range missiles possessed by Iranian-backed Hezbollah. Located within an existing Israeli air force base and operating under Israeli military directives, the base's opening sent a message that any attack against Israel is indirectly an intrusion into a U.S. defense system as well.[85] When Israel bombed the Iranian embassy in Damascus, killing two Iranian generals, on April 14, 2024, the system was tested. The Islamic Revolutionary Guard Corps (IRGC), a branch of the Iranian military, launched retaliatory attacks against Israel and the Israeli-occupied Golan Heights with drones, cruise missiles, and ballistic missiles, together with the Islamic Resistance in Iraq, Hezbollah in Lebanon, and the Yemeni Houthis. Israel shot down most – not all – of the incoming weapons. Moreover, this relative success relied on cooperation with U.S., British, French, and Jordanian air forces, plus French warships for radar coverage, whom the Iranians had warned in advance.[86]

Not only did the interceptions reflect the limited extent of Israel's ability to deflect such attacks, even when aided by the combined efforts of Western nations and with lengthy warning in advance. It also highlighted both Israel's increasing dependency on U.S. support – and conversely, the inadequacy of that support. Despite the massive U.S. aid and the effective multilateralization of critical aspects of defense, Israel was not invulnerable and its liabilities were growing more costly and complicated. While most of the incoming weapons – 99% as Western media intoned relentlessly – had indeed been shot down, this had been at great cost. Israel spent some 4–5 billion shekels ($1.1–1.4 billion) to intercept Iran's flurry of drone and missile strikes, as estimated by General Reem Adminaoch, a former Israel economic adviser to the army. "One Arrow missile used to intercept an Iranian ballistic missile costs $3.5 million, while the cost of one David Sling missile is $1 million, in addition to the sorties of aircraft that participated in intercepting the Iranian drones," Adminaoch added. These estimates cover only the interception of what the Iranians launched; but neither the damage and injuries that were marginal "this time."[87] Meanwhile, a senior researcher in an Israeli security think tank told the *Wall Street Journal* that the costs "were enormous" and comparable to what Israel had spent during the 1973 Arab-Israeli War.[88]

Furthermore, Iran had demonstrated that, despite advance warning, it was nonetheless able to penetrate not just Israeli defenses, but those of the combined West. An estimated nine Iranian missiles that breached Israel's air defenses hit two Israeli air bases, while five ballistic missiles struck the Nevatim Air Base and another four hit the Negev Air Base. In each case, the damage was marginal.[89]

As far as Iran was concerned, it had achieved its objective. First of all, it had cautioned Israel about the impending attack, to minimize collateral damage that could be exploited for a disproportionate retaliation. Overtly, it had demonstrated its military capacity while seeking to avoid unwarranted civilian casualties and unnecessary infrastructure damage. The tacit signal was more significant. It sought to demonstrate what Iran *could* do, yet refrained from doing; this time. After all, Nevatim is not just one of the largest air bases in Israel, hosting stealth fighter jets, transport aircraft, tanker aircraft and machines for electronic reconnaissance/surveillance. It was also the home of the Wing of Zion; that is, Israel's main government transport aircraft, tasked with transporting the president and prime minister overseas during international visits. The message was: We can reach your country, your leaders, your military, your people, and your critical infrastructure, when and if we want to. We do not seek escalation. But we will defend our nation from your aggression.

It was an unambiguous set of signals that could have been used for de-escalation by the United States and Israel. Yet, neither chose such tact. Instead, Israel sent its own signal just months later. Instead of an enduring ceasefire agreement that would have resulted in the release of the Israeli hostages, PM Netanyahu greenlighted still another targeted assassination, to "eliminate" Ismail Haniyeh, the pragmatic political leader of Hamas and its principal negotiator. Moreover, the assassination was conducted in Iran and on the very day of the inauguration of its new, reform-minded president, Masoud Pezeshkian. In other words, the purpose of the assassination was to undermine the release of the Israeli hostages; to kill ceasefire talks; to sabotage possible peace prospects with Hamas; to spark regional escalation and use it as a pretext for a war against Hezbollah and expansion into southern Lebanon, up to the Litani River; to violate Iranian sovereignty in order to engage Iran's Revolutionary Guards Corps; and to sabotage the Pezeshkian presidency prior to his rule, to expand distance between Washington and Tehran.

Seldom has any hope of hope been strangled in so many ways, in such a short time.

Long before October 7, secretary of defense Lloyd J. Austin III had affirmed that the U.S. "commitment to Israel is enduring, and it is ironclad." In summer 2023, Biden seconded him. And hours after the Hamas offensive,

Austin pledged Israel America's "ironclad support."[90] By now, the phrase is an essential part of the liturgical rhetoric that the White House cultivated with its major strategic and non-NATO partners, despite the dark track record of elevated military assistance from Afghanistan and Iraq to Ukraine and even darker in Gaza. But in the long view, it is quite consistent with U.S. policies in the region at large. The challenge was to reconcile America's "special relationship with Israel" with the interests of the regional countries.

Chapter 4
PERILS OF MILITARIZATION

It was a catastrophe without comparison. Israeli journalist Gideon Levy tried to speak on the phone with his friends in Gaza until his heart just gave way. He felt overwhelmed by the sheer extent of devastation. The dead, the wounded, the buildings destroyed, the mosques demolished, the factories gone, the educational institutions leveled:

> It was a war that was no war, in which Israel met virtually no resistance, no counterattack worth speaking of. It was just a wild onslaught upon the most helpless population in the world, besieged and jailed, with nowhere to run, not even into the sea. White phosphorous shells scorching living flesh, Flechettes flinging their nails far and wide, manned and unmanned aircraft discharging missiles, disproportionate bombing and shelling. Hundreds of innocents were killed for no other reason other than they were Gazans. The people of Gaza, many of them born to 1948's refugees, who had already suffered one tragedy by Israel's hand, now faced the next chapter in the tragic saga of their lives: an aimless, futile, criminal, superfluous offensive.[1]

Some knew it as the Battle of al-Furqan, others as the Gaza Massacre, whereas Israel called it Operation Cast Lead. It sounded decisive, yet somehow sanitized the smell of death. This wasn't the 2023–2024 Gaza War, however. It was the 2008–2009 Gaza War, which lasted just three weeks, not months. But since it occurred in the aftermath of the West's financial crisis, the atrocities and war crimes were buried behind headlines about recession, mass layoffs, and white-collar blunder. It took place almost 15 years ago. But like a musical section introducing the theme, it heralded a dark opera or cantata. It was a prelude to what would be perfected following October 7 – wholesale death and devastation. It heralded an endgame in which there would be no winners.

But how did unilateral militarization sideline multilateral diplomacy in Israel? Was the obliteration of Gaza a proof of its success or failure?

SOURCES OF ISRAEL'S MILITARY SUPREMACY

Today, Israeli military is intertwined with the U.S. military-industrial complex. Thereby, it is subject to the kind of pressures that complex is coping with. In addition to basic military spending, there is another side to the perils of militarization. American defense innovation suffers from cost pressures; the decline of the U.S. industrial base and its ability to support defense needs; the bias for short-term policies; the erosion of domestic defense innovation; and growing competitive challenges from other nations. As a result, the Pentagon is eager to exploit other viable sources of military innovation among its major NATO and non-NATO allies, such as Israel, particularly after the demise of the Soviet Union. The relative decline of U.S. defense technology leadership reflects the broader erosion of American innovation overall.[2] By the 1970s and '80s, Western Europe and Japan had caught up with the U.S. on the global innovation frontier. The subsequent U.S.-led IT revolution of the 1990s seemed to slow down innovation convergence, but only until the bubble burst in the early 2000s. Indeed, the technological advancement of large emerging economies, such as China, and major transitional economies like Russia, has even more clearly delineated different nations' impacts in global innovation.[3] Hence, America's interest in the Israeli military and its surveillance innovation.

Israel's National Security

In 1953, Israel's first prime minister, David Ben-Gurion, crafted a strategy to respond to the national security challenges of the young country. It laid down the pillars of Israel's national security doctrine until the 1967 War.[4] Subsequently, there have been a number of new formulations, yet none of these have matched the scope and influence of the original document.[5]

According to Ben-Gurion's "The Military and the State," Israel's Arab neighbors had not accepted Israel's right to exist and were determined to finish Israel's destruction.[6] What worked against Israel was these countries' demographic size and resources, which would allow them to acquire advanced weapon systems and military capacity over time. But Israel had its own advantages. While its small size did not allow strategic depth, it could move troops fast from one location to another. Thanks to immigrants, it benefited from more qualified human capital. And unlike the large but disunited

Arab world, Israel was a singular actor as long as it was united internally. Hence, the need for an advanced air force and intelligence that could keep its neighbors in check; expansive Jewish immigration to build a larger qualified population; coupled with requisite educational and science systems; mandatory military service and huge reserves that could be mobilized rapidly; and an overwhelming ethos of unity that would ensure that the small "nation in uniform" would be more effective than a simple sum of its parts. Despite his ideological differences with revisionist Zionism, BG's grand strategy was predicated on Ze'ev Jabotinsky's "Iron Wall." Israel would build such a strong security state that eventually Arabs would have to be resigned to its presence in the Middle East.[7]

Since Israel would not be able to halt Arab wars, effective deterrence was vital to keep the enemy at bay and wars less frequent. If that failed, Israel needed an early warning system to respond to the challenge in time. In case of conflict, decisive victory was necessary. The more stunning the triumph was, the more it would buy time to address the next attack. Furthermore, there were three additional caveats regarding external circumstances. Israel needed to align with a major power to secure advanced weapon systems and upgraded military capacity. Hence, the early partnership with France and subsequently with the United States. Building on the French-Israeli cooperation, the second factor was "nuclear ambiguity." Israel would develop nuclear capacity as soon as possible but never officially disclose its existence or size. Unofficially, it would signal and occasionally inflate both. Indeed, the shrewd use of signaling was an inherent part of the deterrence. This ultimate deterrence would be used only when all other alternatives had been exhausted, which almost happened in October 1973.

That gave rise to the other side of the nuclear opacity: the Begin doctrine which deemed that Israel will never allow its enemies to acquire nuclear weapons. Hence, Begin's 1981 air strike on Saddam Hussein's Osirak nuclear reactor to block Iraq's nuclear ambitions. Finally, a third element was needed in the region. Even in the case of a war with its proximate neighbors, Israel could cultivate alliances with *their* neighbors. In the postwar era, this "alliance of the periphery" was premised on cooperation with Türkiye and the Shah's Iran, and Ethiopia. Hence, the logic: the enemy of my enemy is my friend, which could be used to weaken and divide the prime adversary.

Following the 1967 War and the subsequent 1973 Yom Kippur War, the regional status quo changed. As the Allon Plan was not codified by the Labor governments, the fate of the occupied territories became the primary risk, especially after the 1979 Israel-Egypt peace treaty and the reluctance of the Likud governments to define Israel's ultimate borders. Until then, the PLO and its reluctance to recognize Israel had been seen as the main obstacle to peace. Now, with the aggressive expansion of the settlements, the Begin government refused to recognize the Palestinian case, even after Arafat had recognized the right of Israel to exist in 1988. In the absence of viable, peaceful alternatives, Palestinians had few alternatives but to fight back, which Israel sought to crush with disproportionate force. Hence, the First Intifada (1987–93), the rise and fall of the peace process, the Second Intifada (2000–2005), and a series of Gaza Wars paving the way to October 7, 2023.

From the 1967 War to October 7, the occupied territories had provided greater strategic depth, but at the cost of peace and stability. Israeli educational and science systems remain impressive, but the former is eroding, while its science systems suffer from brain drain. The ethos of unity prevailed, but the actual unity was gone. Israel was more polarized than ever before. Overall, this reflected social differentiation that is typical of most post-industrial societies. By the 2000s, sociologists saw Israel as a melting pot of more than half a dozen social segments, including the previously hegemonic secular Ashkenazi upper middle class, the national religious, the traditionalist Mizrahim (Orientals), the Orthodox religious, the Arabs, the new Russian immigrants, and the Ethiopians. None of these groups were homogeneous, and most of them harbored deep political and ideological divergences (e.g., "hawks" vs. "doves"). Yet, each held on to a separate collective identity and often waged a cultural war against the others.[8] Though characteristic of advanced economies, such "identity politics" posed a special challenge in Israel where it undermined the ethos of unity critical to the national security strategy.

Furthermore, there was an Iron Wall on the borders, coupled with a Separation Wall and checkpoints in the West Bank. Yet, peace and security were even more elusive than before. Then October 7 mocked the much-touted deterrence. The "ironclad ties" remain with the U.S., but the Gaza War demonstrated their limits. Alliances in the periphery were once augmented with normalization efforts with the Gulf states, but all have been alienated by Israel's conduct of the war in Gaza, including Egypt and Jordan. The ties with Türkiye are frozen. Iran, which Israel lost as an ally with the Islamic Revolution, is now a highly consequential regional adversary.

Israeli capabilities remain impressive, but there are increasing doubts as to whether they are sufficient. And they are synonymous with neither a political solution nor an enduring peace. In the long-term, the economic costs of those capabilities are likely to prove untenable.

Israel's Qualitative Military Edge

In 2009, Dan Senor and Saul Singer published their bestseller, *Start-up Nation: The Story of Israel's Economic Miracle*, seeking to explain how Israel, despite its wars, "produces more start-up companies on a per capita basis than large, peaceful, and stable nations and regions like Japan, China, India, Korea, Canada, and all of Europe?"[9] Actually, both authors were born Americans. Senor was a high-profile neoconservative, ex-spokesman for the Coalition Provisional Authority in Iraq, longtime Republican operative and one-time Mitt Romney advisor. Singer was his brother-in-law and a former adviser in U.S. Congress, who immigrated to Israel in the mid-'90s. In their view, the key to Israeli success was largely internal and all about the persistence of battlefield entrepreneurs "seeding a culture of innovation."[10]

What *Start-up Nation* downplayed was the "qualitative military edge" (QME), which for over half a century had paved the way to Israel's high-tech triumph and has been legislatively institutionalized. Independently of Israel, the concept of QME originates from the Cold War. Since countries of the Warsaw Pact had a numerical advantage over the U.S. and allied forces stationed in Europe, America sought to maintain a qualitative edge in defense systems. After the Six-Day War, the Johnson administration became resigned to the prospect of an increasing drift of the Arab States toward Moscow. Hence, its 1968 approval to sell Phantom fighters to Israel, replacing the French Mirages that had triumphed in the Six-Day War. With the Yom Kippur War, the QME concept became specifically applied to Israel in relation to its Arab adversaries. As U.S. Secretary of State Alexander Haig put it in 1981, "a central aspect of U.S. policy since the October 1973 war has been to ensure that Israel maintains a qualitative military edge."[11]

The QME is predicated on the idea of technological, tactical, and other advantages, based on advanced technology that allows Israel with its small population to deter its Arab adversaries with their huge populations. Conceptually defined by Israel's first prime minister Ben-Gurion in 1953, the notion of qualitative superiority is a core component of Israel's defense to maintain a military edge over regional adversaries.

For decades, successive administrations, in cooperation with Congress, have taken measures to maintain Israel's QME. That's why U.S. arms sales policy has permitted Israel first regional access to U.S. defense technology. When both Israel and an Arab state operate the same U.S. platform, Israel has first received a more advanced version of the platform or the ability to customize the U.S. system. When Israel has objected to a major defense article sale to an Arab military – for instance, the 1981 sale of Airborne Early Warning and Control System aircraft (AWACS) to Saudi Arabia – Congress has at times promoted and legislated conditions on the usage and transfer of such weapons prior to or after a sale.[12] In 1992, after the U.S. announced a sale to Saudi Arabia of F-15 fighters, the Bush Sr. administration offered Israel Apache and Blackhawk helicopters. In 2007, when the Bush Jr. administration sold Saudi Arabia Joint Direct Attack Munitions (JDAMs), it agreed to sell more advanced JDAMs to Israel, again to preserve its QME. Just three years later, the Obama administration sold an additional 20 F-35 aircraft to Israel, following a sale to Saudi Arabia that included F-15s. In 2013, when the Obama administration sold the UAE advanced F-16 fighters, it provided Israel with KC-135 refueling aircraft, anti-radiation missiles, advanced radar, and – for the first time to another country – the sale of six V-22 Osprey tilt-rotor aircraft.[13]

If President Johnson's Phantom deal first extended the QME into the U.S.-Israel bilateral ties, Reagan was the first president to commit to Israel's QME, which every subsequent administration has repeated. The commitment to maintain Israel's qualitative military edge was formally written into law in September 2008.[14]

One implication is that those weapons that Israel used to obliterate Gaza into nothingness were predicated on cutting-edge technological innovation in the United States, which was thus complicit in the Strip's genocidal atrocities.

The Costs of Military Supremacy

In Israel, the defense industry is a pivotal employer, a major supplier of the Israeli Defense Forces (IDF) and has been a leading exporter worldwide. Amounting to $28 billion in 2023, its defense expenditure, despite the small Israeli economy, ranks 15th worldwide, ahead of Canada (population of 40 million), Spain (40m) and Brazil (215m). The industry originates from secret weapons factories of small arms and explosives in the pre-state era. In this early era, the key player was the Israel Military Industries (IMI, or "Ta'as"), which was founded in 1933 and is today headquartered in Ramat Sharon, an affluent suburb north of Tel Aviv. During and after the 1948 War, the Jews used arms produced domestically, surplus U.S. machinery and wartime surplus aircraft, tanks and artillery. The nascent industry excelled in upgrading such equipment, as evidenced by the Uzi submachine gun, a minor export success at the time. The absence of peace contributed to the expansion of the industry. In the late 1950's, IMI began collaboration with the Israel Defense Forces (IDF) aiming to develop the most technologically advanced small arms systems for troops fighting in urban areas and harsh environments. The distinct existence of the state-owned IMI ended in 2018, when it was taken over by Elbit Systems.

From the 1950s to the 1967 War, France served as Israel's primary military supplier. By the mid-to late 1970s – that is, prior to the broad alignment with the U.S. – indigenous suppliers were delivering an increasing share of the IDF's major weapons systems. These systems featured the Reshef missile boat, the Kfir fighter plane, the Gabriel missile, and the Merkava tank. The Kfir was based on plans of the French Mirage III acquired clandestinely through a Swiss source. It was powered with a U.S. General Electric J79 engine, yet embodied Israeli-designed and Israeli-produced components for the flight control and weapons delivery systems. Israeli products proved attractive, but its international isolation limited sales potential. The pressure by Arab countries played a part in decisions by Austria and Taiwan not to buy the Kfir and in Brazil's decision not to purchase the Gabriel missile for its navy. By contrast, South Africa, despite the UN arms embargo against arms shipments to the Pretoria government, acquired six Reshef missile boats, more than 100 Gabriel missiles, radar and communications systems, while upgrading its British-built Centurion tanks with Israeli assistance. Total employment in the domestic defense sector peaked around the mid-1980s.[15]

Israel's military cooperation with the United States took off amidst the Yom Kippur War. During its aftermath, U.S. military aid to Israel soared. Following Netanyahu's first cabinet, the crumbling peace process and the Second Intifada (2000–2005), military expenditure began to climb again. It doubled during the Netanyahu cabinets. Nonetheless, its share steadily decreased as a percentage of GDP from 15 percent in the early '80s to close to 5 percent in the '90s (Figure 4-1).

Figure 4-1   Israel's Military Expenditure

(*Blue*) In millions of US$ at current prices and exchange rates. (*Red*) As percentage of gross domestic product. *Source: Data from SIPRI*

With barely 10 million people, prior to October 2023 the Israeli military had 170,000 active personnel and 465,000 reservists. By comparison, Europe's largest military, France which has almost 70 million people, has 208,000 active military personnel, but barely 24,000 reservists. With extensive reserve duties, Israeli male recruits serve 32 months and women for two years; far longer than their peers in other countries. This way Israel can mobilize tens of thousands very fast. In this sense, it is a "people's army" but one that has proven very costly in terms of missed economic opportunities. In the late 1960s, Israel played a major role in the creation of the Singaporean military. Both are small countries surrounded by more populous and ethnically different nations. Each has invested significantly into defense. Both had little land and natural resources. Yet, they chose very different growth trajectories.

Unlike Israel, Singapore, under the leadership of Lee Kuan-Yew, opted for a multicultural nationhood, to avoid the kind of race riots that threatened to divide the country in the mid-1960s. By contrast, Israel's secular-democratic state did not ensure equal rights to its Arab citizens; not even to Jews with Mizrahi background. Furthermore, unlike Israel, Singapore chose to stress economic development as its central objective, thereby reinforcing internal integration and cultivating friendly trading ties with its far bigger neighbors and beyond them. By contrast, Israel made national security its central tenet at the expense of economic development. As a result, funds that could have fostered unity and balanced regional development have been steered to security and suppression in the occupied territories. Meanwhile, it has suffered from international isolation and grown massively reliant on U.S. military aid and money flows by American Jewry, particularly revisionist Zionists.

The net effects are reflected in military expenditure. In Israel, the expenditure has been consistently more than twice as high as Singapore's. Thanks to its massive immigration, Israel's population is today almost 40 percent higher relative to Singapore. That might explain some of the difference. However, military expenditure as a percentage of GDP tells the story. In Israel, it soared to more than 30 percent of the GDP by the mid-1970s. Thereafter, it decreased to 10 percent in the 1990s and 5 percent in the 2000s. By contrast, the figure was its highest – about 5 percent – until the mid-1980s but has declined since 2000 to about 2.7 percent of the GDP. In brief, the discrepancy between the Israeli and Singaporean ratio peaked at 25 percent; and even today Israelis invest twice as much into defense as Singaporeans. Unlike Israel, Singapore moved from Third World to First World status in just a generation. Unlike Israel, Singapore did it without U.S. military aid and external fundings, which never comes without strings attached (it opted for foreign investment by major Western economies). The net effect? Singaporean per capita income is today twice as high as that in Israel.

At the aggregate level, the five biggest military spenders in 2023 were the United States, China, Russia, India and Saudi Arabia, which together account for 61 percent of world military spending. But aggregate figures ignore the military burden *per capita*. Obviouslly, big countries have bigger defense budgets. But some small countries carry an even higher burden. Israel is a case in point. It ranks second in the per capita spending. Aside from Ukraine that Israel supplies and Singapore, whose military it once built and still supplies, the list includes mainly the Gulf states, including Qatar, UAE, Saudi Arabia and Kuwait. Even in 2023 Israel's spending was 50 percent more than that of Ukraine. Though the country is no longer in war with its Arab neighbors and has had no such war in decades, its military spending continued to climb. Then Israel's large-scale Gaza offensive caused monthly military expenditure to almost triple to $4.7 billion in the month of December 2023; that's $56 billion in annual terms, or a tenth of the country's GDP.

The Burden of Israel-U.S. Military Ties

In Israel, even "peace" – bearing in mind incessant friction with Hezbollah in the north, with Palestinians in the occupied territories, and a massive military-industrial-surveillance complex deployed to manage this untenable system – is very costly. During the past decade, Israel's military spending as a share of GDP amounted to 5.3 percent; that's almost twice as high as the average of developed countries in the period. Back in the 1970s, it had registered at around 20 to 30 percent, whereas in the past two decades, it has been around 4 to 6 percent.

The longstanding per capita burden and missed opportunity costs of peace are huge. Israel's share of world population is 0.1 percent. Yet, its share of world military spending amounts to a stunning 1.1 percent. That's a whopping *11 times* its demographic role in the world.[16] An increasing number of Israelis wonder if their wars are just U.S. proxy wars in which their heroic task is to die to the last Israeli to maintain the occupation.

From this perspective, Israel's extensive military ties with the United States undermine rather than foster its national security. The official purpose of the latter is peace. By contrast, the U.S. military support is predicated on a continued and exhaustive strategy of tension, which is then deployed as the rationale for new arms sales, which, in turn, ensure the expansion of the Pentagon and its global defense contractors. In view of Big Defense, peace is bad business, whereas lasting conflicts and simmering hotspots are good for business.[17] Both the U.S. and Israel face an untenable future, due to their dependency on military expenditure, which is undermining the welfare state in Israel and what's left of it in the U.S. Worse, when the indebtness in America results in a national crisis, U.S. military aid will be significantly reduced and Jewish-American financial transfers will take a hit as well.

One doesn't have to be a peace activist or a cynic to connect the dots. Along with Ukraine and Taiwan, Israel is a textbook case of the operations of Big Defense, thanks to the revolving doors between the Pentagon, defense contractors and think tanks. Indeed, State Secretary Antony Blinken, National Security Adviser Jake Sullivan and Defense Secretary Lloyd Austin have all been connected with the Center for a New American Security (CNAS) and other think tanks, consultancies and lobbies that sell access to the White House. While in the Pentagon, Austin bought arms from Raytheon; as Raytheon's board member, he sold weapons to the Pentagon; as Defense Secretary, he oversees purchases from the contractors, and so on and so forth. It is a veritable, lucrative and huge merry-go-round racket, ridden with moral hazard and conflicts of interests, but one that's global, increasingly lethal and complicit in genocides.[18]

EXPORTING WEAPONS AND SURVEILLANCE
From Agricultural Aid to Arms Transfers and South Africa

During his visit in April 1976, Israeli TV showed South Africa's prime minister John Vorster arriving at the airport to be greeted by Israel's PM Yitzhak Rabin with a warm hug. Next, Vorster was taken to Yad Vashem, the Holocaust Memorial in Jerusalem. Actually, the South African should have been arrested and prosecuted, according to Israeli law, as a Nazi collaborator. Why wasn't that the case?

In World War II, Vorster had fought in the pro-Nazi *Ossewabrandwag*. Subsequently, he claimed he had been anti-British rather than pro-Nazi, which did not prevent him from implementing and maintaining South Africa's apartheid policy since 1948. Like his precursor, Vorster sympathized with Israel, which white South Africans considered another apartheid state.[19] In his view, both countries represented white civilization. South Africa had its blacks; Israel, its Palestinians. Both had to cope with savages and that required force. Most importantly, the two shared a common interest that overrode other considerations: international arms transfers. Only a year before Vorster's photo-op in Yad Vashem, Israel and South Africa agreed on a secret defense co-operation pact. It was convenient at a time when both were unable to source weapons and defense technology on the international market, due to arms embargoes. Officially, each denied the existence of the pact until 2010, when the relevant documents were declassified, including Israel's offer to sell nuclear warheads to South Africa.[20]

South Africa was not an exception, but a rule. Israel also sold napalm and other weapons to El Salvador during its counterinsurgency wars between 1980–1992 that killed more than 75,000 civilians. In 1994, Israeli-made bullets, rifles and grenades were allegedly used in Rwanda's genocide which killed at least 800,000 people. In 2023–2024, the Gaza War was just the latest test laboratory for the Israeli arms industry. Nevertheless, the timeline matters. Until the 1960s, Israel was still known for the secular socialism of its pioneering generation and development aid to agricultural experts in many African countries of which Golda Meir was so proud. By the 1970s, things were rapidly changing as Israel was already gaining dark notoriety for its Messianic settlers, clandestine weapons sales and military advisors in the developing economies of Africa, Asia and Latin America. The longer the Israeli occupation has prevailed, the greater capabilities Israel has acquired in counter-insurgency operations, which now complement the classic staple of its arms transfers, often tested in the occupied territories.

Israeli Arms Suppliers and the Periphery Doctrine

International arms transfers are dominated by the United States, the world's largest arms supplier. In Israel, its origins can be dated from the 1950s when Paris and Tel Aviv shared a joint challenge. With a disintegrating overseas empire, France was struggling to sustain its Arab colonies in northern Africa. Meanwhile, Israel saw itself threatened by the Arab world. When the two aligned, France became Israel's main arms supplier and subsequently a partner in the 1956 War. There were 140,000 Jews in Algeria. Some joined the indigenous FLN fighting for independence but most sided with the French and the secret paramilitary group, OAS. The military alliance with France led the Israelis to also learn more about the *guerre revolutionnaire*, which was applied in Algeria following the French defeat in Indochina.[21] Some of the ideal tenets of the doctrine were developed by David Galula, a French military officer and scholar of Jewish descent. Galula argued that it was the absence of an appropriate counterinsurgency doctrine that accounted for the debacle of "French pacification" in Algeria, particularly for the brutality that failed to win hearts and minds in Algeria, alienated support in metropolitan France while discrediting French prestige abroad.[22] The U.S. intervention in Vietnam where Americans replaced the French in the 1950s, was inspired by the brutality of the *de facto* French counterinsurgency in Algeria and, Galula might well say, has today contributed to the failures of Israeli military practices in the occupied territories, just as it did later to U.S. operations in Afghanistan and Iraq.

In the mainstream narrative, most of Israel's initial arms sales were to Third World countries. Due to the financing challenges of the clients and competition from new Third World arms producers such as Brazil and Taiwan, Israel engaged in joint ventures and coproduction that allowed it to break into the more lucrative American and Western European markets. By the early 1980s, more than 50 countries on five continents had become customers for Israeli military equipment.[23]

The France-Israel alliance was aligned with the broader "periphery doctrine" that was developed against Arab encirclement by Reuven Shiloah, the first director of the "Central Institute for Coordination" (Mossad) in 1949–1953. A close advisor to Ben-Gurion, Moshe Sharett and several other early Israeli leaders, Shiloah developed the periphery doctrine, or the purposeful effort of creating ties between Israel and the countries beyond the immediate circle of hostile neighbors (Israel's proximate Arab neighbors, Egypt, Jordan, Syria, and Lebanon refusing to recognize the State of Israel and boycotting it); that is, countries like Turkey, Iran, Ethiopia, Sudan and eventually some African nations as well.[24] Over time, the periphery strategy called for ties with the Phalangists in Christian Lebanon, royalists in Yemen, rebels in Southern Sudan, and Kurds in Iraq. Hence, its encouragement of non-Arab and non-Muslim minorities in the Middle East – the Lebanese Maronites, the Druze, and the Kurds – to seek political independence in cooperation with Israel. Following decades of military cooperation with the U.S., Israel's regional strategy shifted in the 2010s, when the Netanyahu cabinets have been increasingly guided by what some call a "reverse periphery doctrine," promoting relations with those Gulf monarchies that share Israel's security and economic interests.[25] That was very much in the U.S. interest in the region.

Military Ties with Autocratic Democracies

Thanks to the secular-socialist image of its founding generation, Israel could initially seek alignments with developing economies from Asia to sub-Saharan Africa. Building on increasing cooperation with the U.S. and its military aid, these efforts to win friends in the Third World gave way to military collaboration with some of the most ruthless regimes beyond the Middle East, as Israel was used to cement ties with the kind of dictators America needed but with whom it could not officially align.

In Asia, these involvements started with military cooperation with Burma (present-day Myanmar) in the late 1950s, before General Ne Win's coup and the country's international isolation, and with Lee Kuan Yew's Singapore in the early 1960s, as Israelis built the foundations of the city-state's defense. By the 1970s, these engagements deteriorated to collaboration with the likes of Taiwan's Generalissimo Chiang Kai-shek, South Korea's general Park Chung Hee, and the Philippines under Ferdinand Marcos. In General Suharto's Indonesia Mossad operated under commercial cover, while U.S. Skyhawks planes were sold from Israel to Indonesia. When the CIA launched its Operation Cyclone in Afghanistan against the Soviet Union, Israel was one of the countries supporting the armed struggle of the Muslim jihadists. Israelis trained the Sri Lankan army in counterinsurgency. Due to their role in the Non-Alignment Movement, India and China resisted Israeli courting until the end of the Cold War. In sub-Saharan Africa, Israel first established relations with Ethiopia and Liberia in 1957, followed by the Congo, Nigeria, the Ivory Coast and Tanzania at the turn of the 1960s. By the Six-Day War, Israel had diplomatic contacts with much of sub-Saharan Africa as long as the countries were in the pro-West camp. In Africa, Israel's activities were influenced and financed largely by the U.S. and other major Western powers, such as West Germany and France. Hence, too, the major role of the CIA in financing Israel's African "foreign aid" operations in the late '60s. Israel's ties with the continent declined following the 1967 War, with a broader collapse after the 1973 war and the OPEC oil boycott.[26] What survived was Israel's alliance with apartheid South Africa. In the 1980s, the country was believed to be one of Israel's principal trade partners. With the "Jerusalem-Pretoria Axis," South Africa emerged as "Israel's second most important ally, after the U.S."[27] But as declassified files show, during the Cold War, Israel did not serve just U.S. interests, ideally it sought to sell arms to all parties. Angola is a textbook case illustrating how the arms, diamonds and oil business can thrive as long as politics, human rights and corruption can be ignored.[28]

But as Israel kept its control over the occupied territories, it became isolated in the rest of the world. The exception was the U.S.-dominated Western Hemisphere, particularly Latin American dictatorships under the U.S.-led Operation Condor. This circle of military leaders – including General Augusto Pinochet in Chile, General Romeo Lucas Garcia of Guatemala, Roberto D'Aubuisson of El Salvador, Paraguay's General Alfredo Stroessner, and Nicaragua's Anastasio Somoza – admired Israel's ruthless military efficiency, particularly its counterinsurgency operations. "In Central America, Israel is the 'dirty work' contractor for the U.S. administration," wrote Knesset member Matityahu Peled in the mid-1980s, on the eve of the First Intifada.[29]

In Haiti, President Duvalier loved to carry his ubiquitous Uzi. In Argentina, "generals Viola, Videla, Valin, and Galtieri became gracious hosts to Israeli military and civilian leaders, and their names grew familiar to their Israeli counterparts during the years of military rule."[30]

In a sense, these ties climaxed in the 1980s with Israel's role in the controversial Iran-Contra affair, when senior Reagan administration officials covertly facilitated the illegal sale of arms to Iran, subject to an arms embargo, hoping to use the proceeds to fund the Contras, an anti-Sandinista rebel group in Nicaragua. The postwar clandestine relationship between Israel and Iran dates from the 1950s and involved the Shah and most major Israeli political leaders from David Ben-Gurion and Golda Meir to Yitzhak Rabin, Shimon Peres, and Menachem Begin. Though linking a wide range of activities, including close cooperation between Israel's security operatives and Iran's hated SAVAK, the Iranian secret police and intelligence service, it was mainly about oil-for-arms to Israel. In the early postwar era, the bilateral relationship aimed to weaken Egyptian President Nasser's grip on the region and limit Soviet influence, with the encouragement of the White House. And so it was that in 1982, the U.S. supported Israel's plans to supply arms and military instructors for an (ultimately unrealized) coup attempt against Khomeini. The Khomeini Revolution resulted in the severance of formal ties with Israel, but it did not close all channels to Tehran. Nor did it halt Iran's interest in acquiring American arms, insofar as this was at the time largely unavoidable, given its prior holding of American weaponry. Once again, Israel served as a matchmaker, paralleling the role it played in the days of the Shah.

With the end of the Cold War, Israel's military ties with and through the U.S. seemed to diminish, but they did not disappear. With the U.S. post-9/11 wars, many of the military involvements revived and surged, particularly with the booming Israeli military and surveillance exports. Everything old was new again. In the post-9/11 wars, Washington would ultimately spend over $8 trillion in military expenditure. It was a veritable bonanza and Israel had no intention of not participating in it. And as the U.S. public had had enough of defense spending and the cost-of-living crises, U.S. forces largely withdrew from the past war arenas. But as the old theaters closed, new and far bigger ones were initiated with proxy wars, first in Ukraine and Gaza. Meanwhile, the stage had been set with the "pivot to Asia" since the early 2010s for a looming Taiwan crisis to challenge China, and with some nine locations for rotating batches of U.S. military in the Philippines to weaken China, prior to the actual crisis. Following in the footprints of the Pentagon and the U.S. Big Defense, Israeli arms giants planned to boost their margins in each case.

International Arms Transfers

Though there are almost 70 major arms exporters globally, the five largest ones – the U.S., France, Russia, China and Germany – account for 75 percent of all arms exports.[31] In military expenditure, Israel ranks 15th. But in arms exports, as measured by the share of global arms exports, it is 9th in the world, right after the UK and Spain.[32] Israel's arms imports soared when it created its special relationship with the United States. Hence, the dramatic surge from the late 1960s to the '70s. As the U.S. became Israel's court supplier following the Yom Kippur War, Israeli defense contractors could capitalize more on exports. What also mattered was the diminished threat of war with Israel's Arab neighbors, especially subsequent to the peace treaty with Egypt. The predominance of arms imports marks the period when Israeli wars were mainly about survival. By contrast, the predominance of exports, except for during the crisis periods, marks the subsequent period. Israeli crises have been the effects of the cycles of counterinsurgency in the occupied territories (Figure 4-2).

Figure 4-2   Israel's Arms Exports and Imports, 1960–2022

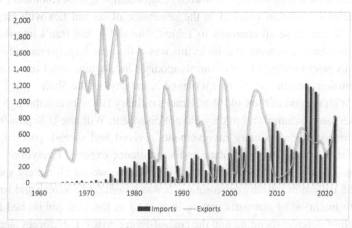

SIPRI trend indicator values. *Source: SIPRI*

In 2023, the arms revenue of the seven companies in the world's top-100 arms-producing and military services companies based in the Middle East went up by 11 percent to $17.9 billion. It was the largest regional annual percentage increase in arms revenue. Several of these giants were headquartered in Israel, which benefited from record arms sales for two consecutive years. Defense exports totaled $12.5 billion, almost double the figure between 2011 and 2016. Business was booming. In addition to the proxy war in Ukraine,

Israeli weapons were in high demand in Gulf countries. However, its export future was in the Asia-Pacific region, the largest purchaser of Israeli defense goods, accounting for almost a third of its total exports, followed by Europe and the Gulf states.[33]

The aggregate arms revenue of the three Israel-based companies among the top-100 worldwide rose by 6.5 percent to $12.4 billion in 2022. The group was led by Elbit Systems (ranked 24th) with revenue of $5 billion, thanks to increased sales of artillery systems to European countries, particularly to arm the proxy war in Ukraine. It was followed by the state-owned Israel Aerospace Industries or IAI (35th) with $4.1 billion, a historical high, as its arms order backlog soared to $15.6 billion. In relative terms, Rafael (42nd) expanded even faster, with arms revenue of $3.4 billion. In its facility in Germany, Rafael produced anti-tank missile launchers that Germany and the Netherlands supplied to Ukraine. In the past half a decade, the main recipients of Israeli arms exports feature India (37% of Israel's total exports), Philippines (12%) and the U.S. (8.7%). Unmanned aerial vehicles (UAVs) and drones made up the largest chunk of exports (25%), followed by missiles, rockets, and air defense systems (19%), exports of radar and electronic warfare systems (13%) and cyber-intelligence systems (6%). Manned aircraft, avionics, observation systems, weapons launchers, communication systems, vehicles, maritime systems, ammunition and services accounted for much of the rest.[34]

As an arms importer, Israel was ranking 15th in the world. Its main suppliers featured the U.S. (69% of Israel's total imports), Germany (30%) and Italy (0.9%). Imported weapons, particularly U.S. combat aircraft, have played a major role in Israel's military actions against Hamas and Hezbollah. By the end of 2023, pending deliveries of major arms to Israel included 61 combat aircraft from the U.S. and four submarines from Germany.[35]

However, in February 2024, Israel's protracted brutal war on Gaza led UN experts to warn that transfers of weapons or ammunition to Israel that would be used in Gaza were likely to violate international humanitarian law and should cease immediately.[36] By late March, Canada halted all arms shipments to Israel. By late April, France banned Israeli companies from participating in the annual Eurosatory arms and defense industry exhibition. Yet, Israel's two greatest arms suppliers, the U.S. and Germany, barked a lot but didn't bite. In public, there was vocal criticism. In the shadows, it was largely business as usual. To paraphrase the lyrics of *Damn Yankees*, what Israel wanted, Israel got. Furthermore, Israel could no longer regard critical imports as self-evident, not even from India which accounted for almost half of its total military sales worldwide. Then in February 2024, India's water transport union's 14,000 workers, including 3,500 at most major ports, heeded the call by their Palestinian peers and refused to handle weapons destined for Israel.[37]

The full negative fallout has yet to be fully accounted; presumably some of Israel's clientele are immune to the widespread public abhorrence of genocidal atrocities in Gaza. One of them was Morocco, one of the Arab countries that normalized relations with Israel as part of the Abraham Accords in 2020 – in part, thanks to U.S. recognition of Morocco's claim to Western Sahara, and in part as a result of longstanding overt and particularly covert cooperation with Israel (ever since the mid-1960s assistance of Mossad in the murder and disappearance of Mehdi Ben Barka, the Moroccan anti-imperialist revolutionary).[38] In July 2024, Israel Aerospace Industries (IAI) announced an agreement worth $1 billion over five years with Morocco, which preferred the Ofek 13 satellite to those of Airbus and Thales, its previous suppliers in the field. It was the latest deal added to the many signed by Israel with Morocco.[39] The deepening of Israel's intelligence-sharing ties with Morocco dated from the 1960s, when Mossad reportedly assassinated Mehdi Ben Barka, the revolutionary opponent of French imperialism and King Hassan II.[40]

During the most devastating days of the Gaza War, IDF spokespersons spoke about "targeted killing" and "smart bombs." This was mainly for international PR and public consumption. In reality, much of the destruction was brought about by American munitions that likely dated from the 1950s. In early 2023, the U.S. began shipping hundreds of thousands of 155mm shells from emergency storehouses in Israel to Ukraine. With the Gaza War, the price of these artillery shells surged fourfold.[41] From the perspective of U.S. Big Defense, it was a dream come true, with assembly-lines running day and night. In their view, it was nothing personal; just business. Those who survived the genocidal atrocities had a very different take.

THE OCCUPIED TERRITORIES AS TEST LABORATORIES

Israeli Drone Hegemony

That Israel's weapons exports were tested on civilian Palestinians was the "dirty secret of Israel's weapons exports."[42] Take, for instance, the Heron TP "Eitan" drone, Israel's largest unmanned aerial vehicle (UAV) that was brought into service in 2007. Produced by the state-owned Israel Aerospace Industries (IAI), the Eitan was first used during Operation Cast Lead in the 2008–2009 Gaza War for attacks against civilians. In the process, of the 353 children killed and 860 injured, 116 died from missiles launched by drones.[43]

After the war, IAI benefited from a surge in orders of Heron variant drones from at least 10 countries.

Today, Israel is the world's largest exporter of military drones: in 2017, it was estimated to be behind nearly two-thirds of all UAV exports over the previous three decades. Elbit, the maker of the Iron Sting, provides most of the land-based equipment procured by the Israeli military and about 85 percent of its drones.[44] Following the 2014 Gaza war, its export market expanded significantly, too. The Hermes 450 and Hermes 900 were used extensively in Operation Protective Edge, during which 37 percent of fatalities were attributed to drone attacks.[45] Subsequently, Elbit entered into contracts for the new Hermes 900 drone with more than 20 countries worldwide, including the Philippines, India, Canada, Brazil, Chile, Colombia, the European Union, Mexico, Switzerland and Thailand. The same excitement accompanied Rafael's new David's Sling air defense system, which Israel sold to Finland, America's new NATO partner, an eager buyer despite the genocidal atrocities in Gaza in December 2023.[46]

Figure 4-3   Israeli Drones

IAF Eitan (Heron TP) UAV (drone), Israeli Air Force, Independence Day 2017 (MathKnight and Zachi Evenor)

Source: Wikimedia Commons

In Israel, recent sales have been fostered by new regulations allowing sales of more weapons to a greater range of countries without licenses and with lesser oversight. Since the early days of the Gaza War, Gazan health officials had "observed severe burns on the bodies of Palestinians who were killed and wounded by Israel's bombs – whether caused by an unknown weapon or not – is something they have not seen in previous conflicts."[47] The incendiary bombs, the Iron Sting's debut and the new Spark drone indicated that Israel is testing new weapons in the conflict on Palestinians. Moreover, in some cases, privatization has extended to Israeli weapons the kind of crowdfunding that has long benefited the Jewish settlements. Since October 7, 2023, the drone startup XTEND, which has already made use of military contracts and venture capital, has sought out charitable donations. "Join Us in Supporting Israel's Defense," reads the text on the website, right above a "DONATE" button. It is one of similar efforts soliciting charitable, tax-deductible donations to bolster Israeli national security, thanks to the broad leeway of U.S. law governing charitable contributions to non-profits operating overseas.[48] As test laboratories, the occupied territories have given a boost not just to Israeli military and surveillance industries, manufacturing exports and software capabilities. In the process, military doctrines have evolved, too.

"World's Most Powerful Cyberweapon": NSO's Pegasus

In the past half a decade, UAVs and drones made up the largest share of Israel's arms exports, whereas cyber-intelligence systems (6%) accounted for a far smaller chunk.[49] Nevertheless, Israeli analysts have claimed that their country hosts the world's second-largest cybersecurity cluster, with 12 percent of the 500 largest global cybersecurity firms, after 32 percent in San Francisco metropolitan area. In the past decade, Google and Microsoft were the most active buyers of Israeli companies. In hardware: Apple, Broadcom, Qualcomm, and Nvidia design chips in Israel; Google and Amazon follow suit. Intel has been designing CPUs and other chips in Israel for decades.[50] As Israeli start-ups are usually acquired by U.S.-based firms or go public in Nasdaq, Israel-made innovation serves "made in America" objectives. While both the U.S. and Israel have conducted pioneering cyber campaigns to obstruct Iran's nuclear program, Israeli cyber offerings have proved very attractive around the world, particularly among the autocrats and amid "dirty wars."

In October 2018, Jamal Khashoggi, an influential Saudi journalist in the West, was reportedly killed and dismembered inside a Saudi consulate in Istanbul.[51] The digital trail was soon traced to the Israeli cyber-intelligence firm NSO Group and its famous/infamous proprietary spyware, Pegasus, which can be deployed for remote zero-click surveillance of smartphones. Officially, NSO's clients were authorized governments using the technology to fight terror and crime. Yet, it was reportedly used by Israeli police for warrantless domestic surveillance, targeted rights activists and journalists, state espionage and as an instrument in the Khashoggi murder.

Pegasus spyware is classified as a weapon by Israel, so any export of the technology must be approved by the government. After the death of Khashoggi, Saudi Arabia lost access to Pegasus. After a call by Saudi Crown Prince Mohammed bin Salman (MBS) to then-PM Netanyahu, Saudis were reauthorized to use the system. As the investigative reports by the Project Pegasus global consortium showed, Israel encouraged the NSO to sell the spyware to the UAE, Bahrain, Oman and Saudi Arabia. Spyware sales played a key role in Netanyahu's diplomacy, with NSO signing deals in India, Hungary and Poland in the wake of warming bilateral ties with Israel. The spyware played a central yet clandestine role in Israel's normalization efforts in the Gulf and the effort to contain Iran's nuclear program. In Africa, it was used to spy on U.S. State Department officials while talks were under way for sales to the CIA, the DEA, and Pentagon's command in Africa. The FBI was interested as well, but Pegasus was too controversial in America, so NSO offered the G-men a new spyware, Phantom. Two other Israeli cyber companies, Quadream and Cellebrite, were also peddling their spyware in Saudi Arabia.

The path to the accords was paved by the "world's most powerful cyberweapon."[52] When NSO and Candiru, whose systems had been used in dozens of countries, were put on the list of U.S. sanctions, Israeli companies Intellexa and Cytrox joined them in 2023. "If the U.S. really wanted to stop the spread of Israeli offensive cyber systems," Israeli lawyer and human rights activist Eitay Mack argues, "it would impose sanctions on the Israeli defense officials who grant export licenses to these firms. But human rights are not a primary U.S. interest."[53]

In the past, cyber experts joined Israel's military, intelligence and police agencies to make use of their talent. Now these specialists exploit their capabilities in military and intelligence, tested in occupied territories, to sell them in commercial markets and, when possible, in more shadowy markets because "that's where the money is."

Algocide: Artificial Intelligence, Human Attrocities

In 2021, Brigadier General Y.S. published *The Human Machine Team*, which he pledged would "address national security challenges and threats, lead to victory in war." Humans are the bottleneck that prevent the creation of tens of thousands of targets in context, he wrote. The solution? A human-machine team that "is capable of learning and drawing conclusions from big data in order to make predictions, and from these predictions creating targets and also answering the question of whether the targets are relevant in real-time."[54] Despite using a pen name, the author kindly included in the book his email address: Yossi.human.machine@gmail.com. Amid the Gaza bombings, it was traced to Yossi Sariel, the commander of Israel's legendary intelligence Unit 8200. Israel's mass assassination factories deploying AI for maximum devastation were premised on the human-machine team's program, Lavender.

Reportedly, the Lavender program was deployed particularly in the early days of the Gaza War, when it excelled in abject destruction. Marking all suspected military operatives of Hamas and Islamic Jihad, even the low-ranking ones, it targeted them and their homes, and thereby all proximate civilians, women and children alike.

In the past, comparable targeting was subjected to protocol constraints to minimize collateral damage. After October 7, the Israeli military gave officers sweeping approval to embrace the Lavender kill lists, fully knowing that the system made "errors" in about 10 percent of cases and occasionally targeted individuals who had little or no connection to militants. As the attacks usually took place at night when entire families were present, civilian collateral damage was maximized. To foster devastation, additional automates, such as "Where's Daddy?," were deployed to trace the targets and conduct bombings when they arrived in family residences. Still another AI system, "The Gospel," zoomed into buildings and structures where militants operated. By contrast, Lavender put people first. Reportedly, for every Hamas operative marked by Lavender, it was permissible to kill up to 15–20 civilians. Backed with AI, the Israeli military purposely used "dumb bombs" hitting these homes.[55]

The military AI arms race reflects a rivalry to develop and deploy lethal autonomous weapons systems (LAWS). Established in 2017, Google's Project Maven sought to give the Pentagon real-time battlefield command and control. As she came to understand the destructive potential inherent in Maven, Laura Nolan, an Irish software developer, resigned from the project and joined the International Committee for Robot Arms Control (ICRAC), a founding member of the Campaign to Stop Killer Robots. In 2021, she warned about the dehumanizing technology and the moral distance it enables. If dehumanization is defined as "the failure to acknowledge the humanity of others" then "dehumanization can be the first step towards war, genocide, and other atrocities."[56] At the same time, the Israeli government and military launched Project Nimbus, as Google Cloud Platform's AI tools were expected to give the Israeli military and security services critical intelligence and surveillance capabilities, particularly in the occupied territories. As Israel's atrocities surged in Gaza, so did protests in Google against technologies that "empower genocide."[57]

In *Modernity and the Holocaust* (1989), sociologist Zygmunt Bauman argued that the technical-administrative success of the Holocaust was due, at least in part, to the skilful utilization of "moral sleeping pills" made available by modern bureaucracy and modern technology. "The natural invisibility of causal connections in a complex system of interaction, and the 'distancing' of the unsightly or morally repelling outcomes of action to the point of rendering them invisible to the actor," were most prominent among them. In turn, these were coupled by "the method of making invisible the very humanity of the victims."[58] Moral distance is facilitated by moral indifference, especially when it seems to be fostered by a sense of the perpetrator's nvisibility.

In the 20th century, the Holocaust typified such moral distance, but it is in no way unique. In the early 21st century, algocide plays a similar but far more effective and lethal role. A simple definition of an algorithm is that it is a finite set of instructions carried out in a specific order to perform a particular task. In turn, genocide is a combination of the Greek term for "genos" (people) and the Latin suffix -caedo (act of killing): geno-cide. By the same token, algocide can be defined as a deliberate effort to use the algorithms of artificial intelligence in genocidal atrocities. In this sense, AI is an algorithmic instrument and likely to be surpassed by technological innovation and even greater modes of destruction, over time.

What makes AI a supreme facilitator in this lethal process is the moral distance it achieves between the killer and the target. In mid-1970s Israel, I used to know a kibbutznik who served in Sayeret Matkal, one of the country's elite special forces, and another who was a fighter pilot. One engaged in physical close combat; the other fought his wars in sterile isolation. The former still suffers from a variety of post-traumatic stress disorders (PTSD) and an internal struggle, trying to legitimize his lethal encounters in special operations, not all of which he is proud. The latter has moved on into the lucrative high-tech sector, with seemingly few moral pangs. The former dealt with physical, face-to-face combat. The latter thrived in what he used to call, "video-game-like battle environments." Like gravity, morality weakens with distance.

All high-tech wars' abstract results may lead to less ethical decisions because the human consequences of those decisions seem distant, but ultimately the reality of what they have done seeps in, as indicated by studies measuring the trauma of drone operators engaged in assassinations. Moral distance is more effectively compounded by certain psychodynamic forces, particularly "splitting" which allows a person to view people and things in absolute, Manichean terms as black and white, evil and good. Hence, the need for dehumanization and demonization, to reinforce splitting. To fight another human being is ethically challenging to rationalize; but to fight a "human animal" is framed as a moral necessity, whether in Nazi operations to "cleanse" the German body politic from Jews and other "sub-humans," or in Gaza operations in which civilian massacres were legitimized not by "ethnic cleansing," but as vital to peace and stability. If everybody in Gaza is a potential mass-murderer and the idea of collective punishment applies, moral distance operates by refuting itself: it is not just militarily expedient to use AI to exterminate hundreds; it is a moral responsibility. I do good by eliminating evil. That's how I can best serve the most moral army in the world. And so, mass extinction is perversely legitimized as an ethical duty.

A few months prior, Israeli weapon manufacturers' booths at the Dubai Airshow had still been vacant. But just days after the Lavender disclosure, the largest arms trade show in Asia, Singapore Airshow, featured the Israeli pavilion and its 11 companies, including the big three: Israel Aerospace Industries, Elbit and Rafael. They were augmented by Aeronautics, Controp, Bird Aerosystems, Skylock, Sentrycs, Orbit, Steadicopter and the state-owned Tomer whose offerings include the Jericho missile that can carry a nuclear warhead. There was great interest in their new weapons systems – both in defensive interceptors and offensive attack drones and the tiny, high-tech loitering munitions that had proved so lethal in Gaza and Lebanon. To many, the Singapore trade show demonstrated that "the Gaza War was a selling point for Israeli arms makers."[59]

DOCTRINES OF DEVASTATION

Varieties of Necrotization

In the early 2000s, Cameroonian historian Achille Mbembe used the cases of Palestine, Africa, and Kosovo to illuminate how zones of death evolve into primary form of resistance.[60] The "necropolitics" created what Mbembe calls deathworlds, or new forms of social existence in which "vast populations are subjected to living conditions that confer upon them the status of the living dead."[61] These zones have long been the daily life of subjugation in the occupied territories. But the scope of such deathworlds is far more extensive. It could be called *necrotization*.

Necrotization seeks to transform a world of life into a world of death because that is what displacement, dispossession and devastation ultimately require. It is not personal. It is the collective psychological obliteration of those who have nothing to lose, and therefore refuse to move away, fight for their homes and risk nothingness for being. Necrotization turns homes full of life into craters of lethal quiet as it transforms buildings, schools and universities into rubble and ruin, poisons the water, the air, the very earth upon which the victims stand, with the purpose of making them move away. Necrotization can target a nation's politics, its polity. It can zoom in on an entire society and its culture. An economy can be necrotized, and so can an entire population and the land it inhabits, even its entire ecology. In an algorithmic genocide or algocide, ultra-modern information and communication technology facilitates a necrotization process that is capital-intensive, stunningly rapid and lethally effective.

In the Gazan mass bombardments, targeting was subject to artificial intelligence, which necrotized the intended targets by accepting certain probabilities of error, allowing algorithms to dictate not just who will die, but also to take out others in their proximity as well. From drones to cyberweapons and artificial intelligence, the doctrines and technologies of devastation have played a central role in warfare and in genocidal atrocities. But in the final analysis, they are instruments deployed to certain ends. While the path leading to the 2023–2024 Gaza War is littered with massacres ever since Mandatory Palestine, these trajectories moved to a new stage some two decades ago with the Dahiya doctrine. This isn't a new phenomenon unique to Israel, either. It has a long history in "scorched earth" wars – in the postwar era particularly from Nazi Germany to British and French counterinsurgency doctrines and America's calculated destruction in North Korea and Vietnam. What made it different was Israel's frankness about its ultimate ends, its effort to systematize devastation and its inclusion of methods that are usually considered war crimes.

The Dahiya Doctrine: From Beirut to Gaza

A mainly Shia Muslim suburb, Dahiya is located south of Beirut. It is a residential and commercial area with malls, retail stores and *souks* or market bazaars. In 2006, it was Hezbollah's stronghold. In the war of that year, following the group's rockets on Israeli border towns, Israel's military focused on major civilian targets in Lebanon, including infrastructure and public works, ports and factories, power systems, civilian homes and industrial plants, even ambulances. UN Emergency Relief authorities called Israel's offensive "disproportionate" referring to the "horrific" leveling of "block after block" of buildings in Beirut. They regarded it as a "violation of international humanitarian law". A third of those killed were children, while 900,000 Lebanese were displaced.[62]

The military strategy focusing on civilian infrastructure destruction was first outlined in 2005 by Gadi Eisenkot. It was based on the idea that the IDF would have to severely damage Dahiya to create effective deterrence against Hezbollah.[63] Eisenkot's predecessor had been compelled to quit for having been "too cautious."[64] The assumption was that the deployment of disproportionate power would end Hezbollah for good, or at least for a sustained period. Hence, Eisenkot's new strategy of disproportion. In the Dahiya doctrine, the army deliberately targets civilian infrastructure to wreak massive suffering on the civilian population, thereby establishing an effective deterrence. Following the 2006 Lebanese War, the same doctrine was deployed in the 2008–2009 Gaza War. As Eisenkot saw it,

> What happened in the Dahiya quarter of Beirut in 2006 will happen in every village from which Israel is fired on. . . . We will apply disproportionate force on it and cause great damage and destruction there. From our standpoint, these are not civilian villages, they are military bases.[65]

A central element in the Dahiya doctrine relates to the purpose of ending the conflict in the shortest possible time.[66] Furthermore, Eisenkot pledged that "in the next clash with Hezbollah, we won't bother to hunt for tens of thousands of rocket launchers and we won't spill our soldiers' blood in attempts to overtake fortified Hezbollah positions. Rather, we shall destroy Lebanon and won't be deterred by the protests of the 'world.'"[67] Replace the terms "Hezbollah" with "Hamas" and "Lebanon" with "Gaza," and the implications are unambiguous. In effect, the implication was Eisenkot's precise intention (Figure 4-4). "Implementing the Dahiya strategy in Gaza," he added, "would have made it clear to Hamas that we do not intend to hit them proportionally."[68]

Despite broad international opposition against such doctrines, Eisenkot was appointed as a minister without portfolio in Netanyahu's war cabinet following October 7, 2023.

In the past, Israel's wars were with sovereign governments in state-to-state wars. But since the 1982 Lebanese War, insurgency has been Israel's primary challenge. New kinds of threats required a new military approach. Though critics continue to claim that the Israel/Palestine conflict can only have a political solution, Dahiya proponents did not necessarily agree. Destroy the enemy's infrastructure, polity and society and there will be a significantly weakened negotiating partner. The Messianic far-right extended the implication further: Abject destruction equals no enemy to talk with. No enemy, no conflict. As a politician, Eisenkot was not such an extremist. He supports Israeli democracy and a two-state solution. But as a military strategist, he opened the Pandora's Box that the Messianic far-right soon embraced as its own.

Figure 4-4 Dahiya Doctrine: Gaza, 2023

Palestinians inspect the ruins of the al-Amin Muhammad Mosque destroyed by the Israeli bombing of Khan Yunis, in the southern Gaza Strip, on October 8, 2023.

Source: Wikimedia Commons (Photo by Mahmoud Fareed \ WAFA)

But why did the wider international debate on Israel's genocidal atrocities begin only with its ground assault in Gaza after October 7, 2023? That is, almost two decades after the development and implementation of the Dahiya doctrine, amid the ruins and rubble of that devastated neighborhood in Beirut? The military strategy was known, it had often been stated explicitly. It was premised on the wholesale decimation of civilian infrastructure, presumably to pressure "hostile regimes." Although genocide has its legal definition, it can be identified only *ex post facto*. It suffers from an "asymptotic" challenge. It relies on a threshold beyond which the doctrine crystalizes as genocide. However, when the situation crosses that threshold, it has already become genocide *de jure*. A genocide is declared a genocide only after innocents have been butchered. If a meteorological report could

be released only after a tornado, it would be useless. Second, if organizational changes serve as evidence of shifts in sovereignty, then changes in the
organizing normative framework, organizational structure, and the symbolic
performance of power serve as indicators for a change in the legal likelihood
of genocide, even if no formal declaration of genocide is made. A major shift
of national security doctrine or military strategy is a case in point of such
organizational changes.[69]

Following the application of the Dahiya doctrine in the 2008–2009
Gaza War, critics characterized Eisenkot's doctrine as "state terrorism."[70] In
the view of the UN, it was a "carefully planned" assault intended "to punish,
humiliate and terrorize a civilian population."[71] What the Dahiya doctrine
achieved in Gaza was abject devastation, but its cruel logic impacted Israel
itself as well.

The Hannibal Directive

In December 2023, 12 bodies of hostages were repatriated to Israel,
including three killed by friendly fire by the IDF. The hostages had been
trying to be rescued. Unarmed and shirtless, they were waving a makeshift
white flag when they were killed.[72] What made some Israelis uneasy with the
incidents of friendly fire and reports of Israeli soldiers caught in contested
areas was the Hannibal Directive. This is a controversial procedure intended
to prevent the capture of Israeli soldiers by enemy forces by neutralizing the
hostages themselves. Introduced in 1986, amid the Lebanese War, after a set
of abductions of IDF soldiers in Lebanon and subsequent prisoner exchange,
it was suppressed by Israeli military censorship, and disclosed to the public
only in 2003.[73]

Many civilian casualties were blamed on the directive's implementation in the 2014 Gaza War, and it was officially revoked in 2016 by IDF Chief
of Staff Gadi Eisenkot, the architect of the Dahiya doctrine.[74] But it has not
disappeared. Amid the Hamas offensive, the IDF was ordered to prevent "at
all costs" the abduction of Israeli civilians or soldiers. Among other events,
early suspicions of its implementation were reinforced by a tank fire incident in Kibbutz Be'eri near the Gaza Strip, where a tank commander was
ordered to break into a kibbutz home where Hamas held 13 Israelis hostage;
even at the cost of their lives.[75] In mid-summer 2024, the official IDF probe
acknowledged the decision to fire tank shells at a kibbutz home where Israeli
hostages were held. Between October 7 and 8, 101 local residents and visitors
were killed, while 30 more were kidnapped to Gaza. It was Brig. Gen. Barak
Hiram who gave the controversial order to fire a tank shell at a Kibbutz Be'eri

house where Hamas held hostages. A proponent of Greater Israel, Hiram represents a new generation of the IDF. "The Bible is the source of our life and of our right to this land," he told new recruits in 2022. Ahead of the ground operation in Gaza, Hiram also made clear that a dialogue with Palestinians was waste of time. "If we backslide and try to hold all kinds of negotiations with the other side, we are liable to fall into a trap that will tie our hands and will not allow us to do what's needed, which is to go in, maneuver and kill them."[76]

Another case underscores the subtle linkages between the Hannibal Directive, alleged misconduct and the far-right Jewish settlement movement. Take for instance Col. Nissim Hazan, who lives in a Jewish settlement in the West Bank; he fired a shell at another kibbutz home killing 12 of the 14 hostages held by Hamas. Hazan said he "had no choice," adding that the failures of October 7 do not matter because the Gaza War "is very healthy for us militarily."[77] In the recent investigations, the IDF has acknowledged that the mission to defend the residents of Be'eri failed. What it downplayed was that its conduct of the operation made the failure worse. Hundreds of soldiers from various units were near the kibbutz yet did not enter it; the troops evacuated wounded soldiers, seemingly indifferent to the fact that civilians were being killed in their homes and kidnapped to the Gaza Strip; they did not help civilians who managed to rescue themselves; and the soldiers fought in an area full of civilians with disregard for their endangerment. Even then, the IDF called the shelling decision "professional and responsible."[78]

Speaking about the Israeli airstrikes, Lieut. Col. Nof Erez said that drills had been conducted for the directive over the past 20 years, but this time was different. As he put it in November 2023: "It was a 'mass Hannibal.'" Indeed, "there were many openings in the [Gaza] fence. Thousands of people in many different vehicles, both with hostages and without hostages."[79] By July 2024, documents and testimonies left little doubt that the Hannibal order was deployed at three army facilities infiltrated by Hamas, endangering civilians as well. The message conveyed at 11:22 AM on October 7 across the Gaza Division network was understood by everyone: "Not a single vehicle can return to Gaza." It wasn't the first such order. There was "a host of orders and procedures laid down by the Gaza Division, Southern Command and the IDF General Staff up to the afternoon hours of that day, showing how widespread this procedure was, from the first hours following the attack and at various points along the border."[80]

After October 7, other allegations charged that the IDF, armed with the directive, had targeted Israeli civilian hostages for the first time and on a mass scale. In the aftermath of October 7, news reports on location showed hundreds of burnt vehicles placed outside the city of Netivot in southern Israel, contending that the collected vehicles were destroyed in the Hamas-led attacks on Israeli military targets and civilian towns. Reflecting the disruptive devastation that accompanied the offensive, they were depicted as the net effect of Hamas's "human animals." Some cars had "blood stains or ashes that were difficult to collect for various technical reasons that have to do with the way these individuals were killed." So, due to the absence of body parts or remains of many of those killed in the massacre, ZAKA, the civil extension of emergency response in central Israel, decided to bury the vehicles (Figure 4-5). Rabbi Yaakov Roja, the ZAKA's rabbinic authority, proposed the idea.[81]

Figure 4-5   Who Scorched the Cars?

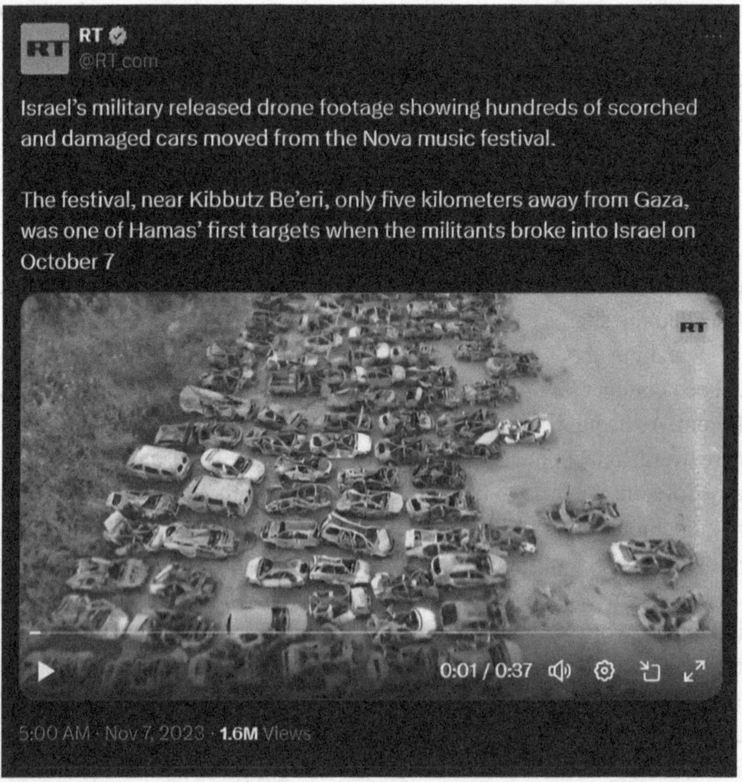

RT ✓
@RT_com

Israel's military released drone footage showing hundreds of scorched and damaged cars moved from the Nova music festival.

The festival, near Kibbutz Be'eri, only five kilometers away from Gaza, was one of Hamas' first targets when the militants broke into Israel on October 7

0:01 / 0:37

5:00 AM · Nov 7, 2023 · 1.6M Views

Source: Screen capture of X/Twitter by RT, on November 7, 2023

But how did the perished die? Did Hamas militants deploy explosives and fire to destroy the cars, even if every second mattered and their primary objective was to hijack up to 250 people, including military personnel and sensitive documentation? What was the exact role of the Hannibal Directive among those Israelis who were killed on October 7? And why the decision to bury the cars, for the first time since the establishment of Israel, if the idea was to find out the truth on the perished? Obviously, it was important to respect the religious tradition, presumably, "to preserve the sanctity of the deceased," as the 80-year-old ultra-Orthodox Roja stressed – but these were primarily cars, not people, albeit some bore traces of human blood. However, Roja wasn't just one of the leading members of the Israeli chief rabbinate, but lieutenant colonel in the IDF. As a man of faith, his actions were dictated by the Jewish halakha. As a soldier, he was commanded by the IDF, which reportedly resorted to the Hannibal orders on October 7.

The mounting evidence on the deployment of the Hannibal Directive suggests that at least some of the most jarring images of charred Israeli corpses, homes reduced to rubble and burned-out hulks of vehicles presented to Western media were, in fact, "the handiwork of tank crews and helicopter pilots blanketing Israeli territory with shells, cannon fire and Hellfire missiles."[82] According to *Ha'aretz*, Israeli police investigation confirmed that Israeli Apache helicopters killed numerous Israeli citizens at and around the Nova electronic music festival. Subsequently, the police slammed the claim.[83] Bluntly put, were the cars buried out of respect for the dead, or to bury the crime evidence?

Mass Assassination Factories

After October 7, the magnitude of Israel's counter-offensive reinforced the view that population displacement, i.e. ethnic cleansing, if not genocide, was the tacit political purpose behind the military strategy. Only two days after the Hamas offensive, IDF spokesperson Daniel Hagari stated that "the emphasis is on damage and not on accuracy."[84] Indeed, following October 7, the Israeli army expanded its authorization for bombing non-military targets, thereby loosening constraints regarding expected civilian casualties. For the first time, it used artificial intelligence (AI) to generate more potential targets than ever before.

It was only by mid-December 2023, after two months of steady Israeli bombing and devastation in the largest civilian centers of the Gaza Strip, that the U.S. intelligence community acknowledged what had been evident since day one to the human targets – and to a horrified world public able to watch the strikes via social media. Nearly half of the air-to-ground munitions that Israel had used in Gaza had been unguided, otherwise known as "dumb bombs" while the rest were precision-guided munitions. Unguided munitions are less precise and pose a greater threat to civilians, especially in the densely populated Gaza.[85]

These ground realities were known well before the U.S. intelligence report, thanks to Israeli investigative journalism, which indicated that the Gazan targets struck by Israeli aircraft were of four types. "Tactical targets" featured armed militant cells, weapon warehouses, rocket launchers, anti-tank missile launchers, and so on. "Underground targets" focused mainly on the Hamas tunnels under Gazan neighborhoods, including under civilian homes. "Power targets" included high-rises and residential towers in the heart of cities, and public buildings such as universities, banks, and government offices. Finally, "family homes" featured attacks to destroy private residences to assassinate a single resident suspected of being a Hamas or Islamic Jihad operative.[86]

Tactical targets comprised classical military targets. When underground targets were dug under civilian homes, aerial strikes on such targets could result in the collapse of the homes above or in close proximity to the tunnels. Such deaths and injuries seem to have been regarded as "unavoidable collateral damage." While Israelis have argued that hitting power targets by such an attack will generate "civil pressure" on Hamas and serve efforts at regime change, on closer scrutiny such stated objectives either reflect inflated hopes or poor pretexts for an intended devastation. For all practical purposes, destroying residential, corporate and public buildings without any regard for the lost civilian lives effectively obliterated the Palestinian infrastructure throughout the Gaza Strip, leaving nothing whatsoever to return to. In that sense, the facilitated goal, effective if unspoken, seems to have been the removal of Palestinian presence from the territory altogether – not just those elements of the infrastructure that made their survival possible, but all traces of their culture and history, through the destruction of universities, muse-ums, mosques and churches; that is, everything. Out of sight, out of mind. Finally, despite the stated purpose of limiting attacks against family homes, or operatives' homes, mounting evidence indicated that many families that were killed had no operatives belonging to Hamas or other targeted militant groups. In each case, the underlying assumption was that civilian survivors would resign to their fate and leave the Gaza Strip rather than stay and fight back. That is an assumption that has been proven flawed, time and time again, ever since Israel's retaliatory raids in the early 1950s.

The tacit objective in Israel's Gaza War was not just to destroy Hamas but to encourage the surviving Gazans to leave – or die.

WAS OCTOBER 7 AVOIDABLE?

Right after the brutal Hamas-led attack of October 7, Israeli authorities vehemently condemned what they called "our September 11" and a "surprise attack." The hard questions were conveniently ignored. Was it a "surprise"? Was it Israel's Pearl Harbor event or something very different? With all its military might, how did Israel fail to see the writing on the wall? Why were the strategic border communities neglected? Why were the Israeli hostages effectively abandoned? And why was the abundant intelligence on the impending Hamas attack deliberately ignored?

The Neglected Gaza Envelope

When Israel was established, its leaders considered as strategic what were then its border areas. Adjacent to the Gaza Strip, these are the populated areas in Israel's Southern District located within 7 km of the border and thus within the range of mortar shells and Qassam rockets. If these areas are strategic to national security, why were they so vulnerable on October 7?

Some of these settlements were created at the eve of the 1948 Arab Israeli War, including Sa'ad and Nirim, the two kibbutzim. The bigger ones were established soon after the 1949 Armistice Agreement, including Sderot, a development town for Mizrahi immigrants, and the military Nahal Oz, designed to become a civilian settlement and serve as a first line of defense against possible Arab incursions. In practice, many of these localities were neglected, while some, particularly the immigrant development towns, felt shunned. When Israel occupied the Gaza Strip in 1967, border threats diminished until the First Intifada in the late 1980s and the rise of Hamas. After Israel's unilateral withdrawal from the Gaza Strip in 2005, cross-border shelling and rocket attacks into Israel increased accordingly.

To protect these areas, which now became known as the Gaza Envelope, the Knesset enacted a law to assist the "confrontation-line communities." But when these measures expired in 2014, the district command of the IDF *cut* the associated budgets. Yet, the 2014 Gaza War caused a substantial adverse impact on the proximate settlements, due to rocket and mortar attacks, tunnels, intrusions, even incendiary kites. The war was followed by another wave of violence in 2018. And on October 7, many communities in the Gaza Envelope were infiltrated, with hundreds of Israelis butchered and kidnapped.

Instead of protecting its citizens, Israel had retreated from its traditional security obligations to the adjacent Israeli communities. As evidenced by the national budget for the Gaza Envelope localities in 2014–2024, these communities were, as critics said, "slated for abandonment following the November 2022 elections." In effect, the per capita budgets approved for the years 2023 and 2024 were almost *a third lower* than that of 2022.[87] This was a reflection of a broader problem. Officially, the settlement division of the World Zionist Organization (WZO) was intended to support the development of Israel's rural and underprivileged areas through funding new communities and regional development. Yet, already a decade earlier, the division had been charged for having become "a private slush fund for the settler movement."[88]

So, well before October 7, the Gaza Envelope of adjacent Israeli communities was effectively neglected by the government. However, the huge military border barrier prevailed. The initial Gaza-Israel barrier was built in tandem with the peace process in 1994, while the enhanced high-tech security system ensued in 2006, after Israel's unilateral withdrawal and at the cost of $220 million. The 65-km barrier featured a 7-meter wall with sensors, remote-control machine guns and barbed wire in the areas taken from adjacent kibbutzim. Patrolled from the air and on the ground, the barrier was soon known as the Iron Wall and was repeatedly touted as a seal of security by the Netanyahu cabinets. Yet, that protection was as elusive as the Maginot Line of walls and armed defenses built after World War I to protect the French, but easily outflanked by the German forces. In a matter of minutes, Hamas proved that the barrier is not impregnable, and walls are not insurmountable, just as fortifications can be undermined by tunnels. Between 2017 and 2021, to counter the many tunnels Palestinians dug for infiltration, Israel also constructed an underground border wall, equipped with sensors several meters in depth along the entire border.[89] In Israel, the high-tech security barriers were portrayed as impenetrable. And yet, the IDF was tricked by Hamas's messaging, over-relied on a remote-controlled surveillance systems and weapons that were swiftly disabled by drones and snipers, enabling its infiltration and onslaught. Furthermore, the builder of the barrier had warned already in 2018 that it absolutely required a military presence. It was not designed to prevent mass assault on its own.[90]

Unsurprisingly, the Hamas offensive caused a full breakdown in trust between the localities and the state, with residents reluctant to return to homes until security was fully ensured. Subsequently, the government did approve a 5-year $4.9 billion plan to rehabilitate and redevelop the Gaza Envelope while calling for significant tax cuts. Such pledges added to the rising debt burden amid a war that cost over $255 million per day. As a result, the residents could not help but wonder whether they should trust such pledges.

As regional escalation spread to northern Israel, it shared the Gaza Envelope's challenges, now facing the rockets of the Hezbollah. By summer

2024, local leaders were warning the Netanyahu cabinet they planned to leave if the situation wouldn't improve. "Where is the government?" asked the chief of the regional council, Moshe Davidovitch. "Even a banana republic does not work like this," he added. "The government is destroying the North."[91]

Abandoned Hostages

On June 1, 2024, some 120,000 Israelis rallied in Tel Aviv demanding an immediate hostage deal, denouncing their government and calling for the dismissal of Prime Minister Benjamin Netanyahu and for early elections.[92] It was the largest mass demonstration since October 7. The protesters fought back a sound cannon by the police as multiple officers were hurt. Similar mass protests were held at numerous locations around the country. The demonstrations had escalated ever since the terrifying Hamas attack because, so it seemed, the hostages were not a cabinet priority.

On October 7, 2023, as part of the overall offense, Hamas-led Palestinian militant groups abducted 251 people from Israel to the Gaza Strip, including children, women and elderly. Almost half of the hostages were foreign nationals or had multiple citizenships. The next day, Prime Minister Netanyahu appointed ex-military commander Gal Hirsch to coordinate the cross-governmental response to abducted civilians and soldiers. Internationally, the appointment was portrayed as the PM's proactive move to ensure the timely release of the Israeli hostages. Little did they know. As brigadier general, Hirsch had commanded an IDF division during the 2006 Lebanon War, which saw the first test of the Dahiya doctrine, premised on the destruction of civilian infrastructure. Hirsch was seen as responsible for the blunder enabling an abduction by Hezbollah militants and the battles of Bint Jbeil and Ayta ash-Sha'b, which the IDF failed to occupy, despite heavy casualties. Following a barrage of criticism, Hirsch was forced to resign.[93] After years of career rehabilitation, he joined Likud at the behest of Netanyahu and became the party favorite for the role of the national police chief in 2021; until he and his business partners were indicted for tax evasion of $1.9 million in a case concerning arms sales to Georgia.[94]

Why did Netanyahu appoint as his hostage tsar a general who had already blundered one high-profile abduction affair, failed to protect his soldiers and was indicted for corruption?

Unsurprisingly, the families of the hostages concluded that, to the Netanyahu government, the fate of the hostages was secondary to the ground assault. That realization led to bitter and divisive mass demonstrations against the government and for the release of the hostages. In July 2024, after a ceasefire and months of wheeling and dealing, an estimated 116 people were still believed to be held hostage or captive by Hamas and other armed groups in Gaza, including 43 whose deaths had been confirmed by Israeli authorities. At least 79 of those held in captivity were believed to be civilians. According to the Hostages and Missing Families Forum in Israel, signs of life had been received from 33 hostages as of 18 May.[95]

If the hostage families and ordinary Israelis despised a government that seemed to ignore the fate of the abducted, they found it far harder to digest the idea that this government may have been responsible for the deliberate killing of their loved ones. Just days after October 7, early reports and interviews suggested that the IDF had detailed *prior* knowledge of the Hamas offensive three long weeks beforehand, based on information from military intelligence's Unit 8200. Highlighting the extent to which the IDF's Gaza Division was aware of a potential attack on Israel's southern border communities, the document, which was ignored by senior officials, detailed a series of exercises conducted by Hamas' elite Nukhba units in the weeks prior to its publication. One of the most shocking sections of the IDF report featured instructions relating to the taking of hostages, the number of which was estimated to be between 200–250, coming close to the actual 251 captives.[96] Does this enumeration in the report reflect extraordinary foresight? Or does it – since its findings were blatantly ignored prior to October 7 – illustrate a deliberate intention to allow a certain extent of devastation, in order to create a transformational event that would legitimize a broad-scale invasion and, ultimately, a war of obliteration? Such considerations, of course, have been quickly torpedoed as "conspiracy theories." However, as long as credible investigations are deferred or suppressed in advance (e.g., the burying of burned and demolished cars during October 7), legitimate concern prevails on the causes of devastation on October 7.

If the writing was on the wall, why was it ignored?

Ignored Intelligence

After October 7, an Egyptian intelligence official said Israel had ignored repeated warnings that "an explosion of the situation is coming, and very soon, and it would be big." Netanyahu denied receiving any such advance warning. Yet, the Egyptian confirmed that the Israeli PM had received direct notice from Cairo's intelligence minister. Similarly, Michael McCaul, head of Foreign Affairs Committee of the House told reporters of the alleged warning.[97]

The inconvenient fact was that Israeli intelligence authorities had been aware of the threat for months yet ignored it. In November 2023, the *New York Times* reported that "Israel knew Hamas's attack plan more than a year ago." Code-named Jericho Wall, the 40-page blueprint outlined a lethal invasion. The document had been circulated widely among Israeli military and intelligence leaders, but experts determined an attack of that scale and ambition was beyond Hamas's capabilities.[98] The *Times* report reverberated internationally. But it wasn't a scoop. Soon after October 7, Israeli media released *several* reports indicating that many intelligence analysts' warnings were ignored. What was new in the *Times* piece was the document verifying the story.

Furthermore, there was a potentially explosive issue behind the Israeli deaths: not about the numbers, but about the perpetrators. Not about "friendly fire," which is not uncommon amid fierce battles, but about the consequences of the Hannibal Directive, which many Israelis have charged is being a rule demanding that they kill their fellow soldiers and family members, presumably in the interest of a "greater good." As we have seen, the Hamas-led offensive was compounded by what some Israeli soldiers subsequently called a "mass Hannibal."

Just days after October 7, testimonies from members of the mainly female lookout units bolstered accusations that Netanyahu's leadership fatally misread the dangers from Gaza. In a TV segment, two soldiers, Yael Rotenberg and Maya Desiatnik, recounted their experiences in the months before the attack. Rotenberg frequently saw many Palestinians dressed in civilian clothing near the border fence with maps, scrutinizing the ground around it and digging holes. Once, when she passed the information on, she was told they were just farmers, and there was nothing to worry about. "It's infuriating," said Desiatnik who served in Nahal Oz, where 20 other women border surveillance soldiers were murdered by Hamas. "We saw what was happening, we told them about it, and we were the ones who were murdered."[99]

Underpinning all these ignored warnings was the IDF's assumption that Hamas lacked the capability to attack and would not dare to do so. It was fostered by two factors. First, gender bias. The longer the militarization has prevailed in Israel, the more the country's gender gap – that is, the difference between women and men as reflected in social, political, and economic attainments – has deepened. Today, Israel's gender gap ranks at the level of El Salvador and Uganda.[100] What, after all, did the "girls" of the lookout units know? Furthermore, the idea that Hamas lacked capability to attack was predicated on the belief they were "human animals," as the Netanyahu and the cabinet ministers called Hamas operatives. And sub-humans cannot think out-of-the-box.

In reality, based on *1–2 years of evidence*, Hamas militants had trained for the *blitz* attacks in at least six sites across Gaza in plain sight and less than 1.5 km from Israel's heavily fortified and monitored border, as even the mainstream CNN concluded barely a week after October 7.[101] Worse, many testimonies by Israeli witnesses to the Hamas attack indicate that the Israeli military killed its own citizens struggling to neutralize Palestinian gunmen, in accordance with the Hannibal Directive. As one witness said to Israel Radio: "[Israeli special forces] eliminated everyone, including the hostages."[102]

Convenient Narratives and Inconvenient Truths

By May 2024, new evidence indicated that Israel's intelligence failure was the net effect of a "chain of failures" that pervaded the entire security sector, both in the Shin Bet and the IDF. The common denominator was the fallacy that Hamas was only able of firing long-range rockets against Israel. Whatever did not fit this theory was rejected. So, the warnings of the IDF female spotters were systematically ignored. What they saw as an impending mass attack, intelligence officers dismissed as "routine Hamas training." Second, after the Gaza war in 2021, it was decided to cease intelligence-gathering on Hamas' tactical array and the intermediate ranks of its military arm, and to focus only on few individuals. Opposing views to this intelligence concept were marginalized. These failures were coupled with a sense of disdain in the intelligence culture, which viewed the border fence, together with the underground border barrier, between Israel and Gaza, as denying Hamas the possibility of invading Israel. The "Iron Wall" was impenetrable. In reality, Hamas operatives breached the border barrier at 44 different points. Intelligence practices were turned upside down. In the north, intelligence-gathering of Hezbollah was left on the tactical level in the hands of the division. In the south, the command thought Hamas was incapable of launching an invasion into Israeli territory, certainly not on a mass scale.[103]

In this view, the intelligence failure on October 7 can be attributed primarily to the rejection of external warnings, denial of internal evidence, suppression of tactical intelligence, autocratic culture, and inflated perception of the effectiveness of the separation barriers. The ongoing investigation of the military is likely to stress similar factors. But was that the full story or a part of the story? In effect, what was *the* story? In the early narrative, "intelligence failure" was framed as the prime narrative. But the thesis is hard to argue when tactical intelligence was delivered exceptionally well, despite reduced resources, outlining the threats in detail weeks and weeks before the attack, including the almost exact number anticipated to be abducted. There are too many anomalies and happy coincidences in the current narratives.

If "intelligence failure" is not the story, is it the "neglect of intelligence evidence"? But was that neglect really due to the new intelligence concept that failed? Taking into consideration the cumulative pile of evidence on the impending attack and the repeated warnings well prior to October 7, including those by policy authorities in adjacent Arab countries, it is challenging to buy into the conventional wisdom. It leaves open the question, was the "neglect of intelligence evidence" just unprofessional conduct – or deliberate?

In the United States, September 11, 2001 provided the kind of catastrophic and catalyzing event – like "a new Pearl Harbor" – that the leading neoconservatives, gathered around the Project for the New American Century in 2000, envisioned as critical to achieve massive rearmament in America and that subsequently served as a flawed pretext for the war against Iraq and global war on terror.[104] In Israel, the Hamas offensive was immediately followed by a coordinated nationwide outcry that "October 7 is our September 11" by PM Netanyahu, who had built his rise to power in the 1990s in cooperation with the very same U.S. neoconservatives.[105] With October 7, he used the Hamas offensive to legitimize the subsequent ground assault, which many in his war cabinet hoped would result in ethnic expulsions that would open Gaza for Jewish resettlement. Meanwhile, his Messianic far-right cabinet partners used the fog of war to disguise their effort at the effective annexation of the West Bank.

The point is not to argue that one or another of these narratives is conclusive. Too much evidence is still missing. The point is that the current "facts" include many anomalies that conventional wisdom shuns, but alternate narratives can explain. Conventional wisdom may be convenient, but it is seldom either persuasive or final.

Part II

THE TRANSFORMATION OF ISRAEL

Chapter 5

ZIONISM, DEMOCRACY AND A JEWISH NATION

When I first met Amos Oz amid the 1982 Lebanese War, which we both condemned, he was an internationally renowned novelist and a co-founder of the "Peace Now" movement. Prior to my move to New York City, I had just translated the kibbutznik's book on the settler-induced divisions, *In the Land of Israel* (1983), to my native Finnish language. What we talked about were his writings in 1967, when he already sensed what loomed ahead, characterizing the radicalized Jewish settlers as "neo-Nazis." For those who identified with the painful legacy of Jewish history and the existence of Israel but not with ethnic supremacy doctrines, colonial subjection and expansion, the Six-Day War posed a challenge. Occupation made Oz uneasy, not triumphant.

Until then, Israel had fought for its survival. Now it prepared to embark on colonial expansion. Just weeks after the war, Defense Minister Moshe Dayan reneged on the idea of returning territory in exchange for peace. The terms of his address left Oz breathless. He did not translate Dayan's term "living space" in Hebrew. He used its German version, *"Lebensraum,"* Nazi Germany's pretext for expansion and atrocities in occupied Eastern Europe. It was a term that should have raised harrowing memories. Yet Dayan relied on it as a pretext for colonization. As Oz saw it:

> Living space means one thing: disenfranchising the foreigner, the inferior "savage" and making place for the superior and the civilized—the powerful....
>
> Not for that did we fight. Israel's living space is entirely before it: the wastelands of the Galilee and the Negev. We have no living space in the West Bank of the Jordan, because it is populated by a nation living on its land, even though it is currently a nation routed in battle. The expression "living space" defiles our war. Our enemies were seemingly correct when they suspected...

that behind the peace declarations upon our tongues lurked a need for expansion and annexation.[1]

Fighting for existential survival is one thing. Fighting for colonial expansion and annexation is something very different, whether in the name of national security, divine redemption or *Lebensraum*. The difference between these two stances reflects the slide of labor Zionism that was typical of the pre-1967 era into the revisionist Zionism that has prevailed since then. The transition has gone hand in hand with very different views on the state of Israel, secularism and fundamentalism, as well as on democracy and autocracy.

BUILDING A NATION

The Pre-State Waves of Jewish Immigration

Jewish immigration to Palestine began in the 1840s with the liberalization of the Ottoman domestic policy. The majority of immigrants came from the Russian Empire and Eastern Europe and settled among existing Arab communities. Between 1840 and 1880, the Jewish population in Palestine climbed from 9,000 to 23,000. In Arab Palestine, it was a fraction of the total.[2] In the late 19th century, the rise of the Zionist movement sped up Jewish migration to Palestine in several waves (*aliyah*, lit. "ascent"). The First Aliyah (1882–1903) followed pogroms in Russia in the early 1880s.[3] These Jewish immigrants founded separate settlements, particularly the cooperative agricultural *moshavot*. In that period, 35,000 Jews came to Palestine, but the rough conditions caused half of them to leave. Some 15,000 established new rural settlements, and the rest moved to the towns. It was the beginning of the pre-state *Yishuv* (lit. "settlement" of the Jewish people in Palestine) It also marked the onset of segregation between Jews and Arab; the polarization into "us" and "them."

After the notorious pogroms in Czarist Russia, the Second Aliyah (1904–14) ensued with up to 40,000 immigrants to Palestine, many of them socialist Zionists. It accelerated nation-building giving birth to the labor movement and the first major Jewish city, Tel Aviv, founded on the outskirts of the ancient port city of Jaffa, now seen as a suburb of Tel Aviv. These Jews launched the first agricultural collectives, the *kibbutzim*, and the Jewish self-defense organizations. They published Hebrew newspapers and created political parties, laying the institutional foundations for the pre-state. In this period, 40,000 Jews immigrated, but again harsh conditions led many to leave. Though socialists, these Jews, too, worked and lived separately from the surrounding Arab communities.

Amid the fog of World War I and the ongoing demise of the old European empires, the fate of Arabs and Jews in Palestine was decided in clandestine great power pacts, many of which were mutually conflicting. The 1915–16 Hussein-McMahon correspondence indicated an undertaking for a united Arab state in exchange for the Great Arab Revolt against the Ottoman Empire in World War I. Yet, in the secret 1916 Sykes-Picot Agreement the UK and France defined their mutually agreed spheres of influence in the eventual partition of the Ottoman Empire. It was followed by the 1917 Balfour Declaration, which pledged to establish a "Jewish national home" in Palestine. The clandestine plans, hollow pledges and broken promises set the stage to the subsequent Jewish-Arab violence, which the former colonial powers then attributed to Jews and Arabs. Meanwhile, Americans, too, began to seek a presence in the Gulf as well.

In the Third Aliyah (1919–23), 40,000 Jewish immigrants came from Russia, Poland and Hungary. They built roads and towns, and drained marshes. The powerful General Federation of Labor (Histadrut) and its institutions were founded as well as the Haganah, the core of Israel's Defense Force (IDF). Agricultural settlements expanded; industrial enterprises ensued. With expansion, rising tensions between Jews and Arabs erupted in the Jaffa riots in 1921.[4] Palestinian Arabs saw Jewish colonies increasingly as a threat, "as shown by the correlation between outbreaks of the conflict and waves of immigration."[5]

With 82,000 immigrants, the Fourth Aliyah (1924–29) was the first Jewish mass immigration to Palestine. Coming largely from Poland, these middle-class immigrants brought some capital with which they established small businesses and workshops. There were few alternative destinations after the quotas of the U.S. Immigration Act (1924).[6] As Arab-Jewish tensions escalated, the British-appointed Shaw Commission identified the cause of the 1929 Palestine violence as "the Arab feeling of animosity and hostility towards the Jews consequent upon the disappointment of their political and national aspirations and fear for their economic future." The Shaw Commission was critical of Jewish immigration and land-purchase policies that, it argued, gave Jews unfair advantages. Struggling to find a balance, it saw the status quo as untenable and expected economic pressure upon the Arab population to increase.[7] Yet, the rise of Nazism in Germany and fascism in Italy generated ever-more desperate Jewish immigrants waves seeking refuge in Palestine, thus paving the way to the 1936–1939 Great Palestinian Revolt. It began as a general strike but evolved into an armed insurrection, which the British crushed harshly, causing 10 percent of the adult Palestinians to be killed, wounded, imprisoned or detained.[8]

Triggered by the Great Depression, Hitler's rise to power in Germany and the darkening clouds in Europe, the Fifth Aliyah (1929–39) brought nearly 250,000 Jews, many of them professionals, mainly from Germany and Poland. The massive wave sparked the 1936–39 Arab Revolt in which hundreds of British and Jews were killed or injured, while thousands of Arabs perished. With successful industrial takeoff, rural migrants would find jobs in the new urban hubs. In Palestine, that logic effectively failed the rural fellahin who were first rendered landless in their home regions, then found themselves jobless in the emerging metropolitan centers.[9] Compounding the friction, the increasing plight of the peasant migrants occurred in tandem with the rapidly rising Jewish immigration waves. Though suppressed brutally by the British, the revolt did contribute to the British "White Paper" (1939) restricting Jewish immigration and land-buying.

Finally, the Sixth Aliyah (1939–48), the last pre-state immigration wave, comprised almost 140,000 Jews, mainly Holocaust survivors, though every fifth came from Arab countries. To Palestinian Arabs, it was a nightmare, especially after the unilateral declaration of Israel's Independence. What some call the Great Aliyah (1948–51) took off as almost 690,000 Jewish immigrants flocked to Palestine, effectively doubling the Jewish population in three years. Half were Holocaust survivors from the postwar Europe; another half were Jews from Arab countries, particularly from Syria, Iraq and Yemen. In the decade following the Suez War (1956) and the French colonial rule in North Africa, another 465,000 Jews arrived, with more than half from Eastern Europe and the rest from North Africa. After the Six-Day War (1967), still another wave of almost 230,000 immigrants came to Israel, this time mainly from developed countries.

Ashkenazi Elite, Sephardi/Mizrahi Majority

Since 1948, Israel has absorbed more than 1.9 million Jewish immigrants. In the pre-state Zionist movement, it boosted a leadership that was initially German-Jewish, even though most of the supporters were Russian and Eastern European Jews. Both were *Ashkenazim;* that is, Jews of mainly European descent. Indeed, the pre-state Jewish community, *Yishuv,* was the creation of Eurocentric Jewry.

In the pre-state Yishuv, the Ashkenazim came to occupy the key positions of power. After the establishment of Israel, many new immigrants were still of Ashkenazi descent coming from the West, including France,

Argentina, the U.S., Canada, the UK, and South Africa. But their numbers were soon offset by Jews from the Arab countries. As Palestine was swept by war, their position had become vulnerable as a result of persecution, confiscations and riots. In the mainstream narrative, the story is often depicted as a kind of mirror-image of the ethnic cleansing of Palestinian Arabs by Israel. The actual narrative is more complex.

For ideological motives (the "in-gathering of exiles") and more pragmatic ones (the need for immigration and low-cost labor), the Zionist movement proactively pushed for Jewish emigration from Arab states in which many Jewish communities had lived in relative peace for centuries, occasionally by questionable methods. Following the creation of Israel, the deterioration of the regional status quo led to the mass emigrations of Jews from their Arab homelands. In the official narrative, this is a triumphant story of integration and modernization. Certainly, the ostensible ability of the new state to absorb huge immigration flows in the first decade of its existence was impressive. That, however, cannot conceal the fact that many new arrivals from the Arab countries found themselves treated as more "primitive," "second-class citizens" in Israel. I recall a conversation with a dear friend, an Israeli Jewish woman who was originally born in Kurdistan. In many ways, she found herself at the bottom of the tacit "color hierarchy," yet managed to rise from poverty into the middle class. She was warm, smart but also street smart and could easily beat most macho males in a game of Shesh Besh. Yet, even two decades after immigration, her recollections were painful. "It was so humiliating," she said. "[The Ashkenazis] saw us as primitives, as animals. So, they sprayed our bodies with pesticide, destroyed our family structure and imposed their secularism on us."[10]

Often, the net effect was bitterness and resentment regarding the official Zionist ideology and how it actually operated; both of which were associated with the then-dominant Labor Party. Take, for instance, Operation Ezra and Nehemiah (1951–54), which airlifted some 120,000–130,000 Iraqi Jews to Israel. By all indicators, it was among the most pivotal events of the Jewish exodus from the Muslim World. Yet, the official triumphant story is contradicted by many bitter and at best bittersweet accounts, memoirs and nuanced histories, including those by Avi Shlaim and Naeim Giladi. One of the "new historians," Avi Shlaim recalls these experiences in *Three Worlds: Memoirs of an Arab Jew* (2023). His parents had many Muslim friends in Baghdad and little interest in Zionism. When anti-Semitism surged, the Zionist underground did not seek to contain the flames but instead fanned them. Nevertheless, when Iraqi Jews fled to Israel, they faced an uncertain future under the Eurocentric Ashkenazi elite. In the process, their history was rewritten to serve a Zionist narrative.[11] The story of Naeim Giladi is even more controversial. Starting as an idealistic, Zionist Iraqi Jew, he was mugged by realities and morphed into an anti-Zionist. Disillusioned by the institutionalized racism and Zionism's cruelties, Giladi concluded that Israel's prime interest in Jews from Islamic countries was as a supply of cheap labor. While Ashkenazi Jews occupied privileged positions in urban Israel, the "Oriental" Jews were needed to farm the lands of Palestinians driven out by Israeli forces. Furthermore, he attributed the 1950–51 Baghdad bombings to "Zionist agents" to spread fear among Iraqi Jews and thus to promote their exodus to Israel.[12] The stance is controversial but not unique. It is shared by some Israeli historians, British journalists, even the former CIA station chief Wilbur Crane Eveland, a major postwar critic of U.S. policies in the Middle East.[13]

Of the 820,000 Jewish refugees between 1948 and 1972, 586,000 were resettled in Israel. They were *Sephardim* (lit. "Jews of Spain"), although the term came to cover the Jews of the Middle East and North Africa. As ethnic distinctions grew more intricate, the term *Mizrahi* (lit. "communities of the East") was used to refer to Jews from the broader Middle East.

When the Soviet Union collapsed, many Jews left for Western Europe and North America, but most – almost 1 million – immigrated to Israel in the 1990s. Of these immigrants, almost three-fourths originated from Russia and Eastern Europe. Most were Ashkenazim (Figure 5-1).

Figure 5-1   Immigration to Israel by Country, 1948–Present

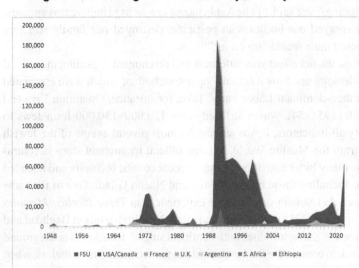

* Without Russia and former Soviet States

Source: Jewish Virtual Library

Contradictions of Zionism

From the first Zionist congress at Basel in 1897 to David Ben-Gurion's unilateral declaration of independence in 1948, the objective of the Zionist movement was to establish a Jewish homeland. Subsequently, the Zionist movement has sought to consolidate that objective. When the architect of political Zionism, Theodor Herzl, wrote his visionary *Der Judenstaat* (1896), he saw the Zionist movement as a response to enduring antisemitism. His objective was the "restoration of the Jewish state."[14] Born into a prosperous secular Jewish family, the Austro-Hungarian Herzl worked for the Viennese newspaper *Neue Freie Presse* as its Paris correspondent. Confronted with antisemitic events in Vienna and reporting on the Dreyfus trial in France, Herzl revised his views on antisemitism. Jewish assimilation did not work. The only solution to historical persecution was the creation of a Jewish state. Despite their diversity, all basic forms of Zionism – labor, revisionist, cultural, religious, and practical – agreed on that basic denominator, in one way or another.[15]

All these Zionists groups hoped to establish *Eretz Israel* ("Land of Israel") as a national homeland of the Jews. The differences centered on the question of *how* that state should be restored. In the late 19th century, most Zionists saw Palestine, then a part of the Ottoman Empire, as the natural destination, due to its central role in ancient Jewish history. But some, including Herzl, considered the challlenge of antisemitism so overwhelming that they were willing to consider other options, such as certain parts of present-day Uganda or Kenya, Argentina, today's Iraq (ancient Mesopotamia), and Sinai. After some scrutiny, these alternatives were rejected, as the idea of the "ingathering of exiles" in their historic homeland prevailed. To the faithful, it was a non-negotiable objective; to the pragmatic, it was a convenient myth that served to mobilize the masses.

From the beginning, Zionism has been marked by two primary contradictions, however. The first is the ambivalence between what was basically a secular project and its quest for legitimacy via historical, even biblical rights. Historian Ilan Pappé likes to call it a "bizarre mixture" because most advocates of Zionism, "don't believe in God, but they do believe God nonetheless promised them Palestine."[16] Yet, it was precisely as such – that is, as an internally inconsistent contradiction that Zionism was seen to serve a useful function. That's what political myths do. They are not based on scientific argumentation, but on loaded slogans aiming to mobilize the proponents.

As long as the labor governments were in power in Israel, the secular-democratic narrative reigned. But ever since the first Likud governments in the late 1970s, secular objectives have been infused with religious ideas.

The settlements in the occupied territories are a case in point. With labor coalitions, efforts at "national security" predominated over the fantasies of "national redemption." As the distinction between the biblical *Eretz Israel* and the secular Land of Israel has dimmed, the latter has been linked with expansionist Greater Israel ideologies. Concurrently, the idea of Israel as a secular, democratic state has given way to the idea of a religious Jewish nation-state. In the process, the perceived dimensions of *Eretz Israel* have shifted. According to the Jewish tradition, God promised the holy land to the descendants of Abraham, but apparently God diplomatically avoided a precise definition of the land and its borders. The bible features a dozen or so somewhat different boundaries. In turn, the Greater Israel dreams by the pre-state terror group, Irgun, the precursor of the present-day Likud, features boundaries that include the pre-1967 Israel, the occupied territories, a slice of Egypt-controlled Sinai, the southern part of Lebanon and a northern part of Saudi Arabia, Jordan and Syria, even a slice of Türkiye and western Iraq. It was only in the postwar era that Likud, eager for government responsibility, gave up the early claims for parts of Saudi Arabia, Iraq, Syria (except for Golan Heights) and Türkiye. (Figure 5-2)

Despite the egalitarian ideals of the early labor Zionists, the second primary contradiction centers on the nature of the Zionist movement as a colonial enterprise. Herzl's pamphlet *Der Judenstaat* was initially subtitled: "Address to the Rothschilds." Hoping for sponsors, he wrote it as a speech to the mighty Rothschild family banking dynasty.[17] To his chagrin, however, Baron Edmond de Rothschild rejected the plan. The financier thought it threatened the Diaspora Jewry and thereby the settlements he was financing in Palestine. Herzl argued that the "state of the Jews" could only exist with the support of a European colonial power: "We should form a portion of a rampart of Europe against Asia, an outpost of civilization as opposed to barbarism."[18] Herzl saw himself as a Zionist Cecil Rhodes, the proponent of British colonialism and imperialism. Among the revisionist Zionists, this emphasis has been even stronger. Ze'ev Jabotinsky considered Zionism an offshoot of the Western civilization against the Arabs: "Zionism is a colonizing adventure and it therefore stands or falls by the question of armed force."[19]

Like other forms of settler colonialism, the first contradiction has fostered doctrines of Jewish supremacy, whereas the second contradiction highlights the inherent tension between Israel's early ideals and its effective role as a U.S. client state in the early 21st century.

Figure 5-2   Greater Israel by Irgun in the Early 1930s

An Irgun poster published around 1947. The title is from Genesis 15:18: "Unto thy seed have I given this land, from the river of Egypt unto the great river, the river Euphrates." The map features all of mandatory Palestine and Transjordan. At the bottom, there are quotes from Ze'ev Jabotinsky: "The river Jordan has two banks: one is ours, and so is the other" and "Let my right hand wither if I forget the east side of the Jordan."

Source: Palestine Poster Project

The Rise of Labor Zionism

In the late 19th century, the dream of a more just world united those who saw the Jewish future in socialist and Zionist terms. As a onetime friend and collaborator of Marx and Engels, whom he introduced to communism, Moses Hess was an early champion of socialism and what would become known as Zionism. If the world was split between labor and capital, he argued, it was also marked by the divide of antisemitism. The only way to resolve the "last national question" was by means of a socialist state in Palestine.[20] Although socialist ideas appealed to many Jews, it was the French debacle of the century that would fuel the rise of Zionism across the old continent.

Despite science and progress and dreams of universal emancipation, the Dreyfus affair, a political scandal dividing the Third French Republic from 1894 until 1906, rocked Jewish communities across Europe. If a Jewish officer could be wrongly charged for treason and secular France of *liberté, égalité, fraternité* was not immune to antisemitism, what country was? The affair had a direct impact on Theodor Herzl, the architect of political Zionism. Initially, he saw Jewish finance as the precondition for sovereignty. The instrument Herzl first envisioned was "the Jewish Company," in part emulating the chartered land-acquisition companies of the European colonial powers. Herzl's role was vital in the creation of the World Zionist Organization in 1897 and its Basel Program "to establish a home in Palestine for the Jewish people, secured under public law."[21] After alternative destinations, including Argentina and Uganda, had been put aside, the strategic objective became to accelerate immigration flows to Palestine.

Opposing bourgeois capitalism, socialist labor Zionists like Ber Borochov, Chaim Arlosoroff and Berl Katznelson wanted to establish an agricultural economy on the basis of equality. They saw the land in almost mystical terms, as a way to remake Hebrew Jews through manual work. Yet, the First Aliyah remained relatively small as most Jews in Eastern Europe sought immigration to America. It was the widespread pogroms in Russia and Eastern Europe and the subsequent Second Aliyah that brought to Palestine the socialist Zionists of the first kibbutzniks and nation-builders.

In the interwar period, labor Zionists were joined by religious Zionists who opposed secularism and revisionist Zionists who saw class struggle as secondary to national struggle. As doors closed in isolationist America and conditions deteriorated in Europe, ideology was no longer the guiding principle in Jewish immigration; despair and urgency were. In Europe and Palestine, labor Zionists were fully in charge. But in the United States where antisemitism was not as lethal, Jews benefited from social mobility which made them more responsive to the revisionist ideals marking the liberal middle-class and Jewish militancy. With the Fifth and Sixth Aliyahs during and after World War II, Israel had to absorb hundreds of thousands of immigrants, many of whom were impoverished Holocaust survivors, and build state institutions for the rapidly-rising population.

But the socialism that labor Zionists espoused differed critically from Western European social democracy.

CONSOLIDATING THE JEWISH NATION

From Class to Nation

Though labor Zionism originated from Jewish socialism in Russia and Eastern Europe, neither Ben-Gurion nor Golda Meir, the two most influential postwar labor Zionists, championed class struggle. They did not advocate the kind of socialization of production forces that marked the postwar Soviet Union and its client states. They were not in the privileged position of Western Europe's social-democratic parties, which operated in developed, post-industrial economies. Their first priority was to build a nation and to create institutions to govern the land. Hence, the pragmatic effort at class *cooperation* to achieve industrial capitalism. This task had already been acknowledged by Ben-Gurion in the early 1920s:

> The possibility of conquering the land is liable to slip out of our grasp. Our central problem is immigration … and not adapting our lives to this or that doctrine. … We are conquerors of the land facing an iron wall, and we have to break through it. … The creation of a new Zionist movement, a Zionist movement of workers, is the first prerequisite for the fulfillment of Zionism.[22]

By the same token, neither Marxism nor liberalism was acceptable for the labor Zionists. The former categorized the agents of history as classes; the latter, as autonomous individuals. In labor Zionism, the classes and the individuals would have to cooperate for the benefit of the (Jewish) nation-state. Founded in 1920, even the Histadrut, the powerful General Federation of Jewish Labor, sought to "conquer labor" from the Palestinian Arabs. And even though the word "Jewish" was excluded from its full name, it did not give full membership to Arab workers until 1959.[23]

Ironically, the faster agricultural Israel evolved, the sooner came the industrial takeoff, which eventually marginalized the role of agriculture in the economy. Furthermore, the massive flows of immigrants from Europe came from countries that had industrialized or were industrializing by World War I. Even as the young Israel invested in basic state institutions and physical infrastructure, it benefited from relatively qualified human capital, from whence the temptations of revisionist Zionism. This was neither socialism nor nationalism. It was, as Zeev Sternhell called it, "nationalist socialism,"[24] in which the state had primacy over civil society, and the state, in turn, built on the supremacy of the nation. It was organic nationalism in which the nation was seen as a body, and the body was more important than its parts, the individuals.

As the Fourth Aliyah brought many middle-class Jews to Yishuv, Ben-Gurion still hoped to keep them within the labor Zionist camp. That's why it was necessary to get rid of "the class concept that obscures the national character of our movement."[25] While labor Zionists rejected the classic definition of class struggle, they kept the *term* to preempt the left from claiming a monopoly of the socialist heritage. Hence, the reinterpretation of class struggle as a nationalist concept. To these Zionists, class warfare was not about class antagonism, but about class collaboration to improve Jewish workers' living standards in the interest of the entire nation. Their version of class warfare did not aim to subvert the capitalist order, but to set it up. Paradoxically, class warfare became an organizing myth to gain the acceptance of Jewish middle-classes, to divert them from the temptations of bourgeois revisionism.

As the labor Zionists built the foundation for a Western democracy in which political parties dominated, the parliament became relatively weak whereas the executive branch proved extraordinarily strong. The system benefited labor coalitions for three decades. But then, ever since the Likud governments took over, the system has benefited the hard-right. And when and if far-right majority governments come to dominate in Israel, classes and individuals will be subject not just to the nation, but to a *Jewish* nation-state; and ultimately, a Jewish theocracy. In the postwar era, it was a fringe idea. Today it is a possibility, thanks to the rise of revisionist Zionism.

Revisionist Zionism, Fascism and Liberalism

In the pre-1948 era, revisionist Zionist militants led by Ze'ev Jabotinsky stirred America's conscience by placing controversial newspaper ads, lobbying conservative and liberal members of Congress, and staging dramatic protest rallies. Through these high-profile tactics, they attracted a wave of support from an extraordinary cross-section of Americans, as Jabotinsky "left behind the seeds of a movement that would one day profoundly affect the destiny of American Jewry."[26] But the militants also launched a shadowy underground division to smuggle weapons into Palestine. Jabotinsky's revisionism stressed the Jewish right of sovereignty not just over the British Mandate but over the entire Land of Israel which to them meant a Greater Israel (compare Figure 5-2). Usually, Jabotinsky is portrayed as a nationalist and a liberal democrat, who supported a free market with minimal government intervention.[27] Yet, his political stances and activities reflect a progressive slide from economic liberalism and forceful nationalism to neoconservatism and autocratic militancy.

Since the Jewish population was only a fraction of that of the Arabs in Mandatory Palestine (1920–1948), the revisionists emphasized the importance of armed struggle over any sort of democratic process. That gave rise to their paramilitary Irgun and its spinoff, the Stern group, which paved the way to the postwar political careers of Likud's prime ministers Menachem Begin and Yitzhak Shamir, respectively. Chaim Weizmann, the liberal president of the World Zionist Organization, leaned on Britain and the U.S. and Ben-Gurion sought support wherever it was available. By contrast, Jabotinsky and his revisionists saw Italy and Mussolini as their ideological soulmate and possible patron.

Fluent in Italian, Jabotinsky had studied in Rome in the late 1890s.[28] In the 1920s and 1930s, he saw Italy and Mussolini as the prime ideological inspiration for the revisionists. Just as Mussolini's rise was predicated on the defeat of Socialists and Liberals, so would the Revisionists have to raise their flag of sovereignty by beating down the labor and political Zionists. In 1934, Mussolini allowed Jabotinsky to set up a Betar Naval Academy in Civitavecchia, not far from Rome, where Jewish cadets were trained by the Black shirts. The cooperation ended in 1937 when Mussolini aligned Italy with Nazi Germany (Figure 5-3).[29]

Figure 5-3   Jabotinsky and Mussolini, Revisionism and Fascism

(*Left*) Mussolini and Hitler in 1937. (*Right*) Jabotinsky in the British Army, around 1915–1916. *Source: Wikimedia Commons*

Another revisionist faction, the ultra-right Brit HaBirionim (lit. "the Strongmen Alliance" of a "Covenant of Outlaws"), fully embraced Italian fascism. Founded by Abba Ahimeir and his ideological peers, it touted "revisionist maximalism," including the idea that Jabotinsky, like Mussolini, should be referred to as *Il Duce*. In 1930, the faction planned to create a fascist Jewish state in Palestine.[30] It conducted minor political operations until its 1933 assassination of Chaim Arlosoroff, the socialist leader of the Yishuv.[31] In Tel Aviv, Arlosoroff's funeral attracted up to 100,000 mourners. The assassination deepened the breach between the Zionists and the distinctly fascist revisionists.

As Jews in wartime Poland joined the partisans to fight Hitler and the antisemitic Polish regime, Jabotinsky's revisionists opted for the reverse, forging an alliance with the conservative and antisemitic Polish regime. Ultimately, the ploy aimed at regime change in Palestine. Backed up with weapons from the Polish regime, Menachim Begin hoped to take over the pre-state institutions in Tel Aviv in 1939. In turn, Irgun was to take over the Government House in Jerusalem and declare a provisional government. Eventually, Jabotinsky gave up this plan that amounted to a coup against labor and political Zionism.[32] Following the establishment of Israel, Begin led the Herut Party, the precursor of today's Likud, while Ahimeir became a member of the editorial board of its daily.[33] Most revisionists, including Jabotinsky and his successors, supported the revisionist maximalists' promotion of force to achieve Greater Israel. It was neoconservatism half a century before Chile and Pinochet, with Israeli characteristics. It is this ethno-nationalism that explains why Jabotinsky and his successor Menachem Begin were more willing to work with Poland's antisemitic nationalists as opposed Polish socialist partisans (and why contemporary Netanyahu cabinets have formed ties with states in which nationalism goes with antisemitism). What made the ethno-nationalism so powerful as a unifying force was the mass persecution of Jews in the 1930s. It thrives amid divisions.

These political doctrines form the foundations of the contemporary Jewish hard-right. They are also the fountains of its far-right extremism, including rabbi Meir Kahane's Kach party, which the Knesset criminalized in the 1980s, and his successors among the settler zealots, such as the Otzma Yehudit (Jewish Power) Party and its leader, Itamar Ben-Gvir. It was this kind of revisionism that also appealed to Benzion Netanyahu, a disciple of Ahimeir and onetime assistant to Jabotinsky's personal secretary and the revisionists' onetime U.S. point man, and eventually to his son, Benjamin Netanyahu.

Americanizing Zionism

Historically, most Jewish immigrants did *not* settle in Israel, however. By far the greatest proportion immigrated to the United States. As in Israel, the early Zionist movement in America was led by Jews of German descent. Yet, starting with the Russian pogroms, Eastern European Jews immigrated to America *en masse* between 1880s and 1910s. There were 5 million Jews in the U.S. around 1950 as opposed to just over 1 million in Israel. As the demographics of American Jewry began to mature following the removal of the U.S. immigration restrictions of the mid-1920s, the numbers of those in Israel climbed to U.S. levels in the 1990s. With the collapse of the Soviet Union and the mass inflows of Russian Jews to Israel, the number of Jewish immigrants to America increased in tandem. Today, the U.S. and Israel host over 7 million Jews, each. Together, they account for the majority of the world Jewry (Figure 5-4). Along with the U.S. government and its "special relationship" with Israel since the 1970s, American Jews have played a central role vis-à-vis Israel, particularly as donors.

Figure 5-4   Jewish Population in the United States and Israel

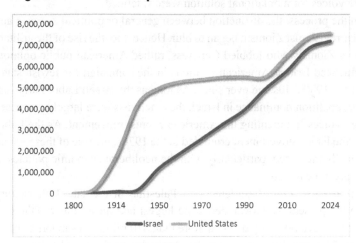

Source: Data from Jewish Virtual Library; author

The World Zionist movement was initially dominated by Jews of German descent. With the pogroms and massive migration inflows, the movement was transformed by the rise of Nazism and World War II. Until then, Zionists were building a "Jewish National Home" in Palestine. That period ended in 1942, when the U.S. Zionists convened in the posh art deco dining halls of New York's Biltmore Hotel explicitly calling for the creation

of a "Jewish Commonwealth integrated in the structure of the new democratic world." The delegates agreed that

> the United States constituted the new Zionist "battleground" and
> that Washington would have the paramount say in the struggle
> for Jewish sovereignty. Henceforth the Zionist movement would
> strive for unqualified Jewish independence in Palestine, for a state
> with recognized borders, republican institutions, and a sovereign
> Army, to be attained in cooperation with America.[34]

It was a virtual coup d'etat. The new Yishuv-based practical Zionists
led by Ben-Gurion pushed aside the more moderate and diplomatic older
generation of political Zionists led by Chaim Weizmann, who could only
bristle at the Biltmore program. Weizmann's gradualism, the quest for
peaceful partition and talks with Britain were out. Ben-Gurion's pursuit of
immediate statehood, a Jewish state in all of Palestine, and armed resistance,
if necessary, were in.[35] In the process, socialist Zionists, such as Hashomer
Hatzair, could only vote against assertive unilateralism, whereas other progressive voices for a binational solution were sidelined.

In the process, the distinction between general or political Zionism and
muscular revisionist Zionism began to blur. Hence, too, the rise of the militant
American Zionists who lobbied Congress, rallied American public opinion,
and influenced British-American relations in the campaign for Jewish statehood in the 1930s–40s and ever since. As long as the Israeli Labor Party sustained its coalition dominance in Israel, these activists were largely dismissed
as fringe voices fragmenting the American Zionist movement. As the Labor
hold on the Israeli government crumbled in the 1970s, the role of these voices
dramatically increased, particularly with the neoliberal economic policies of
the Netanyahu cabinets.

From early Zionist settlement in Palestine in the late 19th century
through the present, American Jews, the largest and most affluent Diaspora
community, have officially donated more than $30 billion to support projects
in Israel. This relationship pattern has been derisively called "checkbook
Zionism," or what has here been termed proxy Zionism. What started as a
partnership of the practical Zionists and the checkbook Zionists or the absen-
tee payers took shape in the early decades of the 20th century, particularly
through the United Jewish Appeal (UJA) in America and the Jewish Agency
in Israel, until it began to falter in the 1980s.[36]

It is this historical transformation – the Great Conjuncture, as it is
called here[37] – that also changed the traditional pattern of American giving

to Israel. That's why the cracks in the relationship grew increasingly after the 1967 War and more prominently in the 1980s and early 1990s, due to the occupied territories and the settlement expansion, with the result being a drop in UJA campaign receipts year after year. This change did not herald diminishing American interest in Israel overall. In reality, Americans were not less interested in Israel but changing how they gave. Rather than giving through the traditional organizational channels, increasing numbers of American Jews were choosing to donate to new organizations that afforded them more opportunity to decide how their funds would be used. At the eve of the 2020s, the number of organizations raising funds for projects in Israel had reached nearly a thousand extending from mainstream causes like hospitals, museums, *yeshivot*, and universities to more boutique causes, such as Jewish settlement-related issues. So, in part, the change in giving reflected the rising affluence of American Jewry and the increasing differentiation of the funding organizations. In part, it illustrated the interests of revisionist proxy Zionism stressing settlement expansion, historical Jewish revisionism. resettlement of occupied territories and so on. These are highly sensitive and contested issues that big federated philanthropic organizations seek to avoid, unlike dedicated niche organizations that do not shun controversies.

WHAT IS ISRAEL?

The Failure of the *Judenstaat*

When Herzl wrote his *Judenstaat* (*The Jewish State*, 1896) amid the Dreyfus affair, he and his contemporaries saw antisemitism as an eternal curse, which cried for an enduring solution, which to them meant a Jewish state. Herzl's initial objective was sovereignty anywhere. In 1903, he was still peddling a Uganda Scheme, endorsed by the British colonial secretary. Other Zionists supported Argentina, Cyprus, present-day Iraq, Mozambique and the Sinai as locations for the future Jewish state.[38] When the Zionist movement consolidated on Palestine as the preferred location, Herzl and his successors were inspired by the biblical prophecy of *Kibbutz Galuyot,* or "the ingathering of exiles" in the Land of Israel. And so, foreseen by the Prophets, this idea became central to Zionism, with Israel's "Law of Return" deeming that "every Jew has the right to come to this country as an *oleh* [immigrant]."[39] To appeal to most Zionists, Herzl took a core idea in Religious Zionism, like Georges Sorel once seized upon the idea of violence, to inspire the Jewish masses. Zionism needed a powerful myth, and biblical redemption would do.

In the view of the Zionists, the ingathering of exiles would end the expulsions and persecution that had cast such a dark shadow over Jewish history. Yet, that precisely has *not* happened. The Israeli historian of Nazi Germany, Moshe Zimmermann, argued in the aftermath of October 7 that the Hamas offensive was no Holocaust. Whether the Hamas offensive is seen as a modern-day pogrom, as Zimmermann argued, or a reflection of liberation struggle, as the proponents of Hamas would argue, what really matters is that the *raison d'être* of Zionism was predicated on the idea that Israel is the only safe heaven of world Jewry; and thus only in Israel, Jews can feel safe and secure. Yet, the ability of Hamas to undermine that illusion so thoroughly, even after 75 years of Israeli existence, suggests that the Zionist project has failed.

Here is what we need to think about: How did it come about that Zionism disappointed and that the Zionist state – or its prophets, from Herzl onward – is incapable of meeting the goals it set for itself? The event of October 7, a pogrom on the soil of Israel, in the State of Israel, is a turning point in our assessment of the success of Zionism, and a turning point in the Israeli-Palestinian conflict.[40]

In Herzl's stated view, antisemitism marked all societies in which Jews were a minority. Only sovereignty, which to him implied an adequate Jewish majority, would ensure a life without persecution to the Jews. Yet, Israel has failed to deliver such security. Ever since its creation, it has been effectively at war. Nor has its establishment mitigated antisemitism. On the contrary, Israel's conduct appears to contribute to increasing Jewish insecurity not just within Israel, but among the Diaspora, not to mention the Middle East at large. Even though almost half of world Jewry now resides in Israel, this has not nullified antisemitism. On the contrary, it is actually fostering a new antisemitism around the world. Worse, the drive to transform the democratic Jewish state into a religious autocracy is contributing to the outflow of the best and the brightest from Israel.

Nonetheless, both the Israeli right-wing and its Messianic far-right saw things very differently: not as a "failure" of Zionism, but as an incomplete realization of Zionism. The Hamas offensive succeeded because the Iron Wall is not yet strong enough. Consequently, what is needed is *more* suppression of dissidence internally and *greater* fire-power externally.

Universalist Diaspora, Nationalist Israel

As it began to emerge in the 1980s, this trajectory was opposed by some progressive Jewish leaders, such as Nahum Goldmann (1896–1982), the founder of the World Jewish Congress and its president (1951–78). Known as a strong proponent of Zionism, Goldmann also believed in the idea of a Jewish Diaspora, but saw neither as enough on its own. He saw the two as complementary. As a champion of multilateralism and international cooperation, he often criticized Israel's excessive reliance on military might. For the same reason, he argued that Israel had to recognize the Palestinians as a people, and vice versa. In 1970, when Egypt's president Gamal Abdel Nasser invited him to talks, the effort was halted by Israel's Labor government. In 1974, when he tried to contact PLO leader Yasser Arafat, Israeli government saw it as high treason, which he thought foolishly short-sighted. And when in 1982 Goldmann appealed to Prime Minister Begin not to reanimate antisemitism and anti-Zionism with the Lebanese War, the Likud leader ignored the call, unleashing a new wave of both antisemitism and anti-Zionism.[41] The unwillingness to engage in peace talks in 1970 was followed by the Yom Kippur War; in 1974, by decades of international terrorism; and in 1982, by the Sabra and Shatila massacre and the devastating South Lebanon conflict that would last until 2000 contributing to the rise of Hezbollah in the north and Hamas in the south, and Palestinian Intifadas in the West Bank.

Obviously, neither the historical emancipation of Jews outside Israel nor Jewish nationhood are solutions against persecution. However, the two are not mutually exclusive, but complementary stances to the kind of discrimination and atrocities that haunt minorities around the world. If Hitler's Judeocide was an overwhelming proof that assimilation has its limits, Israel's destabilization in the Middle East is testimony to the limits of Jewish nationhood. At the broadest level, antisemitism is hardly a European privilege. In one form or another, intolerance of difference is hardly a European monopoly. What made the old continent different was the longstanding Christian persecution of Jews that went hand in hand with the progress of modernity since the 15th century, the rise of romantic ethno-nationalism and scientific racism in the 19th century, and the cruel efficiency marking Europe's mass-industrial attempt to exterminate its Jewry in the 20th century. In marked contrast, Jewish communities lived in relative peace in the Muslim countries.

On the Israeli side, the challenge is that the Sorelian myth of the ingathering of exiles is not a myth at all to many of the country's conservative, far-right and Messianic Jews. To them, it marks the initial stage of national redemption. It is this lingering unresolved tension between religion and nationality that rabbi Zvi Yehuda Kook, the Messianic spiritual leader of the Jewish settlements in the West Bank, saw as the beginning of the redemption.[42] By summer 2024, apocalyptic concerns for Israel's future and regional escalation fueled extraordinary Messianic fervor among the far-right, who now saw the Gaza War as the 21st century biblical war between Gog and Magog and October 7 as the birth pains and prelude to national redemption. The darker the future seemed, the lighter it would be. Hence, too, the visit of Israel's far-right security minister Ben-Gvir to the Al-Aqsa Mosque compound in August 2024. It was quickly denounced by Washington and Brussels. It was considered insensitive, provocative and self-defeating. But they missed the point. The greater the catastrophe, the more glorious the redemption. Ultimately, all the Messianic far-right could offer was a vision of hell that was depicted as rejuvenation.

The Zionist Cultural Wars

Following the Cold War, the polarization between the peace advocates of the Israeli Labor coalition and the hawks of the revisionist right-wing has been reflected in the cultural wars between the post-Zionists and neo-Zionists. With the rise of the new historians and the peace process, the former challenged the old dogmas of official Zionism, while the latter called for a more inclusive and international self-definition. As far as the new augurs were concerned, the objective of Zionism – the creation of the modern state of Israel – had materialized in 1948. With its ideological mission fulfilled, Zionism per se was history. Post-Zionism was the new reality.

Like postmodernism in Western academia, post-Zionism in Israel emerged mainly in the universities and intellectual circles. One of its more influential proponents has been Avraham Burg, who sees Herzlian Zionism as a dated scaffolding that should be removed. Growing up as the son of Yosef Burg, the longtime minister of the National Religious Party, the veteran Israeli politician is a former speaker of the Knesset, chairman of the Jewish Agency and interim president. By 2007, he warned that "to define the State of Israel as a Jewish state is the key to its end." Instead, French civic nationalism might be an example to follow.[43]

In 2023, just two months before October 7, Burg joined more than 1,500 U.S., Israeli, Jewish and Palestinian academics and public figures who signed an open letter stating that Israel operates "a regime of apartheid." It called on Jewish groups to speak out against the occupation in Palestine. Burg has argued that Israel is moving toward fascism and violence, due to a continuing trauma from the Holocaust. He was inspired by the French precedent of civic nationalism; that is, by its efforts to distinguish civic nationalism from ethnic nationalism.[44] Efforts to define Israel by Jewishness, Burg argued, are a dead-end and recipe to far-right religious terror.[45]

If post-Zionism thrived in the largely secular Tel Aviv, it was soon offset by conservative and religious neo-Zionism in Jerusalem. Backed up by Israeli right-wing sponsors and American neoconservative money, neo-Zionism seemed exclusionary, nationalist, and occasionally supremacist, evolving in parallel with and opposition to labor and left-wing post-Zionism.[46] With the emergence of the peace movement and post-Zionism, new right-wing NGOs, such as Im Tirtzu, and religious networks like Arutz Sheva surfaced to present "pro-settlement views," as opposed to the "leftist post-Zionism" with its "self-hating Jews." Arutz Sheva is an Israeli media network identifying with Religious Zionism. Promoting the settler movement, it seeks to counterbalance what it regards as "negative" and "defeatist" post-Zionism. Founded in 2006, Im Tirtzu has been intertwined with networks of other groups in Israel and the United States, including think tanks, holding companies, funds, exporters, Christian-Zionist ministries, lobbies, and consultants (Figure 5-5).

Figure 5-5   Neo-Zionist Im Tirtzu and U.S. Neoconservative Funding

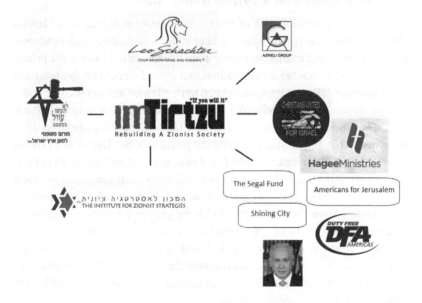

Im Tirtzu's networks feature Israeli think tanks, such as the Legal Forum for the Land of Israel, and the Misgav Institute for Zionist Strategies (which would later gain notoriety for its promotion of ethnic cleansing). The latter has received funding from the Azrieli Group, a real estate holding company;

Leo Schachter, Israel's second-largest exporter of processed diamonds originating from Brooklyn, New York; a fund headed by businessman Yotam Bar-Hama; and the Forum for Religious Zionism. Until the early 2010s, the largest donor was the John Hagee Ministries (JHM), through its Christian-Zionist arm, Christians United For Israel (CUFI). After excessive politicization, JHM ceased its funding. The losses were soon offshet by Shining City, a U.S. organization closely linked with PM Netanyahu.[47] Emulating Nazi propaganda, Im Tirtzu was charged for fascist practices, which led it to file a lawsuit. In court proceedings, Zeev Sternhell, an expert on fascism, testified that Im Tirtzu's activities did rest on fascist principles.[48]

Supported by abundant funding, neo-Zionist NGOs have sought to marginalize post-Zionist thinking, particularly in Israeli universities, targeting their human rights centers, legal clinics, anti-apartheid movements, Nakba day, peace activists, and so on. Following October 7, they have had a central role in marginalizing, neutralizing and, in some cases, criminalizing dissidence in Israel in the name of "national security."

The Struggle over a *Jewish* Nation-State

In the UN partition plan of 1947, Israel had been defined as a "Jewish state." The term was embraced a year later in its Declaration of Independence, which had no explicit reference to the term "democratic," even if the principles it espoused – not the actual realities that ensued – could be characterized as "democratic." By contrast, the related term, "Jewish and democratic state" is far more recent. It was officially added in the amendment to Israel's *Basic Law: The Knesset*, which was passed in 1985, officially legislated in 1992 and amended in 1994, typically, amid the peace process. But as that process crumbled, so has the idea of "Jewish and democratic state" eroded over time.

By the 2014 Gaza War, Israel's political institutions seemed to be under a process of erosion. In the occupied territories, democracy has been non-existent almost from the beginning. Ruled by occupation force, Palestinians have minimal rights. In the past, Israelis spent years in the military to protect the nation from existential threats. Today, they serve in order to prolong the very occupation that is posing an existential threat to Israel. What used to be a Jewish and democratic state is at risk of turning into a Judeo-state, with other minorities as *de facto* second citizens.

The legislative history of the Jewish nation-state bill began in 2011, when the then-chair of the Knesset's foreign affairs committee, Avi Dichter, the former director of Shin Bet who had been charged with extrajudicial killings and human rights violations during the Second Intifada, filed the Nation

Bill, a proposal to define the nature of the state of Israel as the state of the Jewish people.[49] Tacitly, it was an effort to redefine the designation "Jewish and democratic state" in the Israeli basic laws.[50] Dichter was known for being blunt. After October 7, he endorsed the forced displacement of civilians from the northern Gaza Strip, acknowledging that "we are now rolling out the Gaza Nakba...Gaza Nakba 2023. That's how it'll end."[51]

In the original legislation, "Jewish" highlighted the unique nature of the Israeli state, while "democratic" underscored the secular nature of the state. From the beginning, there has been a tension between these two terms. To some in the Likud coalition, Israel is Jewish first and only then democratic. In 2017, a special joint committee headed by MK Amir Ohana, the first openly gay Likudnik, was formed to champion the bill. Supporting the exemption of Netanyahu from prosecution in the corruption investigations, Ohana had been in the PM's circle. Upon presenting the reformed bill, he described it as "the law of all laws."

> It is the most important law in the history of the State of Israel, which says that everyone has human rights, but national rights in Israel belong only to the Jewish people. That is the founding principle on which the state was established.[52]

There were Orwellian echoes in the idea that everyone has human rights, but some have them just more than others. Despite its potential harm to Israeli democracy and minorities, particularly its Arab citizens, the reformed bill was approved in 2018, after some dilution. Most Israelis supported the law, while a third opposed it. Most Israelis also felt that equality for all Israeli citizens should have been explicitly covered by law. The Arab members of the Joint List tore the printed text of the law while decrying "Apartheid" in the Knesset. The PLO secretary-general Saeb Erekat called it a "dangerous and racist law" which "officially legalizes apartheid and legally defines Israel as an apartheid system."[53] To the far-right Messianic Jews, the new bill was a window of opportunity. They dream of making the Judaic halakha Israel's legal code. Among others, Bezalel Smotrich has long campaigned for the Ministry of Justice "to restore the Torah justice system."[54]

Not every Israeli agreed with such views. But few criticized them as vehemently as the former deputy mayor of Jerusalem, Meron Benvenisti, who warned that Israel had become a "a master-nation democracy; in German, a *'Herrenvolk* democracy.'" As he put it, "We are a country that behaves like a full-blooded democracy, but we have a group of serfs, the Arabs, to whom we do not apply democracy. The result is a situation of extreme inequality."[55] Meaning the "master race," the term *Herrenvolk* originated from 19th century colonial discourse that legitimized colonialism and endorsed white Europeans' supposed racial superiority. In such a sham democracy, only one ethnic group has voting rights, while another is disenfranchised. One ethnic group dominates, and the other is repressed.

Herrenvolk democracy is a racial ideology that marked America's segregationist South, apartheid South Africa, and the pre-1980 Rhodesia (present-day Zimbabwe).[56] This supremacy doctrine has also proved very appealing to Jewish supremacists particularly, but not exclusively to the Messianic far-right.

FROM DEMOCRACY TO AUTOCRACY

The Quest for "Judicial Reforms"

After the far-right election victory in late 2022, the Netanyahu cabinet's newly-appointed justice minister, Yariv Levin, claimed that "judicial activism" had ruined public trust in the legal system and made it impossible for the government to rule effectively. Sensing a historical opportunity to remake the Israeli legal system, the new government would seek to "reform" Israel's judiciary.

Levin's draft proposal pushed for sweeping changes in the judiciary, executive and legislative processes and functions. It sought to change the process for choosing judges by giving the government control over the selection and dismissal of all judges, including those in the Supreme Court. It tried to restrict the Supreme Court's capacity to strike down laws and government decisions by requiring an enlarged panel of the court's judges and a "special majority" in order to do so. It would allow the Knesset to overrule the Supreme Court by a majority voting against the Court, and had an "override clause" that would enable the Knesset to re-legislate laws unless all justices agreed unanimously to strike them down. It would allow ministers to select and fire justices' legal advisors and decide whether or not to adhere to legal advice. It would prevent the court from using a test of "reasonableness," which precluded the courts from hearing petitions or appeals against governmental and administrative decisions seen as "unreasonable."[57]

Opposition leader Yair Lapid called Levin's reform draft "a letter of intimidation," contending that the Netanyahu cabinet threatened to "destroy the entire constitutional structure of the State of Israel." Speaking against the proposed reforms, Lapid warned of an impending "political coup" and pledging that the opposition would reverse the reforms. "Like a gang of criminals," the government has "put a loaded gun on the table."[58]

Unlike many other democracies, Israel does not have a constitution. Along with New Zealand, San Marino, Saudi Arabia, and the United Kingdom, Israel is one of few countries operating according to an uncodified constitution. In the 1950 Harari Decision following Israeli independence, the Knesset opted to legislate the constitution in a piecemeal fashion.[59] Between the 1950s and late 1980s, it passed nine Basic Laws. Many of these laws center on individual liberties, but also on the principal state institutions and civil rights. Some were earlier protected by the Supreme Court. In particular, *The Basic Law: Human Dignity and Liberty* ensured the Supreme Court had the authority to disqualify any law contradicting it, and protection from Emergency Regulations.[60]

These rights are critical to dissidents in Israel, Israeli Arabs and civil rights in the occupied territories. In this perspective, the proposed judicial reforms can be seen as an attempt to hammer out a Jewish democracy at the expense of secular civil rights, including a *de jure* apartheid rule opposed to such *de facto* practices in the occupied territories.

Ben-Gurion's Concern with an Official Constitution

As Israel's first prime minister, David Ben-Gurion had a critical role in setting up the newly created country's institutions, infrastructure, and key policies. Why did he not push for a strong constitution? In part, this was due to great disagreements among different political groups. The ultra-pragmatic BG, as he was called, shunned the idea of an official, explicit constitution because it was likely to bring the tensions out in the open. Moreover, he thought that a formal constitution might permit the Supreme Court to overrule his centralized social-democratic policies and thus undermine his efforts at a majoritarian election system. He saw himself building a nation from scratch. He needed consolidated, centralized sovereignty to do the job.

What Ben-Gurion failed to foresee was that one day his adversaries, led by the successors of Menachem Begin and his Herut Party, would exploit the loopholes that the Labor governments left behind, to remake the judiciary. Worse, BG inadvertently contributed to such efforts. To stress sovereignty while blurring its content, he used the term *mamlakhtiyut*, which is typically translated as "statism" or "etatism," both of which fail to convey the nuanced origins of the term. BG chose the term to associate the State of Israel with its glorious historical past as a biblical Hebrew kingdom. By the same token, the term (*Melech*, lit. "King") allowed him to distinguish between the "Jewish nation" and the formal Israeli state.[61] Conversely, it has allowed his far-right-wing fans to link those two meanings by blurring the distinction. The net effect has been the ethnicization of the concept; that is,

Jewish nation + Israeli state = Jewish nation state of Israel

Ben-Gurion seized *mamlakhtiyut* to associate but not to link modern sovereignty and statehood with the perceived glory of past Hebrew kingdoms. By contrast, the Messianic far-right seeks to link, not just to associate, the mythological past, the idealized present and the apocalyptic future. The terms are the same, but the coded meanings radically different. Stressing an exclusionary ethno-nationalism, the ensuing concept rejects all non-Jewish groups from its scope, including Israeli Arabs, Palestinians, Druze and other non-Jewish minorities. Furthermore, as Ben-Gurion left the door open to a mystical, ethno-nationalist interpretation of Jewish sovereignty, his effort to avoid an explicit constitution went hand in hand with his reluctance to define Israel's *ultimate* borders. He saw expansion as an instrument for national security, whereas his ethno-nationalist successors regard it as an inherent part of national redemption. He knew that the international community would oppose such a project, which is perceived as neo-colonialism. His ethno-nationalist successors couldn't care less how the world sees their project. Since it is divinely ordered, secular international opposition is immaterial.

The separation between the legislative and executive branches is relatively weak in Israel since the government tends to hold a majority – however fragile – in the Knesset. The Supreme Court is effectively the last institution having the power to limit government actions and legislation passed by a parliamentary majority. That's why Levin and the Netanyahu cabinet hoped to take that power away from the judiciary and shift it to the government. To succeed, they first had to subvert Justice Aharon Barak's constitutional revolution.

Toward Constitutional Counter-Revolution

Over a century ago, American historian Charles Beard demonstrated that the U.S. Constitution was framed by the class interests of its elite, thereby reflecting a counter-revolution of sorts. Though highly popular in the first half of the 20th century, it has been targeted since the Cold War and McCarthyism and remains highly controversial today.[62] Due to the absence of such a constitution in Israel, the Likud governments have sought to surpass it via a body of rulings serving the same purpose. This is, in effect, a legal counter-revolution, aiming to protect the economic interests of those forces that finance Likud's conservative leaders, the Messianic far-right and the settlers. Until the proposed judicial reforms, all legislation, government orders, and administrative actions of state bodies in Israel were subject to judicial review by the Supreme Court. Between 1992 and 1999, *in parallel with the peace process*, Supreme Court Justice Aharon Barak, in a series of rulings, developed something of a doctrine, or "Constitutional Revolution," as he called it. This transformation, he argued, came about with the adoption of the Basic Laws focused on human rights in the Knesset and by the Supreme Court. The revolution raised these laws – including the right to equality, freedom of employment and freedom of speech – to a position of normative supremacy, thus granting the courts rather than just the Supreme Court the ability to strike down legislation deemed inconsistent with the rights embodied in the Basic Laws. As the net effect, Israel morphed from a parliamentary democracy to a constitutional parliamentary democracy, in which the Basic Laws were seen as its constitution.[63]

Over a decade later, in parallel with the failure of the peace process, the proponents of judicial reform wanted to bury Barak's "constitutional revolution." Hence, the Netanyahu cabinet's constitutional counter-revolution.

Interestingly, the draft of the proposed judicial reforms came from the Misgav Institute for Zionist Strategies. The think tank was Israeli but it was also American, with many American-Jewish members and Israeli settler hawks.[64] As its first major project, it drafted the versions of reforms first submitted to the Knesset in the 2000s. It was the same institute that also advised the Israeli government on Gaza, arguing right after the Hamas attack that the war offered a "rare opportunity to evacuate the entire Gaza Strip" and ethnically cleanse Gaza (Figure 5-6).[65]

After the electoral triumph of the Israeli far-right, the Netanyahu cabinet began to push the highly controversial judicial reforms in January 2023. The effort was led by Netanyahu's deputy PM and minister of justice, Yariv Levin, and the chair of the Knesset's constitution committee, Simcha Rothman. Like Netanyahu, Levin is a veteran Likud politician, a scion of a far-right family. His maternal uncle was a conservative member of the first Knesset and the commander of the cargo ship *Altalena*. In June 1948, the ship was loaded with fighters of the far-right terrorist group Irgun and a huge cache of military equipment. A violent confrontation ensued between the newly created Israeli Defense Force led by Ben-Gurion, and the Irgun headed by Menachem Begin. It was a clash the revisionists never forgave. The Levins were on the defeated Irgun's side, and decades later Begin served as the honorary guest holding the baby, Yariv, at his circumcision ceremony. As a rising Likud star, Levin fought against Israeli withdrawal from Gaza in 2005. He opposes the creation of a Palestinian state and the two-state solution, supports settlers and believes Jews have the right to remain in all parts of the land of Israel.

Figure 5-6 Judicial Reforms and Ethnic Cleansing

(*Above, left*) A scanned copy of the cover page of "Constitution of Israel proposed by the Institute for Zionist Strategies" (Sep 2010). (*Above, right*) A scanned copy of the position paper of the Misgav Institute for National Security and Zionist Strategy advocating for the "relocation and final settlement of the entire Gaza population" (Oct 2023). *Source: Wikimedia Commons*

Simcha Rothman was Levin's mirror image on the side of the religious militants. He is a Knesset member of the far-right Religious Zionist Party and the chair of its constitutional committee. Born into a Jewish-American family from Cleveland, Ohio, he lived in Bnei Brak, the center of orthodox and haredi Judaism east of Tel Aviv. A critic of Netanyahu's corruption trial, Rothman represented the militant, anti-Arab party promoting far-right Kahanism and Jewish supremacy and supporting the annexation of the occupied territories to Israel. In late 2023, he called for "resettling" Gaza's refugees; that is, for ethnic cleansing in the Strip.[66]

When the dynamic duo, Levin and Rothman, unveiled the government plan for a legislative overhaul of the country's judicial system, all hell broke loose.

Mass Protests Against Judicial Reforms

The champions of Israel's often-controversial policies like to say that Israel is the only democracy in the Middle East, discounting the elections being held in countries such as Türkiye and Iran. In reality, Israel's democracy ranking has eroded in the past decades. According to popular democracy indices, the Middle Eastern and North African countries with highest scores feature Israel, Tunisia and Iraq. Nonetheless and unsurprisingly, given it is an occupying state, Israel is seen as a "flawed democracy" ranking behind almost half a hundred countries and at par with Panama, Colombia and South Korea, another U.S. client state.[67] Israeli voters are painfully aware of Israel's democratic erosion, now in their own regard. As a result, the proposed judicial reforms were opposed by most Israelis in massive protests, which began soon after as the cabinet introduced the reform package.

Starting in Tel Aviv's Habima Square, the site of the 2011 cost-of-living protests, the anti-reform demonstrations garnered some 20,000 protesters, with smaller rallies of thousands in Jerusalem and elsewhere. The first protest was organized by "Standing Together," a grassroots Arab-Jewish movement, though it did not address Palestinian interests. In just a week, the number of the protesters grew eight-fold to some 150,000 people while demonstrations spread in Israeli cities. By mid-March, up to 260,000 people were demonstrating in Tel Aviv (Figure 5-7).

Figure 5-7   Israeli Mass Protests against Judicial Reforms

Israeli mass protests against the proposed "judicial reforms" in Tel Aviv, March 4, 2023. *Source: Wikimedia Commons (photo by Amir Terkel)*

When Netanyahu's defense minister and Israel's consul general resigned in response to the proposed judicial reform, hundreds of thousands of Israelis protested in 150 locations. President Herzog called Netanyahu to halt the legislative process and the national labor federation Histadrut announced a general nationwide strike. By mid-June, massive nationwide protests were the new norm, as hundreds of IDF reservists, organized by the *Brothers in Arms* movement, joined the protests, as well as 200 high-tech companies, followed by the Israel Business Forum, a group of the 50 largest corporates representing most private-sector employees. Concurrently, these protests spread to New York City.[68]

In the past, Israel's judiciary had regularly upheld policies, practices and laws that helped enforce the "system of apartheid against Palestinians," including upholding administrative detentions, green lighting the destruction of villages and imposing restrictions on family reunification. But on some occasions, the Supreme Court had intervened to protect Palestinian rights. With the judicial reforms, even this "slim and inconsistent" protection was expected to disappear. The proposed overhaul had chilling implications for Palestinian rights.[69]

Given that the far-right cabinet held a 64-seat majority in the 120-seat Knesset prior to the Gaza War, opposition parties could do little within the legislature to stop judicial reform. A month before October 7, the Supreme Court heard the case. But then, as the protests were about to collapse the Netanyahu cabinet and result in new elections, on October 7 the Hamas offensive began. Following a year of protests against the judiciary reforms and three months of anti-government demonstrations amid the Gaza War, the Supreme Court struck down the bill.[70] Though celebrated as a triumph for democracy in Israel and abroad, the vote was tight (8-7) at the historic 13-hour hearing. Moreover, the justices also ruled that the Supreme Court has the power to overturn the Basic Laws (12-3).[71]

It was the Supreme Court's way to uphold its independence and power in the Israeli democracy. But the tight vote reflected significant support for the judicial reforms even in the High Court of Justice itself. As far as the Netanyahu cabinet was concerned, even though it was unable to implement its judicial reforms in the fog of the war, it would continue the two-decade long struggle for its bill. The timing failed, not the proposals. The glass was half-full. Their time would come later.

And when Israel's military advocate general Yifat Tomer-Yerushalmi ordered masked military police investigators to arrest soldiers suspected of sexually abusing a Palestinian detainee in a notorious detention facility, she was summoned to the Knesset foreign affairs and defense committee, so that she could be put in her place. The underlying objective was to target her and the military police, so that they would be deterred and not open another investigation against soldiers. Meanwhile, attorney general Gali Baharav-Miara was also under assault. The efforts to uphold the rule of law and the counter-efforts to suppress such attempts in the name of national security are not random events, but an integral part pf the ongoing judicial coup by the far-right cabinet, to achieve amid the Gaza War autocratically what they failed to accomplish at a time of peace democratically. Indeed, it is typified by the takeover of the police by national security minister Itamar Ben-Gvir.

SUBVERSION OF THE JEWISH-DEMOCRATIC STATE

One way to look at the progression of this quasi-official state violence is as a narrative describing the rise of the Messianic far-right into power. In their journalistic investigation, Ronen Bergman and Mark Mazzetti outline how, after 50 years of failure to stop violence and terrorism against Palestinians by Jewish ultranationalists, "lawlessness has become the law."[72] While that is an apt description of the far-right's grip of critical sectors of the Israeli society, it doesn't adequately explain the existing tensions between the civil bureaucracies and the apocalyptic reformers.

There is an alternative way to depict that progression. Instead of aiming to integrate the lawful and the lawless, the state bureaucracy and the state violence, it tells the story as a rising tension between these *dual* realities; that is, the official, normative state and its darker side, the prerogative state. Obviously, the narrative of the dual state is less convenient, not least because of its dark track record in Nazi Germany. But as we shall see, it is better equipped to narrate the institutional story of cutting-edge capabilities coupled with their degradation under subversion, corruption and Messianism.[73]

As long as the dual state prevailed, the civil servants of the normative state were still able to keep the Messianic far-right of the prerogative state at bay. To the latter, the Gaza War was a historical, divinely-ordered opportunity not just to take over and annex the occupied territories but also to dominate the government and its executive bureaucracies.

Emergence of the Dual State

At the eve of World War II, Ernst Fraenkel fled from Nazi Germany to the United States, where he published his master treatise, *The Dual State* (1941). It was an analysis of the political system of the Nazi state, which he saw as "a contribution to the theory of dictatorship."[74] Fraenkel knew the system intimately. In the Weimar Republic, he had been a leading socialist jurist, and as a lawyer, he had represented political defendants in court, mainly Jews targeted by the Nazi regime. Eventually, as a dissident, he worked in the underground with several resistance groups until his immigration in the late

1930s to America.[75] What worried Fraenkel was the gradual perversion of the democratic institutions of the Weimar Republic from 1918 to 1933. During that period, the Nazi Party took power as Hitler was able to use emergency powers to undermine constitutional governance and suspend civil liberties.

How could it happen? How could democracy collapse and Germany end up under one-party dictatorship? Fraenkel's simple response was: the dual state. Democratic institutions remained, but mainly as pale shadows, as façades rather than effective institutions. In fact, the Nazi state had two sides. One featured the *normative* state, which was "an administrative body endowed with elaborate powers for safeguarding the legal order as expressed in statutes, decisions of the courts, and activities of the administrative agencies." It represented the rule of law. The other side of the dual state referred to the *prerogative* state; that is, a "governmental system which exercises unlimited arbitrariness and violence unchecked by any legal guarantees."[76] It excelled in unrestrained artificiality, including violence, unimpeded by any rule of law.

Fraenkel showed the constant friction between the traditional judicial bodies representing the normative state and the agencies of the prerogative state, the instruments of the dictatorship. As the resistance of the traditional law-enforcing bodies was weakened by 1936 – in just three years after the triumph of Hitler's Nazi Party in a presumably democratic election – Fraenkel showed how the decisions of the courts reflected the progress of Nazi radicalism in Germany. It was not the courts' purpose to foster extremist radicalism, but as they did tolerate such legal revisionism, these courts were virtually digging their own graves.

In the postwar era, the idea of the dual state influenced the postwar debates about the Third Reich. But Fraenkel's theory was not just about Nazi Germany. It was about the potential of political regression in industrialized democracies and thereby about Israel as well. Contemporary Israel is not Nazi Germany and the early 2020s aren't the early 1930s. Nor has Israel's constitutional framework been replaced by the "leader principle" (*Führerprinzip*) as the basis of executive authority. And yet, there are distressing parallels.

From Weimar Germany to Israel

While it had first emerged as a fringe movement in the 1970s, the rise of the Messianic far-right had been fostered by the Likud coalitions' settlement expansion since the 1980s. After the failure of underground violence, these groups chose to march into and infiltrate the very same democratic institutions they despised, particularly after the Oslo Accords in the 1990s.

Through these decades, they were reinforced by massive U.S. military aid and Jewish-American financiers, particularly donors representing revisionist Zionism.

In Germany, Nazis benefited from the *Völkisch* ideology – that is, the German ethnic nationalist movement – which served as a glue tying together different social and economic groups. In Israel, Jewish ethno-nationalism, in varying degrees, has had a similar role as a glue for political, social and cultural cohesion. In Germany, the *Völkisch* nationalists saw the Jews as "aliens" who belonged to a different *Volk* – in the sense of "folk" or "race" – from the pure Aryan Germans and thus had no business in the new Germany. In Israel, the Jewish far-right perceives the Arabs as aliens in the Jewish state thus favoring the expulsion of the Palestinians but tolerating Israeli Arabs to preserve a semblance of an effective democracy. German expansionism was legitimized with notions like *Lebensraum* that, in practice, translated to the ethnic cleansing and genocidal atrocities of *Generalplan Ost*, seeking to enslave much of Eastern Europe. In Jewish ethno-nationalism, "Greater Israel" was the apocalyptic ideology fueling the settlements and efforts to expand Israel's boundaries, resulting in ethnic expulsions and atrocities, all in the name of "national security."

The *Völkisch* precedent had relied on the idea of "blood and soil," fueled by the organicist metaphors of a singular, unified and racially pure social body. It was essentially a frustrated rebellion of lower-middle-class Germans who were sidelined and ignored by the ruling elite of German junkers, industrialists and military, and laboring poor whose socialist leaders had been taken down. The values of romantic nationalism and idealized agrarianism were typical to Germany where industrialization and urbanization, which had uprooted an entire generation of Germans, was still relatively recent. In Jewish ethno-nationalism, it is the mythologized God-given Eretz Israel, the Land of Israel, that ensures collective singularity and racial purity. For all practical purposes, this ideology relies on the longstanding resentment by poorer Jews from Arab countries, assertive religious Jews and the ultra-orthodox, the Messianic far-right, coupled with free-market conservatives, ideological Likudniks and the settler zealots. Among the Messianic far-right, the *Völkisch* "blood and soil" meant Jewish supremacy coupled with the Eretz (Land) of Israel.

For years, historians of Nazi Germany like Moshe Zimmermann have drawn upon the legacy of Weimar Germany to understand the endangerment of Israeli democracy by authoritarian, nationalist and racist forces, "to determine where on the chronological calendar of the Weimar Republic we in Israel were situated. Now, in 2023 we are wondering: Are there not features of the regime in Israel that are familiar from German history after 1933?" In this trajectory, the Israel of the Messianic far-right has a prominent role. As fueled by its underlying forces, "the story of 'Greater Israel' and the settlements is the story of a society that is becoming a hostage to biblical romanticism that is sweeping the whole society to perdition."[77]

With the election triumph of the Messianic far-right in fall 2022, the contours of the new order have become clearer. For all practical purposes, the Messianic far-right saw the normative state as an unwarranted obstacle to more effective, autocratic governance. The administrative body of the Israeli state was all nice and fine, but these elaborate powers that were designed to safeguard the legal order were ill-suited to the national security contingencies that were posing existential threats to Israel. Statutes, court decisions and administrative activities had their role, but decision-making had to be more effective. The enemies of Israel were no democracies. They didn't have to wait for court orders. The Jewish state required institutions that served the Jewish people, not its enemies. With the 2018 Jewish nation-state, the prerogative state began to play an ever-greater role in Israel at the expense of the normative state. Responding to this effort at a "judicial regime coup," hundreds of thousands of Israelis stormed the streets protesting it, a protest which eventually was diluted by demonstrations related to the Israeli hostages and the Gaza War. Yet, most Israelis had voted for the parties that made up the Messianic far-right, which was now firmly in place. And its strategic objective was to subvert the normative state by the exercise of "unlimited arbitrariness and violence unchecked by any legal guarantees" – in the name of a state of emergency, as too many times before.

Chapter 6

THE FALL OF ISRAELI POLITICS

At 1:00 AM on September 25, 2008, Professor Zeev Sternhell opened the door of his home in Jerusalem to enter an inner courtyard. The internationally-renowned 73-year-old expert on fascism had survived the Holocaust era and fought in several Israeli wars, but now he faced a different threat. As he turned the handle, the pipe-bomb went off. The explosion did not kill him but injured him. At the site, police found fliers offering $25,000 to anyone who would kill members of Peace Now movement he supported. The incident, Sternhell said, "goes to illustrate the fragility of Israeli democracy, and the urgent need to defend it with determination and resolve."[1]

More than a year later, Jack "Yaakov" Teitel, a Florida-born ultra-orthodox Jew, was arrested for perpetrating the attack. The arrests for suspected murders, bomb attempts, and for potentially catastrophic mortar plans began over a decade before. Living in a settlement that had been expropriated from the Palestinians, he started by murdering a Palestinian taxi driver and a West Bank shepherd in 1997. After Israel's unilateral disengagement from Gaza, he began to escalate, targeting a proximate Jewish settlement, police officers and a Christian monastery, while testing a shipped booby-trapped package. After the Sternhell assassination attempt, he was detained on suspicion of murdering two police officers in Jordan Valley, planning to bomb a gay bar in Jerusalem and flying a remote-controlled toy plane with explosives into Tel Aviv's gay pride parade. He dreamed of firing a mortar against the Al-Aqsa Mosque. By the time police retrieved his DNA traces at Sternhell's home, his lethal trajectory had lasted almost 12 years.[2]

In the court, Teitel's legal defense was provided by Honenu, a controversial organization protecting far-right Israelis accused of serious crimes against Arabs and Israeli security forces. Having raised funds for Kahane-inspired Yigal Amir, who assassinated prime minister Yitzhak Rabin in 1995, Honenu had assisted Ami Popper, accused of the murder of seven Palestinians; the members of the Bat Aying Underground, seeking to blow up a Palestinian girls' school in 2002; three Israelis for the murder of an

179

Arab teenager, and a number of Jewish supremacists of the anti-assimilation Lehava organization for arson at a Jewish-Arab school. One of Honenu's vocal attorneys was Itamar Ben-Gvir, the present Netanyahu cabinet's minister of national security, whom Israelis had ranked as the worst-performing member before October 7. In particular, Ben-Gvir was under heavy criticism for the record number of murders under his watch.[3]

By the 2014 Gaza War, Sternhell feared the collapse of Israeli democracy, which he compared with Vichy France in the 1940s. Seeing the "signs of fascism in Israel" reach a new peak, he warned that the time to reverse the trend was running out.[4]

How did Israeli politics decline into such extremes?

CLASSES AND CLEAVAGES

Complexities of Israeli Politics

Every modern society has segments – economic, social, religious and so on – with different interests that divide them into specific groups. Based on shared social and economic backgrounds, these interests translate into political cleavages shaping party systems and voting blocs, while accounting for the dominant internal conflicts in these countries. The "frozen party systems" reflect historical socio-economic divisions. They are often political manifestations of class conflicts.[5] Over time, such divides change; sometimes dramatically and often around new cleavages like clashes over integration and multiculturalism, environment and climate change, globalization and localism, and so on. Interestingly, growing inequality in many countries has not led to renewed class conflicts, but to new divides over identity and integration.[6]

The fluidity and complexity of Israeli politics and its parliament, the Knesset with its 120 members, reflects the country's extraordinary economic, ethnic, religious, and educational diversity. Yet, this diversity has common denominators. Most parties portray themselves as Zionist, despite great differences in how they define the term. *Effectively*, there are four to five pivotal party blocs: labor Zionists who dominated Israeli government coalitions around 1948 to 1977; right-wing Zionists who have led the country thereafter; and religious Zionists who have moved from moderation to assertiveness, while capitalizing on their leverage in coalition governments. Though a minority in Knesset, coalitions need them for majority. In the past two decades, Israeli politics has also seen the rise of centrists presenting themselves as moderate-secular alternatives, and Messianic far-right and ultra-orthodox parties.

If Zionism is what unites big party systems in Israel, the blocs are differentiated by multiple cleavages, including unique immigration patterns. Then there is the exceptional role of the Jewish religion. Historical legacies also feature the postwar dominance of the strong labor party and the right-wing backlash since the 1977 elections. These legacies, in turn, are associated with high levels of inequality among Jews themselves, compounded by neoliberal policies since the 1980s. There is also the persistent influence of the Israel-Arab conflict, the role of the large Arab minority within Israel and the large number of Palestinians in the occupied territories.

In the postwar era, the voters of the left-wing parties comprised working class and lower-middle-class voters. Since then, the voters of labor and allied parties have become associated with voters representing higher social classes. The reverse applies to the postwar voters of right-wing parties who used to be associated with higher-education and higher-class. Since then, they have also linked with lower-social class voters (Figure 6-1).

Figure 6-1   Israeli Election Results, 1949–2022

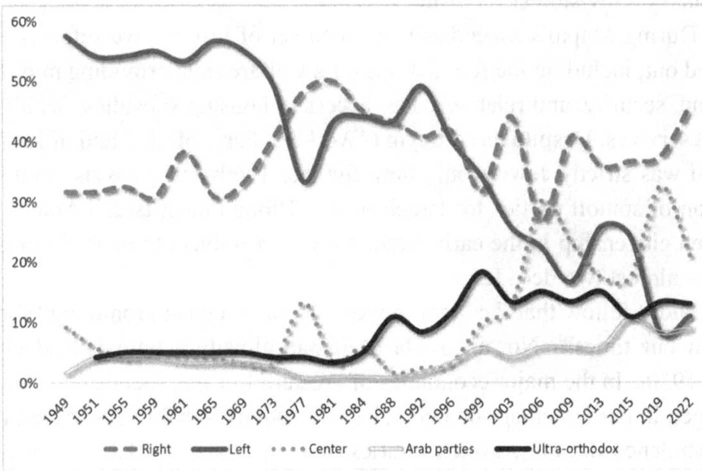

Source: Data from the WID database; updated by author.

In Israel, the transformation of these cleavage structures helps to explain the drastic transformation of politics. It shows how Labor Party trajectories and its stalwarts, such as David Ben-Gurion and Golda Meir, gave way to Likud's right-wing coalitions, from Menachem Begin to Benjamin Netanyahu; how these blocs have in turn given rise to centrist blocs, led by Benny Glantz and Yair Lapid; and how extremists, such as Bezalel Smotrich and Itamar Ben-Gvir, have emerged from the Messianic far-right.

Postwar Labor Governments' Versions of Socialism

Founded in 1930 as a merger of non-Marxist Zionist-Socialists and their more moderate peers led by David Ben-Gurion, *Mapai* was the leading core of the pre-state Yishuv and Israeli politics until its reincarnation as the modern Israeli Labor Party in 1968, which ruled with its dominant coalitions until the pivotal 1977 election. This hegemony rested particularly on the *Histadrut*, the powerful trade federation that prevailed over the nascent Jewish state's economy, infrastructure and society.

In the pre-state era, Histadrut also founded the first defense groups, *Hashomer* for settlement defense and *Haganah*, the paramilitary organization that gave rise to Israel's Defense Forces (IDF). Until 1945, Haganah relied on moderate self-restraint (*havlagah*), which triggered the splits of the more assertive and hard-right Irgun, headed by the subsequent Likud head Menachem Begin and Avraham Stern's Lehi ("Stern Gang"), led later by Yitzhak Shamir, Begin's successor in the 1980s. Conducting assassinations and bombings against the enemies, the two groups were seen as terrorists by the British, Arabs and moderate Jews alike. Both were inspired by Ze'ev Jabotinsky's revisionist Zionism.[7]

During Mapai's ascendancy, a broad set of progressive reforms were carried out, including the foundations for a welfare state providing minimum income, security, and relatively free access to housing subsidies, health and social services. Despite its acronym ("Workers' Party of the Land of Israel"), Mapai was strictly Jewish-only until the late 1960s but gave rise to a succession of spinoff parties for Israeli Arabs. Though most Israeli Arabs were granted citizenship in the early Israel, they were subject to martial law until 1966 – almost two decades.

Did it follow that the labor movement was socialist promoting "socialism in our times"? No, as Golda Meir had already acknowledged in the early 1950s. In the major economies of Western Europe, socialist parties had emerged in parliamentary democracies and countries that had achieved their independence decades, even centuries ago. In Israel, the labor movement not only built the nation but the foundations of Israeli capitalism, typically amid massive immigration inflows yet with minimal initial resources. Public intervention intensified mainly in times of pressing national crises.

The trajectory of the Israeli labor movement was unique. In contrast to the social-democratic parties of Western Europe, it had to build companies and serve as a large employer. To sustain jobs for Jewish immigrants, it shunned Arab labor. As a capitalist employer, it encouraged private investment to create more jobs, whereas the European labor movement saw itself in a class struggle against its employers. Even as such policies deepened the breach between the Israeli labor and its socialist roots, they generated great support for the labor movement. By the same token, it came to dominate the Zionist movement, particularly under Prime Minister Ben-Gurion's priorities, which were marked by national, not class goals.[8]

How the Occupation Undermined Labor Governments

The success of the labor movement was the cause of its fall. As Israel's rapid economic growth began to stabilize in the 1960s, the key institutions consolidated. But when the young work force wanted a socialist party to protect their interests in the industrializing economy, the nationalist socialism of the labor movement failed. Some of its spinoffs, such as the leftist Mapam, did maintain such stances, but they remained relatively small and mainly in the opposition. As nation builders, Labor governments promoted the nation. As the economy differentiated further and the mass society segmented, the immigration divides were compounded by ethnic differences among the Ashkenazim, Sephardim and Mizrahim. The consequent economic polarization, reflected by labor unrest, was reinforced by the varieties of religious streams. Fragmentation undermined the idea of a unified sovereignty, represented by the white Ashkenazi elite.

Driven by Histadrut and its Mapai core, the left wing attracted more than half of the Israeli vote until the late 1960s and the Six-Day War. But instead of peace and prosperity, the victory resulted in a War of Attrition and the almost-catastrophic Yom Kippur War, which was blamed on the labor coalition. While advocating a two-state solution, it permitted the rise of the Messianic far-right settlements due to what it regarded as "national security" considerations. It was this hesitation that cost its future. When the Labor governments returned under the leadership of Yitzhak Rabin and Shimon Peres, the peace process was revived in the 1990s. But by then, they relied on a fragile majority coalition. Moreover, Rabin's assassination did not result in the restoration of a strong labor coalition. It paved the way to the rise of the right-wing Likud under Benjamin Netanyahu.

The debate on the decline of Israeli labor dominance is long-lasting.[9] Usually, the losses are attributed to the rise of neoliberalism and attendant decline of social democratic parties in Western Europe. Certainly, the changing cleavage structures do matter, but they do not explain the timing of the fall since 1977. The decline is also explained by the inability of the labor alignments to attract labor voters, its failures to stay attuned to demographic shifts, and so on. Yet, the record shows that the Labor government was actually strengthened in 1973 but fell dramatically in 1977, as a result of the Yom

Kippur War, itself the direct effect of the prior War of Attrition and continued occupation. Finally, labor's fall has been explained, particularly among the Likud, by the failure of the Oslo Accords to make Israelis feel more secure. Yet, Rabin and the peace process, despite the brittle political majority, had enjoyed great popular support until his assassination. The sense of insecurity ensued only a few years later with the Second Intifada and the rise of Hamas, which Netanyahu's Likud tacitly supported to weaken the Palestinian Authority and to undermine the peace process. The greater the instability and the volatility, the greater the perceived political benefits to the Likud.

In the long view, the labor hegemony was dented by cleavage shifts within the Israeli economy and polity, coupled with the failure of the labor governments to take a clear stand on the occupied territories and the Messianic settlers. In 1949, the labor (46) and the left (25) had over 70 seats in the 120-member Knesset. Despite holding a near monopoly, the alignment still held over 60 seats in 1973, with labor actually increasing its voice at the expense of the left. Yet today the labor coalition has lost *more than 90%* of its representation (Figure 6-2).

Figure 6-2　Decline of Labor Dominance

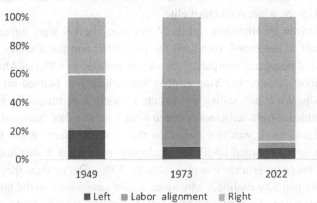

Sources: Author, data from Israel's Knesset

RISE OF THE RIGHT, FAR-RIGHT AND CENTER

The Rise of the Right

By the time the right-wing Likud coalition took power in 1977, Menachem Begin had struggled for political legitimacy and rehabilitation from his terrorist past for three long decades. Under his leadership, the

Likud – and its prior political forms, such as Herut (1948–65), and Gahal (1965–73) – expanded its support. It was fueled by liberals, who opposed socialism and wanted to reduce all government interference in the economy, by the economic interests of entrepreneurs, by white-collar employees and professionals, and by conservative populists who promised to increase benefits to the lower-middle-class and working poor. To characterize it simply as right-wing would be misguided. Most conservative parties stress economic policies but shun explicitly "revanchist" objectives, which is what the Likud did until the 1980s. To describe the party as far-right would be misguided as well. To capture the support of the neglected Jews from the Arab countries and the religious voters, both of whom were dependent on social transfers, Begin initially pushed free-market initiatives, but stressed social responsibility. Such a mixture of internally inconsistent policies was untenable over time. When neoliberal economic policies took over in the mid-1980s, so did assertive geopolitics that the religious supported for Messianic reasons and the Jews from Arab countries believed were vital because "the Arabs only understand force." Like Begin and Shamir, Netanyahu proved masterful in capitalizing on the politics of resentment.

The rise of the right-wing coalition also reflected hardening sentiments after several wars, including the rise of religious conservatives, who began to shift their allegiances from the Labor toward Likud, and the associated emergence of the Messianic settlers who opposed labor's secularism and the peace process. Moreover, it was driven by the backlash of Jews from Arab countries; that is, the alienation of Mizrahi voters from Iraq, Morocco, Libya, Iran, Iraq and Yemen, who felt they had been second-class citizens under the thumb of Mapai's coalition, widely perceived as representing the condescending white Ashkenazi elite. Furthermore, it evidenced the inability of the center parties to garner a significant percentage of the vote. Finally, it reflected increasing U.S. military aid to Israel and the parallel neoliberal policies after the mid-1980s economic stabilization.

The Begin government's economic policies reflected an effort at broad conservative reforms to satisfy all these diverse constituencies. Hence, the large budget, rapid acceleration of inflation, increased balance of payments deficits, coupled with rising foreign debt. Unsurprisingly, the adverse trends were accompanied by slow economic growth. The right-wing dominated, independently or together with labor in periodic "national unity" governments, except for the brief hope for peace in the 1990s occasioned by the Oslo Accords I-II. Concurrently, the Center and the Arabs remained in the margins. The role of the religious and ultra-orthodox began to climb after the 1982 Lebanese War, with successive Palestinian uprisings and the rapid settlement expansion, particularly under the Likud. Yet, they remained a negligible force during the period.

It was then, too, that extra-parliamentary forces began to pressure Israeli democracy. Like the Weimar democracy, Israel's parliamentary institutions fell under the increasing weight of extremist movements. But where Weimar Germany witnessed a struggle between the far-right Nazis and far-left Communists, Israel, in the absence of popular socialist militancy, saw a struggle between far-right ultra-religious movements and their American-Jewish sponsors, and the more moderate labor supporters and secular centrists.

Israeli Kahanism, American Money

When the far-right rabbi Meir Kahane set his eyes on the Israeli Knesset, he was endorsed by rabbi Zvi Yehuda Kook, his ardent admirer.[10] Though Kook had been a staunch supporter of the National Religious Party, he broke with them in 1974 when they entered the Rabin government over his opposition.[11] The rabbi's support mattered. He was the spiritual leader of the radical settler group, Gush Emunim. Yet, Kahane's Kach party remained on the fringes until the conservatives replaced the labor coalition in the government. It was then that the U.S. arms transfers and the number of Jewish settlers in the West Bank – many of whom were Jewish-American immigrants – began to soar, amid the divisive 1982 Lebanese War.

When Kahane ran in 1984, the elections authorities tried to ban him. Until then, neither a quasi-fascist in the Israeli parliament nor racial law proposals had been conceivable in Israel. Hence, the absence of laws to ban them. When Kach gained its only-ever seat in the elections, the fierce rabbi refused to take the Knesset's traditional oath of office insisting on an added Biblical verse. He advocated the observance of the Torah and halakha (Jewish law). Since such hate was still resisted by the Israeli lawmakers, Kahane was boycotted across the aisles, even by the conservatives and the orthodox, his most loyal constituency in America, resulting in his often speaking to an empty assembly. The Israel Broadcasting Authority shunned coverage of his activities, but then, the rabbi's most controversial activities had always taken place in the shadows. In 1985, the Knesset responded indirectly by passing an amendment to the Basic Law, banning "undemocratic" parties that "incited to racism."

Despite its rising popularity with the onset of the First Intifada, Kach was banned from entering the 1988 elections, a move that Alan Dershowitz, the high-profile neoconservative American-Jewish lawyer, characterized as "anti-democratic."[12] In Kahane's view, "Judaism is diametrically at odds with Western democracy":

Western democracy has to be ruled out. For me that's cut
and dried: there's no question of setting up democracy in Israel,
because democracy means equal rights for all, irrespective of
racial or religious origins. Therefore, democracy and Zionism
cannot go together. And Israel's Declaration of Independence,
which proclaimed this state to be a Jewish state, is a totally
schizophrenic document. You just can't, on the one hand, want
a Jewish state and at the same time give non-Jews the right to
become a majority....[13]

Identifying the central contradiction not just between secular Zionism
and orthodox Jewishness, Kahane saw Israeli democracy as a part of the
problem because it would allow the relative rise of political power by Israeli
Arabs, due to their faster birth-rates. Worse, if the Palestinians of the West
Bank and Gaza were to be included, Kahane argued, the Jewish state would
no longer remain Jewish. A two-state solution was no solution to him because
it permitted a Palestinian state. But nor was a singular state because it would
result in an Arab majority over time. Kahane offered a simple and brutal
way out. The only way to ensure racial purity in Israel was ethnic expulsion,
which he turned into a political platform. In the Knesset, he tried to transfer
the Arab population out of Israel, revoke Israeli citizenship from non-Jews
and ban Jewish-Gentile marriages and sexual relations. If the Jewish state
was to be truly *Jewish*, it had to be "pure in race." In the occupied territories,
Kahane's sermons of hate and activism attracted far-right and ultra-orthodox
settlers, the Mizrahi Jews from Arab countries, and conservative Jews identifying with Jabotinsky's revisionist legacy. The reasons were different, but
Kahane couldn't have cared less. It was the net effect that mattered.

In his U.S. lobbying campaigns, Kahane netted millions of dollars from
wealthy American donors. Over time, he had attracted an odd mix of wealthy
fans, including former Haagen-Dazs ice-cream president Reuben Mattus,
with the 1987 Tony award winner Jackie Mason, and with mob attorney
Barry Ivan Slotnick, who helped him forge a close relationship with Joseph
Colombo Sr., then-head of the Colombo crime family. His political success
in Israel was the direct outcome of his ability to raise significant funds from
wealthy American Jews via Kach International, the Institute for the Authentic
Jewish Idea and Jewish Overview. By the late 1980s, these organizations
allowed him to bring to Israel about $500,000 ($1.6 million today) *annually*,
which he used to set up more than 50 branch offices in the small country.[14]

Kahane's organizations launched charitable tax-exempt foundations
in the U.S., facilitating the sending of hundreds of thousands of dollars to

Kahane's movement in Israel, despite federal tax codes barring such charitable tax-exempt foundations from using contributions to finance political campaigns. Shuttling across America four or five times a year raising funds, Kahane shrewdly tailored his message to his audiences. But the central theme prevailed: "Arabs must leave Israel because they are a threat to the state's existence. If they do not leave willingly, they should be deported at gun point."[15]

The Romance with the Center

Only months after Prime Minister Yitzhak Rabin and PLO's leader Yasser Arafat signed the Oslo Accords in the White House, Rabin was assassinated by an orthodox Jewish zealot closely linked with Kahanist extremists. In Israeli politics, it heralded a shift. With the failure of the Madrid Peace Conference and the fall of the peace process, Ariel Sharon's national unity government began the construction of the Separation Barrier in the West Bank. Beloved by the hawks but haunted by the specter of the Sabra and Shatila massacre that took place under his watch in the 1982 Lebanon War, Sharon's rule compounded the turmoil of the Second Intifada which he had provoked. But by the early 2000s the turmoil led him to rethink Israel's policies, especially after some of his closest friends, some of whom were war heroes, told him that the Israeli occupation was the primary obstacle to lasting peace. Seeking a legacy as a peacemaker, Sharon built a political consensus for a unilateral withdrawal from Gaza. In polls, it was welcomed by most Israelis but cursed by the far-right and the ultra-orthodox. Like with Rabin, some rabbis prayed for the Angel of Death to kill Sharon.[16]

Sharon resigned as head of Likud and dissolved parliament, launching a new centrist party, Kadima ("Forward"). It wasn't the first centrist party in Israel. The precedents included the Shinui (1976–77), Ezer Weizman's Yahad (1984), and the Center Party (1999–2001). Of these, Shinui represented the most typical middle class-driven centrism in Israel. It was a Zionist and secular, free market liberal party. But by the same token, neither Shinui nor its successors could resist the excesses of neoliberal economics. Worse, secular centrism faced headwinds at a time when the settlers and Messianic far-right were on the rise and were the only parties that could create majority coalitions strong enough to rule. Indeed, Kadima proved to be the most popular centrist party in Israel's history, paving the way to successors like Ehud Barak's Independence (2011–12), Tzipi Livni's Hatnua (2012–19), Kulanu (2014–20) and Yair Lapid's Yesh Atid (2012–present). As Likud's support declined, Kadima's soared in polls. Sharon's plan was to leave the West Bank, with a maximum number of settlements under Israeli control. It left most settlements intact but gave isolated Palestinian villages access to large urban centers, thanks to an intricate system of underpasses and tunnels. It was a variation of the old Allon Plan.[17]

Just months before his expected election triumph to ensure a mandate to implement these changes, Sharon suffered two strokes. The first was a minor one. The second stroke killed him. As Sharon sank into coma, his deputy, former mayor of Jerusalem Ehud Olmert, replaced the bulldozer general. In the subsequent elections, Kadima, even without Sharon, still garnered 30 percent of the vote, beating both Likud (27%) and Labor (23%). It was a vote for peace, calling for further withdrawal from the West Bank.

For a while, a new Palestinian uprising was deferred, thanks to Israeli suppression, Palestinian weariness, and President George W. Bush's explicit support for a two-state solution. But Olmert had none of Sharon's clout and he was overwhelmed by the 2006 Israel-Hezbollah War and haunted by corruption allegations that eventually resulted in a conviction, setting the stage for Likud's return. In the 2009 election, Likud recaptured its lead (41%), Kadima was humiliated (23%) and Labor was beaten back (17%). With Sharon gone, his longtime nemesis Netanyahu retook his place as Likud's leader.

Following Sharon and Olmert, the next centrist challenge came with the 2011 cost-of-living crisis and the subsequent founding of Yesh Atid ("There is a Future"), another centrist, liberal Zionist political party, led by former TV journalist Yair Lapid, the son of the ex-Shinui party politician. Emulating Tony Blair and Barack Obama's "Third Way" ideas, Yesh Atid offered centrist populism to its middle- and upper-middle class constituencies, with anti-incumbent messaging, calls for cleaner politics and moderation in economic and security issues. A decade later, hungry for governmental responsibility, Lapid joined the far-right cabinet of Naftali Bennett in 2021. In this quest, he was drawing from Netanyahu's blueprint of deploying American strategists in Israeli elections. For a decade, Lapid's guru had been Democratic political consultant Mark Melmann. A onetime adviser of John Kerry, Melmann had worked for the biggest Israel lobby, AIPAC, seeking to disrupt Iran's nuclear program and opposing Democratic progressives like Bernie Sanders and Jamaal Bowman. Melmann believed that, with Lapid, Naftali's government could restore Israel's bipartisan place in U.S. politics.[18] In practice, the cabinet survived a year.

In the 2022 election, Lapid's party won 24 seats, its best result yet. But after it failed to form a government and returned to the opposition, the stage was set for Netanyahu's far-right cabinet. In Israel, "Third Way" politics can be challenging: too conservative for the labor, too soft for the right, and too-everything for the Messianic far-right.

U.S. NEOCONSERVATISM, JEWISH-AMERICAN FUNDS

The Netanyahus' Revisionist Roots

For years, hundreds of thousands of Israelis have demonstrated against their prime minister Benjamin Netanyahu and his cabinets, and since 2023 particularly against its proposed judicial reforms, the handling of the Israeli hostages held by Hamas and the Gaza War overall. The demonstrations started as "Bring Them Home Now" hostage protests, which remained the primary concern, yet broadened to anti-war protests. The Netanyahu cabinet hit hard Israelis who posted or expressed such sentiments by suspending and censuring such individuals from work and school. Nonetheless, by mid-April 2024, tens of thousands of Israelis – 100,000 according to the organizers – were protesting at *weekly* anti-government, hostage release rallies in Tel Aviv, Jerusalem and other major locations across the country, despite efforts by the government to stifle rallies and the army to limit public gatherings.[19] Amid the summer heat, as the war continued, so did the weekly mass protests, marred by increasing police violence.[20] Nothing like this had happened before in Israel, especially in the middle of a war. But power ensured Netanyahu's political survival and legal immunity. To avoid prosecution, he needed to stay in power and keep the Gaza War going. Born in Israel but growing up in Philadelphia, Benjamin "Bibi" Netanyahu (1949–) is the longest-serving prime minister in Israel's history. He sees himself as an activist of Zion, like his grandfather Nathan Mileikowsky. While Netanyahu's grandfather and father had a marginal role in revisionist Zionism, he put himself into its center.

Nathan Mileikowsky, the Russian-born rabbi and early Zionist champion, was known for his advocacy against socialist Zionism and anti-Zionists. After migration to Israel, he raised funds abroad for the pre-state Yishuv and cooperated with rabbi Abraham Isaac Kook, the founding father of Religious Zionism whose son, rabbi Zvi Yehuda Kook, is the revered spiritual father of Israel's settlers and the Messianic far-right. One of Mileikowsky's sons was Benzion Mileikowsky (who later adopted his father's pen name as his last name), a medieval historian and onetime deputy assistant to Ze'ev Jabotinsky, the pioneer of revisionist Zionism. Benzion ("the son of Zion" in Hebrew) befriended revisionists such as Abba Ahimeir, who wanted to create a Jewish fascist state in Palestine and who was one of the likely assassins of the Zionist labor leader Haim Arlosoroff. But eventually Benzion opted for an academic career in America, returning to Israel only in the '70s. Benjamin Netanyahu, his son, is the product of both worlds.

Building on his master treatise, *Origins of the Inquisition in 15th Century Spain*, Benzion saw Jewish history as a series of holocausts. He had a not-so-scientific tendency to incorporate evidence that supported his thesis and to suppress anything that didn't. By the same token, he shunned the long period of Spanish history of *Convivencia* (Spanish, "living together") from the Muslim Umayyad conquest of Hispania in the early 8th century until the expulsion of the Jews in 1492. In the different Moorish Iberian kingdoms, the Muslims, Christians and Jews lived in relative peace. This period of religious diversity and tolerance – captured wonderfully by Maria Rosa Menocal in *The Ornament of the World: How Muslims, Jews and Christians Created a Culture of Tolerance in Medieval Spain* (2002) – differed drastically from the subsequent Spanish and Portuguese history when Catholicism became the sole religion in the Iberian Peninsula, following expulsions and forced conversions.[21]

Benzion Netanyahu fully shared Jabotinsky's insistence on the creation of an "Iron Wall" between Israel and its Arab neighbors. The Oslo Accords, Netanyahu's aging father complained, were "the beginning of the end of the Jewish state." After Israel's disengagement from Gaza, he supported its reinvasion, "even if it brings us years of war." And to the end of his long life, he stuck to the European orientalist bias – "The tendency to conflict is the essence of the Arab. He is an enemy by essence. . . . His existence is one of perpetual war."[22]

Netanyahu and Israel's Hard Right

Benjamin Netanyahu is his own man, but he was heavily influenced by his father. Like his older brother Jonathan, the celebrated hero of the Entebbe operation that cost his life, Bibi served with distinction in Sayeret Matkal, an elite reconnaissance unit of the Israeli military. After studies at MIT and working as a consultant for the Boston Consulting Group, his political career began in the late 1980s, when he served as Israel's permanent UN representative, at which time I met him in New York City. These were the formative years of the U.S. neoconservative movement, many of whose ideas he shared. Israel's ambassador to the U.S., Moshe Arens, a scientist, veteran Likud politician and ex-Irgun operative, paved Netanyahu's path to the corridors of power in Washington. In New York City, Netanyahu also befriended rabbi Menachem Schneerson, whom he saw as "the most influential man of our time."[23] Courted by Israeli politicians and every U.S. president from Richard Nixon to Joe Biden, Schneerson was a Messianic mystic who made his Chabad-Lubavitch movement a worldwide force, while linking the fate of Israel, world Jewry and the United States. Some of his adherents regarded him as the Messiah. Netanyahu courted him for the same reason as American presents: *Moshiach* or not, the rebbe delivered the support of huge crowds in Israel, the United States and the Diaspora.

Seemingly unassuming, shrewd, fast and smart, and well-trained in American-style communications, Netanyahu was a natural to succeed Likud's old guard; that is, Menahem Begin, the former leader of the terrorist Irgun group, and Yitzhak Shamir, the ex-head of the terrorist Stern group. He knew his moment had come, even if he would first have to overcome Likud dinosaurs like Shamir, and the Likud princes: "The dinosaurs are dying out and the princes are too blue-blooded to fight for the crown. I'll get there."[24] (Figure 6-3).

Figure 6-3 Netanyahu's Web of Revisionist Zionism

Netanyahu's leadership in Likud started in the aftermath of Rabin's assassination, thanks in part to the incendiary political climate his campaign permitted to fester in 1995; and in part to hiring Arthur Finkelstein to run his campaign. The legendary Republican political operative had sold presidents Nixon and Reagan to America. He was known for his repetitive, hard-edged campaigns, which idolized his candidates by tarnishing their adversaries.[25] In Israel, the scaremongering worked. By early 2024, Netanyahu had led half a dozen Israeli cabinets in 28 years.

From the start, Netanyahu's career has been overshadowed by dark money controversies. The corruption charges began in 1997, when police recommended his indictment on corruption charges for influence-peddling.[26] Investigations into the murky dealings began in 2016, following a dozen debacles, three attorney generals and two state comptrollers.[27] After a three-year investigation, he was indicted and faced trial in 2020, with 333 prosecution witnesses. The long list excludes many debacles by his wife Sara and her adviser, and his son Yair. Netanyahu remains haunted by a litany of bribery, fraud and breach of trust charges.[28] In his position as PM in 2009–2016, Netanyahu made decisions that have significant implications for national security, yet without orderly decision-making process, decisions that allegedly enriched him. One of these decisions involved the purchase of submarines and vessels from German shipbuilder Thyssenkrupp in a deal valued at $2 billion. In June 2024, the state commission investigating the affair sent five warning notices to parties who may be harmed by the investigation.[29] In addition to Netanyahu, those notices went to former military and Mossad leaders, including Yossi Cohen who had used "Mafia-like" pressure against the leaders of the International Criminal Court.

The problems went even further. Since the start of his career, Netanyahu's selected aides had to be approved by Sara, according to their loyalty rather than expertise, a highly controversial practice that would later be extended to some appointments involving even military and intelligence authorities. Meritocracy was nice, loyalty was everything.

What accounts for his staying power? In the long view, Israel's shift to the right since the late 1970s, the Messianic doctrines seeking to legitimize occupation, the hardening of political divides after Rabin's assassination and the crumbling of the peace process, Likud's longstanding cooption of Jews of Middle Eastern ancestry and religious Jews, and perhaps most importantly, Netanyahu's ultra-rich Republican sponsors in America ranging from the late Las Vegas casino tycoon Sheldon Adelson to the Falic family, owners of a chain of 180 Duty Free Americas stores, Irving Moskowitz who had funded settlements since 1969 with a lucrative bingo parlor, and many others in his "millionaire list." Ben-Gurion may have invented *hasbara* (lit. "explanation"), the Israeli version of public diplomacy to explain its case, but Netanyahu has been its most efficient practitioner. However, as the gap between the rhetoric and realities deepened, he became the ultimate oracle of what critics see as a parallel universe of hollow propaganda.

Likud's "Clean Break" from the Oslo Accords

Ideologically, Netanyahu's rise went hand in hand with the rise of neo-conservatism in the U.S. and Israel. In Israel, Irving Moskowitz, was among the major U.S. billionaire settlement funders contributing to the blueprint for financial proxy revisionism. These can be defined as wealthy Jewish-American financial philanthropists who support revisionist Zionism and its tenets, including Jewish settlements in the occupied territories, Messianic religious schools and universities, Jewish far-right groups and paramilitary activities.

Historically, American Jewry has had a critical role as the financial sponsor of Israel. But until the 1970s, most money flows targeted traditional philanthropic concerns in America and Israel, from social charities and educational institutions to hospitals and health services and so on. As long as labor governments held power in Israel, practical and political Zionists played a key role in the control of these financial flows by financial philan-thropists in America, eager to foster economic and social development in Israel. When Likud coalitions took over, the traditional Jewish philanthropic areas central to Jewish-American financiers prevailed. However, financial proxy revisionists began to shift some of their monies from traditional areas to settlement expansion and efforts at the annexation of occupied territories, as well as neoliberal economic policies, ethnic nationalism and autocracy and so on. Effectively, such financing has supported regime change in Israel from mainstream parties to the Messianic far-right, from secular Jewish democracy to ethnic autocracy, and so on.

Of course, Moskowitz was not only Netanyahu's donor and one of the many in his "millionaire list." He was also an associate of the right-wing Ariel Center for Policy Research, a hardline advocacy group espousing the Likud line on Israeli security.[30] In the United States, Moskowitz was among the funders of major neoconservative think tanks promoting the War on Terror and hardline Israel-centric Middle East policies, including the Hudson Institute, the neoconservative American Enterprise Institute (AEI), and the Jewish Institute for National Security Affairs (JINSA).

Since 2018, the hawkish bipartisan JINSA has championed a U.S.-Israel mutual defense pact, which led to a draft discussed by Netanyahu and Trump's secretary of state, Mike Pompeo. At the time, it was not implemented; but it seems to remain in the background and ideas of the draft have been included in various versions of the so-called "grand bargain" that the Biden admin-istration hopes to implement in the region.[31] Moskowitz also donated to the Center for Security Policy (CSP), supported by the U.S. Big Defense and led by an anti-Muslim conspiracy theorist. Sponsoring the far-right Western

Center for Journalism, he was a big sponsor of American Crossroads, a U.S. Super PAC (political action committee) raising funds for Republican Party candidates. Founded by Karl Rove, Republican political consultant behind Bush Jr.'s presidential campaign and one of the architects of the Iraq War, it has pioneered many new fundraising venues (Figure 6-4).

Along with other pivotal financiers, Moskowitz contributed to the rise of neoconservatism in America, and to the rise of the movement's many Jewish leaders who shared the ideas of revisionist Zionism, including Paul Wolfowitz, Richard Perle, Robert Kagan, William Kristol, and so on. Led by Kristol and Kagan, neoconservatives founded their think tank, Project for the New American Century (PNAC) with a view to sustaining America's unipolar moment for decades to come. Whatever was in the interest of Israel according to Netanyahu's Likud was in the national interest of America. They were also members of the "blue team," which pushed for a confrontational policy

Figure 6-4   Moskowitz's Money Networks

toward China and a strong military and diplomatic endorsement for Taiwan, shifts that would mark the subsequent Trump and Biden administrations. It is this policy that has dictated the Biden administration's approach to October 7 and the Middle East at large.

The rise of neoconservatism in the U.S. went hand in hand with the emergence of Netanyahu's Likud in Israel. It resulted in a neoconservative policy document, *A Clean Break: A New Strategy for Securing the Realm,* described as "a kind of U.S.-Israeli neoconservative manifesto."[32] It was released by the Institute for Advanced Strategic and Political Studies (IASPS), an Israel-based think tank that Moscowitz sponsored. The report was published in

1996 by American-Jewish neoconservatives led by Richard Perle, President Reagan's uber-hawk, presumably at the behest of the new Israeli prime minister, Benjamin Netanyahu. It called for a muscular U.S. Middle East policy to defend Israeli interests, including the removal of Saddam Hussein from power in Iraq (which ensued in 2003), a proxy war in Syria (which ensued in 2011), rejection of any Israeli-Palestinian solution that would include a Palestinian state (one of the Trump administration's motives for pursuing the 2020 Abraham Accords), and an alliance between Israel, Türkiye and Jordan against Iraq, Syria and Iran (tacit efforts remain). The final report included ideas not just from neoconservatives, but from their Likud affiliates.[33] Certain parts of the policies set forth in the report were rejected by Netanyahu. But he shared its overall thrust.

Neoconservative interventions were marked by a continued "strategy of tension" that Netanyahu contributed to in Israel. It was sustained by ceaseless instability, a perceived common enemy ("Palestinians," "Arabs"), and the ever-deeper U.S.-Israeli ties, which ensured huge inflows of military aid and ever-increasing economic assistance by American Jewry. Membership in the neoconservative club had its benefits: it made Netanyahu rich. Despite his lofty legal fees, Netanyahu's personal wealth was estimated at $14 million over half a decade ago. Unofficial estimates suggest the total could be several times more. Yet, during the pandemic financial crisis, he gifted himself with hundreds of thousands of dollars' worth of retroactive tax exemptions at the expense of the state treasury.[34]

The negative tradeoff of Likud-led policies has been high: severe economic polarization within Israel, suppression in the West Bank and Gaza, and chaos and destruction in the neighboring Arab states and beyond.

If bingo parlors were among those who funded Netanyahu's early career, it was Vegas casinos that propelled his leadership in the 2010s.

The Agenda of Casino Mogul Sheldon Adelson

For some two decades until his death in 2021, when *Forbes* estimated his net worth at $35 billion, Sheldon Adelson was a major sponsor of Netanyahu and kingmaker among the Republicans who helped fund Trump's drive to the White House. In addition to his daily newspaper in the U.S., the *Las Vegas Review-Journal*, the Vegas casino mogul and political donor wanted to shape pro-Likud views in Israel as well, so he purchased an influential daily, *Israel Hayom*, and a weekly, *Makor Rishon*, associated with conservative right and Religious Zionism.[35]

In Adelson's view, "the Palestinians are an invented people. The purpose of the existence of Palestinians is to destroy Israel." The idea of a two-state solution had to be rejected, even if that would undermine Israeli democracy. Or as he put it, "So Israel won't be a democratic state, so what?" Like the anti-Arab rabbi Kahane, he thought that any solution leading to a Palestinian state was synonymous with "committing demographic suicide." What Israel needed was a "big wall" around itself, saying, "I would put up a big wall around my property."[36] Adelson was shrewd enough to use coded signals. Jabotinsky's solution against the Palestinian Arabs had been an "Iron Wall" and talks based on military muscle.

Netanyahu's efforts to drag Washington into a war against Iran got Adelson's full backing. At the peak of his power, Adelson not only made and broke U.S. Republican and Israeli politicians. He was collaborating with CIA in efforts to blackmail Chinese officials gambling in his Macau casinos.[37] The Jewish-American mainstream, including the Israeli lobby, was too soft, he thought. Sissies don't protect Israel; tough Jews do. Adelson walked the talk. In 2017, he had the Israeli-American Council hijacked with a hard-right agenda.[38] But nothing lasts forever. Leaked transcripts from a graft probe showed that Sheldon and Miriam Adelson, the owners of the *Israel Hayom*, lamented the PM's wife's control over major government decisions. Adelson told investigators that Sara "would tell my wife that 'if Iran were to attack [Israel], it would be on your head, because we did not advertise favorable photos of her.'"[39] The relationship devolved from steadfast friendship into "constant complaints" and even "screams on the phone" on the part of the Netanyahus, mainly Sara, to the point where Miriam Adelson would disconnect.

Having long boosted rabbi Meir Kahane's disciples in Israel, Adelson was also a major funder of Jewish settlements in the occupied territories. In 2019, a U.S. appeals court revived a $1 billion lawsuit by Palestinians seeking to hold Adelson and other pro-Israel defendants liable for alleged war crimes and support of Israeli settlements.[40] The plaintiffs, including 18 Palestinians and Palestinian-Americans as well as a Palestinian village council, alleged a conspiracy among defendants to expel non-Jews from the disputed territories, and accused them of committing or aiding in genocide and war crimes. Other defendants included billionaire Larry Ellison, Bank Leumi BM and Bank Hapoalim BM, construction and support companies such as Hewlett Packard Enterprise Co. and Volvo AB, 13 nonprofits, and the United States.

In the view of the D.C. Circuit Court of Appeals, the only political question concerned who had sovereignty over the Israeli-occupied territories but courts could rule on whether the defendants conspired to expel non-Jews or committed war crimes "without touching the sovereignty question, if it concluded that Israeli settlers are committing genocide."[41] On the Palestinian side, the *Tamimi opinion* has been seen as consequential because the judge allowed the case to proceed and analyzed it based on a close reading of the law, rather than the politically-charged context. Since the case was not dismissed, it theoretically allows courts to rule on the merits of Palestinian human rights claims instead of continuing to dismiss such claims on non-justiciable grounds.[42] Yet, expectations should be tempered. The question of Palestine is highly unlikely to be properly adjudicated until the U.S. elevates the role of international law in its courts and rejects the current double standard in which the court invokes the "political question doctrine" to basically avoid the rule of law.[43]

In June 2024, Miriam Adelson, the casino tycoon's widow, pledged to spend millions of dollars to support Trump in the upcoming general election. In return, she pursued U.S. recognition of Israeli sovereignty over the West Bank, with neither Palestinian Authority nor peace accords. That ranked at the top of her list: "Israel annexing the West Bank and the U.S. recognizing its sovereignty there."[44]

The Kohelet Policy Forum: U.S. Funds, Israeli Neoconservatism

In 2018, the Knesset passed the highly controversial "nation-state law" stating that only Jews had the right to self-determination in Israel and Arabic was downgraded to a language with "special status." The bill had been outlined years before by Moshe Koppel, the chair of the Kohelet Policy Forum (KPF).[45] "With tactics imported from the U.S. Capitol Hill,"[46] the KPF became a formidable presence in Israeli politics in just one decade, influential among the lobbyists, parliamentary advisers, MKs and ministers. Avraham Diskin, Avi Bell and Eugene Kontorovich led the neoconservative think tank along with Koppel. The ex–New Yorker Koppel, a mathematics wizard, founded Kohelet in 2012. In just a decade, its roster of scholars soared from six to over 160. By 2019, he could say that "we're the brains of the Israeli right wing."[47] Like many other transplanted Americans, Koppel lived in an upscale West Bank settlement in violation of international law. When the Trump administration announced the U.S. no longer considered Israeli settlements in the occupied West Bank a violation of international law, Secretary of State Mike Pompeo delivered a video message, thanking the KPF for supporting the new doctrine.[48]

Koppel also sat on the board of the Tikvah Fund, a KPF donor whose leader has contributed to Netanyahu's campaign finance, funding conservative and settlement organizations in Israel. For a decade, the Forum wielded increasing influence on Israel's decision-making centers, with neoconservative, settlement-supporting politics and free-market economics. KFP was also behind the key policy papers buttressing the attempted 2023 judicial reform.[49] Totaling several million dollars, its largest donations were made anonymously and sent through a U.S. nonprofit organization called American Friends of Kohelet Policy Forum (AF-KPF). These money flows seemed to originate mainly from two Jewish-American billionaires and philanthropists, Arthur Dantchik and Jeffrey Yass. After college, Dantchik moved to Las Vegas making a living gambling and playing poker, like Jeffrey Yass who also was a professional gambler. The two co-founded Susquehanna International Group (SIG), overseeing the firm's global private equity, venture capital investments, commodity trading business, and international activities. They shun publicity. Through the SIG's Chinese arm, the two made fortunes on Chinese blockbuster companies, including ByteDance, the parent of TikTok.

With a net worth of $7.5 billion, Dantchik is an active supporter of Israeli causes. And so is Yass, with net worth estimated at $29 billion. Between 2010 and 2020, his Claws Foundation gave more than $25 million to the Jerusalem-based Shalom Hartman Institute and to the Kohelet Policy Forum, the driving force behind the judicial reforms, and to U.S. libertarian think tanks like the CATO and Ayn Rand Institute. Yass, who avoided $1 billion in taxes while largely escaping public scrutiny, poured his money into campaigns to cut taxes and support election deniers.[50] As the anti-judicial reform mass protests escalated, KPF began to soften its stance, calling for a partial compromise, while Dantchik withdrew from donations to think tanks in Israel.[51]

However, the primary conduit for funds to Kohelet had already changed in 2021, when more than 90 percent of its $7.2 million in income came from the Central Fund of Israel, a family-run nonprofit that gave $55 million to more than 500 Israel-related causes. The fund was run by Marcus Brothers Textiles on Sixth Avenue in Manhattan, which sponsors highly controversial settlement projects in the West Bank, while supporting the far-right activists' Honenu and Im Tirtzu. The latter is supported by the Likud and seeks to delegitimize alternative Zionist voices and peace movements while sponsoring neo-Zionist cultural wars. The former is notorious for defending Jewish far-right extremists charged with violence against and killings of Palestinians (Figure 6-5).

Figure 6-5   Kohelet and Some of Its Spinoffs

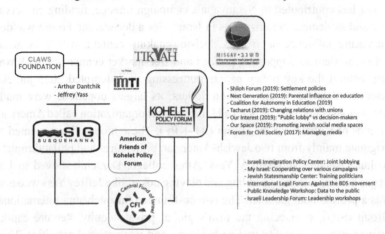

Until the mass protests against the judicial reforms that the KPF had outlined – what the demonstrators called the "judicial regime coup" – its executive director, Meir Rubin, was able to keep a relatively low profile. The purpose of Kohelet was to influence policy and that purpose was accomplished: "We run the Knesset."[52] As Kohelet's success attracted excessive adverse attention to the controversial think tank, it had to figure out a way to disappear while continuing its high-level influence campaigns. Hence, its spinoffs, clones, partners and joint initiatives blurring the association with the original Kohelet, while sustaining its influence networks. These have been recently augmented by webs of hard-right and far-right networks of NGOs, think tanks, initiatives and media (Exhibit 6-1).

In the early days of the Gaza War, the key role among these spinoffs belonged to the Misgav Institute, which was established on the remains of the nonprofit that created the Institute for Zionist Strategies, founded in 2004. As Kohelet's people took over its leadership, the new incarnation became infamous after October 7 for promoting ethnic cleansing in Gaza to build a thriving property market in the Strip.[53]

As Kohelet's star dimmed as the consolidated force of Israel's hard-right, its role as an organization faded. But that was only a prelude to its new chapter, via its spinoffs, clones and their successors and parallel offsetting forces. What united them all were the intimate economic, ideological and geopolitical ties with the corresponding master organizations in the United States, ranging from the hard-right Heritage Foundation, Hudson Institute and various NATO affiliates to the Center for Strategic and International Studies, the Center for a New American Security, and the like.

Exhibit 6-1   Kohelet's Spinoffs and Clones

In the past few years, Kohelet has cloned a web of think tanks, NGOs and associations with a direct link to Kohelet or its officials, or both. Another web was linked to the KPF indirectly, via partnerships with the same officials and donors; that is, Israeli Immigration Policy Center, My Israel, and so on. Additionally, its former members founded several clones, including the Shiloh Policy Forum, which KPF supported by paying salaries; the Civil Society Forum; the Israeli Immigration Policy Center; additionally, the KPF trained anti-LGBTQ groups. The co-founders of Next Generation – Parents for Choice in Education were KPF researchers, and there were still other NGOs linked with the KPF, such as Coalition for Autonomy in Education, Choosing Educations, Tacharut the Movement for Freedom of Employment working against the labor federation Histadrut; Our Interest – Your Lobby, and Hamerchav Shelanu ("Our Space").

At the height of its influence, the Forum had the ear of Likud governments, the rising conservative star ex-Minister Ayelet Shaked and many others. It wrote position papers for the far-right former PM Naftali Bennett and the Likud MK Nir Barkat, a high-tech millionaire, who subsequently was outed in the Pandora Papers debacle. Barkat was the Knesset's richest politician, who expanded his support in Jerusalem by endorsing gender-segregated buses. However, the position papers that KPF drafted for him focused on economic development in the settlements. The goal was to make Barkat the PM and Netanyahu appointed him his minister of economy in the far-right cabinet.[54] After advising Libya, presumably since 2005. Michael Porter, the competitiveness guru of American business, was consulted on how to transform Jerusalem into a world hub of outsourcing and biotechnology. "Even when politics fails," Porter said, "the connection between Jewish and Arab businessmen succeeds. At the end of the day, the way Israelis and Arabs do business is not so different."[55] For all practical purposes, Barkat's Startup Jerusalem initiative aimed at replicating the dual economy in business networks. In other words, Jewish innovation in Jerusalem would, in part, rely on outsourced, low-cost manufacturing in the occupied territories.

Kohelet was the largest organization of its kind in Israel, but not the only one. In the far-right of Netanyahu's coalition – Religious Zionism, Otzma Yehudit, and Noam – several NGOs have significantly increased their influence. Komemiyut (founded in 2006) is one of the older groups with Bezalel Smotrich, the self-proclaimed anti-Arab fascist, as one of its founders. It is known for its anti-gay "Beast Parade" and rabbi Dov Lior, the idol of Yigal Amir, who assassinated Prime Minister Rabin in 1995 and the Kahanist Baruch Goldstein, who carried out the prior massacre of Muslim worshipers. Known for his racist comments, Lior preaches Jewish purity and believes that the killing of non-Jews during wartime is sanctioned by halakha. Regavim (2016) seeks to influence government policy with alumni in key positions. Smotrich is also a leader of this group, known for employing drones and aerial photography to closely monitor construction by Palestinians and Arab citizens of Israel. Messianic orthodox are the key constituency of Torat HaMedina (2018) advocating for a Halakha State; that is, for a fundamentalist Jewish rather than a secular democratic Israeli state. The Movement for Governance and Democracy (2019) seeks to exert a radical impact on legislation. Still others, including Hazon and Gvanim (2007) advocate anti-LGBTQ+ sentiments, championing the Judaization of specific regions or launching religious settlers in mainly secular neighborhoods.[56]

TOWARD THE MESSIANIC FAR-RIGHT

Rise of the Far-Right and Ultra-Orthodox

In the past two decades, Israel's conservative mainstream has taken a giant step toward the hard-right, including the far-right. In part, the shift was enabled by the zeitgeist, particularly the rise of U.S. neoconservatism and its import variations in the Israeli right. In significant part, it involved the expansion of American-Jewish money inflows to Israel, preceded by the migration of a chunk of America's Jewish ultra-rich from Democrats to Republicans. In Israel, the shift was shaped by coalition politics at the cabinet level. The crumbling peace process, the concomitant border wars, uprisings in the occupied territories and the vicious cycle of Gaza Wars, played a critical role. There was a series of converging adversities, some of which may have been orchestrated to annex the territories. Until the early 2020s, the far-right groups had been shunned. Then Netanyahu opened the cabinet doors to them.

Through the Cold War, the National Religious Party (NRP) represented the religious Zionist movement. Until 1992, it was part of every government coalition. Created by the 1956 merger of two old religious parties, Mizrachi and Hapoel HaMizrachi, the secret to the NRP's success was not its religious constituency, but political mathematics. Since neither Labor in its glory days nor Likud through most of its history has achieved a strong majority in the 120-seat Knesset, NRP has enjoyed extraordinary leverage. Though its share of the Israeli electorate amounted to just about a tenth, it was vital to any coalition, which gave it disproportionate bargaining power.

Focusing largely on economic and social matters and the status of Judaism in modern Israel, NRP initially served as Labor governments' partner. Things began to change after the Six-Day War, which many of its members saw not just as a military triumph, but as a miracle. At the time, the young Turks of the party, Zevulun Hammer and Yehuda Ben-Meir, still demanded greater attention to socio-economic challenges that were burdening the religious in Israel. When the settler movement took off in the 1970s, it was not seen as extremism, but as still another sign of a path leading to national redemption. With the right-wing' courting it, the NPR left the godless socialists of Labor and aligned with Likud.

Following new wars, insurgencies and uprisings, the religious groups went through a transformation and fragmentation of their own. As the moderates lost, the hawks gained in the 1980s, even if many didn't accept the ethnic cleansing of rabbi Meir Kahane's Kach, the terrorism of the Jewish Underground, and settler violence. At the same time, internal divides deepened within the party between the largely Ashkenazi leadership and the

Sephardi and Mizrahi constituencies. Polarization led to the rise of orthodox parties, such as the short-lived Mizrahi Tami party and the more-enduring Shas, representing Sephardi and Mizrahi Haredi Jews. If the turn to the right in the 1977 election was the Mizrahi Jews' first voter rebellion, the rise of Shas in the 1980s was the second one. As it went on to become a major political party, it distinguished itself from the Ashkenazi-dominated Orthodox Jewry.

Furthermore, many were alarmed by the peace process of the 1990s, the unilateral withdrawal from Gaza and the subsequent efforts to withdraw from the West Bank. These forces further radicalized those who saw Israel as a divine creation and the settlements as God's work. In the fog of the pandemic years, the new major bloc of Israeli politics – the alliance of the far-right and the ultra-orthodox – gathered its forces in the face of general malaise, economic stagnation, turmoil in the blockaded Gaza and volatility in the West Bank. The net effect was the most far-right cabinet in Israel's history.

In the 2022 elections, Netanyahu's Likud captured 46 percent of the vote. That was almost as much as Begin had achieved after the peace treaty with Sadat in 1981 (50%). No major secular opposition was viable because the centrist Kadima (21%) and the left (11%) had barely a third of the vote, while Arab parties remained on the margins (9%). By contrast, the ultra-orthodox were now a major player (13%), thanks to Religious Zionism (Tkuma) and the far-right Otzma Yehudit, the successor of Kahane's forbidden Kach party, which joined forces within the Likud. Although they captured barely 5 percent of the vote, their sympathizers were the new silent majority. Altogether, the religious far-right was now almost as powerful as the center (18%). More importantly, due to sheer demographics, the religious far-right population was growing twice or thrice as fast as the rest of the Israeli population. Absent no major changes, the future could belong to them (Figure 6-6a).

From the Fringes to the Cabinet

After the election triumph, the far-right Itamar Ben-Gvir delivered a glowing tribute to rabbi Meir Kahane, the late Jewish-American rabbi known for his racist and violent anti-Arab ideology and support of the mass expulsion of Palestinians. Despite U.S. State Department's public criticism of Ben-Gvir for praising Meir Kahane, Netanyahu made him minister of national security. But it was a game of mirrors. While the State Department publicly expressed moral disgust, it had removed the racist Kahane Chai group from its list of "foreign terrorist organizations" half a year earlier. The move had facilitated the Israeli far-right's electoral triumph.[57] The Biden administration sought moral distance from the hatemongers it was enabling. It was extraordinary hypocrisy, at the expense of the lives of the Palestinians and Israeli dissidents.

Figure 6-6 Messianic Far-Right

(a) Rise of the Messianic Far-Right

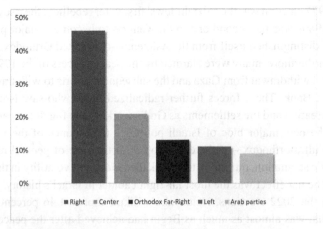

The share of votes received by different political blocs in Israel.

(b) Far-Right Members of Netanyahu Cabinet

| Itamar Ben-Gvir | Bezalel Smotrich | Israel Katz |

Source: (a) Data from Yonathan Berman (1949–2019); author (2019–2), based on official election results. (b) Wikimedia Commons

In the early '70s, the settlers were still few and largely in the margins of society. In December 2023, they entered the Israeli cabinet and vital government agencies. As the new leadership began to move Israel from a parliamentary democracy to a religious autocracy, Tamir Pardo, a former chief of Mossad (2011–2016), charged Prime Minister Netanyahu with bringing parties "worse than the Ku Klux Klan" into the government[58] (Figure 6-6b).

Far-right parties like Otzma Yehudit ("Jewish Power") are ideological successors of rabbi Meir Kahane's Kach party. Its leader, Itamar Ben-Gvir, first gained national notoriety in 1995 by brandishing a Cadillac hood ornament that had been stolen from Prime Minister Yitzhak Rabin. "We got to his car, and we'll get to him too," Ben-Gvir said.[59] Weeks later, Rabin was assassinated. A son of Iraqi Jewish immigrants, Ben-Gvir grew of age in a secular family but embraced religious far-right views during the First Palestinian Uprising (1987–93). As a teenager, his mother had been active in the Irgun, a paramilitary right-wing group that the British and Labor Zionists had considered a terrorist movement. As Netanyahu's minister of national security, Ben-Gvir espoused Kahanism. He lived in a settlement that was illegal by international law and has called for expulsions of Arab citizens of Israel. In January 2023, his provocative visit to the Temple Mount, the locale of the Al-Aqsa Mosque, contributed to turmoil, as did subsequent efforts to replicate such visits.[60] When Ben-Gvir entered Netanyahu's government, he got what he wanted: the newly created national security ministry. His mandate included overseeing the Israel Border Police in the West Bank. A fox took over the henhouse.

Another fatal decision of the Israeli government was the post-October 7 pledge by the energy minister, Israel Katz, a veteran Likud politician. As Katz stated: "Humanitarian aid to Gaza? No electrical switch will be turned on, no water hydrant will be opened and no fuel truck will enter Gaza until the Israeli abductees are returned." He added, "No one will preach morals to us."[61] For two decades, Katz had promoted plans to substantially raise the number of Jewish settlers in the Golan Heights. He fought against Israel's Gaza withdrawal, while lobbying to have $32 billion set aside for incentives and subsidies for settlers in the West Bank. After years of wheeling and dealing, the Israeli police proposed to indict him for favoring high-level Likud members and their princeling children in his ministry. Yet, he was not prosecuted.[62]

Netanyahu's minister of defense was Bezalel Smotrich, a vehement opponent of a Palestinian state and self-proclaimed fascist, racist and homophobe, who lives in an illegally built West Bank settlement. In 2021, he declared that Israel's first prime minister, David Ben-Gurion, should have "finished the job" and kicked all Palestinians out when Israel was founded. In his view, members of Israel's Arab minority communities are citizens, but only "for now."[63] The leader of the National Religious Party – Religious Zionism – was born in an Israeli settlement in the Israeli-occupied Golan Heights and grew up in an illegal settlement in the occupied West Bank. Smotrich's extremist politics aimed at replacing the secular rule of law with traditional Jewish law. In spring 2023, when he took over a large chunk of the administration of the West Bank, he did not condemn settler violence. Instead, he urged Israel to react "in a way that conveys that the landlord has gone crazy" and called for "striking the cities of terror and its instigators without mercy, with tanks and helicopters."[64] It became his rallying cry after October 7.

In Smotrich's view, Arabs owned no land. Jews were the landlords. Palestinians were just short-term tenants. Jews stayed; Palestinians were visiting. Judea and Samaria were God's gift to the Jewish people. So, when Netanyahu entrusted him with the administration of the occupied West Bank, it was a signal to Palestinian Arabs: *Leave!*

A Center-Right Alternative

In May 2024, Smotrich and Ben-Gvir were slamming the Netanyahu cabinet for negotiating a "reckless" hostage deal. They threatened to leave the cabinet. Despite widespread international protests, the two wanted Netanyahu to destroy Rafah. Responding to the far-right threats, National Unity Minister Gadi Eisenkot, an observer in the war cabinet, counter-slammed the "political blackmail."[65] Minister-without-portfolio Benny Gantz went further. He gave the PM a deadline of June 8 to derive a comprehensive strategic plan for the "day after" Hamas in Gaza, threatening to leave the government if this did not happen.[66]

The political drama was overshadowed by the grand bargain talks between Washington and Riyadh to get Israel to approve the two-state solution in return for normalization of the Saudi-Israeli ties. Hence, the vocal frictions within the Israeli war cabinet, as the conservatives, religious, far-right and opposition sought to position themselves amid the U.S. pressures. In this battle, Benny Gantz and his opposition forces were seen as a possible alternative to Netanyahu.

Like so many other Israeli leaders, Gantz got into politics from the military. Born into a family of Holocaust survivors, he grew of age in a cooperative agricultural community, rose rapidly in the IDF, finished a course in the U.S. Army Special Forces and fought in the Second Intifada and two Lebanese wars. He commanded the IDF in the 2012 and 2014 Gaza wars. Launching his Resilience Party, Gantz pledged to strengthen Jewish settlements in the West Bank and vowed Israel would never leave the Golan Heights. He did not endorse the two-state plan but supported a unilateral launch of a Palestinian entity on 65 percent of the West Bank. It was still another variation of the '70s Allon Plan. Gantz wanted to neutralize the Palestinian threat, but under Israeli terms. He saw the West's main challenges as "extremist Iran, Islamic terror, and regional instability."[67]

Instead of running on his own, Gantz launched a new Blue and White alliance in early 2019 with the centrist Lapid and moderate liberal and center-right forces. By the fatal 2022 election, Netanyahu was breaking bread with the far-right and ultra-orthodox, whereas Gantz had formed a joint list with a center-right party that was joined by former IDF chief of staff Gadi Eisenkot, Gantz's successor at the IDF who had developed the devastating Dahiya doctrine. The alliance won 12 seats in the election. After October 7, 2023, Netanyahu and Gantz announced they would launch a war cabinet in which Gantz would serve as minister without portfolio – as he did, until he had had enough and gave his ultimatum to Netanyahu.

As U.S. pressure against the Netanyahu cabinet mounted, Gantz believed Washington would welcome him as the man of the hour. From the standpoint of the Palestinians, he was simply another version of Israel's iron fist. The Saudis could deal with Gantz, as long as there was a semblance of a two-state solution on the table.

What was certain, as his biographer put it, was that on the day Netanyahu would finally leave his job, "his ultimate legacy will not be a more secure nation, but a deeply fractured Israeli society, living behind walls."[68]

Toward a Resuscitated Left?

On the morning of October 7, after Hamas invaded the Gaza envelope, Yair Golan jumped into his small Toyota Yaris, rushing to the area where more than 260 young people were being mown down in hails of gunfire, according to Israel by the "human animals" of Hamas. However, as early Israeli media reports demonstrated and as the ongoing investigation by the IDF attests, Israel's own Hannibal Directive – that is, efforts to preempt hostage-taking by letting the hostages be killed – played a central role during and immediately after October 7.[69] Knowing the territory, Golan was able to find and rescue many who had fled from the music event and were hiding in fields and bushes, thanks to WhatsApp location messages sent to him by the youths or their parents.[70] His laconic heroism impressed the jaded Israelis.

Golan is a reserve major general who represented the left-wing Meretz party and had served as deputy minister of economy. Until recently, the fragmentation of the left has undermined the return of left-wing cabinets. At the end of May, Israeli labor elected Yair Golan as its leader with 95 percent of the vote. "What is called the Israeli left is experiencing a terrible crisis, a massive collapse," Golan says. "Now it needs to be resuscitated."[71] He carries some baggage, though it may also work for him. He was to become the IDF chief of staff in 2016, until his Holocaust Day speech. Wearing the red paratroop beret, Golan said that the occasion should lead Israelis to deep soul-searching about "how we, here and now, treat the stranger."

If there's something that frightens me about Holocaust remembrance it's the recognition of the revolting processes that occurred in Europe in general, and particularly in Germany, back then – 70, 80 and 90 years ago – and finding signs of them here among us today in 2016.[72]

Golan felt that the IDF should hold to a high moral standard, particularly in its dealing with the Palestinians. As a net effect, the Israeli right-wing, far-right and the ultra-orthodox practically exploded and Golan lost the chief of staff position. As a left-wing Zionist, he hopes to unify the fragmented labor, ensure secular education and end right-wing corruption. He believes in the two-state solution but would prefer to keep most settlement blocs in return for land swaps.

Golan's mandate is to unify the left to crush the right. It's a tall order from a single-digits starting-point. At the turn of July 2024, he was able to have Israel's Labor Party and the left-wing Meretz to fuse into a new party, "The Democrats." In the 2022 election, Meretz won just 3.2% of the vote, failing for the first time to pass the electoral threshold (3.25%), while the Labor Party barely passed (3.7%). So, the merger was dictated less by ideological agreement than the will to survive. What is new about the Democrats is that it is likely finally to generate a single united party. Even together, the two represented barely 7 percent of the 2022 vote, which left them behind the Likud (23%), the centrist Yesh Atid (18%), the Messianic far-right RZP-Otzma (11%), Benny Gantz's National Unity (9%) and the Sephardi and Mizrahi Jews' Shas (8%). Immediately after October 7, the Likud would have crushed its rivals, but after months of a poorly-managed unpopular war that had entangled the IDF into genocidal atrocities, public sentiment had shifted drastically, due to the Netanyahu cabinet's failure to have the hostages released; its prolonged war and the consequent economic weakening; increasing friction with Israel's critical military ally, the United States; and the continued displacement of tens of thousands Israelis in northern Israel and the Gaza Envelope. Nonetheless, any Labor Party opposition, whatever its name, faces a hard uphill battle and nasty headwinds, to restore its position in the Knesset, even in part.

The Diminished Peace Prospects

The stagnation of the peace process since the late 1990s has fostered two major secular trends in Israeli politics, as self-identified by the constituencies. The Israeli right has steadily expanded, rising from 39 to 68 percent after the Hamas offensive. At the same time, the once-so-powerful left has steadily declined from its already diminished 29 percent to 11. With the end of the Second Intifada, the center surged to its 2014 peak at 32 percent, but has decreased to 24 percent since then. Focusing on Jewish Israelis, these polls overstate the right-wing supremacy. But the polls do highlight the role of those right-wing parties that are likely to rule the cabinet. Most Israeli Arabs support Arab lists that reflect left-to-labor forces

Typically, uprisings and wars have augmented the right-wing Likud's support, as long as it has been seen as successful in pacifying the external threats. Conversely, the opposition forces have been able to capitalize on the right-wing's liabilities politically but have failed to build away from them. Even a hypothetical combination of center-left forces has been on decline since the mid-2010s. What this implies is that a historical bloc that could end Likud supremacy in Israel would have to be built, at least in part and in the beginning, on the internal divides of the right. The latter comprise a complex mix of ideological Likudniks, free-market conservatives, the religious and the ultra-orthodox and the far-right. Hence, the efforts by Gantz, Lapid and others to build on an expanded center, augmented by moderate conservatives, social liberals and religious constituencies (Figure 6-7).

Figure 6-7   Israeli Politics, Prospects for Peace

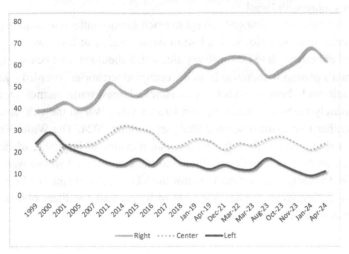

"Do you describe yourself as right, moderate right, center, moderate left?" (%); Jewish Israelis, combined moderate + firm

Source: Data from Dahlia Sheindlin, 1999–2024; Peace Index, Tel Aviv University; author

Ever since the Second Intifada, the prospects for permanent peace between Israel and the Palestinians have been distant. Despite a temporary rapprochement in the early and mid-2010s, these hopes deteriorated as Israeli cabinets shifted further to the far-right ever after 2017 – years before October 7. In the aftermath of the unilateral withdrawal from Gaza, every fourth Israeli believed in peace prospects, meaning 60 percent didn't. In 2023, every ninth Israeli believed in peace, but three of four didn't.[73] Months of war have led larger political blocs within Israel to sympathize with stances that make common cause with the left. And their numbers are far more impressive. Some surveys suggest a slight recovery for the left. But not much has changed as of yet.

Within a month of the outbreak of the Gaza War, the Jewish Federations of North America raised more than $600 million for Israel. An additional $400 million comprised an estimate of donations raised in multiple campaigns by other Jewish communal and private organizations.[74] In the past, Americans used to be strongly supportive of Israel. In 2023, 54 percent of Americans still sympathized more with Israelis, but over 31 percent sympathized more with Palestinians. The latter figure doubled before Israel's Gaza War. The biggest changes in attitudes have occurred among young Americans. Almost every second registered voter in America between the ages of 18 and 29 sympathizes more with the Palestinians, compared to every fourth who sympathizes more with Israel.[75]

But have times changed enough to reach a major inflection point in public opinion in Israel? No. Such a U-turn would require at least two things: A full and effective halt to U.S. military aid, which should at least be contingent on Israel's phased withdrawal from the occupied territories, coupled with an economic trade boycott with the EU, Israel's largest trade partner. Despite increasingly vocal opposition against Israel's Gaza War in the U.S. and the EU, neither requirement seemed likely in summer 2024. The White House continued to ship weapons for the war that it criticized in public, while the largest European economies continued to trade with Israel whose war they criticized vocally. Neither the U.S. nor the EU wanted to sink the boat that was struggling under the heavy weight of its excessive military obligations and an untenable economic status quo.

Chapter 7
ISRAEL'S ECONOMIC EROSION

After the first month of Israel's Gaza War, Prime Minister Benjamin Netanyahu vowed that the state of Israel would provide help to every Israeli affected.

> My directive is clear: Open the taps and channel funds to whoever needs them. Just like we did during COVID. In the past decade, we have built here a very strong economy and even if the war exacts economic prices from us, as it is doing, we will pay them without hesitation.[1]

What Netanyahu did not provide were the actual figures. Yet, half a year *before* the Gaza War, 280 senior economists in Israel had warned that the government's budget allocations to the ultra-religious Haredi groups, in exchange for their coalition support, "will transform Israel in the long run from an advanced and prosperous country to a backward country."[2] The economic backlash associated with the proposed judicial overhaul had led to a massive capital flight and sharp decline in foreign investment, resulting in currency depreciation, a sluggish stock market, a slowdown in tax revenues, and rising public debt.[3]

The Gaza War compounded the risks. Adding to its active military force of 150,000, Israeli Defense Force (IDF) summoned 360,000 additional reservists, 8 percent of Israel's workforce, for the war. As the net effect, the Israeli economy would have to cope with the most adverse impact since the late 1970s, which had at that time resulted in a lost decade.

In June 2024 after months of war, some analysts predicted the impact would be a déjà vu of the 1970s. In reality, what followed the Yom Kippur War in Israel was a tragedy that transformed the country and its future. What ensued with the Gaza War was a catastrophe as Israel obliterated the Gaza Strip. In the absence of a major change in Israel's economic direction and priorities, what looms ahead could prove far worse to both Israel and the occupied territories.

ECONOMIC RESILIENCY TESTED, AGAIN

Structural Transformation

Major Western European economies – the United Kingdom, France, Germany and Italy – had experienced their industrial takeoffs and drive to technological maturity by World War I. In the postwar era, roughly from 1945 to 1973, they enjoyed a strong economic expansion, thanks to huge reconstruction and recovery programs and the subsequent post-industrialization. After the twin energy crisis of the '70s and the subsequent stagflation, the postwar Keynesian era of full employment and stable prices gave way to monetarist doctrines and neoliberal economic policies, including privatization, liberalization and deregulation. Despite the globalization decades, the expected transition to sustainable growth has been slow and overshadowed by financialization; that is, the expansive role of the financial sector. In the process, the kind of growth accelerations that were typical to industrialization have given way to growth decelerations as these major economies are maturing economically and graying demographically, while struggling to cope with climate change.[4]

In Israel, these trajectories have been similar in patterns, yet compressed in time, due to the country's unique history. Advanced economies had industrialized by 1914, when the major immigration waves to pre-state Israel began to intensify. As the West began the shift from industrialization to post-industrialization after World War II, Israel was still a poor, agricultural economy amid a devastating war, even if it benefited from qualified human capital, thanks to immigration from industrialized Europe.

If the preconditions for the industrial takeoff emerged in the pre-state Yishuv, the actual takeoff ensued in the first postwar decades, when Israel's national institutions, infrastructure, and military were established. At the same time, the young state invested significantly in an impressive public education system and a high-class science system, both of which played a vital role in its speedy transition from the process of takeoff to the drive to technological diversification and maturity.

Under Likud coalitions, the country suffered great volatility as it shifted to neoliberal economic policies. The eclipse of the Cold War and booming globalization drove substantial financialization, whereas the quest for sustainable growth and development lagged behind. What made Israel different from Western Europe was that these transitions occurred faster and more disruptively, amid huge immigration waves, particularly from Russia, greater economic polarization, as well as friction and uprisings in the occupied territories (Figure 7-1).

Figure 7-1   Israel's Structural Transformation

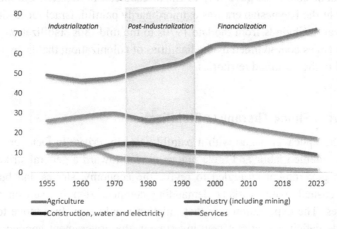

Main sectors, selected years (%)

Source: Data from World Development Indicators

Rapid, Postwar Catch-Up Growth

Having industrialized before World War I, Western Europe's advanced economies were moving toward post-industrialization and services in the postwar period. By contrast, Israel was amid its industrial transition. Starting from a far lower point, it nonetheless benefited from significant human capital, thanks to the immigrants from Europe and Holocaust survivors.

Fueled by catch-up growth, the transition from agriculture to industry was fast. From the founding of Israel in 1948 to the Yom Kippur War in 1973, the Israeli economy grew at a very rapid rate. During this period, real GNP increased at an annual rate of 10.4 percent, one of the highest in the world. Accelerated growth translated to a steady rise in *average* per capita incomes as rapid catch-up growth allowed per capita incomes to grow at faster rates than in the richer economies.

Despite rapid growth, prices remained relatively stable, with strong increases in labor and capital driving the rapid economic growth. Meanwhile, the Israeli population soared nearly fourfold, from 870,000 to 3.3 million. Interestingly, capital stock grew nearly twice as fast until 1967. These strong economic trends crumbled with the Yom Kippur War in 1973, which resulted in great loss of life and injury. As government spending on the military increased, tax revenues were penalized by the reduced economic activity, and the balance of payment was ailing. And things got a lot worse after the 1974 oil crisis.

Subsequently, Israel joined the great shift from industry to services, as a blue-collar-centered labor force gave way to white-collar employees, while labor coalitions gave way to Likud cabinets. In Western Europe, the demise of the Keynesian era was extraordinarily painful. Israel faced similar structural headwinds from the late 1970s to the mid-'80s stabilization, with its challenges compounded by the liabilities of colonization; that is, by rising turmoil in the occupied territories.

From Shock Therapy to Stabilization

The upheaval began with a painful austerity crisis. In October 1977, the discontented labor and trade unions moved toward a general strike. As Begin's government struggled to revive the economy, strikes and buying sprees ensued, with workers demanding compensation for sudden price increases. The expectation was that inflation would soar. In a move to cut the trade deficit and attract new investment, the government announced it would float the Israeli pound, abolish most controls on foreign currency and cancel export incentives. It also announced several tax reforms, including an increase of the value-added tax to 12 percent on all goods and services. Speaking on primetime TV, Prime Minister Menachem Begin pled with Israelis, already battered by inflation, to accept the increases by behaving with "commonsense and national feeling."[5]

To militant labor, it was Chile, Israeli style. Instead of Pinochet and Milton Friedman, Israel had Begin's austerity. The jaded leaders of the 1.1-million-member Histadrut labor federation set up a "war room" to coordinate their campaign for wage increases to offset the expected cost-of-living increase. If necessary, they would respond with a general strike.

Given the desperate status quo, the Begin government might have been overthrown had the national focus stayed on the domestic economy. But it didn't. After the Yom Kippur War, Egypt's President Sadat, eager to leverage his new political capital, expressed willingness for peace negotiations, which subsequently consumed the nation's attention. In the course of the next five years, the Likud government managed to achieve the worst possible economic and geopolitical outcome. As the promising peace talks were limited to Egypt, a series of new wars ensued and they were no longer about national survival, but about continued colonization. Meanwhile, Begin's fast-changing finance ministers – Simha Erlich, Yigal Hurvitz and Yoram Aridor – failed to subdue inflation. Then came shock therapy.

After the 1967 Six-Day War, the young Israel was bursting with a sense of invincibility, optimism, and hope. Following the Yom Kippur War, however, a weary country struggled with a sense of vulnerability, pessimism and resignation. The contrast was dramatic. It was the net effect of the War of Attrition and the Yom Kippur War, converging with the eclipse of catch-up growth. For the Israeli economy, the post-1973 years were a lost decade, with stalled growth and soaring inflation plus rising government expenditures. In Western Europe, the strong postwar expansion collapsed with the 1974 energy crisis. In Israel, the pattern was similar, but more extreme. In both cases, governments sought to continue past policies, without adequate increases in economic growth and productivity. The equation was untenable. In Israel, the U-turn came with a bank stock crisis, coupled with hollow guarantees that the bank-share prices would rise indefinitely, until the bubble party burst in 1983.[6] As a recovery plan was implemented, Israel's banks were nationalized.

The macroeconomy was a different story. With growth stalling, inflation soared to an annual rate of 450 percent, projected to zoom to 1,000 percent by year-end 1985. After gradual piecemeal measures failed, the government of Shimon Peres executed a stabilization plan aiming at "sharp disinflation."[7] Coupled with the subsequent introduction of market-oriented structural reforms, including privatization, the aggregate economy revived – at the cost of rising polarization.[8]

Since the 1985 Stabilization Plan, the status quo of the Histadrut, the powerful labor organization, had become shaky. Ensnared in debt, it had resigned to the layoffs and wage-freezes with "understanding." Until then, the labor federation had provided health insurance to much of the population. As health minister in the Rabin government, Histadrut's head Haim Ramon was pushing for national health insurance, which would effectively cut the tie between the members of Histadrut and the main health fund. When the Labor Party refused to go along, Ramon resigned, ran independently, won a majority in Histadrut and cut the tie while the Rabin government put a restored national health bill through the Knesset. As Histadrut lost its health monopoly, its membership plunged from 1.8 million to 650,000 in 1995.[9] As it lost its dues, the sharp deficit increase forced the federation to sell off assets, which effectively dismantled the institution. Without its crown jewels, a powerful institution that used to control a fourth of the economy was bankrupt.

Neoliberalism and Globalization

With the end of the Cold War, Israel's economy was transformed by two major developments. In just a few years, the implosion of the Soviet Union brought over a million new immigrants to the country. Many were highly educated, leading to the scientific and technical sector boosting the burgeoning technology sector. For a fleeting period, the economy also bene-fited from the peace process until the adverse turn in the early 2000s, when the crash of the technology boom went hand in hand with the onset of the Second Intifada. Ironically, the terror attacks of 9/11 in America benefited the Israeli economy due to the huge demand for defense and security products. Three decades of massive U.S. military aid had greatly expanded the Israeli defense sector, while restricting its civilian diversification. Why take risks in emerging civilian industries when the money was in the weapons and surveil-lance industries? In the West, the 2008 financial crisis proved painful, but the Israeli economy weathered it fairly well. Unlike most of the West, Israel was a net lender. Also, the banks' risky behavior had been limited by decoupled commercial and investment activities, which reduced financial risk-taking and volatility.[10]

Despite its ongoing friction with Hezbollah in Lebanon and insurgen-cies in the West Bank and Gaza, modern Israel is usually portrayed as an advanced economy with a sophisticated welfare state, a powerful military and a substantial high-tech sector. In reality, Israel was a latecomer to the Organisation for Economic Co-operation and Development (OECD), which it joined only in 2007. In relative terms, the role of its welfare state has been more than halved in the last decades. Furthermore, the high-tech sector and its start-ups have benefited a relatively small segment of the society and remain critically dependent on the symbiosis with the United States.[11]

2011 Cost-of-Living Crisis and Its Aftermath

On July 14, 2011, Daphni Leef, a 25-year-old video editor, had to vacate the central Tel Aviv apartment where she had lived for three years, due to renovations in the building. Rental prices in the Tel Aviv metropolitan area had skyrocketed. Since average salaries were lower than those in the high-income West, many Israelis were penalized by the relatively high costs of consumer goods, which impacted even basic necessities. Leef had had it. She set up a tent in the Habima Square, a major cultural space, while launch-ing a Facebook page inviting other Israelis to join the protest. Hundreds of Israelis joined her with their tents.[12] Responding to her call, protesters gathered around Rothschild Boulevard in Tel Aviv, but also in Zion Square in Jerusalem, the southern Be'er Sheva and the northern cities.[13]

As the protests broadened into a mass movement, they focused on social justice, challenging the social and economic status quo. Seeking to contain the discontent, the government announced a series of measures "to solve the housing shortage."[14] But it was too little, too late for the protesters who participated in mass rallies in major cities across Israel, attracting 200,000 to 350,000 people (Figure 7-2).

Figure 7-2   Israeli Housing Protests

Israeli housing protests in Tel Aviv, August 6, 2011
Source: Wikimedia Commons

By September, the "March of the Million" witnessed 460,000 people taking to the streets across the country, with some 300,000 in Tel Aviv alone.[15] In addition to the rising cost of housing and living, the mass protests were sparked by government corruption, the widening gap between rich and poor, and rising poverty rates. In part, these mass protests mimicked the urban protests of the Arab Spring, which were in full swing by fall 2011. In part, they evolved in parallel with the Occupy Movement, which started in downtown Manhattan but soon diffused to almost 1,000 cities across over 80 countries.[16] In part, too, they were compounded by largely domestic economic challenges, coupled by high military expenditures that had penalized Israeli welfare, especially since the 1980s. Moreover, in the 20th century, population increase had supported growth acceleration, but now it seemed to drive growth deceleration. Israel's young age cohorts were relatively educated yet dissatisfied with what they saw as shrinking opportunities. Furthermore, discontent was also rising among the religious Haredi Jews, along with high jobless rates among Israeli Arabs. It was the Israeli middle class and working labor that continued to feel the bulk of the tax-paying burden. In this view, the 2011 mass protests against the high costs of living were the first major middle-class revolt in Israel.

Did the 2011 mass protests change the status quo? A decade after Daphni Leef and her fellow activists began their protest movement, Israeli housing prices nearly doubled, with no signs of slowing.[17] Worse, the rising prices went hand in hand with declining housing affordability and an eroding middle class. While some of these forces were attributed to international pressures, in Israel the status quo was particularly challenging due to the double whammy of high inequality and high concentration of wealth.

Rising Income and Wealth Inequality

Thanks to the Likud coalitions' neoliberal economic policies, Israel has exceptionally high inequality compared to other OECD countries, despite its early social egalitarian ideals. After a remarkable recovery from the pandemic, the risk balance in Israel was tilted to the downside.[18] The Gaza War compounded the risks. In Israel, the rise in income was relatively rapid following independence, as measured by *average* per adult income. Despite significant immigration waves, it had almost tripled from 1950 to the early 1970s. That period was followed by a rather stagnant phase, roughly from the Yom Kippur War (1973) to the aftermath of the Lebanese War (1982–85). The upswing prevailed until the end of the global technology boom in 2001. Growth was restored by 2004 and sustained until October 7, except for the severe COVID-19 recession.

The Israeli performance is impressive relative to that of the broader region, despite the presence of several energy-rich Gulf countries. Between 1950 and 1977, per adult national income in the Arab Middle East caught up with the Israeli level, mainly as the effect of the rising leverage of the OPEC and the stagnation of Israeli income. After the '70s, OPEC's Gulf states saw some of their profits disappear into the Latin American bubble. Then after 1980, there has been a progressive divergence between the two. However, it would be very naïve to see this divergence as a simple difference between GDP potential *in* Israel and the Arab states. Of course, GDP and GDP per capita income are very rough and elusive indicators. Social indicators suggest more nuanced differences, as does the dramatic rise of Israeli inequality and poverty.

Furthermore, external maneuvers played a vital role in wreaking havoc in Arab states, which played to the advantage of Israel. In the 1980s, the Iran-Iraq War, which benefited mainly U.S. Big Defense and geopolitics, undermined the rise of both states' economies, while the Persian Gulf War drove Iraq to an edge of an economic abyss. In Egypt, Sadat's assassination led to the Mubarak regime and general impoverishment. Smaller economies – Jordan and Syria – had to navigate amid these centrifugal forces. Lebanon was devastated by a prolonged civil war. After three decades of economic exhaustion, two decades of U.S. post-9/11 wars ensued, including the fragmentation and decline of Libya and Iraq, while the Arab Spring led to instability across the region and especially Syria's devastating civil war, unleashing a massive refugee crisis from the Middle East to Western Europe. At the same time, Israel benefited from multibillion U.S. military aid annually.

Accordingly, by 2022, Israeli per adult national income was about $74,500, whereas the corresponding average level in Arab Middle East was below $40,000. In other words, the Israeli average had risen almost twice as fast. This imputed comparative success was also in part derived from the offshoring of the Palestinian challenge into the neighboring Arab states.

In a small country historically proud of its egalitarian ideals, at least as it concerned its Jewish majority, one might presume that rapid economic growth had lifted all boats, particularly since the 1980s. Yet, the realities are almost precisely the reverse, as evidenced by the shares of the ultra-rich (top-1% of the population), rich (top-10%), middle-class (middle-40%) and the working labor (bottom-50%). Despite the rapid increase in national income, the rich (48% of the national income) have retained their share, whereas the middle-classes (39%) and particularly the working labor (13%) have been kept down (Figure 7-3).

Figure 7-3   Rise of Israeli Inequality Since the 1980s

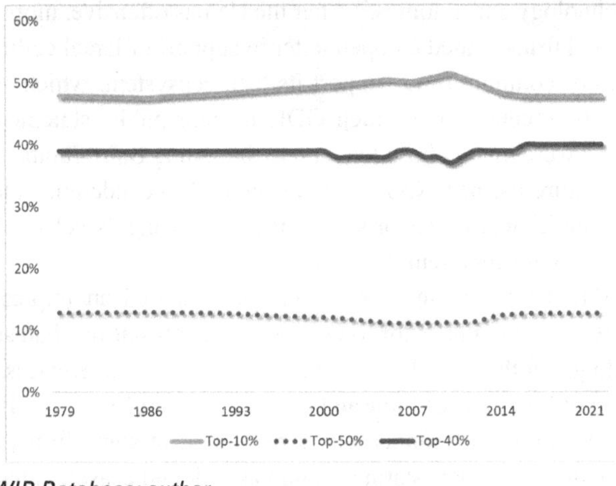

Source: WID Database; author

The evolution of Israel's wealth inequality mimics these trends and milestones. But unlike income inequality, which is more attuned to periods of growth and recessions, wealth inequality has climbed quite steadily from the mid-1990s and accelerated since the turn of the 2010s. The bigger national cake has not ensured the well-being of the majority. Despite promises of a "shared future," the top 10% possess almost two-thirds of national wealth, the middle-classes nearly a third and the working labor just a fraction (4%).

THE DISCONTENTS OF THE ISRAELI ECONOMY

Assets and Liabilities of Israeli High-Tech

In the 1950s, Israel was still a developing economy in which agricultural exports predominated. Today, it is a small high-tech power in which advanced technology reigns. The sector is critical to its long-term productivity, growth and living standards. It is seen as one of the most prolific centers of high-tech innovation with an export-oriented high-tech cluster.[19] This rests on entrepreneurial start-up companies and venture-capital (VC) firms, which have proved resilient. Despite its small size, Israel has more companies listed on the U.S. stock exchanges than any other country except the United States and Canada. Building on information and communication technology (ICT), the cluster emerged in the 1990s with hardware design, computer software, data communications, electro-optics, and network/Internet security. For over a decade or two, the sector has been diversifying, with greater focus on life sciences industries, especially biotechnology and agribiotech.[20]

Yet, ICT remains the sector's center, not least because its critical core: military technology and avionics.[21] After the Hamas offensive, more than 500 venture capital firms signed an open letter in support of Israel calling for the global investor community to support its tech ecosystem, which accounted for almost 20 percent of the Israeli GDP. In their public statements, these VC firms that were mainly based in Israel – including Bain Capital Ventures, Bessemer Venture Partners, GGV Capital and 8VC – condemned the "senseless and barbaric acts of terrorism" while supporting Israel's role in the "global innovation ecosystem."[22]

In 2021, the Israeli tech ecosystem had secured an impressive $27 billion in VC investments. Prior to October 7, Israeli startups had seen a dip in VC funding, but that largely echoed global patterns. Nonetheless, with the mobilization of hundreds of thousands of Israeli reservists, some 10 percent of Israel's technology personnel was conscripted; in some firms, up to 30 percent.[23] With Israel's devastating ground assault and ceaseless hammering of civilians in Gaza, Israel's technology cluster showed its more vulnerable side: its high degree of globalization left it exposed to the international environment. After half a year of Israel's wreaking destruction on Gaza, sentiments were shifting among foreign investors active in Israeli technology. The number of foreign VC funds plunged, and the industry was set back by a decade. Since these foreign investors were responsible for more than 80 percent of the capital flowing into Israeli technology, the continuous decrease in the number of active investors caused great unease even beyond the sector. The big question was whether the decline was temporary and would reverse after the end of hostilities, as the optimists thought, or whether it would prove longer-lasting, especially if international boycotts and sanctions would spread, as the pessimists argued.

In late summer 2024, investors, after moving much of their capital abroad, were hoping for a permanent ceasefire in Gaza, the release of hostages and de-escalation in the north. They were on the fence. Furthermore, while the economy seemed resilient, this was in part a mirage. It wasn't the result of productive economic activity. Rather, the IDF served as a quasi-Keynesian shock absorber, along with the government. Consumption wasn't fueling the economy, but rather the IDF payments and the government's financial aid. They kept spending humming, coupled with the massive governmental buying of arms and military equipment from businesses. By contrast, the civilian economy – consumption, exports, investment and business production – had shrunk, thanks to lingering uncertainty and the huge number of employees on reserve duty. The net effect was rising debt and a march toward recession.

The technology sector was also sensitive to overall patterns in Israel's international trade. Apart from its access to fresh produce suffering from the hostilities in the border areas, Israel is significantly dependent on imports. These have become increasingly vulnerable due to the prolonged Gaza War in southern Israel, increasing hostilities with Hezbollah in northern Israel, rising tensions in the West Bank, lingering and persistent Houthi attacks in the Red Sea, and beyond, the Turkish boycott, fears of regional escalation and international tensions in general. One third of all Israeli imports come from the European Union and more than a quarter from Asia, both of which are critical of the Israeli offensive. Moreover, imports from Asia made the threats to the trading route in the Red Sea particularly significant for Israel. While the U.S. remained by far the biggest export destination for Israeli goods, accounting for 14 percent of the total, this contribution was predicated on the absence of major boycotts and sanctions against Israeli exports.[24]

The bottom line for Israel's technology sector is the fact that the longer the Gaza War prevailed, the greater the challenges would prove to Israeli productivity, growth and living standards. Today, there are some 440 R&D centers in Israel owned by multinational corporates, led by U.S. giants such as Microsoft, Apple, Google, and Amazon.[25] In early 2024, only every tenth reported severe consequences from the ongoing conflict, whereas the majority saw just limited impact from war. But not every company was as confident. After a month of hostilities, Tomer Simon, the chief scientist of Microsoft Israel's R&D Center, wrote to Israel's National Security Council, expressing concern for the future of Israel's high-tech sector. Warning that multinational companies may close R&D activities, he noted that for every tech job, there were five more created that drive Israel's economy. "There is a great danger here," he cautioned. "Israel cannot return to just producing oranges. Without high-tech we will return to being a third world economy."[26]

Intel's Second Thoughts

The longer the Gaza War prevailed, the worse has been the collateral damage in the Israeli economy, including its strategic and critical technology sector. The Israeli story of Intel, the pioneer of the U.S. Silicon Valley, is a case in point. Despite three months of devastation in Gaza, the subsidiary celebrated 50 years of Intel Israel's innovative contributions to life-changing technologies, from the Centrino chip, which enabled the world to use WiFi, to Intel's Core™ processors and artificial intelligence (AI). Israel Intel employs 11,700, jobs with two of three working in advanced development, and its exports amount to $9 billion. Intel Israel's development and manufacturing centers in Haifa, Petah Tikvah, Jerusalem and Kiryat Gat are "vital to Intel's success and play an active role in most areas of the company's global operations."[27]

In late December 2023, Intel still confirmed it would invest $25 billion in total in the construction of a new chip factory in Kiryat Gat. The new plant was expected to join a set of factories that Intel is launching, mainly in the U.S. Planning to start operating within four to five years, the plant would include chip manufacturing using innovative ultraviolet (EUV) lithography technology.

Yet, half a year later, Intel halted the construction of its factory in Israel. In part, this reflected preparation to new trade wars as the jobs of several senior officials at Intel Israel were transferred to Intel's new factory in Ohio, as part of the U.S. program to encourage the launch of chip factories in America. "Israel continues to be one of our key global manufacturing and R&D sites, and we remain committed to the region," Intel said in its official release. "Our decisions are based on business conditions, market dynamics, and responsible capital management."[28]

It was just business, as they say. And the first rule of business, particularly chip business, is peace and stability creating foundations for growth and development. War, friction and disruption do not foster such an environment. Time would tell whether Intel's decision reflects cyclical fluctuations or a structural shift. It matters because Intel is not just any firm. It is an anchor company that gives rise to a huge ecosystem of hardware, software and services. Even more importantly, it is central to AI and thereby to the most advanced military technologies.

How critical is the Israeli advanced technology sector for taxes? Roughly, a *fourth* all tax payments in Israel stemming from companies and salaries came from the high-tech sector. Moreover, the salaried employees in the high-tech sector accounted for nearly two-fifths of salary income tax payments.[29] Taking into consideration the global ecosystems of the high-tech sector, any major international boycott of the Israeli technology has the potential to disrupt its operations and thereby tax revenues to the state and the public sector, which are critical to the increasingly polarized society.

From "Brain Gain" to "Brain Drain"

From the pre-state Aliyah waves to mass immigration after independence, Israel has benefited from a highly educated and scientifically trained labor force.[30] Unfortunately, nothing good lasts forever. If the net benefits of human capital flight for the receiving country are described as a "brain gain," the net costs for the sending country are characterized as a "brain drain."[31] In its early decades, Israel was a net beneficiary of brain gain, perhaps up to the mass inflow of Russian immigrants in the 1990s. However, as a small relatively open economy, it is highly exposed to global economic integration, compounded by its deep ties with United States since the 1980s. And in the past two decades, America has served as the prime attractor of Israeli talent.

By the early 2000s, some Israeli social scientists warned that talent emigration was "far more severe than has been suggested." By then, the probability of emigrating from Israel was 2.5 times higher for educated individuals (individuals with a bachelor's or higher degree) than those with less education.[32] As such, the emigration of Israeli academics was an inherent part of a worldwide phenomenon that had intensified at the end of the Cold War, when relatively open borders and graying demographics in advanced economies made technological innovation pivotal to their growth and productivity.[33]

In 2013, the Nobel prize for chemistry was won by three Americans, two of whom were Israeli-born immigrants to the United States. Yet, while the brain drains from most countries to the U.S. had fallen, Israel's academic brain drain to the U.S. had become unparalleled, with 29 Israeli scholars in the U.S. for every 100 remaining at home in 2008. That was several orders of magnitude more than the 1.1 Japanese or the 3.4 French scholars for each 100 remaining in their respective home countries.[34] A rising share of Israeli graduates were leaving, particularly those who studied in the leading Israeli institutions of higher learning and in the fields regarded critical for economic growth and security. By 2014, for every Israeli that held an academic degree who returned to Israel from abroad, 2.8 left. By 2017, this figure had climbed to 4.5 emigrants per returnee. In effect, the rising discrepancy seemed to go hand in hand with increasing insecurity, the drift to the hard-right in Israel, and upheavals in the occupied territories.

In recent years, Israel's primary export locomotive has been its high-tech sector. Fewer than 3 percent of all employee positions in Israel are in high-tech manufacturing fields, yet these accounted for more than 40 percent of Israel's entire exports in 2015 (Figure 7-4a). Israel's research universities are among the world leaders in many fields, but the crème de la crème in the West are almost invariably American universities. Israeli universities encourage their best students to do their PhDs or their post-docs in leading U.S. research universities. In relative terms, no other country even approaches Israel in terms of the share of its population who are temporary scholars in the U.S. (Figure 7-4b). One implication is that emigration by a critical mass out of the total, even just a few tens of thousands could have, as Dan Ben-David has argued, "catastrophic consequences for the entire country."[35]

Figure 7-4   Talent Emigration from Israel

(a) High-Tech Manufacturing

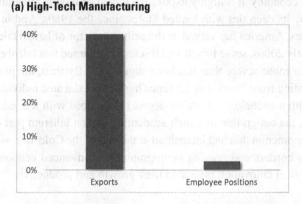

(b) Temp Foreign Scholars in U.S. Universities

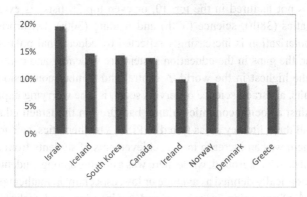

(a) As % of Israel's exports and employee positions; (b) Per 100,000 in home country, average for 2015–17.

Source: Dan Ben-David, Shoresh Institution and Tel-Aviv University, (a) data from Israel's Central Bureau of Statistics; (b) data from Institute of International Education

In January 2023, the presidents of Israel's universities issued a joint statement warning that the government's plan to weaken the judicial system could cause a serious blow to academia resulting in further "brain drain." In particular, the weakening of the justice system would likely lead to an international boycott of Israeli academia, with "international colleagues not coming to Israel, with restrictions on access to international research foundations, with foreign industries reluctant to cooperate with Israeli academics and with the exclusion of Israeli researchers from the international community of research and education."[36]

In the long view, continued brain drain is likely to have an adverse impact on Israel's labor productivity, which will cause the country to lag further behind the lead economies. Lingering economic polarization will virtually ensure that the most educated segments of the society will have to bear the greatest income-tax burden, the impact of which was starkly evidenced by the 2011 cost-of-living crisis protests. Furthermore, wars and conflicts maintain a continued occupation that reinforces migration outflows, while adding to the income-tax burden and reducing prospects for investment in higher education. Some 10 percent of Israeli citizens already have dual citizenship, facilitating their departure.

If Israel is to excel in science and technology *in the future*, one might expect the country to rank among the highest in the OECD PISA (Program for International Student Assessment) rankings measuring 15-year-old school pupils' scholastic performance on mathematics, science, and reading.

In the latest report, Asian countries rank highest, along with Nordic states. Yet, Israel is not featured in the top 10, or even top 20 lists, as evidenced by mathematics (38th), science (37th) and reading (30th). Unsurprisingly, economic polarization is increasingly reflected by educational polarization. In particular, the gaps in the education system are widening and continue to be among the highest in the world. A central and somber conclusion from the test results, as Israeli science observers see it, is "the worrying expansion of gaps against a socio-economic-cultural backdrop in the Israeli education system. In all three literacy areas tested in PISA – mathematics, science, and reading – there was an increase in the achievements of students from a relatively established background, while there was a decline among students from a socio-economically defined as average or low, especially in mathematics."[37]

Instead of investing in science and engineering, and technological innovation, which account for Israel's innovation success, spending has been steered into the endless swamp of the occupation and the needs of colonial settlers, some of whom dream of dismantling the state and the restitution of a fundamentalist theocracy. By nature, highly educated talent believes in universal values, openness and tolerance; that is, ideals that far-right and the ultra-orthodox consider "subversive."

The Welfare State Under Threat

According to its Declaration of Independence (1948), Israel was founded to be or at least to become a welfare state:

> The State of Israel will be open for Jewish immigration and
> for the Ingathering of the Exiles; it will foster the development of
> the country for the benefit of all its inhabitants; it will be based on
> freedom, justice and peace as envisaged by the prophets of Israel;
> it will ensure complete equality of social and political rights to all
> its inhabitants irrespective of religion, race or sex. . . . [38]

What was left unsaid was *how* Israel would become a welfare state amid wars and seemingly endless friction, massive immigration flows, inadequate economic endowments and absent natural resources. Nonetheless, Israel committed a substantial share of its economic resources to welfare systems. Only defense exceeds its welfare spending. Through its first decades in particular, it was one of half a dozen welfare-states with the highest per capita rate of welfare spending. Between 1960 and the early 1980s, during its formative years of rapid growth, Israel's public spending climbed fast, doubling from about 20 percent to almost 40 percent relative to the GDP. It did "foster the development of the country," but not necessarily "for the benefit of all its inhabitants." It supported all Israelis, but the primary beneficiaries were the European-born Ashkenazim rather than the Sephardim and Mizrahim from the Middle East and North Africa.

Had these trends been consolidated, appropriate redistribution policies could have achieved a more egalitarian balance. But occupation policies were premised on big allocations into defense, which trumped the need for welfare spending. Furthermore, the shift to Likud governments undermined welfare-state driven development for the decades to come. Israel's public spending, as a percentage of total spending, was challenged in the 1980s. In the subsequent decade, it was reduced to a level typical of many Western European economies. In the past two decades, this rate has eroded further. Israel's welfare state was a major budget priority until the aftermath of the Six-Day War and Likud's 1977 election triumph. However, the occupation of the Palestinian territories led to far-reaching changes in Israeli economy, politics, and security. One of the prime victims was welfare spending on Israelis.

Most Israeli governments have adhered to the commitment to care for the more vulnerable segments of the society, to ensure reasonable living conditions, help children in distress, and attach central importance to education. Nevertheless, the same governments have resolved disagreement over distribution of limited budgetary resources by reducing welfare expenditures. As perceptive welfare analysts have argued:

> Not one of Israel's governments formulated a comprehensive welfare policy, or ever put together a binding document which set down the overall welfare rights of Israel's citizens, on the one hand, and clarified the resources that would finance those rights, on the other. All of them, without exception, adhered to the practice by which elected officials were able to use the tool of welfare for cynical political purposes.[39]

The paradoxical net effect is that, inadvertently, Israel became a society with abundant welfare institutions but without a welfare policy. Moreover, defense spending trumped welfare policies. Furthermore, following settlement expansion, welfare policies have been secondary to "national security" considerations. And if current trends prevail, the future is even murkier. When rising polarization is ignored, whether it is due to class, ethnicity or religion, the gap between the rich and the poor and poverty rates are likely to continue to climb – as evidenced by deepening breach between secular Israelis and the ultra-orthodox Haredim.

THE HAREDI CHALLENGE

Secular Versus Orthodox and Haredi Israel

Unlike most Israeli Jews who are secular and serve in the military, orthodox Jews have a stricter interpretation of religion, the *halakha* (Jewish law) and traditions. The ultra-Orthodox *Haredim* differ further from modern values and practices. The Hebrew term (the Biblical verb, *hared*) is featured in the Book of Isaiah (66:2) referring to "[one who] trembles" at the word of God. It is used to distinguish Haredi Jews from other Orthodox Jews. Today, Haredim play a role in the Israeli government. Not so long ago, some had little interest in secular institutions. And few of them, a tiny anti-Zionist minority, saw the Israeli regime as a religious blasphemy. The most extreme version of these ultra-orthodox Haredi is the group Neturei Karta or the "Guardians of the City" in Mea Shearim, one of the oldest Jewish neighborhoods outside of the Old City in Jerusalem.[40] It used to be led by rabbi Amram Blau, who was initially active in the ultra-orthodox *Agudat Yisrael* movement, like his brother. But by the 1930s, he, with fellow rabbis, founded the fiercely anti-Zionist Neturei Karta. After the Yom Kippur War, I met their unofficial spokesman, rabbi Moshe Hirsch (1927–2010).

Rabbi Hirsch saw the "Zionist entity" as a blasphemy. Originally from New York City, he had attended rabbinical academy in New Jersey. Upon migration to Jerusalem, he never became an Israeli citizen in what he considered "a Palestinian occupied territory." As Hirsch saw it, "the establishment of the secular state of Israel had nothing to do with divine intervention." That is why he and Neturei Karta opposed Israel and its very existence. "Israel is an abomination. We advocate its peaceful dismantling. Jews are strictly forbidden from re-establishing sovereignty in Israel until the arrival of the Messiah. The founding of a Jewish state is a rebellion *against* God, blessed be his name. The re-establishment of Israel can only occur with divine intervention through the Messiah." The ultra-orthodox lived in close proximity to secular Jews whose lifestyles had been under rapid modernization. Weren't the ultra-orthodox youths intrigued by secular jobs, street cafes, and consumer gadgetry? "Our men and women are not interested in 'secular' matters," the rabbi smiled. "They have dedicated their life to serving God and understanding divine mysteries. What you call 'modern' is regarded as blasphemy here. Why should our youth care for it? They know the truth."

What is the truth? "Our people know they live a life of Heaven here in Mea Shearim. What's outside, that's Hell."

In the mid-1970s, these extreme views on modernity represented an odd fringe in the margins of the Israeli civil society. Nonetheless, Hirsch established ties with Fatah, the PLO and Yasser Arafat who made the rabbi his advisor on Jewish Affairs.[41] But Neturei Karta was just a tiny bloc of believers. At the time, I wondered whether such absolute Messianic *certitude* would one day penetrate the wider Israeli society? And what if that fundamentalism would also pervade the political realm?

In the 1970s, most ultra-orthodox still grouped around the Agudat Yisrael (lit. "Union of Israel") movement. Originating from Upper Silesia in Poland, it grew to be the umbrella party of Haredim in Israel until the 1980s, when it split along ethnic lines into the Ashkenazi Degel HaTorah, often allied with Agudat Yisrael (under the name United Torah Judaism, UTJ), and the Sephardic and Mizrahi Haredi party known as Shas. Together, Shas (8% of current Israeli vote), UTJ (6%), coupled with the Messianic far-right alliance (11%), represent about a quarter of the Israeli electorate that is vital for the right-wing Likud coalition.

But the religious participation has come with a price that secular Israel is no longer willing to pay.

Secular Jews, Haredim and Fiscal Nightmares

In their relatively open communities, the values and interests of secular Israelis are not that different from those in the developed Mediterranean Europe. In the largely closed communities, however, the Haredim follow their spiritual leaders, who encourage the male youths to study and devote their life to Torah and the females to embrace their life as housewives and mothers of large families. Where secular Israelis orientate toward democratic practices, Haredim are socialized via communal activities. After schooling, the Haredi yeshivas preempt the draft. The anti-market education is geared *not* to prepare them for life in the secular, modern world. And that means low-paying jobs, even poverty, compounded by the Haredi wives' lifelong pregnancies and thus absence from the labor force.

So, how do these families survive? In the postwar era, the state supported efforts to rebuild the lost community of Torah students. With their bargaining power in Labor and Likud coalitions, religious parties succeeded so well that among Haredi men, fully half do not participate in the workforce. According to critics, a Haredi family in which the father doesn't work can receive four times the total financial help given to a non-Haredi Jewish family. From the point of view of the economy and policy, the net effect has been perverse. To allow these students to feed their families while they learn, Haredi political parties have put in place over the years a vast system of government subsidies, stipends and other benefits that have transformed their community in two ways. Today, it is effectively a community that lives at the expense of other people (read: the secular tax-paying middle class), and that systematically disincentivizes its young men from joining the workforce.[42] In the past, the system worked because economic growth was relatively higher and the Haredi community relatively smaller. Prior to October 7, secular long-term growth was already slowing in the maturing economy, while the community was getting bigger, making the system untenable and a source of substantial secular-religious friction over time. Meanwhile, the long-term structural deceleration of the economy has been amplified by adverse short-term cyclical pressures associated with the protracted Gaza War.

To sustain what secular observers regard as a vicious cycle of religious learning, low-skill jobs and relative poverty, the Haredim have a huge, vested interest in supporting the kind of political influence that can retain their fiscal benefits in the government institutions. In light of the rapidly-rising share of the Haredim in the Israeli population and their unavoidable increase in political power, "the burden on the welfare state will further intensify and the distribution of the benefits will turn even more tilted in favor of the Haredi population."[43] Paradoxically, the dramatic rise of the ultra-orthodox is steadily undermining the welfare society that enabled it. Since 2018, collected tax income has fallen short of public expenditures by nearly 5 percent in the general population, but over 66 percent in the Haredi sub-population. The Haredim depend on public transfers to make up this difference.[44]

In May 2023, as the mass protests against the judicial reforms escalated and the Knesset prepared to vote on the 2023–24 budget, the Finance Ministry forecasted that the far-right Cabinet's approval of funds to meet the Haredi coalition demands could result in Israel's economy losing *more than $1.8 trillion by 2060*, due to the increase of the demographic segment – the ultra-orthodox Haredim – which is lacking basic skills and resisting integration into a modern labor market.[45] The sum is nearly *four times* the current annual GDP. The Ministry warning was followed by an open letter of 280 Israeli economists, including former senior Bank of Israel and Treasury officials who advised that Israel is slowly but surely downgrading itself into a third-world developing economy. The Haredi budget allocations were posing an "existential threat to Israel's future."[46]

After October 7, senior economists wrote another open letter to Prime Minister Netanyahu and Finance Minister Smotrich. "The severe blow inflicted on Israel," they warned, "requires a fundamental change in the order of national priorities and a massive diversion of budgets in order to deal with the damage caused by the war, aid the victims, and rehabilitate the economy. . . . Cosmetic changes within the existing budget do not come close to the required scope of expenditure."[47]

Thanks to the far-right Netanyahu government, the enacted provisions in the Knesset's fiscal budget of 2023–2024 will increase – not reduce – the benefits to the Haredi population. It all adds up to massive collateral damage that is fully unwarranted. Will things change in the future? Perhaps, but trends are on the downside. In most OECD countries, the fertility rate – the average number of children that are born to a woman over her lifetime – is barely 1.7. With an average of three children per woman, Israel has the highest fertility rate among the OECD economies. Today, the median age exceeds 44 years in Europe. In Israel, it is 30 years, barely higher than in India (29.5).[48]

Over the past two decades, the growth rate of the ultra-orthodox population has been the *highest* among the sub-populations in advanced economies. In relative terms, this is about the same as in Ethiopia. It is driven by high fertility, young age at marriage and a great number of children per family.[49] In 2023, nearly 14 percent of the total Jewish population were Haredim. Driven by demographics, that share could increase to 16 percent in 2030. It is likely to surpass that of Israeli Arabs by the early 2040s; and later in the 21st century, the Haredi population could be at par with that of non-Haredi Jews in Israel (Figure 7-5).[50]

If secular Israel were to give way to a Haredi Israel, it would mean economic suicide.

Figure 7-5   Israeli Population Forecast, by Population Groups

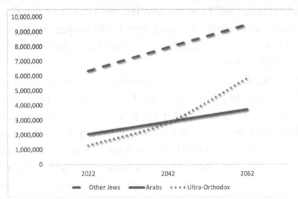

Source: Report on Annual Statistical Ultra-Orthodox (Haredi) Society in Israel, based on data by the Central Bureau of Statistics (CBS)

By August 2024, the ultra-orthodox demonstrators were clashing openly with police outside army bases in Israel. Despite a Supreme Court ruling deeming that the draft exemptions previously enjoyed by the ultra-Orthodox were illegal, the Israeli army authorities anticipated that some 70 percent of the ultra-orthodox candidates would not show up for the first day in the process. Both the Shas party's Torah sages and the leader of the non-Hasidic Ashkenazi community, Rabbi David Landau, had ordered their followers not to come to the draft office for the initial screening, much less actually serve. Among the ultra-Orthodox groups, the forced imposition was described as "a Holocaust of young ultra-Orthodox men."

THE GAZA WAR AND ISRAEL'S ECONOMY

October 6, 1973 Versus October 7, 2023

Soon after October 7, the Biden administration began to transfer massive amounts of weapons to Israel. Some saw the transfers as reminiscent of Nixon's frantic rearmament drive in fall 1974. But the comparison was misguided. Half a century ago, Israel was in an existential battle for survival, battling against Egypt in Sinai and Syria in the Golan Heights – against an Egyptian army of 600,000 to 800,000 troops and Egypt's 150,000 troops and their combined 3,400 tanks. Caught by surprise, Israelis were taking heavy hits. Although the attack was expected, its timing and combined military force overwhelmed even the sober leadership, which led Golda Meir and Moshe Dayan to activate nuclear preparation.

Now, fast forward to the aftermath of October 7, when Israel was battling Hamas's al-Qassam Brigades and its some 30,000–40,000 fighters who had no tanks. Hamas did have its missiles, but Israel had its effective interceptors. Hamas was able to kill more than 1,100 people, mainly civilians, in the course of that initial assault, but even that was a third of the total Israeli deaths in the Yom Kippur War.

And yet, the U.S. government responded as if the sky was falling. Even as President Biden *in public* appealed to Israel not to be "consumed" by rage in its response, he declared himself a "Zionist" while greenlighting a colossal, historical arms drive to Israel. Deliberately shrouded in secrecy, the drive took off when it was clear Israel no longer faced an immediate national threat. In the course of the Gaza War, that became the White House blueprint: washing its hands in public while escalating arms transfers in the dark. By December 2023, Israel had received over 10,000 tons of arms in 244 cargo planes and 20 ships from the U.S. That's more than 15,000 bombs and 50,000 artillery shells in just the first six weeks. The net effect was to be expected – horrific obliteration. If it could be said that Hamas had anticipated Israel's ferocious reaction, if not its full magnitude, it could also be said that the latter would have been impossible without the decision of the White House to enable and facilitate such obliteration.

The rearmament drive was purposely kept in the dark, presumably to avoid public scrutiny; and the anticipated result prevailed. During the first five months, the U.S. approved over 100 military sales to Israel, yet publicly disclosed only two. Meanwhile, weapons were also transferred in undisclosed amounts from the U.S. military stockpiles in Israel. If Israel was not facing a battle for survival and if it soon became clear that the effective objective of the war was not just to "destroy Hamas," but to destroy the Palestinian civilian and infrastructural presence in Gaza, why did the White House knowingly enable genocidal atrocities, which could have been avoided if U.S. arms transfers and overall military aid had been withheld?

Since most of these arms were purchased with U.S. taxpayers' money through the U.S. Foreign Military Sales (FMS) program, American citizens effectively funded most of the carnage. Like the Iron Dome, Gaza's obliteration was designed by Israel but "made in America." The financial flows that made possible the destruction comprised $3.8 billion U.S. annual military aid, plus over $14 billion to buy more weapons. It was an extraordinary racket, perhaps the most extreme disruptive form of corporate-enhancing warfare in America in such a short span of time.

Corporate Warfare, Civilian Nightmare

Of the more than 60 companies profiteering from the genocidal atrocities in the Gaza Strip, most were defense contractors, including the U.S. Big Defense (Boeing, General Dynamics, L3, RTX or Raytheon), whereas a tenth comprised primarily U.S.-based airlines, shipping and logistics firms. In terms of their country of origin, every second was American and every fourth Israeli, respectively. Fewer than every tenth came from European Union, mainly Germany, the UK and Asia (Figure 7-6).[51]

Figure 7-6   Gaza Profiteers

(a) The Producers

AeroVironment	Corsight AI	Mercedes-Benz Group	BAE Systems	HD Hyundai
Agilite	Elbit Systems	Renk Group	JC Bamford Excavators	Toyota
AM General	Emtan Karmiel	Rheinmetall AG	Rolls-Royce	DJI
Boeing Co	InfiDome	ThyssenKrupp		
Caterpillar	Israel Aerospace Industries			
Colt Manufacturing	MDT Armor (Shladot)	Leonardo		
Day & Zimmermann	NextVision			
Flyer Defense	Paz Oil	Aimpoint AB		
Ford Motor	Rafael	Nordic Ammunition		
General Dynamics	SK Group			
General Electric	Smartshooter			
General Motors	SpearUAV			
Ghost Robotics	XTEND			
Google/Alphabet				
L3 Harris Technologies	CAL Cargo			
Leupold & Stevens				
Lockheed Martin				
Northrop Grunman				
Oshkosh				
Palantir Technologies				
Plasan				
RTX (Raytheon)				
Shield AI				
Skydio				
Textron				
Valero Energy				
Woodward				
Atlas Air				
Boeing				
Kalitta Air				
National Airlines				
Western Global				
Hoplite Group				
Sigmatech				

(b) The Final Product

Sources: (a) Who Profits; American Friends Service Committee; Database of Israeli Military and Security Export; (b) Close-up of a photo of Gaza City, Oct 9, 2023 / Wikimedia Commons

How did these companies contribute to the "war effort"? In addition to its well-known civilian side, Boeing was among the largest weapons manufacturers. In Gaza and Lebanon, the Israeli Air Force deployed its F-15 fighter jets and Apache AH-64 attack helicopters in most attacks, demolishing entire families in seconds.[52] They were also used in the notorious bombing of the Jabalia refugee camp, in which hundreds of Palestinians perished. The camp hosted 110,000 people in 1.4 square kilometers, which is more than four times the average density in Manhattan.[53] In turn, Caterpillar's D9 armored bulldozers, which are deployed to demolish Palestinian homes in the West Bank, were reportedly used to crush displaced Palestinians in Beit Lahia's Kamal Adwan Hospital courtyard.[54]

General Dynamics manufactures the massive 2,000-pound MK-84/ BLU-109/GBU-31 bomb, notorious for its damage. Its purpose in the densely populated urban areas is abject obliteration. The explosion of a 2,000-pound bomb is said to mean "instant death" for people within 100 feet, with lethal fragments extending for up to 1,200 feet. According to CNN, Israel had dropped hundreds of these 2,000-pound bombs on Gaza by late December. Nothing like this had been seen since Vietnam. In the first month of the war alone, these General Dynamics bombs caused more than 500 impact craters over 12 meters (40 feet) in diameter. They are four times heavier than the largest bombs the U.S. dropped on ISIS in Mosul, Iraq.[55] These massacre machines targeted civilian hubs.

And then there was the legendary RTX, formerly known as Raytheon, supplying the Israeli Air Force with guided air-to-surface missiles for its F-16 fighter jets, cluster bombs and bunker busters, which were deployed systematically to hammer Gaza's civilian population and infrastructure. By investing in offensive arms bound to Israel, Wall Street was effectively violating its own rules. Many multibillion-dollar investors in the defense industry claim to adhere to internationally-agreed-upon frameworks such as the Universal Declaration of Human Rights and the UN Guiding Principles, which urge businesses to "avoid infringing on the human rights of others and should address adverse human rights impacts with which they are involved." In practice, these defense companies the financiers invest in enabled Israel's campaign in Gaza, including genocidal atrocities.[56]

In turn, the Israeli Elbit-made MPR 500 multi-purpose bombs played a central role in Gaza. Designed for use in "densely populated urban warfare," they were perfect for the job. These bombs contained 26,000 controlled fragments for "high kill probability," as Elbit proclaimed in its marketing.[57] It was also its Hermes 450 drones that attacked three vehicles of the humanitarian organization, World Central Kitchen, near Deir al-Balah in the central Gaza, causing the death of seven aid workers who were managing food shipments.[58]

The UK-based BAE Systems, one of the world's largest weapons producers, manufactured the M109 howitzer, a 155mm mobile artillery system, which the Israeli military deployed extensively, firing tens of thousands of 155mm shells into the Gaza Strip. Documented by Amnesty International, the IDF used white phosphorus artillery shells in densely populated civilian areas in Gaza, many of which may be considered unlawful indiscriminate attacks.[59] What makes white phosphorus so harmful to humans is that it is very difficult to extinguish. Sticking to skin and clothing, its smoke is also harmful to the eyes and respiratory tract. It can cause deep and severe burns, penetrating even through bone.[60]

White phosphorus munitions were used in Vietnam and more recently in Gaza; in the former, it was presumably used against Viet Cong guerrillas, whereas in the latter densely populated civilian areas were the primary targets (Figure 7-7).[61] By December 2023, Israel also used U.S.-supplied white phosphorus munitions in an October attack in southern Lebanon in what Amnesty International regarded as a war crime. The controversial munitions were hardly new in Gaza. Between December 2008 and January 2009, the IDF "repeatedly exploded white phosphorus munitions in the air over populated areas, killing and injuring civilians, and damaging civilian structures, including a school, a market, a humanitarian aid warehouse and a hospital."[62]

Figure 7-7   White Phosphorus Bombs from Vietnam to Gaza

(a) Vietnam, 1966

(b) White Phosphorus injuries, Gaza 2009

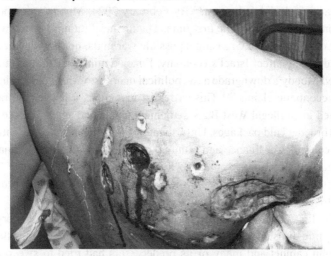

(a) A U.S. Air Force Douglas A-1E Skyraider drops a white phosphorus bomb on a Viet Cong position in South Vietnam in 1966. (b) Gazan youth undergoing hospital treatment for white phosphorus injuries, 2009

Source: Wikimedia Commons

The Costs of the War

Based on preliminary figures by the Finance Ministry, the Israeli financial newspaper *Calcalist* reported in late 2023 that the war with Hamas in the Gaza Strip would cost up to a whopping *$51 billion*. Half of the cost was attributed to defense expenses, which were soaring to $255 million per day. The rest came from a loss of revenue, compensation for businesses and rehabilitation. Equal to 10 percent of gross domestic product (GDP), the estimate had several caveats. The assumption was that the war would last 8–12 months, and that it would be limited to Gaza, without full participation by Lebanon's Hezbollah, Iran or Yemen. The 350,000 Israelis who had been drafted as military reservists would soon return to work. This was an "optimistic" estimate, however. Even without major escalation, the costs of the regional spillovers were likely to prove substantial. As the conflict lingered, drafted reservists could not return to work *en masse*. Besides, more than 125,000 Israelis had been displaced who would not return home without sufficient security guarantees – which seemed not to be forthcoming in the foreseeable future.[63]

Two months into the war, the Finance Ministry projected that the ongoing war would cost Israel around $13.8 billion in 2024, assuming that the high intensity fighting in Gaza would come to an end in the first quarter of the new year, which didn't happen.[64] By February 2024, Moody's dropped the rating on Israel's debt for the first time. The financial ratings agency warned that the ongoing war in Gaza and a possible war in the north with Hezbollah could adversely affect Israel's economy. Finance minister Bezalel Smotrich slammed Moody's downgrade as a "political manifesto" that "did not include serious economic claims."[65] This extremist ideologue, a lawyer by training who lived in an illegal West Bank settlement, again and again pledged "bigger and broader" aid packages. Unfortunately, Smotrich had no credentials in either economics or finance and minimal credibility among market analysts. Even the finance ministry could no longer deny realities, when the Israeli Statistics Bureau reported that in the fourth quarter of 2023 the economy shrank by 20 percent on an annualized basis.[66]

The first year of the most far-right government in Israel's history was an economic disaster. Worse, it heralded a set of inconvenient truths that the Netanyahu cabinet and many of its predecessors had tried to sweep under the carpet. After several dramatic transformations, the Israeli economy had arrived at a fatal impasse.

Neoliberal and Alternative Narratives

In the early weeks of the Israeli ground assault, international observers presumed that Israel's economy would suffer a short-term hit but recover fast as it had done before. Surely, they contended, the future would be a replica of the past! But as the Gaza War dragged on, the tone reversed. The assumption then became that Israel was heading to another lost decade, somewhat like after the 1973 Yom Kippur War. *Bloomberg Businessweek* called it a cautionary tale. In this essentially neoliberal narrative, war spending was seen as an anomaly that must in due time give way to a return to the free-market economics.[67] In reality, war spending has overshadowed the history of Israel from the pre-state years to the present, while its embrace of neoliberalism in the 1980s resulted in the kind of extreme polarization that proved to be the worst among all OECD economies. Hence, the two narratives, the neoliberal story by the *Bloomberg Businessweek* and its alternative:

Neoliberal Narrative	**Alternative narrative**
The insistence that Israel should never again be caught flat-footed led to a huge ramp-up in defense spending, which averaged almost 29% of gross domestic product in 1973–75.	Wrong. Israel's ramp-up in defense spending began with the 1950s "border wars," and the escalation ran in parallel with the U.S. military ties that soared with Nixon's rearmament in 1973–75.[69]
The side effects were devastating. The government deficit blew out to 150% of GDP, fueling 500% annual inflation. The period, known in economic circles as "the lost decade," ended in the 1980s when the country enlisted outside specialists to help draft tough reforms that slashed state spending, stabilized the shekel and attracted foreign investment.[68]	The effort to overcome war spending through austerity failed. Hence, the out-of-control deficits and hyper-inflation. The net effect was "a lost decade" resulting from shock therapy and stabilization that broke the post-war economy, brought to power the hard-right Likud, leading to new wars and an Intifada, while "stabilizing" the economy at the cost of ever-deeper polarization.

In the neoliberal narrative, the war spending is necessary but temporary; cyclical, not structural. The trick is to return to the good old pre-October 7 economy. There are parallels, the narrative contends, between the post-1973 and the likely post-2024 Israeli economy. In the 4th quarter of 2023, it suffered a 21.7% annualized drop in economic output. While like the war in 1973, the war in Gaza is now the most expensive in the country's history and its cost could soar to more than $67 billion through 2025. Before the war, defense spending was at an all-time low of 4.5% of GDP, but it is set to double in 2024. Consequently, the decisive test in the neoliberal narrative was the government's ability to lower the defense-spending-to-GDP ratio back to reasonable levels within several years. Otherwise, Israel would slide back into another lost decade. Like conventional wisdom, the neoliberal narrative offered a seemingly persuasive and credible argument. But just like the narrative of the "lost decade" itself was ridden with cracks and holes, their war spending tale left out some inconvenient truths.

In reality, the war spending was unwarranted and avoidable. Unwarranted: The reluctance to withdraw from the occupied territories and complete the peace process set the stage for October 7.[70] Avoidable: The Israeli communities adjacent to the Gaza Strip were purposely neglected. Nevertheless, the key role belongs to the warnings of the impending Hamas offensive that were systematically ignored or downplayed by military and intelligence authorities.[71] Before October 7, war spending as a percentage of GDP was on decline, but aggregate war spending was not. Its escalation began with the Netanyahu cabinets and the associated crumbling of the peace process begun in the 2000s, which has only intensified since the 2014 Gaza War. More importantly, much if not most military spending, coupled with foreign economic assistance particularly via American Jewry, went effectively into the settlements, whose very presence continued to escalate new uprisings and new wars.[72]

In this view, the decisive test is not the government's ability to lower the defense-spending-to-GDP ratio back to reasonable levels within several years, but *how* it would be done. "More of the same" is no solution when it is fostering polarization that is dividing Israel to the point of civil friction. The decisive test would have been to put the peace process on track, thereby enabling engagement in truly multilateral diplomacy to contain the external threats, and thus prevent secular risks. This would have enabled investment in Israel and Israelis, preempted the devastating brain drain, and rebuilt welfare and social security in a nation in which poverty is spreading. Instead, Gaza remained the "world's largest open-air prison."

From the standpoint of the Likud coalitions that have dominated Israeli governments since the 1980s, the "threat of Gaza" kept the U.S. military aid humming, served to weaken the Fatah-dominated Palestinian Authority and offered one possible pretext for a conflict with Iran. It also fostered the semblance of a common enemy which reinforced the internal political unity that was vital because of the creeping economic polarization. From the Gazans' perspective, there was nowhere to go. They couldn't go to the West Bank. Egypt had never granted citizenship to the Palestinian refugees who had fled there. Jordan, Lebanon and Syria had enough challenges of their own. Most importantly, Palestinians knew, by experience, that if they left, there would be no return. That was the catch. So they clung to their homes in Gaza. But by 2024, even those were largely gone.

The End of the Road

Whether Israel would need months or years to figure out how to defend its borders, that task will be both unviable and impossible as long as Israel refuses to determine *where* those borders are, in cooperation with Palestinians. Its violent quest for "security" will not bring lasting peace; mutual trust might.

At the end of May 2024, Israel government bond yields hit a 13-year high, which did not bode well for the future. As the risk of the 10-year dollar bonds was priced higher than in countries like Peru and Hungary, the state had to pay higher interest. Meanwhile, 130 Israeli senior economists gave their harshest warning as of yet, slamming the Netanyahu cabinet's unsustainable policies that imposed a heavy economic and military burden on just one part of the population. They had a point. Along with the unresolved Palestinian conflict and untenable settlement expansion, it was the Israeli government's economic policy that was now jeopardizing Israel's survival. Or as the economists put it: "Without a change in the existing course, these processes endanger the existence of the state."[73]

For some four decades, Israel's economic policies have sped up the polarization of its society. The war budget assigned a disproportionate, increasing burden of the military reserves on the working population. It continues to allocate a significant chunk of the budget to Haredi institutions, which shun the market economy while permitting the exemption from conscription for a growing part of the population (read: the Likud cabinets' ultra-orthodox constituencies).

In the absence of international pressure, particularly U.S. influence, the current trends are likely to prevail. As a result, many of those bearing the economic and security burden will continue to emigrate from Israel, including the best and the brightest. Since the remaining population will be less productive, the burden on them will increase, which will over time set the stage for a vicious circle, with the migration of the brightest fostered by the deterioration of the most vulnerable. In the short- to medium-term, the route to a sustainable path would be for the government to end incentives for non-work, reform the Haredi education system, reduce disparities in the security burden and preempt constitutional changes threatening civil rights in Israel. Israel's secular challenge remains that these reforms are precisely those that the Likud-led governments have opposed. Furthermore, even if such short- and medium-term guidelines were adopted, they would have little effect on the increasing polarization in Israel and the unsustainable settlement policies.

Signals indicating a shift in international public sentiment have increased with the protracted war. Starting in March 2024, USS, the biggest British private pension fund, reduced exposure to Israeli stocks and debt following pressure from its members, dumping over $100 million of Israeli assets.[74] Fitch ratings downgraded Israel to "A," stressing a negative outlook. Though widely condemned by the Netanyahu cabinet, it was still a conservative response to rapid shifts in the economic landscape, including the continued war, the associated geopolitical risks underpinning the negative outlook, elevated regional tensions which – if materialized – would further damage Israel's credit profile. Worse, Fitch expected that "the government will permanently increase military spending by close to 1.5% of GDP versus pre-war levels. Israel is likely to maintain a stronger presence along its borders than in the past, amid plans to widen mandatory draft and to increase domestic military production, which would also add to spending."[75]

In the second quarter of 2024, Israel's economy grew at a much slower pace than forecast, as the protracted Gaza War continued to take a heavy toll on exports and investments. On a per capita basis, the GDP actually contracted. The war has forced the largest military mobilization since 1973, while more than 100,000 remain displaced. It is an untenable equation. In such a status quo, "staying the course" will effectively bankrupt the economy. The greatest national security threat in the history of Israel is its grossly disproportionate stress on militarized national security, reinforced by America's basically military foreign policy.

Part III
REPERCUSSIONS IN THE MIDDLE EAST AND BEYOND

Part III

Chapter 8

THE STRUGGLE FOR A SOVEREIGN PALESTINE

In 1969, Golda Meir, the iconic Israeli Labor leader, whom Ben-Gurion once called "the only man" in the Israeli government, was asked whether the emergence of the Palestinian fedayeen was an important new factor in the Middle East.

> Important, no. A new factor, yes. There was no such thing as Palestinians. When was there an independent Palestinian people with a Palestinian state? It was either southern Syria before the First World War and then it was a Palestine including Jordan. It was not as though there was a Palestinian people in Palestine considering itself as a Palestinian people and we came and threw them out and took their country from them. They did not exist.[1]

The view was shared by many Labor Zionists and by most Israeli conservatives who still dreamed of Greater Israel.

The first Palestinian attacks against Israel commenced in the 1950s, when Yasser Arafat's launched his Fatah. Then the Palestine Liberation Organization (PLO) was founded and Arafat replaced Ahmed Shukeiri as its leader, months before Meir's interview. In those tumultuous years, Meir was often asked if she still stood by the comments; she did. In 1972, just days after she repeated her response,[2] Palestinian militants infiltrated the Munich Olympic Village, killed members of the Israeli team and took others hostage. At Meir's order, Israel retaliated by bombing ten PLO bases in Syria and Lebanon. Subsequently, Mossad executed most of the militants and PLO operatives who had played role in the Munich massacre. The greenlight came from a committee led by Meir.

Yet, Meir's public comments and private thoughts were two different things.

UNEVEN ECONOMIC DEVELOPMENT

Golda's Hesitation

As an old political fox, Golda had already expressed readiness to accept the establishment of a Palestinian state in the West Bank in 1970, according to declassified files. In a "top secret" discussion, she stated unambiguously and in her typical style:

> My mind is open to [the establishment of a Palestinian state].
> I am ready to listen as to whether there is a glimmer of hope for an independent Arab statelet in Samaria and Judea, and maybe Gaza too.... If they call it Palestine, so be it. What do I care?[3]

Meir seemed to be open to potential political arrangements for a Palestinian state, whether it was a state that is member of a confederation with Israel, Jordan, or both, or as a completely independent country. The timing matters. The meeting took place in the aftermath of "Black September"; that is, the month-long conflict between the Jordanian kingdom and the PLO, which was then banished to Lebanon. Yet, the Iron Lady said that "if [Arafat] becomes prime minister of Jordan, we will negotiate with him. Arafat as the head of a terrorist organization—no. But if he becomes head of a government that he'll represent as a Palestinian, then fine." Nonetheless, Meir felt uneasy with such scenarios, saying that such arrangements would be created to destroy Israel. Former military leader Yigal Allon stressed that "I don't suggest encouraging a Palestinian state. Rather, in the long term, a peace contract that will keep options open."[4]

Golda Meir was a figure of historical stature. But Golda (née Mabovitch) was nonetheless a captive of her times. Born in Kiev, her earliest memories involved pogroms. The idea that Israelis would one day engage in pogroms of their own against vulnerable Palestinians was inconceivable to her. In public, she rejected the idea of Israel's ethnic cleansing of Palestinians in 1947–1948, attributing such things to Arab propaganda.

Ultimately, the secret 1970 discussion, which took place on the eve of Yom Kippur, did not result in a peace effort. The hesitation set the stage for a fatal war just three years later; Allon's subsequent peace plan that never became effective; Defense Minister Dayan's covert efforts to support the expansion of Jewish territories in the occupied West Bank; and the Labor regime's drastic plunge and hard-right Likud's dramatic rise in the 1977 election, followed by several major wars.

Nonetheless, neither the wider Israeli public nor the international community knew about these internal debates that could have reversed the course of history and spared the lives of generations of Israelis and Palestinians in the region.

Furthermore, not everybody agreed that disproportionate devastation – Jabotinsky's "Iron Wall" – was the path to peace in the Middle East. These included Efraim Halevy, the former head of the Mossad and a hard-headed pragmatist. Knowing that Israel will never have peace until Palestinians are treated as equals and with dignity, Halevy has argued that those who were seeking peace in the Middle East should "take the opportunity of a seriously weakened Hamas to reflect on how we might bring it into the political process instead of just confronting it with tanks in the back alleys of Gaza."[5] But Halevy did not make those comments after October 7. He had urged Israel and the U.S. to bring Hamas into the political process in 2009.

As long as mutual recognition remains ignored, denied or repressed, peace will remain a distant prospect in Israel/Palestine. Furthermore, this polarization has long been amplified by the steep economic gap between the colonizers and the colonized.

Palestine's Dual Economy

Even during the period of the British Mandate, the Palestinian economy was no longer a singular, homogeneous whole. It was a dual economy, with distinct Arab and Jewish economic sectors within a single country, divided by different levels of development, technology, supply and demand.[6] In the past, Jews had worked and lived relatively peacefully in the Arab countries. But ever since the 1880s, when the Jewish immigration waves began to increase, the polarization between Arab and Jewish Palestine had been compounded by the Jewish sector prioritizing Jewish labor. As Jewish immigration waves expanded, the Jewish and Arab populations and geographies were splitting into two separate and unequal economies.

With the establishment of Israel, the new Jewish state was left with a substantial Arab population (170,000) in areas under its control. As these areas were largely under military government, their economic integration was initially limited. Things began to change only in the 1960s with the lifting of the military government. It was then that the Arab sector *within* Israel became more integrated with that of the Jewish economy, despite enduring social gaps. Concurrently, Palestinian agricultural land within Israel was taken over by the Jewish state, while Arabs were reduced to wage labor in the Jewish sector, often physically distant from their homes. In 1965 the Israel Land

Administration (ILA) began the demolition of houses in Arab villages that had been abandoned in the course of the 1948 Arab-Israeli war. In practice, the ILA employed the Israel Archaeological Survey Society (IASS) in these efforts to clear the country of deserted villages. So, most of the abandoned Palestinian villages disappeared as a result of a purposeful plan originating with the ILA, thereby ensuring the refugees had no homes to return to, and indeed, erasing their existence from historical documentation. The demolition of houses in the Latrun enclave, a strategic hilltop overlooking the road between Tel Aviv and Jerusalem, and the Golan Heights after the 1967 War was to a great extent a continuation of the pre-1967 operation. In practice, the IASS archaeologists carried out the ILA's initiative while subordinating their scientific agenda to that of the governmental bodies with which they cooperated.[7]

In development, even minor differences in initial conditions can have a great impact on future outcomes. Sensitivity to those conditions makes development highly path-dependent. The uneven economic development in the post-1949 West Bank and Gaza relative to Israel proper is a case in point. In the first two decades of its existence, Israel's GDP increased at a rate of 10 percent per year, with the rate of investment growth at nearly 6 percent. The influx of wage earnings gradually raised the economic status of Israel's Arab population. But a significant differential prevails between the two demographics, due to social and economic discrimination.[8]

Following the 1949 Armistice Agreements, the West Bank was occupied and subsequently annexed by Transjordan; the Kingdom of Jordan. At the same time, the age-old economic links between the West Bank and the Gaza Strip suffered a total break. Although the West Bank lagged behind the Jewish areas in economic development, it was ahead of the East Bank. Moreover, a significant share of Palestinian refugees fled from the newly established Israel to the East Bank, which penalized its development. Hence, the postwar West Bank's curious mix of "relative prosperity and acute industrial underdevelopment."[9]

After the 1948–49 Arab-Israeli War, the Gaza Strip became an Egyptian-administered territory. Following the 1967 Six-Day War, it came under Israeli occupation. Due to the great inflow of refugees into Gaza, now cut off from the West Bank, the Strip hovered at the edge of collapse. Still, Egypt chose not to annex the territory. Instead, it would hold it "in trust for the Palestinians, pending the establishment of their state." Nor was Gaza integrated with Egypt's economy. In the absence of natural resources, most people, half of whom were refugees, were employed in agriculture. Industrial development was minimal. Hence, the low living standards.

The primary economic catalyst involved the UN troops and particularly the employees of the UN refugee relief agency (UNRWA) stationed in the Strip. Created as a purely temporary measure, UNRWA's mandate has been subject to renewal every three years ever since. In the absence of peace in the region, it remains a lifeline to the Gazans. Nonetheless, the prevention of autonomous economic development virtually ensured that even prior to 1967, per capita income in the Strip was only *half* of that in the West Bank.[10]

Israeli Occupation and Partial Integration

During the first decade following the 1967 War, Israel's Labor coalition dominated policies in the West Bank and Gaza. East Jerusalem was effectively annexed. While the Labor leaders shunned official annexation of the occupied territories, they did not withdraw from them. Though they prioritized the Allon Plan, they permitted the rise of the far-right Messianic settlers. Viewing the issue of territories through the prism of national security, they limited Jewish settlements to less-populated areas to preempt potential friction with Palestinians.

Promoted by Moshe Dayan, an "open bridges" policy was implemented with Jordan permitting relatively free movement between the West Bank and Jordan.[11] The consequent partial economic integration was premised on the exports of Israeli goods to the occupied territories, and the export of labor from the territories to Israel, with Israelis capitalizing on Palestinian consumers and workers. Effectively, it fostered *dependent* development in which Israel took advantage of Palestinian low-cost labor, while Palestinians came to rely on Israeli industrial goods. Independent Palestinian enterprise and development was perceived as something of a national security threat. Even then, Israel's annual GDP growth hovered around 6 percent, but the rate in the occupied territories was twice as high, insofar as it was starting from an exceptionally low point. Another implication was that as the rate of investment climbed within Israel, it would remain low in the territories where industrial takeoff, due to Israeli policies and restrictions, remained an empty dream.

After the Israeli occupation, the West Bank and Gaza Strip's external trade, previously limited mostly to neighboring countries of comparable wealth and level of development, was soon reoriented toward Israel, an economically more advanced country with a GNP about 20 times as large. At first, this growth in the West Bank/Gaza Strip was accompanied by a rise in private investment as a share of GDP from about 14 percent in 1969 to 30 percent in 1979, with real private investment growing at an average of

25 percent a year. Though seemingly impressive, most of it was devoted to residential construction. By contrast, real investment in machinery and equipment grew by less than 1 percent a year, decreasing to 5 percent from about 10 percent of GDP. In other words, the West Bank was integrated into the Israeli economy in terms that supported investment and growth in Israel, while undermining private investment in the occupied territories.[12] Dayan's objective was to retard development in the occupied territories. In fact, economic dependency served as a cornerstone of Israel's military occupation. Both its military and the powerful labor federation Histadrut perpetuated the postwar status quo. Starting with a 1970 cabinet decision, a military administration would supervise the employment of Palestinian Arabs. Of the 11 percent that was taken from the wages of each Palestinian worker for National Insurance, only 1 percent was slated for work accidents, employer bankruptcy and a birth in an Israeli hospital that was a rarity for Palestinians. The rest went to a special "Equalization Fund," presumably to supply the Palestinians with social and cultural services. In practice, these monies were used to finance the occupation. The workers paid the full National Insurance tax, yet they did not benefit from most of the rights that this tax is supposed to cover, such as unemployment compensation, old-age pension, disability benefits, and so.[13]

For the occupied territories, Israel was an economic colossus, whereas for Israel the territories represented less than 7 percent of its gross national income. With jobs, the standard of living began slowly to rise in the territories. In 1968, some 10,000 laborers, most with official permits, crossed the Green Line; that is, Israel's *de facto* borders between 1949 and the Six-Day War in 1967, to work in Israel. By 1977, there were 66,000 such laborers, with a third lacking official permits. At the end of the period, the gross national income (GNI) in the territories exceeded its gross domestic product (GDP) by 35 percent, thanks mainly to labor earnings in Israel.[14] More than a third of the territories' GDP originated mainly from labor earnings in Israel. Some Palestinians made money, but in Israel and under Israeli terms. It wasn't autonomous development. It was dependent development.

With the transition from Labor to Likud coalitions in 1977, the occupied territories were in for a rollercoaster. At first, Likud's policies sped up the integration of the territories into Israel, both economically and politically. But as Likud-supported settlement expansion escalated, economic integration faded.[15]

In the occupied territories, rapid growth plunged from 12 to 4 percent, while GDP growth plunged to close to zero by the mid-'80s, paving the way for the First Intifada. Investment declined further and unemployment began to climb. While in the West Bank, growth was fueled by the migrant workers who represented 37 percent of the labor force; in Gaza, the comparable figure was even higher, close to 50 percent. For Israel at that time, the need for Palestinian labor was marginal; in the territories, that labor's earnings were a critical source of growth, a vital lifeline for survival.[16]

This was a period of deepening geopolitical ties between Israel and the United States, and by the same token, increasing economic integration. If the U.S. is viewed as the core economy, Israel can be seen as its sub-core, whereas the occupied territories represent a colonial, peripheral economy. The economies of the West Bank and Gaza Strip were at once both an integral part of a larger economy dominated by Israel, and an economy distinct from that of Israel; in brief, separate and unequal. In the first two decades of Israeli occupation, the territories were suppressed by high economic, administrative, political and cultural barriers working against industrial development, as the prime effect of the Israeli policy was to keep the West Bank and Gaza as markets for Israeli products and suppliers of cheap labor to Israel.

Where the Israelis saw themselves as a benign hegemon contributing to peace and stability in the occupied territories, Palestinians saw them as imposing a settler colonialism that was more akin to that in Algeria and Vietnam. Finding no peaceful ways to regain their territories, they opted for other means.

MODERNIZATION AND ISLAMISM

Between 1949 and 1956, the Arab intrusions into Israel and Israel's retaliatory responses set the patterns of conduct that would characterize Arab-Israeli conflict for decades to come. And so did Israel's use of disproportionate force in the West Bank, including the 1952 reprisal operation on the village of Beit Jala resulting in blown houses and dead civilians, and the notorious 1953 Qibya massacre, leaving behind destroyed houses, a school and a mosque and 69 dead, two-thirds of whom were women and children.[17]

In Gaza, autonomous Palestinian military activity was not viable under the Egyptian administration. In the West Bank, the popular National Guard formed a spearhead against Israel along the armistice line. Without a group of their own, the members of the Muslim Brotherhood joined Fatah and the Marxist Popular Front for the Liberation of Palestine (PFLP). In the two decades following the UN partition plan and the 1967 War, the Brotherhood did not engage in major military activity against Israel, either in the West Bank or Gaza. But things were changing. The Muslim Brotherhood had long spearheaded the liberation movements, while seeking a balance in the transition from tradition to modernity.

Al-Banna's Islamic Modernization

Having grown weary of British imperialism, Hassan Al-Banna (1906–49) was concerned by efforts to modernize and secularize Egypt at the expense of Islam.[18] Born in the rural Nile Delta, he was a son of a muezzin and mosque teacher and imam. In 1923, he moved to Cairo amid rising pressures of modernization and Westernization. Ever since the late 19th century, Western sociology and its pioneers—from Marx and Tönnies to Durkheim and Weber—had sought to understand the often-violent transition from rural tradition and religious community to modernity and secular urbanity. But unlike Marx's Britain, Durkheim's France and Weber's Germany, Egypt was colonized and underdeveloped.

Al-Banna had nothing but disdain for Egypt's liberal ruling regime. Nor was he sympathetic to Turkey's Ataturk, who saw modernization as identical with Westernization, or liberal oligarchs, who also identified Westernization with modernity. He sought an alternative path to modernization and material development. Along with his friends, he took an oath to become "troops for the message of Islam . . . brothers in the service of Islam; hence we are the Muslim Brothers." As such, modernization was not the issue, but its Western version was.[19]

Western modernizers saw tradition as a hindrance to modernity. Hence, their efforts to accelerate the transition to a secular modernity. By contrast, Al-Banna's modernization built on traditional communities and their associated social networks, in particular those around mosques, and on Islamic welfare agencies and neighborhood groups. What accounted for success here was not anti-modernization, but a peculiar mix of tradition and modernity, enabled by faith-based communities facing shared challenges across the region.[20]

Islamic modernization did not have to be mutually exclusive with Western modernity or Islamic tradition. Many movements in non-Western societies have displayed strong anti-Western, even anti-modern themes, yet they have been distinctively modern. There is no single "right" modernity. The multipolar world economy stands on a more inclusive modernity.[21]

Indeed, it was the mix of tradition and modernity that accounted for the popularity of the Muslim Brotherhood, not only among the poorest and most vulnerable but also in the civil society, from educated civil servants and white-collar workers to professionals. As its branches grew from 150 in 1936 to 1,500 in 1944, the Brotherhood in Egypt increased to an estimated 100,000–500,000, diffusing from northern Africa to Palestine in 1946, and subsequently to Sudan, Saudi Arabia, Syria, and Lebanon.[22] But when it sent volunteers to fight against Israel in 1948, it was targeted by the Egyptian monarchy. A year later, Al-Banna was assassinated by King Farouk's secret police, but his martyrdom compounded the Brotherhood's clout. It is this friction between pan-Arab nationalism and pan-Islamism that still divides the Middle East.[23]

Qutb's Islamism

With the UN Partition, the establishment of Israel and its effective control of most of Palestine, the Muslim Brotherhood in Palestine was transformed. Moreover, with the annexation of the West Bank to Jordan in 1950, the West Bank and Jordan's Brotherhood merged. Meanwhile, the Brotherhood's influence in Egypt and Gaza declined, due to King Farouk's suppression. That paved the way for Sayyid Qutb (1906–1966), who advocated the establishment of an Islamic caliphate.

An outspoken critic of Western civilization, selfish individualism and materialism, Qutb fought secular modernization and championed Islamic revival. Raised in a politically active, landowning family, he received a British-style education in Cairo and made a name as a literary critic while working for Egypt's Ministry of Education. Between 1948 and 1950, he was in Colorado on a scholarship to study the U.S. educational system. He was not impressed by America. Qutb was interested in and enjoyed some of Western music, literature and Hollywood, but he was far more critical of Western culture than al-Banna. The status symbols that Americans obsessed over, he saw as manifestations of greed. American ideas of equality were a sham. He was a man of color and was treated accordingly in the segregated America. And his conservatism led him to denounce America's endless infatuation with sex and its seductive women temptresses.[24] He saw Western civilization as a regime of imperialist control and discipline.[25] Following his return to Egypt, he attacked the West's secular materialism, economic inequities and brutal racism. When he denounced secularism, he did not effectively condemn the West's individual freedoms; but he saw them as a tacit tradeoff. Secularism was inherently "oppressive" because it undermined freedom of religion by constraining all religious practice into the private realm. To a devout Muslim, faith was about community; the most important freedom of all. The distinction between private and public dimension sabotaged the foundation of faith.[26] Embracing Islamism, he resigned from the civil service, joined the Brotherhood in the early 1950s and became one of its leading figures.

When Nasser and the Free Officers overthrew Egypt's pro-Western government, Qutb and the Brotherhood welcomed the coup. Although Nasser would often consult Qutb, his secular socialist nationalism was on a collision course with Islamism. As the relationship soured, Nasser initiated a crack-down against the Brotherhood and jailed Qutb. Although Qutb never gave up the idea that Islam would have to be built on modernization, he began to propagate a radical embrace of Islam.[27]

Although Qutb was executed in 1966, his ideas appealed to Brotherhood's members in Egypt and across the Middle East, and through his brother, particularly in Saudi Arabia. One of these ardent followers was Ayman al-Zawahiri (1951–2022), subsequently a leading figure in the Egyptian Jihad, which was behind the 1981 assassination of President Sadat. Subsequently, Zawahiri became a close associate of al-Qaeda leader, Osama bin Laden, whom he succeeded in 2011, until a U.S. drone strike killed him, too.

FROM ARMED STRUGGLE AND PEACE TALKS TO WAR

The Rise of Arafat's PLO

In the Palestinian view, the June 1967 War was a Second Nakba. Of the one million Palestinians in the West Bank and Gaza, some 280,000–325,000 were displaced with most settling in Jordan. More than 700,000 remained in the occupied territories. In the Golan Heights, over 100,000 fled. Israel allowed only the remaining residents of East Jerusalem and the Golan Heights to receive Israeli citizenship. After the 1967 War, the number of Palestinian refugees increased by more than 50 percent.

The Palestinian armed struggle was first associated with Fatah ("victory"); the acronym of the Palestinian National Liberation Movement (*Harakat al-Tahrir al-Watani l-Filastini*). Launched in 1959 by Arafat and other Palestinian refugees from Gaza who studied in Cairo and worked in the Gulf states. Fatah formed the secular, nationalist and socialist core of the Palestinian liberation movement. It joined the Palestine Liberation Organization (PLO), an umbrella organization of major militant groups that was founded in 1964 by the Arab League to be a representative of the Palestinians. The PLO aimed at Arab unity and the liberation of Palestine. Initially led by Ahmad al-Shukeiri, a lawyer who had struggled for a Palestinian state since the 1940s, the PLO was supported by Gamal Abdel Nasser, Egypt's popular leader.[28]

As hundreds of thousands of Palestinians sought refuge in Jordan, they soon found, as their parents had after 1948, that Israel would not permit their return. At the time, the PLO was effectively an umbrella of eight organizations headquartered in Damascus and Beirut. Meanwhile, the small and fragile

Hashemite Kingdom struggled to cope with massive economic pressures as the PLO carved itself into a "state within a state" in Jordan. Starting with the "Black September" of 1970, the Jordanian civil war between Arafat's PLO and King Hussein's armed forces killed hundreds of Jordanians, but among the Palestinians thousands perished and still more were injured. Eventually, the conflict climaxed in Jordan's expulsion of the PLO to Lebanon in July 1971.

In short order, Palestinian terrorism went international, Lebanon saw the onset of a 15-year long civil war, and Syria served as a base for new militant groups. In 1988, the PLO declared a State of Palestine comprising the internationally recognized Palestinian territories, including the West Bank and Gaza; in 1993, the PLO rejected terrorism and recognized the State of Israel.[29] A year later the Palestinian Authority (PA) was officially formed. In 2012, the UN voted to recognize the State of Palestine as a non-member UN observer state. As of June 2024, the State of Palestine is recognized as a sovereign state by 145 of the 193 member states of the United Nations.

But despite its rising international political clout, the PLO has found itself marginalized as the Islamist movements have gained momentum in the occupied territories. While Israel maintained an official support for the two-state solution, it did nothing to bring it into being, with the Oslo Accords regarded by most parties as long dead. Its coffin was nailed when the Israeli Knesset voted overwhelmingly against Palestinian statehood in July 2024. Importantly, it was backed not only by the Likud coalition and its Messianic far-right supporters, but by members of Benny Gantz's center-right party, whereas Yair Lapid's center-left party left the plenum to avoid backing the measure. Only members of Labor, left, and Arab parties continue to support the two-state solution. In other words, in the Israeli parliament, barely 10 percent of the representatives support solidly Palestinian statehood, whereas 25 percent are hedging their bets. Three of four want a solution that allows Israel to retain the occupied territories but preferably without the Palestinians—which, in turn, is predicated on ethnic expulsions or "voluntary transfers."

The Rise of Hamas

After years of debates on the role of Islamic revival and moral change as opposed to armed struggle and secular modernization, the Brotherhood, under the pressure of its young militants, began to move toward armed struggle against Israel. In 1967, the leaders of the Brotherhood in Arab countries greenlighted the participation of its Jordanian arm with Fatah, while financial support was garnered from Brotherhood's members in the Gulf. But this phase came to an abrupt end with the Jordanian civil war.[30] Subsequently, the Brotherhood in Jordan focused mainly on advocacy, whereas its Palestinian arm adopted a different stance under Israeli occupation.

Between 1967 and 1987, in just two decades, the number of mosques in the West Bank and Gaza more than doubled from 600 to 1,350. As Israeli occupation grew more brutal and settler violence took off, so did the Islamist movement in Palestinian mosques and universities. One of the Brotherhood leaders was Sheikh Ahmed Yassin (1937–2004), a militant Islamist born in Ashkelon in Mandatory Palestine. His family fled to Gaza, settling in al-Shati refugee camp after his village was ethnically cleansed in 1948.[31] A quadriplegic and nearly blind, Yassin viewed armed struggle as the only viable venue for resistance, and as a "religious duty." Educated at home, Yassin read widely and delivered weekly sermons after Friday prayers, drawing large crowds. In 1973, he participated in setting up the Brotherhood's Palestinian branch and subsequently established the Islamic charity, Mujama al-Islamiya, in Gaza.[32] And so, the Palestinian Brotherhood moved toward military activity, securing funds externally to buy weapons, bringing together a mix of older moderates and younger militants in the early 1980s.[33]

Regionally, the Islamists' support was fueled by the Iranian Revolution in 1979 and the Afghan fedayeen battle against the Soviet Union, supported by U.S. weapons, training and finance. When Israeli authorities found out about the Brotherhood's weapons purchases, Yassin and his companions were imprisoned in 1984. But a year later, he was released in a prisoner exchange. As the First Intifada began in Gaza in 1987, Yassin co-founded the paramilitary wing of the Palestinian Muslim Brotherhood, which soon became known as the Islamic Resistance Movement (Hamas). Just two years later, Israel conducted another mass campaign of arrests and Yassin was imprisoned for life for ordering killings of alleged Palestinian collaborators. But he would soon return to the limelight.

From Interim Peace to Provisional War

In the late 1980s, Israeli analysts saw the future of the West Bank and Gaza economies in terms of three scenarios: the status quo with the existing barriers (conservative option), a modified status quo with some barriers removed (reformist option), and unrestricted development as a separate Palestinian entity (radical option). At the time, the Likud seemed to favor the conservative option, whereas the reformist option prevailed among the Labor coalition. The radical option was marginal because it lacked adequate political support.[34]

The scenarios assumed a gradual process in which the past served as a recipe for the future. But Israeli analysts were in for a surprise. When the First Intifada took off in 1987, the conservative scenario reigned. As the peace process took off in the 1990s, the reformist scenario seemed invincible and the radical scenario within reach. With the failure of the peace process and the inception of the Second Intifada, which many attributed to Sharon's calculated provocation, a U-turn ensued, as the conservative option was deemed the only realistic alternative.

In September 1993, Israeli Prime Minister Yitzhak Rabin and Yasser Arafat signed the first peace agreement between Israel and the PLO. In reality, the success of the Oslo process was due to secret negotiations not in or by the U.S., but via a direct dialogue between Israeli and Palestinian leaders in Oslo, Norway. The Oslo Accords—the Oslo I Accord, signed in Washington, D.C. in 1993 and the subsequent Oslo II Accord, signed in Taba, Egypt, in 1995—were interim agreements between Israel and the PLO. As part of the Oslo Accords, the occupied West Bank was divided into three areas; that is, A, B and C that would be under Palestinian, joint and Israeli control, respectively (Figure 8-1).

Figure 8-1   West Bank After Oslo Accords

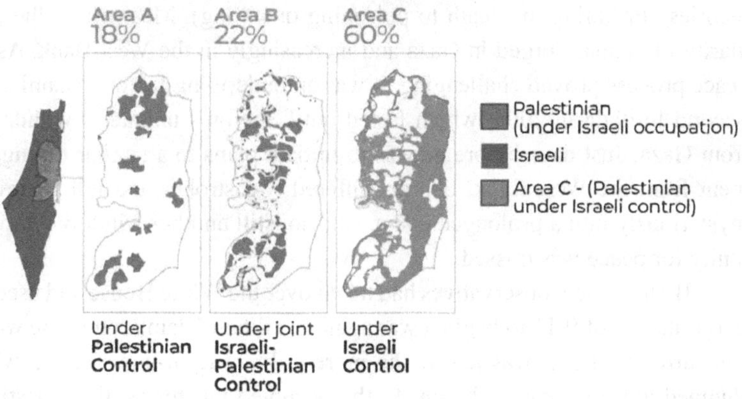

Area A 18%   Area B 22%   Area C 60%

- Palestinian (under Israeli occupation)
- Israeli
- Area C - (Palestinian under Israeli control)

Under Palestinian Control   Under joint Israeli-Palestinian Control   Under Israeli Control

Source: Al Jazeera

The Oslo Accords marked the conclusion of the long peace process based on Resolution 242 In 1967, which supported future negotiations involving Israel's return of captured territories, in exchange for peace with Arab states (the "land-for-peace" principle), and the Resolution 338 of the UN Security Council ending the Yom Kippur War in 1973. Half a decade later, these were followed by the U.S.-brokered 1978 Camp David Accords between Israel and Egypt. Initially, the predominant U.S. and Israeli view was that Palestinian "autonomy" would not necessarily lead to "statehood." U.S. officials' views changed after Fatah opted for diplomatic engagement by renouncing "armed struggle" and accepting the UN Security Council Resolutions 242 and 338. It was a pragmatic shift following a series of political and military setbacks in Lebanon and Jordan. Importantly, the timeframe coincided with the First Intifada, which raised widespread unease in Israel that its control over the West Bank and Gaza might prove unsustainable.[35] Due to the U.S. rethink, the PLO's shift and Israeli concern at the spread of the Intifada, political space opened for a diplomatic process, setting the stage for the Oslo talks. As the negotiations were premised on negotiations between Rabin's government and the PLO, the agreements and the peace process stood on thin ice. With Rabin's assassination, it began to give in.

Most Palestinians in the occupied territories supported the peace process, which contributed to the suspension of the Intifada. However, militants were aligning behind the Islamic resistance of Hamas rather than the PLO, whose aging leaders had been marginalized in Tunis. As the prospects of peace talks faded away, volatility increased in the occupied territories. The ailing Arafat saw the PLO's dominance fall, failed to unify the factions of the movement and passed away in 2004 (with persistent though unverified theories attributing his death to poisoning or killing). Meanwhile, the popularity of Hamas surged in Gaza and increasingly in the West Bank. As the peace process proved challenging, it was an underlying factor sustaining the Second Intifada in 2000, which lasted until Sharon's unilateral withdrawal from Gaza. Just days before he was to initiate plans to a similar disengagement from the West Bank, Sharon suffered two strokes and fell somewhat mysteriously into a prolonged coma. And so, still another window of opportunity for peace was missed.

By then, neoconservatives had taken over the White House and used the terror attacks of 9/11 to begin a war against militant Islam around the world. Concurrently, Israel was led by the more militant right-wing Likud, which shunned any two-state solution. In the occupied territories, the Palestinian movement was shifting toward Hamas and Islamic resistance—thanks in part to the Netanyahu government.

Netanyahu, Hamas and Divide-and-Rule

When the peace process began in Oslo, the Izz al-Din al-Qassam Brigades of the restructured and reorganized Hamas mobilized their armed struggle. When the Oslo Accords were signed in the White House, Hamas launched its political office. The prosperous Gulf regimes, particularly Saudi Arabia, Kuwait and UAE, saw in Hamas a way to support Palestinians while keeping distance from the PLO. Arafat's miscalculation—his decision to support Iraq's invasion of Kuwait in August 1990—undermined his clout in the Gulf states. As Hamas intensified operations against Israelis in the late 1990s, including the first Hamas suicide bombings since 1993, Israel took its revenge instead on the Palestinian Authority (PA). Ironically, Israeli authorities tacitly supported the rise of Hamas, when their main antagonist was still the PLO. And so it was that PLO operatives in the occupied territories faced brutal repression, while the Islamists could operate in Gaza.

It was the old British divide-and-rule ploy with Israeli characteristics. Like the CIA, which had used the fedayeen against the Soviet Union in Afghanistan, Israelis thought they could exploit Islamists against the PLO.[36] But just as the U.S. did not anticipate Osama bin Laden's 9/11 terror attacks after Afghanistan, Israelis did not expect the hand they had fed with to be bitten.

Despite a long sentence, Sheikh Ahmed Yassin was released from Israeli prison in 1997 as part of a deal with Amman, following Mossad's failed assassination attempt of Hamas leader Khaled Mashal in Jordan. Netanyahu allowed the Hamas leader to return to Gaza as a hero in late 1997, relying on the Islamists to sabotage the Oslo Peace Accords. The rise of military action by the al-Qassam Brigades was "facilitated by the release of dozens of cadres who had been active in the Qassam Brigades from PA prisons in the West Bank and Gaza Strip. These cadres quickly set about preparing for a new phase of military action. In the West Bank, the recently freed Ibrahim Hamid helped to reconstitute military cells. Meanwhile, the Israeli occupation authorities released Salah Shehadeh, the founder of military action in Gaza."[37]

In Gaza, Yassin intensified attacks on Israel, including suicide bombings. Although he had survived a prior Israeli missile attack, in 2004 an Israeli helicopter gunship fired a missile at him after Fajr prayer in Gaza City. Condemned internationally, the brutal attack killed the wheelchair-ridden Yassin, his bodyguards and nine bystanders. Nonetheless, he had been far more pragmatic about Palestine than was generally acknowledged. As he once said,

We have to be realistic. We are talking about a homeland
that was stolen a long time ago in 1948 and again in 1967. My
generation today is telling the Israelis, "Let's solve this problem
now, on the basis of the 1967 borders. Let's end this conflict by
declaring a temporary ceasefire. Let's leave the bigger issue for
future generations to decide." The Palestinians will decide in the
future about the nature of relations with Israel, but it must be a
democratic decision.[38]

After Yassin's massacre, over 200,000 Palestinians attended his funeral
procession. The effect of the assassination was precisely the reverse of that
Israel had hoped for. It strengthened Hamas, broadened its base and hardened
its stance. To Netanyahu's Likud, which saw Hamas mainly as an instrument
to undermine the PLO, that was irrelevant. As he had said to Likud's Knesset
members as recently as March 2019, "anyone who wants to thwart the establishment of a Palestinian state has to support bolstering Hamas and transferring money to Hamas. This is part of our strategy: to isolate the Palestinians
in Gaza from the Palestinians in the West Bank."[39]

Hamas was manna to Netanyahu. But it did not come from heaven.
Netanyahu stirred the turmoil through intermediaries, delivering hundreds
of millions of dollars of covert financial aid to Hamas, while his cabinet
looked the other way. The lives lost in suicide attacks in Israel and the far
greater numbers of Palestinians killed by Israelis served the bigger cause of
the Greater Israel.

TOWARD THE ENDGAME

Democracy Under Attack

Despite Sharon's unilateral disengagement from the Gaza Strip in 2005,
Israel continued to control its airspace, territorial waters and the movement
of goods and people in and out of Gaza. Hence, the status of Israel as nonetheless effectively an occupation power continued, in view of the UN and
international watchdogs. That said, the withdrawal did set the stage for the
first Palestinian election in a decade.

The original election had taken place in 1996, when the peace process
still fueled the PLO's predominance, while its main adversary, Hamas,
refused to participate, due to the former's "unacceptable negotiations and
compromises" with Israel. Postponed for years as a result of disagreements

between the two adversaries and the Second Intifada, the elections took place
in 2006. The results reflected the new facts on the ground. In the 2006 legislative elections held in the Palestinian territories—that is, the West Bank,
including East Jerusalem, and the Gaza Strip, which have been occupied by
Israel since 1967—Hamas, under the name "Change and Reform," won a
clear majority in all occupied Palestinian territories, capturing over 44 percent
of the vote as opposed to 41 percent by the ruling Fatah, or 76 of 132 seats
in the Palestinian Legislative Council (PLC), the unicameral legislature
of the Palestinian Authority. That was enough to run the government
without forging a coalition. Besides Rafah, Hamas predominated in Gaza.
Importantly, except for Tulkarm, Jenin and Bethlehem, it also controlled

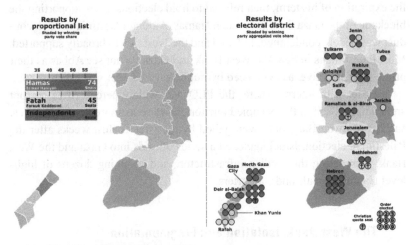

most of the West Bank (Figure 8-2).

Figure 8-2   2006 Palestinian Legislative Election
Source: Al Jazeera (January 2006)

Before the 2006 elections, Israel had been concerned that Hamas might
win enough seats to gain a foothold in the Palestinian leadership. However,
U.S. president George W. Bush was reluctant to exclude Hamas from the
electoral process. Associating democracy with the West, Bush presumed that
democratic elections would result in a pro-Western government. Moreover,
Arafat's successor Mahmoud Abbas felt confident that Fatah would win the
election. As a net consequence, Hamas's triumph "was seen as an affront to
the central premise of the Bush administration's policy in the Middle East."[40]
The result was a triple-whammy. Israel felt vindicated, the U.S. humiliated,
and the EU lost.

As Ismail Haniyeh, the political leader of Hamas, prepared to take power in all the occupied territories where it now predominated in both the West Bank and the Gaza Strip, it quickly became clear that the West supported democracy, but only if elections result in an outcome that is in the interest of the West. Hamas's triumph wasn't a part of that picture. Following the crackdown by Hamas's leadership on Fatah, which had not taken its electoral defeat easily, Israel and the Middle East Quartet—the U.S., Russia, UN and EU—introduced economic sanctions against the Palestinian Authority, Hamas's parliamentarians and Palestinian territories. Since then, no new Palestinian elections have been held.

After January 2009, the PLO's Mahmoud Abbas stayed president after the expiration of his term, then refused to hold elections, even supporting the blockade of the Gaza Strip to weaken Hamas. Among Palestinians, such conduct was widely condemned. In Israel and the West, it was broadly supported. Most Palestinians in both the West Bank and Gaza do not see Abbas as their prime representative, as evidenced by public surveys ever since then.

Beset with internal strife, the PLO was widely perceived as corrupt and compromised in the occupied territories, while its more popular figures, such as Marwan Barghouti, were jailed by the Israelis. Just weeks after the Palestinian election, Israel launched a series of raids into Gaza and the West Bank, hammering the civilian infrastructure and detaining dozens of high-level Hamas officials and supporters.

The West Bank: Isolation and Fragmentation

Following the occupation of the West Bank in the 1967 War, Israel adopted an Open Bridges policy, aiming to maintain mobility and exchange with Jordan. Defense Minister Moshe Dayan hoped to exploit partial integration as leverage in future talks. Since then, partial integration has been replaced by isolation and fragmentation.

The Separation Wall is usually associated with the Second Intifada and the Likud. In fact, the idea of a physical barrier between the Israelis and the Palestinians was first introduced by Prime Minister Rabin in 1992 after the killing of an Israeli teenage girl in Jerusalem. Rabin sought to suppress violence from spreading to major Israeli cities. With Gaza in turmoil in late 1994, Rabin said that "we have to decide on separation as a philosophy. There has to be a clear border."[41] What he likely meant was an effective border that would be secure and internationally recognized as *de jure*.

And so, in parallel with the peace process and in contradiction to any spirit of it, the first sections of the Wall were built. After Rabin's assassination, subsequent governments implemented more systematic construction plans, though not without substantial delays. In efforts to legitimize the Wall, Israeli governments have credited it for the decline in suicide bombings and other Palestinian intrusions. By contrast, Israeli security agencies attribute the decline of the attacks to increased pursuit of Palestinian militants by the Israeli army and intelligence, Hamas's increased political activity, and a truce among Palestinian militant groups in the occupied territories.[42]

Today, the length of Israel's Separation Wall in the West Bank amounts to more than 708 kilometers. That is more than twice the length of the border between the Israel-controlled West Bank and Jordan's East Bank. The Wall's purpose is to provide "a response to the threats posed to the state of Israel and protect its population from the threat of terror and criminal activity." Some parts comprise up to 9 meters of high concrete wall, and heaps of barbed wire, while others feature a multi-layered fence system with intrusion detection equipment.[43] Moreover, the Wall itself contributed to the continuing Israeli land grab in the occupied territories. It does not run along the Green Line, or the internationally recognized 1967 boundary. A whopping 85 percent of the Wall falls *within* the West Bank, encroaching on Palestinian lands (Figure 8-3a).

Figure 8-3   Isolation and Fragmentation

(a) The 2020 Separation Wall   **(b) Israeli Checkpoints**

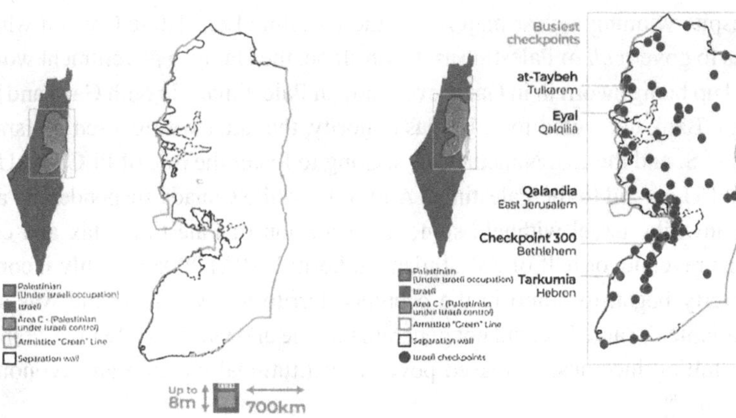

Source: Al Jazeera

Palestinians see the Wall as a reflection of Israeli apartheid. If the pre-1977 occupation encouraged partial integration, the Wall promotes partial disintegration that has reduced Palestinians' economic, social and political freedoms, caused losses of land, caused challenges in accessing medical and educational services in Israel, restricted access to water sources, and had devastating economic effects. It has turned Palestinian mobility within and out of the territories into an hours-long humiliating journey. The Kafkaesque system of surveillance, control and suppression is the subject of Ameen Nayfeh's *200 Meters* (2020) which revolves around a Tulkarm family separated by the Israeli wall, and its absurd consequences. Already in 2004, the International Court of Justice (ICJ) found, in its advisory opinion, that the barrier violates international law and should be torn down. Unsurprisingly, the non-binding opinion was ignored. By 2013, the World Bank estimated that the Wall, coupled with "checkpoints and movement permits," caused up to $185 to $229 million in costs.[44] With constrained mobility within the territories and to Israel, many Palestinians rely on agriculture. Yet, the harm to the farming sector has had "drastic economic effects on the residents, whose economic situation is already very difficult, driving many families into poverty."[45] By the early 2020s, there were over 700 road obstacles across the West Bank, including 140 checkpoints, which severely limited mobility of some 70,000 Palestinians who had Israeli work permits but who had to get across these checkpoints in their daily commute (Figure 8-3b).

The Gaza Strip: From Economic Blockade to Devastation

The 2006 democratic election resulted in an odd stalemate paralysis. Despite winning a clear majority to the Palestine Legislative Council which was to govern *all* of Palestine as it then stood, the Haniyeh government would end up being sworn in in Gaza, even though Palestinians in both Gaza and the West Bank had voted for a Hamas majority, the latter was ignored by Israel, the U.S. and the EU. Nonetheless, seeking to foster the role of PLO, the U.S. and EU cut aid to the Palestinian Authority, while Canada suspended its aid. Meanwhile, Israel withheld some $475 million of Palestinian tax and customs revenue, or half of Palestinian Authority's (PA) 2005 monthly income. Poverty began to climb in the occupied territories. Whatever aid was still available, it came late, did not generate income and was less effective. Hence, the falling incomes, increased poverty, institutional collapse and economic decline.[46]

With the economic dead-end and political in-fighting, the friction between Fatah and Hamas burst into an open military conflict in June 2007. Following Hamas's takeover of Gaza from Fatah, Israel and the U.S. imposed a ground, air, and maritime blockade, and announced it would allow only humanitarian supplies into the Strip. Meanwhile, some sanctions were lifted on the West Bank to boost Fatah's lingering regime. After the U.S. ended its 15-month economic and political boycott of the Ramallah-based PA, it kept the Hamas-led Gaza under sanctions and blockade. The EU followed in its footprints while Israel finally transferred hundreds of millions of dollars in tax revenues it had seized to Abbas, not to Hamas, the clear winner of the second Palestinian elections. The new round of divide-and-rule was all in the name of promoting freedom and democracy.

Foreshadowing the Gaza War of 2023–2024 when Israeli leaders implausibly insisted their objective was to destroy Hamas while causing minimal damage to the civilian population, Israeli authorities in 2008 maintained that the Gaza blockade was necessary to weaken the ruling Hamas militant group, whereas Palestinian civilians were not targeted. What actually happened was very different—as intended. Israel's blockade was a *deliberate* attempt to push the area's economy "to the brink of collapse," according to a U.S. diplomatic cable released by Wikileaks. In other words, not only Israel but the United States understood that the policy was taking a heavy toll on the area's civilian population. Behind the façade, the Bush administration was colluding with Israel, while Israeli officials repeatedly told American diplomats outright that the embargo sought to damage the Gazan economy:

> Israeli officials have confirmed to Embassy officials on multiple occasions that they intend to keep the Gazan economy functioning at the lowest level possible consistent with avoiding a humanitarian crisis....
>
> As part of their overall embargo plan against Gaza, Israeli officials have confirmed ... on multiple occasions that they intend to keep the Gazan economy on the brink of collapse without quite pushing it over the edge....
>
> Gaza should receive just enough money for the basic needs of the population but ... is not interested in returning the Gazan economy to a state of normal commerce and business.[47]

It was these ruthless decisions that set the stage to Israel's genocidal atrocities in Gaza 15 years later, and to U.S. complicity in the massacres. The objectives were reminiscent of those of Imperial Britain in India in the late 19th century and again in 1943, causing famines in Bengal in which millions perished. Furthermore, that economic blockade was augmented by physical destruction and devastation, or what Israel called Operation Cast Lead, also known as the Gaza Massacre (2008–2009). The three-week armed conflict between Israel and Hamas caused a drastic humanitarian crisis and degradation of infrastructure and basic services.

Hamas's Armed Struggle, Tunnels and Missiles

In November 2012, the state of Palestine was tacitly recognized by the UN General Assembly with the status of a non-member observer state, perceived as a step towards the recognition of Palestinian statehood. "The moment has arrived for the world to say clearly: enough of aggression, settlements and occupation," Palestinian President Abbas said. But he warned that "the window of opportunity is narrowing and time is quickly running out."[48]

What complicated the status quo was the issue of contested representation. While Hamas had triumphed in the democratic elections, Fatah leaders, who were supported by the West, continued to speak in the name of the Palestinian Authority. Meanwhile, armed resistance was escalating and Israel's countermeasures grew increasingly lethal and disproportionate. In brief, there was a stark disconnect between the world of ostensible diplomacy and the world of effective realities.

Hamas's leadership was dispersed between three geographical areas: the West Bank, the Gaza Strip, and exile communities, largely in Jordan, Lebanon, and Syria. With some 30,000 troops, its military capacity—the Qassam Brigades—was developing rapidly. Hundreds of Hamas cadres underwent military training in Iran via Damascus. Weapons shipments reached Gaza via land from Sudanese ports to the Egyptian Sinai, entering Gaza through tunnels and via sea, with smuggled arms arriving by boat to the Gaza coast or via Sinai to the Strip through tunnels. Despite Israeli restrictions, the Hamas confrontations (2008–2009, 2012, 2014) indicated the Brigades were "developing missiles, launchers, explosive devices, and drones that are more accurate, longer-range, and more capable of impacting the occupation forces' fortifications." By the 2014 War—that is, a decade before October 7—the range of these rockets already covered most of Israel.[49] In addition to the Qassam missiles, Hamas was developing explosive devices, hand grenades and drones. The idea of manufacturing unmanned aircraft to carry out intelligence and combat missions dated back to 2006.

Initially, the Hamas tunnels grew from smuggling tunnels connecting the Gaza Strip to Egypt at least since the early 1980s to a tunnels network, with the rise of the hard-right and pro-settler Likud coalitions in Israel. Israel's anti-tunnel efforts had already intensified during the Second Intifada, when the IDF launched numerous raids to prevent the Palestinian use of underground warfare by destroying over 100 tunnels by June 2004.[50] Another momentum ensued in 2007, when the tunnels again grew dramatically not just in size, but in sophistication and in strategic importance, as the net effect of the Egyptian and Israeli economic blockade to crush the Hamas electoral triumph in the Palestinian election.

During the 2014 confrontation between Hamas and Israel, Hamas is said for the first time to have used a large network of combat tunnels. Two years later, Ismail Haniyeh, the Hamas leader, suggested that the tunnel network was twice the size of the 75-mile-long complex of Củ Chi tunnels built by the Việt Cộng during the Vietnam war.[51] After the 2014 Gaza War, Israel discovered 62 miles or 100 km of tunnels, one-third of which accessed Israeli territory. The tunnel system ran beneath many Gazan towns and cities, including Khan Yunis, Jabalia and the Shati refugee camp.[52] Tunnel warfare was not about "terrorism" as it was designated in the U.S. and Israel, in an effort to deflect the popular support behind these battles. In the postwar era, it has been one of the most lethal and complicated forms of Palestinian exercise of its right to military resistance, marking particularly U.S. efforts to defeat the struggles for national sovereignty and insurgencies in Vietnam, Afghanistan, and Iraq.

In the U.S. post-9/11 wars in particular, urban warfare has brought tunnel warfare back into the spotlight, as these two combat modes are likely to continue to merge and influence each other.[53] Coupled with numerous attacks launched from the sea, Qassam's use of tunnels had dramatically changed the rules of engagement a decade prior to October 7. After the 2021 Gaza War, Hamas leader Yahya Sinwar said Hamas has 500 km of tunnels in the Gaza Strip and that only five percent of the tunnels had been damaged in the clashes. Emulating Hezbollah in southern Lebanon, Hamas deployed Iranian and North Korean knowledge to build its tunnels as well. Nicknamed "Hamas Metro" by the IDF, it is significantly smaller than Hezbollah's underground Inter-Regional Metro but has proved equally lethal. Like Hezbollah tunnels, the Hamas Metro features underground command and control rooms, weapons and supply depots, field clinics and specified designated shafts used to fire missiles of all types. The hidden and camouflaged shafts cannot be detected above ground. And like Hezbollah, Hamas used Iranian and North Korean knowledge, and likely Hezbollah's extensive experience as well, to build its tunnels.

Oddly enough, despite years of time to prepare for the tunnel threat, Israel's hard-right leaders ignored it. At the eve of October 7, both the army and the civilians were effectively unprepared for the looming blow. Israel was prepared, but for the wrong war. It focused on land and air, even cyber defenses; but not underground war. The threats were known, but they were neglected and downplayed. Several years before October 7, Maj. Gen. (res.) Itzhak Brik had warned that—thanks to the patient strategy of Iran and its "proxies," including Hezbollah and Hamas, in Israel's proximity—there were probably more than 200,000 rockets and missiles, large and small, aimed at

Israel's major population centers and strategic targets, and at vital defense and civilian infrastructure (energy systems, natural resources, electricity, fuel, natural gas, water, transportation, communication, public health and safety institutions). "The hazard posed by these missiles has turned Israel into the world's most threatened country," Brik argued.

Yet over the decade in which this terrifying deployment took shape around us, Israel's political and security leadership fell into a deep sleep. It did not prepare either the Israeli Defense Forces or the country in general for the threat emerging before our very eyes—neither in terms of offensive capabilities, nor in terms of the ability to prepare and protect the home front to absorb thousands of missiles strikes every day.[54]

Brik and other like-minded military strategists urged Israelis not to believe the IDF's triumphant media briefings and mainstream analysts' misguided reassurances. The two were not preparing Israelis for a glorious victory, but distracting them from the impending failure. There was no solution to Hamas' tunnels.[55]

And Hamas had still other assets. In July 2024, Hamas dossiers detailing intel on thousands of Israeli soldiers and their families was leaked online. The purpose of the reports, which had circulated online for a number of months, was illustrated by the cover title: "As revenge for the killers of [the] children of Gaza." The dark web was rife with Israelis' data that could be used for attacks.[56]

Calm Before the Storm: The 2018–2019 Gaza Border Protests

The irony is that, despite all the tough rhetoric from the inception of its creation, Hamas has several times signaled efforts at peace talks. After his proposals for long-term ceasefire agreements were rejected by Israel, Sheikh Ahmed Yassin, the founder of Hamas, had already gone further in an interview by the Egyptian *al-Ahram* newspaper in 1999: "We have to be realistic. We are talking about a homeland that was stolen a long time ago in 1948 and again in 1967. My generation today is telling the Israelis, 'Let's solve this problem now, on the basis of the 1967 borders.'"[57] As Yassin's proposal was ignored by Israel, the Second Intifada, a more violent one, began, and the wheelchair-bound Yassin himself was assassinated after morning prayers in Gaza by the Hellfire missiles of an Israeli AH-64 Apache helicopter gunship. By 2014, Israel's state comptroller released a report criticizing the then-Netanyahu cabinet citing the total absence of consideration of political options as alternatives to Israel's 2014 Gaza War. By March 2017, Israel's former head of Mossad, Efraim Halevy, wrote that it was "time for Israel to talk to Hamas."[58] Typically, he published the piece in the *Washington Post*, not in Israeli media, to push for a U.S. intervention. But neither Netanyahu nor Trump had any interest in peace talks. After several rejected proposals, Hamas rewrote its charter just weeks later to accept a Palestinian state in the 1967 borders without recognizing Israel.[59] The move was historically reminiscent with the one Arafat's PLO used in the late 1980s to open a dialogue with the U.S. and foster a more peaceful solution. To Netanyahu, the new charter was just an antisemitic ploy, while the Trump administration neglected still another historical opportunity.

As Palestinian leaders got nowhere given Israel's reluctance to engage in peace talks, ordinary Palestinians tried something new and untested—Gandhian non-violence.

With the continued economic blockade of Gaza, new Israeli wars, continued settlement expansion in the West Bank and requisite military raids, settler violence and lingering uprisings, things went from bad to ugly in December 2017, when President Trump announced that the U.S. recognized Jerusalem as the capital of Israel.[60] Trump's declaration was followed by an avalanche of demonstrations throughout the West Bank and Gaza against the blockade of Gaza and the moving of the U.S. Embassy in Israel from Tel Aviv to Jerusalem. Opposition to such moves united Fatah and Hamas. By early 2021, the two also agreed to jointly conduct the long-overdue elections in Palestine, in accordance with the Oslo Accords. But neither popular unity nor democratic elections in Palestine were in line with the U.S.-Israeli agenda. The former threatened to strengthen Palestinian resistance, which both wanted to weaken, and the latter risked bridging the divide between Fatah and Hamas which they tacitly encouraged. Hence, the severe pressure by both the U.S. and Israel, which eventually led Abbas to cancel the planned election.[61]

Meanwhile, there was a spontaneous effort to engage in mass protests, but this time largely in line with the Gandhian principles of non-violence. From March 2018 to December 2019, a series of Friday demonstrations—the Great March of Return—took off in Gaza, near the Israel border. The demonstrators protested against Israel's land, air and sea blockade of the Gaza Strip and the Trump administration's recognition of Jerusalem as the capital of Israel. They demanded that the Palestinian refugees should be allowed to return to the lands they were displaced from in present-day Israel. Though smaller groups occasionally tried to breach the fence throwing stones and

Molotov cocktails, the protests were by far mostly peaceful. Israelis shot and killed 223 Palestinians, most of whom were walking peacefully towards the Gaza barrier fencing them in, putting paid to the notion of using Gandhian protest tactics against Israel. According to Israeli rights organizations every fourth was a child; only every seventh was deemed a "militant." An estimated 9,000–13,000 Palestinians were injured. On the Israeli side, just half a dozen were injured.[62]

There is a historical precedent to these protests and the use of disproportionate power to crush them. After the Nazi *Kristallnacht* in November 1938, Mahatma Gandhi urged German Jews to adopt his Satyagraha, peaceful protest, to fight the Nazi violence. In the consequent debate,[63] Jewish theologian-philosopher Martin Buber, an early supporter of a binational state in Palestine and admirer of Gandhi, observed that if the Jews would lie down in front of the Nazi tanks, the German tanks would simply drive over them. Traditional pacifism did not work with such abuse of power. Distressingly, the lesson that the Israeli government conveyed to the Gazans during the protests of 2018–19 was that peaceful non-violence would not work with Israel. The takeaway: there was no alternative to violence.

PALESTINIAN ECONOMIC DEVASTATION

The Fall of Gaza, Stagnation of the West Bank

In 1994, amid the peace talks in Oslo, Palestinian per capita income, adjusted to purchasing power parity, was barely 15 percent of the Israeli level. The hope that peace would bring stability and raise living standards in the West Bank and Gaza died with the assassination of Prime Minister Yitzhak Rabin by a far-right religious law student. This triggered still another cycle of devastation. In 2017, Palestinian per capita income had climbed to 16.2 percent relative to the Israeli level. After more than two decades, that's an advance of barely 1 percentage point. So, what about the progress in the ensuing five years? Despite all the hoopla by the Trump and Biden administrations that the Middle East was at the "cusp of peace and prosperity," Palestinian per capita income had fallen further behind. Even before October 7, it was 12.9 percent compared to the Israeli level. That's over 2 percentage points lower than where it was *over two decades ago*. In brief, the idea that Palestinians were somehow benefiting from Israeli domination was just cynical misinformation. Living standards in the West Bank and Gaza were falling relative to Israeli levels, while those in Gaza were plunging relative to the West Bank (Figure 8-4).

Figure 8-4   Economic Divergence

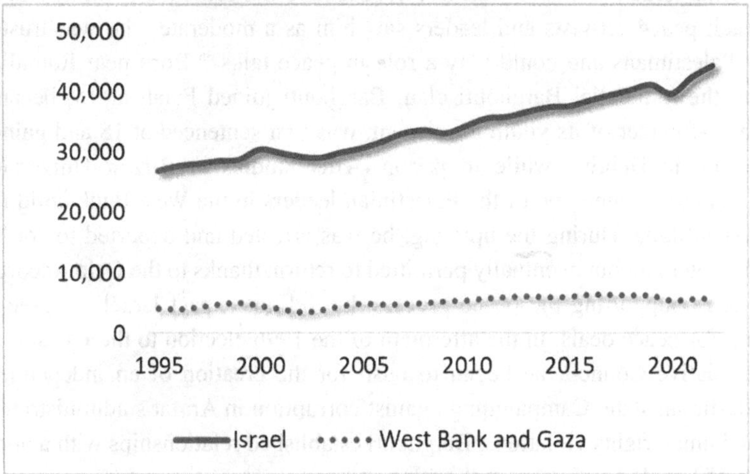

Per capita income in Israel and West Bank/Gaza, 1995–2023
GDP Per Capita PPP: Israel Vs West Bank and Gaza (1995–2023).
Source: Data from World Bank

It could have been otherwise. The past three decades have left the West Bank and the Gaza Strip a pale shadow of what they *could* have been, if the peace process had been a given a chance. Under an economic blockade and systemic de-modernization by Israel *and* the United States and European Union, living standards in Gaza have dramatically fallen behind those in the West Bank. In 2022, over a year before October 7, per capita income in the West Bank was *four times higher* than in Gaza., while unemployment and poverty rates were far higher in Gaza as well.[64] This largely reflects the Israeli blockade of Gaza following the political takeover by Hamas in 2007 and the recurring wars. It was compounded by donor financing that had shifted toward the Palestinian Authority, which controlled the West Bank. Ominously, just a month before October 7, even the IMF issued a warning about the dire outlook for the Palestinian economy.[65]

Struggle for Palestinian Leadership: Barghouti, Abbas, Haniyeh and Sinwar

Even today, Marwan Barghouti, who may be the most popular among Palestinians along with Ismail Haniyeh, remains convicted of killing and injuring Israeli civilians, with five consecutive life sentences. Unlike Likud, Israeli peace activists and leaders saw him as a moderate who was trusted by Palestinians and could play a role in peace talks.[66] Born near Ramallah into the influential Barghouti clan, Barghouti joined Fatah at 15, became the co-founder of its youth movement, was first sentenced at 18 and gained fluency in Hebrew while in prison. After studies in Birzeit University, Barghouti became one of the Palestinian leaders in the West Bank amid the First Intifada. During the uprising, he was arrested and deported to Jordan for incitement but eventually permitted to return, thanks to the Oslo Accords. Though supporting the peace process, he did not expect Israel to agree to land-for-peace deals. In the aftermath of the 1996 election to the Palestinian Legislative Council, he began to push for the creation of an independent Palestinian state. Campaigning against corruption in Arafat's administration and human rights violations, Barghouti established relationships with a number of Israeli politicians, authorities and members of the peace movement. When the Camp David summit failed to bring about the peace deal, Barghouti became disillusioned.[67]

Providing tacit support to Hamas, Netanyahu cabinets' strategic goal became to undermine PLO's popular young leaders such as Barghouti, while supporting their older, compromised incumbents. Hence, too, the first Israeli effort to blow Barghouti to pieces in a missile attack. After that failure, the IDF chose the lesser evil by arresting Barghouti. It hoped to neutralize the leader Western media called "Palestine's Nelson Mandela." Following Israel's devastating 2014 Gaza War, Barghouti urged the Palestinian Authority to immediately end security cooperation with Israel and called for a Third Intifada against Israel. Today, he is seen as a viable Palestinian leader even by the European Union. Unlike any other incumbent Palestinian leader, Barghouti could bring Palestinian people together in an enduring peace deal, a process that China's intermediation made more viable in summer 2024.[68] Yet, most Likud supporters and far-right and ultra-religious leaders do not want a unified Palestinian front. In February 2024, amid the Israel-Hamas war, when Hamas called for Barghouti's release, he was placed in solitary confinement. A month later, he was reportedly beaten by prison guards.[69] That doesn't bode well for his future.

Mahmoud Abbas had been among the first to call for talks with moderate Israelis in the late 1970s. Unlike many of his peers, he focused mainly on diplomacy rather than militancy and was the PLO signatory on the 1993 Oslo Accord.[70] When Israel and the U.S. refused to deal with Arafat in the early 2000s, Abbas became the preferred "anti-Barghouti" alternative. Largely for the same reason, his pragmatism attracted the ire of Palestinian Islamic Jihad and Hamas. After Hamas's 2006 electoral win, the antipathy turned into open warfare in Gaza, and Gaza fell under Hamas while the PLO sought to keep Hamas out of the West Bank. In return, Hamas operatives and many Palestinians saw Abbas, and particularly his two wealthy sons, as corrupt and complicit in Israeli suppression.[71] By contrast, Israelis continued to suspect Abbas's credibility and commitment to cooperation. Despite his old age, Abbas was reluctant to renounce his role as the head of PA. To him, Palestinian statehood was too close to give in.

Ismail Haniyeh, born in Al-Shati refugee camp in Gaza in the early 1960s, represented Hamas's political bureau. His parents had fled from their home near the present-day Israeli city of Ashkelon amid the 1948 War. After working in Israel and his studies, he led the students' Muslim Brotherhood. A midfielder in the Islamic Association soccer team, he was a team player. When he graduated, the First Intifada began. And when the Israelis killed Ahmed Yassin, Haniyeh had been in charge of his office. He has survived Israeli efforts to eliminate him and the Hamas leadership, leading the movement from the Gaza election win to 2017. When he was elected chairman of Hamas's political bureau, he relocated to Qatar. After October 7, an Israeli airstrike killed 14 members of his family. Subsequently, another half a dozen of his kin has been killed.[72]

In Gaza, Yahya Sinwar, the mastermind of the October 7 offensive, has become a key decisionmaker, even as he operates from somewhere in the Gaza tunnel infrastructure. Like him, Sinwar's family fled from Ashkelon. Coming of age in Khan Yunis, he had first been arrested by the Israelis in the early 1980s. In the subsequent years, he responded to brutality with brutality. When Sinwar took over Hamas in 2017, he cultivated collaborative ties with Hezbollah and Iran. With an Israeli bounty on his head, he was in constant movement hiding in tunnel networks. He knew his time was likely to come – just as he knew others were waiting for their turn to continue his work for the liberation of Palestine. Like many other Hamas leaders, he had spent much of his life in Israeli prisons, which fostered his character, persistence and brutality, and resilience.[73]

Despite the calls by Israel and the West for a "reformed PLO leadership," most Palestinians support the Hamas offensive, even at the risk of their lives. In a hypothetical presidential competition between Barghouti and Mahmoud Abbas from Fatah, and Hamas's political leader Ismail Haniyeh, the U.S.-led

West supported mainly the ailing, almost 90-year-old Abbas, while Haniyeh was considered a fugitive terrorist and Barghouti a jailed murderer. But as May 2024 polls suggest, Palestinians supported Barghouti (42%), by a wide margin, against Haniyeh (27%), and Abbas (5%) (Figure 8-5).

Figure 8-5 Palestinian Leaders

(a) Organizational Leaders: Barghouti, Haniyeh, and Abbas

(b) Factional Leaders: Dahlan, Sinwar, Barghouti, Mustafa

(c) Palestinian Polls

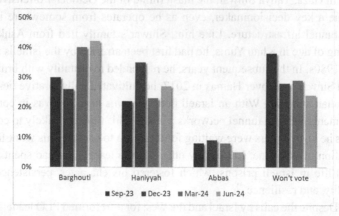

"In a competition between Marwan Barghouti, Ismail Haniyeh, and Mahmoud Abbas, you would vote for:"

Source: (a+b) Wikimedia Commons; (c) "Public Opinion Poll No (91)." The Palestinian Center for Policy and Survey Research (PSR), March 20, 2024, p 17.

When the Palestinians were asked to name their preferred candidate—whether representing an organization or a faction—to be president of the PA after Abbas. Marwan Barghouti came first, with 27% of the public mentioning his name, followed by Ismail Haniyeh (14%), Mohammed Dahlan (8%), Yahya Sinwar (7%), and Mustafa Barghouti (2%). The poll also showed that satisfaction with Hamas's performance was increasing (75%), followed by Sinwar (65%), as opposed to Fatah (24%), Abbas (10%) and new prime minister Muhammad Mustafa (9%).[74]

The former World Bank economist Mustafa enjoyed the support of Abbas and the West, but not of most Palestinians. A longtime supporter of non-violent resistance and a two-state solution, Mustafa Barghouti is also a veteran critic of the PLO and PA for corruption. A veteran Fatah leader, Mohammed Dahlan had a central role in the Oslo talks and the head of Gazan security forces, but he has been criticized for corruption and blamed by Abbas for Arafat's poisoning. The U.S. sees Dahlan as a potential future replacement for Palestinian President Abbas.[75]

As far as Palestinians are concerned, any just representation of Palestine would have to include both Hamas and PA, both Marwan Barghouti and Ismail Haniyeh. Abbas is widely rejected. By contrast, Dahlan and Mustafa were the likely potential successors to Abbas.

The Beijing Declaration: Unifying the Palestinian Front

On July 23, 2024, altogether 14 Palestinian factions, including rivals Hamas and Fatah, agreed to end their divisions and form an interim national unity government, thanks to Beijing's intermediation (Figure 8-6). After a breakthrough deal between Saudi Arabia and Iran, it was China's second major contribution to peace in the Middle East. In the past, Egypt and other Arab countries had tried but failed to reconcile the two leading factions. The Beijing meeting took place in tandem with efforts by international mediators to achieve a ceasefire deal in Israel's Gaza War. Thanks to the Beijing Declaration, Palestinians were now in a position to heal and unify their ranks, if the national unity government prevailed.[76]

Despite the calls by Israel and the U.S. for a "reformed PLO leadership," most Palestinians in both Gaza and the West Bank continued to support the Hamas offensive, even at the risk of their lives. Their first choice is peace. But in light of Israel's obliteration war in Gaza and its *de facto* effort to annex the West Bank, they believed only armed struggle could save them from ethnic expulsions, which the members of Israel's Messianic far-right pledged almost daily.

Figure 8-6   Beijing Declaration: Palestinian Signatories

Source: Al Jazeera, Wikimedia Commons; author

In the foreseeable future, a Palestinian national unity government is critical. After the obliteration of Gaza, it must pick up the pieces from the ruble and ruin, manage the affairs of Palestinians in Gaza and the West Bank, oversee reconstruction and prepare conditions for elections. But would the Fatah-Hamas deal prevail? Skeptics expected the West to kill any effort at a national unity government, as it has done since the onset of the peace process in the 1990s.

In the months prior to the Beijing Declaration, Chinese officials had ramped up advocacy for the Palestinians in international forums, calling for a larger-scale Israeli-Palestinian peace conference and a timetable to implement a two-state solution. The alternative was lethal: regional escalation of Israel's obliteration war from Gaza and the West Bank to Hezbollah in southern Lebanon, or a fatal confrontation with Iran.

Just days after the Beijing Declaration, Israel delivered its responses by assassinating Fuad Shukr, Hezbollah's top military commander, in a strike on Beirut's southern suburbs. Worse, right thereafter, in a stunning development that threatened to reshape the 9-month war in Gaza, multiple Iranian television channels reported the assassination of Hamas political leader Ismail Haniyeh in Teheran, while he was a guest of the government, attending the inauguration of Iran's new president. In just a few days, the Netanyahu War cabinet had managed to drastically up the stakes of re-escalation of hostilities against Gaza, southern Lebanon and Iran.

The Costs of Occupation

By the end of May 2024, Spain, Norway and Ireland had formally recognized a Palestinian state in a coordinated effort by the three Western European nations to add international pressure on Israel over the civilian death toll and humanitarian crisis in the Gaza Strip. The goal was "to help Israelis and Palestinians achieve peace," said Spanish Prime Minister Pedro Sánchez.[77] The Netanyahu cabinet did not share that view. Israel's foreign minister Israel Katz recalled Israel's ambassadors to Oslo, Dublin and Madrid and ordered a formal reprimand to the three countries' envoys in Israel. The White House said President Joe Biden "believes a Palestinian state should be realized through direct negotiations between the parties, not through unilateral recognition."[78]

That sounded good in theory. In practice, such talks were not viable as long as Israel and the U.S. insisted that Hamas, which Gaza considered its democratically-elected representative, and PLO's Barghouti, who was supported by most Palestinians, could have no role at the negotiating table. It was comparable to a situation in which the Palestinians would express their sincere desire for direct talks, as long as Netanyahu would first be executed and Biden confined to jail.

Behind the facades of these "peace process games," the costs of the occupation continued to soar and the devastation to spread.

Over the period from 2000 to the present, Israel, the United States and their allies have turned a developing regional economy into a fragmented, grim enclave of diminished hope. Between 2000–2002, the adverse impact was dramatic as the West Bank's already fragile and vulnerable economy contracted by a whopping one third. After the Second Intifada, Israel enforced stringent measures in the occupied Palestinian territories. With the economic blockade of Gaza, the overall impact was disastrous for some 15 years, long before October 7.

Even with high dependence on employment in Israel and its settlements, the West Bank's regional economy had experienced two decades of jobless growth, fostering an average of 18 percent unemployment from 1995 until 2020. Without jobs in Israel and in the settlements, its unemployment rate could have been 16 percentage points higher and at par with the extremely high rate in Gaza. The cumulative economic cost of the stricter Israeli measures imposed in the period 2000–2019 is estimated at *four and a half times the size of the West Bank regional economy* in 2019.[79] Since the GDP for the West Bank and Gaza in 2019 was $17.1 billion, the sum total implied is more than $75 billion.

In terms of poverty alleviation, the cost due to occupation is also substantial, typically with the poorer segments of the population disproportionately affected. Without the tighter Israeli restrictions imposed after the Second Intifada, the 2004 poverty rate in the West Bank could have been less than 12 percent, or only one third of the observed more than 35 per cent. As a result, the real minimum cost of eliminating poverty in the West Bank soared from $73 million (constant 2015 U.S. dollars) prior to the second uprising (1998) to $356 million in 2004, and to $428 million in 2007. Based on more than half a decade of factual evidence on the costs of occupation, the UNCTAD conclusion prior to October 7th was unambiguous:

> The evolving and cumulative cost of occupation cannot be reversed without ending the occupation, in line with relevant United Nations resolutions. All mobility restrictions in the occupied Palestinian territory need to be lifted, and the contiguity of its constituent parts, including East Jerusalem, needs to be re-established. Palestinian public and private operators should be allowed to function in Area C, which represents at least 60 per cent of the West Bank. The United Nations maintains its position that a lasting and comprehensive peace can only be achieved through a negotiated two-state solution.[80]

After half a century of elevated exploitation, Israel's occupation turned a potentially vibrant developing regional economy into a fragmented ghetto of devastation, particularly in the past quarter of a century. And that was *before* the destruction and chaos unleashed after October 7.

By 2021, Gaza's economy was on the verge of collapse, while the ailing West Bank was struggling, even before the global pandemic.[81] It was then that the Strip and the West Bank suffered the COVID-19 nightmare. Despite intimate proximity, Israel and Palestine were worlds apart during the pandemic. It was a crisis, but also an opportunity; a historical moment to build new bridges, by support and sympathy. Yet, that's precisely what did not happen. While Israel was praised as a vaccination leader, Palestinians were forced to adopt crude survival measures and endure economic privations. Worse, Israel utilized the pandemic to tighten surveillance and control over Palestine and the Palestinians. Still worse, by undermining access to infrastructure vital for water, sanitation and hygiene, the occupying power left Palestinians vulnerable amid the crisis of a century.[82]

The lesson was not lost in the West Bank and the Gaza Strip. Over half a century of PLO's armed struggle wasn't enough. The peace process didn't work. Decades of Hamas's harsh battles didn't do the job. Efforts to reason fostered a "normalization" process that effectively ignored Palestinians. Peaceful Gandhian non-violence went nowhere. Pandemics that should have united the colonizer and the colonized in compassion, left the most vulnerable at the mercy of Malthusian "war, famine and disease."

So, perhaps the lesson was to hit back so hard that it could no longer be ignored.

FANTASIES AND REALITIES

By February 2024, Ambassador Lana Nusseibeh of the United Arab Emirates (UAE) stressed there must be an "irreversible progression" toward a two-state solution in the Arab-Israeli conflict before there is a regional commitment to the reconstruction of Gaza. Reflecting broader sentiments in the region, the UAE's UN ambassador added that "we cannot keep refunding and then see everything that we have built destroyed."[83] The patience of the Gulf countries, including the signatories of the Abraham Accords, was at its end. So, Saudi Arabia, the UAE, Qatar, Jordan, Egypt, and the Palestinian Authority agreed to move forward with plans to present a joint political vision for rehabilitating the Gaza Strip and establishing a Palestinian state after the Israel-Hamas war. To preempt such schemes, PM Netanyahu's office presented its own vision of "Gaza 2035" in May.

The Gaza 2035 Plan: A Hard Sell of Historical Magnitude

Purporting to revitalize the Gazan economy, Gaza 2035 depicted the existing Gaza as an "Iranian outpost" that "thwarts any future hope for the Palestinian people." Highlighting the Strip's role in the historical Baghdad-Egypt trade routes and Yemen-Europe trade routes, it proposed to reintegrate Gaza into the regional economy.[84] In most corners of the world, it is peace and stability that have brought about economic development and prosperity. The Gaza 2035 plan turned the building blocks upside down. Attract the massive infrastructure investment, and peace and development will follow. The precondition for progress was blindness to realities. Deflecting responsibility for historical economic and human costs onto Iran, the Plan sought to encourage American support for the destruction of the Iranian nuclear facilities, while the Gulf states and Egypt would pressure Israel's adjacent neighbors to join the scheme (Figure 8-7).

Figure 8-7   The Gaza 2035 Plan

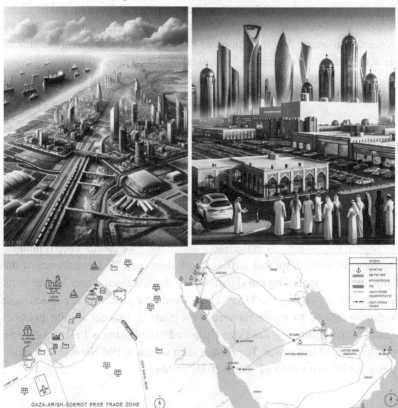

GAZA-ARISH-SDEROT FREE TRADE ZONE

Source: "Gaza 2035," Israel PMO, March 2024.

Rebuilding Gaza would proceed in three steps. During the first year of the humanitarian aid phase, Israel would create safe areas free of Hamas control, starting in the north and spreading toward south. A coalition of Arab countries—that is, Saudi Arabia, UAE, Egypt, Bahrain, Jordan, and Morocco—would apportion and supervise humanitarian aid in these areas that Gazans would run under the supervision of the Arab states. Israel could still premise humanitarian aid on the supposed extermination of Hamas. During the second phase of 5 to 10 years of rehabilitation, Israel would take over the responsibility for security, while the Arab coalition would create a multilateral Gaza Rehabilitation Authority (GRA), to oversee the reconstruction and the Strip's finances. The GRA would be run by Palestinians who will be responsible for the safe areas, in coordination with a "Gaza Marshall Plan" coupled with deradicalization. The GRA wouldn't include members of

Hamas, which Israel wants gone, or the Palestinian Authority (PA), which Israel wants to be "reformed." In Israel's view, Palestinians cannot rule; they have to be ruled.[85] Self-governance would follow in the long-term, but Israel would retain the right to act against "security threats." Eventually, the Palestinians would manage Gaza independently and join the Abraham Accords.

The Plan downplayed the true costs of the massive but necessary rehabilitation of the ecological devastation.

The key to Gaza 2035 was massive infrastructure investment, which would be the adjacent Arab countries' responsibility. Why would they be interested? The wider regional plan was to ramp up mega-projects such as NEOM in Saudi Arabia, Saudi Crown Prince Mohammed bin Salman's zero-carbon city called "The Line," located at the northern tip of the Red Sea. Gaza would serve as a vital entrepôt for the export of Gazan goods, Saudi oil and other raw materials from the Gulf. A massive free trade zone (FTZ) would couple Sderot-Gaza-El Arish, allowing Israel, Gaza, and Egypt to take advantage of the location jointly. In the process, Israel would get a prime seat in the regional mega-hub. The newly discovered gas fields north of Gaza, whose planned use Israel would control in the name of security, would help support the burgeoning industry. The idea of solar energy fields to be built in Sinai along with desalination plants was a carrot to Egypt, which Israel's Gaza War had alienated. The goal was to make the FTZ into a competitor to cheap Chinese manufacturing in electric vehicles.

But here is the reality: while the Gulf states and Israel's Arab neighbors had benefited billions of dollars in development, thanks to Chinese initiatives, they had lost hundreds of thousands of lives and hundreds of billions of dollars in economic costs, due to the U.S. post-9/11 wars. The Biden White House made U.S. participation in the regional security arrangements dependent on the role of Saudi Arabia and the Arab coalition in its front against China. In the Middle East, that made little sense. China was the greatest buyer of oil and natural gas and a major trade partner of the regional states, which benefited from the New Silk Road investments by China.[86]

For Israel, the major advantage, other than security in the south, was normalization with Saudi Arabia. Major advantages for the Gulf states included the NATO-like defense pacts with the U.S. and unfettered access to Gaza's Mediterranean ports through railways and pipelines. The assumption was that if such an intervention would prove successful in Gaza, it could be repeated in Yemen, Syria, and Lebanon. In other words, the ultimate objective of the plan was to absorb the Axis of Resistance in the region by extending infrastructure investments and U.S. military domination across the region.

After decades of devastation by the collusion of U.S. and Israeli military might, it was a hard sell of historical magnitude in the region.

So, if these were the Israeli aspirational fantasies of Gaza in mid-2024, what were the realities?

The Realities of Gaza

In the Gaza Strip, the scale, impact and pace of destruction proved overwhelming in a matter of days. It was far worse than anything seen since Dresden or Rotterdam during World War II, when some 25,000 homes were demolished in each city. In Gaza 70,000 housing units—three times more—were destroyed and over 290,000 partially damaged. Due to the destructive power of weapons in the early 21st century, calls have increased for a new war-related concept to be included among the list of crimes against humanity; that is, domicide (Figure 8-8).

Domicide ("domicile" plus "-cide") means the deliberate and systematic destruction of homes and basic infrastructure in a manner that makes them uninhabitable.[87]

From October 2023 to late May 2024, the number of lost buildings in North Gaza and Gaza City doubled to 70–75 percent of the total. In the south, Deir El-Balah and Khan Younis lost more than half of the total and even Rafah in the Egyptian border suffered almost 40 percent of the total.

As the evidence of the domicide continued to accumulate, concerns in the Israeli government grew accordingly. If domicide would be acknowledged as a crime against humanity, "international legal authorities will no longer be looking to accuse a brigade commander of destroying a neighborhood but will aim the arrows of prosecution at the leadership of the army or of the state."[88] By the end of summer 2024, Gaza had been reduced to an estimated 42 million tonnes of rubble. Removal will take years and cost as much as $700 million. The challenge will be complicated by unexploded bombs, dangerous contaminants and human remains under the ruins. Preliminary estimates suggest that rebuilding Gaza could cost far more than $80 billion, when taking into account hidden expenditures, such as the long-term impact of a labor market devastated by death, injury and trauma.[89] Meanwhile, food shortages, crumbling infrastructure, a failing medical system, flowing sewage, waste buildup, and summer heat had turned Gaza's humanitarian crisis into a serious epidemiological threat, due to polio and feared outbreaks of hepatitis A, infectious diseases, intestinal disease and respiratory diseases like measles and whooping cough.

Figure 8-8   The Gazan Domicide

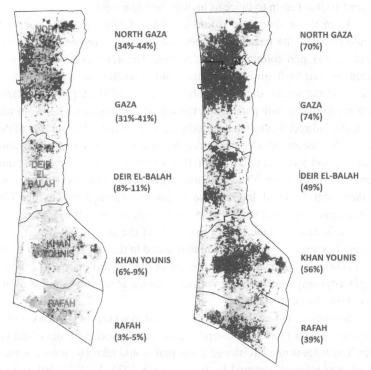

NORTH GAZA (34%-44%)	NORTH GAZA (70%)
GAZA (31%-41%)	GAZA (74%)
DEIR EL-BALAH (8%-11%)	DEIR EL-BALAH (49%)
KHAN YOUNIS (6%-9%)	KHAN YOUNIS (56%)
RAFAH (3%-5%)	RAFAH (39%)

(*Left*) 16%–21% or up to 61,200 buildings in the Gaza Strip were likely damaged between October 7 and November 10, 2023. (*Right*) 58% of buildings were likely damaged or destroyed by May 20, 2024.

Analysis based on Sentinel-1 radar, OpenStreetMap and Microsoft building footprint data.

Source: Jamon Van Den Hoek PhD, Corey Scher; conflict-damage.org

By then, there were more than 40,000 Palestinian fatalities, while over 92,400 had been injured. The number of unaccounted amounted to 10,000–20,000; many of whom were believed to be buried under the rubble. In other words, official death tolls are deceptive. Furthermore, the epidemiological threats are likely to further deplete the Palestinian population, thanks to the Malthusian "ministers of depopulation." Some 495,000 Palestinian faced catastrophic levels of food insecurity and nearly 2.0 million or 90 percent of Gaza had been displaced. Thousands remained missing in Gaza and hundreds in the West Bank.[90] However, the final count would be far worse. By May 2024, some 30 percent of the deaths in Gaza were *un*identified. Since two of every five buildings in the Gaza Strip had been destroyed in the first quarter of 2024, the number of bodies still buried in the rubble was estimated to exceed 10,000 (or up to twice as high by late summer).[91]

Even if the Gaza War would end immediately, many *indirect* deaths would ensue in the near future from causes such as reproductive, communicable, and non-communicable diseases. The total death toll would be expected to be high, given the intensity of the conflict; destroyed health-care infrastructure; severe shortages of food, water, and shelter; the population's inability to flee to safe places; and the loss of funding to UNRWA. In recent conflicts, indirect deaths have varied around 3–15 times the number of direct deaths. So, assuming a conservative downside risk of 4:1, direct deaths of 38,000 could translate to about 186,000, or 7.9 percent of the entire population in the Gaza Strip.[92] The conclusive final count depends on the accuracy of the model deployed. In Gaza, the 4:1 ratio was comparable to East Timor, where armed struggle endured 25 years lasting until 1999. At the other extreme is Sierra Leone, where over half of the population was displaced during its violent 11-year war, which resulted in the staggering ratio of 16:1. In the Gaza Strip, more than 80 percent of the 2.4 million people had been displaced; many, several times. As a net effect, a 16:1 ratio would translate to up to 608,000 indirect deaths.

Moreover, the economic costs will be staggering. UN Development Program (UNDP) has used several scenarios to assess the costs of the Gaza War. The longest one envisioned a war that would take 10 months or longer, which had already occurred by mid-summer 2024. In 2023, Palestine lost almost 9 percent of its GDP and was estimated to lose another 26 percent in 2024. If the war continued longer, the GDP loss in the ongoing year could exceed 29 percent.[93] The ecological costs of the Israeli obliteration will haunt Gaza for years to come. By late April 2024, Israel's devastation had created 37m tons of debris. That's an average of 300kg of rubble a square meter of land. Worse, these piles and heaps of debris and wreckage were laced with unexploded bombs, which could take up to 15 years of extensive work to remove, assuming the availability of 100 trucks on a daily basis.[94] Taking into consideration the fact that on average about 10 percent of weapons fail to detonate when fired, huge demining teams would be warranted, for years.

Usually, war is defined as a violent conflict between states or nations. *The Gaza War was not a war.* It was collective punishment compounded by genocidal atrocities and massive displacement; that is, obliteration. Obliteration can be defined as total destruction of something so that nothing remains of it. In this sense, it implies abject devastation. Another sense of the term suggests a more figurative eradication for removing something from memory. Hence, the obliteration of museums, libraries, institutions of learning, arts and culture. Finally, obliteration also refers to a concerted effort to reverse development and thus entirely undermine all economic progress. In this sense, it is synonymous with de-development and un-development. In Gaza, for the first time in history, de-development went hand in hand with the most advanced destructive technology, fueled by artificial intelligence. The strategic purpose was abject obliteration.

In this view, the Gaza 2035 plan was an aspirational PR ploy designed to blur the realities of devastation in the Strip.

Chapter 9

FROM ULTRA-APARTHEID
TO GENOCIDE

"The violence and the destruction in Palestine and Israel did not begin on October 7, 2023," said South Africa's justice minister, Ronald Lamola, in the packed, ornate hall of the Peace Palace in The Hague. "The Palestinians have experienced systematic oppression and violence for the last 76 years." As the opening arguments got underway in January 2024, South Africa made its case against Israel at the International Court of Justice (ICJ). Lamola acknowledged the brutal horrors committed by Hamas on October 7, but made it very clear that "no attack, no matter how severe, can justify this violence."

South Africa's justice minister was seconded by attorney Adila Hassim whose arguments centered on Israel's genocidal intent. "Genocides are never declared in advance," Hassim said to the judges and audience in the packed, ornate hall of the Peace Palace (Figure 9-1). He continued, "but this court has the benefit of the past 13 weeks of evidence that shows incontrovertibly a pattern of conduct and related intention that justifies as a plausible claim of genocidal acts."[1]

Had Israel had something to do with South Africa's apartheid? Why was a country that was born in the shadow of the Holocaust accused of genocide? And were the atrocities in Gaza a genocide, or just a "nightmare"[2] as some Western observers argued?

Figure 9-1 Justice in The Hague

South Africa's genocide case against Israel at the International Court of Justice, The Hague on Friday 12 January 2024.

Source: Wikimedia Commons

THE GENESIS OF ULTRA-APARTHEID IN PALESTINE

Apartheid South Africa and Zionism

Racial discrimination against black people in South Africa began with large-scale colonization over four centuries ago. By the early 19th century, Imperial Britain and British settlers began to colonize the frontier regions. The new colonial rulers built on prior legislation, which led to a divide between the English common law and the existing law in South Africa and its legislative autonomy. It was this divide that enabled the sanctification of racial discrimination and the ensuing inequality. In 1833, the Slavery Abolition Act eradicated slavery across the British Empire. Ostensibly, it should have superseded prior legislation in South Africa, but it didn't. To comply with the Slavery Abolition Act, the South African legislation was broadened to include Ordinance 1 (1835) and Ordinance 3 (1848), respectively, giving rise to an indenture system and other legislation limiting the freedoms of unskilled workers, and between "races."[3]

As industrial takeoffs accelerated in in the late 19th century Europe, South Africa industrialized on the back of mining and infrastructure

288 THE FALL OF ISRAEL

investment. The Mineral Revolution was a revolution by, of and for the white colonial settlers. Following the European powers' scramble for Africa, the Anglo-Zulu War and two Boer Wars, the Boer republics were incorporated into the British Empire. Meanwhile, South Africa began to introduce more segregationist policies towards non-whites. The goals were reflected by the Afrikaans term *apartheid* ("separateness," or "apart-hood").[4]

After the 1948 all-white elections, the National Party enforced white supremacy and racial separation. When the South African republic was established in 1961, it withdrew from the British Commonwealth, with black opposition driven underground and eventually into guerrilla warfare. A year later, the UN General Assembly passed resolution 1761 in response to South Africa's racist apartheid policies. The resolution requested member states to break off diplomatic relations and to cease trading with South Africa (arms exports in particular), and to deny passage to South African ships and aircraft. It also set up a special committee against apartheid calling for a boycott of South Africa. Though initially ignored by the West, it would find allies in the West, including the UK-based Anti-Apartheid Movement. By 1973, the UN General Assembly had agreed on the International Convention on the Suppression and Punishment of the Crime of Apartheid (ICSPCA). In the process, "apartheid was declared to be a crime against humanity, with a scope that went far beyond South Africa."[5] Popular uprisings ensued in black and colored townships in 1976 and 1985. However, it wasn't until the mid-1990s that the last vestiges of apartheid were abolished, and a new constitution was promulgated into law enshrining democratic equality: one person, one vote.

Similarly, in the Middle East, the occupied territories controlled by Israel saw two major uprisings, or intifadas. Yet, the end of Cold War did not result in the abolishment of Israeli apartheid, despite increasing efforts and obvious parallels. Following the Yom Kippur War, the UN General Assembly's Resolution 3236 recognized the Palestinian people's right to self-determination, inviting the Palestine Liberation Organization (PLO) to participate in international diplomacy. The oil crisis in 1975 paved the way to resolution 3379, which stated that "Zionism is a form of racism and racial discrimination." In the UN, Israeli ambassador Chaim Herzog, the future president of Israel, stated the decision was "devoid of any moral or legal value."[6] Then, he tore the resolution in half. Like biblical sins, these sentiments tend to diffuse over generations. Since 2021, Herzog's son Isaac has been Israel's president. After the Hamas offensive, he said there were "no innocent civilians in Gaza" charging its residents of collective responsibility.[7] And when South Africa's genocide launched its case against Israel in the ICJ, he declared it a "blood libel" against Jews[8] and later would go on to shred the UN Charter with a paper shredder in protest of the UN General Assembly vote to boost the status of the Palestinian mission.

At the end of the Cold War, Resolution 3379 was revoked by the UN Resolution 46/86 introduced by U.S. President George H. W. Bush. "To equate Zionism with racism is to reject Israel itself, a member of good standing of the United Nations," Bush said. "By repealing this resolution unconditionally, the United Nations will enhance its credibility and serve the cause of peace."[9] And yet, for all practical purposes, the result has been precisely the reverse. It contributed to Israel's sense of impunity, the rise of its Messianic far-right and the obliteration of Gaza.

But Bush's UN address wasn't just about Zionism and racism. It was about wheeling and dealing. The revocation was Israel's precondition for participation in the Madrid Conference of 1991, which paved the way to the Oslo Accords.

Ultra-Apartheid in Israel

A decade prior to October 7, former Israeli security chief Yuval Diskin warned that "in the occupied territories all the conditions are there for an explosion."[10] In 1993, PM Yitzhak Rabin had entrusted him to establish ties with the Palestinian security forces as part of the Oslo Accord. Subsequently, he served prime ministers Ariel Sharon, Ehud Olmert and Benjamin Netanyahu as the director of internal security, Shin Bet (2005–2011). By the early 2010s, Diskin was harshly criticizing Netanyahu's leadership in Israel, warning that "alongside the State of Israel, a *de facto* State of Judea is being formed" in which "there are different standards, different value systems, different attitudes towards democracy, and two legal systems." Meanwhile, the settlers' and their sympathizers' "anarchistic, anti-state, violent, and racist ideologies are treated tolerantly by the Israeli legal and judicial system."[11]

Israeli apartheid was no allegation. It was daily reality for most Palestinians in the occupied territories, just as it once was for blacks in South Africa.

The apartheid association between South Africa and Israel is not something new, however. After the UN vote on apartheid, South Africa's prime minister Hendrik Verwoerd was particularly annoyed by Israel's vote against South Africa's segregation. "Israel is not consistent in its new anti-apartheid attitude," Verwoerd lamented. "They took Israel away from the Arabs after the Arabs lived there for a thousand years. In that, I agree with them. Israel, like South Africa, is an apartheid state."[12] Of course, Verwoerd was making a political point, but the argument had validity. In effect, martial law had been imposed on the Arab citizens of Israel from 1948 to 1966, and it continues to be intermittently enforced to the present. Effectively, military government imposed various restrictions on Palestinians, including on their mobility, with security checkpoints set up to enforce these permits allowing entry. Meanwhile, requests for government services for Arab Israelis were directed to military courts instead of civil courts.[13] These measures were subsequently adopted in the occupied territories, particularly the West Bank.

Subsequently, the UN adopted the (non-binding) Declaration on the Elimination of All Forms of Racial Discrimination, sponsored mainly by the Arab League, the Soviet bloc and many new African states. From the nationalist Palestine Liberation Organization (PLO) to the Marxist Popular Front for the Liberation of Palestine (PFLP), Palestinian resistance intensified following the Six-Day War. Its messaging linked Israel with apartheid.

However, there were several major differences with classic apartheid as enforced in South Africa and that of Israel in the occupied territories. Sociologist Elia Zureik, one of the first to use the term "apartheid" in scholarly scrutiny of the situation of Israeli Arabs and of Palestinians in occupied territories, argued that irrespective of size, "the dominant segment is the 'majority' as it has the organized power to initiate policies to dominate, exploit and control the 'minority.' Such policies can be formal and legal as in South African apartheid, or informal and semi-legal as in Israel's treatment of the (Israeli Arabs) Palestinians, and the Palestinians under occupation in the West Bank and Gaza."[14]

Second, in apartheid South Africa, a white minority dominated a black minority, whereas in Israel a Jewish majority discriminates against a Palestinian minority, keeping the Palestinians under military occupation. Moreover, under Israeli occupation, apartheid rests on ethnic identification. In South Africa, the objective of apartheid was to sustain a system of racial segregation in which one group is deprived of political and civil rights, exploiting the low-cost labor of the under-privileged group for the benefit of the privileged group. This is reminiscent of Israeli occupation from 1967 to the First Intifada in 1987 and, to a lesser degree, the present West Bank, whereas Israel has regarded the Gaza Strip as a "hostile state" since 2007.

But what makes Israeli apartheid different is its ultimate purpose: ethnic cleansing. This kind of apartheid is not just instrumental. Nor is its goal just to exploit low-cost labor. Since the UN Partition Plan, its ultimate purpose has been the Judaization of Arab Palestine. Apartheid is an instrument to that final goal. Apartheid South Africa was willing to live with segregated, exploited and underprivileged black people. Since the late 1970s, the Israeli system has slowly but surely sought to use segregation as an interim instrument to ethnically cleanse the occupied territories through Palestinian displacement, dispossession and, when regarded as necessary, abject devastation. In this sense, it is not just apartheid. It is *ultra*-apartheid. In Latin, ultra means "beyond, or "on the far side of." In this sense of going beyond the norm, ultra-apartheid officially shuns classic apartheid, yet benefits from the low-cost labor of the under-privileged group while ultimately seeking its obliteration.

Segregation: From South Africa to Israel

When I first visited the West Bank and the Gaza Strip in summer 1973 at the eve of the Yom Kippur War, senior Israeli army officers in both territories spoke excitedly about the prospects for Palestinian autonomy and progress toward a lasting peace. By contrast, Palestinians compared such proposals to South Africa's efforts to set aside segregated black territories, or Bantustans, which seemed to undermine any prospects of enduring peace.

Israel's occupied territories and South Africa's Bantustans share similar fragmented enclaves, separated or walled areas, discontiguous parts, and highly restricted mobility, with economic inequality and social segregation as the common denominators. Typically, when the UN voted against apartheid in South Africa, only a few countries – the United States, Western Europe and Japan and their client states – voted against the resolution or abstained. Similarly, four decades later, when the UN voted for the Palestinian statehood, the configuration was the same, with the decolonized Global South supporting the resolution (Figure 9-2).

Figure 9-2   Segregation: From South Africa to Israel

(a) South Africa's Pre-1996 Bantustan   Israel's Occupied Territories

(b) Against Apartheid System

Apartheid Convention, 1973   International recognition of Palestine, 2012

Sources: (a) Creative Commons Attribution-Share Alike 4.0 International license; UN Office for Coordination of Humanitarian Affairs. (b) Creative Commons Attribution-Share Alike 3.0 International license; Wikimedia Commons (ICSPA-members)

Under the Likud and Netanyahu governments, Israel has been morphing into an apartheid state with its occupied territories into Palestinian Bantustans. In 2021, Human Rights Watch warned that Israel had crossed the apartheid threshold.[15] A year later, Israel's former attorney general, Michael Ben-Yair, said that "my country has sunk to such political and moral depths that it is now an apartheid regime." In August 2023, the former speaker of the Israeli parliament, Avraham Burg, and the renowned Israeli historian, Benny Morris, were among more than 2,000 Israeli and American public figures who signed a public statement declaring that "Palestinians live under a regime of apartheid."[16]

And a month before the October 7 offensive, Mossad's ex-chief Tamir Pardo said that Israel's mechanisms for controlling the Palestinians, from restrictions on movement to placing them under military law while Jewish settlers in the occupied territories are governed by civilian courts, matched those of the old South Africa. "There is an apartheid state here," since "two people are judged under two legal systems."[17] The violent far-right does not disagree. Nor does it consider racism something negative. Promoting merciless anti-Arab violence in the West Bank, Meir Ettinger, the grandson of rabbi Meir Kahane, calls openly for the demolition of the secular state of Israel and the creation of a fundamentalist Torah state. His grandfather pushed for racist legislation, which conservative politicians then likened to the Nuremberg Laws. Ettinger readily acknowledges that "the system of laws he envisions fairly closely resembles the laws of the Third Reich. 'We are racists. Period.'"[18]

Yet, the Democratic Biden administration continued to build on Trump's Middle East policies, which effectively ignored the Palestinians' apartheid nightmare

How did the Palestinian stagnation compare with that of black South Africans in the days of institutionalized racism? "I have witnessed the systemic humiliation of Palestinian men, women and children by members of the Israeli security forces," Desmond Tutu, the Nobel Peace laureate, said in a statement. "Their humiliation is familiar to all black South Africans who were corralled and harassed and insulted and assaulted by the security forces of the apartheid government."[19] The simple answer is that South African blacks who lived under apartheid had more to hope for than Palestinians. During the period of apartheid (1948–94), the per capita income of South Africa's blacks relative to that of the whites climbed from 8.6 to 13.5 percent. Compared with South African blacks, the Palestinians' starting point relative to the Israelis was almost twice as high in percentage terms. But even before October 7, 2023, it had plunged to a lower level than that of South Africa's blacks at the close of the apartheid era. This reversal took place under the watch of the Trump and Biden administrations (Figure 9-3).

Figure 9-3   Incomes of South African Blacks and Palestinians

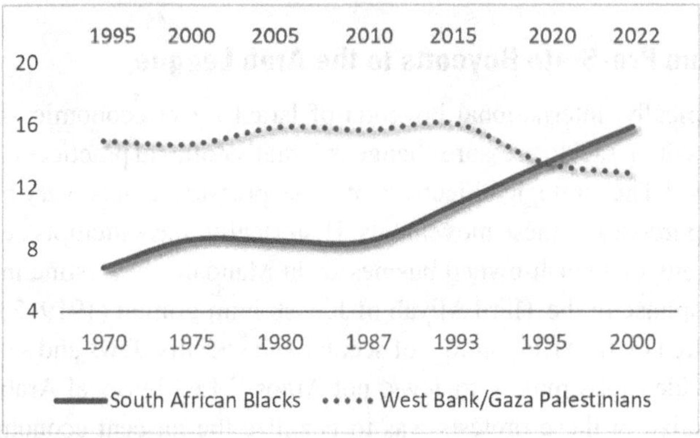

(*Blue line*) Black per capita incomes relative to white apartheid South Africa (1970–2000). (*Red line*) Palestinian per capita incomes in West Bank/Gaza relative to Israelis (1995–2022)

Source: Data from World Development Indicators (World Bank)

Until October 7, Israeli per capita income (which disguises its extreme polarization) has been at par with that of the UK and higher than in Italy, in absolute terms. By contrast, Palestinian per capita income was estimated at $5,700, which is lower than that of Nigeria and Cambodia; barely ahead of Myanmar. Israelis and Palestinians live in close physical proximity to each other, but inhabit two different worlds, as comfortably as if London were next to Yangon.

Ultra-apartheid is among the nightmares that paved the way to the genocidal atrocities.

INTERNATIONAL BOYCOTT EFFORTS

After a month of the Gaza War, a new app surfaced calling on people not to buy products from companies that support Israel. It offered to "simplify the process of scanning barcodes and searching for products that is listed for the boycott movement. It makes your shopping goes easily when you know what brand you don't want to buy, and the app helps you with that, just scan the product and the app will tell you."[20] By April 2024, there had been over 1 million downloads of the app on Google Play alone. The boycott app reflected broadening discontent not just against Israel's method of war, but against its continued occupation of Palestinian territories. Efforts at international boycott of Israel are as old as the country itself. With the obliteration of Gaza, the boycott efforts broadened and deepened.

From Pre-State Boycotts to the Arab League

Typically, international boycotts of Israel reject economic and social dealings with Israel to pressure change in Israel's political practices and policy measures.[21] The strategic objectives of these pressure groups vary according to basic purposes of these movements. Historically, such attempts began with the boycotts of Jewish-owned businesses in Mandatory Palestine in 1922. It was a response to the Third Aliyah of Jewish immigration (1919–23), which was marked by the rising inflow of secular and socialist Jews and settlements that provided jobs mainly to Jews, not Arabs.[22] Led by local Arab leaders, the objective in these protests was to penalize the nascent economy of the pre-state Yishuv. With the subsequent immigration waves, communal strife escalated, resulting in calls for broader boycotts by local Arab political, business and labor leaders.

In the aftermath of the great immigration waves of the Fifth and Sixth Aliyah (1924–29, 1929–39), coupled with illegal immigration since the rise of Nazism and Fascism in Europe, local calls for boycott grew louder as they became promoted by the Arab League, the regional group of the Arab world. At its inception, it had half a dozen member states; today, there are 22 members. Founded in December 1945, the League's boycott of Israel began amid its inception and before Israel formally came into existence. The objective was to isolate Israel economically in the region, in order to penalize its economic and military capabilities.

As these efforts seemed to intensify in parallel with the OPEC oil embargo in the mid-1970s, the first cracks in the boycott front surfaced with Israel's peace treaty with Egypt (1979 and Jordan (1994), and the onset of the peace process. With the Oslo Accords, the Gulf countries (GCC) ended their participation in the Arab boycott, though noting that full elimination of the boycott depended on the evolution of the peace process and cooperation between Israel and Arab countries. In 1998, Gil Feiler could still start his *From Boycott to Economic Cooperation* with confidence: "The longest functioning example of economic sanctions being applied against any state – the Arab boycott of Israel – appears to be disintegrating. The boycott was always an integral part of the Arab-Israeli conflict, and, at least until the 1970s, was designed to help bring about the demise of Israel as a state."[23]

In the Middle East, optimism can be fleeting. When the peace process hit the wall, wars in Gaza, uprisings in the West Bank and Hezbollah rockets from southern Lebanon escalated; so did new efforts to boycott Israel. They faced high hurdles, however. One of them was Citibank, just as it had once been in South Africa.

In early March 2023, two Israeli brothers were killed in a terror attack near Huwara, a Palestinian town. In a matter of hours, violent settlers rampaged through the town, set homes and cars on fire, killed one Palestinian and injured several badly. Minister Smotrich attributed the blame to Huwara, a "village that is beset by terror" adding, "the village of Huwara needs to be wiped out." He suggested "the state of Israel should do it."[24] In brief, the way to suppress terrorism was to level Arab villages terrorized by the settlements. Days later, Citibank leadership held cordial meetings in public with Smotrich to calm the markets after the adverse impact of the Silicon Valley Bank and Signature Bank collapses. By contrast, the International Monetary Fund, the U.S. Chamber of Commerce and others refused to meet Smotrich due to his pro-genocide statements. But Citi had no such compunction; it had a record of apartheid cooperation.

According to the standard story, Citibank re-entered South Africa in summer 1994 with a representative office that was converted to a full branch a year later. Since then, it grew to become the country's largest foreign bank and the sixth largest commercial bank.[25] But its earliest presence in South Africa went back to 1920 when National Bank of New York first opened an office in Capetown. In 1958 the bank opened for business in Johannesburg and remained active on the ground up until 1987 when Citicorp sold its South African subsidiary. Instead of withdrawing from the country amid international pressure, Citi was the last holdout. As the sole American bank with operations in South Africa, it served as a central symbol of U.S. involvement in apartheid. Though one of the original sponsors of the Sullivan Principles, a code of conduct for American companies in South Africa a decade before, Citi stayed. It ceased operations only days after the Ford Motor sold its South African operations. The withdrawal had nothing to do with the ethical principles Citi claimed to support. As the spokesman for Citicorp, the bank's corporate parent, said. "This was a business decision based on all the factors involved."[26]

As in South Africa in the past, Citibank is today heavily invested in Israel's infrastructure as the largest American banking institution in the country. In 2013, it launched the Citi Tel Aviv Accelerator to support and invest in Israeli start-ups specializing in financial tech, cybersecurity, and AI. It encouraged multinational corporations to "set up shop" in the Israeli market by providing connectivity and local presence. Supported by the Israel Innovation Authority, Citibank established Citi Innovation Labs in 2021 to leverage its position in the global financial markets in support of Israel's start-up sector. More recently, it has entered the lucrative U.S. military aid market, facilitating billions of dollars into Israeli military weapon funding. In 2023, Israel's Defense Ministry used Foreign Military Financing (FMF) from the U.S. to secure a loan from "a small consortium led by Citibank" that allowed for the purchase of F-35 fighter jets from Lockheed Martin, the U.S. defense contractor. Israel is responsible for paying interest on the loan using their national funds. U.S. Defense Department will repay Citibank directly for the loan, using the available and future-year Foreign Military Financing appropriations for Israel.

For Citi, the money was good and with the Hamas offensive business was booming. In South Africa, Citi had held its own until the eclipse of its apartheid. Why should Israel be any different? That's the challenge of international boycott movements in a nutshell.

Boycott, Divestment and Sanctions (BDS) movement

When anti-apartheid veterans met Palestinian activists at the 2001 World Conference Against Racism in South Africa, they proposed the kind of campaigns that had been deployed to defeat apartheid there. By 2005, several Palestinian civil society groups issued a "Call for BDS"; that is, a Boycott, Divestment and Sanctions (BDS) movement. The BDS movement called for internationally imposed "broad boycotts and divestment initiatives against Israel similar to those applied to South Africa in the apartheid era."[27]

The BDS movement was modeled after the British Anti-Apartheid Movement (1959–94). Associating their protests against Israel with the struggle of South Africans against apartheid, the BDS and other boycott movements sought international support for "non-violent punitive measures against Israel unless and until it changes its policies by ending its occupation and colonization of all Arab lands and dismantling the [Separation] Wall." It sought for "recognition of the fundamental rights of the Arab-Palestinian citizens of Israel to full equality." It appealed for "respecting, protecting and promoting the rights of Palestinian refugees to return to their homes and properties as stipulated in UN [General Assembly] resolution 194."[28] These three goals center on ending the occupation, and securing the rights of Israel's Arab-Palestinian citizens and Palestinian refugees' right of return. The first two paralleled the anti-apartheid struggle, the third one reached beyond it. Despite sympathy for the BDS movement, international critics focus mainly on the occupied territories, as evidenced by the 2015 European Commission's product-labeling notice, the UN Human Rights Council resolution focusing on a database of companies in these territories, the 2016 UN Security Council Resolution 334 to enforce the withdrawal of the settlements, and so on.[29]

Despite the rising popularity of the BDS movement and traditional forms of boycott efforts ranging from commercial relations and diplomatic ties to multilateral organizations, the economic effects have been marginal until recently. In 2015, a report by the think tank RAND estimated that an effective BDS campaign against Israel could cost the Israeli economy a cumulative $47 billion over a decade.[30] After being targeted by the BDS, many companies – Veolia, Orange, G4S, General Mills and CRH – have withdrawn from Israel. Furthermore, those companies that have stated their commitment to human rights – Siemens, Hewlett-Packard (HP), AXA, Puma, and Carrefour – have become increasing BDS targets, particularly in Europe. Already prior to October 7, BDS divestment campaigns have managed to force European private banks like Nordea and Danske Bank and billionaires such as Bill Gates and George Soros to sell their shareholdings in companies that are direct targets of BDS (Figure 9-4).

Figure 9-4   Guide to BDS Campaigns

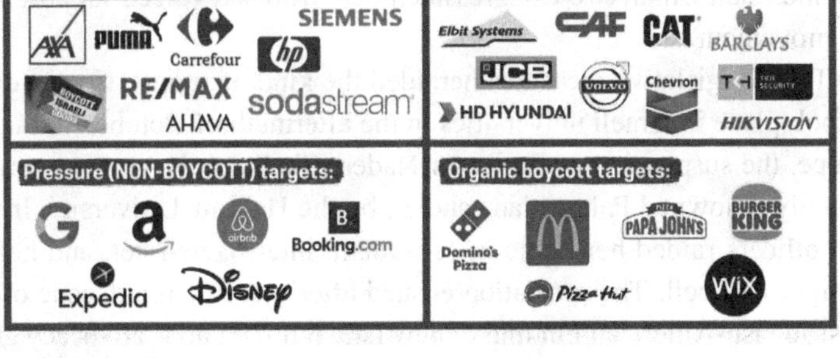

Source: BDS, Apr 23, 2024

During the Gaza War, social media sites, particularly X (formerly Twitter), TikTok, Facebook and others, featured users deploying the hashtag #BDSMovement, who are naming brands with ties to Israel and calling for boycotts: McDonald's was targeted after a location in Israel offered free food for the Israeli military, as were other global fast-food chains such as Domino's Pizza and Burger King. Some boycotted Starbucks after the company sued its labor union over a union social media account posting support for Palestinians. In March 2024, Starbucks' Middle East franchisee laid off roughly 10 percent or 2,000 workers at its restaurants throughout the region, grappling with boycotts of the brand over the Israel-Gaza war. Meanwhile, McDonald's announced that the boycott campaign had resulted in financial losses of approximately $7 billion. A month later, after months of dramatically declined revenues in the Middle East, the fast-food giant bought all 225 restaurants from its Israel franchise. It faced condemnation for providing free meals to the Israeli military, which was accused of engaging in war crimes against Palestinians in Gaza. Protests in the Middle East started in Lebanon and Egypt, spreading to Türkiye, Pakistan, Malaysia and other countries. Even 30 years of operations in Israel did not spare the brand.[31] McDonald's owns only a tenth of its outlets; it prefers franchises. For now, the umbrella brand distanced itself from its Israeli operation, perhaps hoping that the end of the war would result in "business as usual."

While the Palestinian-led BDS sees itself as a human rights movement, Israel has charged it with antisemitism, conflating it with anti-Zionism. Accordingly, the movement is one of the prime targets of the Israel lobby in the United States and Israel has spent millions of dollars to neutralize BDS and have it banned.[32] In 2016, Israel's Ministry of Strategic Affairs allocated some $100 million to oppose BDS-related activities.[33] A year later, the Knesset also passed a law allowing the government to block entry into the country of nonresidents calling for a boycott against Israel or Israelis in West Bank settlements, or persons who are associated with organizations that do so. In 2019, this law was used to deny entry to U.S. representatives Rashida Tlaib and Ilhan Omar, two Congressmembers who had voiced support for the BDS movement.[34]

These legislative measures heralded the kind of suppression of dissent that took place in Israeli universities in the aftermath of October 7. Take, for instance, the suspension of Professor Nadera Shalhoub Kevorkian, an internationally renowned Palestinian scholar, by the Hebrew University. In April 2024, officers raided her home in Jerusalem, interrogated her, and held her overnight in a cell. The escalation ensued after more than a decade of revisionist Jewish-American funding of new Israeli think tanks, advocacy groups and media that championed tougher measures against "leftists," "peaceniks" and other "self-hating Jews."[35] Since then, there has been increasing concern among progressive Jews in America that Israeli students are leading the censorship enterprise "at the forefront of Israeli McCarthyism."[36]

International University Protests against the Gaza War

In April 2024, genocidal atrocities in the Gaza Strip coupled with increasing suppression of dissent, even in academia. Protests spread rapidly onto university campuses in the United States and in a number of other countries, as a part of broader international protests against Israel's Gaza War. In the United States, the escalation began with an encampment protest at Columbia University, which called in the NYPD to suppress campus protests for the first time since the 1968 Vietnam demonstrations. These protests soon spread across several universities on the East Coast, while protest camps were erected on more than 40 campuses. An estimated 97 percent of the demonstrations were peaceful, whereas police responses were often characterized as disproportionate and violent.[37]

Following dramatic scenes involving protesters and police in U.S. colleges, a growing student movement to occupy university campuses expanded throughout the world. Among others, student groups in the UK, France, Canada, Netherlands and Australia erected "solidarity encampments," triggering a variety of responses from university authorities and local law enforcement. Similar movements were also seen in India, Mexico, Lebanon and other nations in the Global South.[38] Typically, the greatest concentration of the university protests took place in the West, particularly in those countries that supported Israel and its Gaza War, directly, indirectly and clandestinely (Figure 9-5).

In most U.S. protests, student demands mimicked those of the BDS movement, including severing financial ties to Israel. They targeted companies engaged in and profiting from the war, including U.S. tech giants like Google, Amazon and Microsoft. In many cases, students also demanded academic boycotts of higher-learning institutions in Israel and disclosure of investments. In particular, they wanted the termination of vendor contracts with active roles in the Israeli occupied territories and the Gaza War, including Cisco, Lockheed Martin, Caterpillar and General Electric.[39]

In 1968, student protests had had a hard impact on Columbia University, as applications, endowments, and grants plunged in the subsequent years. But the demonstrations did change Columbia's relationship with U.S. military, ending federal sponsorship of classified weapons research and severing ties

**Figure 9-5   2024 Protests against the
Gaza War on University Campuses**

Universities in the United States with Israel–Hamas war protests in April 2024. Columbia University is marked in red. Other colleges that had encampments are marked in green, and non-encampment protests are marked in blue.

Source: Wikimedia/OpenStreetMap

with the Institute for Defense Analyses (IDA), the university's interface with the U.S. military-industrial complex.[40] Distressingly, President Biden condemned the protests, calling them antisemitic while criticizing those who "don't understand what's going on with the Palestinians."[41] Among the protesters, the perception was that the president, "Genocide Joe" as they called him, was beholden to the sources of his campaign finance and effectively out of touch with the atrocities in the Gaza Strip and Israeli apartheid in the occupied territories.

What made these student protests very different from those of their predecessors was that they had no personal stakes in the issue and were acting out of purely moral concern. Furthermore, they featured both Palestinian and Jewish students. In the aftermath of October 7, progressive Jewish peace activists called for an immediate ceasefire and justice for Palestinians. Voicing sentiments reflecting those of the organization "Not in Our Name," they protested in sit-ins across America, including on Capitol Hill. To them, the essence of Judaism was social justice. Cognizant of the Jewish history of persecution, they refused to ignore its lessons. By their participation in these demonstrations, all students – Jews and non-Jews alike – risked their professional futures, missed graduation ceremonies and were often targeted by critics, media, and even violently by law enforcement agencies. Instead of being applauded for their civil courage and integrity, many were charged with incitement and antisemitism. The unspeakable implication was that they should have celebrated the perpetrators of genocidal atrocities and their co-perpetrators who were complicit in these crimes against humanity, as effectively were the bystanders who were looking the other way in order to appear neutral.

Israeli and International Companies in the Occupied Territories

In addition to those Israeli companies, defense contractors, financial institutions and universities that have been targeted in boycott and sanction campaigns for years, recent boycott efforts have increasingly centered on companies that play a critical role in the occupied territories, especially in the West Bank and East Jerusalem. Under international law, Israeli settlements, their maintenance and expansion are illegal activities, which give rise to individual criminal liability as war crimes and crimes against humanity under the Rome Statute of the International Criminal Court.

Israeli, European, and international business enterprises, operating with or providing services to Israeli settlements, play a critical role in the functioning, sustainability and expansion of illegal settlements. Since the late 2010s, the UN Human Rights Office of the High Commissioner (OHCHR) has used independent international fact-finding missions to investigate the implications of the Israeli settlements on the civil, political, economic, social and cultural rights of the Palestinian people throughout the occupied territories, including East Jerusalem. These reports do not cover all companies operating in the occupied territories. However, they do include the major ones that play the most critical roles (Figure 9-6).

The overwhelming majority of these firms are headquartered in Israel. There are more than 110 such companies. Since the first OHCHR report in 2020, some are no longer involved in the listed activities, such as General Mills and its Israeli subsidiary, which likely divested following a campaign to get the company to stop manufacturing its Pillsbury products on stolen Palestinian land. In addition to a broad variety of Israeli companies making money on the illicit territories, several international companies prevail in these areas, including Airbnb and Expedia (U.S.), Booking.com and Tahal Group (Netherlands), J.C. Bamford Excavators and Opodo (UK). Still others operate through their parent organizations, including Motorola and Booking Holdings (U.S.), Egis (France), and Altice (Luxembourg), and licensors or franchisors, such as Greenkote (UK).

Figure 9-6 Israeli and International Companies in the Occupied Territories

Companies in Settlements

A. Business enterprises no longer involved in listed activities:
Amnon Mesilot Ltd.
Ashtrom Properties Ltd
Avgol Industries 1953
Bank Otsar Ha-Hayal
Brand Industries Ltd.
Citadis Israel Ltd.
Darban Investments Ltd.
Energy Renewable Energies
General Mills Inc.
General Mills Israel
Indorama Ventures P.C.L.
Jerusalem Economy Ltd.
Municipal Bank Ltd.
Pelegas Ltd.
Zorganika Ltd.

B. Business enterprises involved in listed activities
Airbnb Inc.
American Israeli Gas Corp
Amir Marketing and Investment Inc.
Amos Hadar Properties and Investments
Angel Bakeries
Archivists Ltd.
Ariel Properties Group
Ashtrom Industries Ltd.
Bank Hapoalim B.M.
Bank Leumi Le-Israel B.M
Bank of Jerusalem Ltd.
Beit Haarchiv Ltd.
Bezeq the Israel Telecom
Booking.com B.V.
C Mer Industries Ltd.
Café Café Israel Ltd.
Caliber 3
Cellcom Israel Ltd.
Cherriessa Ltd.
Chish Nofei Israel Ltd.
Comasco Ltd.
D.B.S Satellite Services Ltd.
Delek Group Ltd.
Delta Israel Brands Ltd.
Dor Alon Energy in Israel 1988 Ltd.
Egis Rail
Egged Transportation Ltd.
Electra Afikim
EPR Systems Ltd.
Extal Ltd.
Expedia Group Inc.
Field Produce Ltd.
Field Produce Mktg. Ltd.
First International Bank of Israel
Galshan Shvakim Ltd.
Hadiklaim Israel Date Growers
Hot Mobile Ltd.
Hot Telecom Systems
Mivne Real Estate
Israel Discount Bank
Israel Railways Corp.
Italek Ltd.

J.C. Bamford Excavators
Kavim Public Transportation
Lipski Installation
Matrix IT Ltd.
Mayer Davidov Garages
Mekorot Water Company
Mercantile Discount Bank
Merkavim Transportation Tech
Mizrahi Tefahot Bank
Modi'in Ezrachi Group
Mordechai Aviv Tassiot
Motorola Solutions Israel
Naaman Group Ltd.
Nof Yam Security
Ofertex Industries 1997
Partner Communication
Paz Oil
Pelephone Communications
Proffimat S.R.
Rami Levy Chain Stores
Rami Levy Hashikma
Re/Max Israel
Shalgal Food Ltd.
Shapir Engineering
Shufersal Ltd.
Sonol Israel Ltd.
Superbus Ltd.
Supergum Industries 1969
Tahal Group International
TripAdvisor Inc
Twitoplast Ltd.
Unikowsky Maoz Ltd.
Zakai Agriculture Know-how
ZF Development
ZMH Hammerman Ltd.
Zriha Hlavin Industries

C. Business enterprises involved as parent companies:
Alon Blue Square
Alstom S.A.10
Altice International Ltd.
Ashtrom Group Ltd.
Booking Holdings Inc.
Delta Galil Industries
ODIGEO S.A.
Egis Group
Electra Group Ltd.
Export Investment Co
Hadar Group
Hamat Group Ltd.
Kardan N.V.
Mayer's Cars and Trucks
Motorola Solutions Inc.
Natoon Group
Villar International Ltd.

D. Business enterprise involved as licensors or franchisors
Greenkote P.L.C.

European creditors *

Loans and underwriting services to selected companies, by creditor parent:
BNP Paribas
HSBC
Deutsche Bank
Société Générale
KfW
Barclays
Crédit Agricole
Santander
ING Group
UniCredit
Banco Bilbayo Vizcaya Argetaria
Commerzbank
Groupe BPCE
Skandinaviska Enskilda Banken
NatWest
Standard Chartered
Intesa Sanpaolo
Crédit Mutuel
La Caixa
Danske Bank
Swedbank
Landesbank Baden Württemberg
DZ Bank
Nordea
BayernLB
Rabobank
Landesbank Hessen-Thüringen
Svenska Handelsbanken
KBC Group
DNB
Lloyds Banking
Raiffeisen Banking
Norddeutsche Landesbank
Hamburg Commercial Bank
Erste Group
Paragon Bank
La Banque Postale
BNP Finance
Banco de Sabadell

European investors *

Share and bondholding in selected companies, by investor parent:
Government Pension Fund Global
Crédit Agricole
Deutsche Bank
Groupe BPCE
Legal & General
Allianz
Deka Group
Nordea
AB Industrivärden
BNP Paribas
DZ Bank
Schroders
Swedbank
"Algemeen Burgerlijk Pensioenfonds"
HSBC
Janus Henderson
Intesa Sanpaolo
Barclays
AMF Pensionsförsäkring
Skandinaviska Enskilda Banken
Svenska Handelsbanken
AXA
Alecta
Abrdn
"Pensioenfonds Zorg en Welzijn"
Sjunde AP-fonden
M&G
Baillie Gifford
La Banque Postale
Storebrand
Aviva
Flossbach & von Storch
"Pensioenfonds Metaal en Techniek"
Bpifrance
Första AP-Fonden
B-Flexion
Ackermans & Van Haaren
Independent Franchise Partners
Crédit Mutuel
Man Group
Royal London
Rothschild
"Pensioenfonds van de Metalektro"
Fjärde AP-Fonden
Banco Mediolanum
AKO Capital
Aegon
Tredje AP- Fonden
KBC
Anima

*OHCHR update of its database, UN Human Rights Office of the Commissioner, June 30, 2023

** European Financial Institutions' Continued Complicity in the Illegal Israeli Settlement Enterprise, Don't Buy into Occupation, December 2023.

According to *Don't Buy into Occupation* (DBIO), a coalition of 25 Palestinian, regional and European organizations, in the early 2020s almost 800 European financial institutions, including banks, asset managers, insurance companies, and pension funds, had financial relationships with more than 50 businesses that were actively involved with Israeli settlements. All of these companies were involved in activities that raise particular human rights concerns, which constitute the basis for inclusion in the UN database of business enterprises. The list had almost 40 major European creditors, including BNP Paribas, HSCBC and Barclays, and 50 European investors, including Crédit Agricole, Deutsche Bank and Allianz (see Figure 9-6).

In the past decade, the Israeli government has invested hundreds of millions of dollars in PR struggles against the international boycott movement. Though controversial, the latter has attracted many Israeli Jews as well. Despite different political motivations, they are united by the quest for peace and the conclusion that international pressure is necessary to achieve change in Israel. In 2012, Avraham Burg, the former chair of the Knesset and interim president of Israel, endorsed a boycott of Israeli settlement products. Personally, he boycotted all products produced in the settlements, refusing to cross the Green Line; that is, the pre-1967 borders. Such products were not "made in Israel" and should not be mislabeled that way. Colonizing Palestinian lands has made Israel "the last colonial occupier in the Western world."[42] Burg's views were echoed by *Ha'aretz* journalist Gideon Levy, who also supported boycotting Israel, stressing that it was "the Israeli patriot's final refuge." As far he was concerned, "the change won't come from within."[43]

International boycotts are painful, but they cost less than human massacres and the economic expenditures of forever wars. They are neither antisemitic nor anti-Israel. They target the occupation, the settlers and their allies in Israel and elsewhere, and their violence. Yet, the likelihood that most Israelis would adopt Gideon Levy's view of Israeli boycotts is minimal, thanks to the parallel universe created by decades of massive U.S. military aid and money flows by American Jewry. If the status quo is untenable and change won't come from within, then change must come from without.

THE CASE FOR GENOCIDE

South Africa's Genocide Case Against Israel

Two weeks after October 7, Brazilian President Luiz Inácio Lula da Silva said that what was happening in the Middle East "isn't a war, it's a genocide that has killed nearly two thousand children."[44] By February 2024,

Israel had displaced most of Gaza's 2.3 million Palestinians while obliterating their infrastructure. The overwhelming majority of the tens of thousands killed and over 100,000 wounded were women and children. But were the atrocities in Gaza a genocide?

In January 2024, when South Africa presented its opening arguments against Israel at the International Court of Justice (ICJ), the legal team charged Israel with genocidal acts, rhetoric and incitement. "Recognizing the ongoing Nakba of the Palestinian people," they saw "Israel's genocidal acts in the context of its' 75 years of apartheid." They asked the ICJ judges to impose binding preliminary orders on Israel, including an immediate halt to Israel's military campaign in Gaza.[45]

Ever since the inception of its ground assault in Gaza, Israel has fervently denied all genocide charges. In a video statement released prior to the ICJ proceedings, Prime Minister Netanyahu defended his country's actions, claiming they had nothing to do with genocide. "Israel has no intention of permanently occupying Gaza or displacing its civilian population," Netanyahu thundered. "Israel is fighting Hamas terrorists, not the Palestinian population, and we are doing so in full compliance with international law." He said the Israeli military was "doing its utmost to minimize civilian casualties."[46] This has been Israel's standard response ever since the inception of the ground assault in October 2023, amid Israeli forces leveling Gaza and displacing its residents in violation with international law.

In an official statement posted on X/Twitter, the spokesperson for Israel's foreign ministry claimed that South Africa was "functioning as the legal arm of the Hamas terrorist organization," and "utterly distorted the reality in Gaza," ignoring the "the fact that Hamas terrorists infiltrated Israel, murdered, executed, massacred, raped and abducted Israeli citizens, simply because they were Israelis, in an attempt to carry out genocide."[47] Such statements certainly reflected the views of the Israeli government's key constituencies and of those Israelis who found it incomprehensible that their country could ever be accused of the kind of genocidal atrocities that marked the Holocaust. And it was certainly not the first time that Israeli right-wing politicians exploited the legacy of the Holocaust for their own purposes. Typical of the rhetoric of Menachem Begin, these statements intensified in the 1980s when Likud politicians initiated their concerted efforts to take over most of the occupied territories. By the early 1980s, Nahum Goldmann, former head of World Jewish Agency and World Zionist Organization, had had enough of such pretexts. He warned about the weaponization of the Holocaust to legitimize Israeli atrocities: "We certainly must refrain from using the argument of the Holocaust to justify whatever we may do. The use of the Holocaust as excuse for bombing of Lebanon, for instance, as Menachem Begin does, is a kind of [sacrilege], a banalization of the sacred tragedy of the [Holocaust], which must not be misused to politically doubtful and morally indefensible policies."[48]

During the 1982 Lebanon War and again in the course of the 2023–2024 Gaza War, mounting evidence of genocidal atrocities seemed to mock Israeli denials regarding such massacres. In the view of the international community, it was almost as if the Israeli government and most Israelis, despite the atrocities' substantial global exposure, were living in a parallel universe. Nonetheless, politics overshadowed the quest for the UN genocide convention from the beginning.

Lemkin's Mission, Politics, and Genocide Convention

The history of the legal definition of genocide is intertwined with the life of Raphael Lemkin (1900–1959), a Polish-Jewish lawyer who played a critical role in the establishment of the Genocide Convention. Born in a large farm near Wolkowysk, Lemkin understood very early in life that the suffering of the Jews in eastern Poland was part of larger and more systemic pattern of injustice and violence in history and around the world. Squeezed between the Nazi extermination and the approaching Soviet forces amid World War II, he fled Europe and found asylum in the United States. Many of his relatives were not as lucky; 49 died in the Holocaust.[49]

In *The Axis Rule in Occupied Europe* (1944), Lemkin coined the term genocide from the Greek *genos* (family, clan, tribute, race, stock, kin) and -*cide* (Latin for -cidium, killing). Following World War II, he worked on the legal team of the U.S. prosecutor at the Nuremberg Tribunal. He felt it was not effective because it did not prosecute the Nazi atrocities targeting ethnic and religious groups. *That* became his life mission; an effort at an *international* convention to preempt the rise of "future Hitlers."[50]

Ostensibly, this objective was realized in December 1948, when the just-created United Nations approved the Genocide Convention, based largely on his proposals. But amid the Cold War, diplomatic concessions sidelined historical facts. Early drafts included political killing, which was opposed by the Soviet Union and some other nations, so the notion was removed in a diplomatic compromise. The drafts also featured acts of cultural genocide, but these were opposed by European colonial powers – UK, France, Netherlands, Belgium, Denmark and some settler countries, including the U.S., Canada, Australia and New Zealand – so this concept was shelved as well, even though Lemkin considered colonial acts inherent in genocide.[51] And so it was that addressing the some five centuries of colonial atrocities ranging from Spanish conquistadors and British East India Company to American Indian Wars was effectively suppressed because, to quote Wittgenstein, "whereof one cannot speak thereof one must be silent." The price of the Genocide Convention was the exclusion of the colonial genocide atrocities that resulted in the institution of that convention.

Suppression of the Holocaust

When I grew up in Scandinavia in the postwar era, we had a small library. But it probably had most early works – non-fiction, fiction, memoirs – on the Holocaust, including Primo Levi, Elie Wiesel, Nelly Sachs, and André Schwarz-Bart. It also featured works of antisemitic literature that paved the way to the Holocaust, from *The Protocols of the Elders of Zion* (1903), the fabricated text purporting to disclose a Jewish plot for global domination, Henry Ford's *International Jew* (1920), Hitler's *Mein Kampf* (1925) and, of course, William Shirer's *The Rise and Fall of the Third Reich* (1960). I read them all as a teen. At the time, the proliferation of Holocaust literature in the United States was still a more marginal phenomenon. In a famed 1957 survey, sociologist Nathan Glazer concluded that the Jewish genocide "had remarkably slight effects on the inner life of American Jewry."[52] Until the 1967 War, the Holocaust was largely shunned in American life, including American-Jewish life. Even over a decade later, when I wrote a preface to *Se questo è un uomo* ("If This Is a Man") by Primo Levi, the Jewish-Italian partisan and Holocaust author, it was apparently an anomaly, even then. In the early 1980s, when Levi tried to generate interest in his work abroad, he discovered that several international editions had been partially censored, except for in tiny Finland where a young author saw Levi as a refraction of Kafka; as Josef K., the central character of Kafka's *The Trial*.[53]

When I arrived in New York City in 1986, I met Nobel laureate Elie Wiesel, with whom I would keep in touch for years. I asked Wiesel about the odd response in America to the Holocaust. "Both World Wars and the Holocaust took place in Europe," Wiesel said. "Europeans have a deep sense of history. America does not. Without that sense of history, the sense of tragedy is thin as well."

In the postwar era, there were few or no monuments on the Holocaust in the United States. They were politically inconvenient in the postwar era. Through World War II, the "free world" included the U.S., its European allies, the Soviet Union and China. With the Cold War, old friends became enemies, while old enemies – Germany, Japan and Italy – became new allies.

As a net effect, wartime history was an inconvenient reminder of history. Furthermore, as many Jews had fought with the Soviet Union and in the socialist partisan movements, they were seen as the kind of subversives who were targeted in the McCarthyite 1950s.

Even when the philosopher Hannah Arendt published *Eichmann in Jerusalem* in 1963, she could rely on only two English-language studies, Gerald Reitlinger's *The Final Solution* (1953) and Raul Hilberg's master treatise, *The Destruction of the European Jews* (1981) whose publication by Princeton Arendt herself had undermined just a few years before. Similarly, Yad Vashem had declined to participate in the projected publication.[54]

Things changed dramatically after Israel's triumphant Six-Day War in 1967. The membership of Zionist organizations that had plunged after the war years soared, as Washington, Pentagon and American Jewish elites sort of "re-discovered" Israel. As Norman Finkelstein has expressed it: "Paradoxically, after June 1967, Israel facilitated assimilation in the United States: Jews now stood on the front lines defending America – indeed, 'Western civilization' – against the retrograde Arab hordes. Whereas before 1967 Israel conjured the bogy of dual loyalty, it now connoted super-loyalty. After all, it was not Americans but Israelis fighting and dying to protect U.S. interests. And unlike the American GIs in Vietnam, Israeli fighters were not being humiliated by Third World upstarts."[55]

Though controversial in the U.S., Finkelstein's argument is very much in line with historical facts.

Weaponization of the Holocaust

If the triumphalism of the 1967 War legitimized Israel and its new role as the defender of democracy and freedom in the Middle East, the 1973 War highlighted the vulnerability of the small nation and revoked a new sense of the Holocaust, thereby legitimizing the massive U.S. military assistance to Israel and the ever-deeper bilateral ties. One of the side-effects was what Finkelstein called "the Holocaust industry"; that is, the exploitation of the legacy of the Holocaust for political and economic gain and to further Israeli interests. Though contested and controversial, the argument underscores the liabilities inherent in *any* enterprise to exploit historical suffering for ulterior objectives. In this view, the evocation of the Holocaust in the aftermath of October 7 built on a longstanding, half-a-century-old narrative of weaponization.

On October 30, 2023, after the deeply polarized 15-member UN Security Council had failed to adopt any resolution on the Gaza War, the

Israeli UN Ambassador Gilad Erdan and his team marched into a session wearing a yellow Star of David that read "Never Again," presumably in honor of those killed on October 7. "Some of you have learned nothing in the past 80 years," Erdan thundered, denouncing the Security Council for "staying silent" over the Hamas attacks: "Some of you have forgotten why this body was established."[56]

This odd masquerade wasn't just for the international community. Following in the footprints of Netanyahu, Erdan had started his political career opposing the Oslo Accords and the withdrawal from Gaza. As a Knesset member, he had fostered Israel's ties with Evangelical Christians, held several ministerial posts and led Israel's fight against the Boycott, Divestment and Sanctions (BDS) movement. Like some other high-profile Likudniks, he had long been jostling to succeed Netanyahu. But not everybody in Israel bought his showmanship in the UN. Behind the façade of unanimity, officials in Israel's ministry of foreign affairs criticized the "cheap gimmick," and the chair of Israel's Holocaust Museum, Yad Vashem, reprimanded him in public.[57]

If weaponizing is defined as exploiting something for the purpose of attacking a person or a group, Erdan was weaponizing the Holocaust to legitimize Israel's genocidal atrocities in Gaza. Moreover, as he made his gimmick the center of international attention, he dragged attention away from the lives of the hostages. Furthermore, cognizant of the fact that Netanyahu's successor would have to appeal to Israel's Messianic far-right, he used a coded visual. Neither he nor his team relied on the Star of David alone. It was inscribed with the words "Never Again," presumably in reference to the yellow star Jews were forced to wear by the Nazis (Figure 9-7). Though the phrase is often associated with the lessons of the Holocaust and other genocides, it was popularized in Israel by rabbi Meir Kahane in his 1971 book, Never Again! and by his Messianic far-right, anti-Palestinian successors. Those were the domestic constituencies he needed to be among Netanyahu's potential successors.

Figure 9-7 Weaponizing the Holocaust in the UN

Source: Close-up of screen capture of UNTV/CNN.

Mossad's ICC Meltdown

In late May 2024, the prosecutor of the International Criminal Court (ICC) in The Hague, Karim Khan, said he would file applications for arrest warrants against Prime Minister Benjamin Netanyahu and Defense Minister Yoav Gallant, as well as against the leader of Hamas in Gaza, Yahya Sinwar, the chief of its political bureau, Ismail Haniyeh and the head of its Qassam Brigades, Mohammed Deif. The news caused outrage among the Likud coalition and the Biden administration. "The ICC prosecutor's application for arrest warrants against Israeli leaders is outrageous," Biden said in the statement. "What's happening is not genocide."[58]

By ICC indicators, of course, it was. But the U.S. position was that it wasn't. So it couldn't be, officially. Instead, in the West and particularly by the Biden administration, it was portrayed as a kind of distressing confluence of unforeseen forces, a bit like how climate denialists describe every instance of global warming not as global warming, but as a mysterious weather anomaly.

What made Khan's decision without precedent is that it was the first time an ICC prosecutor sought arrest warrants against the leader of a Western ally. If anything, the ICC, Khan and his predecessor, Fatou Bensouda, had an odd track record. For a decade or two, the ICC has largely gone after the poorest countries in Africa, which had suffered the worst and longest from colonial massacres and plunder. Apparently, there were no such instances of criminality in the West.[59] From Washington's standpoint, Khan had lost sight of his "place." Highly respected in the international legal community, Khan, a

British lawyer of Pakistani descent, relied on evidence indicating that Israel's prime minister and defense minister had deliberately directed attacks against a civilian population and deployed civilian starvation as a method of warfare, as well as direct extermination and/or murder, all of which are crimes under the Rome Statute that established the ICC. If arrest warrants were to be issued, Netanyahu and Gallant would not be able to travel to the more than 120 ICC member countries without risking arrest. While neither the U.S. nor Israel are among the court's members, the Palestine Authority was, and hence the prosecutor had jurisdiction over the Israeli-Palestinian dispute.

The ICC move represented a historical low in Israel's international standing. For decades, Israeli leaders had enjoyed diplomatic impunity in the international system, with Washington using its veto at the UN Security Council extensively to prevent condemnation of Israel. Khan's move ended that period. Furthermore, Israeli authorities feared that the ICC decision could result in an avalanche where pent-up streams of opposition could converge; that is, lawsuits by international organizations and NGOs against Israel in foreign courts, new ICC warrants relating to the devastating Gaza bombings, targeting of other high-ranking officials and so on.

What made the ICC move even more damning was the Mossad-gate it unleashed. Soon after Khan issued his decision, the *Guardian* in Britain revealed that Mossad director Yossi Cohen had been personally involved in a secret plot to pressure Khan's predecessor, Fatou Bensouda, to drop the Palestine investigation into Israel's alleged war crimes and crimes against humanity in occupied territories.[60] In the process, Cohen had recruited the ex-president of the Democratic Republic of Congo into the effort, along with a controversial Israeli billionaire who had made his fortunes by exploiting Congolese cheap labor. It was a stunning display of shrewdness countered by incompetence and bad judgement, and it undermined Mossad's reputation. Reportedly, Israeli intelligence had some 60 people under surveillance – half of them Palestinians and half from other countries, including UN officials and ICC personnel. Presumably, Shin Bet installed NSO's Pegasus spyware – which had previously been used in the infamous Khashoggi murder[61] – on the phones of multiple Palestinian NGO employees, and two senior Palestinian Authority officials. The prior Trump campaign against the ICC was a joint operation in which sanctions were adopted against Bensouda and her top officials because Trump feared U.S. armed forces could be prosecuted. To Netanyahu cabinets, the ICC was a source of great unease. After all, the International Court of Justice (ICJ) is a UN body that deals with the legal responsibility of nation states, whereas the ICC is a criminal court that prosecutes individuals, targeting those deemed most responsible for atrocities.

Effectively, Israel had run "a decade-long secret 'war' against the ICC deploying its intelligence agencies to surveil, hack, pressure, smear and allegedly threaten senior ICC staff in an effort to derail the court's inquiries."[62]

As the Israeli cabinet officials vehemently denied the disclosures and the Bensouda debacle, the newspaper *Ha'aretz* now reported how these same authorities not only confirmed the findings the newspaper had already learned back in 2022, but also how Israeli government officials had used emergency powers to prevent the story from being published at the time.[63] When Cohen's predecessor, Tamir Prado, was asked to comment on the debacle, the ex-Mossad chief said laconically: "It sounds like Cosa Nostra–style blackmail," adding, "I don't think that Israel or its emissaries should be using blackmail and threats against a prosecutor in the court in The Hague, which the Jewish people were key to establishing after the Holocaust in World War II."[64]

As the Netanyahu cabinet struggled to extinguish multiple fires at the same time, it was tripping over its own feet and pouring oil onto new fires.

STARVATION SCHEMES

When in May 2024 the International Criminal Court (ICC) Prosecutor Karim A.A. Khan initiated the case of genocide against Israel, at the top of his list was to address starvation of civilians as a method of warfare as a war crime. Khan noted that the effects of the use of starvation as a method of warfare, together with other attacks and collective punishment against the civilian population of Gaza, were acute, visible and widely known, and had been confirmed by multiple witnesses interviewed by his office, including local and international medical doctors. They featured malnutrition, dehydration, profound suffering and an increasing number of deaths among the Palestinian population, including babies, other children, and women.[65]

Israel quickly disputed and downplayed the allegations, as did conservative mainstream media in the United States and Western Europe. Was there a famine in Gaza? Was starvation used as a weapon of war?

Israel's Red Line for Starvation

Measured by kilocalories (kcal) per person per day, the daily calorie intake is a rough indicator that does not measure the number of calories actually consumed or the differences of calorie intake between different socio-economic classes. In practice, people in the wealthy West consume more calories than those in the developing Global South. In the United States, the daily intake on average exceeds 3,900 kilocalories (kcal) per day. In Israel and Western Europe, it amounts to 3,700 kcal. Having overcome poverty, even China with its 1.4 billion people achieves over 3,400 kcal; or 10 percent more than Brazil and Saudi Arabia. In India, the average is climbing toward 2,600 kcal, whereas African nations consume the least, around 1,600–2,800 kcal.

The average daily calorie intake critical to survival is estimated at 2,100 kcal per day; about the same as the current level in Yemen. According to the international Integrated Food Security Phase Classification (IPC), acute food insecurity proceeds in five phases: minimal, stressed, crisis, emergency, and catastrophe/famine. In the case of a famine, at least two out of every 10,000 people die of starvation or disease in famine conditions; every third is acutely malnourished, there is total loss of income; and every fifth family faces extreme food shortages. As a case of extreme deprivation, famine is reflected by starvation, death, destitution. Malthus called it a "war of extermination."[66] By all estimates, the situation in the Gaza Strip in 2024 was "the most intense man-made famine since the Second World War."[67]

Yet, in February 2024, more than two of three Israelis opposed humanitarian aid to Palestinians starving in Gaza. And in late June 2024, conservative tabloids in the West explained "Gaza's supposed famine" as "Hamas propaganda."[68] Is that what it was?

In the Yemen War, food insecurity, like the cholera epidemic that began in October 2016, translated to hunger and the decimation of farm communities, with the targeting of civilian, agricultural and fishing sites. It was an intended consequence of the military campaign.[69] In Gaza, the population faced starvation and famine as a net effect of Israeli airstrikes, which had demolished food infrastructure, from bakeries to mills and food retail, and the blockade, which ensured the scarcity of vital supplies and aid. By May 2024, some 85 percent of children under five in Gaza spent days without food, while more than half a million Gazans were starving. For months, these manufactured steps that were paving the way to the Gaza famine were downplayed in international media.[70] This was a calculated effect of decisions taken over a decade ago.

With the inception of its blockade in 2007, the Israeli government estimated exactly how many daily calories were needed to prevent or to cause malnutrition in Gaza, in its *Food Consumption in the Gaza Strip: Red Line* document.[71] It was compiled after a cabinet decision, which authorized the tightening of the closure on Gaza after Hamas took control of the Strip. Defining Gaza as a "hostile territory," it imposed "severe sanctions in the civilian sphere." The key assumption was that a daily shipment of 106 trucks to the Gaza Strip per business day would suffice for supplying its residents with their "daily humanitarian portion," including basic food, medicine, medical equipment, hygiene products and agricultural inputs.[72] Not only did the document use a higher calculation of 2,279 calories per person, it also took into account domestic food production in Gaza.[73] To maintain the "basic fabric of life" in the area, Israel would allow in 106 trucks with food and other essential goods every day. To circumvent the blockade, Palestinians brought in tonnes of goods through smuggling tunnels dug under Gaza's border with Egypt. According to Wikileaks, Israel told U.S. officials in 2008 it would keep Gaza's economy "on the brink of collapse" while avoiding a humanitarian crisis.[74]

Prior to the cabinet decision, more than 400 trucks entered the Strip daily. By 2023, a minimum of 500 to 600 trucks was required daily to feed millions of Palestinians in Gaza – most of them refugees – on the brink of starvation. After October 7, about 30–50 truckloads of aid entered the Strip in the first month of war; the rest of the year up to 100.[75] Between October 7 and summer 2024, the truckloads climbed to 200 in spring 2024. The number of trucks was at best about half of what was required. Worse, the assumption that those loads would be distributed equally across the Strip was an illusion. With up to 2 million people displaced and ongoing bombardment, much or most of the aid failed to reach those who needed it the most.

Starvation in Historical Comparison

The Israeli military was not the first to estimate calorie counts for the purpose of survival or extinction. Following an intense drought and crop failure in the Deccan Plateau in 1876, the Great Southern India Famine lasted for two nightmarish years spreading northward. As Britain's famine commissioner, Sir Richard Temple persisted on laissez-faire efforts to constrain grain trade, while insisting on limiting rations and relief qualification. Like the Nazi concentration camp *commandants* later, Temple sought to determine the minimum amount of food for survival, to save the maximum amount of British monies. In the labor camps he set up, inmates were given fewer daily calories than initially in Buchenwald six decades later.[76] Temple estimated the adequate calorie intake per day in Madras in 1877 to be around 1,627 kcal. In reality, it wasn't adequate for work and survival. The net effect? The excess mortality related to the famine has been estimated at 8.2 million deaths.[77] Such figures are not history. In 2020, after half a decade of continuing civil war, the calorie intake in Yemen was estimated at barely 1,340.[78] That's 20 percent less than in Madras some 150 years ago. Or almost at par with the calorie level of the Nazi concentration camps in 1940; at the beginning of World War II, when the German economy was still humming strong.

What about the Gaza Strip?

Measured in terms of total food deliveries into the Strip since October 2023, the figure was about 860 kcal.[79] A third less than in the Nazi camps over eight decades ago. As the German invasion of the Soviet Union failed and the tide of World War II shifted, the Nazi camps deteriorated, with the daily intake shrinking to 700 kcal in 1944. That daily calorie level would have been almost three times the intake of 245 kcal in northern Gaza in the first half of the year 2024,[80] when the *New York Post* announced that there was no famine in the Strip. In turn, the Nazi siege of Leningrad from fall 1941 to January 1944 was one of the longest and most destructive sieges in history, which caused 600,000 to 2 million Russians to perish. The average daily ration was 300 calories, containing virtually no protein. While it is considered extremely low, it was 20 percent higher relative to Palestinians in northern Gaza.[81]

Shockingly, an even lower calorie count was verified in the Warsaw Ghetto hunger study, undertaken by Jewish doctors in 1942. Determined to starve the ghetto in just months, the Nazis only permitted a daily intake of 180 calories per prisoner, withholding vaccines and medicine necessary to prevent the spread of disease in the dense ghetto. Hence, the thriving black market, which supplied about 80 percent of the ghetto's food and a network of 250 soup kitchens.[82] As such, 180 kcal is less than 9 percent of what's needed for daily life (Figure 9-8).

Figure 9-8   Daily Calorie Intake in Extreme Situations: Selected Examples

Source: Food and Agriculture Organization of the United Nations (2023) and other sources; Gaza estimates from Oxfam

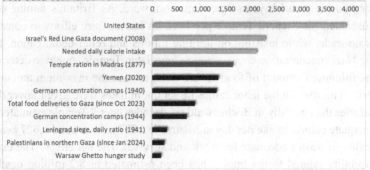

THE CONDITIONS OF GENOCIDE

Israel and Genocide Convention

Effective since 1951, the Genocide Convention (Resolution 260, III) defined genocide as "any of the following acts committed with intent to destroy, in whole or in part, a national, ethnical, racial or religious group, as such: Killing members of the group; Causing serious bodily or mental harm to members of the group; Deliberately inflicting on the group conditions of life calculated to bring about its physical destruction in whole or in part; Imposing measures intended to prevent births within the group; Forcibly transferring children of the group to another group.[83]

"Killing members of the group... " From the Holocaust to the massacres of the Yazidis by ISIS, recognized genocides feature an almost uniform pattern in which adult men and adolescent boys are singled out for murder in the early stages. In Nazi Germany, mass killings by gunshot morphed to gas chambers, which were more effective and industrialized – a sort of a rapid path from craftmanship to mass production, which in this case translates to the mass production of death. In Gaza, October 7 was followed by the Israeli Defense Forces' (IDF) expanded authorization for bombing non-military targets, the loosening of constraints regarding expected civilian casualties – amounting to more than 38,000 in early July 2024 – and the use of artificial intelligence (AI) to generate more potential targets than ever before.[84]

"Causing serious bodily or mental harm... " The second prohibited act comprises a broad variety of *non*-fatal genocidal acts, such as torture and other cruel, inhuman, or degrading treatment or punishment, including the torture and humiliation of male prisoners. When committed with the requisite intent, the objective is to cause serious bodily or mental harm to members of the target group. In both Gaza and the West Bank, the brutal bullying, lawless harassment, collusion of police, military and settlers, and inhuman treatment are all reminiscent of segregation and suppression of blacks in apartheid-era South Africa. From the Israeli human rights groups to the former intelligence leaders of Mossad and Shin Bet, the system of apartheid has been acknowledged as a vital existential risk to the future of Israel/Palestine. After October 7, the system escalated dramatically.

"Physical destruction in whole or in part... " The third condition refers to deadly circumstances that do not support prolonged life. In Gaza, Daniel Hagari, the IDF spokesperson, stated that early on the emphasis of the Israeli ground assault "is on damage and not on accuracy." Since October 7, the strategic objective, which the Biden administration has tacitly accepted, has been to destroy Gaza's infrastructure; *and* the deliberate destruction of the

Palestinian conditions of life, which the Biden administration opposed in rhetoric but effectively permitted in practice. The Palestinians were being pressured to leave Gaza to survive, as stated by the secret memorandum of the Israeli Ministry of Intelligence after October 7.[85] In these operations, Israel was exploiting starvation as a weapon of war with dark precedents in Nazi Germany and Imperial Britain.[86]

"Preventing births..." The fourth condition is aimed at preventing reproduction in the protected group, encompassing acts affecting reproduction and intimate relationships, including involuntary sterilization, forced abortion, the prohibition of marriage, and long-term separation of men and women intended to prevent procreation. Building initially on the Holocaust evidence, this condition envisions a fairly long period from segregation and racial acts to mass extinction. Today, the effectiveness of destructive weapons is such that the killing of a nation can take place more efficiently. In Gaza, this translated to the deliberate targeting of hospitals, among other such services, with the World Health Organization (WHO) warning that women and newborns were bearing the brunt of the escalation of hostilities, particularly the 50,000 pregnant women.[87]

"Forcible transfer of children..." The final prohibited act refers to destruction of the group as a cultural and social unit. It occurs when children of the protected group are transferred to the perpetrator group to be exploited as cheap labor or assimilated. In the case of Gaza, such forcible transfers were not common as there was no interest in assimilation. Due to the system of ultra-apartheid and dehumanization that's pervasive to it, Palestinians are effectively regarded as sub-human. Early on, there were numerous reports of preventable deaths for lack of oxygen and ventilators; and of over 1,000 children that had undergone leg amputations in Gaza, according to UNICEF, some without anesthesia.[88] Yet, that turned out to be just a prelude to far worse. Hence, the UN decision in early June 2024 to add Israel to its blacklist of countries that have committed abuses against children in armed conflict. According to "Children in Armed Conflict" report, more grave violations against children were committed in Gaza, the West Bank and Israel than anywhere else in the world, including peer countries like the Democratic Republic of Congo, Myanmar, Somalia, Nigeria and Sudan.

Article 3 of the Genocide Convention defines the crimes that can be punished under the convention: (a) genocide; (b) conspiracy to commit genocide; (c) direct and public incitement to commit genocide; (d) attempt to commit genocide; and (e) complicity in genocide.[89] According to the Genocide Convention, the specific intent defines the purpose of committing the acts "to destroy in whole or in part, a national, ethnical, racial or religious group, as such." It is this specific intent that is seen as critical to distinguishing genocide from other international crimes, such as war crimes or crimes against humanity.

United States, the "Unnamed Co-Conspirator"

The Gaza catastrophe offers abundant evidence of genocidal intent. Although the rulings of the International Court of Justice (ICJ) are sometimes ignored, they do have symbolic weight. South Africa filed its case against Israel in late December 2023 when it asked the ICJ for an urgent order declaring that Israel was in breach of its obligations under the 1948 Genocide Convention in the ground assault in Gaza. At the ICC, the case was without a precedent in terms of its magnitude, deliberateness, even its transparency, but technically genocide cases have been notoriously difficult to prove, which certainly motivated the Netanyahu war cabinet's calculations.

The Genocide Convention was created in part to avoid future Holocausts, and Israel itself emerged in part as a result of the Holocaust. The world economy may be increasingly multipolar, but American hegemony continues to influence international multilateral organizations such as the ICC, even though the United States is not a state party to the Rome Statute of the International Criminal Court, which founded the ICC in 2002. Israel is not a member of the ICC and rejects its jurisdiction as does the United States. Furthermore, Israel is a major non-NATO ally of the U.S., which is thus complicit, as the Lemkin Institute for Genocide Prevention has argued.[90]

When South Africa launched the proceedings against Israel, the U.S. State Department said the U.S. has not observed acts in Gaza that constitute genocide. As U.S. Secretary of State Antony Blinken put it, "We believe the submission against Israel to the International Court of Justice distracts the world from all of these important efforts. And moreover, the charge of genocide is meritless."[91] In response, 77 groups – representing tens of thousands of lawyers, civil society leaders, and activists from six continents – filed a case in the United States District Court for the Northern District of California against President Biden, Secretary of Defense Lloyd Austin, and Secretary of State Blinken for their alleged "failure to prevent and complicity in the unfolding genocide against Gaza." Besides the human rights organizations, the lawsuit was promoted by Josh Paul who had resigned from the U.S. State Department over arms shipment to Israel; genocide and Holocaust scholars spearheaded by international lawyer William Schabas; and Jewish Voice for Peace. The case was dismissed with a ruling that while "it is plausible that

Israel's conduct amounts to genocide," U.S. foreign policy was a political question over which courts lacked jurisdiction.[92]

In South Africa's case against Israel, the United States remains, as Jeremy Scahill put it, "the unnamed co-conspirator."[93] If South Africa laid a meticulous case detailing Israel's genocidal intent, the inconvenient fact is that the U.S. not only supported it but enabled it all. Without U.S. military aid, finance, training, and diplomatic protection, Israel's genocidal atrocities would not have been viable. One net effect involved elevated threat levels, as evidenced by the warning of the *Annual Threat Assessment*. Inspired by the Hamas attack against Israel, both al-Qaeda and ISIS had directed their supporters to conduct attacks against Israeli and U.S. interests. The intelligence community feared that the Hamas attack was "encouraging individuals to conduct acts of antisemitic and Islamophobic terror worldwide and is galvanizing individuals to leverage the Palestinian plight for recruitment and inspiration to conduct attacks."[94] At the same time, the FBI believed that the threat of Islamic terrorist attack inside the United States had increased to its highest point since 9/11.

The ICJ Condemnation of Israel's Occupation

In mid-July 2024, the International Court of Justice (ICJ) concluded Israel's presence in the Palestinian occupied territories was "unlawful" and called on it to end and for settlement construction to stop immediately. According to the 15-judge panel, Israel's "abuse of its status as the occupying power" renders its "presence in the occupied Palestinian territory unlawful."[95]

For decades, Israel has regarded the United Nations and international tribunals as unfair and biased, or outright antisemitic. While it did not send a legal team to the hearings, it did submit written comments, claiming that the questions put to the court were prejudiced, failing to address Israel's national security concerns. Israeli officials argued that the court's intervention could undermine the peace process, which has been stagnant for more than a decade. In reality, the ICJ legal opinion addressed the most substantial issues of Israel's occupation and placed them in historical context, which hardly made those questions prejudicial. Moreover, there was a strong case to be made that Israel's national security challenges, particularly since the late 1960s, stemmed precisely from its occupation, which undermined Israeli security and had severely destabilized peace and development in the West Bank and the Gaza Strip.[96] Furthermore, the accusation that the ICJ intervention would undermine the peace process came straight from a parallel universe. The process had been torpedoed by Israel, due to its continued refusal to execute the provisions of the Oslo Accords. Occurring almost in parallel with the release of the ICJ opinion, the Knesset vote to condemn Palestinian statehood – supported by the overwhelming majority of the political parties – suggested that Israel had the full ability but little political will to implement the policies required by the peace process.

Condemning the ICJ ruling, Prime Minister Benjamin Netanyahu stated that "the Jewish people are not conquerors in their own land – not in our eternal capital Jerusalem and not in the land of our ancestors in Judea and Samaria. No false decision in The Hague will distort this historical truth and likewise the legality of Israeli settlement in all the territories of our homeland cannot be contested."[97] But no biblical narratives can replace historical truths and the simple fact that the continued occupation was illegal.

The ICJ opinion was non-binding, but it reflected a wide international outrage regarding the Gaza War and had huge symbolic value. Issuing a sweeping condemnation of Israel's rule over the lands it captured 57 years ago, the ICJ identified a wide list of policies that violated international law, including the building and expansion of Israeli settlements in the West Bank and east Jerusalem, exploitation of the area's natural resources, the annexation and imposition of permanent control over Palestinian lands and discriminatory policies against them.

The resounding *breadth* of the opinion was something no party to the conflict had anticipated. In its view, Israel could not claim any sovereignty in the territories it continued to occupy in violation of international law and Palestinians' right to self-determination. The ICJ opinion was likely to foster Israel's international condemnation, boost the movements for boycotts, divestment and sanctions against Israel, and increase the number of countries willing to recognize the state of Palestine.

In its title, the ICJ opinion referred to the legal consequences arising from the policy practices of Israel in "the Occupied Palestinian Territory, including East Jerusalem." Instead of referring to the Palestinian occupied territories in plural, it highlighted the integrity and contiguity of the Palestinian territory. Yet by 2024, East Jerusalem was effectively annexed, the West Bank was about to be effectively annexed, and the Gaza Strip was devastated. All of this, according to the ICJ opinion, was illegal. That was clear. But what the international community would do about such gross illegality was not clear at all.

Chapter 10

PROSPECTS OF REGIONAL ESCALATION

After the Hamas offensive on October 7, the influential Republican senator Lindsay Graham was asked whether he wanted the U.S. and Israel to bomb Iran. Even in the absence of direct evidence of any Iranian involvement, Graham responded: "Yeah." The answer stunned the CNN interviewer. She asked the question again and got the same response.[1] To leave no doubts about his intentions, Senator Graham flew to Tel Aviv where he joined a delegation of U.S. senators. He warned that any escalation of the war would exact a cost from Tehran: "If Hezbollah enters the fray, this war will enter Iran's backyard. There won't be two fronts; there will be three."[2]

Days later, Rep. Michael McCaul, the Republican chair of the House Foreign Affairs Committee, said his panel was drafting legislation to authorize the use of military force "in the event it's necessary," due to a wider proxy war with Iran. McCaul's comments came on the 21st anniversary of the enactment of a measure that had authorized the misguided 2003 U.S. invasion of Iraq.

Ever since October 7, concerns have been amounting over regional escalation and possible global reverberations. But such escalation was one of a set of possible scenarios. It could take place in many ways and the outcome could prove good, bad, ugly – or very ugly.

Depending on Gaza's trajectory after the 2023–24 War, there are several possible scenarios for the future. Some are more probable than others, but all feature possible regional escalation.[3]

THE ECLIPSE OF AMERICAN HEGEMONY

The U.S.-Saudi Alliance

American hegemony in the Middle East dates from a historical deal that has shaped U.S. regional policies since the end of World War II. In February 1945, the ailing U.S. President Franklin D. Roosevelt met Joseph Stalin and

Winston Churchill in the Yalta Conference, where the Big Three discussed the postwar reorganization of Germany and Europe, basically dividing their spheres of influence in the old continent. After Yalta, Roosevelt rushed to meet Saudi King Ibn Saud aboard the USS *Quincy* in the Suez Canal. With a historic handshake, the two agreed on a secret deal, which required Saudi Arabia to supply oil to the U.S. in exchange for American military protection of the Saudi regime. Just months before his death, Roosevelt managed to negotiate the U.S.-Saudi bilateral alliance – Gulf energy for U.S. dollars and military protection – which has fueled Western capitalism ever since then (Figure 10-1).[4]

Figure 10-1 U.S.-Saudi Alliance

U.S. President Franklin D. Roosevelt and King Ibn Saud of Saudi Arabia, on board the U.S. Navy heavy cruiser USS *Quincy*, on February 14, 1945. Photograph by U.S. Army Signal Corps; Naval History and Heritage Command under the digital ID USA-C-545 (cropped). *Source: Wikimedia Commons*

In May 2017, the United States sealed a multibillion arms deal with Saudi Arabia, in a move that was seen to cement its decades-long alliance with the world's largest oil exporter. It was timed to coincide with President Trump's maiden trip abroad. The agreement, which is worth nearly $110 billion immediately, $350 billion over 10 years, was hailed by the Trump White House as "a significant expansion of ... [the] security relationship" between the two countries. Meanwhile, Saudi Arabia was promoting a broad-based push for economic reform, and as part of that effort, signed a flurry of deals with private U.S. companies worth tens of billions of dollars.[5]

Nonetheless, as Crown Prince Mohammed bin Salman (MBS) saw it, America was no longer the only game in town. Riyadh needed arms and development. The White House excelled in the former, but China represented the latter, and it was the latter that was critical to MBS's Saudi Vision 2030; the huge state-led diversification initiative to reduce Saudi reliance on oil revenues, while fostering its economic sustainability in the future. Furthermore, as beneficial as these bilateral ties with the U.S. have been, they have never been equal. When the White House pressed Saudi Arabia to end its oil price war with Russia, President Trump gave Saudi leaders an ultimatum: Cut oil supply or lose U.S. military support. As a result, "the prospect of losing U.S. military protection made the royal family 'bend at the knees' and bow to Trump's demands."[6] Usually, such pressure was applied in the shadows. Trump did it in public. In the Middle East, it was a chilling reminder of a history of U.S. interventions, and the huge economic costs and lost human lives these destabilizations have caused.

Regime Change and Destabilization

For all practical purposes, the U.S.-Saudi pact, which Roosevelt negotiated in 1945 and Nixon renewed in the 1970s, has prevailed. In the Middle East at large, the U.S. approach has been predicated on strategic alliances and, whenever such alignments have not been viable, on regime change. The list of interventions in the region is long and exceedingly dark. In March 1949, the CIA sponsored the coup d'etat by Col. Husni al-Za'im, which undermined democratic rule in Syria. In 1953, the CIA, in cooperation with British intelligence, helped the Shah to remove the democratically elected prime minister Mohammed Mossadegh, which destabilized Iran's development for decades, paving the way for the 1979 Islamic revolution. During the 1958 Lebanon crisis, President Eisenhower applied a doctrine whereby the U.S. would intervene to protect regimes it regarded as threatened by international communism. Both Eisenhower and President Kennedy greenlighted efforts to neutralize Egypt's pan-Arabist president, Gamal Abdel Nasser. In the Kennedy era, the CIA also planned a coup against Abd al-Karim Qasim's Iraq.

With the 1970s energy crises, the U.S. proclivity for interventions intensified. During the Yom Kippur War, President Nixon authorized a strategic airlift to deliver weapons to Israel, which led to decades of massive military aid to Israel, despite its continued settlement violations in the occupied territories. Meanwhile, the CIA armed Kurdish rebels fighting Iraq's Ba'athist leadership. Under Reagan, Washington sent troops to Lebanon during its civil war until the Beirut barracks bombing led to American withdrawal. Amid the 1980s Iran-Iraq War, U.S. warships protected Kuwaiti oil tankers against Iranian attacks, while pressuring Tehran to a ceasefire with Iraq. At the same time, U.S. Big Defense was arming both sides of the lethal war. In 1986, Reagan bombed Libya in response to terrorism.

After the Cold War, the U.S. led a coalition to remove Iraq from Kuwait in the Gulf War. In 2003, the illegal U.S. invasion of Iraq toppled the government of Saddam Hussein, unleashing a decade of instability and giving rise to the brutal Islamic State. In 2011 the U.S. participated in a Western coalition that exceeded its UN Responsibility to Protect (R2P) mandate by launching a military intervention in Libya that toppled Gaddafi and went on to initiate covert operations elsewhere in the Middle East. When Syria was swept by a civil protest, the U.S., France and the UK augmented it into a proxy war.[7] Meanwhile, the U.S. effort to reshape the geopolitical trajectories in the region continued from Turkey and Iran to the disastrous civil war in Yemen.

Historically, these many and exasperating regime-change operations date from 19th century imperialism and 20th century colonialism. In the George W. Bush era, such destabilization was an explicit neoconservative objective. In the Obama era, it was implicit in the U.S.'s assertive liberal internationalism. In the Trump-Biden-Harris era, the neoconservative goals prevailed, even during Israel's genocidal atrocities against Gaza in 2023–24.

Economic and Human Costs of the Post-9/11 Wars

Altogether, America's post-9/11 wars' economic and human costs amount to $8 trillion.[8] In the past two decades or so, the losses of American lives – military and contractors – in these war zones has exceeded 15,000; that's five times the number of 9/11 victims in whose name the Global War on Terror was launched. And these figures pale in comparison to the lost lives in the war theaters where most people – civilians, local military and police, and opposition fighters – had little to do with the 9/11 tragedies. In Iraq, over 300,000 people lost their lives; in Syria, 266,000; in Afghanistan, 176,000; in Yemen, 112,000; in Pakistan, 67,000.[9]

The total of more than 900,000 people is *60 times* the number of the U.S. losses in post-9/11 wars; and *300 times* the number of the 9/11 victims. The U.S. estimates are conservative, however. The UN and other international and local groups put the final tally at more than 1.1 million lost lives.[10]

What is extraordinary is not just the empirical under-estimation of lost lives, but the discounted value of human life in these estimations. Iraq had suffered severely from the sanctions placed on the country following the 1991 Persian Gulf War. Reportedly, half a million [Iraqi] children had died, more than in Hiroshima. When the then-U.S. UN ambassador Madeline Albright was asked whether the price was worth it, she responded: "I think that is a very hard choice, but the price, we think, the price is worth it."[11] Subsequently, those words would haunt her obituaries, but they do reflect thinking in the White House.

When the Biden administration withdrew American troops from Afghanistan in 2021, no peace premium ensued. Instead, American forces were mobilized into other conflict theaters elsewhere in the world. Even in the Gaza War, while Israel carried out the attacks, it could only do so with American financing, training and arms. America was overstretched. Hence, the Biden administration's reliance on multilateralism, as long as it was led by the United States. But today, the world has other alternatives than the U.S. – ones in which economic development rather than arms sales has a central place.

A REGION IN FLUX

Rise of the Global South

The Gaza War could not have happened in a worse historical moment for the West. It took place amid a broad yet precarious shift from globalization to global divides between the West and the emerging multipolar world, following the pandemic-induced global depression and the proxy war in Ukraine. In 2018, President Trump had launched protectionist tariffs against China and other major trading economies.[12] As a consequence, world trade shrank and recovery floundered at the eve of the pandemic depression. The Biden administration had an opportunity to implement a full reset.[13] Instead, it embraced Trump's protectionism, with the European Union and Japan following in its footsteps. Hence, the compounded dire global outcomes in world trade, investment and migration in the early 2020s. It was a fragile time of already-diminished economic prospects, when global cooperation against the perils of extreme climate should have been the primary agenda around the world.[14]

Overall, the collateral damage has long been particularly challenging in developing economies that have served as war theaters, particularly in the Middle East. With the post-9/11 wars and the West's aggressive interventionism during the Arab Spring, the number of forcibly displaced has doubled in a decade. By summer 2024, the number of globally displaced exceeded 120 million, which is almost twice as high as it was after two world wars, the Holocaust, Hiroshima and Nagasaki in 1945.[15] The U.S. post-9/11 wars alone displaced some 48–59 million people, which "raises the question of who bears responsibility for repairing the damage inflicted on those displaced."[16]

The number of refugees hosted by countries in the Middle East and North Africa – or the Arab world – stood at 2.4 million at the end of 2022, with Lebanon (818,900), Jordan (697,800), Egypt (294,600) and Iraq (273,700) hosting 87 percent of all refugees in the region. These impoverished countries, some of which were already both war-torn and war-devastated, are largely the same countries to which Israel wanted to offshore Gazan Palestinians. Preceding the Gaza War, the dire status quo is reflected especially by the forcibly displaced (that is, refugees, asylum-seekers, other people in need of international protection and internally displaced people), dependent on the UN Refugee Agency (UNHCR). The ground zero of the migrant crisis is centered in the Middle East, which is also largely the origin for the refugees who fled to Europe (Figure 10-2).

Figure 10-2   Refugees, People in Refugee-like Situations, by Country of Asylum

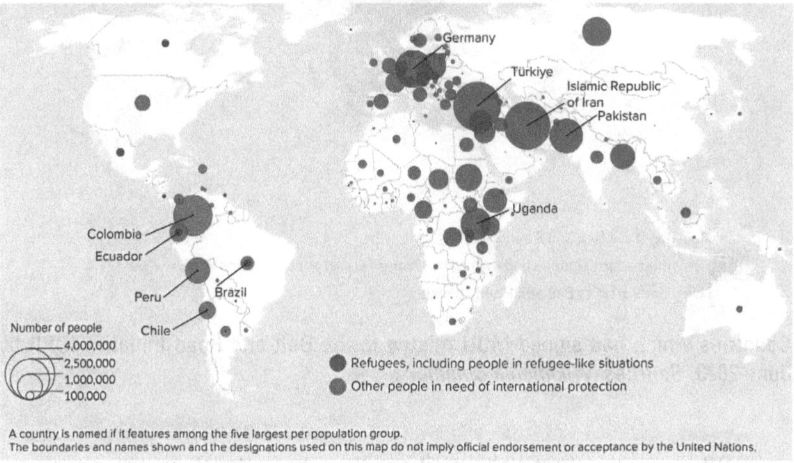

Source: Global Trends UNHCR, June 2023

Besides the U.S. post-9/11 wars, devastating military interventions and attendant migration crises, Israel's Gaza War took place at the crossroads of the post-industrial economies (Global North), and the emerging and developing economies (Global South). Spearheaded by China, the latter represents the interests of the countries therein, stressing the role of peace, stability and development, as evidenced by the rise of the New Silk Road, or the China-led Belt and Road Initiative (BRI). Launched in 2013, it is a colossal effort to energize, sustain and extend global economic integration across the indus-trializing developing economies. The ultimate value of the BRI, targeted for completion in 2049 with the 100th anniversary of modern China, is estimated at $4 to $8 trillion.[17] While the door of these initiatives has been open to the West, the U.S. administrations, unlike some of America's trade partners and allies, have stayed outside the new supranational organizations that most economies in the Middle East support (Figure 10-3). Unsurprisingly, U.S. administrations have portrayed the BRI as a "debt trap." Yet, such claims have been debunked, including by researchers in the U.S.-based Johns Hopkins and the UK-based Chatham House.[18]

Figure 10-3   The 21st Century Silk Road

Initiator of the Belt and Road Initiative

Countries which signed cooperation documents related to the Belt and Road Initiative

Only participate in Belt and Road summit

Countries which had signed MOU related to the Belt and Road Initiative (BRI) by June 2023. *Sources: Wikimedia Commons*

What was the West's alternative to these huge development initiatives? Setting aside the rhetoric of the Global North's "like-minded democracies," the net effect has been NATO's effective expansion to the Middle East and Asia. The consequent geoeconomic fragmentation is least likely to foster development worldwide, and particularly not in the Middle East. By 2023, even the IMF had to acknowledge the heavy penalty of unilateralism, uni-polarity, protectionism and xenophobia on global economic integration. It declared that the world was facing the risk of geoeconomic fragmentation. The deeper the fragmentation, the greater the costs.

Emerging market economies and low-income countries, including those in the Middle East, were expected to be most at risk.[19] In these dire circumstances, Chinese development, multipolarity and intermediation heralded a potential new beginning in the region.

China, Development and Multipolarity

A symbolic milestone was reached in 2009, when China surpassed the United States as the world's biggest energy consumer. Subsequently Beijing also supplanted the U.S. as Saudi Arabia's largest crude oil client. Moreover, China has been Iran's leading customer for oil exports and its largest trade partner, despite the West's sanctions against Tehran. In 2016, President Xi Jinping's three-nation tour in the Middle East codified China's presence in the Middle East as a major energy buyer, importer, infrastructure builder, and peace broker. That contrasted dramatically with the U.S. history of regime changes.[20]

In the past decade, Washington has seen China largely in terms of threats to be contained rather than opportunities to be pursued; that is, as a win-lose proposition. In turn, Beijing regards such win-lose perceptions as a relic from the Cold War era. With regard to the Middle East, the regional roles of these two great powers, despite some parallels, are complementary: similar and different. Following World War II, Washington secured its energy imports while in a position of overwhelming economic, political and military superiority. By contrast, China initially built its energy resources as the world's most populous yet poor, war-devastated economy. When Roosevelt made his energy deal with Saudi Arabia, America was the overwhelmingly superior military power and Americans enjoyed higher per capita incomes than their peers in all other major Western economies. By contrast, when China was still a net exporter of oil in the mid-1990s (it became a net importer by the end of the decade), its military expenditures were only 2 percent of military expenditures worldwide. When China joined the WTO in 2001, its economy was a tenth of the world GDP, and Chinese incomes were only a tenth relative to the U.S. Geopolitically, U.S. interventions in the Middle East build on the legacies of Western imperialism and colonialism. By contrast, the Chinese stance rests on non-interference, stabilization, and development. The contrast is sharp and stark.

Historically, China and the Arab nations share a history of imperial disintegration, colonial humiliation and a struggle for sovereignty and territorial integrity. Modern relations between China and the Arab world go back to the 1955 Bandung conference of the Non-Aligned Movement, with economic cooperation beginning to intensify with the opening of the Sino-Arab Cooperation Forum in 2004. In the following decade, these ties broadened on the back of economic exchange. The China-led BRI has the potential to contribute dramatically to economic development in the region. Such initiatives hold great potential for mutually beneficial cooperation between Washington and Beijing that American foreign policy realists from Kissinger to Brzezinski understood well. That is why the late Zbigniew Brzezinski proposed that in the short term, China should be encouraged to pursue a geostrategic outlook that favors stability over conflict as it embarks on its BRI initiative, adding "and that requires a geopolitically global American-Chinese accommodation." This is precisely what Washington has shunned for more than a decade. Conversely, Brzezinski warned about "the most dangerous scenario," which he saw as "a grand coalition of China and Russia."[21] Which is precisely what Washington has achieved in the past decade.

In an increasingly complex Middle East, where the spread of conflict has been facilitated by the rise of religious sectarianism, all global actors are impacted by memories of colonial brutality compounded by American involvement since the mid-1970s and particularly by the post-9/11 wars. Furthermore, U.S. efforts to contain China's rise seek to undermine the very initiatives that could contribute to peace and development in the region. The Chinese approach differs diametrically from U.S. policies of regime change as evidenced by Beijing's successful intermediation between Riyadh and Tehran; and most recently, the agreement by the Palestinian Fatah and Hamas to seek an interim national unity government. Moreover, China has historically supported the self-determination of the Palestinian people and peace through development. Starting with the Oslo peace process, China has increased its trade with and investment in Israel. In the aftermath of October 7, China engaged in a cautious balancing seeking to maintain its Israeli ties, while pushing for ceasefire and de-escalation in all occupied territories and the region at large. By contrast, the U.S. has sought to penalize Sino-Israeli cooperation, which it fears could undermine its bilateral military cooperation with Israel. Since the Gaza War, China has sought to de-escalate tensions, seeking to serve as a neutral broker, whereas U.S. credibility has imploded in the Arab world, due to its complicity with Israel's genocidal atrocities. Regional surveys suggest China's favorability in the region is three times higher than that of the U.S. In economic relations it is seen as more than twice as attractive than the U.S.[22]

In Washington, the tendency remains to see the Middle East and other world regions in win-lose terms. In Beijing, the prevailing view is to look at the world and its regions in multipolar terms that take into account the interests of *both* the Global South *and* the Global North. Unlike U.S. regime change, it shuns solo acts disguised as dialogue, such as Washington's effort at a "grand bargain" in the Middle East.

The Not-So-Grand Bargain

As the Biden administration's frustration with the Netanyahu cabinet steadily increased and international indignation mounted in spring 2024, opposition leader Benny Gantz, Netanyahu cabinet's minister-without-portfolio, flew to Washington in an "unauthorized visit" to meet Secretary of State Antony Blinken and other senior U.S. officials, effectively sidelining PM Netanyahu. For some two years, the Biden administration had been in talks with Saudi leaders urging Riyadh to establish diplomatic ties with Israel. On the one hand, Saudi Arabia has joined the BRICS alliance, remains one of China's largest oil suppliers and is now selling oil in multiple currencies. On the other hand, it remains the world's second-largest arms importer and 75 percent of those weapons come from the U.S. Riyadh has been negotiating a security pact with the U.S., modeled loosely on the U.S.-Japan mutual security pact.

Saudi Arabia was hedging its bets between the U.S. and China. It wanted the best of the two worlds: weapons from the U.S. and development and diversification assistance from China. Tellingly, Saudi holdings of U.S. treasuries peaked in early 2020 and have declined since then. However, after October 7 and the devastating Israeli counteroffensive, the talks stalled – hence the U.S. pressure for a ceasefire in Gaza and the restoration of the Palestinian Authority (PA) under the kind of "reformed leadership" that Washington and Riyadh could deal with; that is, an imposed PA without leaders who are popular among the Palestinians themselves. In return, Crown Prince Mohammed bin Salman was seeking a U.S.-Saudi mutual defense pact and cooperation on a civilian nuclear program in the kingdom. This was the "grand bargain" the U.S. administration was touting.

Preceded by Israel's peace treaties with Egypt (1979) and Jordan (1994) and the Oslo Accords with the PA (1993–95), the grand bargain was predicated on the Abraham Accords, which reflected Arab-Israeli normalization, particularly between Israel and the UAE and Bahrain. With the U.S. as the behind-the-façade architect, deals with Morocco and Sudan were announced between September 2020 and January 2021, respectively. Prior to the Gaza War, Israel was supposed to agree to minor concessions for the Palestinians; at least for appearances sake. However, after October 7, the Palestinians could no longer be sidelined.[23] At the same time, the bilateral trust between Israel and the Gulf states had eroded.

Furthermore, the Biden administration's grand bargain was no win-win deal. It was predicated on the marginalization of China in the Middle East. The objective of the U.S. grand bargain was to normalize ties between Saudi Arabia and Israel, which was expected to then bring into the U.S.-led regional club the remaining Arab states and, ultimately, to suppress the axis of resistance. To the White House, Saudis were a critical part of a new chessboard in which the U.S., Saudis and Israel would share the strategic objective of containing Iran. Hoping additionally to contain China as a regional actor, the Biden administration wanted to use the Saudi deal to limit the kingdom's cooperation with Beijing on trade, technology and military matters, insisting that the Saudis would continue to trade oil in dollars rather than in local currencies, including the Chinese yuan. This reflected the U.S. concern that bilateral trade deals in local currencies could eventually undermine the U.S. dollar as the *de facto* global currency.

In particular, the White House wanted to alienate Israel from technology trade with Beijing and Chinese investments in Israel, particularly the automated container terminal in Haifa, where the U.S. Sixth Fleet is a regular visitor. Opened by the Shanghai International Port Group in fall 2021, the Haifa terminal has an annual handling capacity of one million ships. In the Middle East, the BRI has huge investments in ports in Saudi Arabia, Oman and Egypt. Washington relied on India to disrupt the China-Israel ties. By 2023, Indian billionaire Gautam Adani controlled 70 percent of the Israel's Haifa port, thanks to the U.S.-Indian effort to create an "Indo-Abrahamic bloc." The objective was to cut Beijing out from the Middle East and to strangle China's rise in Asia. In the process, Adani's past was conveniently ignored. As one of Prime Minister Modi's oligarch billionaires, his career has been trailed by allegations of fraud, stock manipulation and U.S. investors' charges of "pulling the largest con in corporate history."[24] With the diffusion of Chinese innovations in the Middle East, such as 5G, artificial intelligence (AI), and unmanned systems, U.S. efforts to contain that spread have accelerated; a trend illustrated by the Microsoft-G42 deal, in which the U.S. tech giant agreed to invest $1.5 billion in the Abu Dhabi-based technology holding company. In Washington, it was seen as an AI collaboration blueprint to insulate the region from China.

The primary strategic objective of the grand bargain was to consolidate U.S. hegemony in an era when it could no longer rely on unipolar economic and geopolitical supremacy. But this wasn't fully aligned with the interests of the Gulf states, not to mention the other Arab states and the axis of resistance countries. Most Arab countries wanted to foster security cooperation with the U.S., but they also hoped to sustain economic development cooperation with China. Their economic status quo had become untenable. Instead of conflict and instability, they needed peace and development. They had left Cold War behind. Unfortunately, America hadn't.

UNTENABLE STATUS QUO

U.S. Foreign Assistance in the Middle East

The U.S. priorities in the Middle East are not restricted to the Saudi deal, having recently been shaken by Riyadh's agreement to sell oil in yuan. They are reflected by U.S. foreign assistance, most of which has been in military aid. It has been designed to support countries that serve to maintain American hegemony in the region. Since 1946, the U.S. has provided $373 billion in foreign assistance to the Middle East, which makes it the largest regional recipient of U.S. economic and security assistance around the world (Figure 10-4a). For years, the bulk of the U.S. foreign aid, mainly in the form of State Department-managed military assistance, has been directed to just a few countries: Israel, Egypt, Jordan and more recently Iraq (Figure 10-4b).

**Figure 10-4   U.S. Foreign Assistance
in the Middle East and North Africa**

(a) U.S. Foreign Aid by Region: 1946–2020*

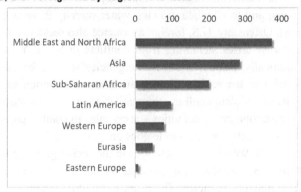

* Current U.S. dollars in billions, obligations.

(b) U.S. Foreign Aid to MENA Countries: 1946–2020*

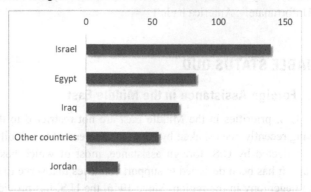

* Current U.S. dollars in billions, obligations.

Source: Funding administered by/appropriated to the State Department, USAID, and Defense Department and recorded, by law, in USAID's "Greenbook."

Bilateral assistance to regional countries seeks to reinforce longstanding U.S. foreign policy goals, presumably to contain Iranian influence, counterterrorism, and to promote Israeli-Arab peace. More recently, it has been touted as a U.S. response to emerging challenges, such as "strategic competition" with Russia, and to contain China, a perceived risk to America's global hegemony, and to alleviate growing water scarcity in some parts of the Middle East. Ostensibly, U.S. foreign assistance also seeks to ameliorate major humanitarian crises stemming from conflicts in Syria, Yemen, and elsewhere – ironically, insofar as these emergencies seem to be associated with U.S. policies in the region. The equation is too common to ignore: strategy of tension – violent conflict – humanitarian crises – reconstruction. Conversely: clandestine proxy activities – arms sales to conflict participants – infrastructure contracts. And the circle goes on.

In other words, Washington's activities in the region give rise to emergencies that the U.S. assistance can alleviate so that its regional activities can give rise to new emergencies. These are not tautological word-games. The bulk of U.S. activities in the region reflect the need of its military-industrial complex for new conflicts, which require arms transfers that provide contractor opportunities that lead to new crises, and so on. The point is not the conflict resolution about which all participants pontificate. The intent is to have no resolution to the conflict so that arms transfers will continue to prevail.

For fiscal 2024, overall aid requested for the region amounted to $7.6 billion, or about 11 percent of the U.S. State Department's international affairs budget request.[25] It is overtly preferential. As we have seen, U.S. military aid for Israel has been designed to maintain Israel's "qualitative military edge" over neighboring militaries.[26] Egypt and Jordan signed peace treaties with Israel in 1979 and 1994, respectively. U.S. military aid to these two countries is designed to encourage continued Israeli-Arab cooperation on security issues, while facilitating interoperability between the U.S. and its Arab partners in the U.S. Central Command (CENTCOM) area of responsibility.

After the implosion of the Soviet Union, the United States, as the sole remaining superpower, enjoyed its unipolar moment in the Middle East. But that unipolar era is fading. In the past decade or so, the economic rise of China has reverberated in the region, in part because it is not predicated on the kind of regime change favored by the U.S. and the previous European colonial powers. Similarly, in the past two decades, Russia has emerged as a major low-cost military power.[27] Hence, the untenable status quo in each major aid-recipient country in the region.

Egypt: An Unsustainable Status Quo

For more than four decades, successive administrations have justified U.S. assistance as an investment in regional stability. Nonetheless, U.S. military aid to Egypt finances the procurement of weapons systems and services from U.S. defense contractors. Through 2023–24, there was great concern in Cairo that Israel would bomb Egypt's wall along the border with the besieged Gaza Strip, compelling the Palestinians to flee to Egypt, as part of a covert plan to resettle Gaza. In view of the critics of President Abdel Fattah el-Sisi, the Israeli offensive also created a pretext for political and security repression prior to the Egyptian presidential election, ensuring his third term until 2030.

Based on its geopolitical importance, large population and diplomatic posture, postwar Egypt has been pivotal to U.S. interests in the region. When the Free Officers took power in the 1950s, both presidents Eisenhower and Kennedy courted Nasser until Cairo's turn to pan-Arabism and Moscow for military armament. Following Sadat's 1979 peace treaty with Israel, the pivot toward the U.S., and the subsequent rise of President Mubarak and his security apparatus, U.S.-Egyptian ties have prevailed. During these decades, Egyptian presidents have all been military men: Gamal Abdel Nasser (1954–1970), Anwar Sadat (1970–1981), Hosni Mubarak (1981–2011), and Abdel Fattah el-Sisi (2013–present). The only exception occurred in 2011–13, when the Arab Spring led Muhammad Morsi and the Egyptian Muslim Brotherhood to power. Democratically elected, it opposed the military-backed single-party rule and supported civil and sharia (Islamic) law. Unsurprisingly, it was overthrown by the Mubarak-era security apparatus that bought el-Sisi to power with U.S. support.

The bilateral tie is vital to Washington because Egypt controls the Suez Canal, one of the world's critical maritime chokepoints linking the Mediterranean and Red Sea. Since 1946, the U.S. has provided Egypt with over $87 billion in military and economic assistance, mainly after 1979.[28] With almost 110 million people, Egypt is by far the most populous country in the region. From the 1950s to 1970s, it had a pivotal political and military role in the Middle East. Today, that clout has faded. Yet, Egypt remains a major actor in the Arab world. It also has common interests with Israel in the face of Islamist militancy and instability in the Sinai Peninsula and Gaza Strip.

The Gaza War caught Egypt in a particularly challenging time with its economy and government finances struggling amid severe pressures. This was due to deficit spending and external shocks, such as to food security as a result of Russia's invasion of Ukraine and rising global interest rates. Between 2016 and 2022, the IMF extended $20 billion in credit to Egypt, and Gulf states lent Cairo tens of billions of dollars in the past decade. But the aid – whether by the U.S., the Gulf states or the IMF – is no longer unconditional. In particular, the IMF's $3 billion fund facility was premised on a set of reforms, such as the privatization of state-owned and military-run corporations.[29]

With its ailing economy and increasing aid conditionality, the el-Sisi government was squeezed by domestic opposition, regional constraints and U.S. pressures. After October 7, 2023, the government faced a rising domestic chorus against Israel and Egypt's bilateral cooperation with its occupation amid the ongoing genocidal atrocities in Gaza. Hence, Egypt's decision to intervene in support of South Africa's case against Israel at the International Court of Justice. In the absence of Israel's full withdrawal from the occupied territories, the bilateral trust with Israel has been eroding for decades. Today it is sustained mainly by U.S. aid, which is vital to Cairo. Meanwhile China's multibillion-dollar economic cooperation initiatives are fostering rather than undermining Egyptian development.

Jordan: Between a Rock and a Hard Place

A month after the inception of Israel's Gaza War, King Abdullah II of Jordan warned that "Gaza and its people] continue to face death and destruction in an ugly war that must stop immediately. Or our region will spiral into a major conflict whose price innocent people from both sides will pay, and whose repercussions will affect the whole world."[30] In December 2023, he was echoed by Foreign Minister Ayman Safadi, who said Israel's war against Palestinians met the "legal definition of genocide." To make things more uncomfortable, Amman faced growing calls to cancel the country's peace treaty with Israel, while Hamas, which has had offices in the country since the 1990s, gained new popularity. Abdullah's concern was that the war could spread from Gaza to the West Bank. Amman saw Israel's attempt to displace Palestinians as a "declaration of war"; an extraordinary shift since the normalization of bilateral ties in 1994.

Unlike Egypt, Jordan is the primary state interlocutor with the Palestinians due to its historical ties with the West Bank. However, the Hashemite Kingdom has also long been a U.S. partner in the Middle East. Hosting some 3,000 U.S. troops, it has partnered in global counterterrorism operations. The stated objective of U.S.-Jordanian military, intelligence, and diplomatic cooperation is to encourage political moderates and to reduce sectarian conflict and terrorist threats in the region. Continued instability in neighboring Iraq and Syria, due to past U.S. interventions, underscores Jordan's strategic importance to and increasing dependency on the U.S.

Successive U.S. administrations have acknowledged Jordan's central role as a U.S. partner. With total bilateral aid to Jordan amounting to $26.4 billion in 2020, the U.S. was seeking $1.5 billion in annual economic and military aid for Jordan, at least until 2029. Washington also provided Jordan with security assistance, border security and loan guarantees. Jordan's leadership is squeezed by its large Palestinian population and Arab citizens sympathetic to their cause. With a population of just 11.2 million, Jordan's GDP is barely $53 billion. Yet, it hosts around 2.2 to 3 million Palestinians. These post-1948 and post-1967 refugees are among the net effects of Israel's occupation. Jordan has long encouraged the U.S. to play a more assertive role with Israel, to force it to settle the Palestinian refugee crisis, and implement the two-state solution with little success.

In the absence of Israel's full withdrawal from the occupied territories, the bilateral trust with Israel has been eroding for two decades. Today it is sustained mainly by U.S. aid, which is vital to Amman. Over the decade preceding October 7, China signed agreements for infrastructure projects in Jordan worth over $7 billion, including plans to build a national railway network, an oil pipeline to link Iraq and Jordan, and a new Jordan-China university. In one way or another, such initiatives have been targeted by U.S. pressure. Such a grand bargain may be in the interest of some in Washington, but it is not in the interest of many in Jordan.

THE AXIS OF RESISTANCE

In his 2002 State of the Union address, President George W. Bush (in)famously targeted what he termed the "axis of evil," an iconic turn of phrase put in his mouth by the neoconservative scriptwriter, David Frum, who equates criticism of Israel with antisemitism. It was a shrewd notion that purposely lumped together very different countries (Iraq, Iran, North Korea) and implicitly associated them with the World War II allies' enemies, the "axis powers" (Nazi Germany, Mussolini's Italy, and Imperial Japan). In Israel and the United States, the Axis of Resistance is habitually defined as the war by "Iran and its proxies" against "Western interests." That is a gross simplification, which conveniently obscures the misguided and catastrophic U.S. war against Iraq, which fostered the rise of the regional opposition in the first place. Furthermore, one of the key targets of the Axis has been the Islamic State (ISIS), ever since the brutal group took over nearly a third of Iraq, thanks to the massive failure of the U.S. war against Iraq, and following that, during the Syrian proxy war, in which ISIS sought to exploit the Western-promoted destabilization of the Assad regime. Such proxy battles go back to Afghanistan in the 1980s, when the CIA's Operation Cyclone armed, financed and trained the Islamic fedayeen against Soviet interests, which subsequently gave rise to al-Qaeda and its Iraqi offshoot, ISIS.

And so it was that soon after Bush's address, regional observers turned the term around and began to refer to the "Axis of Resistance" in the Middle East. For all practical purposes. it has been fostered by the U.S. post-9/11 wars, particularly in Iraq, the Iran-Saudi Arabia proxy conflict, the shadow war by Israel and the U.S. against Iran, the Syrian proxy war, the longstanding Israel-Hamas war and the 2023–24 Israel-Gaza war. In many of these conflicts, an important role belonged to Russia, a longtime partner of several countries in the Middle East (Figure 10-5).

Targeting Iran

Ever since the Islamic Revolution in 1979, when President Carter froze billions of dollars in Iranian assets, Washington has sought to restore the status quo ante of the Shah that had made Iran safe to American capitalism. In the 1980s, U.S. intelligence and logistics played a vital role in arming Baghdad in the Iran-Iraq War, perhaps the most lethal conventional war between developing countries yet, with total casualty estimates up to 1 to 2 million.[31] In 1988, the U.S. launched an attack against Iran, presumably in retaliation for Iran's laying mines in areas in the Gulf. In the mid-'90s, the

Figure 10-5   The Axis of Resistance and Iran's Influence

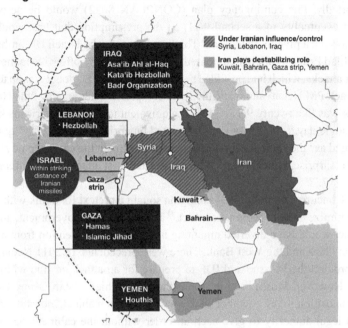

Source: Master Strategist/Axis of Resistance, CC BY-SA

Clinton administration declared a total embargo on dealings with Iran. In 2002, President Bush included Iran in his "axis of evil" speech. Subsequently, intelligence and regime change activities intensified, as the U.S. and Israel cooperated in training secessionist forces in Iran's Kurdistan province.[32] In 2007, U.S. reportedly vetoed an Israeli plan to bomb Iranian nuclear facilities.[33] Yet, during the next three years, the U.S. and Israel deployed the Stuxnet virus, the world's first offensive cyber weapon, to ruin almost a fifth of Iran's nuclear centrifuges. In 2015, years of challenging talks resulted in a nuclear deal (Joint Comprehensive Plan of Action, JCPOA) between Iran, the U.S. and a set of world powers. Despite Iran's verified ongoing adherence to it, the Trump administration pulled the U.S. out of the deal in 2018. As tensions escalated, the U.S. assassinated Iran's most important and popular general, Qasem Soleimani, in a deadly drone strike in January 2020.[34] What was less noticed was that Iran's subsequent retaliatory strike indicated greater than expected weapons capabilities.[35]

While the covert war in the shadows has prevailed since the Islamic Revolution, U.S. regime change efforts moved to a new stage during the Bush administration. Since 2003, the U.S. Army has conducted an analysis called TIRANNT (Theater Iran Near-Term) for a full-scale war with Iran. Reportedly, this contingency plan (CONPLAN 8022) would be activated in the eventuality of a second 9/11, on the presumption that Iran would be behind such a pivotal operation.[36] That's one reason why Israeli UN ambassador Gilad Erdan explicitly compared Hamas's October 7 offensive to the 9/11 terror attacks, which had provided the pretext for the U.S. global war on terror. In Israel, PM Netanyahu made the same comparison, adding that "the Hamas attack was like twenty 9/11s"; that is, equivalent to 50,000 Americans killed in a single day.[37] As if by a jointly-scripted blueprint, "Israel's 9/11" quickly emerged as "the short-hand reference point to explain the catastrophic shock, horror, surprise and enormity of the Hamas terrorist attack Israel suffered on October 7."[38]

Concurrently, many in Washington sought a pretext for a link with Iran, to legitimize a major regional conflict.[39] To Netanyahu's government, an Iran conflict would have diverted mounting negative public attention from atrocities in Gaza and the West Bank. There were precedents. In 2011 Netanyahu had ordered the Mossad and IDF to prepare for an attack on Iran within 15 days. However, Mossad's chief Tamir Pardo and chief of staff Benny Gantz, the opposition's key member in Netanyahu's war cabinet, questioned the PM's legal authority to give such an order without the cabinet's approval. Then, Netanyahu had backed off.[40] But Iran remained on the government's agenda and seems to have been part of Israel's Gaza War agenda. A month after the Hamas offensive, Netanyahu's Mossad chief David Barnea stated that Iran had stepped up terror worldwide." If Israelis or Jews are harmed, he added, Israel's would go after Tehran's "highest echelon."[41]

In April 2024, Israel bombed the Iranian embassy in Damascus killing 16 people including the targets, half a dozen high-level officers of the Islamic Revolutionary Guard Corps (IRGC). The Iranian response came on April 14, after two weeks of great unease in the region, with Iran giving full public notice that it was on its way. The IRGC launched a broad retaliatory attack against Israel and the Israeli-occupied Golan Heights with successive waves of drones, cruise missiles, and ballistic missiles. Tehran designed it carefully as a show of force that would not trigger a wave of escalation. It caused minimal damage in Israel but, as Israel would later acknowledge, despite containment efforts by the U.S., British, French and Jordanian, some of Iran's ballistic missiles penetrated Israel's defenses, and hit the Nevatim Air Base in southern Israel. Iran's attack was unprecedented in that it targeted Israeli territory as a warning shot, making a strong point without occasioning any casualties. Israel's combined domestic defenses and international defenders had proved inadequate against Iran's capabilities. It demonstrated Tehran's ability to counteract Israel's huge air superiority, even while lacking a modern air force of its own. Finally, it highlighted Israel's dependency on major Western powers to protect itself – and the inadequacy of that protection. Israel's muted response suggests rising concern over its presumed impunity concerning military strikes on Iran.

Before October 7, China had been Iran's biggest trade partner for more than a decade. The long-standing ties revolved particularly around the oil trade. In 2020, the bilateral ties reportedly entered a new stage with a 25-year agreement whereby China planned to invest $400 billion in Iran's economy over that time period, in exchange for oil from Iran. Any Israeli or American attack against Iran would be seen as a strike against Chinese sovereignty as well.

Syria: Lingering Proxy Wars

Addressing a party gathering in Damascus in December 2023, Syrian President Bashar al-Assad credited Palestinian resistance for "shattering" Israeli hegemony and challenging the dominance of the Zionist narrative on a global scale. In his view, the Gaza War exposed Israel's "terrorist reality" to the world.[42] By April 2024, Israeli air strikes on Syria's northern province of Aleppo had killed more than 40 people, most of them soldiers, including members of Hezbollah.

Governed by President Hafiz al-Asad from 1970 until his death in June 2000, Syria is a prominent player in the Middle East. Like many other states in the Middle East, the country was founded following centuries of Ottoman rule. After over two decades as a French mandate, it gained *de jure* independence as a democratic parliamentary republic in 1945. Four years later, its democratically elected government suffered a coup d'état, the first military regime change in modern Syria. Ostensibly led by the Army's chief of staff, Husni al-Za'im and other military leaders, the coup was engineered by the U.S. It was a test case for America's "capacity for exerting a democratizing influence on Arab countries."[43] Za'im ratified the construction on Syrian territory of the Trans-Arabian Pipeline, banned the Communist Party and signed an armistice with Israel.[44]

The overthrow destabilized Syria, setting the stage for successive military coups between 1949 and 1971. That contributed to the demise of Syrian democracy and the rise of pan-Arabism, ironically, the two things U.S. regime change was supposed to preempt. In 1958, Syria entered a brief union with Egypt. A new era dawned in 1963, when still another coup brought to power the socialist Ba'ath party. It consolidated the one-party state that ran the country under emergency law from 1963 to 2011, even longer than the rule of Generalissimo Chiang Kai-shek in Taiwan. As constitutional protections for citizens were suspended, internal power struggles in the Ba'ath party led to new coups until 1966 and 1970, when General Hafiz al-Assad seized power. Assad assigned Alawite loyalists to key posts in the armed forces, intelligence, bureaucracy, and the ruling elite. His "Alawi minority rule" finally consolidated power.

After the Cold War and the death of Hafiz al-Assad in 2000, his son Bashar al-Assad inherited the presidency and the autocratic system. Syria was suspended from the Arab League for over 11 years as multiple countries converged in an effort to overthrow the Assad government. The brutal proxy war killed a total of 580,000 to 620,000 people, causing the displacement of 6.7 million internally and 6.6 million external refugees. Taking into consideration the size of Syria's population, it was a catastrophe of extraordinary magnitude. During the Cold War, Syria had aligned with the Soviet Union. Since then, Russia had been Syria's ally. In the civil war, Moscow's support was critical to Bashar's surviving the struggle against Islamist extremists, such as ISIS and al-Qaeda's affiliate al-Nusra, which effectively collaborated with the U.S. against the Syrian government.

The Golan Heights, which Israel has occupied since 1967, remains one of the most intractable issues in the Arab-Israeli dispute. Since October 7, Syria has been on Israel's horizon, due to Iranian targets in the country, while the U.S. has maintained control over Syrian oil in eastern Deir Ezzor province. At the same time, Syria's allies, Iran and Russia, have charged Israel with flagrant violations of Syria's sovereignty, as it was regularly bombing the country at will and with impunity. Just days before October 7, President Bashar al-Assad visited China hoping to end over a decade of diplomatic isolation under Western sanctions. In turn, China had offered to help reconstruct the war-battered country. Though smaller than those of traditional donors, China's humanitarian aid in Syria has increased markedly, through the Belt and Road Initiative.

Yemen: Houthi Strikes over the Red Sea

In a speech, Abdul Malik al-Houthi, the leader of Yemen's Iran-aligned Houthis or Ansar Allah (helpers of God), said the group will "seek to escalate more and more if the barbaric and brutal aggression against Gaza does not stop, along with the siege of the Palestinian people from whom they deny aid and medicine."[45] Controlling Yemen's capital and most populous areas, the Houthis have attacked international shipping in the Red Sea since November

2023 in solidarity with Palestinians, drawing U.S. and British retaliatory fire since January 2024. Demonstrating the fragility of global energy security, the attacks were disrupting maritime trade in one of the world's busiest corridors. The net effect? Freight firms felt forced to reroute around the Cape of Good Hope to avoid the Suez Canal.

Located in the southern end of the Arabian Peninsula, Yemen borders Saudi Arabia to the north and Oman to the northeast, sharing maritime borders with Eritrea, Djibouti and Somalia. With a long coastline of 2,000 kilometers and 35 million people, it is one of the poorest countries in the world. In the 19th century, it was divided between the Ottoman and British empires. In 1962, a coup established a republic in North Yemen, whereas South Yemen's independence ensued in 1967. In long-isolated North Yemen, most people lived on subsistence agriculture. With oil discoveries on the Arabian Peninsula, living standards climbed, thanks to remittances from the Yemenite migrant labor working in Saudi Arabia. After the Cold War, the two states united in 1990, with Ali Abdullah Saleh as president. Since Yemen did not join the U.S.- and Saudi-led effort to oust Iraq from Kuwait, some 800,000 Yemenis were expelled from Saudi Arabia. With the demise of remittances, the net effect was massive unemployment and poverty. The Saleh regime did bring some stability to the north. It was a narrow oligarchy of military and security officers, tribal sheikhs, and northern businessmen. With elevated polarization, "the steep pyramid of patronage, power and privilege" diverted for private gain the public funds that could have been used for nation-building.[46]

As natural gas failed to offset the loss of oil revenues, explosive population growth reinforced immiseration. The Saleh regime became contested by the Houthis in the north and a secessionist movement in the south, with the revival of al-Qaeda, and the Yemenite Spring in 2011. Following Saleh's resignation, Yemen was engulfed in a civil war with the Presidential Leadership Council, the Houthi movement, and the separatist south. In 2015, Saudi Arabia launched airstrikes against the Houthis, claiming they were being aided by Iran. The Saudi coalition included Gulf countries, plus Jordan, Morocco, Sudan, Egypt, and Pakistan, with U.S. assistance in intelligence, targeting, and logistics.[47] As a result of the ensuing famine, more than 50,000 children in Yemen died from starvation in 2017. Critics charged the Saudi campaign for genocide, particularly its blockade of Yemen. It was compounded by a cholera outbreak affecting more than 1 million people. By the end of 2021, the war in Yemen had likely caused over 377,000 deaths, with roughly 70 percent children.[48]

Two years before October 7, the Houthis had fired on Saudi refineries in the Abqaiq-Khurais attack. As a result, Saudi Arabia's oil production was cut by half during the repairs. Indeed, the Houthis' lethal capacity has been systematically underestimated in the West. Following October 7, the Houthis targeted Israeli territory and commercial vessels transiting the Bab al Mandab Strait. Initially, the U.S. Navy tried to intercept Houthi-launched projectiles and prevent Houthi seizures of vessels. As these measures proved inadequate, the U.S. launched Operation Prosperity Guardian, a coalition formed to patrol the Red Sea. Nonetheless, the lingering Houthi attacks diverted traffic from the Red Sea, driving up shipping firms' costs, insurance premiums, and ocean freight rates.[49] And while the U.S. denied that the Houthis attacked USS *Eisenhower* on June 22, 2024, the aircraft carrier left the Red Sea a day later, after serving for months to thwart the Yemeni Houthi group's attacks on commercial shipping.

A month later, an explosive-laden drone launched by the Houthis in Yemen struck an apartment building in Tel Aviv, killing an Israeli man and wounding several others. Though identified, the drone was not shot down by air defenses and sirens were not activated due to human error. A day later, Israeli Air Force jets struck the weapons depots, a power plant and oil refinery facilities near Hodeidah, the Yemeni Red Sea port, causing extensive damage, killing half a dozen and injuring more than 80 people. It was the first time Israel struck in Yemen. In view of the Netanyahu cabinet, the disproportionate outcome reflected a typical Israeli deterrence: massive disproportionate response against civilians/civilian facilities. Yet, the success of the Houthi strike – at some 1,700 km from Israel – sent a message adding to that of the Iranian strike in April. Israel is vulnerable. In turn, the expected Houthi retaliation efforts against Israeli targets could raise the risk of an outbreak of a multi-front, high-intensity war. Like Khomeini's supporters preceding the Islamic revolution in Iran, the Houthis' politically marginalized followers are attracted by the group's struggle for economic development, social justice and Islam. Like the Palestinians in Gaza, they have the least to lose and heaven to win. Meanwhile, China has gradually increased its economic role in Yemen investing in the country's underdeveloped oil sector. When the hostilities end, development could surpass decades of destructive wars.

THE CHALLENGE FACING HEZBOLLAH

Lebanon: A Sectarian Balance at Risk

With barely 6 million people and a GDP half that of Jordan's, Lebanon today is a pale and fragmented shadow of the old "Paris of the Middle East." Teetering at the edge of bankruptcy, it struggles not to morph into a failed state. After World War I, the 1916 Sykes Picot agreement had allowed Britain and France to divide the Ottoman Empire's Arab provinces into zones of influence, with France taking over present-day Lebanon. Except for the cosmopolitan Beirut, the Maronite Christian enclave of Mount Lebanon was cobbled together with the mainly Muslim coastal cities, once a part of Ottoman Syria. In 1943, when Lebanon gained independence from France, the presidency was to be reserved for a Maronite Christian, the prime minister's post for a Sunni Muslim, and the speaker of parliament for a Shi'a.[50]

Despite the 1958 U.S. marine invasion, the Christian dominance crumbled under the pressure of a series of events, particularly the influx of mainly Sunni Muslim Palestinians fleeing to Lebanon during the 1948 War, the Palestinian militias residing in Lebanon in the 1970s and 1980s, and the subsequent mobilization of Lebanon's marginalized Shi'a Muslim community. This had led to a lingering civil war lasting from 1975 to 1990. In the early 1980s, Iran-backed militants later to be known as Hezbollah began to contest Israel's military presence in the largely Shi'a southern Lebanon. The U.S. brought forces to the conflict which were withdrawn after the 1983 deadly bombing of the Marine barracks in which over 240 Americans perished. Overwhelmed by the lethal spillovers of the Israel/Palestine conflict, the fragile mosaic that once was Lebanon fell apart as 150,000 people died in the hostilities. Today, two-thirds of the population is Muslim, equally divided among Sunnis and Shi'as, while less than a third comprise Christians, mainly Maronite Catholics.[51]

Marking the end of the long civil war in 1990, the Taif Accords formalized a new, even more fragile national status quo among the sectarian groups. After its participation in the U.S.-led coalition forces in the Persian Gulf War, Syria joined the process as something of an arbiter between rivals. With its militias dismantled and the Lebanese Armed Forces re-established, Hezbollah rejected disarming, given its role as resistance to Israeli military presence in southern Lebanon.[52] But instability lingered. In 2005, the assassination of Sunni former prime minister Rafik Hariri triggered huge street protests. A year later the Hezbollah-Israel War claimed almost 1,200 lives with Israel's first deployment of its fatal Dahiya doctrine, "designed to punish, humiliate and terrorize a civilian population," as the Goldstone Report later concluded.[53] The doctrine got its name when Israel dropped 23 tons of high explosives in a single raid on the Beirut Shia-dominated civilian southern suburbs of Dahiya.[54]

Following the 2006 Lebanon War, the 2007 North Lebanon conflict, the 2008 clashes in Lebanon and the Syrian civil war spillovers, every fourth resident in Lebanon was a refugee from Syria by the mid-2010s. In fall 2019, a mass protest uniting Lebanon's different sectarian groups triggered one of the "most severe crises episodes globally since the mid-19th century."[55] A year later, one of the largest non-nuclear explosions ever recorded shook the port of Beirut killing almost 200 people. That's where Lebanon stood at the eve of the Israel Hamas War: at the edge of a sectarian abyss, still suffering from the 1970s spillovers of the Israel-Palestine conflict. But for now, as a result of Israel's genocidal assault on Gaza, the diverse population has unified. In due time, hostilities would end. What then? Between 2000 and 2014, Lebanon received $20 million in aid from China. Following Lebanon's liquidity crisis since 2019, its government has looked to China for economic investments. That's what Beirut desperately needed, after half a century of devastating conflicts. But it wasn't a scenario supported by Israel. Likud cabinets wanted a "security zone" of their own up to the Litani River. In turn, Washington shunned Chinese economic presence in the fragile country.

The Power of the Party of God

Amid increasing speculation over regional escalation, major think tanks and over 100 leading Israeli military and government officials completed a report in early 2024 that had been three years in the making. Envisioning a final showdown, it concluded that the Israeli home front was effectively unprepared for an all-out war with Hezbollah that could prove far more costly than anticipated. It reflected Israelis' realization of the likely high costs and devastation of taking on Hezbollah, or the "Party of God," which is centered in southern Lebanon and has conducted numerous attacks against Israeli and Western targets.[56] In the U.S. view, Hezbollah is Iran's proxy force enabling Tehran's power projection across the region, thereby posing a risk to American interests and those of its allies.[57] But the linkage is self-serving and both Iran and Hezbollah are often demonized because they challenge the dark U.S. track-record in the Middle East.

Hezbollah was built by Iran's Islamic Revolutionary Guard Corps (IRGC) to foster a unified resistance against Israel in Southern Lebanon.[58] It was also shaped by the struggle against the Southern Lebanon Army (SLA) and the Israeli military between 1985 and 2000, and by its participation in Lebanese politics ever since 1990. Ironically, Hezbollah emerged as an unintended effect of the Israeli presence in Lebanon. "When we entered Lebanon," former Israeli PM Ehud Barak has acknowledged, "there was no Hezbollah. We were accepted with perfumed rice and flowers by the Shia in the south. It was our presence there that created Hezbollah."[59] After 2012, Hezbollah participated in the brutal Syrian proxy war supporting Bashar al-Assad's government against the proxy jihadi forces armed and supported by the U.S., France and others, and in Iraq fighting against the Islamic State. By its own testimony, it has up to 100,000 fighters.[60]

The history of Hezbollah is intertwined with that of Hassan Nasrallah, a Lebanese cleric and its secretary-general, who joined the group in 1982 and became its leader after an Israeli airstrike killed his predecessor, Abbas al-Musawi, a decade later. Led by Nasrallah, Hezbollah began to acquire longer-range rockets. By 2006, it possessed about 100 long-range missiles, including the Iranian-made Fajr-3 and Fajr-5. The latter had a range of 75 km, enabling it to strike the Israeli port of Haifa, while the Zelzal-1 had an estimated 150-km range, allowing it to reach Tel Aviv. Already by then, it was a military force to be reckoned with.[61] Like Ayatollah Khomeini's Iran, Nasrallah's Hezbollah focused on political participation, but also domestic socio-economic injustice. That resonated in Lebanon, torn by decades of civil strife, crumbling infrastructure and rudimentary social services. When Israel ended its 18-year occupation and withdrew from Lebanon under Hezbollah pressure, that, too, enhanced Hezbollah's popularity.

Hezbollah has been funded by Iran, Lebanese business groups and individual donors, and by taxes paid by the Shia Lebanese and diaspora and other Muslim countries. Its popularity goes beyond the Shi'a base. Participating in politics since 1992, it draws popular support from a huge network of schools, clinics, youth programs, and other social services. It entered the cabinet for the first time in 2005, with 1–3 three seats in each Lebanese government since then. It has also fought for the untapped offshore energy reserves. In 2010, it stated that the Dalit and Tamar gas fields, some 80 km west of Haifa claimed to be in an Israeli exclusive economic zone, belonged to Lebanon, and warned Israel against extracting gas from them.[62]

In 2018, U.S. sources estimated Iran's support for Hezbollah at $700 million per year.[63] By October 7, 2023, it likely had at least 60,000 fighters, including full-time and reservists. It had increased its stockpile of missiles to some 150,000.[64] In spring 2024, the concern in both Israel and Lebanon was that Israel's lingering war in Gaza, Hezbollah's strikes in Israel and Israel's retaliatory strikes could lead to a far deadlier and broader conflict across the volatile region. The Netanyahu cabinet's increasing hits against Hezbollah and Iranian targets by summer 2024 suggested that Israel considered the cost of potential escalation lower than the benefits of crippling those targets – and that the White House, though officially "concerned," was playing along.

As Israel was threatening a major strike against Hezbollah, the 22-member Arab League announced it no longer viewed the organization as a "terrorist group" (in 2016 the League had designated Hezbollah a terrorist organization, in line with Saudi Arabia). It was a major policy shift reflecting Arab concerns with Israel's Gaza War and regional escalation and the rapprochement between Riyadh and Tehran. The stakes of any major Israeli operation against Hezbollah increased accordingly.

Nasrallah often highlights Hezbollah's advanced weaponry but he tends to be mum on its highly developed below-ground infrastructure of tunnels.

The Hezbollah Inter-Metro Tunnel Networks

What made Hezbollah a particularly risky challenger was not just its missiles, but its capabilities in underground warfare, which Israel first discovered during the 2018 conflict when the IDF exposed half a dozen tunnels dug from Lebanon into Israel. The largest tunnel featured air-conditioning, phone lines, and rail tracks. It was 260 feet deep, equivalent to a 22-story building, over 3,000 feet long, and extending nearly 250 feet into Israel. It served as a platform for cross-border invasions. Until then, the Israeli military had thought that the rocky terrain of southern Lebanon hindered the development of an extensive Hezbollah tunnel network. Realities proved them wrong.[65]

After the Second Lebanon War of 2006, in which Israel drastically raised the stakes by adopting the Dahiya doctrine of mass devastation, Hezbollah concluded that it needed to prepare for an existential struggle with Israel. And so, it is thought that, with support from Iran and North Korea, it began to build an "inter-regional" tunnel network.

Why North Korea? In the 1950s, when the U.S. bombardment destroyed 90 percent of North Korean cities, its leadership saw itself in an existential dilemma in which the U.S. nuclear deployment could not be excluded (Washington was had already used biowarfare against North Koreans), the only way out was to build tunnels for military use. Hezbollah's network was far more extensive than the "Hamas Metro." Initially, Hezbollah's tunnel construction benefitted from the experience of Palestinian fighters who had dug tunnels in southern Lebanon before Israel's 1982 invasion. While the building and cooperation may date from the late 1980s with North Korean advisors, it intensified after the 2006 War.

Far more than a network of offensive and infrastructure local tunnels, in or near villages, it is a network of tens of kilometers of regional tunnels that extend and connect the Beirut area (Hezbollah's headquarters) and the Beqaa area (logistical rear base) to southern Lebanon (divided into two "lines of defense"). Let's call it the "Hezbollah Inter-Metro." Extending potentially into Israeli territory, its cumulative strength is thought to reach up to hundreds of kilometers, with underground command and control rooms, weapons and supply depots, field clinics and specified designated shafts that are hidden and camouflaged. These are used to fire missiles of all types and cannot be detected above ground. The Hezbollah inter-Metro network also features several types of tunnels. Tactical tunnels are based near Lebanese villages and used mainly by infantry to move secretly, attack and return to rearm and rest. Proximity tunnels are similar but designed to move fighters near the Israeli border for attack. Finally, explosive tunnels are traps filled with explosives and placed in strategic positions to be remotely detonated when IDF troops approach.

An Israel-Hezbollah War Scenario

Following the Hamas offensive, a total of up to 250,000 Israelis were officially evacuated or self-evacuated along the southern border with Gaza and the northern border with Lebanon. The lingering war and hostilities in several fronts continued to keep nearly 100,000 Israelis internally displaced, including 80,000 from along the northern border with Lebanon. Between October 7 and the end of June 2024, Hamas fired 12,000 rockets at Israeli targets while Hezbollah launched more than 8,000 rockets and other explosives into Israel. That was the new normal that everybody dislikes. Until it no longer is.

In the Israel-Hezbollah War scenario projected here, still another Hezbollah retaliatory strike begins, featuring massive fire, with up to 3,000 rocket launches causing havoc across Israel.[66] In one day, Hezbollah launches as many rockets as it had in the past 120 days altogether. Aiming to cause immense devastation in Israel, Hezbollah and its allies in Gaza, Iraq and Yemen spread fire and bloodshed across Israel, particularly greater Tel-Aviv-Yaffo and Haifa as well as strategic targets like Dimona (in these scenarios, Jerusalem is largely spared, due to its immense religious significance), causing thousands of casualties on both the frontlines and the home front, unleashing widespread public panic. At the same time, Hezbollah is hammering the Israeli air force to disrupt and limit its ability to operate from its bases. Heavy and precise missiles are directed towards takeoff routes at steady intervals in concerted efforts to prevent their recovery. Concurrently, indiscriminate fire is directed towards hangars storing F-16, F-35, and F-15 planes, the bulk of Israel's main air power, thanks to U.S. military aid, technology and finance. The strategic goal of the early multi-front attack is to demolish the IDF's air defense systems. Hence, the precision-guided munitions and low-signature weapons, such as loitering munitions, drones, and standoff missiles, to physically strike and destroy Iron Dome batteries.

Today, estimates of Hezbollah's expanded array of missiles amounts to 120,000 to 200,000. In a bid to contain the massive momentum of the early attacks, Israel resorts to a huge counter-response of Iron Dome interceptors and David's Sling missiles. At first, it seems to boost the morale of the civil defense – until it no longer does. Israel's Iron Dome anti-missile batteries risk being overwhelmed in the opening strikes of the war. Complicating the challenge are Hezbollah's increasing and lethally effective use of drones, including kamikaze weapons, which Israel's existing air defenses have struggled to contain. After a few days of waves of missiles and interceptors on over-drive, the stockpiles of the interceptors and missiles are depleted, leaving Israel exposed to new waves of thousands of rockets and missiles without effective defense.

In the first days of the War, Hezbollah fighters are joined by pro-Iranian groups from across the region, including pro-Iranian militias in Syria and Iraq, Hamas and Islamic Jihad in Gaza, the Houthis in Yemen (these scenarios downplay the potential role of Turkiye in a major regional escalation). Israeli facilities are struggling to cope with precise missiles with hundreds of kilograms of explosive warheads, including cruise missiles, as they begin to hammer power plants, electricity and transportation infrastructure, communications, government offices, and water desalination and transmission facilities. Local authorities' sites become targets for widespread cyber-attacks, harming and paralyzing the functioning of the economy and society. As the seaports of Haifa and Ashdod are paralyzed, international trade dries up. Meanwhile, dozens of Iranian-made suicide drones fly at very low altitudes towards high-quality targets deep within Israel, directed at weapon factories, IDF emergency warehouses, and hospitals, which are soon overwhelmed with casualties beyond what medical teams can handle, far more than even after October 7. Traffic light control systems collapse and traffic flow become challenging and dangerous. Compounding the devastation and confusion, Hezbollah sends hundreds of Radwan commandos to seize towns and villages, and IDF posts along the Lebanese border. As the IDF is forced to fight within Israeli territory, efforts are diverted from operations on the ground in Lebanon to take control of launch areas.

On the home front, the public struggles to receive timely and credible information about the war, while hostile psyop floods mainstream mass media and social media with disinformation and fake news. The ultra-rich 1% of Israelis seize their private planes and grasp one of their several passports, while the rich 10% try to follow in their footsteps. Meanwhile, the best and the brightest struggle to find refuge abroad only to find that all flights have been canceled. Confronted with the chaos, Israelis can no longer trust in official sources and spokespeople. The internally displaced try to find a safe zone in Israel but there no longer are any. As anxiety and panic mount, so do ever-larger casualties, massive infrastructural damage, power and water supply disruptions, delays in rescue and relief forces to destruction zones, and difficulties in accessing essential services such as food and medicine. The PM family members pledge retaliation from wherever they are. But it's too little too late. Hezbollah has brought Gaza into Israel.

Throughout the conflict, Hezbollah will try to unleash fires in every possible arena of the total war, including through incitement, encouragement of an uprising in the West Bank and among Israel's Arab citizens. After about three weeks of fire and bloodshed, the unprecedented scale of damage in both Lebanon and Israel will lead to an end of the conflict in a stalemate, amid pressure from the international community.

A similar war scenario was outlined by Maj. Gen. (res.) Itzhak Brik several years before October 7. Unlike the right-wing cabinets, Brik stressed the ingenuity of Iran's patient, long-term strategy aiming to entrench its deployment of missiles around Israel while avoiding creating tension before the job is done. The scenario built on more than 200,000 rockets and missiles by Iran, Hezbollah in Lebanon, Hamas and Islamic Jihad in the Gaza Strip, the Houthis in Yemen, and Shi'ite militias in Yemen, Syria and Iraq. Brik blamed the Likud cabinets for "diverting the attention of our political and security leadership from the main issue: massive preparation of both the IDF and the home front for the existential threat that's burgeoning around us."

> In this equation, Israel has a very serious problem because it has no solution for 3,000 missiles of various sizes that would attack it daily – hundreds of them precision missiles, each carrying hundreds of kilograms of explosives.
>
> If missiles were to land every day on population centers in the Tel Aviv metropolitan area, in Haifa Bay, Be'er Sheva and Jerusalem, and if they were to hit strategic, security and civilian targets (such as power stations, water facilities, airports, and IDF

ground forces and air bases) – they would inflict extremely heavy losses and inestimable damage.[67]

What the extreme war scenarios in Washington underestimated, however, was Israel's likely responses amid a wide and lethal attack. Faced with a seemingly severe destabilization, Israeli leadership may conclude early on it is dealing with an existential struggle for survival and act accordingly. In other words, the idea that Israel would be willing to cope with weeks of daily disruptions without a drastic response is naïve. And should things get worse, Israel is likely to mobilize for a potential nuclear confrontation, as it did in 1967 and 1973.

THE ULTIMATE RISK

Nuclear Ambiguity

The conventional estimate is that Israel's nuclear stockpile comprises some 90 nuclear warheads, which makes the tiny country the world's 9th largest nuclear power. However, unofficial estimates vary. The conventional estimate is at the lower end of a possible range that some analysts suggest could be as high as 200, up to 400 nuclear weapons.[68] The latter would make it the world's 4th largest nuclear power, right after Russia, the U.S., and China, and before France, the UK, India and Pakistan (Figure 10-6).[69]

Figure 10-6   World Nuclear Forces

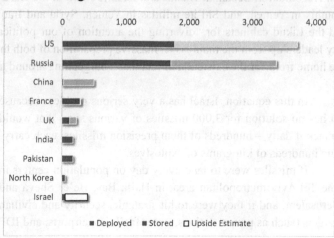

Source: SIPRI, author, January 2024

Most Israelis perceive Iran as the primary nuclear risk. Israel has a broad range of nuclear weapons, while Iran may have enriched enough nuclear material to build them but is thought not to have done so, as of yet. Such weapons, were they to exist, would be deeply underground, possibly inaccessible even by a nuclear strike. In such scenarios, large civilian hubs would not be collateral damage, but intended mass targets. According to some projections, nuclear weapon detonations in Iran's densely populated cities would likely result in millions of dead, with tens of millions of injured and without adequate medical care, a devastating loss of municipal infrastructure, long-term disruption of economic, educational, and other essential social activity, and a full breakdown in law and order. These nightmares include thermal burn and radiation patients who would have to suffer their extreme pains without any treatment.[70]

Officially, Israel has a long-standing policy of nuclear ambiguity. While it has used psychological warfare leaks to signal its disproportionate nuclear deterrence, it neither officially confirms nor denies that it possesses nuclear weapons.[71] In public, the standard statement has been that "Israel will not be the first country to introduce nuclear weapons to the Middle East."[72] Yet effectively, the Israeli policy is more preemptive by nature.

The country first flirted with the nuclear option at the eve of the 1967 War, concerned that it might lose.[73] Since the early 1960s, Israel has relied on what investigative journalist Seymour Hersh has described as the Samson Option. The term refers to the biblical figure of Samson who pushed apart the pillars of a Philistine temple bringing down the roof. In the process, he killed not just his enemy, the Philistines, but himself as well. It suggests an ultimate deterrence strategy of massive retaliation.[74] In October 1973, amid the Egyptian-Syrian invasion, Golda Meir and Moshe Dayan mobilized nuclear warheads for possible use, which led to president Nixon's massive rearmament drive and the rapid deepening of the bilateral military ties.[75]

The Begin Doctrine

In 1981, Israel destroyed Iraq's nuclear reactor Osirak as the Begin government initiated its war on Lebanon. Despite public criticism by the Reagan administration, the U.S. and Israel signed a strategic memorandum of understanding and began to deepen bilateral ties in defense. The Osirak attack gave rise to the Begin nuclear doctrine, which allows no "hostile" regional state to possess nuclear military capability.

Begin described the strike as an act of "anticipatory self-defense at its best." He framed it as a long-term national commitment.

We chose this moment: now, not later, because later may
be too late, perhaps forever. . . . Then, this country and this people
would have been lost, after the Holocaust. Another Holocaust
would have happened in the history of the Jewish people. Never
again, never again! . . . We shall not allow any enemy to develop
weapons of mass destruction turned against us.[76]

In a sense, the Begin doctrine reflected the right-wing Likud's offensive view of national security. But it also represented continuity and can be
dated to the early 1960s Operation Damocles, Mossad's covert campaign to
assassinate Nazi Germany's rocket scientists working for Egypt to develop
bombs using radioactive waste.[77] The legendary head of Mossad, Isser Harel,
recruited former Nazis to provide intelligence on Arab countries. When I met
Harel in the mid-1970s, he denied all such stories. Subsequently, he confirmed
them. One of these hired hands was the legendary Waffen-SS commando
Otto Skorzeny, who had served as adviser to Egypt's President Nasser. There
is a straight line from Operation Damocles to Israel's 1981 attack on Iraq's
Osirak nuclear reactor and the subsequent targeted killings of Iranian nuclear
scientists, particularly since 2010.

A month after the Hamas offensive of October 7, Netanyahu's heritage
minister Amichai Eliyahu suggested that one of Israel's options in the war
against Hamas was to drop a nuclear bomb on the Gaza Strip. As the story
spread internationally, it was quickly disavowed by PM Netanyahu, but
he did not fire his minister. The far-right Eliyahu objected to allowing any
humanitarian aid into Gaza, saying, "we wouldn't hand the Nazis humanitarian aid because there is no such thing as uninvolved civilians in Gaza.[78]

In a way, Eliyahu got what he wished for. By late April 2024, Israel had
dropped more than 70,000 tons of bombs over Gaza, surpassing the bombing
of Dresden, Hamburg, and London combined during World War II.[79] That
amounts to more than 30 kilograms of explosives per individual on mainly
women and children. Furthermore, the weight of the U.S. nuclear bombs
dropped on Hiroshima and Nagasaki in Japan was estimated at about 15,000
tons of explosives. Even before the Rafah offensive, Gaza had been bombed
almost five times more than that. Reflecting extraordinary brutality and blind
disregard to human life, it was a shocking war crime with no parallel in recent
and in fact, in the entire human history. What made it all the more stunning
was the Biden-Harris complicity coupled with the hollow assurances that "we
are working 24 hours a day for peace" with the whole world watching – the
other way.

The Deterioration of Israel's Military Sovereignty

Ever since Iraq's demise, Iran has been Israel's primary nuclear concern. In June 2024, the U.S. and Israel were busy assessing new intelligence about Iranian nuclear models. The purpose of the modeling was the concern that the West's intelligence was a signal about Iran's nuclear weapons ambitions, whereas other officials said it was a "blip" that did not represent a shift in Iran's policy and strategy towards weaponization. Having previously stated that it ended weaponization work in 2003, Iran has repeatedly denied wanting nuclear weapons, and the validity of that denial has been repeatedly confirmed by American intelligence reports. Nonetheless, a month later, U.S. Secretary of State Antony Blinken said, without evidence, that Iran's breakout time – the time needed to produce enough weapons grade material for a nuclear weapon – "is now probably one or two weeks." The assumption – or at least the claim – was that Tehran has continued to develop its nuclear program. "Where we are now is not in a good place."[80]

For decades, most security analysts took at face value the conventional wisdom that Iran would not dare to attack Israel directly and that Israel's nuclear weapons would only be deployed to deter attacks. That bubble was burst after the Israeli bombing of the Iranian Embassy in Damascus killing two Syrian generals. On April 13, 2024, Iran's military, in cooperation with the Lebanese Hezbollah, the Yemenite Houthis and Iraq's Islamic Resistance launched retaliatory attacks against Israel with suicide drones, cruise missiles and ballistic missiles. Most of these were contained; but as addressed earlier, not all. And in this containment, the critical role belonged to the West's multinational intervention; not to the IDF. The outcome did not underscore Israel's success, but rather its failure in containment. This was no surprise to many observers, including those in Israel.

The concern about Israel's liabilities was a motive for the statement by Israel's former PM Ehud Olmert, in the aftermath of October 7. "Israel cannot and should not stay in Gaza. But when Israel's allies ask: What's next? Netanyahu and his government of bloodthirsty messianic thugs have no answer." What Olmert proposed was a plan "based on a NATO intervention force, and restarting two-state negotiations."[81] In fact, this vulnerability was foreseen by Reuven Shiloah, Mossad's first director, already at the turn of the 1950s, when he struggled – unsuccessfully – to have Israel join NATO.[82]

The U.S. War Games: A 2027 Israel-Iran Nuclear Confrontation

So, the question remains: how would Israel respond to a conventional "existential crisis" with Iran? In late 2023, the hypothesis was tested in a high-level U.S. war game in which participants included members of U.S. executive branch, Republicans and Democrats in the Congress, leading academics, think-tank experts and Pentagon officials. The game starts in 2027 with Israeli intelligence reports that Iran is mating nuclear warheads to its long-range missiles. Consequently, Israel targets Iran's key nuclear and missile sites with U.S. standoff hypersonic missiles. That is followed by devastating conventional missile strikes against Israel with thousands of casualties, to which, in this projected 2027 scenario, Israel retaliates with aerial strikes. Iran responds by striking key Israeli nuclear and government buildings and withdrawing from the Nuclear Non-Proliferation Treaty (NPT), thereby signaling its readiness to deploy nuclear weapons. Washington urges Israel to stop escalation. But in an emergency that is perceived as existential for national survival, Israelis have little interest in U.S. concerns. Isolated and unable to halt Iran's possible nuclear strike, the Israeli PM greenlights a non-lethal nuclear demonstration detonation over a remote location in Iran, coupled with conventional strikes and cyber-attacks against the main Iranian nuclear facilities and military sites. Instead of overwhelming Iran, these assaults strengthen resolve in Tehran, which begins preparing a new response. Then, Israel launches a nuclear strike of 50 weapons against 25 major Iranian military targets, including Russian air defense sites (which would be a rather surprising strategic move because it could draw in both Russia and the U.S., the world's greatest nuclear powers). Yet – in the U.S. scenario that *presumes* Iran's offensive nuclear capabilities by 2027 – Iran manages to launch a nuclear strike against an Israeli air base with an American military presence.[83]

Intriguingly, initially the U.S. participants presumed that self-restraint would prevail in this high-level war game. Yet, the simulation's cold logic compelled them into a sequence of steps that quickly went nuclear. Assuming that a severe conventional confrontation would soon drive Israel and Iran at the edge of a nuclear crisis, what would be the *consequences* of such an escalation?

Projected Human Costs of an Israel-Iran Nuclear Confrontation

In one of the most comprehensive scenarios of the consequences of an Israel-Iran nuclear confrontation, Israel's hypothetical nuclear forces were presumed to entail at least 200 boosted and fusion weapons, with yields from 20 Kt to 1 megaton, with an array of delivery capabilities. In turn, Iran was predicted to have some 10-20 nuclear weapons over time, mainly fission devices, in the range of 15–30 Kt and with more limited delivery capabilities.[84] Addressing solely the nuclear exchanges, this scenario assumed multiple strikes by Israel in Iranian cities with some 1 to 2 million people, such as Arak, Ahvaz, Bandar Abbas. Esfahan, Kermanshah, Mashad, Shiraz, Tabriz, and particularly Tehran with its 8.3 million residents. In turn, single strikes by Israel would hit cities with up to 1 million people, such as Arak, Ardabil, Hamadan, Karaj, Kerman, Qazvin Rasht, Reza Iyeh, Yazd, and Zahedan. Iran would rely on single strike against Be'er Sheva and Haifa, respectively, and a double strike against Tel Aviv and its 1.4 million people. The assumption was that Jerusalem would be sidelined, due to its large Muslim population and holy sites.[85]

In addition to the stunning human toll, the presumed likely targeting by both nations of densely populated urban areas would result in devastating loss of critical industrial infrastructure and huge economic decline, coupled with highly damaging mental health and societal chaos, plus extremely destabilizing ripple effects throughout the region and the rest of the world. Iranian cities would suffer high level of fatalities, without the ability to treat massive numbers of burn patients, huge logistical issues with trauma mass casualties, and relative unfamiliarity with radiation victim treatment. Large numbers of surviving thermal burn patients, many of them with concurrent trauma injuries, would be in desperate need of medical care, which won't be available.

The concentration of over 8 million residents in Tehran would result in a large number of both fatalities and injuries. The percent of fatalities would increase from 44 to 67 to 86 percent of the city's population with the use of multiple 100 Kt, 250 Kt, and 500 Kt devices, respectively. There would be 1.5 million victims of thermal burns from either the 100 Kt or 250 Kt multiple weapon attacks, and from 750,000 to 880,000 severely radiation-exposed patients. After detonation, the thermal burn victims would likely receive no care, while the radiation victims would have to live with their severe pain in the hours and days after the attack. The survivors would be the living dead.

In contrast to the broad expanses of Iran, Israel is small and narrow, with its population centered in just a few urban areas and thus highly vulnerable to nuclear warfare. The assumption is that Iran could deliver five 15 Kt devices through Israeli defenses, with detonations on three urban targets using four 15 Kt devices, and one strategic site in its Negev nuclear center (read: in the proximity of Dimona). Even these relatively small weapons would cause great destruction. In the city of Be'er Sheva, half of the residents would be killed with a single weapon, with another sixth of the population being injured. Similar fatality and injury ratios would be seen in Haifa with over 40,000 trauma victims. In contrast to the 75–95% fatality outcomes for Iranian cities with the larger nuclear weapons, two 15 Kt devices used on Tel Aviv would result in 17% of the population being killed; that's almost a quarter of a million people. Even with the relatively small 15 Kt devices, over 100,000 people would suffer thermal burn injuries. Another 100,000 could receive potentially fatal doses of radiation from the two fallout plumes. Some 115,000 would sustain significant trauma injuries. The radiation plume extending from Tel Aviv would cover more populated areas in Israel, even reaching into populated areas of the West Bank. In Iran's single-strike cities the number of total casualties – that is, fatalities and injured – would amount to 7.9 million people, whereas in its double-strike cities the figure would soar to 29 million; that's almost 37 million altogether. In two Israeli single-strike cities and the dual strike Tel Aviv, the total would amount to almost 640,000 people.

"Nuclear Winter" with Biblical Characteristics

The described nuclear scenario was developed a decade ago. The lethal power of both Israel and Iran is today far greater. Furthermore, then Iran's population was 77 million and Israel's barely a tenth of that. Today, the comparable figures are 90 million and 9.3 million, respectively. In metro Tehran, the number of residents today exceeds 9.6 million; and in Tel Aviv 1.4 million, respectively. Adding the inner and outer metropolitan areas in close proximity to Tel Aviv–Yafo, the full Tel Aviv metropolitan area has 4.2 million residents. It is not just the center of Israeli finance and technology, but almost 60 percent of Israeli GDP. In other words, with a population that's only half relative to Tehran, its metro economy amounts to more than 75 percent of Iran's *entire* economy. That makes metro Tel Aviv the preferred target in any major nuclear, conventional and cyber confrontation.

Whatever happens in such nuclear scenarios, their impact won't be confined to the primary targets. In the early 1980s, scientists in the United States and Soviet Union demonstrated that a major nuclear war could unleash a "nuclear winter." In this theory characterizing the anticipated climatic effects of nuclear war, the basic idea is that the fires unleashed by the nuclear weapons would result in black, sooty smoke from cities and industrial facilities that would be heated by the sun and lofted into the upper stratosphere, diffusing globally, enduring for years. The consequent cool, dark and dry conditions at earth's surface would prevent crop growth for at least one growing season, leading to mass starvation over most of the world, coupled with massive ozone depletion, causing enhanced ultraviolet radiation. Even if the nuclear attack would be regional or locational, more people could die in the adjacent non-combatant areas than where the bombs were dropped, due to these indirect effects.[86]

With the proliferation of nuclear technology in the volatile Middle East, the likelihood of a catastrophic nuclear war, whether by purpose or accident, is elevated, even if it would result in utterly unacceptable outcomes in Israel and Palestine, the Middle East and the world at large.[87] Ultimately, the Samson Option remains at the heart of Israel's deterrence strategy of massive retaliation with nuclear weapons. As a "last resort," Samson will bring down the roof and kill himself and the Philistines who capture him. It is a version of the Wagnerian *Götterdämmerung*, "Twilight of the Gods," overshadowed by chaos, violence and destruction.

A nuclear confrontation remains one possible scenario of regional escalation – not the most probable one but certainly the most devastating option. In these considerations, the potential of widespread regional collateral damage has been largely absent. Such a scenario will be preceded by lethal conventional strikes. Yet, such assaults have not had adequate impact on the other components of the Axis of Resistance: Hezbollah in southern Lebanon, Ansarallah (the Houthis) in Yemen, or the supporting forces in Syria and Iraq. Furthermore, the deployment of major conventional fire power is likely before full nuclear mobilization. Yet, the temptation to resort to ultimate weapons to contain ultimate risks is real. Since the reverberations would be felt around the world, the question is how far would Washington, Brussels and Beijing go to preempt such a scenario.

State of Regional Escalation

Amid the ceasefire talks on July 31, 2024, Israel assassinated Ismail Haniyeh, the political leader and chief ceasefire negotiator of Hamas. Haniyeh was killed in his accommodation in a military-run guesthouse in Tehran, after attending the inauguration ceremony for Iran's new president Masoud Pezeshkian. It was Prime Minister Netanyahu's last-minute effort to undermine Hamas, force the reform-minded Pezeshkian to join the hardliners and extend the Gaza War into southern Lebanon, even at the risk of regional escalation.

Though officially portraying itself as a neutral broker in the Middle East, the head of the U.S. Central Command rushed to meet with his IDF colleague to prepare against an anticipated Iranian retaliation. The Pentagon announced the deployment of an additional squadron of F-22 Raptors, while 4,000 marines and 12 ships were deployed to the region. Raising the stakes, U.S. Defense Secretary Lloyd Austin ordered the deployment of USS *Georgia*, a nuclear-powered submarine, to the Middle East.[88] The rare move to publicly announce the deployment of the nuclear submarine reflected the concern of the Biden administration that it was losing control in the Middle East.

Why was the three-phase Israel–Hamas war ceasefire proposal such a nightmare to Netanyahu and his far-right cabinet? The proposed prisoner exchange and armistice proposal to end the Israel–Hamas war was drafted by mediators from Egypt and Qatar on May 5, and endorsed by Hamas a day later. Struggling to redefine the Israeli cabinet's obstinate hesitancy as thoughtful accommodation, President Biden tried to sell it as an "Israeli proposal." In fact, the proposal outlined in three stages, starting with a six-week ceasefire, the release of all Israelis being held in Gaza in exchange for some Palestinian detainees, a permanent ceasefire, Israel's withdrawal from Gaza, and a reconstruction process lasting from three to five years.[89]

When Netanyahu rejected the Gaza ceasefire in late June, it was still another blow to the U.S.-backed proposal, but hardly a surprise. Fighting for political survival, Netanyahu played for time, expecting Trump to win the U.S. presidency against the incumbent Vice President Kamala Harris in November, which he hoped would result in a carte blanche for Israel to "neutralize" Gaza, annex the West Bank, extend Israel's northern presence up to the Litani River in southern Lebanon and to destabilize Iran. So, when Netanyahu greenlighted the Haniyeh assassination in late July, he tried to create new facts on the ground for the continuance of the war. Hence, the Biden administration's effort to rush U.S. military assets into the region with attempts to contain Iran's expected retaliation by pushing the ceasefire with the entire U.S. military and diplomatic arsenal. In the big picture, all these efforts built on the expectation that a major Hezbollah scenario could cause Israel weeks of extraordinary pain and chaos, while a major conventional war between Israel and Iran would trigger a nuclear confrontation in the region.

Unlike the United States, Beijing is sidelining military maneuvering by promoting peace and development in the region. In addition to investing significantly in countries in which the U.S. is known for its military aid and regime change operations, Beijing has defused tensions between Iran and Saudi Arabia, unified Palestinian forces and launched a historic partnership with Egypt. But in mid-August, Beijing sent an even stronger signal about its commitment by establishing a Second Silk Road in the region on the brink of all-out war. It was aligned with a long-term strategy. China has exclusive rights to several Iranian oil and natural gas fields. As part of a 2016–2017 agreement, Beijing cautioned it would regard any foreign attack on these areas as attacks on its own sovereign territory. Two years later, Iran joined China's Belt and Road (BRI) initiative. In March 2021, the two countries signed a 25-year strategic cooperation agreement worth $400 billion. The launch of another Silk Road ensued after major Chinese investments in Saudi Arabian stocks and the signing of memorandums of understanding worth $50 billion with six major Chinese financial institutions.

Meanwhile, the Biden administration resorted to covert efforts to "pacify" the Houthis in Yemen that failed as a group of 70 Israeli Special Forces and American mercenaries were killed during a clandestine operation, thanks to exposure by Russian satellites.[90] Furthermore, U.S. attempts to use a carrot for ceasefire and a stick for deterrence underscored American vulnerabilities in the region. Over time, the U.S. had established 63 U.S. bases, garrisons, and shared facilities. These bases, garrisons, and shared foreign facilities vary from small combat outposts to massive air bases in more than a dozen countries, including Israel, its proximate neighbors (Egypt, Jordan, Syria, Lebanon), the Gulf states (Bahrain, Kuwait, Oman, Qatar, Saudi Arabia, UAE), as well as Iraq and Yemen. Between October 7, 2023, and June 2024, U.S. and allied forces had been attacked more than 170 times: over 100 times in Syria, 70 in Iraq, and once in Jordan, which in January ignited a round of escalatory U.S. counterattacks against Iranian-allied targets that led Iran to rein in its proxies.[91] As Israel subsequently broadened its Gaza War, with provocative attacks in Lebanon, Iran, and Yemen, Iran's partners resumed attacks on U.S. outposts across the region killing or wounding almost 150 U.S. personnel on the regional bases. In the process, not only did the Biden administration initially deny or downplay U.S. presence in the region; U.S. outposts have also become sites of secret sexual assault and a ready source of weapons, ammunition, and equipment for criminals and militants, particularly in Iraq and Syria.

Despite the U.S. withdrawal from Afghanistan in 2021 and a drawdown of forces in Iraq, there were still an estimated 30,000 to 45,000 U.S. troops stationed in the Middle East, according to Pentagon figures.[92] American soldiers are the region's "sitting ducks."

Chapter 11
WHAT IS THE WAY FORWARD?

In the aftermath of October 7, I was in touch with Jonathan Kuttab, a Christian Palestinian and international human rights attorney. For decades, Kuttab advocated the two-state solution. He headed the legal committee negotiating the Cairo Agreement of 1994 between Israel and the PLO, signed by Yitzhak Rabin and Yasser Arafat. Today, he believes the two-state solution is no longer viable because "the extent, depth, and longevity of the occupation has created new facts on the ground." As a result, the proposed compromise – the two-state solution – is not possible, even if Israel and the Palestinians were fully committed to it.[1]

Usually, the Israel/Palestine conflict is portrayed in terms of two scenarios: a two-state or a one-state solution. The proponents of the former argue that the resolution of the conflict is premised on the establishment of two nation states, a Jewish and an Arab state. The champions of the latter believe that a singular state should be established between the River Jordan and the Mediterranean. The two frameworks imply that the support for one or the other solution is the outcome of public debate by the key stakeholders; that is, Israel and the Palestinian Authority, the United States, the European Union, Russia and the leading Arab countries. Typically, the debate excludes the viewpoint of those Arab nations, such as Iran, that resist the West's dictates and those that in the past have supported pan-Arab solutions, like Nasser's Egypt, Gaddafi's Libya and so on.

Some depict the two-state solution as a bi-national state, based on the hope it could serve as a homeland for both Jews and Palestinians. Others argue that it can only have room for either Jews or Palestinians. Based on the findings of *The Fall of Israel*, the actual solution has already taken place – not after October 7, but in the 1950s. Since the 1970s, the peace prospects touted by Washington have served mainly as a façade for a process that is now approaching its endgame.

THE ELUSIVE PEACE PROCESS

The Peace Process and U.S. Hegemony

Despite more than half a century of American diplomacy in the Arab-Israeli conflict, there has been hardly any progress in the so-called "peace process." In 2020, political scientist Ian S. Lustick, a perceptive veteran observer of the Middle East, reframed the story. His revised narrative is about the primary stakeholders, the sequence of the peace process cycles, the influence of the Israel lobby, and the consequent cumulative frustration. The net outcome depicts a carousel that's always in movement yet going nowhere. What the main stakeholders – the Israeli government, U.S. administration, the Palestinians and the peace process industry – want is a two-state solution or quiet absorption of Palestinian territories into Israel. What they need is to be protected from international criticism (in Israel's case) or Israel lobby attacks (in the U.S. case) or to be assured of necessary economic support (for both Israel and the Palestinians).[2] To bear in mind: this was an analysis pre-October 7, before the obliteration of Gaza and the lethal focus on the West Bank.

During the 2023–2024 Gaza War, Lustick either expected a return to the "peace process carousel" or simply suspended the term in his commentaries, despite its centrality in his analysis.[3] Then again, the "peace process" story is a persuasive narrative but what is it that led to its standoff? What maintains the impasse? and what sustains it? After all, the "peace process," as the term is currently understood, evolved with the U.S. interventions when Washington consolidated its partnership with Israel and took a more significant role in the region in economic aid and particularly in arms sales since the 1970s Yom Kippur War, the oil crisis, and the consequent Carter doctrine, which stated that, if necessary, America would use military force to defend its national interest in the Persian Gulf.

> An attempt by any outside force to gain control of the Persian Gulf region will be regarded as an assault on the vital interests of the United States of America, and such an assault will be repelled by any means necessary, including military force.[4]

Drafted by Carter's national security adviser Zbigniew Brzezinski, it was portrayed as a U.S. response to the Soviet invasion in Afghanistan, to keep Moscow away from the Gulf region. In reality, the doctrine emulated Imperial Britain's 1903 proclamation that sought to sustain British naval hegemony in the region.[5] After World War II, U.S. military authorities wanted to sustain American hegemony in the Pacific, which they termed "American Lake." After the twin oil crises, the Gulf got a similar role. A *stated* effort toward peace in Israel/Palestine has been useful to sustain the U.S. hegemony in the region.

Since then, the "peace process" has been underpinned by the great conjuncture; that is, the net confluence of ethnic expulsions, settlement expansion, the U.S.-Israel military ties and Israel's militarization (Chapters 1–4). These structural forces set the stage for a sequence of wars, conflicts and friction, which are made possible by the influx of U.S. weapons in the region. It is this convergence of forces that has dramatically transformed Israel in the past four decades, in particular aggravating the country's ethnic and religious divides and its economic polarization (Chapters 5–7). These forces have also transformed the occupied Palestinian territories into surreal landscapes of horrific devastation (Gaza) and fragmented zones of turmoil (West Bank), contributing to ultra-apartheid, genocidal atrocities, and regional escalation (Chapters 8-10).

In light of the evidence and economic interpretation advanced in *The Fall of Israel*, what is left after decades of failed policies and unwarranted wars is a two-state solution with one-state realities.[6] In this thoroughly historical view, the fate of the two-state solution is not a question for the future. In reality, it was already resolved by the mid-1950s. Everything thereafter is footnotes.

THE RISE AND FALL OF THE TWO-STATE SOLUTION

Palestine, Partition and the First UN Mediation

After World War II, the UN Partition Plan and Israel's unilateral declaration of independence, a Swedish diplomat and aristocrat, Count Folke Bernadotte, was appointed the UN Security Council mediator in the Arab-Israeli conflict. It was the first official mediation in the UN's history. As he took the job, he was eyed suspiciously by both the Jews and the Arabs in Palestine. In contrast to rumors about the Swede's "antisemitic bias," Bernadotte had during the war years negotiated the release of about 450 Danish Jews and more than 30,000 non-Jewish prisoners from Theresienstadt, the Nazi concentration camp. On the Arab side, such activities sparked speculations on Bernadotte's Jewish bias. In light of historical evidence, both concerns seem to have been immaterial. If anything, the Swede had a knack for focusing on the big picture.

After achieving an initial truce in the 1948 Arab-Israeli War, Bernadotte used it to lay the groundwork for the UN Relief and Works Agency (UNRWA) for Palestine Refugees in the Near East. Ever since then, UNRWA has been a lifeline to generations of Palestinians in the West Bank, the Gaza Strip and the adjacent Arab countries.

Bernadotte knew his job was dangerous and wrote his will before arriving in Palestine. He understood the challenges of a mediator having to navigate among conflicting expectations. "In putting forward any proposal for the solution of the Palestine problem," he wrote in his diary, "one must bear in mind the aspirations of the Jews, the political difficulties and differences of opinion of the Arab leaders, the strategic interests of Great Britain, the financial commitment of the United States and the Soviet Union, the outcome of the war, and finally the authority and prestige of the United Nations."[7]

The "first Bernadotte plan" was submitted in secret to both sides of the conflict in late June, whereas the "second Bernadotte plan" was published in mid-September 1948.

The First Bernadotte Plan

The first plan sought to elicit the two sides' reactions and set a direction. Bernadotte and his deputy Ralph Bunche described it as a "proposal" rather than a "plan." It did not espouse the merits of a two-state solution. It was influenced by Dr. Judah Magnes, a prominent Reform rabbi in both the U.S. and Mandatory Palestine, and an early proponent of a binational state. Distressed by the 1929 Arab Revolt in Palestine, Magnes saw the uprising as an understandable response to rising Jewish immigration and effective segregation in Palestine. He believed Palestine should be neither Jewish nor Arab, but binational with equal rights shared by all.[8] It was not a popular view and Magnes was often criticized, particularly in the Jewish media. When the Peel Commission (1937) proposed partition and population transfers, Magnes was alarmed. More than a decade before Bernadotte's mediation, he foresaw the darkness ahead:

> With the permission of the Arabs, we will be able to receive hundreds of thousands of persecuted Jews in Arab lands. ... Without the permission of the Arabs even the four hundred thousand [Jews] that now are in Palestine will remain in danger, in spite of the temporary protection of British bayonets. With partition a new Balkan is made. ...[9]

Impressed by Magnes's foresight, Bunche, who drafted the Swede's plans, overestimated the support for such views among the Jews and Arabs despite a series of uprisings, continuous friction and the controversy that surrounded the UN Partition Plan. A highly regarded political scientist and diplomat in the segregated America, Bunche had been a key deputy of Gunnar Myrdal, the Swedish pioneer of economic development, whose huge landmark report *An American Dilemma: The Negro Problem and Modern Democracy* (1944) would influence the U.S. civil rights legislation in the 1950s. In the early 1940s, Bunche had worked in the Office of Strategic Services (OSS), the precursor of the CIA, as a senior social analyst on Colonial Affairs. The post paved his transfer to the State Department where his task was to advance U.S. interests in the Cold War. As the UK, France, Netherlands and other colonial powers left their colonies, America sought a permanent foothold in them. In the UN's first mediation process, Bunche was soon seen as Bernadotte's "brains." He was America's face amid decolonization. [10]

Though initially less informed about Palestine than Bunche, Bernadotte was a quick study whose pragmatic realism would occasionally guide Bunche's revisions. Bernadotte had great sympathy for the Arab refugees, which was often attributed to his "pro-Arab inclinations." By contrast, Bunche had been criticized for having "pro-Jewish inclinations."[11] Both were attuned to the regional stances of Britain and the U.S, the old imperial master and the new empire-builder. In May 1948, when Israel declared its independence, the U.S. was still hedging its bets. Truman's international affairs advisers, dominant in the White House, promoted the idea that both the partition resolution and the American trusteeship plan should be abandoned in favor of a new territorial division based on the battle lines, with slight modifications. The Arab side would no longer comprise Palestinian Arabs, but the Kingdom of Transjordan.[12] Conducted in secret, such ideas did not fare well among Palestinians, who desired a state of their own, nor with Ben-Gurion who wanted to use the UN Partition Plan to expand Israel's borders. Subsequently, Truman, despite warnings by his foreign affairs experts, decided to support the partition to boost his domestic election campaign.[13]

Nonetheless, Bernadotte and Bunche still held to the hope that Palestine and Transjordan could be restructured as "a Union, comprising two Members, one Arab and one Jewish," each member with full control over its own affairs, including its foreign relations, with full economic union. Consequently, the first proposal called for a confederation in Palestine rather than a Jewish state and an Arab state.[14] Such views were running behind actual developments, however. Bernadotte and Bunche hoped their proposal would reduce hostilities, but it actually amplified them. Anticipating a shift in Truman's views, Ben-Gurion was not content with the partition map. Since Israel had occupied new districts, he wanted these to be included in the new Israeli state. Meanwhile, Arabs rejected the very idea of a Jewish state.

After years of escalating friction, there was little taste left for a binational state in Palestine. To Ben-Gurion and other Jewish leaders, Zionism meant a single, secular-democratic Jewish state, whereas Jewish terror organizations, the right-wing Irgun and far-right Stern Group, dreamed of Greater Israel. An offshoot of Irgun, the latter would play a key role in the UN partition story. It was launched by Avraham Stern, who grew of age in Poland, as did Menachem Begin, Irgun's leader. Calling their group "Lehi," abbreviation of the "Fighters for the Freedom of Israel," the Sternists, proud of their "acts of terrorism," fought the British through World War II, initially seeking an alliance with Mussolini's Italy and Hitler's Nazi Germany. Both the British and the pre-state Israeli leaders called them the "Stern Gang." To Ben-Gurion, it was a way to create nominal distance from Stern, even though its leaders became an integral part of the Ashkenazi elite in the postwar era.

Things went from bad to worse in summer 1948, when Bernadotte said that the Arab nations were reluctant to resume the fighting in Palestine and that the conflict now consisted of "incidents."[15] Condemning Bernadotte's statement for downplaying the extent of hostilities, Jewish leaders criticized his participation in the talks. In turn, Irgun and Stern portrayed Bernadotte as an existential threat to the nascent Israeli state.

Yet, even in June 1948, Bunche was still trying to fit new realities into a long memo by Magnes touting a "loose federation" between Transjordan's King Abdullah and the state of Israel. A UN commissioner would be appointed to head an Economic Council, responsible for a set of common topics. Several of these insights re-emerged in Bunche's proposals.[16]

The Second Bernadotte Proposal

As the first report failed to achieve wider support, Bernadotte and Bunche worked out a more complex proposal, setting aside the ideas of a confederation, binational state and economic union. In practice Bunche submitted the plan, and the Swede ratified it. This plan "updated" the Partition Plan in accordance with the military situation on the ground, thereby emulating the Israeli demands: "A Jewish State called Israel exists in Palestine and there are no sound reasons for assuming that it will not continue to do so."[17]

Building on half a dozen premises, the second proposal, released on September 16, 1948, offered several "suggestions." It proposed that the existing indefinite truce should be superseded by a formal peace, or at least an armistice. The UN should establish the frontiers between the Arab and Jewish territories. The Negev desert, which Ben-Gurion wanted annexed to Israel, should be defined as Arab territory (which effectively denied Israel's access to the Red Sea). The frontier should run from Al-Faluja, 30 km northeast of Gaza City to Ramla and Lod, which would be in the Arab territory, not part of Israel as the Jewish leaders insisted. Prior to 1947, Galilee had a significant Arab majority, yet the Bernadotte plan defined it as Jewish territory. Haifa would become a free port; and Lydda airport, a free airport. The City of Jerusalem, effectively divided into two, would be placed under UN control with local autonomy for Arab East Jerusalem and Jewish West Jerusalem, with full safeguards for the protection of the Holy Places.[18] It was a suggestion that seemed to satisfy no party in the conflict.

Having witnessed the horrible outcome of the Jewish Holocaust in Europe and hoping to avert a catastrophe in Palestine, Bernadotte proposed that the UN should establish a Palestine conciliation commission, while Arab refugees would have a full right to return to their homes in Jewish-controlled territory.

> The exodus of Palestinian Arabs resulted from panic created by fighting in their communities, by rumors concerning real or alleged acts of terrorism, or expulsion. It would be an offence against the principles of elemental justice if these innocent victims of the conflict were denied the right to return to their homes while Jewish immigrants flow into Palestine, and, indeed, at least offer the threat of permanent replacement of the Arab refugees who have been rooted in the land for centuries.[19]

Israel's negotiators were taken aback by the new proposal, which proposed detaching the Negev and East Jerusalem from their territory. It made Bernadotte the *bête noire* of the Israeli leadership. Israel's strongest champion at the time, the Soviet Union, was livid about the plan and the Stern leaders saw it as confirmation of Bernadotte as an agent of Anglo-Saxon imperialism.

In July 1948, the Israeli military was advancing, but Bernadotte refused to acknowledge its victories. Hence, the Israeli effort to get rid of him. "Our interest requires [an] early termination [of the] Bernadotte mission," said Abba Eban, Israel's UN representative, who began to undermine the Swede's role in the diplomatic backrooms.[20] Meanwhile, thanks to convenient leaks, hostile sentiments were displayed vocally in Israeli media.

This time the report was prepared in secret consultation with U.S. and British emissaries.[21] It reflected their views rather than those of the Soviet

Union, the new superpower. Moscow had recognized the state of Israel both *de facto* and *de jure* a year before, which had helped to keep the proposal from being adopted.[22] During these critical months, Ben-Gurion, Irgun and Stern saw the Soviets as their prime partner, whereas the Americans feared a Jewish state would slide Palestine into an vicious cycle of conflicts.[23] The secret maneuverings were publicly exposed later in October 1948, just days before the U.S. presidential elections, embarrassing U.S. President Harry S. Truman. For reasons of domestic politics, he made a strongly pro-Zionist declaration, which set the stage for the defeat of the Bernadotte plan in the UN (Figure 11-1).[24]

Figure 11-1   Bernadotte Plan (1948) and Armistice Agreement (1949)
Source: Jewish Virtual Library

THE PRELUDE TO THE FOREVER WARS

In the Valley of Hell

On September 17, a day after submitting his second report, Bernadotte was on his way to Jerusalem. After spending a night in Syria, he had left Damascus in the morning to fly to Qalandia airport in Jerusalem. Despite prior warnings of possible gunfire, Bernadotte landed without incident. Following a visit to Ramallah, the convoy headed back to Jerusalem. In these early days,

UN personnel traveled unarmed. Since they represented the world, the UN flag would protect them. Yet, just past Qalandia, they were fired on from a short distance and a bullet hit a disk of the rear wheel.

Sitting in the back seat, Bernadotte was between his Chief of Staff, General Åge Lundström, and French Colonel André Sérot. Sérot had swapped places in the motorcade to join Bernadotte and thank him personally for having saved his wife's life in a German concentration camp. Bunche was scheduled to meet Bernadotte in Jerusalem, from where they would proceed to put the new partition proposal before the UN General Assembly. Delays prevented Bunche from reaching the Jerusalem rendezvous point on time. Sérot took his place next to the Count. They were used to disruptions. Just weeks earlier, they had encountered the Sternists' anti-Bernadotte demonstration, which blocked the way to the Belgian consulate (Figure 11-2).

Figure 11-2   Count Folke Bernadotte in Jerusalem

Folke Bernadotte (second from the right) walking with Israeli liaison officer, Moshe Hillman (right), at the head of the UN Security Council delegation, at the entrance to the Belgian Consulate in Talbiah, Jerusalem. They are followed by U.S. General William E. Riley (left) and French Colonel André Sérot (second from left)

Source: Wikimedia Commons

Despite threats, Bernadotte's convoy met no demonstrations this time. As the men started to relax, the big Chrysler, the last of the three-car convoy, began its final ascent up the narrow road through the Jewish-occupied district of Katamon towards Rehavia and the house of Jerusalem's military governor.

Just two years before, Katamon had been a prosperous, mainly Palestinian Christian neighborhood. During the 1947–1948 hostilities, the local population fled the intense fighting in the area. As they tried to return to their homes, the latter had been taken over by the new Israeli state. Katamon was soon repopulated by Jewish refugees.

As the cars passed a road barrier, raised three times before they could pass, they arrived at the foot of the Hill of Evil Counsel. On this hilltop, the high priest Caiphas presumably betrayed Jesus and handed him over to the Romans for crucifixion. Located at the southeast corner of the Valley of Hinnom, it is also known as Wadi el-Rababa, where children were sacrificed to a false god Moloch, according to the Old Testament. The New Testament knows it as "Gehenna," or "hell," referring to the way God's justice will deal with evil.

As the UN convoy began to slow down, they saw an Israeli army jeep beside an abandoned roadblock. To the jaded men, it was just another checkpoint. Three Israeli soldiers in khaki shorts asked them to stop. Carrying Sten guns, the men strode along the stationary cars. The UN workers groped for their papers. Sitting in the leading UN vehicle, Moshe Hillman, the motorcade's Israeli liaison officer, called out in Hebrew to let them through. "It's OK boys," he said: "Let us pass. It's the UN mediator." He was ignored. Instead, one of the three men ran to the Chrysler, pushed the barrel of his sub-machine gun through the opened rear window, and pumped six bullets into Bernadotte's chest, throat and left arm and another 18 into the body of the French colonel next to him. Rushing out of the first car, Hillman ran back to the Chrysler. When he saw the copiously bleeding bodies, he shouted: "My God, oh my God!" and jumped in beside the driver, shouting to him to speed straight for the Hadassah hospital. Lundström was uninjured. Colonel Sérot fell in his seat. He was dead. Bernadotte bent forward, as if trying to get cover. "Are you wounded?" Lundström asked. The count nodded and fell back. His rows of decorations were torn by the bullets, but he was still alive. As soon as they arrived at Hadassah, he was carried inside. Lundström laid him on the bed, took off his jacket and tore away his shirt. Bernadotte was wounded around the heart. There was a lot of blood on his clothes. As the doctor began to examine Bernadotte, the severely wounded Swede stopped breathing.[25]

Bunche, who was supposed to have been in the car, arrived at the rendezvous point half an hour after the Count had left.[26] But it was he who had drafted the plan that led to Bernadotte's assassination. Later, when Bernadotte's killer found out these realities, he stated that "we killed the wrong man." Unlike Bernadotte, Bunche was the man "with the ideas."[27]

It was 5 pm and a beautiful sunset bathed the Old City as the two-state solution died with the last breath of the UN's first mediator.

The Stern Assassins

To Stern, Bernadotte was "the enemy of all those who – like [Stern] – regarded a pro-Soviet policy as the only guarantee of Israel's survival."[28] Stalin had recognized the Israeli state *de jure*; Truman hadn't. With a truce still in force, these revisionist Zionists thought Ben-Gurion's leadership might agree to Bernadotte's peace proposals, which they saw as a calamity. What they did not know was that Israel's leadership had already opted to reject Bernadotte's plan and choose the military option.[29] Unlike Stern, BG and his military advisers expected a temporary halt in the fighting to serve Israel's interests. They used it to re-equip their forces and train them. Meanwhile, new weapons came from Eastern Europe with Stalin's blessing. Bernadotte was not of interest to Moscow. Pushing the British out from Palestine was. Stalin sought access to the region's natural resources. Meanwhile, the CIA's reports on Czechoslovak military aid to Israel triggered intensified American efforts to find a political solution in Palestine.[30]

A day after the assassination, General Åge Lundström, Bernadotte's chief of staff, assessed that it was "a deliberate and carefully planned assassination."[31] Lundström was right. But the path to the assassination had been paved a month before, when Stern members protested against Bernadotte during his meeting with Israel's first foreign minister, Moshe Sharett. The Sternists were waving placards declaring: "Stockholm is Yours; Jerusalem is Ours!'" Their tone grew virulent as they opted for direct action.

Goldfoot Stanley, a Jewish immigrant from South Africa, had settled in Jerusalem and worked as a foreign correspondent for several Western dailies, including *France Soir* and the *New York Times*. During this period, he joined the Stern. His connections and sources were invaluable to the underground. Contributing to several Stern operations, Stanley had participated in the infamous Deir Yassin massacre in which more than 100 Arab villagers, including women and children, were massacred. In mid-September, Stern leaders got his hint on Bernadotte's itinerary in Jerusalem. The assassination was planned in his apartment.[32]

In practice, Bernadotte's assassination had been approved by Stern's leadership: Yitzhak Yezernitsky (later known as Yitzhak Shamir, Begin's successor as Israel's PM), Nathan Friedmann (subsequently Natan Yellin-Mor) and Yisrael Eldad. It was developed by Yehoshua Zettler, Stern's operations chief in Jerusalem, and the actual shooter was Yehoshua Cohen.[33] After the assassination, the hit team hid for a few days in a local religious community, then fled to Tel Aviv in the back of a furniture truck.[34]

The attribution of the assassination to Stern was disputed for almost 60 years. Nor did the assassins pay for their crime. They were fervent nationalists, representing both far-left and far-right. Yellin-Mor, Stern's far-left operative, had been one of the planners of the Cairo assassination of Lord Moyne, the British minister of state in the Middle East, in 1944. Considering himself a "national Bolshevik," Yellin-Mor was appointed to the first Knesset, where he supported Communist and anti-imperialist causes and became later one of the first to support direct talks with the PLO.[35] Eldad, Stern's far-right ideologue, became an academic. In 1982 he was appointed a lecturer at the controversial Ariel University in the occupied West Bank, which got tens of millions of dollars as donations from the Jewish-American casino tycoon Sheldon Adelson, onetime key financier of PM Netanyahu. His funeral in 1996 was attended by both Netanyahu and the PM's predecessor Yitzhak Shamir.[36]

Like Stanley, Yehoshua Zettler, the architect of Bernadotte's assassination, had participated in the notorious Deir Yassin massacre. [37] Through his life, Zettler was suspicious of Arabs and foreigners in Israel. In his later years, he ran a gas station in Jaffa, from which most Arabs had been expunged. After a long life, he died peacefully at 91 in 2009.[38]

The first public admission of Stern's role in the killing was made on the anniversary of the assassination in 1977, well after the statute of limitations for the murder had expired in 1971. Although Yehoshua Cohen's involvement was an open secret within Stern and other groups, he was never charged, and his role was not made public for over 40 years until it was uncovered by David Ben-Gurion's biographer. Cohen became one of the founders of the Sde Boker kibbutz in the Negev Desert, where David Ben-Gurion later retired and where he became BG's bodyguard and close confidant (Figure 11-3).[39] A few years later, Trygve Lie, the UN's first Secretary General who had appointed Bernadotte to his post, met Ben-Gurion in the kibbutz. To Lie's great surprise, the meeting was attended by Cohen, Bernadotte's assassin. The Norwegian swore he would never return to Sde Boker. Cohen couldn't have cared less. He died peacefully in 1986.[40]

Figure 11-3   The Odd Couple: Former PM with Former Assassin

Israel's former PM David Ben-Gurion and his veteran confidante and bodyguard Yehoshua Cohen, the assassin of Count Folke Bernadotte, strolling arm in arm at Ein Avdat, the largest Wadi south of Kibbutz Sde Boker.

Source: Close-up of Im Tirtzu X/Twitter, on August 8, 2024

False Flag Operation?

Today, the identities of the Bernadotte assassins are known. What is less clear is *who* gave the assignment. On that fateful day of September 17, when Bernadotte crossed over to the Jewish side from Transjordan, he had been protected by the capable soldiers of Transjordan's Arab Legion, trained by Glubb Pasha. On the Israeli side, he was on his own. Though fully informed of threats against Bernadotte's life, Israeli authorities sent no escort.

Following their operations, the Stern group habitually disclosed its role publicly. In the case of Bernadotte, it did not. There were leaflets from an unknown group, *Hazit Hamoledet* (transl. "Homeland Front"), claiming responsibility for the murders. In effect, the name was recycled. It was copied from a wartime Bulgarian resistance group. There was no systematic attempt to identify the source of the leaflets. Stern liked to take the credit. So, why would it *not* claim credit for one of its most successful high-profile operations?

Subsequently, many Stern members were disarmed and arrested, but nobody was charged with the killings, and the case was closed without any of the participants having been identified. Oddly, Israeli police authorities did not cordon off the crime scene or conduct any systematic analysis of the crime scene. Even the car in which Bernadotte was murdered was not examined until after it had been repaired, and the first convoy car was never examined at all. Nor was there any attempt to identify the assassins' jeep. And while Stern suspects were detained after the assassination, they were not treated like other prisoners. As *Time* magazine reported, these prisoners at Jaffa made their own rules, ripped bars from the windows and tore down the steel doors connecting their cells: "The Sternists threw open the door of the jail, disarmed the guards, directed traffic in the square where a great crowd had gathered. Some prisoners strolled off to the beach for a swim. Others relaxed with prison guards over coffee in a nearby café."[41]

In effect, several questions relating to the assassination remain murky. Shortly after the assassination, the U.S. and UK intelligence learned that the Czechoslovak Consulate in Jerusalem had issued visas for the day of the murder to fly the actual assassins to Prague on a Czech aircraft with false passports and false names. At the time, the Eastern European country was Israel's critical arms supplier. American weapons came into the picture only two decades later. The odd story got another twist in 2005, when the British declassified files featured a 1949 letter from the then Belgium Consul General, Jean Niewenhuys, referring to a "reliable source" who acknowledged that the assassins were from Stern, but working for Israel. The files suggested that the real architect of the assassination was Reuven Shiloah, subsequently Mossad's first director, who had been involved in the ceasefire talks with both Bernadotte and his deputy Bunche.[42]

In this view, the Bernadotte Plan – it envisioned an even smaller Israel than the UN plan, sought to internationalize Jerusalem and proposed the right of return to Palestinian Arabs – was far too much in conflict with Ben-Gurion's vision. Indeed, after the assassination, the Swedish government thought that Bernadotte had been assassinated by Israeli government agents.[43]

Israel's PM Ben-Gurion noted in his personal diary that Yehoshua Cohen, who later became his close confidant, was involved in the assassination. But he chose not to arrest the killers and put them on trial.[44] Distrust of Bernadotte's objectives and the absence of any international retribution following his death contributed to "Israel's reluctance to provoke a confrontation with [Stern] that would have revealed the details of the conspiracy."[45]

At the time, Col. Moshe Dayan, Ben-Gurion's key military protégé, served as Israel's commander in Jerusalem. In close cooperation with BG, Dayan would soon plot for border wars to escalate a "second round" of open conflict with Arab countries, to expand Israel's boundaries.

TOWARD THE NEXT BIG WAR

After Bernadotte's assassination, Bunche took his place and negotiated a ceasefire mediating the Armistice Agreements. Between February and July 1949, these were signed between Israel and four Arab states: Egypt, Jordan,

Lebanon, and Syria. For this accomplishment, Bunche was awarded the Nobel Peace Prize in 1950.[46] However, the hostilities did not end. They were left simmering, especially since the Armistice Agreement did not result in permanent borders. In the process, the very content of what today is called the "two-state solution" changed.

No Frontiers, No Peace

In 1947, the UN Partition Plan granted 55 percent of Palestine to the new Jewish state and only 45 percent to a non-contiguous Arab state, with Jerusalem under international control. As the Jews were granted areas in which Arabs still constituted the majority, the facts on the ground were ignored. By 1948, when Israel unilaterally declared its independence, the Jewish pre-state forces had expelled 750,000 Palestinians while capturing 78 percent of the historic Palestine. The remaining 22 percent was split into the West Bank and Gaza Strip. After the 1949 Armistice Agreements, it was *these* facts on the ground – not those prevailing prior to 1947, or in the 1947 UN plan – that would prevail until the 1967 Six-Day War. Moreover, the West Bank was incorporated into Jordan. Egypt kept control of the Gaza Strip. In turn, Jerusalem was now split between the Jews and the Arabs.

In March 1949, Reuven Shiloah, who had been Israel's senior member in the Armistice talks and became Mossad's first director just months later, advised U.S. authorities that Israel would never relinquish any Palestinian land it had seized. The post-Diaspora "ingathering" was not complete, or in Moshe Dayan's blunt language, "we have not yet determined whether...our existing borders [Armistice, not Partition] satisfy us."[47] In the United States, a prophetic analysis by the CIA, "A Long-Range Disaster," foresaw the consequences of Israel's sovereignty without borders:

> The establishment of the State of Israel by force, with intimidation of Arab governments by the U.S. and the USSR [means that] the Israeli battle-victory is complete, but it has solved nothing. If boundaries to an Israeli state, any boundaries, had been set and guaranteed by the Great Powers, peace might return to the area. On the contrary, we have actually a victorious state which is limited to no frontiers and which is determined that no narrow limit shall be set. The Near East is faced with the almost certain prospect of a profound and growing disturbance by Israel which may last for decades.[48]

Although the war had ended, border hostilities hadn't. Between 1949 and the 1956 Suez Crisis, the Arab infiltrations from Egypt, Jordan, Lebanon and Syria into Israel and Israel's harsh retaliatory responses set patterns of conduct that would characterize the Arab-Israeli conflict for decades to come.[49] Moreover, Israeli leaders saw Israel's Arab citizens, Palestinian Arabs who had stayed within Israel, as a potential fifth column. Hence the hope of the IDF chief of staff Moshe Dayan for "another opportunity in the future to transfer these Arabs from the Land of Israel."

> When there is an Arab state...which, with world agreement, is ready to resettle Arabs in other places, then that same agreement will be [extended] to the transfer of this [i.e. Israeli Arab] population as well.[50]

Dayan was not alone with his views in summer 1950. He was seconded by senior cabinet ministers, the head of the military and the Jewish National Fund. His solution would appeal to generations of Israeli leaders, including in the aftermath of October 7, 2023, when it was proposed by the Netanyahu government's intelligence ministry.[51] Ultimately, the logic of such ethnic expulsions is simple. When all or most Arabs have been expunged from Israel, the two-state model loses its rationale.

But how to go about it?

Reprisals for Expansion

After the 1948–1949 War, Israel's armed forces had been demobilized. During the war, the IDF had launched a broad variety of measures to fight infiltration, including patrols and ambushes on both sides of the line, and mine fields. In the process, "the front lines effectively became free fire zones and troops were usually ordered to shoot to kill." These anti-infiltration measures caused "the death of several thousand mostly unarmed Arabs during 1949–56, the vast majority between 1949 and 1952," as historian Benny Morris has argued. Many of these Arabs were not the kind of "infiltrators" as portrayed. Initially, they were hoping to return to or visit their properties. Nonetheless, state-authorized or permitted killing of unarmed civilians "reflected a pervasive attitude among the Israeli public that Arab life was cheap."[52] The "shoot-to-kill zones" prevailed with Egypt until the 1979 peace treaty, and with Jordan until the 1994 treaty. Since the Gaza Strip was never annexed by Egypt, it would pose a more complex challenge, as would

Hezbollah in southern Lebanon. In the 2023–2024 Gaza War, Israelis created such kill zones again, presumably for "security."

Hence, the launch of special elite units to contain cross-border infiltration, pillage and killings. In August 1953, the IDF Commando Unit 101 was founded on orders by PM Ben-Gurion.[53] Led by Ariel Sharon, it was Israel's first special forces unit and got its orders directly from the IDF high command. After a month of training, Sharon's unit infiltrated into the Gaza Strip. The "exercise" resulted in the killing of 20 Arabs and was broadly condemned by foreign observers. But it was just a prelude. The Unit 101 was a unique military solution in which a top-down reprisal policy, developed by BG and Dayan, was executed by bottom-up retaliations under Sharon's command, virtually ensuring the exclusion of political solutions. Curiously, "a policy of deterrence was governed by the tactic of retaliation, which contained the seeds of escalation," as Israeli military expert Ze'ev Drory has argued. "At the same time, a military dynamic unfolded in which the logic of field unit response dictated both military and political policy and caught the imagination of a demoralized and war-weary Israeli society."[54] In this way, a highly controversial revenge tactic of a small commando unit became a reprisal policy of the entire nation, forming the core of a national security strategy that still prevails, thanks to its pioneers, Dayan and Sharon, the two highly controversial proponents of disproportionate retaliation, viewed as furthering not deterrence but expansion.

In the IDF and the Knesset, Dayan (1915–1981) shaped Israel's reprisal policy with Sharon largely in charge of the institutionalized retaliations until the 1973 Yom Kippur War. With the Lebanese War in the early 1980s, Sharon (1928–2014) took over contributing to Israel's military responses until his hospitalization in 2005. Dayan's period was characterized by the quest for wars of expansion and broad cooperation with France, whereas Sharon's period saw the dramatic expansion of the Jewish settlements in the occupied territories, U.S. military aid, and the consequent militarization of Israel. It was this harsh and deadly approach that eventually resulted in the Dahiya doctrine of massively disproportionate response and associated genocidal atrocities, coupled with the Hannibal Directive that caused many Israeli combatants and civilians to perish at Israeli hands during October 7, 2023. and its aftermath (Figure 11-4).[55]

**Figure 11-4   Israel's Military Dynamic:
From Dayan to Sharon to Present**

Ariel Sharon and Moshe Dayan in 1955.
Source: Wikimedia Commons (close-up)

Here's how it all began. In October 1953, Unit 101 raided the village of Qibya in the West Bank. Framed as a response to an attack in which an Israeli woman and her two children were killed, Operation Shoshana inflicted heavy damage as Israeli commandos killed nearly 70 villagers, two-thirds of whom were women and children, while wounding 15. Almost 50 houses were demolished with some inhabitants still inside, along with a school and a mosque.[56]

The brutal reprisal was condemned by the UN Security Council, the U.S. State Department and the international community. Ben-Gurion attributed the massacre to Israeli civilians. It was a lie, which Israel's first foreign minister Moshe Sharett criticized severely in the cabinet. Despite international condemnation, Dayan saw it as a huge success since it seemed to reduce infiltrations from Transjordan. To diffuse the gained experience, Dayan merged and restructured IDF units, promoting Sharon to Lt. Colonel.

After the Qibya controversy, Ben-Gurion resigned from office in early December 1953 and retired to his kibbutz in Negev. Moshe Sharett served as caretaker prime minister until he was sworn in as BG's successor in late January 1954, while retaining his portfolio as foreign minister. Internationally, it brought a sigh of relief. Hawks were out, doves marched into the Israeli government. And that precisely was the intended objective. It was a shrewd sham.

The Missed Opportunity

As Sharett took charge, he was informed that U.S. ambassadors in the region thought the purpose of the deliberate Israeli escalation was to bring about a war, and thereby sabotage U.S. negotiations to establish pro-Western alliances with Egypt, Iraq and Turkey.[57] Sharett seized the moment, seeing it as time to turn Israel away from BG's reprisals and toward peace talks.

Moshe Sharett (1894–1965) belonged to the younger generation of the nation's founding fathers. His family had immigrated from Ukraine when he was a child. As a teen, he had lived two years in an Arab village near Ramallah. He spoke Hebrew but was also fluent in Arabic and Turkish, Russian, English, German and Yiddish. A devotee of Chaim Weizmann's political Zionism, Sharett shared the broad aims of the Zionist movement under Ben-Gurion but disagreed on the methods to achieve them (Figure 11-5). One of the signatories of Israel's Declaration of Independence, he led the Zionist movement's external relations for almost quarter of a century, first in the pre-state Yishuv and then as foreign minister until before the Suez Crisis in 1956.

Figure 11-5   Moshe Sharett's Struggle for Peace

My Struggle for Peace: The Diary of Moshe Sharett, 1953–1956. Edited by Neil Caplan and Yaakov Sharett.

Source: Moshe Sharett and his Legacy (https://www.sharett.org.il/)

Soon after the Qibya massacre, BG's goals dawned on Sharett. Before his retirement, "Ben-Gurion spoke for two and a half hours on the army's preparations for the 'second round.' [He] presented detailed figures on the expansion of the military strength of the Arab countries which [he said] would reach its peak in 1956. . . ."[58] If that was the case, Sharett thought the lesson was to seek for an accommodation with the Arabs while there was still time. By contrast, BG's protégés sought to make it impossible for Nasser and other Arab leaders to come to terms with Israel. When Sharett discovered these provocatory aims in January 1954, over two years before the Suez Crisis, he asked Dayan:

> Sharett: Do you realize this would mean war with Egypt?
> Dayan: Of course.[59]

Sharett struggled to bring about peace between Egypt and Israel. Cairo invited a prominent American Quaker, Elmore Jackson, to undertake a secret diplomatic assignment intended to bring about a political settlement with Israel. Jackson had the backing of the U.S. government, Egypt's President Nasser and his PM, Sharett, and Ben-Gurion.[60] The main issues concerned the resettlement of refugees, and the final demarcation of the armistice lines between Israel and the Arab nations. Meanwhile, Sharett's cabinet learned about progress in the talks between London and Cairo on the withdrawal of the British from Suez. Like Sharett, some cabinet members thought the British departure would allow Nasser to focus on rebuilding Egypt's economy and consider a settlement with Israel. By contrast, the hawks saw it as a threat to be thwarted.

Sharett and Nasser initiated a series of informal exchanges in fall 1954. Unbeknownst to both, the opponents of the British-Egyptian rapprochement went ahead with their ploys. In summer 1954, a series of explosions rocked a number of British and American office buildings in Cairo. A group of young Jewish residents of Cairo was arrested and accused of working for Israeli intelligence. In late September, they were to be put on trial. Just days later, Sharett suspected defense minister Pinhas Lavon and Colonel Benjamin Givli, head of military intelligence, were behind the scheme. The goal was "to break the West's confidence in the existing [Egyptian] regime through the creation of public disorder and insecurity," in order to "prevent economic and military aid from the West to Egypt."[61] It was a classic false flag scheme aiming to keep the British in the Suez Canal by attributing the instability and bombings to the Muslim Brotherhood, Communists and nationalists.[62] Since Lavon denied responsibility for the covert operation, Sharett commissioned a board of inquiry. The consequent findings rehabilitated Lavon. The architects of turmoil likely involved Givli and Shimon Peres, then-secretary general of defense ministry and Israel's future president. Known nonetheless as the "Lavon Affair," the scandal penalized Israel's relations with the UK and the United States for years, while causing huge domestic political turmoil.

In January 1955, the CIA was still facilitating communications between Israel and Nasser. Sharett also saw an emissary of the American Civil Liberties Union (ACLU). Roger Baldwin, who had met Nasser in Cairo, advised him that "Nasser did not agree with those who wish to drown Israel in the Mediterranean. He believes in mutual co-existence with Israel and knows that negotiations must inevitably take place."[63] Meanwhile, Israel's UN representative Abba Eban informed Sharett that "the U.S. was willing to sign an agreement with us according to which we would commit ourselves not to extend our borders by force and they would commit themselves to come to our assistance should we be attacked."[64] To Sharett, it was big news; the critical commitment Israel needed. Egypt was willing to move ahead. The White House was facilitating. The initiative was now up to Israel.

But as Sharett pushed for de-escalation, things fell apart.

When Lavon resigned in February 1955, Ben-Gurion came out of "retirement" and replaced him as defense minister, while BG's acolytes advocated escalatory provocations. Moshe Dayan wanted to hijack planes and abduct Arab officers from trains. IDF chief of staff Mordechai Maklef asked for a free hand to assassinate Syrian President Colonel Adib Shishakli. Lavon went further, proposing to spread suffocating gas in the Gaza Strip and poisonous bacteria in the demilitarized zone dominated by Syria.[65] Yet, Sharett was still able to set up a meeting of senior Egyptian and Israeli officials.

Then, in late February 1955, Arab infiltrators killed an Israeli civilian in Rehovot and BG greenlighted a retaliation in Gaza. Codenamed Operation Black Arrow, Ariel Sharon led a brutal raid in which 42 Egyptian soldiers were slaughtered and 36 wounded. The operation was unanimously condemned by the UN Security Council. Humiliated and disillusioned, Nasser broke off the informal talks and closed the Gulf of Aqaba to Israeli shipping and air traffic while increasing support for Palestinian fedayeen raids.[66] To bypass Sharett's reluctance to greenlight attacks across the border, BG's protégés had small Israeli patrols, mainly Sharon's paratroopers, infiltrate into Gaza and the West Bank. Subsequently, the proxies would claim their attacks occurred within Israel and were committed by Egyptians, Jordanians and the fedayeen.

By early April, the cabinet's hawks torpedoed the U.S. security pact. It had to be rejected, Dayan insisted, because "it would put handcuffs on our military freedom of action."[67] Ironically, the U.S. security guarantee was rejected for considerations of Israel's national security. And so in summer 1955, BG replaced Sharett as prime minister but let him stay as foreign minister. Dayan was reinstalled as defense minister. The Old Man's retirement and succession had been a charade. Seeking to silence the international indignation over the Qibya massacre while implementing his controversial policies, BG exploited Sharett's leadership to deflect criticism so that Israel could move toward the "second round." Operation Black Arrow effectively killed the last hope of peaceful accommodation between Israel and Egypt.

Sharett's peace efforts did not become known until the late 1970s, when his diaries were published in Hebrew. The disclosure of the deliberate provocations, terror for territorial expansion and clandestine subversions shocked Israelis.[68] Sharett felt betrayed. There was an opportunity for peace, but it was missed, on purpose. Many of the diaries were edited by his son, an accomplished soldier who once served in Shin Bet. In 2021, Yaakov said Israel and the Zionist project were born in sin:

> This original sin pursues and will pursue us and hang over us. We justify it, and it has become an existential fear, which expresses itself in all sorts of ways...
> I'm a forced collaborator with a criminal country... Israel is a country occupying and abusing another people.[69]

Yaakov Sharett described himself as an anti-Zionist. Some of the Sharetts had moved from Israel. To the 94-year-old Yaakov, it was a sign of the times.

The Vicious Repercussions

During the prolonged and inconclusive arms negotiations with Washington, Nasser had suggested to British and American negotiators that if no agreement was obtained, he might need to seek arms from the Soviet Union. The Eisenhower administration thought he was bluffing. Washington offered Nasser light weapons for internal security and defense, demanding hard cash. Haunted by Israel's brutal reprisals, Nasser wanted offensive weapons, hoping to use dollars for development. As the White House proved slow to respond, he turned to the East.[70]

It was a major turning point in the Arab-Israeli conflict and the Cold War. The deal was announced in September 1955. Egypt would be supplied with more than $83 million (today, nearly $1 billion) worth of modern Soviet weaponry through Czechoslovakia with Egyptian cotton exchanged for Czech arms. The shock in Washington and in European capitals was seismic, starting with the demise of U.S. support for the building of the Aswan Dam.[71]

For his part, Nasser said that he had tried to build friendly relations with the United States, but "there is always some obstacle between us, and that obstacle is Israel. America helps Israel with money and moral support, and they use the money to buy equipment to be used against us. But when we ask America to supply us with arms for defense, nothing is done."[72] As Sharett's intelligence chief Isser Harel put it bluntly, "now the U.S. was interested in toppling Nasser and his regime but could not yet take the same steps they had taken in Guatemala and Persia [the CIA's orchestrating the fall of Guzmán's left-leaning government in Guatemala in 1954 and Mossadegh's left-leaning government in Tehran in 1953]. It was also possible that the U.S. did not possess the means to do the job in Egypt, so it would be in their interests to let Israel do the job for them."[73]

As far as the American peace emissary Elmore Jackson was concerned, neither war nor armament was an easy decision for Nasser. "The Arabs are asking only that refugees [from Palestine] receive their natural right to life and their lost property which was promised them by United Nations resolutions."[74]

Unbeknownst to the Israeli leadership at the time, the reprisals also buried Operation Alpha, the U.S. State Department's code word for a secret U.S.-British effort to develop proposals for a comprehensive Arab-Israeli peace settlement, instead fostering an anti-Soviet Arab front in the region. In 1955, both countries agreed Israel should cede parts of the Negev to Egypt and Jordan, creating a territorial link between them, resettle 75,000 Arabs in Israel, and establish a state of non-belligerence between Israel and Arab countries.[75]

As the Israeli reprisal policy buried this opportunity for peace as well, BG and Dayan retreated to the border friction and reprisal policy. Indeed, "retaliatory action was, from the start, a political decision formulated as the security strategy of the Israeli state."[76] As planned, it set the stage for the 1956 Suez War. With the British–French–Israeli invasion of Egypt, Israel sought to re-open the Straits of Tiran and the Gulf of Aqaba while the UK and France hoped to overthrow President Nasser and regain control of the Suez Canal, nationalized by Nasser. Shortly after the invasion began, the three countries came under heavy political pressure from both the United States, the Soviet Union, and the UN, eventually prompting their withdrawal from Egypt.

Amid the Cold War, the crisis fostered the role of the U.S. and the Soviets as superpowers, humiliated the UK and France, and reinforced Nasser's standing in Egypt and the Arab world, which emboldened his pan-Arabism. It contributed to the Soviet Union's invasion of Hungary, and the turn of Egypt, Syria and other Arab states toward Moscow for arms and aid. It turned the Cold War far colder, broadening its scope from Europe and Asia, Latin America and sub-Saharan Africa to the broader Middle East, splitting the region and diverting its scarce economic and natural resources from development and modernization to armament and devastation.

The 1956 Sinai War ended the early phase of the Israeli retribution operations. The debacle undermined Israel's blitzkrieg, turning military success into a political nightmare, as Sharett had long warned. The subsequent reprisals were initiated mainly against Jordan and Syria, because at that time the majority of attacks originated from over the Jordanian and Syrian borders. The net effect has been seven decades of unwarranted conflicts:

- The Six-Day War (1967) and the occupation of the remaining Palestinian territories
- the War of Attrition (1970–1973)
- the Black September, or the Jordanian Civil War (1970–1971)
- the Yom Kippur War (1973)
- the Lebanese Civil War (1975–1990)
- the Israel-Lebanon Conflict (1978–2000)
- Fatah-Hamas Conflict (2006)
- Israel's Lebanon War (2006)
- Israel-Iran proxy conflict (since 2006)
- Syrian Civil War (2011–present)
- Israel's Gaza War (2023–2024) and its reverberations in the West Bank and the Golan Heights, southern Lebanon, Syria, Iran and Yemen.

Furthermore, these wars have been punctuated and precipitated by:

- Israel's border wars (since 1949)
- Palestinian low-level insurgency (1967–1971)
- the First Intifada (1987–1993)
- the Second Intifada (2000–2005)
- Israel's post-disengagement incursions into Gaza (2005–2007)
- Periodic *de facto* Intifadas (since 2007)
- successive Gaza Wars (2008–2009, 2012, 2014)
- the Israel-Palestine crisis (2021)
- escalated Jewish settler violence (since late 2000s)

Should Israel's *indirect* influence be included, the scope of hostilities would feature multiple conflicts involving Iran, Iraq, several Gulf states and northern African Arab states, and other world regions from Latin America to sub-Saharan Africa.

Here's the bottom line: Let's add *all* the Israeli and Palestinian casualties – killed and wounded – in the Arab/Palestine-Israel conflicts from 1948 to pre-October 7 in 2023 and compare the total with the Israel Gaza War (Figure 11-6).

Figure 11-6 Total Casualties in Palestine-Israel Conflicts, 1948–2024

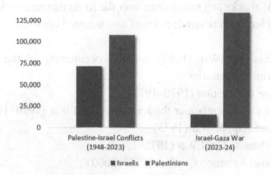

Casualties: Killed and injured by mid-Aug 2024.

Conflicts included: 1948 Arab–Israeli War, 1951–1967 fedayeen attacks, 1956 Sinai War, 1967 Six-Day War, 1967–71 War of Attrition, 1970–71 Black September in Jordan, 1973 Yom Kippur War, 1975–77 Lebanese Civil War, 1978 South Lebanon Conflict, 1982–85 First Lebanon War, 1985–2000 Security Zone in Lebanon, 1984–90 War of the Camps, 1987–93 First Intifada, 1993–2000 Palestinian political violence, 2000–08 Second Intifada 2000–2008, 2006 Second Lebanon War, 2007 Fatah-Hamas Conflict, 2008–2009 Operation Cast Lead, 2012 Operation Pillar of Defense, 2014 Operation Protective Edge, 2021 Israel-Palestine Crisis, 2023–24 Israel's Gaza War

Source: Various sources, author

The number of Palestinian casualties, most of them women and children, in the Gaza War far outweighs the total *cumulative* casualties in *all* the prior conflicts of the past 75 years. By contrast, the number of Israeli total casualties is just a fraction of the Palestinian total in the Gaza War, thanks to the steady flow of advanced U.S. weapons and financing, coupled with billions of dollars of economic assistance by American Jewry.

Israel's Gaza War is a game-changer. As the devastation in Gaza indicates, the Strip will never be the same again. And as the dramatic escalation in settler violence and the effective annexation of the West Bank suggest, the latter's status is at a breaking point. There was a Middle East prior to the Gaza War and there will be one after it. But it is a different, more uncertain and darker Middle East.

A LETHAL IMPASSE

One-State Models

In the West, Israel's peace treaties with Egypt (1979) and Jordan (1994), and the Abraham Accords (2020–2021) with some Gulf states are often portrayed as steps toward a two-state solution. In Israel, they are seen more as bilateral "normalization" deals with individual Arab countries that will over time marginalize or exclude Palestinians from a final peace solution. The Gaza War has jeopardized the future of such normalization agreements, while severely shuttering the existing deals. In the United States, a two-state solution has been the stated American policy for decades, although the White House has failed to take the necessary steps to force Israeli compliance. Without talks between the two sides, and in the absence of a sustained effort by the U.S. to make those negotiations happen and lead to an agreed outcome, faith in such a process, let alone in its outcome, has dwindled in Israel, among Palestinians, in the region and the U.S.

On July 17, 2024, the Israeli parliament made its position crystal-clear, voting by 68 to 9 to reject any creation of a Palestinian state. This vote is consistent with Israeli acceptance of the horrific devastation of the Gaza War and its effort to effectively annex the West Bank. The destruction in the former and the anti-Arab violence in the latter share the same strategic objective: i.e., Israeli-annexed territories devoid of Palestinians, or with minimum Palestinian presence.

At present, the Knesset vote overwhelmingly rejecting a two-state solution would seem to make any options considered heretofore as no longer on the table. However, there have been four generic options for a one-state solution, the debate over which may be extensive but is likely wishful thinking in the context of Israeli intransigence and the strong possibility of a new Palestinian intransigence, given the horrors wreaked upon them: a unitary Israeli state, Palestinian autonomy, federation and confederation. Arguably, negotiations must nonetheless eventually take place, but this is likely to occur at a time when new, decisive facts on the ground emerge. These are the options that over time have been under discussion (Figure 11-7).[77]

In the Middle East, discussion on these models has taken place in historical succession. The first model involves a binational *confederation;* that is, a Palestinian and a Jewish state with a defined and open border between them; and with a joint government in specific areas like external security and foreign trade.[78] This idea was supported by pre-state Jewish binationalists like Judah Magnes who influenced the Bernadotte plans vis-à-vis Bunche's drafts, ultimately leading to the Swede's assassination by the Israeli far-right

Figure 11-7   Israel/Palestine: Four Generic One-State Models

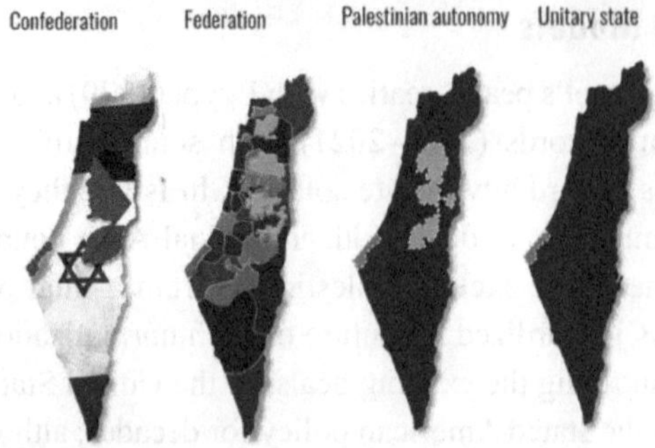

Confederation   Federation   Palestinian autonomy   Unitary state

Source: From Baruch, Pnina Sharvit. 2021. Resolving the Israeli–Palestinian Conflict (INSS) Institute for National Security Studies (Israel)

Sternists in September 1948. That dream of a binational confederation ended with Bernadotte's last breath.

The second solution is a *federal* model; that is, a state divided into Jewish and Palestinian districts that have broad powers at the district level, with the central government retaining authority at the national level. Support for this model is marginal in Israel, though there is a Federation Movement, which envisions the country and the occupied territories in four regions of 30 cantons altogether.[79] Israel has effectively opposed such a federal trajectory since 1948. It was not seen as a realistic option by the postwar Labor regime, whereas the Likud elite sees it as a disguised threat. Their point? Israel is no Switzerland, and Switzerland is not surrounded by the "Arabs." These visions emulate some that were initially developed in the pre-British Mandate era, when the region was still under the Ottoman Empire and Jewish immigration was still relatively low and there was relative peace among the Palestinian Arab majority and the small Jewish minority. After decades of wars, uprisings and resentment, translating such visions into realities in a very different Israel/Palestine is a tall order, yet remains an idea that some binationalists on both sides support today.

The third path involves a state in which the Palestinians have self-rule within an autonomous area. Such scenarios range from the 1970s Allon Plan to the 1990s peace process plans that seem to have crumbled in the past two decades; plans that the hard-right leaders have never really accepted and today reject. Called "Bantustans" by critics who say that in actuality they represent an apartheid regime rather than a form of minority rights, such regions have been perceived as a national security risk by the Likud cabinets since the late 1990s, when Prime Minister Netanyahu formed his first government. To Palestinians, the model has been a nightmare, and the impetus for their ongoing effort for the removal of the Israeli military occupation and for their own self-determination.

Then, there is the fourth scenario, a *unitary* state; that is, a single state in the entire territory with no internal borders. This is the model that Israel seems to be effectively pursuing presently. It would comprise the pre-1967 state, the West Bank and possibly the Gaza Strip. As per Netanyahu's "new Middle East" map presented in his UN presentation two weeks before October 7, this would be effectively a Jewish Israel from the river to the sea.

In the past, most champions of the unitary state represented cultural Zionists (the Brit Shalom or Alliance of Peace in the 1920s and 1930s, humanists such as Judah Magnes) who were against or skeptical of Zionist nationalism. Subsequent proponents of a binational state comprised Jewish intellectuals (philosopher Martin Buber and Hannah Arendt), Israeli left (Hashomer Hatzair, Mapam) and Israeli Arabs. Today, the idea of a unitary Jewish state has become prevalent in both the political right and political center, as evidenced by the recent Knesset vote that overwhelmingly rejected the idea of a Palestinian state. Their argument is that the "democratic character of Israel" can be preserved through such a unitary state. Yet, their initiatives – especially the "judicial reforms" – are undermining the foundations of a Jewish, secular and democratic state. Worse, the Messianic far-right rejects both secularism and democracy, instead promoting a Jewish autocratic – even theocratic – state. Ultimately, such trajectories could undermine Israel's future by amplifying domestic divides (e.g., right vs center-left, secular vs religious, Ashkenazi vs Mizrahi), destabilizing the tax base (e.g., emigration of high-tech talent), bankrupting the economy through protracted multifront wars; and broaden the axis of resistance against the country. Ironically, the triumph of revisionist Zionism could result in its own ultimate meltdown.

While in 1947 Israel officially supported the two-state solution, to Ben-Gurion and the then-dominant Labor hawks, it merely represented an internationally recognized foothold in Palestine that served as a pretext for what would ultimately be a unitary state. Hence Ben-Gurion's ceaseless push for expansion and effectively undefined borders, a long-term project that the Likud regime has embraced.

The key motive is demographic: Adding the Jewish settlers, there are today 9.6 million people in Israel, including 2.1 million Israeli Arab citizens. The number of Palestinians in the West Bank is contested, but most estimations put the figure at 2.5 million and U.S. assessments up to 3 million. In the Gaza Strip, most estimates vary around 2 to 2.3 million. In other words, a full one-state total would mean up to 14.4 million comprising 7.5 million Jews and 6.9 million Palestinian Arabs,[80] whose greater birthrate is likely to significantly impact that relative balance. These numbers exclude Palestinians forced to leave Israel/Palestine since the late 1940s. Nevertheless, such estimates are already a source of great unease among most Israelis. Due to the very high birth rate of Israeli ultra-Orthodox, Jewish and Arab birth rates have been converging. Nonetheless, the full absorption of Palestinian Arabs into a state of Israel would drastically change its "Jewish character," claim the opponents of the Israeli one-state model. Moreover, all things considered, the rising share of the ultra-Orthodox among the Israeli population does not bode well to the "secular and democratic" state either.

Disguised Two-State Solutions

These models are often taken at face value. That's a mistake. In practice, they are disguised two-state solutions because they presume institutional structures, which Israel seeks to control, through fiscal dependency, monetary supremacy, currency dominance, internal security and external military primacy. In a confederation, Israel would reject the idea of shared powers. In a federation, it would oppose independent districts. In both cases, it would resist efforts at refugee solutions through compensation and resettlement. Either of these two models would make Palestinian Arabs the dominant demographic of the ensuing state, which is something Israel has resisted since 1947. Even with Palestinian autonomy, Israel has sought both internal and external control. Sharon's unilateral disengagement from Gaza did not result in a sovereign Gaza. Instead, the Strip was isolated by a high-tech separation barrier, while Israel, taking advantage of surveillance technologies, took control of its land, air, even cyber dimensions. Israeli forces left Gaza, but its control prevailed.

One by one, these models have been proposed – and mugged – by realities: from confederation to federation to autonomy. And that's because each represents either Palestinian equality or some form of quasi-sovereignty while the effective Israeli objective, at least since the 1980s, seems to have been a unitary Jewish state, except for the peace hopes in the 1990s.

Yet, even this model, should it be achieved at the expense of Palestinian loss of territory and lives, will face its own dialectical nightmare over time. It may be contemporary Israel's tacit objective, but it can only be realized with U.S. military aid and by avoiding the kind of international pariah status Israel has been moving toward. Furthermore, the U.S. has its own objectives in the Middle East, for which Israel could prove to be a liability rather than an asset. American hegemony in the region was initially built on Roosevelt's protection-for-oil pact with Saudi Arabia. The Gulf states with their energy resources and untapped reservoirs remain critical to America. When Israeli politics poses a risk to America's grand strategy, the U.S. may seek to distance itself from Israel and marginalize leaders deemed uncooperative (Netanyahu in spring 2024), while supporting those seen as useful (right-center Gantz's meetings in Washington). That said, in the first year of the Gaza War, Congressional support has been Netanyahu's ace in the hole. The question is, for how long can he or his future successors extensively and skillfully play the divide-and-rule game between the White House and the Congress, and between the Republicans and Democrats, with the support of the American Israel Public Affairs Committee (AIPAC) and other prominent members of the Israel lobby.

During the Gaza War, the proponents of Palestinians and Jewish groups for social justice demonstrated against Israel's genocidal atrocities chanting, "From the river to the sea." Perversely, their critics associated the phrase with antisemitism, when it actually referred to a single democratic state for both Jews and Arabs. The real nightmare vision put forward by each side is a one-state model that negates the very existence of the Other. Some Palestinian fringe groups still prefer a one-state model that denies the legitimacy of Israel. But they have neither the means nor the regional or international support to achieve that vision. Neither does Israel have the support to enable a Jewish unitary state, unless both Washington and Brussels are willing to accept the idea of a liquidated Palestine, coupled with potentially devastating turmoil in the region. As Baruch Kimmerling noted two decades ago, the result would be a double politicide: that of the Palestinian polity and, in the long run, that of the Jewish polity as well "because the two are so completely interdependent that destruction of one will necessarily involve the destruction of the other."[81]

In the past decade, international sentiments about Israel/Palestine have shifted. As of June 2024, Israel has been recognized as a sovereign state by 164 of the over 190 UN member states, whereas 145 of these states also recognize Palestine as a sovereign state. The real challenge is that the United States does not recognize Palestine; and as long as the U.S. doesn't do so, nor do the largest European powers – Germany, the UK, France, Italy – and Japan. Should the American stance change, the rest are likely to follow along, unless a breach should emerge between the U.S. and its European allies.

What unleashed the forces of the great conjuncture were those critical years from the late 1940s to late 1950s. It is the sensitivity to these initial conditions that led, through cumulative causation, to a sequence of amplifying events, and through the colonization of the occupied territories, to new wars and uprisings, insurgencies and counter-insurgencies, and regional escalation, virtually ensuring further devastation, with the tacit acceptance of the United States and the West, in the name of the international rules-based order. As the net effect, what is now becoming evident is the fall of Israel, including its economy, polity and society, military and security. In this perspective, the chessboard has been rigged since the late 1940s. Perhaps much of the contemporary debate on the two-state model and the "peace process" is now evoked so ardently because its material conditions were undermined a long while ago.

Two-State Veracities

With the Gaza War, the Strip has been devastated so thoroughly that most of it will be uninhabitable after hostilities. Clearing the area of more than 42 million tonnes of rubble will cost up to $700 million; and its rebuilding up to $80 billion over time.[82] And this is the benign scenario. With the fog of the war, the occupation in the West Bank has effectively shifted from a *de facto* toward a *de jure* annexation. Hence, the dramatic increase in settler violence with the tacit support by military and security authorities. In the 1940s, Yosef Weitz, head of the Jewish National Fund, promoted measures that would drive Arabs out of Palestine; "[The Palestinian Arabs] must be harassed continually" was his mantra.[83] That remains the key motive of the Jewish settlers' anti-Arab pogroms in the West Bank, to expunge Palestinians and thus secure a unitary state without Arabs, with the tacit support of the military and security authorities, and the cabinet.

These shifts have come with a price: the emergence of the Israeli internally conflicted dual state, facing an attendant shrinkage of the rule of law in the normative state and the increasing legal arbitrariness and sanctioned violence by the prerogative state. The rise of the radical right is simply the latest phase in a longstanding process. The zealots' hold over critical state agencies is reflected in the Likud's effort at a judicial coup, but also in the increasing suppression of dissent, historical revisionism in education, routinization of torture, and widespread anti-Arab settler pogroms. The Messianic far-right has seized central elements of the bureaucratic apparatus and its administrative procedures. Hence, national security minister Ben-Gvir's effort to fill the key positions of national police, security and military with like-minded authorities, even at the risk of incompetence, insecurity and escalation.[84] Hence, too, cabinet minister Smotrich's plotting to gain control of the West Bank, evading charges of formally annexing it. These two high-profile ministers are just a tip of the iceberg in the expansive prerogative state.

At the eve of fall 2024, Ronen Bar, the head of Israel's security service Shin Bet, wrote an "emergency letter" addressed to PM Netanyahu, the cabinet and the attorney general, warning that "the Jewish terror leaders want to make the system lose control, the damage to Israel is indescribable." Police incompetence and public legitimacy have led to the expansion of Jewish terrorism, emboldened by "a sense of secret backing" from police. The letter sparked a fiery exchange between Netanyahu and Bar during a prior security cabinet meeting that touched on the deadly settler pogrom in Jit, a Palestinian town west of Nablus:

Netanyahu: "Have we made any arrests?"
Bar: "Two."
Netanyahu: "Why only two? Why not more?"
Bar: "That's the role of the police. There's no police in Israel."[85]

It was a stunning admission and appeal by the head of Israel's internal security. Jewish terror, Bar warned, was jeopardizing Israel's existence, both in the occupied territories and in the volatile border areas. As a textbook example, he mentioned national security minister Ben-Gvir's recent visit to the Temple Mount that could drag Israel "to profuse bloodshed and change the state's face unrecognizably." This anti-Palestinian activity relied on "the use of violence to create intimidation, to spread fear, that is terror." Worse, the nature of Jewish terrorist acts had changed "from focused covert activity to broad, open activity. From using a lighter to using weapons of war... From cutting themselves off from the establishment to receiving legitimacy from certain officials in the establishment."[86]

Step by step, the prerogative state is surpassing the normative state. And given a unitary state, it would effectively overwhelm (though not exclude) the normative state. Indeed, Israel is on the threshold of a significant, reality-changing process that will deliver indescribable damage to itself and likely world delegitimization. Shin Bet expected revenge attacks to ignite "another front in the multifront war we're in, bringing more people into the terror circle to carry out their revenge." Bar foresaw a slippery slope that fostered a sense of governance absence and increasing difficulties in creating vital regional alliances.[87]

There is an inherent linkage between the rise of the dual state in Israel and elevated regional escalation. After a month's lull, Hezbollah began its "initial response" to the assassination of Fuad Shukr, a leading Hezbollah military figure. Reportedly, the response comprised more than 300 rockets yet sought to avoid civilian casualties. Meanwhile, using a total of 100 fighter jets in two waves, the IDF carried out what it claimed to be a preemptive strike, making the stunning yet unverified claim that it had destroyed thousands of launchers targeting Israeli civilians, then contradicting itself by admitting that Hezbollah's intended target was the Mossad headquarters and Intelligence Division base in central Israel.[88] "We identified the Glilot base as the primary target of our operation," Hezbollah's chief Hassan Nasrallah announced. "It houses Unit 8200, which is responsible for intelligence gathering and espionage."[89] The Hezbollah strike ensued, even though in the light of the IDF assertions of the huge numbers of destroyed launchers, such responses should have been impossible. Obviously, military censorship and the Israeli cabinet's media bans undermine any realistic damage estimates.

Yet, the real story is not why Hezbollah targeted the Glilot near Herzliya, Israel's Silicon Valley. Rather, it is that Hezbollah chose *not* to use its precision-guided capabilities to maximize destruction, but only rockets and drones.[90] The intention was to send a message rather than escalation. Both Hezbollah and Israel chose to avoid excessive escalation that could inflame the region, particularly amid ceasefire talks.

Meanwhile, the potential cost of regional escalation rose as Russia began delivering its formidable radars and air defense equipment to Iran. These bolstered Tehran's capacity to withstand any response to its own threatened reprisal over the assassination of the Palestinian negotiator, Ismail Haniyeh (whom the Israelis killed while he was in Tehran attending the inauguration of Iran's new president). In 2016, Iran had acquired advanced S-300 PMU-2 systems from Moscow. Now Russia offered Tehran its long-range, strategic S-400 Triumf air defense missile system.

It was Moscow's signal that Washington was not the only major nuclear power in the region.

AVERTING "THE LONG-RANGE DISASTER"

Eclipse of American Hegemony

Like Russia, Iran and China were concerned about the Ukrainian precedent. Like most crises, the Ukrainian catastrophe was avoidable until its geopolitical trajectory was manoeuvred, at least in part so that peaceful development in conjunction with China could be disrupted.[91] Even as tensions had progressively escalated in the prior half a decade, trade ties between Ukraine and China had steadily increased since President Viktor Yanukovych's state visit to China in 2013. Four years later, Ukraine, then under President Poroshenko, joined China's Belt and Road Initiative (BRI).

In 2019, China overtook Russia as Ukraine's biggest single trading partner. Subsequently, Kyiv and Beijing signed a deal to strengthen cooperation in multiple areas, particularly in infrastructure financing and construction.[92] In 2021, overall trade boomed to $19 billion, having soared 80 percent since 2013.[93] Elected as a peace candidate, President Zelenskyy saw the BRI as an alternative future that would be more peaceful and stable. As he said to President Xi Jinping, Ukraine could become a "bridge to Europe" for Chinese investments.[94] In just a year, major Chinese companies started operations in construction (CPCG, CHEC), food (COFCO) and telecommunications (Huawei). It was an alternate future affording peace and development that appealed to most Ukrainians.

However, this was eyed with increasing concern in the U.S.[95] Washington had worked since the end of the Cold War to transform Ukraine into a client state, pouring billions of dollars into the country. Hence, the crisis escalation. When Zelenskyy flirted with the idea of reconciliation with Russia in 2019, the far right torpedoed it quickly. This was shrewdly exploited by Washington.[96] Since January 2022, Western nations have pledged over $380 billion in aid to Ukraine, including nearly $118 billion in direct military aid from individual countries. Washington accounted for most of the monies.[97]

While U.S. defence contractors have made fortunes "fighting to the last Ukrainian," Ukrainian infrastructure has been devastated and a generation has perished. Over 6 million refugees have fled Ukraine, and another 8 million have been displaced within the country. Having seen the outcome of the proxy war in Ukraine, Arab leaders did not want a déjà vu in the Middle East. Viewed from a historical perspective, the Gaza War can be seen as the logical outcome of the great power dynamic in the Middle East. In the past, this featured the European colonial powers and the Ottoman Empire. Until recently, that dynamic has been fueled mainly by the United States. After President Roosevelt's pact with Saudi Arabia in 1945 the U.S. has served as the region's principal geopolitical architect since the late 1970s, even though its credibility as a "neutral broker" has been contested for decades and it has become complicit with massive policy failures, the unwarranted post-9/11 wars of aggression, and most recently, Israel's genocidal atrocities.

As fraught and unlikely as any landscape of an enduring and equitable peace might seem today, both Israel *and* the Palestinians remain necessary negotiating partners. Burdened by its ongoing economic, political and military degradation – not just since but long prior to October 7 – Israel's liabilities are today more prominent than ever before. By fall 2024, thanks to the protracted war, Israel's real GDP growth rate was eroding. The real decline was steeper, if government interventions were excluded. Consumer spending was resilient, but boosted by public aid to evacuees and reservists. Typical of wartime conditions, inflation was climbing, which required higher interest rates penalizing business and consumer confidence. Low unemployment was historical, but the loss of 100,000 Palestinian workers with minimal foreign hires contributed to the tightness. The net effect was the fall in demand for government bonds, fostered by downgraded credit ratings. These were not just adverse cyclical fluctuations. They reflected rising structural headwinds. It is one thing to have a triumphant six-day war or even a brief low-intensity conflict. It is quite another to subject an already-scarred and polarized economy to a year-long war of obliteration with colonial counter-insurgencies, regional escalation in multi-front conflicts and massive anti-government protests across the country. Israel's economy relies on global economic integration and its military is more dependent on its military suppliers than ever before – hence its overall reliance especially on the United States and the major Western economies. Without this huge support, Israel would collapse. Moreover, the maintenance of Israel's military might is premised on the state of America's military and economy, both of which are under severe erosion. After half a century of massive military spending, more than in any other world region, America has not offered a way forward but has rather penalized the development potential of many, if not most, Arab economies in the region.

Furthermore, America's global hegemonic mission has become increasingly unviable over time. After World War II, the United States accounted for half of the global economy. It had the biggest military by far and was the world's greatest lender. Today America, though still powerful, accounts for about a fifth of the global economy. But now it is the world's greatest creditor, with $35 trillion in gross federal debt (over 120 percent of its GDP, nearly 20 percent higher than amid World War II). That's $270,000 for every taxpayer. Yet, America continues to invest annually almost $1 trillion in military expenditure, or 37 percent of the world total.[98] These monies are predicated on accelerated, unsustainable debt-taking that will cause U.S. debt to soar to almost 170 percent of GDP by the mid-2050s. That's the Greek level prior to the European debt crisis a decade ago. The mounting U.S. public debt will slow its economic growth, push up interest payments to foreign holders of U.S. debt, and pose significant risks to its fiscal and economic outlook.[99]

Armed with this colossal burden, America is marching toward a fiscal crisis that will have huge global reverberations, particularly in those nations such as Israel, whose economy and military are critically reliant on U.S. military aid and economic support. Despite its relatively high living-standards, the high-income U.S. economy no longer benefits from the kind of productivity and growth that would sustain those standards. Hence, the self-defeating addiction to debt and the flag-waving penchant for the kind of xenophobic nationalism and trade protectionism that set the stage for World War II, and the rearmament drives intended to ensure more unwarranted proxy wars.[100]

Multipolar World, Multipolar Peace

In the past two decades, the high-income advanced economies no longer fuel the global economy. It is driven by the large middle-income economies, typified by lower living standards but higher growth potential. Spearheaded by China, these countries feature India, Brazil and Mexico, Russia, Indonesia, Türkiye and others. Since the West's financial recession of 2008–2009, when the major economies were at the edge of default and the emerging economies supported their recovery, these poorer nations have pushed for more inclusive global governance that would be more reflective of the world it claims to represent.[101]

The Middle East is a textbook case. Just as no one nation can any longer fuel the world economy, no single nation can anymore resolve global or even regional challenges. In the region, China has already contributed to stability by mediating the rapprochement between Saudi Arabia and Iran, the two most consequential economic and geopolitical powers in the region; by unifying the Palestinian political front; and by promoting de-escalation.[102] Yet still today, the successors of the old colonial powers seek to ensure disproportionate access to the region's invaluable natural resources.

In an increasingly multipolar world economy, even the most challenging conflicts could be overcome, but only through cooperation between the leading advanced economies and the largest emerging economies. Those who fear such reconciliation like to stress the inherent risks in such endeavors, yet consistently ignore the inherent joint benefits. The latter are so much greater for the peoples concerned yet refused by their domineering elites. In the past decade, China's role has significantly increased in the Middle East. Its approach builds on peace, stability and development, with its diplomatic success in consolidating peaceful rapprochement between Saudi Arabia and Iran and in assembling Palestinian factions into a governing-capable entity. Unlike the United States, it has ties with all stakeholders in the region. But it cannot influence the future without American support. Nor can the two shape the region's constructive development without the facilitation of the international community. The traditional U.S. "shuttle diplomacy" has served mainly as deflection for sustained arms deliveries. UN Security Council initiatives, particularly when they could prove useful, will be vetoed. Put bluntly, post-1945 powers cannot resolve the challenges of the early 21st century. Meanwhile, the stakes continue to rise. Thanks to increasing global integration, regional failures can have severe adverse repercussions around the world.

Such are the primary exigencies and threats posed to the world by the Israel/Palestine conflict that they may be the key to forcing dialogue upon states that are otherwise presently refusing to communicate with each other regarding situations where they are directly engaged. Change will not come from within anytime soon. In the foreseeable future, it can only come from without, if (and only if) the leading countries in the Global North and the largest economies in the Global South can come together for the common good. The need for increasing pressure is imperative, urgent and broad, as particularly manifested in fall 2024 by Israel's foreign minister Katz pressing for measures that implied the kind of Palestinian expulsions in the West Bank that had already devastated the Gaza Strip. [103]

To sideline the new and ongoing scenarios of horrific devastation, what is needed is cooperation based on the least common denominators that could serve as foundational steps for broader and deeper agreements. Such consensus can take time, but deconfliction efforts here can develop trust among former enemies in other theatres.

After a century of failures by the West and half a century of misguided American policies in the Middle East, it is time to try to "cross the river by touching the stones." Unfortunately, time is running out. In Gaza, the horrific devastation has already occurred. Not only that, these genocidal atrocities were and are being committed in real time while the world is watching. The ineffectiveness of the international community's response will virtually ensure that the destruction will continue.

What has happened in Gaza won't stay in Gaza. Perhaps it won't even stay in the region.

ENDNOTES

Chapter 1

1 Kirkpatrick, David D., and Kelly, Kate. 2022. "Before Giving Billions to Jared Kushner, Saudi Investment Fund Had Big Doubts." New York Times, Apr. 10. Nissenbaum, Dion, and Jones, Rory. 2022. "Jared Kushner's New Fund Plans to Invest Saudi Money in Israel." Wall Street Journal, May 8.

2 "Middle East Dialogues: A Conversation with Jared Kushner by Prof. Tarek Masoud." Feb. 15, 2024. Middle East Initiative video [1:29:54]. https://www.youtube.com/watch?v=dtaIHr5S0ts

3 Anderton, Charles H., and Brauer, Jurgen. 2016. *Economic Aspects of Genocides, Other Mass Atrocities, and Their Prevention*. New York: Oxford University Press, p. 25. For a legal analysis, see Pégorier, C. 2013. *Ethnic Cleansing: A Legal Qualification*. New York: Routledge.

4 International Criminal Court. 1998b. "Rome Statute of the International Criminal Court, Article 7." Nov. 10. https://legal.un.org/icc/statute/99_corr/cstatute.htm. Accessed Apr. 10, 2024.

5 Yizhar, S. 1949. *Khirbet Khizeh*. New York: FSG. See Chapter 1.

6 Ibid. See Chapter 8.

7 On the Holocaust and its weaponization, see Chapter 9.

8 Rabin, Yitzhak. 1979. *The Rabin Memoirs*. Berkeley, CA: University of California Press.

9 Shipler, David K. 1979. "Israel Bars Rabin from Relating '48 Eviction of Arabs." New York Times, Oct. 23.

10 Ibid.

11 Begin, Menachem. 1951. *The Revolt*. New York: Henry Schuman.

12 "Letter to the Editors." New York Times, Dec. 2, 1948.

13 Shoshani Neta. 2017. *Born in Deir Yassin* (documentary). See also Aderet, Ofer. 2017. "Testimonies From the Censored Deir Yassin Massacre: 'They Piled Bodies and Burned Them.'" Haaretz, Jul. 16.

14 On the evidence of the classified file, see Hazkani, Shay. 2013. "Catastrophic Thinking: Did Ben-Gurion Try to Rewrite History?" Haaretz, May 16.

15 David, Barak. 2016. "Citing National Security, Israel Likely to Keep Army File on Palestinian Refugees From 1948 Sealed." Haaretz, Sep. 20.

16 On the evidence of the classified file, see Hazkani, Shay. 2013. "Catastrophic Thinking: Did Ben-Gurion Try to Rewrite History?" Haaretz, May 16.

17 See e.g., "'These Matters are Unpleasant.' The Operation of the Ministerial Committee on Access to Restricted Archival Material." Akevot Institute Report, Oct. 2021.

18 Compare Freud, S. 1924e. "The Loss of Reality in Neurosis and Psychosis." *The Complete Psychological Works of Sigmund Freud,* Standard Edition, Vol. XIX, pp. 18–85.

19 Kapshuk, Yoav, and Strömbom, Lisa. 2021. "Israeli Pre-Transitional Justice and the Nakba Law." Israel Law Review 54, no. 3, pp. 305–323.

20 See e.g., Karsh, Efraim. 1997. *Fabricating Israel's History: The New Historians.* London: Frank Cass.

21 This distinction draws from and builds on Shlaim, Avi. 1995. "The Debate about 1948." Int. J. Middle East Stud. 27, no. 3 (Aug.), pp. 287–304. See also Shlaim, Avi. 2004. "The War of the Israeli Historians." Annales 59, no. 1 (Jan.–Feb.), pp. 161–67.

22 Morris, B. 1988. *The Birth of the Palestinian Refugee Problem, 1947–1949.* New York: Cambridge University Press.

23 Pappé, Ilan. 2024. Facebook post. May 16. https://www.facebook.com/pappeIlan/posts/did-you-know-that-70-years-old-professors-of-history-are-threatening-america-nat/877159554454104/

24 Robson, Laura. 2017. *States of Separation: Transfer, Partition, and the Making of the Modern Middle East.* Oakland, CA: University of California Press, pp. 1–2.

25 Ibid., p. 6.

26 "About JNF." See https://www.jnf.org/menu-3/about-jnf

27 Morris, Benny. 2004. *The Birth of the Palestinian Refugee Problem Revisited.* New York: Cambridge University Press, p. 42.

28 Entry for 20 Dec. 1940. See Weitz, Yosef. 1965. *My Diary and Letters to the Children.* Tel Aviv: Massada, II, p. 181.

29 Masalha, Nur. 1992. *Expulsion of the Palestinians: The Concept of "Transfer" in Zionist Political Thought, 1882–1948.* Institute for Palestine Studies, pp. 134–35.

30 Morris 2004, *op. cit.,* p. 314; Masalha 1992, *op. cit.,* p. 188.

31 Masalha 1992, *op. cit.,* p. 188. See also the documentary *Blue Box* (2021) directed by Michal Weits. Weitz was her great-grandfather.

32 Sapir, Michael. 2021. "The JNF is no innocent charity." +972 Magazine, Mar. 4.

33 Khalidi, Walid. 1961. "Plan Dalet: Master Plan for the Conquest of Palestine." Journal of Palestine Studies 18, no. 1 (Autumn, 1988, Special Issue: Palestine 1948), pp. 4–33. See also Khalidi, Walid. 1997. "Revisiting the UNGA Partition Resolution." Journal of Palestine Studies 27, no. 1 (Autumn), pp. 5–21.

34 Pappé, Ilan. 2006. *The Ethnic Cleansing of Palestine.* London: Oneworld Publications.

35 Pappé, Ilan. 2006. "The 1948 ethnic cleansing of Palestine." Journal of Palestine Studies 36, no. 1, pp. 6–20.

36 Morris, Benny, and Kedar, Benjamin Z. 2022. "'Cast thy bread': Israeli biological warfare during the 1948 War." Middle Eastern Studies 59, no. 5, pp. 1–25. Masalha, Nur. 1992. *Expulsion of the Palestinians: The Concept of "Transfer" in Zionist Political Thought, 1882–1948.* Institute for Palestine Studies, p. 175.

37 The 1961 exchanges were republished decades later. Cooke, Hedley V. 1988. "Appendix E: The Spectator Correspondence." Journal of Palestine Studies 18, no. 1 (Autumn), pp. 51–70. See also Khalidi, Walid (1988). "Plan Dalet: Master Plan for the Conquest of Palestine." Journal of Palestine Studies 18, no. 1 (Autumn), pp. 4–19.

38 Al-Wali, Mustafa. 2000. "Eyewitness Accounts of the Tantoura Massacre." Majallat Al-Dirasat Al-Filastiniyya (43); Pappé, Ilan. 2001. "The Tantura Case in Israel: The Katz Research and Trial." Journal of Palestine Studies 30, no. 3 (Spring), pp. 19–39. "Sundance documentary 'Tantura' is a flawed look at 1948 controversy." The Jerusalem Post, Jan. 22, 2022.

39 Forensic Architecture. "Executions and Mass Graves in Tantura, 23 May 1948." May 24, 2023. See https://forensic-architecture.org/investigation/executions-and-mass-graves-in-tantura-23-may-1948

40 Galber interviewed by Shalita, Chen. 2023. "'The Conception That the Conflict Can Be Contained is Obsolete.'" Shomrim – The Center for Media and Democracy, Oct. 16.

41 Masalha, Nur. "The Historical Roots of the Palestinian Refugee Question." In: Aruri, Naseer. 2001. Palestinian Refugees: The Right of Return. London: Pluto Press, pp. 49–50.

42 Davis, Rochelle A. 2011. Palestinian Village Histories: Geographies of the Displaced. Redwood City, CA: Stanford University Press, pp. 237–38.

43 Morris, Benny. 2004. Birth of the Palestinian Refugee Problem Revisited. Cambridge: Cambridge University Press, p. 536.

44 Morris, Benny. 1993. Israel's Border Wars, 1949–1956; Arab Infiltration, Israeli Retaliation and the Countdown to the Suez War. Oxford: Oxford Clarendon Press, p. 11.

45 Shai, Aron. 2006. "The Fate of Abandoned Arab Villages in Israel, 1965–1969." History and Memory 18, no. 2 (Fall/Winter), pp. 86–106.

46 Davis, John. 1970. The Evasive Peace. London: New World Press, p. 69.

47 Cited in John Quigley, John. 1994. "Israel's Forty-Five Year Emergency: Are There Time Limits to Derogations from Human Rights Obligations?," 15 Mich. J. Int'l L. 491.

48 Roberts, Christopher M. 2019. "From the State of Emergency to the Rule of Law: The Evolution of Repressive Legality in the Nineteenth Century British Empire." Chicago Journal of International Law 20(1), Article 1.

49 This is the central argument of Hughes, Matthew. 2019. Britain's Pacification of Palestine: The British Army, the Colonial State, and the Arab Revolt, 1936–1939. New York: Cambridge University Press.

50 Burleigh, Michael. 2013. Small Wars, Faraway Places: Global Insurrection and the Making of the Modern World 1945–1965. New York: Viking, p. 164.

51 Bracha, Baruch. 1993. "Restriction of personal freedom without due process of law according to the Defence (Emergency) Regulations, 1945." Israel Yearbook on Human Rights, pp. 296–323; Yaniv, Avner. 1993. National Security and Democracy in Israel. Boulder, CO: Lynne Riener, p. 175.

52 See e.g., Bull, Anna Cento. 2012. Italian Neofascism: The Strategy of Tension and the Politics of Nonreconciliation. Berghahn Books; and Dossi, Rosella. 2001. "Italy's Invisible Government." University of Melbourne, Contemporary Europe Research Centre.

53 See Ferraresi, Franco. 1997. Threats to Democracy: The Radical Right in Italy after the War. Princeton, N.J.: Princeton University Press; Bull 2012, op. cit.; Ganser, Daniele. 2005. NATO's Secret Armies: Operation Gladio and Terrorism in Western Europe. London: Routledge.

54 Valdes, Juan Gabriel. 2008. *Pinochet's Economists: The Chicago School of Economics in Chile.* New York: Cambridge University Press.

55 Kahane, Libby. 2008. *Rabbi Meir Kahane: His Life and Thought.* Institute for the Publication of the Writings of Rabbi Meir Kahane.

56 Friedman, R. I. 1990. *The False Prophet: Rabbi Meir Kahane – From FBI Informant to Knesset Member.* Brooklyn, NY: Lawrence Hill & Co. See esp. Chapter 5.

57 On the declassified FBI records, see "Informant: Meir Kahane Planned Biological Terror Attack On USSR." Intelwire.com, Oct. 6, 2007.

58 See Kaplan, Morris. 1971. "Kahane Gets 5-Year Suspended Sentence in Bomb Plot." New York Times, Jul. 24; Carmody, Deirdre. 1975. "Kahane Enjoys Freedom as an Inmate." New York Times. Nov. 15.

59 On Kahane's promotion of ethnic expulsion, see Kahane, Meir. 1981. *They Must Go.* New York: Grosset & Dunlap.

60 McQuiston, John T. 1990. "Kahane Is Killed After Giving Talk in New York Hotel." New York Times, Nov. 6.

61 Sullivan, Ronald. 1991. "Judge Gives Maximum Term in Kahane Case." New York Times, Jan. 30.

62 See USA v. Omar Ahmad Ali Abdel-Rahman et al: 93-CR-181-KTD. Retrieved on Mar. 1, 2024. See also Smith, Greg B. 2002. "Bin Laden bankrolled Kahane killer defense." New York Daily News, Oct. 9.

63 Khalidi, Rashid I. 2017. "Historical Landmarks in the Hundred Years' War on Palestine." Journal of Palestine Studies 47(1). This section draws from Khalidi's historical landmarks, which are here defined by old colonial powers (1917–45), the Cold War superpowers (1945–91) and the shift to multipolarity (1991–present).

64 The Declaration was "operationalized" by the confidential 1919 Foreign Office memo in which Balfour confided that, "in Palestine we do not propose even to go through the form of consulting the wishes of the present inhabitants of the country." See memo dated August 11, 1919, cited in Hurewitz, J.C. (ed.). 1979. *The Middle East and North Africa in World Politics,* vol. 2. New Haven, CT: Yale University Press, p. 189.

65 Khalidi, Walid. 1987. *From Haven to Conquest: Readings in Zionism and the Palestine Problem until 1948.* Washington, DC: Institute for Palestine Studies, app. 4, pp. 846–49.

66 For more, see Chapter 4.

67 "Arafat says natural gas field great hope for Palestinian economy." CNN, Sep. 27, 2000.

68 Schwartz, M. 2015. "The Great Game in the Holy Land." TomDispatch, Feb. 26.

69 Nafeez Mosaddeq Ahmed. 2012. "Israel's War for Gaza's Gas." Le Monde Diplomatique, Nov. 28.

70 Schwartz 2015, *op. cit.*

71 Urquhart, C. 2006. "Gaza on brink of implosion as aid cut-off starts to bite." The Guardian, Apr. 16.

72 Compare Davis, Mike. 2001, *Late Victorian Holocausts,* New York: Verso Books, pp. 170–75.

73 "Barak: Hamas Will Pay for Its Escalation in the South." Haaretz, Feb. 29, 2008.

74 "Israel's new war cabinet vows to wipe Hamas off the earth." Reuters, Oct. 12, 2023.

75 On starvation as a weapon of war, genocide and Holocaust, see Chapter 10.

76 On the cost-of-living crisis and mass protests, see Chapter 7.

77 Compare Duddilla, Krishna. 2016. "Leviathan Gas Field, Levantine Basin, Mediterranean Sea." Offshore Technology, Oct.6.

78 "Rethinking Gas Diplomacy in the Eastern Mediterranean." Middle East Report No. 240. International Crisis Group. Apr. 26, 2023.

79 Ibid.

80 For the full argument, see Krasna, Joshua. 2023. "A Long, Hot Summer for Eastern Mediterranean Gas Politics." Foreign Policy Research Institute, Sep. 26.

81 "Suez Canal annual revenue hits record $9.4 billion, chairman says." Reuters, Jun. 21, 2023.

82 Gambrell, Jon. 2021. "Massive cargo ship turns sideways, blocks Egypt's Suez Canal." AP, Mar. 23.

83 Allen, William. 1855. *The Dead Sea, A New Route to India: With Other Fragments and Gleanings in the Past.* London: Longman, Brown & Green, Vol. 1, pp. 319, 342–45.

84 Herzl, Theodor. 1902. *Old-New Land.* New York: Stellar, 2016, p. 39.

85 MacCabee, H.D. 1963. "Use of Nuclear Explosives for Excavation of Sea-Level Canal Across the Negev Desert." Informal Report, Lawrence Livermore National Laboratory. United States Office of Scientific and Technical Information, UCRL-ID-124767, July 1.

86 Compare Gradus 1977, *op. cit.*

87 After the global pandemic, the UAE, the host of Dubai's COP28, distanced itself from the controversial plan, which was vehemently opposed by Israeli environmentalists, due to the EAPC's dark environmental track record. See "Israeli pipeline company signs deal to bring UAE oil to Europe." Reuters, Oct. 20, 2020.

88 "UAE says nixing pipeline agreement won't damage ties with Israel." Times of Israel, Oct. 21.

89 "The Economic Costs of the Israeli Occupation for the Palestinian People: The Unrealized Oil and Natural Gas Potential." UNCTAD. 2019.

90 Ibid.

91 Schenk 2010, *op. cit.*. See also Roberts, G., and Peace, D. 2007. "Hydrocarbon plays and prospectivity of the Levantine Basin, offshore Lebanon and Syria from modern seismic data." GeoArabia 12, no. 3, pp. 99–124.

92 UNCTAD 2019, *op. cit.*

93 Boersma, Tim, and Sachs, Natan. 2015. "Gaza Marine: Natural Gas Extraction in Tumultuous Times?" Foreign Policy at Brookings Policy Report No. 36 (Feb.), p. 13.

94 Ibid.

95 "Options for a policy regarding Gaza's civilian population." Policy Dept. Israel's Ministry of Intelligence, Oct. 13, 2023.

96 Ibid.

97 Ibid.

98 "Israeli officials said in talks with Congo, others on taking in Gaza emigrants." Times of Israel, Jan. 3, 2024.

99 "An Israeli ministry, in a 'concept paper,' proposes transferring Gaza civilians to Egypt's Sinai." AP News, Oct. 30, 2023

100 Gamliel, G. 2023. "Victory is an opportunity for Israel in the midst of crisis." The Jerusalem Post, Nov. 19.

101 Klarenberg, Kit. 2023. "Zionist think tank publishes blueprint for Palestinian genocide." The Grayzone, Oct. 24.

102 Weitman, Amir. 2023. "A plan for resettlement and final rehabilitation in Egypt of the entire population of Gaza." White Paper. Misgav Institute for National Security and Zionist Strategy, Oct. 17.

103 Sheinin, Yacov. 2012. "$10b investment will turn Gaza into the Riviera." Globes, Nov. 12.

104 Ibid.

105 Ibid.

106 Ibid.

107 See the beginning of this chapter.

108 Krauss, Joseph. 2023. "In Israel's call for mass evacuation, Palestinians hear echoes of their original catastrophic exodus." AP News, Oct. 13.

109 Da Silva, Chantal. 2024. "Right-wing Israeli ministers join thousands at event calling for the resettlement of Gaza." NBC News, Jan. 29.

110 Quoted in Ziv, Oren. 2024. "Turning Zeitoun into Shivat Zion: Israeli summit envisions Gaza resettlement." +972 Magazine, Jan. 30.

111 Ward, Clarissa. 2024. "The grandmother who wants to lead Israelis back to a Gaza without Palestinians." CNN, Mar. 20.

112 Izenberg, Dan, Lappin, Yaakov, and Lazaroff, Tovah. 2008. "Daniella Weiss released from house arrest pending trial." The Jerusalem Post, Oct. 6; Lazaroff, Tovah, and Paz, Shelley. 2008. "Sneh to Barak: Jail Daniella Weiss." The Jerusalem Post, Dec. 8.

113 Sharon, Jeremy. 2022. "Settler group openly planning establishment of 3 illegal outposts next week." Times of Israel, Jul. 14; Chazan, Guy. 2023. "Emboldened Israeli settlers seek to tighten grip on West Bank." Financial Times, Nov. 15.

114 Gerlach, David W. 2017. *The Economy of Ethnic Cleansing: The Transformation of the German-Czech Borderlands after World War II.* Cambridge, UK: Cambridge University Press.

115 Aly, Götz. 2007. *Hitler's Beneficiaries: Plunder, Racial War, and the Nazi Welfare State.* New York: Metropolitan.

116 Sadeh, Shuki. 2023. "The West Bank Real Estate Game: Uncovering Subsidies and Land Practices in Settlements." Shomrim, Aug. 3.

117 Mann, M. 2005. *The Dark Side of Democracy: Explaining Ethnic Cleansing.* Cambridge, UK: Cambridge University Press, pp. 9, 31.

118 Compare Lynk, Michael. 2001. "The Right to Compensation in International Law and the Displaced Palestinians." Palestinian Refugee ResearchNet (PRRN), Jan.

119 Refugee repatriation, resettlement and compensation – UNCCP Special Rep. (Johnson) – Proposal/Non-UN document: "The Plan," Proposals for the Implementation of Paragraph 11 of UNGAR 1943(III) of Dec. 11, 1948.

120 See e.g., Hadawi, Samir, and Kubursi, Atif. 1948. *Palestinian Rights and Losses in 1948: A Comprehensive Study.* London: Al Saqi Books, 1988; and Lewis, Frank. 1996. "Agricultural Property and the 1948 Palestinian Refugees: Assessing the Losses." Explorations in Economic History 33.

121 Compare Brynen, Rex. 2008. *The Past as Prelude? Negotiating the Palestinian Refugee Issue.* London: Chatham House Briefing Paper, pp. 17–18.

122 Senechal, Thierry J., and Hilal, Leila. "The Value of 1948 Palestinian Refugee Material Damages: An EstimateBased on International Standards." In: Brynen and El-Rifai 2013, *op. cit.*, pp. 132–58.

123 Kubursi, Atif. "Palestinian Refugee Losses in 1948." In: Brynen and El-Rifai 2013, *op. cit.*, pp. 159–76.

124 See Introduction in Brynen, Rex, and El-Rifai, Roula. 2013. *Compensation to Palestinian Refugees and the Search for Palestinian–Israeli Peace.* New York: Pluto, pp. 1–18.

Chapter 2

1 " Religious Zionist Party MP urges government to occupy Gaza, annex to Israel, demolish all homes." Anadolu Ajansı, Jan. 3, 2024.

2 Sommer, Allison Kaplan. 2023. "Far-right Israeli Knesset Member Zvi Sukkot to Head Subcommittee on the West Bank." Haaretz, Nov. 1.

3 Levinson, Chaim. 2015. "Meet the Jewish Extremist Group That Seeks to Violently Topple the State." Haaretz, Aug. 7.

4 Talal, Hassan bin. 1981. *Palestinian Self-Determination: A Study of the West Bank and Gaza Strip.* New York: Quarter, p. 11.

5 Oren, Michael B. 2003. *Six Days of War: June 1967 and the Making of the Modern Middle East.* New York: Random House, p. 316.

6 "The Six-Day War: Prime Minister Eshkol Reviews Six-Day War." Israeli Foreign Ministry. June 12, 1967. Jewish Virtual Library.

7 On the Allon Plan, see "The Allon Plan (June 1967)." Jewish Virtual Library. Retrieved on Mar. 7, 2024.

8 Pedatzur, Reuven. 2007. "The 'Jordanian option,' the plan that refuses to die." Haaretz, Jul. 25.

9 373. Telegram from the Embassy in Jordan to the Department of State, para. 7–8; Foreign Relations of the United States 1964–1968 Volume XX, Arab-Israeli Dispute, 1967–68. Accessed on May 2, 2024.

10 Berger, Yotam. 2016. "Secret 1970 Document Confirms First West Bank Settlements Built on a Lie." Haaretz, Jul. 28.

11 Aderet, Ofer. 2023. "Israel Poisoned Palestinian Land to Build West Bank Settlement in 1970s, Documents Reveal." Haaretz, Jun. 23.

12 Morris, Benny, and Kedar, Benjamin Z. 2023. "'Cast thy bread': Israeli biological warfare during the 1948 War." Middle Eastern Studies 59, no. 5, pp. 752–76. On the Tatwana poisoning, see "Settlers Suspected of Well Attack." BBC News, Jul. 13, 2004.

13 "HCJ to state: Demolish nine structures in the settlement of Ofra." B'tselem, Feb. 9, 2015.

14 Gorenberg, Gershom. 2006. *The Accidental Empire: Israel and the Birth of the Settlements, 1967–1977.* New York: Henry Holt & Co., pp. 312–18.

15 Shalev, Nir. 2008. "The Ofra Settlement: An unauthorized Outpost." B'Tselem, Dec. 2008.

16 Compare "The Israeli Army and the Intifada: Policies that Contribute to the Killings." Human Rights Watch Report, Aug. 1990.

17 Morris, Benny. 1993. *Israel's Border Wars 1949–1956: Arab Infiltration, Israeli Retaliation, and the Countdown to the Suez War.* Oxford: Clarendon Press. On Israel's reprisal raids and its national security strategy, see Chapter 11.

18 On the Altalena Affair, see Auerbach, Jerold S. 2011. *Brothers at War: Israel and the Tragedy of the Altalena.* Quid Pro, LLC. For an early view, see Lapidot, Yehuda. 1948. "The Irgun: The Altalena Affair." Jun. 20. Jewish Virtual Library.

19 For a more recent assessment, see Shilon, Avi. 2012. *Menachem Begin: A Life.* Yale University Press.

20 Article 78 of the Code allows the sovereign to seize ownerless and uncultivated lands. It was enacted to encourage agriculture in areas that were distant from the center of the Ottoman Empire to elicit tax revenue. By contrast, Israel has exploited it as an instrument of land expropriation. See Ian Lustick, 1981. "Israel and the West Bank After Elon Moreh: the Mechanics of De Facto Annexation." Middle East Journal 4, no. 35, pp. 557–77.

21 See Chapter 1.

22 Hass, Amira. 2012. "From Yamit to the Jordan Valley, the IDF continues to force Arabs from their homes." Haaretz, Apr. 16.

23 Lustick 1981, *op. cit.*

24 Sabatello, Eitan. 1983. *The Populations of the Administered Territories: Some Demographic Trends and Implications.* Jerusalem: The West Bank Data Base Project, pp. 29–30.

25 Lustick, Ian S. 1985. The "Irreversibility" of Israel's Annexation of the West Bank and Gaza Strip: A Critical Evaluation." Final Report, Dartmouth College, Defense Technical Information Center [Unclassified], Oct. 1, p. 9

26 Elon, Amos. 1983. "Stepping up Annexation." Haaretz, Feb. 26.

27 David Shipler. 1982. "Israel Changing Face of West Bank." New York Times, Sep. 12.

28 As documented by Benvenisti and the West Bank Data Base Project in Jerusalem, funded by the Ford Foundation, the Rockefeller Foundation and the American Enterprise Institute.

29 Lustick 1985, *op. cit.*

30 Lustick, Ian S. 1988. *For the Land and the Lord: Jewish Fundamentalism in Israel.* New York: Council on Foreign Relations, esp. Chapter 3.

31 Moreh, Dror. 2015. *The Gatekeepers: Inside Israel's Internal Security Agency.* New York: Skyhorse, p. 171.

32 Hirschhorn, Sara Yael. 2017. *City on a Hilltop: American Jews and the Israeli Settler Movement.* Boston: Harvard University Press, pp. 192–94.

33 "Yatom: Jews Nearly Succeeded in 1984 Temple Mt. Bomb Plot." Haaretz, Jul. 24, 2004.

34 Lustick 1988, *op. cit.*, p. 131.

35 Barthos, Gordon. 1990. "Israeli terror group threatens to kill 12 peace activists." Toronto Star, Jan. 6, p. A2.

36 Gal-Or, Noemi. "Tolerating terrorism in Israel." In: Gal-Or, Noemi (ed.). 2015. *Terrorism in the West: An International Survey.* London: Routledge, pp. 72ff.

37 "Israeli Settlers' Chelsea Boss Backer." BBC News, Sep. 2020.

38 Masalha, Nur. 2000. *Imperial Israel and the Palestinians: The Politics of Expansion.* London: Pluto Press, pp. 123–26.

39 Blau, Uri. 2015. "Haaretz Investigation: U.S. Donors Gave Settlements More Than $220 Million in Tax-exempt Funds Over Five Years." Haaretz, Dec. 7.

40 Pedahzur and Perliger 2011, *op. cit.*, p. 72.

41 Kershner, Isabel. 2015. "Moshe Levinger, Contentious Leader of Jewish Settlers in Hebron, Dies at 80." New York Times, May 18.

42 Hoch, Richard L. 1994. "Sovereignty, Sanctity, and Salvation: The Theology of Rabbi Tzvi Yehudah Ha-Kohen and the Actions of Gush Emunim." Shofar 13, no. 1, pp. 90–118;

43 See e.g., "Accusation of war crimes said lodged against IDF reservists who went to The Hague." Times of Israel, Jan. 29, 2024; "Israel-Hamas war: 'We will fight and we will win,' says Benjamin Netanyahu." News Conference, Oct. 29, 2023.

44 Ben-Johanan, Karma. 2016. "Wreaking Judgment on Mount Esau: Christianity in R. Kook's Thought." Jewish Quarterly Review 106, no. 1, pp. 76–100.

45 Ibid.

46 Inbari, Motti. 2012. *Messianic Religious Zionism Confronts Israeli Territorial Compromises.* Cambridge: Cambridge University Press, pp. 17, 30–32.

47 Lustick, Ian S. 1988. *For the Land and the Lord: Jewish Fundamentalism in Israel.* Council of Foreign Relations, p. 34.

48 Aran, Gideon. 1994. "Jewish Zionist Fundamentalism: The Bloc of the Faithful in Israel (Gush Emunim)." In: Marty, Martin E., and Appleby, Scott (eds.). *Fundamentalisms Observed, Vol. 1.* University of Chicago Press, pp. 265–343.

49 Shahak, Israel, and Mezvinsky, Norton. 2004. *Jewish fundamentalism in Israel.* London: Pluto, p.103; Rachlevsky, Sefi. 2013. "The Extremist Rabbi Who Reigns Unobstructed." Haaretz, Nov. 15; Kaufman, Ami. 2014. "Israeli rabbi: It's okay to kill innocent civilians and destroy Gaza." +972 Magazine, Jul. 22.

50 On the ICC and the Mossad-gate, see Chapter 9.

51 Hamashige, Hope et al. 1996. "Bingo King Aids Israeli Right Wing." Los Angeles Times, May 9.

52 Matthew Dorf, "Is Irving Moskowitz a Hero or Just a Rogue?" Jewish Telegraphic Agency, September 26, 1997. On the alleged worker abuses in the casino, see the Coalition for Justice in Hawaiian Gardens & Jerusalem, stopmoskowitz.org.

53 Hamashige, Hope et al. 1996. "Bingo King Aids Israeli Right Wing." Los Angeles Times, May 9.

54 Sherwood, Harriett. 2011. "Irving Moskowitz demolishes part of Jerusalem hotel to build settler housing." The Guardian, Jan. 9.

55 Pedahzur and Perliger 2011, *op. cit.*, p. 71.

56 "1994: Jewish settler kills 30 at holy site." BBC News. Feb. 25, 1994.

57 Hamashige 1996, *op. cit.*

58 Dorf, Matthew. 1997. "Is Irving Moskowitz a Hero or Just a Rogue?" Jewish Telegraphic Agency, Sep. 26. See also Blumenthal, Max. 2009. "Gambling with Conflict: How a neocon casino king from California funds the Israeli settler movement." Mondoweiss, Jun. 3.

59 Andrew Lawler. 2021. "No Way Out: How the Opening of a Tunnel Blocked the Path to Peace in Jerusalem." Politico, Oct. 2.

60 Blau, Uri. 2009. "U.S. group invests tax-free millions in East Jerusalem land." Haaretz, Aug. 17; Hasson, Nir. 2019. "Settler Group Strengthens Hold on Jerusalem's Christian Quarter After Victory in Court." Haaretz, Jun. 11.

61 Sharrock, David. 1999. 'Inside story: Lost property." The Guardian, Feb. 4. See also Neuman, Tamara. 2018. *Settling Hebron: Jewish Fundamentalism in a Palestinian City.* Philadelphia, PA: University of Pennsylvania Press, pp. 155–56.

62 For more on Moskowitz's economic charm offensives, see Chapter 6.

63 Levy, Gideon. 2010. *The Punishment of Gaza.* New York: Verso. See Introduction.

64 Miller, Elhanan. 2013. "'Sharon was about to leave two-thirds of the West Bank.'" Times of Israel, Feb. 19.

65 Rutenberg, Jim, et al. 2010. "Tax-exempt funds aid West Bank settlements." New York Times, Jul. 6.

66 Blau, Uri. 2015. "Does Your Jewish Charity Donate to the Settlements?" Haaretz, Dec. 8; Blau, Ari. 2015. "Haaretz Investigation: Israeli Corporations Gave Millions to West Bank Settlements." Haaretz, Dec. 15.

67 Kane, Alex. 2021. "Tax-Except U.S. Nonprofits Fuel Israeli Settler Push to Evict Palestinians." The Intercept, May 14.

68 Herman, Alice, et al. 2024. "Pro-Israel money pours in to unseat progressives in congressional races." The Guardian, Apr. 17.

69 Benvenisti, Eyal. 2012. *The International Law of Occupation.* Oxford University Press, p. 236.

70 The Report described such an unauthorized outpost as having four major characteristics: There was no government decision to establish it. It was founded with no legal planning status governing the area it was established upon, to support a building permit. It is not attached to an existing settlement, but at least a few hundred meters distant from it. And it emerged mainly after the mid-1990s. See Sasson, Talia. 2005. "Summary of the Opinion Concerning Unauthorized Outposts." Sasson Report. Israel Ministry of Foreign Affairs, Mar. 10.

71 Israel's Religiously Divided Society. Pew Research Center, Mar. 8, 2016.

72 Hareuveni, Eyal. 2022. "State Business: Israel's misappropriation of land in the West Bank through settler violence." B'Tselem, p. 6.

73 Basic Law: Israel – the Nation State of the Jewish People, Art. 7. Passed by the Knesset on 19 July 2018. English translation available through Knesset website: https://main.knesset.gov.il/EN/activity/Documents/BasicLawsPDF/BasicLawNationState.pdf

74 Hareuveni 2022, *op. cit.*, p. 36.

75 Shezaf, Hagar. 2023. "'There's War, Blood Is Boiling': Settlers Force Palestinians Out of Their West Bank Homes." Haaretz, Oct. 17. See also "The Third Front: Settler Violence in Gaza War's Shadow and the Impact on Area C." Special Report: Settlement Watch Team. PeaceNow, Nov. 2023.

76 "Shin Bet chief said to warn of far-right threats to top general in West Bank." Times of Israel, Dec. 27.

77 See "I Am Shamed by Hebron Settlers' Pogrom." AP/Haaretz, Dec. 7, 2008; 'Olmert: I hate everything Sheldon Adelson loved about Israel." The Jerusalem Post, Jan. 22.

78 See e.g., Frankel, Julia. 2024. "Online fundraisers for violent West Bank settlers raised thousands, despite sanctions." AP, Feb. 23.

79 Murphy, Brett. 2024. "Blinken Says Israeli Units Accused of Serious Violations Have Done Enough to Avoid Sanctions. Experts and Insiders Disagree." ProPublica, May 8.

80 "Arab Students in Israel." Journal of Palestine Studies 10, no. 3 (April 1981), pp. 140–46.

81 On the apartheid rule, see Chapter 11.

82 Molad poll from 2015.

83 This section builds on and updates the report by Gordis, Avishay Ben-Sasson. 2017. Israel's National Security and West Bank Settlements. Tel Aviv: Molad, Dec.

84 Gordis, Avishay Ben-Sasson. 2016. Israel's National Security and West Bank Settlements. Tel Aviv: Molad, p. 15.

85 Heimann, Ariel, and Berkman, Alon. 2024. "Israeli Communities During the Swords of Iron War: Plans, Execution, and Reassessing the Criteria for Evacuation." The Institute for National Security Studies, No. 1838, Mar. 21.

86 See the Fourth Geneva Convention, Part III, Section III, Article 49 Relative to the Protection of Civilian Persons in Time of War. Originating from August 12, 1949, it deems that "the Occupying Power shall not deport or transfer parts of its own civilian population into the territory it occupies." See International Humanitarian Law Databases. https://ihl-databases.icrc.org/en/ihl-treaties/gciv-1949. Retrieved on Apr. 24, 2024.

87 Report of the Independent International Commission of Inquiry on the Occupied Palestinian Territory, including East Jerusalem, and Israel, UN General Assembly 77 Sess., UNN DOC. A/77/328 (Sep. 14, 2022), supra note 3.

88 On the Israeli state as a dual state, see Chapter 5.

89 Levine-Schnur, Ronit, and Megiddo, Tamar, and Berda, Yael. 2023. A Theory of Annexation. SSRN, Feb. 5.

90 Shezaf, Hagar. 2023. "Israeli Gov't Circulates Draft Plan to Transfer Powers Over Civilian Life in the West Bank to Smotrich's Control." Haaretz, Feb. 15.

91 Harel, Amos, et al. 2014. "Security Sources: 100 Followers of Racist Rabbi Are behind Hate Crimes." Haaretz, May 8.

92 Rutenberg, Jim, et al. 2010. "Tax-Exempt Funds Aid Settlements in West Bank." New York Times, July 6.

93 Odenheimer, Natan, et al. 2024. "Israeli Official Describes Secret Government Bid to Cement Control of West Bank." New York Times, June 21.

94 Smotrich, Bezalel. 2017. "Israel's Decisive Plan." Hashiloah, Sep. 7.

95 Hecht, Ravit. 2016. "The Face of Israel's Far Right Wants to 'Abort' Palestinian Hope." Haaretz, Dec. 3.

96 Compare Chapter 1.

97 "Blinken denounces civilian toll in Gaza, says 'far too many Palestinians have been killed.'" CNN, Nov. 10, 2023.

98 Michaeli, Yarden and Scharf, Avi. 2024. "Buffer Zone and Control Corridor: What the Israeli Army's Entrenchment in Gaza Looks Like." Haaretz, Mar. 28. See also "Establishing a 'security zone' in Gaza is a war crime." B'Tselem, Feb. 21, 2024.

Chapter 3

1 Remarks by President Biden on the Terrorist Attacks in Israel. Speech. The White House, Oct. 10, 2023.

2 Ibid.

3 "Nikki Haley writes 'finish them' on IDF artillery shells during Israel visit." The Guardian, May 28.

4 On Danon and the two-state solution, see "Supporters of peace deal have no place in Likud, says MK." Times of Israel, Sep. 4, 2013. On leveling Gaza, see "MK Danon to Ynet: If the soldier isn't returned, 'we should start leveling Gaza.'" Ynetnews. Aug. 1, 2013. On ethnic expulsions, see "Israeli minister supports 'voluntary migration' of Palestinians in Gaza." Al Jazeera. Nov. 14, 2023.

5 Brecher, Frank W. 1991. Reluctant Ally: United States Foreign Policy toward the Jews from Wilson to Roosevelt. Praeger. See Chapters 1–4.

6 On the parallel immigration waves to the pre-state Israel, see Chapter 5.

7 Oren, Michael. 2007. Power, Faith and Fantasy: America in the Middle East, 1776 to the Present. New York: Norton, esp. Chapter 24.

8 Rubenberg, Cheryl. 1986. Israel and the American National Interest: A Critical Examination. Urbana, IL: University of Illinois Press, p. 27.

9 Steinbock, Dan. 2024. The End of Modern Economic Growth. Unpublished manuscript, see esp. Chapter 2.

10 On the UN Plan and the future government of Palestine, see Resolution 181, A/RES/181(II), Nov. 29, 1947. https://web.archive.org/web/20120524094913/http://domino.un.org/unispal.nsf/0/7f0af2bd897689b785256c330061d253

11 Declaration of Establishment of State of Israel. Israel's Ministry of Foreign Affairs website, https://embassies.gov.il/MFA/AboutIsrael/history/Pages/Declaration%20of%20Establishment%20of%20State%20of%20Israel.aspx

12 Truman, Harry S. 1956. Years of Trial and Hope, Vol. 2. New York: Doubleday, p. 158.

13 United States Proposal for Temporary United Nations Trusteeship for Palestine. Statement by President Truman, March 25, 1948. See https://www.un.org/unispal/document/auto-insert-194247/. Retrieved on Feb. 21, 2024.

14 "The United States and the Recognition of Israel: A Chronology," see May 12–14, 1948. https://web.archive.org/web/20121031045628/http://www.trumanlibrary.org/israel/palestin.htm. Retrieved on Feb. 21, 2024.

15 Behbehani, Hashim S. H. 1986. *The Soviet Union and Arab Nationalism, 1917–1966*. London: Routledge, p. 69.

16 Herf, Jeffrey. 2021. "The U.S. State Department's Opposition to Zionist Aspirations during the Early Cold War: George F. Kennan and George C. Marshall in 1947–1948." Journal of Cold War Studies 23, no. 4, pp. 153–80.

17 On the U.S.' Middle East policy, Nixon's petrodollar deal, and China's stance, see Chapter 10.

18 On the reverse course and German reindustrialization, see Steinbock 2024, *op. cit.*, esp. Chapter 5

19 "Unrwa closing Jerusalem headquarters after Israeli settler arson attacks." Middle East Eye, May 9, 2024. See also Tondo, Lorenzo, and Kierszenbaum, Quique. 2024. "Israeli settlers call for UN agency's closure in Jerusalem protest." The Guardian, Mar. 27.

20 "US intelligence casts doubt on Israeli claims of UNRWA-Hamas links, report says." The Guardian, Feb. 22.

21 Ibid. See also "UN humanitarian office reports at least 800 Israeli settler attacks since Oct. 7." Anadolu Agency, May 2, 2024.

22 Wilson, Jason. 2023. "Revealed: how US residents are funding illegal settlements in the West Bank." The Guardian, Dec. 23. See also "Israeli politician calls for captured Palestinian civilians to be 'buried alive.'" Middle East Eye, Dec. 8, 2023.

23 Data from U.S. State Department and UNRWA.

24 Margesson, Rhoda, and Zanotti, Jim. 2024. "The United Nations Relief and Works Agency for Palestine Refugees in the Near East (UNRWA): Overview and the U.S. Funding Pause." Updated. CRS, Feb. 9.

25 Shannon, Vaughn P. 2003. *Balancing Act: US Foreign Policy and the Arab-Israeli Conflict*. Aldershot: Ashgate Publishing. See esp. Chapter 4.

26 On Israel's nuclear program and US foreign policy, see Hersh, Seymour M. 1991. *The Samson Option: Israel's Nuclear Arsenal and American Foreign Policy*. New York: Random House. See also Cohen, Avner. 2005. *Israel and the Bomb*. New York: Columbia University Press;

27 This section on the energy crisis, OPEC and the U.S. draws from Steinbock 2024, *op. cit.*

28 Steinbock, Dan. 2018. "Rise of Petroyuan." Georgetown Journal of International Affairs, Jan. 18.

29 Veigel, Klaus Friedrich. 2009. *Dictatorship, Democracy, and Globalization: Argentina and the Cost of Paralysis, 1973–2001*. Princeton, NJ: Princeton University Press.

30 Tyler, Patrick. 2009. *A World of Trouble: The White House and the Middle East – from the Cold War to the War on Terror.* New York: Farrar, Straus and Giroux, pp. 90–91.

31 Hersh 1991, *op. cit.*, pp. 217–26.

32 How destructive are today's nuclear weapons? The International Campaign to Abolish Nuclear Weapons (ICAN). See https://www.icanw.org/how_destructive_are_today_s_nuclear_weapons

33 For more on Israel's nuclear option, see next chapter.

34 Farr, Warner D. "The Third Temple's Holy of Holies: Israel's Nuclear Weapons." Counterproliferation Paper No. 2, USAF Counterproliferation Center, Air War College, September 1999.

35 "William Rogers (U.S. Secretary of State) to Embassies in Tunis and Nouakchott, August 6, 1973" Declassified/Released US Department of State EO Systematic Review, Jun. 30, 2005.

36 "Foreign Relations of the United States, 1969–1976, Volume XXIII, Arab-Israeli Dispute, 1969–1972 – Office of the Historian."

37 Palestinian Personalities Archived 1999–01-28 at the Wayback Machine Palestinian Academic Society for the Study of International Affairs (PASSIA).

38 "Gerald R. Ford: The President's News Conference," Nov. 26, 1975. See https://www.presidency.ucsb.edu/documents/the-presidents-news-conference-58

39 Jensehaugen, Jørgen. 2018. *Arab–Israeli Diplomacy under Carter: The US, Israel and the Palestinians*. London: I.B. Tauris, p. 178.

40 Brzezinski, Zbigniew. 1983. *Power and Principle: Memoirs of the National Security Adviser, 1977–1981*. New York: Farrar, Straus, Giroux, p. 444; Yergin, Daniel. 1991. *The Prize: The Epic Quest for Oil, Money, and Power*. New York: Simon & Schuster, pp. 140, 702.

41 "Republican Party Platforms: Republican Party Platform of 1980." July 15, 1980. See https://www.presidency.ucsb.edu/documents/republican-party-platform-1980

42 "George Bush: Interview with Middle Eastern Journalists." Mar. 8, 1991. See https://www.presidency.ucsb.edu/documents/interview-with-middle-eastern-journalists

43 "'I have no regrets': Law student confesses to killing Rabin." CNN World News, Nov. 5, 1995.

44 Barnea, A. 2017. "The Assassination of a Prime Minister: The Intelligence Failure that Failed to Prevent the Murder of Yitzhak Rabin." International Journal of Intelligence, Security, and Public Affairs 19, no. 1, pp. 23–43.

45 Parenti, C. 2001. "America's Jihad: A History of Origins." Social Justice 28, no. 3 (85), *Law, Order, and Neoliberalism*, pp. 31–38.

46 Miller, Aaron David. 2008. *The Much Too Promised Land: America's Elusive Search for Arab-Israeli Peace*. New York: Bantam, p. 273.

47 Ibid.

48 Hart, Alan. 1989. *Arafat: A Political Biography*. Bloomington, IN: Indiana University Press, pp. 27, 320, 429–430.

49 Bannoura, Saed. 2009. "Israeli Mossad poisoned Arafat through his medications, says Bassam Abu Sharif." Al Jazeera, Jul. 20; "Cause of Arafat death 'unknown.'" BBC News, Sep. 8, 2005.

50 Froidevaux, P., et al. 2013. "Improving forensic investigation for polonium poisoning." Lancet 382 (9900), p. 1308.

51 Filiu, Jean-Pierre. 2014. *Gaza: A History*. Oxford University Press. See esp. Chapter 3.

52 "George W. Bush: Remarks on the Middle East." June 24, 2002. See https://www.presidency.ucsb.edu/documents/remarks-the-middle-east

53 Steele, Jonathan. 2008. "Israel asked US for green light to bomb nuclear sites in Iran." The Guardian, Sep. 25.

54 Carter, Jimmy. 2006. *Palestine: Peace Not Apartheid.* New York: Simon & Schuster.

55 Mearsheimer, John, and Walt, Stephen. 2007. *The Israel Lobby and U.S. Foreign Policy.* New York: FSG.

56 Settlement data from Peace Now. See https://peacenow.org.il/

57 Rosenbaum, Greg. 2015. "Obama Has a Stronger Record on Israel Than You Might Have Been Led to Think." Haaretz, Jun. 23,

58 Kessler, Glenn. 2010. "Netanyahu: 'America is a thing you can move very easily.'" Washington Post, Jul. 16.

59 Horovitz, David. 2014. "US Congress passes Israel strategic partnership bill." Times of Israel. Dec. 4.

60 Levinson, Charles, and Entous, Adam. 2012. "Israel's Iron Dome Defense Battled to Get Off the Ground." Wall Street Journal, Nov. 26.

61 Rubin, Uzi. 2007. "The Rocket Campaign against Israel during the 2006 Lebanon War." The Begin-Sadat Center for Strategic Studies, Jun. See also "Summary of rocket fire and mortar shelling in 2008." Intelligence and Terrorism Information Center, Jan. 1, 2009.

62 "New Israeli anti-missile system sees success in Gaza, altering war against rockets." The Washington Post/AP, April 10, 2011. See also "Devotion, Zionism and some parts from Toys R Us." Hayadan (in Hebrew), IL: Technion – Israel Institute of Technology, Jul. 9, 2014.

63 Entous, Adam, and Bohan, Caren. 2010. "Obama seeks $205 million for Israel rocket shield." Reuters, May 13. And: Opall-Rome, Barbara. 2012. "U.S. Attaches Strings to Israeli Iron Dome Funds." Defense News, Apr. 30. And: "Israel-Gaza: How much money does Israel get from the US?" BBC News, May 24, 2021. And: Magid, Jacob, and TOI staff. 2022. "US House approves $1 billion for Israel's Iron Dome after months-long delay." Times of Israel, Mar. 10.

64 "New Israeli anti-missile system sees success in Gaza, altering war against rockets." Washington Post, Jul. 12, 2014.

65 Solomon, Daniel J. 2016. "Meet David Friedman, Bankruptcy Lawyer Turned Possible Israel Ambassador." Forward, Dec. 16; Maltz, Judy. 2017. "Inside the Religious West Bank Settlement That Forged President Trump's Israel Policy." Haaretz, Jan. 17.

66 Woodward, Bob. 2020. *Rage.* New York: Simon & Shuster. See Chapter 9.

67 "Hamas one of largest obstacles to Palestinian peace, U.S. tells UNSC." The Jerusalem Post, Oct. 28, 2019.

68 Shear, Michael D., and Demirjian, Karoun. 2023. "Biden Requests $105 Billion Aid Package for Israel, Ukraine and Other Crises." New York Times, Oct. 20.

69 Compare Steinbock, Dan. 2023. "Toward BRICS Currencies in the Post-dollar Era." The World Financial Review, Aug. 23. See also, by the same author: 2018. "The Rise of Petroyuan." Georgetown Journal of International Affairs, Jan. 18; "The Great Dollar Debacle." The World Financial Review, 2018, Oct. 30.

70 Eikenberry, Karl W. 2013. "The Militarization of U.S. Foreign Policy, American Foreign Policy Interests." The Journal of the National Committee on American Foreign Policy 35, no. 1, pp. 1–8.

71 Ibid.

72 Vine, David. 2021. *The United States of War: A Global History of America's Endless Conflicts, from Columbus to the Islamic State.* University of California Press. See Introduction.

73 Salazar Torreon, Barbara, and Plagakis, Sofia. 2023. "Instances of Use of United States Armed Forces Abroad, 1798–2020." CRS, Jun. 7.

74 Pfeffer, Anshel. 2021. *Bibi: The Turbulent Life and Times of Benjamin Netanyahu.* New York: Hurst & Co., p. 240.

75 Eikenberry 2013, *op. cit.*

76 Walter Pincus, "Vast Number of Military Bands May Not Be Music to Gates' Ears." Washington Post, Aug. 24, 2010.

77 "The Foreign Service by the Numbers." American Foreign Service Association. Retrieved on Feb. 9, 2024.

78 See "DoD Personnel, Workforce Reports & Publications." https://www.dmdc. osd.mil. Nov. 3, 2022. See also *The Military Balance 2022* (country comparisons), International Institute for Strategic Studies, Feb. 2022.

79 See "About US," Department of Homeland Security. https://www.dhs.gov/ about-dhs. Retrieved on Feb. 9, 2024.

80 Gelb, Lesley. "GDP Now Matters More Than Force: A U.S. Foreign Policy for the Age of Economic Power." Foreign Affairs 89, no. 6 (Nov–Dec. 2010), p. 39.

81 Sharp, Jeremy M. 2023. U.S. Foreign Aid to Israel. Congressional Research Service. Mar. 1.

82 Vick, Karl, and Klein, Aaron J. 2012. "How a U.S. Radar Station in the Negev Affects a Potential Israel-Iran Clash." Time, May 30.

83 McGirk, Tim, and Klein, Aaron J. 2008. "Israelis Wary of a US Radar Base in the Negev." Time, Oct. 2.

84 Klippenstein, Ken, and Boguslaw, Daniel. 2023. "U.S. Quietly Expands Secret Military Base in Israel." The Intercept, Oct. 27.

85 Compare Zohar, Yaniv. 2017. "Israel and US open first American military base in Israel." AP, Sep. 1.

86 Motamedi, Maziar. 2024. "'True Promise': Why and how did Iran launch a historic attack on Israel?" Al Jazeera, Apr. 14. See also Trofimov, Yaroslav. 2024. "Analysis: Israel Repelled Iran's Huge Attack. But Only With Help From U.S. and Arab Partners." Wall Street Journal, Apr. 14.

87 Quoted by the Israeli daily Yedioth Ahronoth. See also "Countering Iran's overnight attack costs Israel $1.35B: Israeli media." Anadolu Agency & AFP, Apr. 14, 2024.

88 Quoted in Peled, Anat. 2024. "Israel's Cost to Intercept Iranian Drones and Missiles Is Put at Over $550 Million." Wall Street Journal, Apr. 15.

89 Raddatz, Martha. 2024. "Minor damage reported at 2 Israeli air bases." ABC News, Apr. 15.

90 "US Promises Israel 'Ironclad Support' Following Hamas Attack." VOA, Oct. 7, 2023.

Chapter 4

1 Levy, Gideon. 2010. *The Punishment of Gaza*. New York: Verso. See Introduction.

2 Steinbock, Dan. 2014. The Challenges for America's Defense Innovation. Information Technology & Innovation Foundation (ITIF), Nov. 21.

3 Steinbock, Dan. 2015. "American Innovation Under Structural Erosion and Global Pressures." Information Technology & Innovation Foundation (ITIF), Feb. 9.

4 Ben Gurion, David. 1953. "The Military and the State" Maarachot, nos. 279–80 (1981), pp. 2–11. [Hebrew]

5 Rabinovich, Itamar, and Brun, Itai. 2017. *Israel Facing a New Middle East: In Search of a National Security Strategy*. Stanford, CA: Hoover. See esp. Chapter 1.

6 Ben Gurion, *op. cit.*

7 Jabotinsky, Ze'ev. 1923. "The Iron Wall." Razsviet, Nov. 11. Reprinted by the Jabotinsky Institute in Israel.

8 Kimmerling, Baruch. 2001. *The Invention and Decline of Israeliness: State, Society, and the Military*. Berkeley, CA: University of California Press. See Introduction. Though a sociologist rather than historian, Kimmerling is often seen as one of the "new historians" in Israel.

9 Senor, Dan, and Singer, Saul. 2010. *Start-up Nation: The Story of Israel's Economic Miracle*. Council on Foreign Relations. See also Glassman, James K. 2009. "Where Tech Keeps Booming in Israel, a clustering of talent, research universities and venture capital." Wall Street Journal, Nov. 23.

10 Ibid.

11 Secretary of State Al Haig, Statement for the Record submitted in response to Question from Hon. Clarence Long, House Appropriations Subcommittee on Foreign Operations Appropriations, Apr. 28, 1981.

12 Sharp, Jeremy M., et al. 2020. "Israel's Qualitative Military Edge and Possible U.S. Arms Sales to the United Arab Emirates." CRS, Oct. 26, pp. 10–11.

13 Ibid. Israel would eventually cancel its planned purchase of the V-22 due to budgetary constraints.

14 The legal formalization was based on the passage of H.R. 7177, commonly known as "The Naval Vessel Transfer Act of 2008." See "Israel's Qualitative Military Edge: Legislative Background." FDD. See https://web.archive.org/web/20180222065632/http://militaryedge.org/israels-qualitative-military-edge-legislative-background/

15 Metz, Helen Chapin (ed.). 1990. *Israel: A Country Study*. Washington, D.C.: Federal Research Division, Library of Congress, pp. 314–19.

16 Data from Tian, Nan, et al. 2024. Trends in World Military Expenditure, 2023. SIPRI, Apr.

17 On the Ukrainian trajectory, see Steinbock, Dan. 2022. "The Unwarranted War." The World Financial Review, Mar. 9.

18 Compare Steinbock, Dan. 2022. The Center of International Insecurity: Biden Administration, CNAS and WestExec: Revolving Doors, Collusion and Big Defense. The World Financial Review, Jul.–Aug.

19 Quigley, John B. 1990. *Palestine and Israel: A Challenge to Justice*. Duke University Press, p. 149.

20 Polakow-Suransky, Sasha. 2010. *The Unspoken Alliance: Israel's Secret Relationship with Apartheid South Africa.* Jacana Media.

21 Crosbie, E. 1974. *The Tacit Alliance.* Princeton, NJ: Princeton University Press, p. 18.

22 Cohen, A. A. 2012. *Galula: The Life and Writings of the French Officer Who Defined the Art of Counterinsurgency.* Praeger. See also Wall, Irwin M. 2001. *France, the United States, and the Algerian War.* University of California Press. pp. 68–69.

23 Metz 1990, p. 318.

24 See Eshed 1997, *op. cit.,* esp. Chapter 22. See also Beit-Hallahmi, Benjamin. 1988. *The Israeli Connection: Whom Israel Arms and Why.* London: I.B. Tauris, pp. 8–15.

25 Guzansky, Yoel. 2021. "Diplomacy of the Periphery of Israel: Then and Now." Middle East Policy 28 (3–4), pp. 88–100.

26 On Israel's military operations in the Third World, see Beit-Hallahmi 1988, Chapter 1. See also Behr, E. A. 1977. "CIA Reportedly Gave Israel Millions While It Was Paying Jordan's Hussein." Wall Street Journal, Feb. 22.

27 Metz 1990, *op. cit.,* p. 319. See also Karny, Y. "Embracing Apartheid in Public." Davar, Aug. 31 [Hebrew]. See also Marcus, Y. 1982. "Sharon's End." Haaretz, Oct. 1, 1982 [Hebrew].

28 Mack, Eitay. 2024. "Israel's Cold War in Angola." May 9.

29 Peled, M. 1985. "Israel and the Arms Market." Haaretz, Aug. 4 [Hebrew].

30 Beit-Hallahmi 1988, p. 102.

31 Data from Wezeman, Pieter D., et al. 2024. Trends in International Arms Transfers, 2023. SIPRI, Mar.

32 Ibid. These developments have been supported by the privatization of security in Israel, particularly in the past two to three decades. Compare Hever, Shir. 2018. *The Privatization of Israeli Security.* London: Pluto.

33 Fabian, Emanuel. 2023. "Israeli arms sales doubled in a decade, hit new record of $12.5 billion in 2022." Haaretz, Jun. 14.

34 Data from Liang, Xiao, et al. 2023. The SIPRI Top 100 Arms-producing and Military Services Companies, 2022. SIPRI, Dec.

35 Ibid.

36 "Arms exports to Israel must stop immediately: UN experts." OHCHR, press release, Feb. 23, 2024.

37 Kumar, Ashok. 2024. "Indian Port Workers Refuse to Load Weapons for Israel's War." Middle East Monitor, Feb. 20.

38 Bergman, Ronen. 2018. *Rise And Kill First: The Secret History of Israel's Targeted Assassinations.* New York: Random House, pp. 86–94.

39 Elmas, Dean Shmuel. 2024. "Morocco becomes huge customer for Israel's defense industry." Globes, Jul. 10.

40 Bergman, Ronen. 2018. *Rise And Kill First: The Secret History of Israel's Targeted Assassinations.* New York: Random House, pp. 86–94.

41 On America's "Indian explosives," see Yaron, Oded. 2024. "'Indian Explosives': In Gaza, IDF Used 70-year-old Munitions and Shells Intended for Training." Haaretz, Mar. 24. See also MacDonald, Alistair, and Gale, Alastair. 2024. "As Ukraine Plows Through Artillery Shells, One Plan to Send More Fizzles." Wall Street Journal, Jan. 29.

42 Dowling, Paddy. 2023. "Dirty secret of Israel's weapons exports: They're tested on Palestinians." Al Jazeera, Nov. 17.

43 Data from Drone Wars UK; and Defence for Children International.

44 Database of Israeli Military and Security Export (DIMSE).

45 Al Mezan Center for Human Rights (Gaza).

46 "Israel signs agreement to sell David's Sling air defense system to Finland." Times of Israel, Nov. 12.

47 Quoted in Dowling, *op. cit.*

48 Xtend-Support-Israel.com. Retrieved on Aug. 22, 2024. See also Lacy, Akela, and Biddle, Sam. 2024. "The Crowdfunding Campaign for Deadly Israeli Military Drones." The Intercept, Aug. 1.

49 Data from Liang, Xiao, et al. 2023. The SIPRI Top 100 Arms-producing and Military Services Companies, 2022. SIPRI, Dec.

50 Tabansky, Lior. 2022. "How Israel Became a Top Cyber Power." The National Interest, Mar. 21.

51 Stancati, Margherita, and Said, Summer. 2018. "Saudi Arabia Says Evidence Points to Premeditated Killing of Khashoggi." Wall Street Journal, Oct. 25.

52 See Bergman, Ronen, and Mazzetti, Mark. 2022. "The Battle for the World's Most Powerful Cyberweapon." New York Times, Jan. 28. See also "NSO Played Key Role in Israel's Gulf Diplomacy, NYT Finds, Confirming Haaretz Reports." Haaretz, Jan. 28, 2022.

53 Mack, Eitay. 2023. "The Unsavory Marriage Between Israeli Cyberweapons, U.S. Interests and Dictatorships." Haaretz, Aug. 3.

54 Sariel, Yossi. 2021. The Human Machine Team. eBookPro. See Chapter 3 on "Deep Defense."

55 Abraham, Yuval. 2024. "'Lavender': The AI machine directing Israel's bombing spree in Gaza." +972 Magazine in partnership with Local Call, Apr. 3. See also Kruppa, Miles, and Perry, Alex. 2024. "Silicon Valley's Hot Talent Pipeline Is an Israeli Army Unit." Wall Street Journal, Aug. 31.

56 Nolan, Laura. 2021. "No Dehumanising Tech." Stop Killer Robot, May 26.

57 See e.g., "Google fires employee after pro-Palestine protest at Israeli tech conference in NYC." Middle East Eye, Mar. 8, 2024. See also Captain, Sean. 2021. "Meet the ex-Googler who's exposing the tech-military industrial complex." Fast Company, Oct. 8.

58 "See Social Production of moral invisibility" in Chapter 1 of Bauman, Zygmunt. 1989. *Modernity and the Holocaust.* London: Polity.

59 Scharf, Avi. 2024. "At Singapore Airshow, the Gaza War Was a Selling Point for Israeli Arms Makers." Haaretz, Apr. 5. For a comprehensive statement, see Loewenstein, Antony. 2023. *The Palestine Laboratory: How Israel Exports the Technology of Occupation around the World.* New York: Verso.

60 Mbembe, Achille. 2003. "Sign In." Public Culture 15, no. 1, pp. 11–40.

61 Mbembe, Achille. 2019. *Necropolitics.* Durham: Duke University Press.

62 "UN appalled by Beirut devastation." BBC News, July 26. See also Israel/Lebanon: Deliberate destruction or "collateral damage"? Israeli attacks on civilian infrastructure. Amnesty International, Aug. 22, 2006.

63 Compare Eisenkot, Gadi. 2010. "A Changed Threat? The Response on the Northern Arena." Military and Strategic Affairs 2, no. 1 (Jun.), pp. 29–40.

64 "Israel general quits over Lebanon." BBC News, Sep. 13, 2006.

65 "Israel warns Hezbollah war would invite destruction." Reuters, Oct. 3, 2008.

66 Ibid.

67 London, Yaron. 2008. "The Dahiya Strategy" [interview with IDF Northern Command Chief Gadi Eisenkot]. Oct. 6.

68 Ibid.

69 This argument is a variation of one by Israeli legal scholars on *de facto* and *de jure* annexation of the Palestinian occupied territories. See Levine-Schnur, Ronit, and Megiddo, Tamar, and Berda, Yael. 2023. "A Theory of Annexation." SSRN, Feb. 5.

70 Falk, Richard. 2011. "Israel's Violence Against Separation Wall Protests: Along the Road of State Terrorism." Jan. 7. See https://richardfalk.org/2011/01/07/israel%E2%80%99s-israeli-violence-against-separation-wall-protests-along-the-road-of-state-terrorism/ Retrieved on Apr. 15, 2024.

71 Report of the UN Fact-Finding Mission on the Gaza Conflict. UN Office of the High Commissioner for Human Rights. Sep. 25, 2009.

72 "IDF says it mistakenly killed 3 Israeli hostages during fighting." NBC News, Dec. 15, 2023.

73 Leibovich-Dar, Sara. 2003. "The Hannibal Procedure." Haaretz, May 21.

74 Kershner, Isabel. 2016. "Israeli Military Revokes Use of Maximum Force to Foil Captures." New York Times, Jun. 28.

75 Limone, Noa. 2023. "If Israel Used a Controversial Procedure Against Its Citizens, We Need to Talk About It Now." Haaretz, Dec. 13; Haaretz Editorial. 2023. "The IDF Must Investigate the Kibbutz Be'eri Tank Fire Incident – Right Now." Haaretz, Jan. 8.

76 Glazer, Hilo. 2024. "Who Is Barak Hiram, the IDF General Who Ordered Tank Fire on a Kibbutz Home With 13 Hostages Inside?" Haaretz, May 31.

77 Breiner, Josh. 2024. "Fighting in Gaza, IDF Tank Officer Who Shelled Kibbutz House on Oct. 7 Says 'I Had No Choice.'" Haaretz, Jul. 16.

78 On the IDF investigation, see Kubovich, Yaniv. 2024. "Israeli Army Says It 'Failed to Protect' Kibbutz Be'eri Residents in Oct. 7 Hamas Attack." Haaretz, Jul. 11.

79 "Israeli colonel says Hannibal Directive was possibly deployed on 7 October." Middle East Eye, Nov. 21. The original source, Haaretz weekly podcast of Nov. 9, 2023, seems to be blocked. Retrieved on May 15, 2024.

80 Kubovich, Yaniv. 2024. "IDF Ordered Hannibal Directive on October 7 to Prevent Hamas Taking Soldiers Captive." Haaretz, Jul. 7.

81 Klein, Zvika. 2023. "This is why Israel plans to bury hundreds of cars, with ashes and blood stains." The Jerusalem Post, Nov. 22.

82 Blumenthal, Max. 2023. "October 7 testimonies reveal Israel's military 'shelling' Israeli citizens with tanks, missiles." The Grayzone, Oct. 27.

83 "Israel Police slams 'Haaretz' claim IDF helicopter may have harmed civilians on Oct. 7." Times of Israel, Nov. 19, 2023.

84 "'Emphasis is on damage, not accuracy': ground offensive into Gaza seems imminent." The Guardian, Oct. 10, 2023.

85 "Exclusive: Nearly half of the Israeli munitions dropped on Gaza are imprecise 'dumb bombs,' US intelligence assessment finds." CNN, Dec. 14, 2023.

86 Abraham, Yuval. 2023. "'A mass assassination factory': Inside Israel's calculated bombing of Gaza." +972 Magazine, Nov. 30.

87 Konor-Attias, Etty, and Maman, Shani Bar-On. 2023. "Numbers that Reveal Abandonment: Government Allocations to Local Governments in the 'Gaza Envelope.'" AdvaCenter, Oct. 26.

88 Levi, Yonatan, et al. Sep. 2014. *The Secret Budget of the Settler Right.* Tel Aviv: Molad, p. 3.

89 Makovsky, David. 2004. "How to Build a Fence." Foreign Affairs, Mar./Apr. See also "Israel completes 'iron wall' underground Gaza barrier." Al Jazeera, Dec. 7, 2021.

90 TOI and AFP. 2023. "Years of subterfuge, high-tech barrier paralyzed: How Hamas busted Israel's defenses." Times of Israel, Oct. 11. See also Silkoff, Shira. 2023. "Gaza fence was not designed to prevent mass assault on its own, builder said in 2018." Times of Israel, Oct. 19.

91 "'Government is destroying the North.'" The Jerusalem Post, May 16, 2024.

92 "120,000 rally in Tel Aviv to demand hostage deal, denounce gov't; 14 officers said hurt." Times of Israel, Jun. 2, 2024.

93 Harel, Amos, and Issacharoff, Avi. 2008. *34 Days: Israel, Hezbollah, and the War in Lebanon.* New York: St. Martin's, pp. 242–43.

94 "Ex-general Gal Hirsch indicted for tax evasion totaling $1.9 million." Times of Israel, Oct. 21, 2021.

95 Israel/ OPT: Hamas and other armed groups must immediately release civilians held hostage in Gaza. Amnesty International, Jul. 12, 2024.

96 Fink, Rachel. 2024. "Report: New Evidence Reveals IDF Had Detailed Prior Knowledge of Hamas Plan to Raid Israel." Haaretz, Jun. 18.

97 "Egypt warned Israel days before Hamas struck, US committee chairman says." BBC, Oct. 12, 2023.

98 Bergman, R., and Goldman, A. 2023. "Israel Knew Hamas's Attack Plan More Than a Year Ago." New York Times, Nov. 30.

99 "Surveillance soldiers warned of Hamas activity on Gaza border for months before Oct. 7." Times of Israel, Oct. 26.

100 *Global Gender Gap Report 2023.* World Economic Forum, Aug.

101 Murphy, P. 2023. "Hamas militants trained for its deadly attack in plain sight and less than a mile from Israel's heavily fortified border." CNN, Oct. 12.

102 "October 7 testimonies reveal Israel's military 'shelling' Israeli citizens with tanks, missiles." The Grayzone, Oct. 27, 2023, based on Haaretz reporting.

103 Kubovich, Yaniv. 2024. "Haaretz Investigation: Disdain, Denial, Neglect: The Deep Roots of Israel's Devastating Intelligence Failure on Hamas and October 7." Haaretz, May 9. See also Fink 2024, *op. cit.* See also Kubovich, Yaniv. 2024. "Israeli Army Begins Investigation of Failures Leading Up to October 7." Haaretz, Mar. 7.

104 *Rebuilding America's Defenses: Strategy, Forces and Resources for a New Century.* Project for the New American Century, Sep. 2000. On the neoconservative elite and its ideology, see Mann, James. 2004. *Rise of the Vulcans: The History of Bush's War Cabinet.* London: Penguin.

105 On Netanyahu's long and close links with the U.S. neoconservatives since the 1990s, see Chapter 6.

Chapter 5

1 Oz, Amos. 1967. "The Defense Minister / and Lebensraum." *Davar*, Aug. 22.

2 Salmon, Yosef. 1978. "Ideology and Reality in the Bilu Aliyah." Harvard Ukrainian Studies 2, no. 4, pp. 430–66.

3 Aliyah refers to a Hebrew term "ascent," which has a biblical subtext of ascending toward Jerusalem.

4 Huneidi, Sahar. 2001. *A Broken Trust: Herbert Samuel, Zionism and the Palestinians 1920–1925*. London: I. B. Tauris, p. 127 See also Segev, Tom. 1999. *One Palestine, Complete*. New York: Metropolitan Books. pp. 173–90.

5 Zeira, Joseph. 2021. *The Israeli Economy: A Story of Success and Costs*. Princeton, NJ: Princeton University Press. See esp. Chapter 1.

6 Alroey, Gur. 2014. *An Unpromising Land: Jewish Migration to Palestine in the Early Twentieth Century*. Stanford, CA: Stanford University Press, p. 17.

7 Shaw Commission. 1930. Report of the Commission on the disturbances of August 1929. UK National Archives, pp. 50–57. See also Wiener Cohen, Naomi. 1988. *The Year After the Riots: American Responses to the Palestine Crisis of 1929–30*. Detroit, MI: Wayne State University Press.

8 Khalidi, Rashid I. 2017. "Historical Landmarks in the Hundred Years' War on Palestine." Journal of Palestine Studies 47, no. 1, pp. 6–17.

9 Yazbak, Mahmoud. 2000. "From Poverty to Revolt: Economic Factors in the Outbreak of the 1936 Rebellion in Palestine." *Middle Eastern Studies* 36, no. 3, pp. 93–113. Of course, the conventional narrative of smooth and frictionless industrialization and urbanization in the West effectively discounts the violence that occurred with actual industrial takeoffs in cities. See Steinbock, Dan. 2024. *The End of Modern Economic Growth*. Unpublished manuscript.

10 She was hardly alone. Many Mizrahi Jews had to cope with similar treatment. See Wurmser, Meyrav. 2005. "Post-Zionism and the Sephardi Question." Middle East Quarterly XII, no. 2, pp. 21–35.

11 See Shlaim, Avi. 2023. *Three Worlds: Memoirs of an Arab-Jew*. Oneworld.

12 Giladi, Naeim. 1998. "The Jews of Iraq." The Link 31, no. 2, pp. 1–13. See also Giladi, Naeim. 1992. *Ben-Gurion's Scandals: How the Haganah and the Mossad Eliminated Jews*, 2nd Ed. Tempe, Arizona: Dandelion Books. For a conventional Israeli view, see Gat, Moshe. 2013. *The Jewish exodus from Iraq: 1948–1951*. London: Frank Cass.

13 Eveland, Wilbur Crane. 1980. *Ropes of Sand: America's Failure in the Middle East*. New York: W. W. Norton.

14 Herzl, Theodor. 1896. *The Jewish State: An Attempt at a Modern Solution of the Jewish Question*. New York: American Zionist Emergency Council, 1946, p. 69.

15 Elon, Amos. 1975. *Herzl*, New York: Holt, Rinehart and Winston.

16 See e.g., "Conversation with Ilan Pappé: We Don't Have the Luxury to Wait Any Longer." The Palestine Chronicle, Dec. 22, 2013.

17 Herzl 1896, *op. cit.*, p. 96.

18 Bein, Alex. "Biography." In: Herzl, Theodor. 1896. *The Jewish State.* New York: Courier Dover, p. 40.

19 Lenni Brenner, Lenni. 1984. *The Iron Wall: Zionist Revisionism from Jabotinsky to Shamir,* Zed Books, pp. 74–75.

20 Compare Avineri, Shlomo. 1985. *Moses Hess, Prophet of Communism and Zionism.* New York: New York University Press.

21 Epstein, Lawrence J. 2016. *The Dream of Zion: The Story of the First Zionist Congress.* Lanham, MD: Rowman & Littlefield.

22 Quoted in Zeev Sternhell, 1998. The *Founding Myths of Israel: Nationalism, Socialism, and the Making of the Jewish State.* Princeton, NJ: Princeton Univ. Press, 1998, p. 21. See also his "Georges Sorel and the Antimaterialist Revision of Marxism." In: Sternhell, Zeev, et al. 1995. *The Birth of Fascist Ideology: From Cultural Rebellion to Political Revolution.* Princeton, NJ: Princeton University Press,

23 Ben Simhon, Dani. 2004. "The Unmaking of the Histadrut." Challenge Magazine, Issue 88, Nov./Dec.

24 Ibid. See particularly Chapter 5.

25 Ben-Gurion, David. 1932. *From Class to Nation.* Tel Aviv: Ayanoth [Hebrew], 1955, p. 33.

26 Medoff, Rafael. 2002. *Militant Zionism in America: The Rise and Impact of the Jabotinsky Movement in the United States, 1926–1948.* Tuscaloosa, Alabama: University of Alabama Press, p. 3.

27 Kremnitzer, Mordechai, and Fuchs, Amir. 2013. *Ze'ev Jabotinsky on Democracy, Equality, and Individual Rights.* Jerusalem: Israel Democracy Institute, p. 12.

28 Schechtman, Joseph. 1956. *Rebel and Statesman: The Vladimir Jabotinsky Story.* New York: Thomas Yoseloff, pp. 49, 60.

29 Kaplan, Eran. 2005. *The Jewish Radical Right: Revisionist Zionism and Its Ideological Legacy.* Madison, WI: University of Wisconsin Press, pp. 149–56; Heller, Daniel Kupfert. 2017. *Jabotinsky's Children: Polish Jews and the Rise of Right-Wing Zionism.* Princeton, NJ: Princeton University Press. pp. 67–238.

30 Larsen, Stein Ugelvik (ed.). *Fascism Outside of Europe.* New York: Columbia University Press, 2001, p. 377.

31 Black, Edwin. 1984. *The Transfer Agreement: The Dramatic Story of the Pact Between the Third Reich and Jewish Palestine.* New York: Macmillan, pp. 131–44, 379.

32 Brenner, Lenni. 1983. "Zionism-Revisionism: The Years of Fascism and Terror." *Journal of Palestine Studies* 13, no. 1, pp. 66–92.

33 Shindler, Colin. 2006. *The Triumph of Military Zionism: Nationalism and the Origins of the Israeli Right.* London: I.B. Tauris, p. 174.

34 Oren, Michael. 2008. *Power, Faith and Fantasy: America in the Middle East, 1776 to the Present.* New York: Norton, pp. 442–45.

35 Gelvin, James L. 2014. *The Israel-Palestine Conflict: One Hundred Years of War.* Cambridge: Cambridge University Press, p. 122.

36 For an analysis of "checkbook Zionism," see the pioneering account by Fleisch, Eric. 2024. *Checkbook Zionism: Philanthropy and Power in the Israel-Diaspora Relationship.* Newark, NJ: Rutgers University Press.

37 See Part I.

38 Rovner, Adam. 2014. *In the Shadow of Zion: Promised Lands Before Israel.* New York: NYU Press, p. 45.

39 "Israel's Basic Laws: The Law of Return." Jewish Virtual Library, Jun. 5, 1950.

40 Aderet, Ofer. 2023. "The Hamas Pogrom Demonstrates That Zionism Has Failed, Says Israeli Historian Moshe Zimmermann." Haaretz, Dec. 29.

41 Goldmann, Nahum. 1982. "Where Is Israel Going?" New York Review of Books, Oct. 7.

42 Compare Asscher, Omri. 2021. "Exporting political theology to the diaspora: translating Rabbi Abraham Isaac Kook for Modern Orthodox consumption." Meta 65, no. 2, pp. 292–311. On rabbi Kook's apocalyptic visions, see Chapter 2.

43 See Shavit, Ari. 2007. "Burg: Defining Israel as a Jewish state is the key to its end." Haaretz, Jun. 7. On post-Zionism and French civic nationalism, see Burg, Avraham. 2011. "We have to decide if we are a nation of 'blood' or 'culture.'" Yediot Aharonoth, Apr. 22 [in Hebrew].

44 For the classic statement on civic nationalism, see Kohn, Hans. 1944. *The Idea of Nationalism: A Study in Its Origins and Background.* New York: Macmillan. Along with philosopher Martin Buber, Kohn in 1925 founded Brit Shalom (lit. "Covenant of Peace") that sought peaceful coexistence between Arabs and Jews in Israel.

45 "Burg: Israeli fascism result of Shoah trauma." Ynetnews, Jun. 11, 2007. See also Shavit, Ari. June 2007. "Burg: Defining Israel as a Jewish state is the key to its end." Haaretz, Jun. 7.

46 Compare Ram, Uri. 2010. *Israeli Nationalism: Social Conflicts and the Politics of Knowledge.* London: Routledge, p. 112.

47 Shefler, Gil. 2010. "John Hagee to cut Im Tirtzu funding." The Jerusalem Post, Aug. 23. See also Blau, Uri. 2017. "Firebrand Anti-leftist Group, Which Slams Foreign Funding of Israeli NGOs, Received Over $1M From U.S. Donors." Haaretz, Jun. 23; and Blau, Uri. 2017. "U.S. Ambassador's Adviser Ran 'Dark Money' Nonprofit That Donated $1M to Right-Wing Israeli Group." Haaretz, Oct. 6.

48 Hasson, Nir. 2012. "Jerusalem Court Starts Debating Meaning of Fascism as Im Tirtzu Sues Activists." Haaretz, Feb. 12.

49 The full name of the Basic Law proposal was "Israel as the Nation-State of the Jewish People." On the charges against Dichter, see "Matar et al v Dichter." Center for Constitutional Rights. Ccrjustice.org. Retrieved on Apr. 10, 2024.

50 These are the Basic Laws of *Freedom of Occupation* and *Human Dignity and Liberty.*

51 Hauser Tov, Michael. 2023. "'We're Rolling Out Nakba 2023,' Israeli Minister Says on Northern Gaza Strip Evacuation." Haaretz, Nov. 12.

52 "Gutted Jewish nation-state bill heads to first reading in Knesset." The Jerusalem Post, Mar. 14.

53 "Majority of Israeli Jews Support Nation-state Law, Polls Determine." The Jerusalem Post, Jul. 31, 2018. See also Dakwar, Haia. 2018. "Israel's Arab minority rallies against new nation-state law." Reuters, Aug, 12.

54 "Smotrich says he wants to be justice minister so Israel can follow Torah law." Times of Israel, Jun. 3, 2019.

55 Roberts, Sam. 2020. "Meron Benvenisti Dies at 86; Urged One State for Jews and Palestinians." New York Times, Sep. 29.

56 On Herrenvolk democracy, see van den Berghe, Pierre L. 1967. *Race and Racism: A Comparative Perspective.* New York: Wiley.

57 See Sharon, Jeremy. 2023. "Levin unveils bills to remove nearly all High Court's tools for government oversight." Times of Israel, Jan. 11. See also Kingsley, Patrick, and Kershner, Isabel. 2023. "Israeli Parliament Passes Law to Limit Judicial Power." New York Times, Jul. 24.

58 Sharon, Jeremy. 2023. "Justice minister unveils plan to shackle the High Court, overhaul Israel's judiciary." Times of Israel, Jan. 4.

59 "Israel's Supreme Court & the Power of Judicial Review." Jewish Virtual Library. Retrieved on Mar. 16, 2023.

60 Gross, Aeyal. 1998. "The Politics of Rights in Israeli Constitutional Law." Israel Studies 3, no. 2, pp. 80–118.

61 On the term itself, see Kedar, Nir. 2002. "Ben-Gurion's Mamlakhtiyut: Etymological and Theoretical Roots." Israel Studies 7, no. 3, pp. 117–32. On the conflation of the term, see Elazar, Yiftah, and Milikowsky, Natan. 2020. "Ethnicizing the Republic: The Strange Career of the Concept of Republican Citizenship in Israel." Citizenship Studies, Jan. 31.

62 Beard, Charles. 1913. *An Economic Interpretation of the Constitution of the United States.* New York: Macmillan.

63 Barak, Aharon. 1993. "A Constitutional Revolution: Israel's Basic Laws." Constitutional Forum, Yale Law School Legal Scholarship Repository. See also Raice, Shayndi. 2023. "The Judge at the Heart of Israel's Constitutional Crisis." Wall Street Journal, Jul. 30.

64 See "About Us." The Institute for Zionist Strategies. https://www.izs.org.il/board-of-directors/. Retrieved on Mar. 16, 2024.

65 Following the subsequent international controversy, the think tank overhauled its website adopting a new name: the Misgav Institute for National Security & Zionist Strategy. It was led by Meir Ben-Shabbat, who in the late 2010s had served as Netanyahu's national security adviser and played a role in the US brokered Abraham Accords.

66 "Israeli member of Knesset calls for resettling Gaza's refugees to 'solve problem.'" Middle East Monitor, Nov. 23, 2023.

67 Democracy Report 2024. V-Dem: Varieties of Democracy.

68 "Thousands in New York City protest Israel's judicial overhaul as Netanyahu addresses UN." The Guardian. Sep. 22, 2023

69 "Defending the rule of law, enforcing apartheid – the double life of Israel's judiciary." Amnesty International. Sep. 13, 2023.

70 HCJ 5658/23 Movement for Quality Government in Israel v. Knesset. 2024.

71 "Israel's Supreme Court overturns a key component of Netanyahu's polarizing judicial overhaul." AP, Jan. 1, 2024.

72 Bergman, Ronen, and Mazzetti, Mark. 2024. "How Extremist Settlers Took Over Israel." New York Times, May 16.

73 On the emergence of the dual state in Israel, see Chapter 5.

74 Fraenkel, Ernst. 1941. *The Dual State: A Contribution to the Theory of Dictatorship*. Oxford: Oxford University Press.

75 Morris, Douglas G. 2020. *Legal Sabotage: Ernst Fraenkel in Hitler's Germany*. Cambridge: Cambridge University Press.

76 Fraenkel 1941, *op. cit.*, xxiii.

77 Aderet, Ofer. 2023. "The Hamas Pogrom Demonstrates That Zionism Has Failed, Says Israeli Historian Moshe Zimmermann." Haaretz, Dec. 29.

Chapter 6

1 Weiss, Philip. 2008. "Wake Up! (Leftwing Israeli Injured by Pipe-Bomb Warns of 'Disintegration of Democracy')." Mondoweiss, Sep. 25.

2 "Settler suspected of multiple hate crimes." Ynetnews, Nov. 1, 2009. See also James, Randy. 2009. "Accused Jewish Terrorist Jack Teitel." Time, Nov. 3, 2009.

3 "Israelis rate Gallant as best-performing minister, and Ben Gvir the worst – poll." Times of Israel, Sep., 2023.

4 Weitz, Gidi. 2014. "Signs of Fascism in Israel Reached New Peak During Gaza Op, Says Renowned Scholar." Haaretz, Aug. 13.

5 On the postwar cleavage theories, see Lipset, Seymour Martin, and Rokkan, Stein. "Cleavage structures, party systems, and voter alignments: an introduction." In: Lipset, and Rokkan (eds.). 1967. *Party Systems and Voter Alignments: Cross-National Perspectives*. New York: The Free Press, pp. 1–64.

6 Gethin, Amory, et al. 2021. *Political Cleavages and Social Inequalities: A Study of Fifty Democracies, 1948–2020*. Cambridge, MA: Harvard University Press. On the Israeli case, see Berman, Yonatan. "Inequality, Identity, and the Long-Run Evolution of Political Cleavages in Israel, 1949–2019." In: Gethin 2021, *op. cit.*, see Chapter 18.

7 See Chapter 5.

8 Zeira, Joseph. 2021. *The Israeli Economy: A Story of Success and Costs*. Princeton, NJ: Princeton University Press, pp. 268–70.

9 Inbar, E. 2009. *The Decline of the Israel Labor Party*. The Begin-Sadat Center for Strategic Studies. Bar-Ilan University, Feb. 23. See also Rapoport, M. 2020. "What happened to Israel's Labor party?" Middle East Eye, Apr. 30. See also Mor, S. 2020. "Doves' Labor Lost: How Israel's Once-Dominant Party Faded into Insignificance." Mosaic, Aug. 2.

10 On rabbi Meir Kahane and violent ethnic cleansing, see Chapter 1. On rabbi Kook's apocalyptic visions, see Chapter 2.

11 Kahane, Libby. 2008. *Rabbi Meir Kahane: His Life and Thought, 1932–1975, Vol. 1*. Israel: Urim Publications, p. 222.

12 Dershowitz, Alan M. 1992. *Chutzpah*. New York: Touchstone, pp. 191–92.

13 Kahane's interview by Mergui, Raphael, and Simonnot, Philippe. 1985. "Israel's Ayatollahs: Meir Kahane and the Far Right in Israel." Chapter 2 in the authors' *Meir Kahane: le rabbin qui fait peur aux juifs*. Atlantic Highlands, NJ: Saqi Books, 1987.

14 Friedman, Robert I. 1987. "Kahane's Money Tree." New York Times, Nov. 8.

15 Ibid.

16 Weiss, Efrat. 2005. "'We prayed for Sharon's death.'" Ynet News, Jul. 26..

17 On the Allon Plan, see Chapter 2.

18 Schneider, Tal. 2021. "Lapid's US pollster sees 10 years of work come to 'dramatic, emotional' fruition." Times of Israel, Jul. 13.

19 "Tens of thousands at weekly anti-government, hostage release rallies." Times of Israel, Apr. 13, 2024.

20 "Weekly rallies marred by police violence; detained protester threatened by cop." Times of Israel, Jun. 30, 2024.

21 See esp. Castro, Americo. 1954. *The Structure of Spanish History.* Princeton, NJ: Princeton University Press. See also María Rosa Menocal. 2003. *Ornament of the World: How Muslims, Jews, and Christians Created a Culture of Tolerance in Medieval Spain.* Back Bay Books. Initially, Convivencia debate was methodological and philosophical. More recently, it has been overshadowed by politicization. See esp. Fernández-Morera, Dario. 2016. *The Myth of the Andalusian Paradise.* ICI Books. The latter reflects the views of the Spanish far-right.

22 Sheizaf, Noam. 2009. "Netanyahu's Father Discusses the Peace Process: Excerpts from the Exclusive Maariv Interview (Part I)." Promised Land Blog, Apr. 3.

23 Netanyahu, Benjamin. 2009. "Truth vs. Darkness in the United Nations." Chabad.org, Sep. 24.

24 Pfeffer, Anshel. 2018. *Bibi: The Turbulent Life and Times of Benjamin Netanyahu.* London: Hurst & Co., p. 149.

25 Compare "Arthur Finkelstein, Innovative, Influential Conservative Strategist, Dies at 72." New York Times, Nov. 12, 2022.

26 Gellman, Barton. 1997. "Netanyahu's Indictment Sought." Washington Post, Apr. 16.

27 Compare "A Guide for the Perplexed: The Many Affairs Involving Benjamin and Sara Netanyahu." Haaretz, Jan. 11, 2017.

28 Heller, Jeffrey. 2018. "Israeli police recommend bribery charges against Netanyahu." Reuters, Feb. 13. See also Marsden, Ariella. 2023. "Netanyahu's corruption trial resumes under shadow of war." The Jerusalem Post, Dec. 3.

29 Gorali, Moshe. 2024. "Submarine-gate commission: Netanyahu 'endangered the security of Israel and harmed its economic interests.'" CTech Calcalist, Jun. 24.

30 Dorf, Matthew. 1997. "Is Irving Moskowitz a Hero or Just a Rogue?" Jewish Telegraphic Agency, Sep. 26.

31 On the grand bargain, see Chapter 10.

32 Vest, Jason. 2002. "The Men from JINSA and CSP." *The Nation,* Aug. 15.

33 Perle, Richard, et al. 1996. "A Clean Break: A New Strategy for Securing the Realm." Institute for Advanced Strategic and Political Studies, Jul. 2006.

34 See e.g., Amit, Hagai. 2019. "With His 50m Shekel Fortune, Netanyahu Is Israel's Fourth Richest Politician." Haaretz, Feb. 25 [based on the Israeli edition of Forbes]. See also Vidal, Elihay, and Zerahia, Zvi. 2020. "With his millions of dollars in assets, Netanyahu's tax exemptions are a drain on the treasury." Calcalist, Jun. 25.

35 "Sheldon Adelson Expands Israeli Media Empire, Buys Makor Rishon and NRG." The Marker, Mar. 30, 2014.

36 "Adelson: Palestinians an invented people out to destroy Israel." Times of Israel, Nov. 10, 2014.

37 McGreal, Chris, et al. 2015. "China feared CIA worked with Sheldon Adelson's Macau casinos to snare officials." The Intercept, Jul. 22.

38 Shalev, Chemi. 2017. "Adelson Has Hijacked the Israeli-American Community for His Hard-right Agenda; New political pressure group will outflank AIPAC and fragment the Jewish establishment." Haaretz, Nov. 7.

39 "Adelsons tell police Sara Netanyahu is 'absolutely crazy' – report." Times of Israel, Sep. 8, 2019.

40 Al-Tamimi et al v. Adelson et al., D.C. Circuit Court of Appeals, 2019, No. 17-5207.

41 "Palestinians' lawsuit in U.S. vs. Adelson, others is revived." Reuters, Feb. 20, 2019.

42 Jaber, Alma. 2019. "Tamimi v. Adelson: Challenging Israeli Exceptionalism in U.S. Courts." Institute for Palestine Studies, Apr. 10.

43 On this double standard and politicization of courts, see Erakat, Noura. 2009. "Litigating the Arab-Israeli Conflict: The Politicization of U.S. Foreign Courtrooms." Berkeley Journal of Middle Eastern & Islamic Law 2, no. 1, pp. 27–60.

44 Weil, Elizabeth. 2024. "Miriam Adelson's Unfinished Business." New York Magazine, May 20.

45 Slyomovics, Nettanel. 2021. "The U.S. Billionaires Secretly Funding the Right-wing Effort to Reshape Israel." Haaretz, Mar. 11.

46 Rubin, Shira. 2023. "Unsurprisingly, Kohelet also promoted the annexation of the occupied territories." Washington Post, Mar. 24.

47 Segal, David, and Kershner, Isabel. 2023. "Who's Behind the Judicial Overhaul Now Dividing Israel? Two New Yorkers." New York Times, Mar. 20.

48 Ibid.

49 Shai Nitzan, Cohen, and Nataf, Shimon, and Bakshi, Aviad. 2022. "Selecting Judges to Constitutional Courts – a Comparative Study." Kohelet Policy Forum, Jan. 9.

50 Elliott, Justin, et al. 2022. "Meet the Billionaire and Rising GOP Mega-Donor Who's Gaming the Tax System." ProPublica, Jun. 21.

51 Debre, Isabel. 2023. "An American billionaire says he'll stop funding the think tank behind Israel's judicial overhaul." AP News, Aug. 4.

52 Quoted in Sadeh, Shuki. 2018. "The Right-wing Think Tank That Quietly 'Runs the Knesset.'" Haaretz, Oct. 5. Though Rubin claims that he doesn't remember saying such a thing.

53 See Chapter 1.

54 "Jerusalem Mayor Nir Barkat Ranked Israel's Richest Politician." Haaretz, Sep. 2, 2013. See also "Global investigation unveils alleged financial misdeeds by Likud MK Nir Barkat." Times of Israel. Oct. 3, 2021. See also Sadeh, Shuki. 2023. "Kohelet Funded Policy Papers Designed to Help Nir Barkat become Prime Minister." Shomrim, Feb. 9.

55 Hermoni, Oded. 2004. "He Helped Gadhafi – He Can Help Us, Too." Haaretz, Oct. 18.

56 Sadeh, Shuki. 2023. "Not Just Kohelet: Exposing the NGOs that Paved the Way

for Radical Right-Wing Legislation." Shomrim, Aug. 31.

57 "Israel's far-right kingmaker joins memorial for racist rabbi." AP, Nov. 11, 2022. "US removes ultranationalist Israeli group from 'terror' list." Al Jazeera, May 20, 2022.

58 "Ex-Mossad chief: Netanyahu allies worse than KKK, overhaul is his 'master plan.'" Times of Israel, Jul. 27, 2023.

59 Hendrix, Steve, and Rubin, Shira. 2022. "Israel election: A far-right politician moves closer to power." Washington Post, Oct. 28.

60 "Biden's strategy for a far-right Israel: Lay it all on Bibi." Politico, Dec. 20, 2022. See also "Wave of international criticism after Ben Gvir visits flashpoint Temple Mount." Times of Israel. Jan. 3, 2023.

61 "No power, water or fuel to Gaza until hostages freed, says Israel minister." The Guardian, Oct. 12, 2023.

62 "Police: Indict Ex-minister Katz for Cronyism." Haaretz, Mar. 23, 2007.

63 "Levin said to call for judges who 'understand' why Jews don't want to live near Arabs." Times of Israel, May 29, 2023.

64 "Israeli settlers rampage after deadly Palestinian attack in West Bank." France 24, Feb. 26, 2023.

65 Sokol, Sam. 2024. "Smotrich threatens to quit gov't over hostage deal; Eisenkot slams far-right 'blackmail.'" Times of Israel, Apr. 30.

66 Breuer, Eliav. 2024. "Gantz to Netanyahu: If you don't change course by June 8 we will withdraw from the government." The Jerusalem Post, May 19.

67 "Gantz in Munich speech: 'No daylight' with Netanyahu on Iran." Times of Israel, Feb. 17, 2019.

68 Pfeffer 2018, op. cit., p. 386.

69 On the Hannibal Directive and particularly its role on October 7 and in its aftermath, see Chapter 4.

70 Surkes, Sue. 2023. "Ex-deputy IDF head Yair Golan wins plaudits for saving partygoers." Times of Israel, Oct. 23.

71 Glazer, Hilo. 2023. "Can Yair Golan Leverage His Hero Image to Build a 'Fresh, Exciting' Israeli Left?" Haaretz, Dec. 7.

72 Heller, Jeffrey. 2016. "Israeli general assailed for Nazi comparison on Holocaust memorial day." Reuters, May 5.

73 Gallup, Oct. 17–Dec. 3, 2023.

74 "Stand United – U.S. Jewry and Israel During the First Month of the War." The Ruderman Program for American Jewish Studies, Haifa University, Dec. 2023.

75 Anderson, Kerry. 2024. "The Bipartisan Consensus in Favor of Israel Is Broken, But When Will It Change U.S. Policy?" War on the Rocks, Apr. 8.

Chapter 7

1 " PM Netanyahu and Finance Minister Smotrich's remarks." Israel's Ministry of Foreign Affairs, Nov. 2, 2023.

2 "'Backward country': Economists warn government over Haredi budget allocations." Times of Israel, May 21, 2023.

3 Razin, A., and Sadka, E. 2023. Economic Consequences of a Regime Change: Overview. NBER Working Paper No. 31723, Sep. On the judicial reforms, see Chapter 5.

4 The following discussion on the stages of growth, development and modernization in major developed and developing economies draws from Steinbock, Dan. 2024. *The End of Modern Economic Growth. Unpublished manuscript,* see esp. Chapter 3.

5 "Economic Shifts in Israel Prompt Protest Strikes." New York Times, Oct. 31, 1977.

6 Compare Blass, Asher A., and Grossman, Richard S. 1996. "A Harmful Guarantee? The 1983 Israel Bank Shares Crisis Revisited." Research Department, Bank of Israel, May.

7 Bruno, Michael, and Minford, Patrick. 1986. "Sharp Disinflation Strategy: Israel 1985." Economic Policy 1, no. 2, pp. 379–407.

8 On the proponents' views, see Fischer, Stanley. 1987. "Stopping High Inflation: The Israeli Stabilization Program, 1985–86." American Economic Review 77, no. 2, pp. 275–78

9 Ben Simhon, Dani. 2004. "The Unmaking of the Histadrut." Challenge Magazine, Nov/Dec.

10 Benchimol, J. 2016. "Money and monetary policy in Israel during the last decade." Journal of Policy Modeling 38, no. 1, pp. 103–124.

11 Compare Chapter 3.

12 "The real estate protest: sleeping bags in the municipality, tents in the square." Ynet News, July 14, 2011.

13 "Protests are spreading: tents in Beersheva and the north." Ynet News, Jul. 7, 2011 [in Hebrew].

14 Efraim, Omri. 2011. "PM announces new housing plan." Ynet News, Jul. 26, 2011.

15 Kraft, Dina. 2011. "Some 450,000 Israelis march at massive 'March of the Million' rallies across country Israel." Haaretz, Sep. 3.

16 Thompson, Derek. 2011. "Occupy the World: The '99 Percent' Movement Goes Global." The Atlantic, Oct. 15.

17 Ben-David, Ricky. 2021. "Israeli housing prices have nearly doubled in a decade, with no signs of slowing." Times of Israel, Oct. 6.

18 Compare Israel: 2023 Article IV Consultation – Press Release; Staff Report; and Statement by the Executive Director for Israel. IMF, Jun. 15.

19 Steinbock, Dan, et al. 2002. Wireless Valley, Silicon Wadi and Digital Island – Helsinki, Tel Aviv and Dublin in the ICT Boom, OECD.

20 Offenhauer, Priscilla. 2008. *Israel's Technology Sector.* Washington, DC: Library of Congress, Nov.

21 For more, see Chapter 4.

22 Konrad, Alex. 2023. "More Than 500 VC Firms Sign Public Statement in Support Of Israel." Forbes, Oct. 12.

23 Data from Israel Innovation Authority; and Start-Up Nation Central (SNC).

24 Levy, Miki. 2024. "Red Alert in the Red Sea: How the War Is Impacting Israeli Trade." Shomrim, Jan. 24.

25 Data from SNC, op. cit.

26 "Microsoft exec says Israel's tech sector could suffer from war with Hamas." Reuters, Nov. 1.

27 See "About Intel Israel." Intel: https://www.intel.com/content/www/us/en/corporate-responsibility/intel-in-israel.html. Retrieved on Aug. 23, 2024.

28 Shulman, Sophie. 2024. "Intel halts construction of new $25 billion factory in Israel." Calcalist, Jun. 10. See also Kabir, Omare. 2023. "With massive investment, Intel reaffirms confidence in Israel." Calcalist, Dec. 27.

29 High-Tech Sector's Contribution to State Revenues from Individuals and Companies. Department of Chief Economist and Israel Innovation Authority, Aug. 2024.

30 See Chapter 5, esp. "Building the Nation."

31 Baptiste, Nathalie. 2014. "Brain Drain and the Politics of Immigration." Foreign Policy In Focus. Institute for Policy Studies, Feb.

32 Gould, Eric D., and Moav, Omer. 2007. "Israel's Brain Drain." Israel Economic Review 5, no. 1, pp. 1–22

33 Compare Docquier, F., and Lohest, O., and Marfouk, A. 2005. "Brain drain in developing regions (1990–2000)." IZA, Discussion Paper No. 1668.

34 Ben-David, Dan. 2013. State of The Nation Report. Taub Center for Social Policy Studies in Israel, Jerusalem.

35 Ibid.

36 Quoted in Kadari-Ovadia, Shira. 2023. "Israeli Universities Warn Judicial Overhaul Will Lead to 'Brain Drain,' International Boycott." Haaretz, Jan. 23.

37 "PISA test 2023: general decline in the level of education." Madan, Dec. 9, 2023.

38 The Declaration of the Establishment of the State of Israel (May 14, 1948). Jewish Virtual Library. https://www.jewishvirtuallibrary.org/the-declaration-of-the-establishment-of-the-state-of-israel. Retrieved on Mar. 20, 2024.

39 Arian, Ofer. 2018. "A welfare state without a welfare policy: the case of Israel." Israel Affairs, Apr. 23.

40 Inbari, Motti. 2010. Rabbi Amram Blau Founder of the Neturei Karta Movement: An Abridged Biography. Hebrew Union College Annual 81, pp. 11–12.

41 The struggle against Zionism didn't fare well in the tumultuous 1990s, when a Kahane follower threw acid in his face and the rabbi lost an eye. See "Rabbi Moshe Hirsch: Ultra-Orthodox Jewish leader who became an adviser to Yasser Arafat." Independent, May 7, 2010.

42 On the vocal Israeli debate regarding the Haredim; the economy and social transfers, see e.g., Gur, Hativ Rettig. 2023. "Why the new state budget both favors and hurts Haredim ... and deeply threatens Israel." Times of Israel, May 23.

43 Razin and Sadka 2023, *op. cit.*

44 Shraberman, Kyril, and Weinreb, Alexander A. 2024. "The fiscal consequences of changing demographic composition: Aging and differential growth across Israel's three major subpopulations." The Journal of the Economics of Aging 27 (Feb.).

45 Wrobel, Sharon. 2023. "Cabinet approves NIS 13.7b in state funds to meet Haredi coalition demands." Times of Israel, May 14.

46 "Open letter from Israel's academic economists to the Israeli government on the new budgetary allocations and their long-term damage to Israel's future." Economists for Israeli Democracy: https://economists-for-israeli-democracy.com/files/coalition_funds_and_the_damage_to_the_Israeli_economy_eng.pdf

47 "A second open letter concerning the economic harm resulting from the proposed reforms in the judicial system in Israel." Economists for Israeli Democracy: https://economists-for-israeli-democracy.com/files/letter_2023-03-02_eng.pdf

48 Data from the UN, Israel Central Bureau of Statistics, and the OECD.

49 Data by Israel's Central Bureau of Statistics (CBS).

50 CBS data, and Cahaner, Lee, and Malach, Gilad. 2024. *Report on Annual Statistical Ultra-Orthodox (Haredi) Society in Israel.* The Israel Democracy Institute.

51 Data collected via Who Profits; American Friends Service Committee; Database of Israeli Military and Security Export.

52 Bohbot, Amir. 2023. "The IDF's 'crushing force' in Gaza: The bulldozer drivers who crush obstacles and level the way for the fighters." Walla, Nov. 2. [in Hebrew].

53 Graham-Harrison, Emma, et al. 2023. "Cratered ground and destroyed lives: Piecing together the Jabalia camp airstrike." The Guardian, Oct. 31.

54 See Investigate, a project of The American Friends Service Committee: https://investigate.info/company/caterpillar

55 Qiblawi, Tamara, et al. 2023. "'Not seen since Vietnam': Israel dropped hundreds of 2,000-pound bombs on Gaza, analysis shows." CNN, Dec. 22.

56 See e.g., Cleveland-Stout, Nick. 2024. "Wall Street ignores own rules while investing in arms bound for Israel." Responsible Statecraft, May 6.

57 See https://elbitsystems.com/media/MPR-500.pdf#page=2

58 "7 WCK team members killed in Gaza." News release, World Central Kitchen, Apr. 2, 2024.

59 Arms, Alan, and Ristic, Marija. 2023. "Israel/OPT: Identifying the Israeli army's use of white phosphorus in Gaza." Citizen Evidence Lab, Oct. 13. See also "Israel: White Phosphorus Used in Gaza, Lebanon Use in Populated Areas Poses Grave Risks to Civilians." Human Rights Watch, Oct. 12, 2023.

60 "White Phosphorus." WHO News Release, Jan. 15, 2024.

61 Compare Christou, William, et al. 2023. "Israel used U.S.-supplied white phosphorus in Lebanon attack." Washington Post, Dec. 11.

62 Rain of Fire: Israel's Unlawful Use of White Phosphorus in Gaza. Human Rights Watch, Mar. 25, 2009. See also Petras, James. 2010. *War Crimes in Gaza.* Atlanta, GA: Clarity Press, pp. 21–22.

63 "War with Hamas to cost Israel above $50 billion, Calcalist reports." Reuters, Nov. 5, 2023.

64 "War with Hamas to cost Israel at least NIS 50 billion in 2024, says Treasury." Times of Israel, Dec. 26, 2023.

65 Lidman, Melanie. 2024. "Israel's finance minister blasts Moody's downgrade of the country's credit rating." AP News, Feb. 11.

66 "Israel's per capita GDP shrank in 2023." Globes, Feb. 19, 2024.

67 Altstein, Gary and Bronner, Ethan. 2024. "Is Israel Headed for Another Lost Decade?" Bloomberg Businessweek, Jun. 3.

68 Ibid.

69 For the analysis of the rise of Israeli's military expenditure, see Chapter 4.

70 On perspectives regarding the settlements, the U.S. role and the Palestinians, see Chapters 2, 3 and 8, respectively.

71 See Chapter 4, "Was October 7 Avoidable?"

72 See Chapter 2, esp. "Settlements as a Security Burden."

73 Dori, Oren. 2024. "130 top economists warn gov't policy endangers Israel's existence." Globes, May 28.

74 Cumbo, Josephine, and Agnew, Harriett. 2024. "UK's biggest private pension fund dumps £80mn of Israeli assets." Financial Times, Aug. 8.

75 "Fitch Downgrades Israel to 'A'; Outlook Negative." Fitch Ratings, Aug. 12, 2024.

Chapter 8

1 Giles, Frank. 1969. "Golda Meir: 'Who can blame Israel?'" Sunday Times, Jun. 15, p. 12.

2 "Iron Lady of Israeli politics" (1970), in This Week, Thames TV [18:42]. See also Klein, Aaron J. 2005. *Striking Back: The 1972 Munich Olympics Massacre and Israel's Deadly Response.* New York: Random House, Inc., Chapter 1.

3 Aderet, Ofer. 2023. "Golda Meir Was 'Open' to a Palestinian State, Newly Released Archives From 1970 Reveal." Haaretz, Aug. 1,

4 Ibid.

5 As he added, "Recognition of Israel's right to exist was never imposed on the Arab states or even Arafat's PLO as a pre-condition for status as a legitimate partner in negotiations. Surely this is an ideological, not a political, position that must be reconsidered." See Halevy, Efraim. 2009. "Bring Hamas into the political process." Gulf News, Feb. 8.

6 Metzer, Jacob, and Kaplan, Oded. 1985. "Jointly but Severally: Arab-Jewish Dualism and Economic Growth in Mandatory Palestine." The Journal of Economic History 45, no. 2: The Tasks of Economic History (Jun.), pp. 327–45. The Maurice Falk Institute for Economic Research in Israel, Jerusalem, 1985.

7 Shai, Aron. 2006. "The Fate of Abandoned Arab Villages in Israel, 1965–1969." History and Memory 18, no. 2, Special Issue: Home and Beyond: Sites of Palestinian Memory (Fall/Winter), pp. 86–106.

8 Bahiri, Simcha. 1987. *Industrialization in the West Bank and Gaza.* London: Routledge. See Chapter 3.1.

9 Frisch, Hillel. 1983. *Stagnation and Frontiers: Arab and Jewish Industry in the West Bank.* West Bank Data Base Project, Jerusalem.

10 Sandler, Samuel with Frisch, Hillel, "The Political Economy of the Administered Territories." In: Elazar, Daniel J. (ed.). 1982. *Judaea, Samaria and Gaza: Views on the Present and Future.* Washington D.C.: American Enterprise Institute for Public Policy Research.

11 Van Arkadie, Brian. 1977. *Benefits and Burdens: A Report on the West Bank and Gaza Strip Economies Since 1967.* Washington D.C.: Carnegie Endowment for International Peace.

12 Compare Kanaan, Oussama. 1998. "Uncertainty Deters Private Investment in the West Bank and Gaza Strip." Finance & Development, IMF 35, no. 2 (Jun.),

13 Ben Simhon, Dani. 2004. "The Unmaking of the Histadrut." Challenge Magazine, Issue 88, Nov./Dec.

14 Bahiri 1987, *op. cit.* See Chapter 4.1.

15 Ibid. See Chapter 2.

16 Ibid.

17 Morris, Benny. 1997. *Israel's Border Wars 1949–1956: Arab Infiltration, Israeli Retaliation, and the Countdown to the Suez War.* New York: Oxford University Press. On these reprisals and Israel's national security strategy, see Chapter 11.

18 Mitchell, Richard P. 1968. *The Society of the Muslim Brothers.* New York: Oxford University Press, esp. Chapter 1.

19 Ibid., see Chapter 10.

20 Compare with Mura, Andrea. 2012. "A genealogical inquiry into early Islamism: the discourse of Hasan al-Banna," Journal of Political Ideologies 17, no. 1, pp. 61–85.

21 Steinbock, Dan. 2024. *The End of Modern Economic Growth. Unpublished manuscript,* see esp. Chapter 1. See also Eisenstadt, Shmuel N. 2003. *Comparative Civilizations and Multiple Modernities: A Collection of Essays.* Brill.

22 Euben, Roxanne L., and Zaman, Muhammad Qasim. 2009. *Princeton Readings in Islamist Thought: Text and Contexts from Al-Banna to Bin Laden.* Princeton, NJ: Princeton University Press, p. 50.

23 Gerges, Fawaz A. 2018. *Making the Arab World: Nasser, Qutb, and the Clash That Shaped the Middle East.* Princeton, NJ: Princeton University Press.

24 Qutb, Sayyid. 1964. *Milestones.* Kazi Publications, 1993. See also Polk, William R. 2018. "The Philosopher of the Muslim Revolt, Sayyid Qutb." In: *Crusade and Jihad: The Thousand-Year War Between the Muslim World and the Global North.* London: Yale University Press, pp. 370–80.

25 Wright, Lawrence. 2006. *The Looming Tower: Al Qaeda and the Road to 9/11.* New York: Alfred Knopf, p. 8.

26 "The America I Have Seen." 1949. In: Abdel-Malek, Kamal (ed.). 2000. *America in an Arab Mirror: Images of America in Arabic Travel Literature: An Anthology.* Portland, OR: Portland State University. On Qutb's life and works, see Calvert, John. 2010. *Sayyid Qutb and the Origins of Radical Islamism.* Hurst & Co.

27 Qutb, Sayyid. 1964. *Milestones.* Islamic Book Service, p. 1. See also Duvall, Nadia. 2019. *Islamist Occidentalism: Sayyid Qutb and the Western Other.* Berlin: Gerlach Press, pp. 39, 64–65.

28 Sharnoff, Michael. 2017. *Nasser's Peace: Egypt's Response to the 1967 War with Israel*. London: Taylor & Francis. p. 17.

29 On the Israel-PLO recognition, see "Israel-PLO recognition: Exchange of letters between PM Rabin and Chairman Arafat/Arafat letter to Norwegian FM" (Non-UN documents). The Question of Palestine. United Nations, Sep. 9, 1993. https://www. un.org/unispal/document/auto-insert-205528/

30 Hussein, Ahmed Qasem. 2021. "The Evolution of the Military Action of the Izz al-Din al-Qassam Brigades: How Hamas Established its Army in Gaza." Al Muntaqa 4, no. 1 (Sep./Oct.), pp. 78–97.

31 Chehab, Zaki. 2007. *Inside Hamas: The Untold Story of Militants, Martyrs and Spies*. London: I.B. Tauris, p. 15.

32 Ibid. See also Pappé, Ilan. 2017. *The Biggest Prison on Earth: A History of the Occupied Territories*. Oneworld.

33 Hussein 2021, *op. cit.*

34 Bahiri 1987, *op. cit.*, see Chapter 8.1.

35 On the U.S. view of the onset of the peace process, see Zanotti, Jim. 2020. "Israel and the Palestinians: Chronology of a Two-State Solution." CRS In Focus, Jun. 30.

36 Higgins, A. 2009. "How Israel Helped to Spawn Hamas." Wall Street Journal, Jan. 25.

37 Hussein 2021, *op. cit.*

38 Cary, Jeff. 2004. "Hamas Ceasefire Proposal: Peace or Pause?" Washington Institute for Near East Policy, Mar. 16.

39 Weitz, G. 2020. "Another Concept Implodes: Israel Can't Be Managed by a Criminal Defendant." Haaretz, Oct. 9.

40 Goldenberg, Suzanne. 2008. "US plotted to overthrow Hamas after election victory." The Guardian, Mar. 3.

41 Quoted in Makovsky, David. 2004. "How to Build a Fence." Foreign Affairs 83, no. 2, Mar./Apr.

42 Harel, Amos. 2006. "Shin Bet: Palestinian truce main cause for reduced terror." Haaretz, Jan. 2.

43 "Operational Concept." Israel: Ministry of Defense, Jan. 31, 2007. See https:// web.archive.org/web/20130927223855/http://www.securityfence.mod.gov.il/Pages/ ENG/operational.htm

44 "West Bank and Gaza – Area C and the future of the Palestinian economy." World Bank, Report No. AUS292, Oct. 2, 2013, pp. 1–71.

45 B'Tselem. 2007. "Separation Barrier." B'Tselem.

46 "Poverty in Palestine: The human cost of the financial boycott." Oxfam International, Apr. 2007.

47 "Israel pushed Gaza to 'brink of collapse': WikiLeaks." NBC News. Jan. 5, 2011.

48 "General Assembly Votes Overwhelmingly to Accord Palestine 'Non-Member Observer State' Status in United Nations." UN Document, November 28, 2012.

49 Hussein 2021, *op.cit.*

50 Shapir, Yiftah S., and Perel, Gal. "Subterranean Warfare: A New-Old Challenge." In: Kurz, Anat; Brom, Shlomo (eds.). 2014. *The Lessons of Operation Protective Edge*. Institute for National Security Studies (INSS), p. 52.

51 Haddad, Toufic. 2018. "Insurgent Infrastructure: Tunnels of the Gaza Strip." Middle East: Topics & Arguments. 10: 71–85; Mangold, Tom, and Penycate, John. 1986. *The Tunnels of Cu Chi*. New York: Berkley Books.

52 Rubenstein, Daniel. "Hamas' Tunnel Network: A Massacre in the Making." In: Goodman, Hirsh; Gold, Dore (eds.). *The Gaza War 2014: The War Israel Did Not Want and the Disaster It Averted*. Jerusalem Center for Public Affairs. pp. 119–29.

53 On the Israeli efforts to redefine conventional, urban and underground warfare in Western military theory, see Richemond-Barak, Daphné and Voiculescu-Holvad, Stefan. 2023. The Rise of Tunnel Warfare as a Tactical, Operational, and Strategic Issue. Studies in Conflict & Terrorism, Aug. 23, pp. 1–20.

54 Brik, Yitzhak. 2020. "The Iranians Are Lulling Israel's Leaders to Sleep." Haaretz, Jul. 14.

55 Compare Brik, Yitzhak. 2023. "Don't Believe the IDF and Israeli Analysts. There's No Solution to Hamas.'" Haaretz, Dec. 25. Tunnels.

56 Benjakob, Omer and Yaron, Oded. 2024. "Cyber Nightmare: Hamas Has Detailed Intel on Thousands of Israeli Soldiers, Families." Haaretz, Jul. 22.

57 Cary, Jeff. 2004. "Hamas Ceasefire Proposal: Peace or Pause?" The Washington Institute for Near East Policy, Mar. 16.

58 Halevy, Efraim. 2017. "Former Mossad chief: Time for Israel to talk to Hamas." Washington Post, Mar. 17.

59 Hroub, Khaled. 2017. "A Newer Hamas? The Revised Charter." Journal of Palestine Studies. Vol. 46, No. 4 (184), Summer, pp. 100–111.

60 Proclamation 9683 of December 6, 2017, 82 FR 58331.

61 Iraqi, Amjad. 2023. "Israeli arrogance thwarted a Palestinian political path. October 7 revealed the cost." +972 Magazine, Nov. 28.

62 "And now for the whitewashing." B'tselem May 24, 2021; Report of the independent international commission of inquiry on the protests in the Occupied Palestinian Territory, Human Rights Council, Feb. 25, 2019 p.6.

63 See e.g., Lev, Shimon. 2017. "'Can the Jews resist this organized and shameless persecution?': Gandhi's Response to the Holocaust." Café Dissensus, Jan. 20.

64 Data from Ajamieh, Yazan et al. 2023. West Bank and Gaza: Selected Issues. IMF, Sep. 11.

65 Lall, Subir, and Valencia, Fabian. 2023. West Bank and Gaza. Report to the Ad Hoc Liaison Committee, Sep. 8.

66 Issacharoff, Avi. 2012. "In rare court appearance, Marwan Barghouti calls for a peace deal based on 1967 lines." Haaretz, Jan. 26.

67 Beinin, Joel; and Stein, Rebecca L. 2006. *The Struggle for Sovereignty: Palestine and Israel, 1993–2005*. Stanford University Press. pp. 105–106.

68 For more, see the next section, "The Beijing Declaration: Unifying the Palestinian Front."

69 "Will Israel release Marwan Barghouti, the 'Palestinian Mandela'?" Al Jazeera, Feb. 15, 2024; Khoury, Jack; and Breiner, Josh. 2024. "Jailed Palestinian leader Marwan Barghouti 'beaten with clubs' by guards, family claims." Haaretz, Mar. 19.

70 See also Abbas, Mahmoud. 1995. *Through Secret Channels: The Road to Oslo.* Reading, UK: Garnet Publishing.

71 See e.g., Balousha, Hazem. 2013. "Report Highlights Corruption In Palestinian Institutions." Al-Monitor, May 6. See also Schanzer, Jonathan. 2012. "The Brothers Abbas: Are the sons of the Palestinian president growing rich off their father's system?" Foreign Policy, Jun. 5.

72 On the transformation of Hamas, see e.g., Kear, Martin. 2018. *Hamas and Palestine: The Contested Road to Statehood.* London: Routledge. See also Natil, Ibrahim. 2015. *Hamas Transformation: Opportunities and Challenges.* Cambridge Scholars Publishing.

73 For a journalistic portrayal, see Teich, Ira Bernard. 2024. "Unveiling Yahya Sinwar: His character, his impact, his peril." Times of Israel, Feb. 7.

74 Public Opinion Poll No. (92), The Palestinian Center for Policy and Survey Research (PSR), May 26–Jun. 1, 2024.

75 El-Komi, Ahmed. 2020. "Is Dahlan really being lined up by the US to replace Abbas?" Middle East Monitor, Sep. 23.

76 On Beijing Declaration, see Steinbock 2024, *op. cit.* See also "The Beijing Declaration: Step 2 to Large-Scale Peace Talks in the Middle East." China-US Focus, Jul. 31.

77 Wilson, Joseph. 2024. "Spain, Norway and Ireland formally recognize a Palestinian state as EU rift with Israel widens." AP News, May 28.

78 "Norway, Ireland and Spain formally recognize a Palestinian state." NBC News, May 22, 2024.

79 Since 2016, the United Nations Conference on Trade and Development (UNCTAD) has annually reported to the UN on the economic costs of the Israeli occupation for the Palestinian people. This section draws from this series of reports by the Secretariat of the UNCTAD: *Economic costs of the Israeli occupation for the Palestinian people: the toll of the additional restrictions in Area C, 2000–2020.* (Aug. 16, 2022); *Economic costs of the Israeli occupation for the Palestinian people: poverty in the West Bank between 2000 and 2019.* (Aug. 30, 2021); *Economic costs of the Israeli occupation for the Palestinian people: the Gaza Strip under closure and restrictions.* (Aug. 13, 2020); *Economic costs of the Israeli occupation for the Palestinian people: fiscal aspects.* (Aug. 2, 2019).

80 UNCTAD 2020, *op. cit.*, p. 2.

81 Economic costs of the Israeli occupation for the Palestinian people: The Gaza Strip under closure and restrictions. UNCTAD. Aug. 13, 2020.

82 Naser-Najjab, Nadia. 2024. *Covid-19 in Palestine: The Settler Colonial Context.* London: Bloomsbury Publishing.

83 "Emirati envoy conditions Gaza rehab funds on progress toward Palestinian state." Reuters/Times of Israel, Feb. 12, 2024.

84 The Gaza 2035 slides. Prime Minister's Office, May 2024.

85 On Palestinian polls, see Chapter 8.

86 On the U.S. efforts at a "grand deal" based on bilateral normalization, see Chapter 11.

87 "'Domicide' must be recognised as an international crime: UN expert." OHCHR, Oct. 28, 2024; Adequate housing as a component of the right to an adequate standard of living. UN General Assembly, Jul. 19, 2022. Both reports were written by Balakrishnan Rajagopal, the UN Special Rapporteur on the Right to Adequate Housing and a professor of law and development at MIT.

88 Ibid. Dr. Ziv Bohrer, an expert in international law at Bar-Ilan University quoted by Graham-Harrison.

89 Hodali, Fadwa, et al. 2024. "Gaza Reduced to 42 Million Tonnes of Rubble. What Will It Take to Rebuild?" Bloomberg, Aug. 16.

90 Reported impact snapshot: Gaza Strip, OCHA, Jul. 10, 2024.

91 "10 000 people feared buried under the rubble in Gaza." UN Office Geneva. May 3, 2024.

92 Khatib, Rashaa, et al. 2024. Counting the dead in Gaza: difficult but essential. The Lancet, Jul. 5.

93 Data from United Nations Development Programme (UNDP) and Palestinian Central Bureau of Statistics (PCBS) in May 2024.

94 Based on estimates by Pehr Lodhammar, the former United Nationals Mine Action Service chief for Iraq. See Graham-Harrison, Emma. 2024. "Gaza's 37m tonnes of bomb-filled debris could take 14 years to clear, says expert." The Guardian, Apr. 26.

Chapter 9

1 Hauser Tov, Michael, with the AP. 2024. "'Israeli Gov't Is Intent on Destroying Palestinians in Gaza': South Africa Presents Genocide Case at ICJ." Haaretz, Jan. 11.

2 Champion, Marc. 2024. "The Gaza War Isn't a Holocaust. It's Still a Nightmare." Bloomberg, Feb. 22.

3 Clark, Nancy, and Worger, William. 2016. *South Africa: The Rise and Fall of Apartheid* (3rd ed.). New York: Routledge. Chapters 1–2 and Chapters 3–5, respectively.

4 Marks, S., and Rathbone, R. 1982. *Industrialization and social change in South Africa*. New York: Addison-Wesley Longman Ltd.

5 On the postwar apartheid, see Worden, Nigel. 2000. *Making of Modern South Africa: Conquest, Segregation and Apartheid* (3rd Ed.). New York: Wiley-Blackwell.

6 "The United Nations: Israeli Statement in Response to 'Zionism Is Racism' Resolution" (Nov. 10, 1975). Jewish Virtual Library. Retrieved on Mar. 1, 2024.

7 Blumenthal, Paul. 2023. "Israeli President Says There Are No Innocent Civilians In Gaza." Ynet News, Oct. 13.

8 Herzog, Isaac. 2024. "The Case Against Israel Rests on Lies Among them is a quote of mine that South Africa grossly distorted in its presentation to the ICJ." Wall Street Journal, Feb. 11.

9 President Bush's Address to the 46th Session of the United Nations General Assembly in New York City, Sep. 23, 1991.

10 "Former Israeli Security Chief Calls Netanyahu a Poor Leader." New York Times, Jan. 4, 2013. See also "Ex-Israeli Security Chief Diskin: 'All the Conditions Are There for an Explosion.'" Der Spiegel, June 24, 2014.

11 "Ex-Shin Bet chief: Government does not want to deal with Jewish terror." Ynet News, Jul. 8, 2015.

12 Clarno, Andrew James. 2009. *The Empire's New Walls: Sovereignty, neo-liberalism, and the production of space in post-apartheid South Africa and post-Oslo Palestine/Israel*. BiblioBazaar [dissertation], pp. 66–67.

13 Do, Nhat-Dang, and Provence, Michael. 2016. "The Legitimacy of Repression: The History of Martial Law in British Controlled Palestine." Equilibrium 2 (Fall), pp. 17–29.

14 Zureik, Elia. 1979. *The Palestinians in Israel: A Study in Internal Colonialism*. London: Routledge & K. Paul, 1979, p. 113.

15 A Threshold Crossed: Israeli Authorities and the Crimes of Apartheid and Persecution. Human Rights Watch, Apr. 2021.

16 "The Elephant in the Room." Academics4Peace, Aug. 4, 2023.

17 "A former Mossad chief says Israel is enforcing an apartheid system in the West Bank." AP, Sep. 7, 2023.

18 Quoted by Idan Yaron in Glazer, Hilo. 2023. "After a Decade Inside the Most Radical Circles of Israel's Far-right, He's Ready to Tell All." Haaretz, Oct. 6.

19 "Israel reminds me of apartheid – Tutu." News24, Mar. 10, 2014.

20 "No Thanks" app in Google Play. See https://play.google.com/store/apps/details?id=com.bashsoftware.boycott&hl=en_GB. Retrieved on Apr. 23, 2024.

21 Losman, Donald L. 1972. "The Arab Boycott of Israel." *International Journal of Middle East Studies* 3, no. 2, pp. 99–122.

22 On the rise of the Jewish immigration waves, see Chapter 5.

23 Feiler, Gil. 1998. *From Boycott to Economic Cooperation: The Political Economy of the Arab Boycott of Israel*. London: Frank Cass, p. 1.

24 "Israel should 'wipe out' Palestinian town of Huwara, says senior minister Smotrich." Times of Israel, Mar. 1, 2023.

25 Citi Group's South African website: https://www.citigroup.com/global/about-us/global-presence/south-africa

26 Feder, Barnaby J. 1987. "Citibank Is Leaving South Africa: Foes of Apartheid See Major Gain." New York Times, Jun. 17.

27 Ibid.

28 See http://www.bdsmovement.net/call. On the genesis and objectives of BDS, see https://bdsmovement.net/colonialism-and-apartheid/summary.

29 On the EC notice, see http://eeas.europa.eu/delegations/israel/documents/news/20151111_interpretative_notice_indication_of_origin_of_goods_en.pdf. On the UN database, see United States Mission to the United Nations, Remarks on the UN Human Rights Council, Jul. 19, 2018.

30 The RAND report was premised on modeling based on previous international boycotts. See Anthony, C. Ross, et al. 2015. *The Costs of the Israeli-Palestinian Conflict*. Santa Monica, CA: RAND.

31 "McDonald's Loses $7 Billion in Boycott Over Israel Support." Morocco World News, Mar. 15, 2024. See also "McDonald's will buy all 225 restaurants from Israel franchise following pro-Palestinian boycott fallout." CNBC, Apr. 5, 2024.

32 Feldman, David. 2018. "Boycotts: From the American Revolution to BDS." In: Feldman, David (ed.). *Boycotts Past and Present: From the American Revolution to the Campaign to Boycott Israel.* Springer, pp. 1–19.

33 Thrall, Nathan. 2019. "How the Battle Over Israel and Anti-Semitism Is Fracturing American Politics." New York Times Magazine, March 28.

34 Levush, Ruth. 2017. "Israel: Prevention of Entry of Foreign Nationals Promoting Boycott of Israel." Law Library of Congress Global Legal Monitor, Mar. 17, 2017. See also Chokshi, Niraj. 2019. "The Anti-Boycott Law Israel Used to Bar Both Omar and Tlaib." New York Times, Aug. 15.

35 Compare Chapter 6.

36 Klein, Shira, and Sternfeld, Lior. 2024. "Students Are at the Forefront of Israeli McCarthyism." Haaretz, Apr. 17.

37 Beckett, Lois. 2024. "Nearly all Gaza campus protests in the US have been peaceful, study finds." The Guardian, May 10. See also "UN right chief troubled by treatment of pro-Palestinian protesters at U.S. universities." Reuters, Apr. 30, 2024.

38 Marx, Willem. 2024. "Campus protests over the war in Gaza have gone international." NPR, May 3.

39 Egan, Matt, and Maruf, Ramishah. 2024. "What the pro-Palestinian protesters on college campuses actually want." CNN Business, Apr. 26. See also: "Student protesters are demanding universities divest from Israel. What does that mean?" The Guardian, Apr. 25, 2024. See also "'Divest from Israel': Decoding the Gaza protest call shaking US campuses." Al Jazeera, Apr. 30, 2024.

40 Karaganis, Joseph. 1999. "Radicalism and research at Columbia: The legacy of '68." 21stC: Issue 4.1, Columbia University.

41 "What is behind US college protests over Israel-Gaza war?" Reuters, Apr. 25, 2024.

42 Burg, Avraham. 2012. "Avraham Burg: Even I – an Israeli – think settlement goods are not kosher." The Independent, Jun. 7.

43 Levy, Gideon. 2013. "The Israeli Patriot's Final Refuge: Boycott." Haaretz, Jul. 14.

44 "President Lula says war in the Middle East is genocide." Agência Brasil, Oct. 25.

45 Quoted in Hauser Tov/AP 2024, *op. cit.*

46 Statement by the Prime Minister of Israel on X formerly known as Twitter, on Jan. 11, 2024: https://twitter.com/IsraeliPM/status/1745186120109846710?lang=en. Retrieved on May 9, 2024.

47 Statement by the Spokesperson of Israel's Foreign Ministry on X, Jan. 11, 2024. See https://twitter.com/LiorHaiat/status/1745427037039280207?lang=en. Retrieved on May 9, 2024.

48 Chomsky, Noam. 1999. *The Fateful Triangle.* Cambridge MA: South End Press, p. 98.

49 Bartrop, Paul R. 2014. *Modern Genocide: The Definitive Resource and Document Collection, Vol. I.* ABC-CLIO, pp. 1301–1302.

50 Lemkin, Raphael. 1943. *Axis rule in occupied Europe: laws of occupation, analysis of government, proposals for redress.* Clark, N.J: Lawbook Exchange. See also Lemkin, Raphael. 1946. "The Crime of Genocide." American Scholar 15, no. 2, pp. 227–30.

51 Staub, Ervin. 1989. *The Roots of Evil: The Origins of Genocide and Other Group Violence.* Cambridge, UK: Cambridge University Press, p. 8. See also Luck, Edward C. 2018. "Cultural Genocide and the Protection of Cultural Heritage." J. Paul Getty Trust Occasional Papers in Cultural Heritage Policy Number 2, pp. 17–29.

52 Glazer, Nathan. 1957. *American Judaism.* Chicago: University of Chicago Press, p. 114.

53 At the time, I had no idea about the haunting impact of my observations on Levi himself. What Levi "read disturbed and impressed him greatly. Steinbock was the first critic anywhere to see Levi as a refraction of Kafka. 'Primo Levi is Josef K.' So, Levi's fear that Kafka's spirit inhabited his life and writing returned." See Thomson, Ian. 2014. *Primo Levi: A Life.* New York: Metropolitan, p. 663.

54 Aly, Götz. 2002. "History reaches into the present. A conversation with the historian Raul Hilberg" [in German]. Neue Zürcher Zeitung, Dec. 10. See also Popper, Nathaniel. 2010. "A Conscious Pariah." The Nation, Mar. 31.

55 Finkelstein, Norman. 2000. *The Holocaust Industry: Reflections on the Exploitation of Jewish Suffering.* New York: Verso. See esp. Chapter 1.

56 Magid, Jacob. 2023. "Erdan tells UN he'll don yellow Star of David until it condemns Hamas; Yad Vashem fumes." Oct. 31.

57 Ibid.

58 "Biden attacks request by ICC prosecutor for Netanyahu arrest warrant." The Guardian, May 21.

59 Steinbock, Dan. 2023. "The Odd Track-Record Of The International Criminal Court – OpEd." Eurasia Review, Apr. 4.

60 In 2020, Norman Finkelstein had argued that Bensouda "whitewashed Israel." The full story emerged only in 2024, when the Mossad operation was disclosed in public. Compare Finkelstein, Norman. 2020. *I Accuse!: Herewith A Proof Beyond Reasonable Doubt That ICC Chief Prosecutor Fatou Bensouda Whitewashed Israel.* OR Books.

61 See Chapter 4.

62 Davies, et al. 2024. "Spying, hacking and intimidation: Israel's nine-year 'war' on the ICC exposed." The Guardian, May 28. See also Abraham, Yuval, and Rapoport, Meron. 2024. "Surveillance and interference: Israel's covert war on the ICC exposed." +972 Magazine, May 28.

63 Compare Megiddo, Gur. 2022. "How Israeli Security Nixed Haaretz's Report Into Alleged Mossad Extortion of International Court Prosecutor." Haaretz, May 30.

64 Melman, Yossi. 2024. "'Sounds Like Cosa Nostra Blackmail': Former Mossad Chief on Successor's Alleged Threats Against ICC Prosecutor." Haaretz, May 30.

65 Statement of ICC Prosecutor Karim A.A. Khan KC: Applications for arrest warrants in the situation in the State of Palestine. ICC, May 20, 2024.

66 Malthus, Thomas. 1798. *An Essay on the Principle of Population.* London: Penguin Classics. See Chapter VII.

67 The quote is by a leading famine scholar. See de Waal, Alex. 2024. "We are about to witness in Gaza the most intense famine since the second world war." The Guardian, Mar. 21.

68 "There is no Gaza famine, so why is the pro-Hamas media silent about this great news?" New York Post, Jun. 20, 2024.

69 Mundy, Martha. 2018. The Strategies of the Coalition in the Yemen War: Aerial Bombardment and Food War. World Peace Foundation, Oct. 9.

70 "Imminent famine in northern Gaza is 'entirely man-made disaster': Guterres." UN News. United Nations. Mar. 18, 2024. See also "Manufacturing Famine: Israel Is Committing the War Crime of Starvation in the Gaza Strip." B'Tselem, Apr., 2024.

71 "Reader: 'Food Consumption in the Gaza Strip – Red Lines.'" Position Paper. Gisha – Legal Center for Freedom of Movement, Oct. 2012. According to defense ministry, "it was part of a research paper that came up in two discussions and that we never made use of."

72 The summary documents were released only in late 2012 after more than three yeas of legal battle. See "'Red Lines' presentation released after 3.5-year legal battle: Israel calculated the number of calories it would allow Gaza residents to consume." Gisha, Oct. 17, 2012.

73 Based on a 15-slide presentation that was presented during the hearing before the Supreme Court dated January 27, 2008. See AAA 3300/11 Ministry of Defense v. Gisha "Food Consumption in the Gaza Strip – Red Lines" presentation. Unofficial translation by Gisha.

74 "Israel Gaza blockade study calculated Palestinians' calories." Reuters, Oct. 17, 2012.

75 "Israel allows entry of aid into Gaza via Kerem Shalom Crossing, but it isn't enough." Gisha, Jan. 3, 2024.

76 Hall-Matthews, David. 1996. "Historical Roots of Famine Relief Paradigms: Ideas on Dependency and Free Trade in India in the 1870s." Disasters 20, no. 3, pp. 216–30. On the Temple wage, see Linden, Eugen. 2006. The Winds of Change: Climate, Weather, and the Destruction of Civilizations. New York: Simon & Schuster, p. 196.

77 Dyson, Tim. 2018. A Population History of India: From the First Modern People to the Present Day. Oxford University Press. p. 137.

78 Compare Liskey, Amber. 2021. "Bread and Tea: A Look into Yemen's Food Security Crisis." IFRU-Egypt, Jul. 1.

79 "People in northern Gaza forced to survive on 245 calories a day, less than a can of beans." Oxfam International, Apr. 3, 2024.

80 Ibid.

81 Stanner, S. A., et al. 1997. Does malnutrition in utero determine diabetes and coronary heart disease in adulthood? Results from the Leningrad siege study, a cross-sectional study. BMJ 315, no. 7119 (Nov. 22), pp. 1342–48. See also Sparén P., et al. 2004. Long term mortality after severe starvation during the siege of Leningrad: prospective cohort study. BMJ 328, no. 7430 (Jan. 3), p. 11.

82 Winick, Myron. 2014. "Jewish medical resistance in the Warsaw Ghetto." In: Grodin, Michael A. (ed.). Jewish medical resistance in the Holocaust. New York; Berghahn Books, pp. 93–105. See also Winick, Myron. 2005. "Hunger Disease:

Studies by the Jewish Physicians in the Warsaw Ghetto, Their Historical Importance and Their Relevance Today." Lecture at Columbia University, Oct. 27.

83 Rubinstein, W. D. 2004. *Genocide: A History*. London: Pearson Education, p. 308.

84 Compare Chapter 4.

85 Compare Chapter 1.

86 See Postscript: "Starvation in Historical Comparison."

87 "Women and newborns bearing the brunt of the conflict in Gaza, UN agencies warn." Statement. World Health Organization, Nov. 3. 2023.

88 Qiblawi, Tamara, et al. 2024. "Anesthetics, crutches, dates. Inside Israel's ghost list of items arbitrarily denied entry into Gaza." CNN, Mar. 2.

89 Convention on the Prevention and Punishment of the Crime of Genocide. OHCHR, Dec. 9, 1948.

90 "Statement of Mourning for the Gazans and the World." Lemkin Institute, Oct. 29, 2024.

91 "US 'not seeing acts of genocide' in Gaza, State Dept says." Reuters, Jan. 4, 2024.

92 McGreal, Chris. 2023. "US rights group sues Biden for alleged 'failure to prevent genocide' in Gaza." The Guardian, Nov. 13. See also Pazanowski, Bernie, and Thomsen, Jacqueline. 2024. "Israeli Military Aid Package Not Reviewable by Federal Court." Bloomberg Law, Feb. 1.

93 Scahill, Jeremy. 2024. "In Genocide Case Against Israel at The Hague, the U.S. Is the Unnamed Co-Conspirator." The Intercept, Jan. 11.

94 The Annual Threat Assessment. 2024. U.S. Intelligence Community, Feb. 5.

95 Legal Consequences Arising from the Policies and Practices of Israel in the Occupied Palestinian Territory, including East Jerusalem. Advisory Opinion. International Court of Justice, Jul. 19.

96 See esp. Chapter 2 on settlements as a security burden.

97 Quoted in Corder, Mike. 2024. "Top UN court says Israel's presence in occupied Palestinian territories is illegal and should end." AP News, Jul. 20.

Chapter 10

1 "US and Israel should bomb Iran: Senator Lindsey Graham." Middle East Monitor, Oct. 12.

2 Kahana, Ariel, and Reuters. 2023. "US Senator warns Iran that 'if this war grows, it's coming to your backyard.'" Israel Hayom, Oct. 23.

3 Compare Chapter 2.

4 Steinbock, Dan. 2024. *The End of Modern Economic Growth*. Unpublished manuscript, see esp. Chapter 2.

5 David, Javier E. 2020. "US–Saudi Arabia seal weapons deal worth nearly $110 billion immediately, $350 billion over 10 years." CNBC, May 20.

6 Gardner, Timothy, et al. 2020. "Special Report: Trump told Saudi: Cut oil supply or lose U.S. military support – sources." Reuters, April 30.

7 Compare Abrams, A.B. 2021. *World War in Syria.* Atlanta, GA: Clarity.

8 Crawford, Neta C. 2021. "The U.S. Budgetary Costs of the Post-9/11 Wars." Costs of War, Watson Institute, Brown University, Sep. 1.

9 Ibid.

10 On the estimated losses in these U.S. war zones, see:

Iraq: Iraq Body Count Database (CBD), Oct. 2021.

Yemen: "UN humanitarian office puts Yemen war dead at 233,000, mostly from 'indirect causes.'" UN News, Dec. 1, 2020.

Afghanistan: "UCDP – Uppsala Conflict Data Program"

Syria: "Syria war: UN calculates new death toll." BBC, Sep. 24, 2021; and "Over 606,000 people killed across Syria since the beginning of the "Syrian Revolution," including 495,000 documented by SOHR." Syrian Observatory for Human Rights, Sep. 1, 2021.

11 "Madeleine Albright Saying Iraqi Kids' Deaths 'Worth It' Resurfaces." Newsweek, Mar. 23, 2022.

12 Togawa, Shannon, and Kahn, Matthew. 2019. "America Trades Down: The Legal Consequences of President Trump's Tariffs." Lawfare, March 13.

13 Krueger, Anne O. 2021. "Resetting US-China Trade Relations." The Project Syndicate, Feb. 4.

14 Steinbock 2024, *op. cit.,* see Chapter 5.

15 Steinbock, Dan. 2022. "The Unwarranted War." The World Financial Review, March 9. See also Steinbock, Dan. 2023. "The Unwarranted Ukraine Proxy War." The World Financial Review, Jan. 27.

16 Vine, David, et al. 2020. "Creating Refugees: Displacement Caused by the United States' Post-9/11 Wars." Costs of War Research Series, Watson Institute, Brown University, Sep. 21.

17 Steinbock 2024, *op. cit.,* see Chapter 5.

18 Jones, Lee, and Hameiri, Shahar. 2020. "Debunking the Myth of 'Debt-trap Diplomacy': How Recipient Countries Shape China's Belt and Road Initiative." Chatham House, Aug. See also John Hopkins University database built by SAIS-CARI: https://chinaafricaloandata.bu.edu/

19 Aiyar, Sgekhar, et al. 2023. "Geoeconomic Fragmentation and the Future of Multilateralism." IMF Staff Discussion Notes, Jan., pp. 3–4.

20 Steinbock, Dan. 2016. "President Xi in the Middle East: From U.S. Regime Change to Chinese Economic Development." China-US Focus, Feb. 1. See also Chapter 3.

21 Brzezinski, Zbigniew. 1996. *The Grand Chessboard: American Primacy and Its Geostrategic Imperatives.* Updated with a New Epilogue. New York: Basic Books 2016, p. 220. See also Allison, Geraham. 2018. "China and Russia: A Strategic Alliance in the Making." The National Interest, Dec. 14.

22 Arab Barometer in Palestine, Feb. 29, 2024.

23 Wong, Edward, and Nereim, Vivian. 2024. "Israel Resists Grand Bargain as U.S. and Saudis Work on Security Pact." New York Times, May 17.

24 "Adani Group: How The World's 3rd Richest Man Is Pulling The Largest Con In Corporate History." Hindenburg Research, Jan. 24, 2023. See https://hindenburgresearch.com/adani/. See also "US activist investor who accused Adani of 'biggest con in corporate history' dares Indian group to sue." The Guardian, Jan. 27, 2023.

25 The region also receives a sizable portion of annual humanitarian assistance appropriations, which are not included in the region-specific aid figures. See Sharp, Jeremy M., et al. 2023. "U.S. Foreign Assistance to the Middle East: Historical, Recent Trends, and the FY2024 Background Request." CRS Report, Aug. 15.

26 See Chapter 4.

27 Compare Steinbock, Dan. 2014. *The Challenges for America's Defense Innovation*. Information Technology & Innovation Foundation, Nov. 21.

28 Ibid. Calculated in historical dollars, not adjusted for inflation.

29 Sharp, Jeremy M. 2023. "Egypt: Background and U.S. Relations." CRS Report, May 2.

30 Kasim, Salim A. 2023. "King of Jordan says situation in Gaza result of more than 7 decades of Israeli mentality." Anadolu Agency, Nov. 12.

31 Compare Murray, Williamson, and Woods, Kevin. 2014. *The Iran-Iraq War: A Military and Strategic History*. New York: Cambridge University Press.

32 Hersh, Seymour M. 2006. "The Next Act." The New Yorker, Nov. 20.

33 Steele, Jonathan. 2008. "Israel asked US for green light to bomb nuclear sites in Iran." The Guardian, Sep. 25.

34 Steinbock, Dan. 2020. "The Story of Trump's Perilous Iran Escalation." The World Financial Review, Jan. 10.

35 See "Missile Attack on Ain Assad Airbase: End of Empire?" in Chapter 8 of Lama, Fadi. 2023. *Why the West Can't Win: From Bretton Woods to a Multipolar World*. Atlanta, GA: Clarity.

36 See Arkin, William. 2006. "The Pentagon Preps for Iran." Washington Post, Apr. 16.

37 "Israeli ambassador Gilad Erdan calls Hamas attack on Israel 'truly unprecedented': 'This is our 9/11.'" Fox News, Oct. 8, 2023. See also "'Hamas attack was like twenty 9/11s': Israeli PM Benjamin Netanyahu." Times of Israel, Oct. 19, 2023.

38 Sarloff, Robert. 2023. "Why 10/7 Was Worse for Israel Than 9/11 Was for America." The Washington Institute for Near East Policy, Oct. 15.

39 Mitchell, Ellen. 2023. "McCaul preparing authorization of military force against Hamas, Iran proxies." The Hill, Oct. 17.

40 "Ex-Mossad Chief Says He Questioned Legality of Netanyahu's Order to Prepare Iran Strike." Haaretz. May 31, 2018.

41 Fabian, Emanuel. 2023. "Mossad chief vows to target Iran's 'highest echelon' if Israelis, Jews hurt in terror." Times of Israel, Sep. 10.

42 "Bashar al-Assad applauds Palestinian resistance's stand against Israel." Nour News [Iran], Dec. 23, 2023.

43 Wilford, Hugh. 2013. *America's Great Game: The CIA's Secret Arabists and the Making of the Modern Middle East*. New York: Basic Books, pp. 96–101.

44 Little, Douglas. 1990. "Cold War and Covert Action: The United States and Syria, 1945–1958." Middle East Journal 44, no. 1, pp. 51–75.

45 "Yemen Houthi leader says group will further escalate if attacks on Gaza do not stop." Feb. 7, 2024.

46 Burrowes, Robert. 2012. "Why Most Yemenis Should Despise Ex-president Ali Abdullah Saleh." Yemen Times, Feb. 12.

47 "Yemen's Prime Minister Is Preparing to Flee as Separatists Reach Gates of the Presidential Palace." Time, Jan. 30, 2018.

48 "Suspected cholera cases in Yemen surpass one million, reports UN health agency." UN, Dec. 22, 2017. See also "Yemen war deaths will reach 377,000 by end of the year: UN." Al Jazeera, Nov. 23, 2021.

49 Blanchard, Christopher M., and Martin, Abigail C. 2024. "Yemen: Conflict, Maritime Attacks, and U.S. Policy." CRS In Focus, Feb. 7.

50 Traboulsi, Fawwaz. 2007. A History of Modern Lebanon. London: Pluto Press, p. 75. See also Maktabi, Rania. 1999. "The Lebanese Census of 1932 Revisited. Who are the Lebanese?" British Journal of Middle Eastern Studies 26, no. 2 (Nov.), pp. 219–41. See also Barshad, Amos. 2019. "The World's Most Dangerous Census." The Nation, Oct. 17.

51 "Lebanon: Census and Sensibility." The Economist, Nov. 5, 2016.

52 Bahout, Joseph. 2016. The Unraveling of Lebanon's Taif Agreement: Limits of Sect-Based Power Sharing." Carnegie Endowment for International Peace, May 2016.

53 Report of the United Nations Fact-Finding Mission on the Gaza Conflict. United Nations Office of the High Commissioner for Human Rights, Sep. 25, 2009.

54 Hirst, David. 2010. Beware of Small States. Lebanon, Battleground of the Middle East. London: Faber and Faber, pp. 336–37.

55 World Bank. 2021. "Lebanon Sinking (To the Top 3)." Lebanon Economic Monitor (Spring 2021), May 31.

56 The lead writer, Reichman's dean Boaz Ganor, was Netanyahu's longtime security consultant. See Azulay, Yuval. 2024. "'Fire and blood': The chilling reality facing Israel in a war with Hezbollah." Calcalist, Feb. 9.

57 Compare Humud, Carla E. 2023. "Lebanese Hezbollah." CRS In Focus, Jan. 11.

58 Dominique Avon, and Khatchadourian, Anaïs-Trissa. 2012. Hezbollah: A History of the "Party of God." Harvard University Press, pp. 21ff.

59 Norton, Augustus. 2009. Hezbollah: A Short History. Princeton University Press, p. 33.

60 El Deeb, Sarah. 2021. "Hezbollah leader declares his group has 100,000 fighters." Associated Press, Oct. 18.

61 "Analysis: Hezbollah a force to be reckoned with." Agence France Presse, Jul. 18, 2006.

62 H. Varulkar. 2010. "Internal Conflict in Lebanon Over Control of Oil and Gas Resources." MEMRI, Inquiry & Analysis Series Report No. 624, Jul. 12.

63 Engeland, Anisseh Van, and Rudolph, Rachael M. 2013. From Terrorism to Politics. Ashgate Publishing, Ltd., pp. 33–34. See also Karam, Joyce. 2018. "Iran pays Hezbollah $700 million a year, US official says." The National, Jun. 6.

64 Nashed, Mat. 2023. "Can Lebanon's Hezbollah afford to go to war with Israel?" Al Jazeera, Oct. 16.

65 Information on what is here called the Hezbollah Inter-Metro is limited and relies in part on Israeli military and intelligence. It should be taken with a grain of salt. In addition to Israeli and international media, this section draws from Beeri, Tal. 2021. "Hezbollah's 'Land of Tunnels': the North Korean-Iranian connection." ALMA, July. Beeri served for decades in IDF intelligence units.

66 This section draws largely from Azulay 2024, *op. cit.* See also Kabir, Omer. 2023. "Over 15 cyber attack groups affiliated with Iran, Hezbollah or Hamas are operating against Israel, says National Cyber Directorate." CTech Calcalist, Dec. 25. See also Jones, Seth G., et al. 2024. "The Coming Conflict with Hezbollah." CSIS, Mar. 21. See also Beaumont, Peter. 2024. "Israel's Iron Dome risks being overwhelmed in all-out war with Hezbollah, says US." The Guardian, Jun. 23.

67 Brik, Yitzhak. 2020. "The Iranians Are Lulling Israel's Leaders to Sleep." Haaretz, Jul. 14.

68 Kristensen, Hans M., and Korda, Matt. 2024. World nuclear forces. In: SIPRI Yearbook 2024: Armaments, Disarmament and International Security, pp. 271–366. See also Luscombe, B. 2012. "10 questions: Jimmy Carter." Time, Jan. 30. See also Clifton, E. 2016. "Powell acknowledges Israeli nukes." Lobe Log, Sep. 14. See also Kristensen, Hans M., and Norris, Robert S. 2014. "Israeli nuclear weapons, 2014." Bulletin of the Atomic Scientists 70, no. 6, pp. 97–115.

69 Kristensen, Hans M., and Korda, Matt. 2024. World nuclear forces. In: SIPRI Yearbook 2024: Armaments, Disarmament and International Security, pp. 271–366.

70 Dallas, Cham E., et al. 2013. "Nuclear war between Israel and Iran: Lethality beyond the pale." Conflict and Health 7, no. 10.

71 Cohen, Avner. "Israel." In: Born, Hans, et al. (eds.). 2010. *Governing the Bomb: Civilian Control and Democratic Accountability of Nuclear Weapons.* Oxford: Oxford University Press, pp. 152–170.

72 See e.g., Bronner, Ethan. 2010. "Vague, Opaque and Ambiguous: Israel's Hush-Hush Nuclear Policy." New York Times, Oct. 13.

73 Broad, W., and Sanger, D. 2017. "'Last secret' of 1967 war: Israel's doomsday plan for nuclear display." New York Times, June 3.

74 On the Israeli nuclear strategy, see Hersh, Seymour. 1991. *The Samson Option: Israel's Nuclear Arsenal and American Foreign Policy.* New York: Random House. See also Cohen, Avner. 1998. *Israel and the Bomb.* New York: Columbia University Press.

75 See "Yom Kippur War: At the Edge of a Nuclear War" in Chapter 3.

76 Spector, Leonard S., and Cohen, Avner. 2008. "Israel's Airstrike on Syria's Reactor: Implications for the Nonproliferation Regime." Arms Control Today 38, no. 6 (July/August), pp. 15–21.

77 Black, Ian, and Morris, Benny. 1992. *Israel's Secret Wars: A History of Israel's Intelligence Services.* New York: Grove Press, pp. 193–200.

78 Bachner, Michael, and TOI staff. 2023. "Far-right minister says nuking Gaza an option, PM suspends him from cabinet meetings." Times of Israel, Nov. 5.

79 "200 days of military attack on Gaza: A horrific death toll amid intl. failure to

stop Israel's genocide of Palestinians." Euro-Med Human Rights Monitor. Apr. 24, 2024.

80 "U.S. and Israel assessing new intelligence about Iran nuclear models." Axios, Jun. 18, 2024. See also "Blinken says Iran's nuclear weapon breakout time is probably down to 1–2 weeks." CNN, Jul. 19, 2024.

81 Olmert, Ehud. 2023. "Bring in NATO Forces: The Plan Israel Should Present for Postwar Gaza." Haaretz, Nov. 29.

82 On Shiloah's NATO efforts, see Chapter 4.

83 Sokolski, Henry. 2024. "Wargame simulated a conflict between Israel and Iran: It quickly went nuclear." Bulletin of Atomic Scientists, Feb. 27.

84 Cordesman AH. 2007. *Iran, Israel and Nuclear War*. Washington, D.C: Center for Strategic and International Studies (CSIS).

85 The Israel-Iran nuclear scenario of this section draws from Dallas, Cham E., et al. 2013. "Nuclear war between Israel and Iran: lethality beyond the pale." Conflict and Health 7, no. 10. However, as stated in the text, this decade-old scenario, considered conservative even originally, understates the more lethal power of each country today, as well as significant population increases in each.

86 Robock, Alan. 2010. "Nuclear winter." Clim Change 1 (May/Jun.), pp. 418–27.

87 On the likely consequences of a regional nuclear war, see Toon, Owen B., et al. 2007. "Consequences of regional-scale nuclear conflicts." Science 315, no. 5816, pp. 1224–25.

88 Schmitt, Eric, and Cooper, Helene. 2024. "U.S. To Send More Combat Aircraft and Warships to Middle East, Officials Say." New York Times, Aug. 5. See also "US publicly announces submarine move to Middle East amid Israel-Iran tensions." Reuters, Aug. 12.

89 Magdy, Samy, and Callister, Drew. 2024. "Here's what's on the table for Israel and Hamas in the latest cease-fire plan." AP News, May 2.

90 The disclosure came from Douglas Macgregor, a former Pentagon advisor during Donald Trump's administration. See "US colonel claims Israeli special forces, American legionaries killed in Yemen." Turkiye Today, Aug. 10, 2024.

91 Turse, Nick. 2024. "The U.S. Has Dozens of Secret Bases Across the Middle East. They Keep Getting Attacked." The Intercept, Aug. 6.

92 Knutson, Jacob. 2023. "Where U.S. troops are stationed in the Middle East." Axios, Oct. 31.

Chapter 11

1 Kuttab, Jonathan. 2021. *Beyond the Two-State Solution* [self-published]. On his personal journey, see Kuttab, Jonathan. 2023. *The Truth Shall Set You Free*. Hawakati.

2 Lustick seized the theory of Nash equilibrium to show how rational competitors could be trapped into a suboptimal yet painfully stable predicament. See Lustick, Ian S. 2020. "The Peace Process Carousel: The Israel Lobby and the Failure of American Diplomacy." Middle East Journal 74, no. 2 (Summer).

3 See e.g., Lustick, Ian. 2024. "History Tells Us How the Israel-Hamas War Will End." *Time*, Jan. 10. See also "Forum on Gaza with Menachem Klein, Ian Lustick, and Yoav Peled." *Logos*, Mar. 9, 2024.

4 Brzezinski, Zbigniew. 1983. *Power and Principle: Memoirs of the National Security Adviser, 1977–1981*. New York: FSG, pp. 444.

5 Compare Yergin, Daniel. 1991. *The Prize: The Epic Quest for Oil, Money, and Power.* New York: Simon & Schuster, pp. 140, 702.

6 This sort of interpretation goes back to Beard, Charles. 1913. *An Economic Interpretation of the Constitution of the United States*. New York: Macmillan. See also Seligman, Erwin R.A. 1903. *The Economic Interpretation of History*. 2nd Ed. New York: Columbia University Press, pp. 67, 162–63.

7 Bernadotte, Folke. 1951. *Diary of Folke Bernadotte, To Jerusalem*. Hodder & Stoughton, 1951, pp. 114–15.

8 Compare Kayyali, Abdul-Wahhab Said. 1977. *Palestine. A Modern History*. Croom Helm, p. 151.

9 Dr. Judah Magnes in New York Times, July 18, 1937.

10 See Urquhart, Brian. 1993. *Ralph Bunche: An American Life*. New York: W. W. Norton. On Bunche and decolonization, see Hill, Robert A., and Keller, Edmond J. (eds.). 2010. *Trustee for the Human Community: Ralph J. Bunche, the United Nations, and the Decolonization of Africa*. Ohio University Press. See also Raustiala, Kai. 2022. *The Absolutely Indispensable Man: Ralph Bunche, the United Nations, and the Fight to End Empire*. Oxford University Press.

11 Compare Kirkbride, Alec. 1976. *From the Wings: Amman Memoirs, 1947–1951*. London: Frank Cass, p. 55. See also Touval, Saadia. 1982. *The Peace Brokers: Mediators in the Arab–Israeli Conflict, 1948–1979*. Princeton, NJ: Princeton University Press, p. 54.

12 Ilan, Amitzur. 1996. *The Origin of the Arab–Israeli Arms Race: Arms, Embargo, Military Power and Decision in the 1948 Palestine War.* Basingstoke: Macmillan, pp. 20–23.

13 For more, see Chapter 3.

14 Ben-Dror, Elad. 2016. *Ralph Bunche and the Arab-Israeli Conflict: Mediation and the UN 1947–1949.* London: Routledge, pp. 70–71.

15 Quoted in *The Palestine Post*, July 12, 1948.

16 Ben-Dror 2016, *op. cit.*, pp. 70–71.

17 Ibid., p. 68. Ben-Dror's detailed Bunche analysis demonstrates painfully well the gradual transformation of the Partition Plan into something very different.

18 Bernadotte, Folke. 1948. *Progress Report of the United Nations Mediator on Palestine*. United Nations General Assembly Doc. A/648, part one, section V, paragraph 6.

19 Ibid.

20 Ben-Dror 2016, *op. cit.*, p. 86.

21 Ilan, Amitzur. 1989. *Bernadotte in Palestine*. London: Palgrave Macmillan UK, pp. 186–91.

22 Morris, Benny. 2004. *The Birth of the Palestinian Refugee Problem Revisited.* Cambridge: Cambridge University Press, p. 426.

23 On the divisions of the Truman White House at the eve of Israel's independence, see Chapter 3.

24 On President Truman's turn against the UN Partition Plan, see Chapter 3.

25 Hewins, Ralph. 1950. *Count Folke Bernadotte: His Life and Work.* Minneapolis: TS Denison, pp. 223–39.

26 This is the story as subsequently narrated in the Nobel Prize nomination. See Sveen, Asle. 2008. "Ralph Bunche: UN Mediator in the Middle East, 1948–1949." NobelPrize.org. Archived from the original on Dec. 31, 2008.

27 For Yehuda Cohen's comment, see Marton 1994, *op. cit.,* p. 254.

28 Heller, Joseph. 1994. *The Stern Gang: Ideology, Politics and Terror, 1940–1949.* London: Frank Cass, p. 239.

29 Ilan, Amitzur. 1989. *Bernadotte in Palestine, 1948.* New York, NY: St. Martin's Press, pp. 200–201. On the Stern, see Heller, Joseph. 1995. *The Stern Gang: Ideology, Politics and Terror 1940–1949.* London: Frank Cass.

30 Ben-Dror 2016, *op. cit.,* p. 89.

31 "General Lundström Gives Eyewitness Account of Bernadotte's Death." UN Department of Public Information, Press Release PAL/298, Sep. 18, 1948.

32 "Goldfoot Stanley," Stern Group's website in Israel: https://lehi.org.il/en/goldfoot-stanley/

33 Ilan 1989, *op. cit.,* p. 212.

34 "The Assassination of Count Bernadotte." Jewish Virtual Library. Retrieved on Jul. 16, 2024.

35 Semitic Action. 2019. "The Story of Natan Yellin-Mor (Gera)." VISION Magazine, Mar. 8.

36 Stanger, C.D. 1988. "A haunting legacy: The assassination of Count Bernadotte." Middle East Journal 42, no. 2, pp. 260–72. See also Golan, Zev. 2007. *God, Man and Nietzsche: A Startling Dialogue between Judaism and Modern Philosophers.* New York: iUniverse. On Adelson's revisionist Zionism and financing influence in Israeli politics, settlements and occupied territories, see esp. Chapter 6.

37 "2 Ex-Stern Gang Members Admit Murdering U.N. Aide." Los Angeles Times, Sep. 11, 1988. See also "Obituary: Yehoshua Zettler." Daily Telegraph, May 21, 2009.

38 "Obituary: Yehoshua Zettler." Daily Telegraph, May 21, 2009.

39 Marton, Kati. 1994. *A Death in Jerusalem.* New York: Pantheon Books.

40 Hewins 1950, *op. cit.,* pp. 223–39.

41 "Israel: Who's in Charge Here?" Time, Oct. 18, 1948.

42 Suarez, Thomas. 2023. *Palestine Hijacked: How Zionism Forged an Apartheid State from River to Sea.* Northampton, MA: Olive Branch Press, pp. 289–95.

43 Ilan 1989, *op. cit.,* p. 238.

44 Ben-Gurion, David. 1948. *War Diary.* Edited by Rivlin, Gershon and Oren, Elhanan. Tel Aviv: MOD, 1983, 2: 2: 7 [Hebrew], Sep. 19.

45 Stanger, Cary David. 1988. "A Haunting Legacy: The Assassination of Count Bernadotte." Middle East Journal 42, no. 2 (Spring), pp. 260–72.

46 Sveen 2008, *op. cit.*

47 Suarez 2023, see Chapter 8.

48 CIA, "A Long-Range Disaster." Information Report, Mar. 1949 (declassified date illegible, DOC_0000107452).

49 Morris, Benny. 1993. *Israel's Border Wars 1949–1956: Arab Infiltration, Israeli Retaliation, and the Countdown to the Suez War.* Oxford: Clarendon Press.

50 Israeli cabinet meeting of June 18, 1950, as quoted by Morris 1993, *op. cit.*, p. 164.

51 For more, see Chapter 1.

52 Morris 1993, *op. cit.*, pp. 124, 135.

53 "Unit 101." Special Warfare Encyclopedia: https://specwar.info/.

54 Drory 2005, *op. cit.*

55 See Chapters 3–4.

56 Shlaim, Avi. 1999. *The Iron Wall: Israel and the Arab World.* New York: W.W. Norton, p. 91.

57 Sharett, Moshe. 1953–56. *My Struggle for Peace,* 3 Vols. In: Caplan, Neil, and Sharett, Yaakov (eds.). 2019. *The Diary of Moshe Sharett, 1953–1956.* Bloomington: Indiana University, Vol. 1, see entry of Apr. 9, 1954.

58 Ibid., see Oct. 19, 1953.

59 Ibid., see Jan. 31, 1954.

60 Gwertzman, Bernard. 1982. "Go-Between Says Nasser Sought Israeli Pact." New York Times, Nov. 28. See also Jackson, Elmore. 1982. *Middle East Mission: The Story of a Major Bid for Peace in the Time of Nasser and Ben-Gurion.* New York: Norton.

61 The Acts of the Olshan-Dori Enquiry Commission annexed to Sharett's diaries. See Rokach, Livia. 1980. "Israeli State Terrorism: An Analysis of the Sharett Diaries." Journal of Palestine Studies 9, no. 3 (Spring), pp. 3–28.

62 Jackson 1983, *op. cit.,* p. 74. See also Teveth, Shabtai. 1996. *Ben-Gurion's Spy: The Story of the Political Scandal That Shaped Modern Israel.* New York: Columbia University Press. p. 81.

63 Sharett 1953–1956 Vol. 2, see Jan. 25, 1955.

64 Ibid., see Jan. 28, 1955.

65 Ibid., see Mar. 5, 1955.

66 Drory, Ze'ev. 2005. *Israel's Reprisal Policy 1953–1956: The Dynamics of Military Retaliation.* London: Frank Cass, p. 152.

67 Sharett 1953–1956 Vol. 2, see Apr. 14, 1955.

68 Sharett began to keep his diary on Oct. 9, 1953, after BG announced his resignation. *Yoman Ishi* [Personal Diary], 8 Vols. Tel Aviv, 1979 [English version in 3 vols].

69 Aderet, Ofer. 2021. "'Israel Was Born in Sin.'" Haaretz, Sep. 19.

70 Smisek, Martin. 2022. *Czechoslovak Arms Exports to the Middle East:* Vols 1–3. Helion and Company. See esp. Vol. 2.

71 Burns, William. 1985. *Economic Aid and American Policy towards Egypt, 1955–1981.* SUNY Press, pp. 16–17.

72 "Egypt: The Revolutionary." Time, Sep. 26, 1955.

73 Sharett 1953–1956 Vol. 2, see Oct. 3, 1955.

74 Jackson 1983, *op. cit.*, pp. 66, 69.

75 "Operation Alpha (1955)." The Israeli-Palestinian Conflict: An Interactive Database. See also "U.S. Efforts to Obtain a Settlement Between Egypt and Israel; the Beginnings of Operation Alpha, Jan. 1–Aug. 26, 1955," *Foreign Relations of The United States, 1955–1957, Arab-Israeli Dispute, 1955*, Vol. XIV, U.S. Department of State.

76 Drory 2005, *op. cit.,* see Introduction.

77 For an Israeli overview of these four generic models, see Baruch, Pnina Sharvit. 2021. *Resolving the Israeli–Palestinian Conflict: The Viability of One-State Models.* Institute for National Security Studies. Memorandum No. 2017. Dec. Typically, the report was sponsored by the U.S. CIA.

78 Compare Cohen, Jennifer, et al. 2017. *Reimagining Israel/Palestine: Assessing a Confederal Future.* New York: Columbia School of International and Public Affairs.

79 For an overview of their vision, see: https://www.federation.org.il/index.php/en/the-federation-plan.

80 Demographic data from the UN and Israel.

81 Kimmerling, Baruch. 2003. *Politicide: Ariel Sharon's War Against the Palestinians.* London: Verso. See Introduction.

82 Estimates from Hodali, Fadwa, et al. 2024. "Gaza Reduced to 42 Million Tonnes of Rubble. What Will It Take to Rebuild?" Bloomberg, Aug. 16.

83 On ethnic expulsions and Jewish settlement expansion, see esp. Chapters 1–2.

84 Compare Breiner, Josh. 2024. "How Far-right National Security Minister Itamar Ben-Gvir Took Over Israel's Police." Haaretz, Jun. 13. See also Odenheimer, Natan, et al. 2024. "Israeli Official Describes Secret Government Bid to Cement Control of West Bank." New York Times, Jun. 21.

85 TOI Staff. 2024. "Backing Shin Bet chief, Gallant says Ben Gvir endangering Israel's security." Times of Israel, Aug. 23.

86 Bar's letter was released by Israel's Channel 12 News. Quotes are from Lis, Jonathan. 2024. "Shin Bet Chief Warns PM and Ministers: Jewish Terror Is Jeopardizing Israel's Existence." Haaretz, Aug. 22.

87 Ibid.

88 Compare (and contrast) "How Israel's Preemptive Strike Against Hezbollah Unfolded." Haaretz, Aug. 25; and "Hezbollah responds to assassination of Martyr Fouad Shokor." Al Mayadeen, Aug. 25.

89 Saideddine, Wassim. 2024. "Hezbollah chief Nasrallah confirms 'success' in avenging killing of top commander." Anadolu Ajansi, Aug. 26. On the Unit 8200, see Chapter 4.

90 Most analysts in the West missed these implications. Some Israelis didn't. See e.g., Shalom, Amir Bar. 2024. "Why Nasrallah scaled down his Sunday attack, and why Israel had limited its pre-emption." Times of Israel, Aug. 27.

91 This section draws from Steinbock, Dan. 2022. "The Unwarranted War." The World Financial Review, Mar. 9; and Steinbock, Dan. 2023. "The Unwarranted Ukraine Proxy War: A Year Later." The World Financial Review, Jan. 27.

92 "China, Ukraine sign deal to strengthen infrastructure cooperation." Global Times, July 4, 2021.

93 State Statistics Service of Ukraine.

94 "Volodymyr Zelenskyy's first phone conversation with President of China Xi Jinping took place," July 13, 2021: https://www.president.gov.ua/en/news/vidbulasya-persha-telefonna-rozmova-volodimira-zelenskogo-z-69509

95 Steinbock, Dan. 2012. *The Case for Huawei in America.* Huawei America, Sep.

96 As the West Point report puts it, "these groups have bitterly opposed any suggestion of compromise with Russia over Donbas through the Normandy negotiating process ... and oppose concessions floated by President Volodymyr Zelensky." See Lister, Tim. 2020. "The Nexus Between Far-Right Extremists in the United States and Ukraine." CTC Sentinel, April, pp. 30–43.

97 "Ukraine aid: Where the money is coming from, in 4 charts." CNN, Mar. 20, 2024.

98 Data from SIPRI Database.

99 Data from the bipartisan Congressional Budget Office.

100 This argument builds on Steinbock, Dan. 2022. "Great Powers and Globalization: Spotlight on the United States and China." In: Schwerpunkt AuBenwirtschaft. 2021/2022. *Reglobalisation: Changing patterns.* Oesterreichische Nationalbank (ONB) and Werschaftskammer Osterreich (WKO).

101 For the full argument, see Steinbock, Dan. 2024. *The End of Modern Economic Growth.* Unpublished manuscript.

102 Compare Chapter 10.

103 Quoted in Sokol, Sam. 2024. "This is a war': FM urges Gaza-style temporary evacuation of Palestinians in West Bank." Times of Israel, Aug. 28.

ACKNOWLEDGEMENTS

This work has benefited from decades of exchanges with many government leaders, senior officials of government agencies, multinational corporations, international think tanks, development banks, financial institutions and innovation organizations around the world. It builds on my past works and affiliations with India, China and America Institute (U.S.); Shanghai Institutes for International Studies (China); EU Center (Singapore); Harvard Cluster Network (U.S.); OECD Development team; Indian Council on Global Relations, German Institute of Development and Sustainability, several UN agencies, and many others.

For years, my work has centered on economic growth and development in the increasingly multipolar world. *The Fall of Israel* tells the same story, but the painting is different. It shows what happens when development is reversed. The abject obliteration that now prevails in the Gaza Strip is the ultimate end of reversed development.

Although the origins of *The Fall of Israel* go half a century back, I began to write what became the book two days before October 7, due to the 50-year anniversary of the 1973 Yom Kippur War. I expected a new catastrophe to be just a matter of time. These commentaries struck a chord, and were released by *The World Financial Review* (UK), *Consortium News* (U.S.) and *Anti-War* website and re-published in every world region. It was around then that I connected with Diana G. Collier, editorial director of Clarity Press. The ensuing cooperation resulted in the book at hand, thanks to Diana's incredible support and assiduous sparring.

This book would not have been viable without my beloved wife, Donna, who encouraged me to write it, after my near-fatal injury.

During these past months, I have often thought of my friends, the late Amos Oz and the late Yael Dayan, the co-founder and co-leader of Peace Now, the Israeli peace movement. I dedicate *The Fall of Israel* to their memory.

Dan Steinbock
August 15, 2024

ABOUT THE AUTHOR

Dr. Dan Steinbock is an internationally-renowned expert of the multi-polar world economy and the founder of the global consultancy Difference Group Ltd. He has served in the India China America Institute (U.S.), the Shanghai Institutes for International Studies (China), and the EU Center (Singapore) and he has cooperated with several other think tanks around the world. He has lived in Europe, the U.S., Asia and the Middle East, and traveled in most world regions. A senior Fulbright scholar, he came to New York City in the 1980s. Today he spends most of his time in Asia. He has lectured around the world and consulted for multinational companies, multilateral development banks, government agencies, intergovernmental organizations like the OECD, and regional trading blocs, such as the EU, and several megacities. He has given keynotes on the global economy in institutional venues following Nouriel Roubini, Paul Krugman, Alan Greenspan, and Nassim Nicholas Taleb. He has been interviewed by and contributed to most major media worldwide. He has also worked in the *kibbutzim* and been influenced by progressive and peace movements.

INDEX

452

executive gizmo toys, little chrome balls on strings that bounced back and forth, and iron filings that moved in magnetic waves. He loved playing with all those toys while he pondered his next move.

Jack was always kind of evasive and indirect. He found it very difficult to talk about his personal feelings, and maybe that was his attraction to Terry and her church. He saw the church as a way to rediscover his humanity. I suspect that was what he was doing in California.

Jack used to have a lot of parties, and he'd invite mostly people from Terry's church. There would be people of all different colors, people wearing bells, barefoot people with rings in their noses, or elegantly dressed people who looked like La Jolla socialites. Jack liked to play the guitar at his parties. He played country-western, wrote his own songs, and he was really pretty good. During this whole new-age era of self-help and find your true self and all that, Jack had come to the conclusion that if he could be anything he wanted to be, he would be a country-western star.

One afternoon I was at Jack's house on the bluff, sitting in the hot tub with him, when I said, "Jack, you know when I was a kid, I used to drive seventy-five miles so I could surf at this spot right below your house. I bet you've never even been down there."

Jack didn't say anything. He was still lost on Wall Street.

"I think everybody who lives at the beach should know how to surf," I said.

That caught Jack's attention. "Maybe you're right," he said. "I think I'd like to try surfing."

So I led this beefy stockbroker down his own private stairway to the beach. I put him on a long board and started pushing him into a few small waves, which is the best way to help a beginner feel the excitement of riding a wave. But it just wouldn't work. Even while he was getting thrashed around by a wave, Jack was still rolling numbers around in his head and digesting stock reports. He was like a brain without a body. "I guess I'm never going to be a surfer," he finally said.

"That's okay, I'm never gonna be a stockbroker," I said.

Another time, when Jack looked to me like he'd been under way too much stress, I said, "Jack, you need a change. Let's go to

Hawaii. It's a whole different lifestyle over there. It'll be really good for you."

Jack knew the stress was killing him, so he said, "Maybe you're right. I've never been to Hawaii. Let's go."

So I made a phone call and arranged for us to stay at my old friend Mike Horack's place, on the North Shore of Oahu.

The first thing Jack did when we landed at the Honolulu airport was make a phone call to see how his stocks were doing. Then we rented a car and headed for the North Shore.

Mike Horack, who owned a surf shop in Honolulu, had a beautiful house right on the beach, a Hobie Cat, lots of surfboards, and plenty of peace and quiet. It was paradise at Mike's place, except for one thing— Mike didn't have a telephone.

That afternoon Jack started to go into a nervous sweat. At first I figured it was just jet lag and maybe the excitement of being in a new environment. After a little rest he'd be ready to relax and have fun.

But it only got worse. Without a phone, Jack was out of touch with his computers and with the stock market. I knew Jack well enough by now to know that he wasn't having a heart attack; he was having an anxiety attack.

By dusk Jack was shaking violently and vomiting, but Mike Horack and I still had hopes that Jack would feel better after a good night's rest.

At seven the next morning, it was obvious that Jack hadn't slept. His eyes were bloodshot, and his lips were twitching, with flecks of white at the corners of his mouth. He told us, "I'm sorry, but I gotta get outa here."

I said, "Jack, let's go surfing. A little exercise will help you relax."

"I CAN'T RELAX! I GOTTA GET OUTA HERE RIGHT NOW!"

"Okay . . . okay," I said. "I'll take you to the airport, but at least let me drive you around the island first. You should at least see this place before you go."

Jack didn't care, as long as his bags were in the car and he was on the way to the airport. So we drove around Oahu, but the whole way he kept saying, "What time's the plane leave? Will I make it? Do the planes leave on time here?" We had to stop twice to call the airport to make sure we knew what time the plane left. Jack also called New York both times.

When we finally got to the airport and Jack could actually see the planes departing, he started to relax. By ten o'clock, after being in Hawaii less than twenty-four hours, Jack was on his way back to California, to his computers and his gizmos.

But in spite of his odd little quirks, Jack knew how to have fun in his own way. One day Terry was talking about going up to L.A. to see some people about her TV ministry. Right away Jack said, "That's a great idea. I'll take you up there myself."

Jack picked us up at Terry's house in the most ridiculous stretch limousine I'd ever seen. It was at least six feet longer than the standard limo. It had a huge chrome grill and a big chrome maiden on the hood, like the figurehead on a ship's prow. The whole passenger section was filled with big bouquets of flowers. We had champagne, fruit juices— the whole setup just so Jack could show us how he liked to have fun. He brought his guitar along too, and while we were driving north on I-5, Jack sang his country-western songs for us.

When we got to Hollywood Boulevard, around lunch time, Jack opened the sunroof, then said, "Now I'm gonna play you a little song I been workin' on." Just then a big eighteen-wheeler pulled up alongside us. The trucker inside leaned way out his window and stared down through our sunroof. I guess he didn't like what he saw there—people lying in flowers, drinking champagne, singing, and having fun. Anyway, the trucker reached out and threw a big sloppy tuna-fish sandwich through the sunroof. It hit Jack right in the head, fell open, and the soggy tuna oozed down his face and over his guitar.

Jack stopped playing for a moment, like he was thinking. Then he looked up and said to Terry and me. "Folks, I'm gonna name this here song 'Tuna-Fish Sandwich.' "

Jack eventually finished writing that song and recorded it on his own country-western album. I don't think it sold many copies.

As for Terry and me, one day we had a big argument, broke

off our relationship in a flurry, and that was the end of that. But every now and then in a bookstore, I still see a copy of that tape on personal relationships I helped her write. I hope it's doing somebody some good.

In the summer of 1981 I had some money in my pocket and an urge to get out of California for a while. I had a friend who owned a ranch in Costa Rica near Golfito, on the Pacific side, down by the border with Panama. I knew there was an outstanding surf spot, Pavones, not far from his place, and I was curious about it. My friend had invited me down several times, so I finally decided to go.

When I arrived at the ranch, my friend was gone, but he'd left a note telling me to make myself at home and he'd be back in a few days. I went to check out the surf spot, but the waves weren't breaking. I went back to the ranch and, out of curiosity, started looking around the place. There were several workers in the rice fields and cowboys herding cattle. I spotted one worker who looked like he might be an American, so I went over to talk to him and found to my surprise it was Pat Curren, the master designer of the old rhino guns.

"Hey, Doyle," he said, as if he'd just seen me the day before. Actually, I hadn't seen Curren in something like fifteen years. He had aged well, and he looked fit; but after all this time, he still had that intensity in his eyes.

"Curren!" I said. "What are you doing here?"

He shrugged. "Aw, I work around the place in exchange for room and board."

Trying to get more information than that out of Curren was hopeless. His son, Tommy, was the hottest young surfer in California (Tommy Curren dominated professional surfing throughout the Eighties), and Pat was obviously proud of his boy; but other than that, he had no interest whatsoever in what was going on back in the States.

A few days later I saw Curren again. This time he was on horseback, riding into the jungle. He was leading a second horse loaded with two surfboards and provisions, and said he was heading